Industrial
Organic Nitrogen Compounds

MELVIN J. ASTLE
Case Institute of Technology
Cleveland, Ohio

American Chemical Society
Monograph Series

REINHOLD PUBLISHING CORPORATION, NEW YORK
CHAPMAN & HALL, LTD., LONDON

Printed in the United States of America
THE GUINN CO., INC.
New York 14, N. Y.

Photocomposed by THE SCIENCE PRESS, INC., Lancaster, Pa.

GENERAL INTRODUCTION

American Chemical Society's Series of Chemical Monographs

By arrangement with the Interallied Conference of Pure and Applied Chemistry, which met in London and Brussels in July, 1919, the American Chemical Society was to undertake the production and publication of Scientific and Technologic Monographs on chemical subjects. At the same time it was agreed that the National Research Council, in cooperation with the American Chemical Society and the American Physical Society, should undertake the production and publication of Critical Tables of Chemical and Physical Constants. The American Chemical Society and the National Research Council mutually agreed to care for these two fields of chemical progress. The American Chemical Society named as Trustees, to make the necessary arrangements of the publication of the Monographs, Charles L. Parsons, secretary of the Society, Washington, D. C.; the late John E. Teeple, then treasurer of the Society, New York; and the late Professor Gellert Alleman of Swarthmore College. The Trustees arranged for the publication of the ACS Series of (a) Scientific and (b) Technological Monographs by the Chemical Catalog Company, Inc. (Reinhold Publishing Corporation, successor) of New York.

The Council of the American Chemical Society, acting through its Committee on National Policy, appointed editors (the present list of whom appears at the close of this sketch) to select authors of competent authority in their respective fields and to consider critically the manuscripts submitted.

The first Monograph of the Series appeared in 1921. After twenty-three years of experience certain modifications of general policy were indicated. In the beginning there still remained from the preceding five decades a distinct though artibary differentiation between so-called "pure science" publications and technologic or applied science literature. By 1944 this differentiation was fast becoming nebulous. Research in private enterprise had grown apace and not a little of it was pursued on the frontiers of knowledge. Furthermore, most workers in the sciences were coming to see the artificiality of the separation. The methods of both groups of workers are the same. They employ the same instrumentalities, and frankly recognize that their objectives are common, namely, the search for new knowledge for the service of man. The officers of the Society therefore combined the two editorial Boards in a single Board of twelve representative members.

Also in the beginning of the Series, it seemed expedient to construe rather broadly the definition of a Monograph. Needs of workers had to be recognized. Consequently among the first hundred Monographs appeared works in the form of treatises covering in some instances rather broad areas. Because such necessary works do not now want for publishers, it is considered advisable to hew more strictly to the line of the Monograph character, which means more complete and critical treatment of relatively restricted areas, and, where a broader field needs coverage, to subdivide it into logical subareas. The prodigious expansion of new knowledge makes such a change desirable.

These Monographs are intended to serve two principal purposes: first, to make available to chemists a thorough treatment of a selected area in form usable by persons working in more or less unrelated fields to the end that they may correlate their own work with a larger area of physical science discipline; second, to stimulate further research in the specific field treated. To implement this purpose the authors of Monographs are expected to give extended references to the literature. Where the literature is of such volume that a complete bibliography is impracticable, the authors are expected to append a list of references critically selected on the basis of their relative importance and significance.

PREFACE

This book has been written in an attempt to summarize the chemistry of most of the types of organic nitrogen compounds. No single book has appeared in recent years which has accomplished this goal. Many very excellent treatises are available describing the chemistry of amino acids and proteins, alkaloids and heterocyclic nitrogen compounds. Accordingly these compounds are not discussed extensively in this monograph. In order to present a comprehensive survey of nitrogen chemistry it has been necessary to discuss the simple heterocyclic nitrogen ring systems in some detail.

Considerable attention has been given to the patent literature in order to present developments from the industrial laboratories as well as those from other institutions. Reaction mechanisms are discussed whenever they appear useful in understanding the chemistry involved but no attempt is made to make this work an approach to the theory of reactions.

I wish to acknowledge the invaluable help of Miss Marcia Parsons, Librarian at Case Institute of Technology. Miss Parsons did the major part of the literature searching and without her help this book probably never would have been written.

Cleveland, Ohio   MELVIN J. ASTLE
January, 1961

CONTENTS

1. ALIPHATIC AMINES

Amines are derivatives of ammonia in which one or more hydrogen atoms are replaced by alkyl or aryl groups. The nitrogen-carbon bonds are formed by the overlapping of p atomic orbitals which should make the bond angles 90 degrees. Actually these angles are increased to approximately 111 degrees in ammonia and are somewhat larger in amines as a result of the mutual repulsion of the alkyl or aryl groups, especially if they are bulky. Only three of the five electrons on the nitrogen are used in bonding with carbon so that the nitrogen has one unshared pair of electrons which is capable of bonding with electron-deficient atoms or ions.

Amines, because of the unshared pair of electrons on the nitrogen, are bases in that they are proton acceptors or electron donors. Thus amines react with acids to form salts in the same way as does ammonia and water solutions of the amines are basic.

$$: NH_3 + HCl \longrightarrow NH_4^+ + Cl^-$$

$$RNH_2 + HCl \longrightarrow RNH_3^+ + Cl^-$$

$$: NH_3 + HOH \rightleftarrows NH_4^+ + OH^-$$

$$RNH_2 + HOH \rightleftarrows RNH_3^+ + OH^-$$

In the same way amines form salts with Lewis acids such as boron trifluoride by donating the electron pair on the nitrogen to complete the octet of the boron.

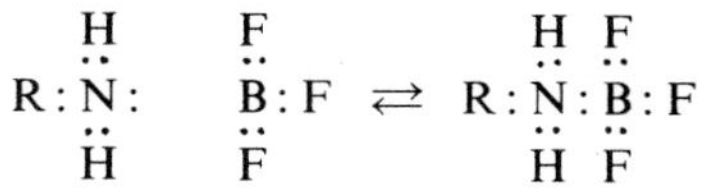

$$
\begin{array}{cc}
\text{H} & \text{F} \\
\text{R:N:} & \text{B:F} \\
\text{H} & \text{F}
\end{array}
\rightleftarrows
\begin{array}{c}
\text{H F} \\
\text{R:N:B:F} \\
\text{H F}
\end{array}
$$

Alkyl radicals are electron releasing so that replacement of the hydrogen atoms of ammonia by these groups should make the electron pair more available for bonding and the basic strength of the amine should be increased. That this is true is shown in Table 1–1.

TABLE 1–1. BASICITIES OF ALIPHATIC AMINES

Compound	pKa
Ammonia	4.8
Methylamine	10.64

1

TABLE 1-1. (*Continued*)

Compound	pKa
Dimethylamine	10.70
Trimethylamine	9.80
Ethylamine	10.67
Diethylamine	11.00
Triethylamine	10.72

The fact that amines are relatively weak bases results from the fact that the amine is found in water solution largely as a hydrated molecule in which the association is caused by hydrogen bonding.

$$
\begin{array}{c}
\text{H} \\
| \\
\text{R}\!-\!\text{N} \text{------} \text{H}\!-\!\text{O} \\
| \qquad\qquad\quad \diagdown \\
\text{H} \qquad\qquad\qquad \text{H}
\end{array}
$$

Very few ammonium ions are formed as a result of a proton transfer.

When all four of the hydrogen atoms of the ammonium ion are replaced by alkyl groups, however, the resulting quaternary ammonium hydroxide $R_4N^+OH^-$ is a strong base comparable to sodium or potassium hydroxide. As would be expected, the primary amines are stronger bases than ammonia and secondary amines are still stronger. The tertiary amines are, however, considerably weaker than secondary amines but are still stronger than ammonia. This has been explained by Brown.[1-8] The bond angles in ammonia are about 111 degrees and the substitution of alkyl groups for hydrogen atoms spreads the angles somewhat more, the amount of spreading depending upon the size of the alkyl groups present. When the amine is converted into an ammonium ion by picking up a proton, or converted to a salt by donating an electron pair to boron trifluoride the tetrahedral structure is achieved with a resulting compression of the bond angle. This sets up considerable strain in the molecule and since dissociation to the free amine and the acid relieves this strain by permitting the return to the unstrained bond angles, dissociation is favored. By increasing the size of the groups substituted on the nitrogen, basicity is decreased still further. It follows that tertiary amines, having more alkyl groups and therefore greater strain in the associated ammonium ion would tend to be the weaker bases. Brown confirmed the theory by investigating the dissociation constants of a large number of amine-alkylboron compounds. With a given alkylboron (trimethylboron) and successive substitution of alkyl groups in the ammonia molecule the inferred order of basic strengths as a result of steric strain should be

$$NH_3 > \quad RNH_2 > \quad R_2NH > \quad R_3N$$

On the basis of the electron releasing ability of the alkyl groups on the nitrogen the order of basicity is

$$R_3N > R_2NH > RNH_2 > NH_3$$

Inasmuch as these two effects act in opposite directions, the resulting basic strength of the amine is a compromise between the two forces so that in most cases the order of basicity with alkyl amines is

$$R_2NH > R_3N > RNH_2 > NH_3$$

The lower molecular weight amines are gases with odors resembling ammonia. They are soluble in water and form salts similar to ammonium salts. The solubility of the amines in water decreases with increasing molecular weight but because of salt formation they are all soluble in dilute acids.

The salts of amines with the hydrohalogen acids all have characteristic melting points even though melting is usually accompanied by some decomposition. The melting points of some of these salts are given in Table 1–2.

TABLE 1–2. MELTING POINTS OF ALKYLAMMONIUM HALIDES

Formula	M.P. (°C)	Formula	M.P. (°C)
CH_3NH_3Cl	226	$(C_2H_5)_2NH_2Cl$	217
$(CH_3)_2NH_2Cl$	171	$(C_2H_5)_3NHCl$	254
$(CH_3)_3NHCl$	275	$C_2H_5NH_3Br$	159.5
$C_2H_5NH_3Cl$	109	$C_2H_5NH_3I$	188.5

Lambert and Strong[9] found that ammonia, primary and secondary amine vapors are associated as dimers at temperatures of 20–130°C but tertiary amines are not. The association is caused by hydrogen bond formation.

Amines up to and including the hexylamines have fishy odors. Trimethylamine is found in the tissues and excreta of fish. Many amines are formed during putrefaction of protein and are responsible for the odors which accompany such processes. Among these are 1,4-butanediamine commonly known by its descriptive name putrescine and 1,5-pentanediamine commonly called cadaverine.

Preparation of Amines

The more general methods for the preparation of amines involve the alkylation of ammonia by alkyl halides, alcohols, or carbonyl compounds in the presence of hydrogen, and the hydrogenation of nitro compounds, nitriles and amides. In addition to these there are specific methods which are useful for the preparation of many amines. In most cases mixtures of primary, secondary and tertiary amines are obtained, but special methods are available which will give essentially pure primary or secondary amines.

Alkylation of Ammonia by Alkyl Halides. Alkyl halides react with ammonia under suitable conditions to form a mixture of primary, secondary and tertiary amines. Alkyl iodides are more reactive than bromides which are in turn more reactive than chlorides. Commercially, only the chlorides can be used economically even though their use requires more drastic reaction conditions. The direct reaction product of an alkyl halide with ammonia is an alkyl ammonium halide.

$$C_2H_5Cl + NH_3 \longrightarrow C_2H_5NH_3Cl$$

With excess ammonia an equilibrium is approached in which the free primary amine is liberated to compete with ammonia for reaction with more of the alkyl halide to form a secondary amine.

$$C_2H_5NH_3Cl + NH_3 \longrightarrow C_2H_5NH_2 + NH_4Cl$$

$$C_2H_5NH_2 + C_2H_5Cl \longrightarrow (C_2H_5)_2NH_2Cl$$

The secondary amine by reaction with more alkyl halide forms a tertiary amine which in the presence of excess alkyl halide may form a quaternary ammonium salt.

$$(C_2H_5)_3N + C_2H_5Cl \longrightarrow (C_2H_5)_4NCl$$

Treatment of the quaternary ammonium salt with moist silver oxide (AgOH) gives the quaternary ammonium hydroxide which is a very strong base comparable to sodium or potassium hydroxide.

It is evident that this method is of value only when the resulting primary, secondary and tertiary amines can be easily separated by distillation or other process. Thus the methylamines cannot be made satisfactorily in this way because of the small differences in boiling points of the products of reaction, (CH_3NH_2, $-6.5°C$; $(CH_3)_2NH$, $7.4°C$; $(CH_3)_3N$ $3.5°C$). The ethylamines on the other hand have been made commercially using this procedure. The use of a very large excess of ammonia favors production of primary amines. If secondary amines are desired the concentrations of alkyl halide and ammonia can be adjusted to give primary and secondary amines and the primary amine formed can be recycled.

The reaction is most satisfactory for the preparation of primary amines from alkyl halides having more than three or more carbon atoms. Under these conditions polyalkylation is limited and the products having widely different boiling points are more easily separated. In general, primary halides react more readily than secondary halides and tertiary halides show a strong tendency to be dehydrohalogenated to olefins.

The reaction conditions will vary somewhat with the nature of the alkyl halide used. Temperatures in excess of 100°C are required when chlorides are used, and since ammonia is a gas it is often desirable to use pressure to increase its concentration in the reaction mixture. This process has been used for the preparation of ethylenediamine. Ethylene dichloride and the equivalent of 65 per cent aqueous ammonia were pumped through nickel pipes maintained at a temperature of 120°C and under a pressure of 160–170 atmospheres. The product consisted primarily of ethylenediamine together with a lesser amount of polyethylenepolyamines.[10]

In many cases alcoholic solutions of ammonia have been used at room temperature. Thus Whitmore and Langlois[11] reacted *n*-butyl bromide with a large excess of ammonia in alcohol at room temperature to give a 47 per cent yield of *n*-butylamine. The reaction required about 2 days. Higher molecular weight alkyl halides react much slower but will give amines by heating with alcoholic ammonia.[12]

von Braun made a rather intensive study of the alkylation of ammonia with alkyl halides using a mixture of liquid ammonia and alcohol.[13] He reports that liquid ammonia seems to favor the formation of primary amines, particularly as the molecular weight of the alkyl bromide is increased. Thus amyl bromide gave a 10 per cent yield of primary and an 80 per cent yield of secondary amylamine. Under the same condition octyl bromide gave approximately equal amounts of primary and secondary amine and *n*-dodecyl bromide gave a 90 per cent yield of primary amine. He also reported that with butyl chloride no appreciable quantity of quaternary ammonium salts was formed and if conditions were right secondary amines could be made the chief products.

Shreve and Rothenberger[14] showed that sodium amide in liquid ammonia gave a larger proportion of primary amine. Shreve and Burtsfield[15] investigated the reaction of a suspension of sodium amide in liquid ammonia on a series of alkyl bromides at –50°C and atmospheric pressure. The product consisted of a mixture of amines and olefins. *n*-Hexyl bromide gave a 74 per cent yield of primary amine, but the yield became smaller with decreasing chain length. The *n*-alkyl chlorides showed a greatly decreased reaction rate compared with the bromides.

A study of the position of the halogen atom in the alkyl halide indicated that only primary halogens react readily. The action of sodium amide in liquid ammonia on 2-bromopentane and *tert*-amyl bromide gave only olefins.

When a tertiary hydrogen atom is on a carbon atom adjacent to the halogen, a 5 per cent yield of amine is obtained and a 57 per cent yield of olefin.

A tertiary hydrogen on a carbon atom at least once removed from the halogen had no appreciable effect on the products obtained. The addition of water to the system has little effect on the total yield of amines but does appreciably increase the yield of secondary amines.

A patent issued to I. G. Farbenindustrie A. G.[16] describes the preparation of dialkylamines from alkyl chlorides having 10 to 18 carbon atoms. A large excess of aqueous ammonia was used under pressure at 120–170°C. The yields of secondary amines were described as good and the primary amines could be recycled.

Quaternary ammonium salts were formed by the reaction of tertiary amines and higher molecular weight 1-chloroparaffins in suitable solvents within relatively narrow temperature ranges. Trimethylamine reacted with decyl- and cetyl chlorides in alcohol at temperatures below 110°C to give quaternary ammonium salts in almost quantitative yields. Above 110°C the yields decreased rapidly. Triethylamine and tributylamine reacted very sluggishly.

The reaction between ammonia and alkyl halides may be influenced by catalysts. Nekrasova and Shuikin[17] found that catalysts based on magnesium oxide were effective. A mixture of primary, secondary and tertiary amines was obtained when ammonia and an alkyl chloride (mole ratio 2.1:1) was passed over the catalyst at 310°C as shown in Table 1–3.

TABLE 1–3. ALKYLATION OF AMMONIA WITH ALKYL CHLORIDES
IN THE PRESENCE OF MAGNESIUM OXIDE

Alkyl Chloride	% Amine		
	Primary	Secondary	Tertiary
Butyl chloride	39.2	18.1	2.7
Hexyl chloride	45.0	13.0	2.5
Heptyl chloride	50.5	9.0	1.5
Octyl chloride	58.0	4.2	0.8
Nonyl chloride	69.0	8.0	—
Decyl chloride	70.6	8.0	—

The yield of primary amines increased very markedly with increasing molecular weight of the alkyl chloride.

The Sharples Chemical Co.[18] developed a process for the conversion of pentyl chlorides to pentylamines. Mixtures of a solution of ammonia in alcohol and the isomeric pentyl chlorides (from the chlorination of pentane) are introduced into an autoclave and anhydrous ammonia is added. The temperature is raised to 160–165°C where it is maintained for 2 hours after which the temperature is again raised until the pressure reaches 400 psi and this temperature is maintained for an additional 2 hours. The pressure is then dropped and the reaction product distilled to remove the ammonia which is absorbed in cold alcohol and re-used. When essentially all of the ammonia has been removed, by-product pentylenes and pentyl alcohols, unreacted pentyl chloride and ethyl alcohol are recovered. The residue in the pot consists largely of the pentylammonium chlorides from which the free amines are liberated by adding sodium hydroxide and distilling the resulting mixture of water and amines. The product consists of three parts of monopentylamines and two parts of dipentylamines with only very small amounts of tertiary amines.

A few additional examples are of interest in the preparation of specific amines from alkyl halides and ammonia.

Hexamethylenetetramine can be used as the source of ammonia. Thus alkyl halides prepared from the corresponding alcohols can be converted to the desired amine by reaction with hexamethylenetetramine followed by the decomposition of the resulting quaternary salt with hydrochloric acid.[19]

Sodium iodide may be added as a catalyst. Thus to an ethanol solution of hexamethylenetetramine and slightly more than 1 mole of sodium iodide, was added 1 mole of an alkyl chloride or bromide and the mixture permitted to stand at room temperature for periods of a few minutes to several weeks. In general the longer the carbon chain the longer is the time required to produce the amine. A 72 per cent yield of methylamine was obtained in 1 week and an 82.5 per cent yield of ethylamine in eight days. An 82 per cent yield of benzylamine was obtained in only 2 hours.[20]

Hydrogen chloride was added to cyclopentadiene at $-20°C$ to give the theoretical yield of 3-chlorocyclopentene which was then added to a solution of ammonia in methanol at $-10°C$ to give 3-aminocyclopentene. This amino olefin was ozonized at $-10°C$ to give glutamic acid.

1,4-Dichloro-2-butene treated with hexamethylenetetramine in chloroform at $60°C$ gives an addition product which is decomposed by hydrochloric acid to give $ClCH_2CH=CHCH_2NH_2Cl$. Under the same conditions 1,4-dichlorobutane gives a poor yield of the amine hydrochloride. 1,4-Dibromobutane gives an excellent yield of $BrCH_2CH_2CH_2CH_2NH_3Br$. 1,4-Dichloro-2-butyne treated with hexamethylenetetramine in methanol and the mixture allowed to stand for several days gives the dihydrochloride of $H_2NCH_2C\equiv CCH_2NH_2$ in excellent yield.[21]

Alkylation of Ammonia with Alcohols. Alcohols react with ammonia in the vapor phase at temperatures of 300–500°C. For the lower molecular weight alcohols, temperatures of 400°C, pressures of about 100 atmospheres and a reaction time of 2 to 3 hours seem to be optimum. A mixture of primary, secondary, and tertiary amines is formed in which the amines seem to exist in equilibrium with each other. It is therefore possible to improve the yield of the desired product by recycling the other two.

Methanol and ammonia (mole ratio of 1:2) are mixed and heated to 350°C under 200 psi pressure and then passed over an alumina catalyst at 450°C. The crude product, consisting of ammonia and a mixture of mono-, di-, and trimethylamines, is difficult to separate because of the similarity in boiling points. Separation by azeotropic distillation with compounds such as xylene is possible. Under the above conditions the product contains about 50 mole per cent monoethyl-, 20 mole per cent dimethyl-, and 30 mole per cent trimethylamine. This ratio may be varied somewhat by controlling the ratio of alcohol to ammonia and by recycling the primary or secondary amines.[22] Uchida and Ichinokawa[23] passed a mixture of methyl alcohol and ammonia (mole ratio 1:1.5) over a catalyst, consisting of an equimolar mixture of magnesium oxide and silica, at 450–500°C to give a product containing 28.8 per cent CH_3NH_2, 57.6 per cent $(CH_3)_2NH$ and 13.6 per cent $(CH_3)_3N$.

The alkylation of ammonia by alcohols has been accomplished in the presence of hydrogen and a hydrogenation catalyst consisting of a mixture of nickel and copper deposited on alumina activated with boric acid. Thus 2 moles of ethyl alcohol, 1 mole of ammonia and 3 moles of hydrogen were passed over the catalyst at 220°C to give a product consisting of ethyl-, diethyl- and triethylamines in the ratio of 1:5:3. The conversion of ethyl alcohol amounted to 52 per cent.

Davies *et al.*[24] passed lower molecular weight aliphatic alcohols together with ammonia and hydrogen in the vapor phase at temperatures of 240–300°C and pressures of 10–25 atmospheres over a formaminate-copper catalyst promoted with an alkaline earth basic compound. Thus *n*-butyl alcohol, hydrogen, and ammonia gave conversions of 96 per cent per pass based on the alcohol, and yields of 97 per cent. The liquid product contained 17 per cent butylamine, 52 per cent dibutylamine and 12 per cent tributylamine.

Ammonia and *n*-butyl alcohol (mole ratio 4:1) were passed over a catalyst consisting of chromic oxide on alumina at 350°C to give a 68 per cent yield of amines.[25] The amines consisted of 74 per cent monobutylamine and 26 per cent dibutylamine. Nickel- or cobalt oxides may be substituted for the chromium oxide and are just as effective in promoting the reaction.

n-Butylamine has also been prepared by passing *n*-butyl alcohol and ammonia (mole ratio 1:4) over alumina or a catalyst composed of Al_2O_3—Fe_2O_3—TiO_2 at temperatures of 375–420°C. The most active catalyst consisted of alumina containing 15 per cent Fe_2O_3. The titanium dioxide-alumina catalyst was very active but rapidly lost its activity. The best conversion to amines was 25 per cent obtained at 390°C. Olefins were obtained in appreciable yields. Hindley and Fisher[26] prepared *n*-butylamine by introducing *n*-butyl alcohol, ammonia and Raney nickel into an autoclave and heating at 195°C for 7 hours. *n*-Butylamine was obtained in 53 per cent yield and essentially no secondary butylamine was formed.

Krishnamurthy and Rao[27] investigated the high pressure ammonolysis of alcohols in the presence of an aluminum oxide catalyst made from aluminum nitrate. The yield of amine increased with temperature up to about 300°C. Above 325°C the alcohols were dehydrated to olefins. Pressures of about 140 psi were used. At a high ammonia to alcohol ratio, primary amines predominated while at low ratios, secondary and tertiary amines were formed. The highest total conversion to amines was about 30 per cent obtained with an ammonia to alcohol ratio of 6. The presence of water in the feed inhibited the formation of amines but water in the catalyst had little effect. The presence of iron, thorium, zinc or molybdenum in the catalyst inhibited the production of amines.

Kozlov and Akhmetshima[28] found that in the reaction of cyclohexanol with ammonia in a flow system, dehydration to cyclohexene can be suppressed by increasing the pressure to 7–10 atmospheres of ammonia. The dehydration becomes very important at 1 atmosphere. Optimum temperatures are 260–300°C. The conversion of cyclohexanol to cyclohexylamine is 70–74 per cent and the yields are 90–95 per cent.

The yields of amines are best when primary alcohols are used. Secondary and especially tertiary alcohols give olefins as by-products.

Popov and Shuiken[29] reacted ethyl, isopropyl and *n*-butyl alcohols with ammonia at 290–450°C in the presence of platinum on silica gel or activated carbon. These alcohols gave a mixture of primary, secondary and tertiary amines in excellent yields. *sec*-Butyl alcohol and cyclohexanol gave relatively low yields of only the primary amine.

Catalytic hydrogenation of a mixture of cetyl alcohol and diethylamine in the presence of Raney nickel at 200°C and a pressure of 82 kg/sq cm gave cetyldiethylamine in good yield.[30]

Popov and Shuiken believe that the alcohols are converted into amines by direct displacements of the elements of water on the catalyst surface without the formation of unstable intermediates such as aldehydes. This view is supported by the fact that acetaldehyde gave no amines, while propionaldehyde, acetone and methylethyl ketone gave low yields of only the primary amines.

Whitehead[31] passed isopropyl alcohol and ammonia over pelletized basic aluminum phosphate at 350°C and 200 atmospheres to give a mixture of propylamines. Eighty per cent of the isopropyl alcohol was converted to products of which 46 per cent was isopropylamines.

Smeykal[32] prepared high molecular weight secondary and tertiary amines by treating aliphatic or cycloaliphatic alcohols containing 8 or more carbon atoms with primary or secondary amines containing not more than 5 carbon atoms. Thus dimethyldecylamine was prepared in 90 per cent yield by passing a mixture of dodecyl alcohol and dry dimethylamine over an alumina catalyst at 360°C and 190 atmospheres.

Arnold[33] describes the preparation of mixed dodecylamines by passing a mixture of ammonia and dodecyl alcohol vapors at atmospheric pressure over a catalyst consisting of a rigid porous gel impregnated with alumina. Temperatures of 250–500°C were used.

Davies *et al.*[34] prepared amines by passing alcohols containing less than nine carbon atoms, together with 2 to 4 moles each of ammonia and hydrogen over a Raney copper catalyst at 240–300°C and at 10–25 atmospheres. The best catalyst is obtained from a copper-aluminum alloy containing 55 per cent copper by treatment with 10 per cent sodium hydroxide until 20–70 per cent of the aluminum is removed. A copper-silicon catalyst has also been used. Thus butyl alcohol, hydrogen and ammonia (mole ratio 1:3:1.25) were passed over the catalyst at 250° and 17 atmospheres to give a product containing 17 per cent butylamine, 52 per cent dibutylamine and 12 per cent tributylamine.

Saturated primary diamines may be prepared by the reaction of a glycol or amino alcohol with ammonia under pressure in the presence of a ruthenium catalyst. Hydrogen is usually present in the reaction mixture.[35]

Reductive Alkylation of Ammonia with Carbonyl Compounds. Alkyl groups may be introduced into ammonia or primary or secondary amines by reaction with aldehydes or ketones in the presence of hydrogen and a hydrogenation catalyst such as nickel or platinum. The reaction involves the hydrogenation of the addition product of the aldehyde with ammonia, or possibly the hydrogenation of the dehydrated product of the addition compound.

$$RCHO + NH_3 \longrightarrow R-\underset{\underset{OH}{|}}{CH}-NH_2 \begin{array}{c} \xrightarrow{(H)} RCH_2NH_2 \\ \nearrow \\ \xrightarrow{(H)} \\ \xrightarrow{-(H_2O)} R-CH=NH \end{array}$$

Secondary and tertiary amines are formed in the same reaction. Schwoegler and Adkins[36] propose that secondary amines are formed by the addition of a primary amine to the intermediate imine followed by hydrogenation with the loss of ammonia

$$RCH_2NH_2 + RCH=NH \longrightarrow R-\underset{\underset{NH_2}{|}}{CH}-NHCH_2R \longrightarrow RCH_2NHCH_2R + NH_3$$

Secondary amines are prepared by treating a ketone with ammonia or an alkylamine and hydrogen over a catalyst consisting of cuprous oxide on calcium or barium sulfate. Thus 2-methyl-4-ethylaminopentane was prepared in 86 per cent yield by heating a mixture of methyl isobutyl ketone with 70 per cent aqueous ethylamine in methanol in the presence of the catalyst at 160° and 1400–1500 psi.

Tertiary amines may be formed by the addition of the secondary amine to the aldehyde and the subsequent hydrogenation of the resulting hydroxy amine. It is obvious that an imine cannot be an intermediate in this reaction.

$$(RCH_2)_2NH + R'CHO \longrightarrow R-\underset{\underset{OH}{|}}{CH}-N(CH_2R)_2 \xrightarrow{2H} R'CH_2N(CH_2R)_2 + H_2O$$

Similar reactions occur with ketones in which a secondary alkyl group is introduced on the nitrogen atom but the method is not successful for the introduction of a tertiary alkyl group on the nitrogen.

Reactions of aldehydes or ketones with ammonia give rise to primary amines and secondary amines in which the two alkyl groups are the same. If an aldehyde or ketone is reacted with a primary amine, unsymmetrical secondary amines may be obtained by the hydrogenation of the intermediate Schiff's base that is formed. In some cases the Schiff's base may be isolated.

$$R-CHO + R'NH_2 \xrightarrow{-H_2O} RCH=NR' \xrightarrow{2H} RCH_2NHR'$$

The action of ammonia and hydrogen on aromatic and polynuclear aldehydes in the presence of Raney nickel gives a mixture of the corresponding amine and alcohol. Thus benzaldehyde gives benzylamine and benzyl alcohol. The amine is usually formed in larger amount. o-Methoxybenzaldehyde treated in methanol with ammonia and hydrogen at 35°C under a pressure of 80 kg/sq cm gives a 64 per cent yield of the corresponding amine.[37]

It has also been reported that a nitro compound can be used in place of the amine[38] because in the presence of the hydrogen and a suitable catalyst the nitro group will be reduced to the amine.

$$C_6H_5NO_2 + 2C_3H_7CHO + 5H_2 \longrightarrow C_6H_5N(C_4H_9)_2 + 4H_2O$$

Aldehydes having no α-hydrogen, such as benzaldehyde, may be hydrogenated in ammoniacal ethanol in the presence of Raney nickel at temperatures below 75°C. By controlling the ratio of aldehyde to ammonia the product may be predominantly primary or secondary amines.[39]

Hydrogenation of ketones in a solution of 17 per cent ammonia in ethanol in the presence of Raney nickel at 20° and a pressure of 1 atmosphere gives the corresponding amine in excellent yield. Methyl benzyl ketone is converted to $C_6H_5CH_2CH(NH_2)CH_3$ in 85 per cent yield. Methyl styryl ketone ($C_6H_5CH{=}CH{-}COCH_3$) yields $C_6H_5CH_2CH_2CH(NH_2)$-CH_3 in 67 per cent yield.[40]

Aldol condensations accompanying the reductive alkylation of ammonia by aldehydes or ketones can be almost entirely suppressed if the ammonia and the carbonyl compound in a suitable solvent are mixed below 0°C and the mixture subsequently hydrogenated in the presence of a catalyst.[41]

In the most satisfactory procedures an ethanol solution of the aldehyde or ketone and ammonia are hydrogenated in the presence of a Raney nickel catalyst.[36,39] Platinum and palladium catalysts are also frequently used. If primary amines are desired, the ammonia is used in considerable excess. For the preparation of secondary amines the mole ratio of carbonyl compound to ammonia is made about 2:1. If the carbonyl compound is used in excess, tertiary amines are formed.

Pressures of 20–150 atmospheres and temperatures of 40–150°C are desirable. At pressures below 20 atmosphere and at temperatures below 40°C, the reaction rate is too slow to be practical. At temperatures of 40–75°C, Raney nickel equal to about 3 per cent of the aldehyde is recommended but if the temperature is raised to 125–150°C only 0.5–1.0 per cent Raney nickel is required.

Secondary amines are also prepared by the hydrogenation of an ethanol solution of a primary amine and an aldehyde or ketone. Conditions are much the same as above except that the mole ratio of reactants is changed.[42,43]

Amalgamated zinc and hydrochloric acid has been found to be an excellent reagent for the reductive alkylation of hindered amines such as mesidine (mesitylamine). Thus N,N-dimethyl-, N-isopropyl-, N-isobutyl-, and N-isoamylmesidine were prepared from the corresponding aldehydes in 18–94 per cent yield.

Reductive alkylation of aromatic primary amines with aldehydes cannot be accomplished satisfactorily in acidic media because the reactants tend to form polymers under these conditions.[44]

Aldehydes having four or fewer carbon atoms are too reactive with ammonia to give satisfactory yields of amines. Formaldehyde reacts with ammonia to give hexamethylenetetramine rather than methylamine. The hexamethylenetetramine can be reduced, however, to give a mixture of methylamine and trimethylamine.

The earlier commercial processes for the preparation of hexamethylenetetramine were batch processes operating at about 20°C and used aqueous solutions of formaldehyde and ammonia as raw materials. The reaction is highly exothermic and difficult to control, especially at the low temperatures required. Higher temperatures resulted in the formation of undesirable by-products. The product was isolated by low pressure crystallization. Recently the trend has been toward continuous processes in which the temperature is controlled by carrying out the reaction at the boiling point of water at reduced pressure. Advantage is taken of the heat of vaporization in order to get better temperature control. In the Meissner process[45] the formaldehyde and the ammonia are introduced as gases into the reactor which contains water. The heat of hydration and heat of reaction are removed by vaporization of water from the reactor. The optimum temperature (50–70°C) of the reaction is controlled by varying the total pressure at which the reaction mixture is allowed to boil, or by controlling the partial pressure by the presence of non-condensable gases. The hexamethylenetetramine precipitates out of the saturated solution as the reaction proceeds. Since the heat of reaction and heat of hydration are sufficient to remove all the water additional evaporator equipment and heat are unnecessary.

Hexamethylenetetramine may be nitrated to give the very excellent explosive known as Cyclonite, Hexogen or RDX. RDX was the explosive used in the blockbuster bombs of World War II. Hexamethylenetetramine is also used in the production of molded plastics, vulcanization accelerators, as a starting material in the production of various pharmaceuticals and in several waterproofing resins and adhesives.

Acetaldehyde, propionaldehyde, and butyraldehyde give, in addition to the corresponding alkylamines, appreciable quantities of heterocyclic amines (substituted pyridines). Thus the reductive alkylation of ammonia with n-butyraldehyde in the presence of a Raney nickel catalyst gives a product containing 32 per cent n-butylamine, 12 per cent di-n-butylamine and 23 per cent 2-n-propyl-3,5-diethylpyridine.[46]

Brimer[47] describes the preparation of n-butylamine from butyraldehyde by a one- or two-step process. A 29 per cent aqueous solution of ammonia is stirred vigorously at 25°C while butyraldehyde is introduced over a period of two hours. The mixture is allowed to settle and the nonaqueous layer containing $CH_3CH_2CH_2CH{=}NH$ and very small amounts of butyraldehyde are charged into an autoclave and hydrogenated at 150°C under 500 psi pressure in the presence of Raney nickel. n-Butyl amine is obtained in 90 per cent yield.

Aliphatic aldehydes containing 5 or more carbon atoms can be converted to primary amines in better than 60 per cent yield in the presence of an excess of ammonia and a nickel catalyst.[48]

Ketones are readily converted to amines by reductive alkylation. Yields of primary amines from acetone are only about 30 per cent but with higher ketones the yields are usually greater than 50 per cent. Thus methyl n-propyl ketone is converted to 2-aminopentane in 90 per cent yield[49] and methyl isopropyl ketone to 2-amino-3-methylbutane in 65 per cent yield.

Secondary amines and, to a lesser extent tertiary amines, are always formed in the reductive alkylation reactions involving either aldehydes or ketones.

In contrast to low yields of amines previously obtained from acetone, investigators at Shell Development Corp. in 1954 reported that the hydrogenation of an equimolar mixture of acetone and ammonia over Raney nickel at 140° C and 740 psi gave a 97 per cent yield of isopropylamine.[50]

Ketimines can be prepared from water-soluble compounds such as acetone and isopropylamine by adding to water made slightly acidic with HCl. The temperature rises to about 50° C during the first 5 minutes. The mixture is permitted to stand overnight.

Water insoluble compounds are refluxed in benzene which removes the water as formed as a water-benzene azeotrope.

The ketimines can subsequently be hydrogenated to secondary amines by hydrogenation at 100° C and 200 psi in the presence of Raney nickel.

Hexadecylamines have been prepared from 9-methyl-7-pentadecanone or the corresponding alcohol by heating in a hydrogen atmosphere with ammonia or an amine in the presence of a hydrogenation catalyst such as the oxides of copper and chromium or copper and aluminum.[51] When ammonia is used the major product is a primary hexadecylamine with only small amounts of secondary and tertiary amines being formed. Typical aminating agents in addition to ammonia are methyl- and ethylamines, ethanolamines, or benzylamine. The compounds formed are reported to be effective as fungicides and insecticides.

Hexamethylenediamine can be prepared by treating cyclohexene in an aliphatic alcohol with ozone and subjecting the resulting product to reductive amination with hydrogen and ammonia or a primary or secondary amine. The reaction with hydrogen and ammonia is carried out at 50° C and a pressure of 200 atmospheres in the presence of a cobalt catalyst.[52]

Cyclopentylamines have been prepared in 67 per cent yield by passing cyclopentanone (in excess) together with hydrogen and ammonia at 150° C over a catalyst consisting of 15 per cent nickel on alumina. The product contains 86 per cent cyclopentylamine and 14 per cent dicyclopentylamine.[53]

Dibenzylethylenediamine is obtained by hydrogenating the condensation product of benzaldehyde and ethylenediamine.

$$2C_6H_5CHO + H_2NCH_2CH_2NH_2 \longrightarrow C_6H_5CH{=}NCH_2CH_2N{=}CHC_6H_5 \xrightarrow[Pt]{H_2}$$

$$C_6H_5CH_2NHCH_2CH_2NHCH_2C_6H_5$$

The hydrogenation is carried out in a hydrocarbon solution in the presence of a platinum or palladium catalyst.[54]

The Leuckart Reaction. This reaction discovered in 1885[55] is a process for the reductive alkylation of ammonia, primary- or secondary amines by aldehydes or ketones in which formic acid or one of its derivatives serves as the reducing agent. Leuckart's work received little attention until Ingersoll and his associates applied the method for the preparation of a series of substituted α-phenethylamines.[56] The reaction is carried out by heating a mixture of the carbonyl compound and ammonia or the amine and formic aid to rather high temperatures. Primary and secondary amines formed in the reaction are obtained as formyl derivatives from which the free amine is recovered by hydrolysis. Tertiary amines are obtained as formates.

$$RCHO + 2HCOONH_4 \longrightarrow RCH_2NHCHO + 2H_2O + NH_3 + CO_2$$

$$RCHNHCHO + H_2O \longrightarrow RCH_2NH_2 + HCOOH$$

The ammonium salt decomposes on heating to ammonia and formic acid and the ammonia adds to the aldehyde to form an addition product which is reduced to the amine with formic acid. Reaction of this amine with more formic acid gives either the salt (with tertiary amines) or the amide. As in the case of reductive alkylation using hydrogen, either the ammonia-aldehyde addition product or the imine, $>C=NH$, formed by dehydration of the product may undergo reduction. Inasmuch as the reaction temperatures required are above that necessary for the dehydration of ammonium formate to the amide, formamide has been considered to be the actual intermediate. However, acetophenone in diethylene glycol does not react with formamide at 120–130°C in 15 hours. Ammonium formate under the same conditions gave a 10 per cent yield of α-phenethylamine in 4 hours.

At higher temperatures where formamide is effective it is probably in equilibrium with ammonium formate.

$$RCHO + HCONH_2 \rightleftarrows RCH=NCHO + H_2O$$

$$HCONH_2 + H_2O \rightleftarrows HCOONH_4$$

The Leuckart reaction is most effective with aromatic aldehydes and ketones which have boiling points of 100°C or higher. Yields are usually in the order of 40–90 per cent. The method is superior to the reduction of aldoximes and ketoximes made from the same carbonyl compounds particularly when functional groups are present which may be removed by hydrogenation. Thus an 82 per cent yield of α-(*p*-chlorophenyl)ethylamine is obtained from *p*-chloroacetophenone by the Leuckart reaction, whereas the reduction of *p*-chloroacetophenoneoxime with sodium and ethanol, sodium amalgam and acetic acid or by catalytic hydrogenation proceeds with the removal of chlorine from the benzene ring.

In addition to ammonium formate and formamide, methylammonium and dimethylammonium formates have been used in some cases as the reducing agents.[57]

Formaldehyde reacts very readily with ammonium formate to give trimethylamine as the major product.[58] It is very difficult to stop the reaction to give methyl- or dimethylamine. The best yields (80 per cent) have been obtained when an excess of formic acid is used with formaldehyde.[59] One mole of formaldehyde and 2–4 moles of formic acid are used for each methyl group introduced indicating that it is mainly the formic acid that supplies the hydrogen for the reduction. The reaction may be carried out on the steam bath.

Long chain primary or secondary amines of 12 to 18 carbon atoms and formaldehyde (mole ratio not less than 1:2) are reduced with formic acid at temperatures of 25–100° C to form the corresponding dimethyl- or methylamines. It is important to maintain an excess of formic acid of 2–5 moles per mole of amine. Thus octadecyldimethylamine is obtained from stearylamine and formaldehyde and laurylamine is converted to dodecyldimethylamine.[60]

Other amines used with formaldehyde and formic acid include ethylamine, piperazine,[61] benzylamines and phenylamines.[62,63] Yields of tertiary amine approach the quantitative in each case. Ethylenediamine and tetramethylenediamine have been completely methylated in 92 per cent yield.

Aniline and compounds having strongly negative groups attached to the nitrogen such as amides, ureas, and hydroxylamine cannot be successfully methylated in this way.

Acetaldehyde heated on the steam bath with ammonium formate and formic acid is not converted to the expected amine. Instead 2-methyl-5-ethyl pyridine is formed.[59] Valeraldehyde reacts with ammonium formate to give triamylamine and with aniline and formic acid to give diamylaniline.[64]

Benzaldehyde heated with ammonium formate at 180° C for several hours gives a 35–40 per cent yield of tribenzylamine together with N,N-dibenzylformamide, dibenzylamine, N-benzyl formamide and benzylamine. As much as 20 per cent of the benzaldehyde is converted to polymeric materials.

In general substituted benzaldehydes react less readily than benzaldehyde itself.

A number of 2-aminoalkanes have been prepared from methyl ketones such as methyl propyl ketone, methyl butyl ketone,[65] methyl amyl ketone, methyl hexyl ketone and methyl cyclohexyl ketone.[66] Diethyl, dipropyl, dibutyl, and diheptyl ketones give primary amines in yields of 40–80 per cent. Alkyl aryl ketones such as acetophenone, propiophenone and isobutyrophenone have also been converted to the corresponding amines.[57,67,68,69]

In early experiments Leuckart and Wallach heated dry ammonium formate and the carbonyl compound to 180–230° C in a sealed tube. Later a mixture of ammonia or substituted amine was used and better yields were obtained. Formamide has also been used but temperatures must be considerably higher and yields are not as high. An ammonium formate-formamide reagent was used by Ingersoll[56] with excellent results.

The most satisfactory reagent seems to be formamide or ammonium formate to which sufficient 90 per cent formic acid is added to maintain a slightly acidic mixture. One to three equivalents of formic acid are usually required.[68] A few reactions are carried out on a steam bath but usually temperatures of 150–230° C are used.

A number of reactions are summarized in Table 1-4.[70]

TABLE 1-4. REDUCTIVE ALKYLATION OF AMINES WITH
CARBONYL COMPOUNDS—LEUCKART REACTION

Aldehyde or Ketone	Reagent	Product	Yield (%)
Formaldehyde	Butylamine/HCOOH	N,N-Dimethyl-butylamine	80
Formaldehyde	Tetramethylene di-amines/formic acid	Tetramethylene-1,4-diaminobutane	92
Formaldehyde	Piperidine/formic acid	N-Methylpiperidine	80
Butyraldehyde	Piperazine/formic acid	N-N'-Dibutyl piperazine	63
Benzaldehyde	Ammonium formate	Tribenzylamine	35–40
		Dibenzylamine	10–15
Benzaldehyde	Piperazine/formic acid	N,N'-dibenzyl-piperazine	84
di-*n*-Heptyl ketone	Ammonia/formic acid	8-Amino pentadecane	40
di-Isopropyl ketone	Formamide/formic acid	2,4-Dimethyl-3-pentylamine	64
Methyl amyl ketone	Ammonium formate	2-Heptylamine	55
Methyl hexyl ketone	Formamide/formic acid	2-Octylamine	60
Phenylacetone	Amylamine/formic acid	N-Amyl-β-phenyl isopropylamine	50–70
Acetophenone	Ethylamine/formic acid	N-Phenyl-α-phenyl amine	70
Laurophenone	Ammonia/formic acid	α-Phenyldodecyl amine	78
Benzophenone	Ammonia/formic acid	Benzhydrylamine	80

Bunnett and Marks[71] report that metal chlorides such as ferric, zinc and magnesium chlorides are catalysts for the Leuckart reaction. They particularly recommend magnesium chloride for the preparation of tertiary amines from ketones and secondary ammonium formates of dialkylformamides. As an illustrative experiment 720 g of 25 per cent aqueous dimethylamine was added slowly to 184 g (4 moles) of formic acid and the mixture distilled to remove 620 g of water. To the dimethyl formamide thus formed was added 199 g (1 mole) of *p*-bromoacetophenone, 46 g (1 mole) formic acid and 30 g (0.15 mole) $MgCl_2 \cdot 6H_2O$. The flask was heated in an oil bath for 6–10 hours at 160° C. The yield of tertiary amine was about 50 per cent in 6 hours.

Bunnett, Marks and Moe[72] found that dialkyl formamides in the presence of formic acid and magnesium chloride were superior to dialkylammonium formates for the preparation of tertiary amines.

Mousseron *et al.*[73] investigated the Leuckart reaction with formamide and N-substituted formamides. Benzaldehyde reacted with diethylformamide to give an 85 per cent yield of N,N-diethylbenzylamine. Under the same conditions *p*-nitrobenzaldehyde gave a 15 per cent yield and *m*-nitrobenzaldehyde a 45 per cent yield of the corresponding N,N-diethylnitrobenzylamine. If formic acid was used the reaction time was reduced but no increase in yield was observed. 2-Hydroxycyclohexanone is converted to a mixture of *cis*- and *trans*-2-dialkylaminocyclohexanols with the *cis* compound the major product. The reaction is claimed to be stereospecific with the formation of the least stable product which in most cases has the *cis* configuration.

Kost and Grandberg[74] using formamide in formic acid propose that the first step in the Leuckart reaction involves the dissociation of the formamide and that the first product is the formyl derivative of the amine. Thus a formamide-formic acid mixture (mole ratio 6:2.5) was prepared by adding ammonia or ammonium carbonate to formic acid and heating to 150° C. A catalytic amount of Raney nickel was added, the mixture heated to 120° C and cyclohexanone was added over a period of 1.5 hours. Heating was continued for an additional 1.5 hours, the mixture was cooled, neutralized with 50 per cent sodium hydroxide, the liquid decanted and the precipitate treated with hot water to give a 98 per cent yield of formylcyclohexylamine.

When the procedure was modified by adding concentrated HCl to the mixture after heating and evaporating to dryness an 85 per cent yield of cyclohexylamine was obtained.

A mixture of urea, cyclohexanone, formic acid and Raney nickel was heated at 110° C for 3 hours during which time a formic acid-formamide mixture was added. Dicyclohexylamine was obtained in 84 per cent yield. The addition of the ketone to hot formamide tends to increase the yield of primary amine. If, however, the formamide-formic acid mixture is added to excess ketone, the secondary amine is the major product and unreacted ketone can be recovered. The addition of nickel accelerates the decomposition of formic acid and decreases the acidity of the medium.

Rikasheva and Miklukhim[75] prepared benzylmethylamine ($C_6H_5CHNH-CH_3$) and benzylamine ($C_6H_5CH_2NH_2$) from acetophenone and benzaldehyde using a 2 to 3 fold excess of isotopically labeled ammonium formate (DCO_2NH_4) as the reducing agent. It was found that the deuterium from the formate attached itself to the carbonyl carbon atom of the ketone or aldehyde but there was no exchange with the reaction solvent. The isotope effect is similar to that observed in the Cannizzaro reaction which favors an intramolecular migration of the deuterium or hydrogen. These investigators believe that a mechanism which calls for the participation by water of hydroxyl groups of other compounds is not correct. They propose that the formamide adds across the carbonyl group to give the intermediate $RR'C(OH)NHCHO$ which reacts with formic acid to give a hydrogen bonded cyclic structure which opens up to give $RR'CHNHCHO$, formic acid and carbon dioxide.

Wallach showed that in the presence of formic acid the alkylation of an amine by a carbonyl compound proceeds at lower temperatures than if ammonium formate or formamide are used alone. This modification of the Leuckart synthesis of amines is frequently referred to as the Wallach reaction. In this reaction a primary or secondary amine, an aldehyde or ketone, and formic acid are heated at temperatures in which carbon dioxide is evolved. The over-all reaction may be written as

$$R_2NH + R'CHO + HCOOH \longrightarrow R_2N-CH_2R' + H_2O + CO_2$$

The Wallach reaction is reviewed in a paper by Staple and Wagner.[76]

Simple aliphatic amines are methylated to the corresponding tertiary amines by warming with formaldehyde in formic acid. Yields are better than 80 per cent. Dimethylbutylamine, dimethylbenzylamine and methylpiperidine are prepared in this way. 1,4-Diaminobutane gives the tetramethyl derivative in 92 per cent yield.[59]

Reduction of Oximes. The reduction of oximes to amines accomplishes much the same purpose as does the Leuckart reaction. Thus aldehydes or ketones can be treated with hydroxylamine to form an oxime which can subsequently be reduced by conventional methods.

Oximes may be hydrogenated to amines in the presence of Raney nickel catalysts in 50–90 per cent yield.[65,77,78,79] A mixture of primary and secondary amines is obtained. Iffland and Yen[80] hydrogenated aliphatic ketoximes at atmospheric pressure over a Raney nickel catalyst to give primary amines in 43–85 per cent yield. No secondary amines were obtained.

Kametoni and Nomura[81] used the Raney nickel alloy and sodium hydroxide to reduce oximes to amines.

Reeve and Christian[82] used Raney cobalt for the reduction of oximes and found it to be just as effective as Raney nickel and perhaps superior when dioxane or alcohol was used as the solvent for the oxime. The hydrogenation was effected at 200–220 atmospheres of hydrogen and temperatures of 80–125° C. The reaction was complete in 10–20 minutes. The yields of amines from such compounds as n-butyraldoxime, benzaldoxime and methyl ethyl ketoxime were better than 90 per cent of which 95–97 per cent was primary amines.

Heptylamine has been prepared from heptaldoxime in 73 per cent yield by reduction with sodium and absolute ethanol.[83]

Lithium aluminum hydride is also an excellent reagent for the reduction of oximes. Thus 2,2-diphenylcyclohexanone oxime has been reduced to 2,2-diphenylcyclohexylamine in 80 per cent yield.[84]

Diamines may also be prepared by the hydrogenation of dioximes or aminonitriles. 2,3-Butanedioxime is hydrogenated in the presence of a platinum catalyst to give an 80 per cent yield of a mixture of dl-2,3-diaminobutane and meso-2,3-diaminobutane. 2-Aminobutyronitrile in ethanol is reduced with lithium aluminum hydride in ether to give an excellent yield of 1,2-diaminobutane.[85]

Reduction of Nitriles. The reduction of nitriles has long been an important method for the preparation of amines. A mixture of primary, secondary and tertiary amines is usually obtained. The reduction may be carried out chemically using sodium and an alcohol or a metal and an acid or by hydrogen in the presence of a catalyst such as platinum or nickel.

The higher molecular weight nitriles were first reduced to amines by sodium and an alcohol and among the first to develop this technique were Krafft and Moye[86] who prepared hexadecylamine by the reduction of palmitonitrile with sodium and ethyl alcohol. This is a practical method for the preparation of amines but has the disadvantage that large excesses of sodium are required which must be disposed of in some manner.

Harwood[87] developed a method which involves forming a dispersion of sodium in toluene and using this dispersion in the reduction of nitriles. The sodium thus dispersed, because of the small particle size, is much more reactive and the amount of metal required can be materially reduced. This method gives almost theoretical yields of primary amines and is particularly effective in the preparation of amines from unsaturated nitriles. The method may be illustrated for the preparation of dodecylamine from lauronitrile.

Twenty grams of sodium is suspended in 300 g of toluene. The suspension is heated to boiling and 36 g of lauronitrile mixed with 65 g of 1-butanol and 300 g of toluene are slowly added. The reaction mixture is then heated for one-half hour at 60°C with stirring, after which time it assumes a jelly-like consistency. After completion of the reaction 300 g of water is added in order to react with the excess sodium and to decompose the alcoholate. Two layers are formed and the aqueous layer is discarded. The other layer is then acidified and the 1-butanol and toluene removed by distillation. The amine is obtained by making the mixture alkaline and distilling.[88]

Dinitriles having 5 carbon atoms in the chain are reduced to a mixture of a pentanediamine and a piperidine. The piperidine is formed by the cyclization of either a monoaminonitrile or the diamine.

To illustrate the procedure, sodium was added to a mixture of glutaronitrile in ethyl alcohol which was then heated on the water bath for 15 minutes. Water was then added and the product recovered by steam distillation. The product contained 20 per cent piperidine and 66 per cent pentanediamine. The slower the reaction was performed the greater the amount of piperidine produced. If a group was substituted on the carbon atom α- to the cyano group, the yield of cyclic products was increased. Alcohols other than ethyl alcohol are used successfully.

The reduction of nitriles to amines with lithium aluminum hydride or other metal hydrides has been described by several investigators.[89,90] The reaction is carried out in ether solution at room temperature or below and yields are in general better than 80 per cent. Octylamine has been prepared in 90 per cent yield by dissolving caprylonitrile in ether, cooling in an ice bath and adding an ether solution of lithium aluminum hydride. When the reaction was complete the solution was washed with water, then with dilute sodium hydroxide and again with water to decompose the metalamino complex formed and the amine was recovered by distilling the ether solution.[91]

2-Cyanocyclohexanone and *trans*-2-cyanocyclohexanol were reduced with lithium aluminum hydride to give *trans*-2-(aminomethyl)cyclohexanol.[92]

Dialkylaminonitriles, $(CH_3)_2N—CH_2CN$ and $(CH_3)_2NCH_2CH_2CN$, have been reduced to diamines in 69 per cent yields. The hydride to nitrile ratio was varied from 1 to 2 with little or no effect on the yield of diamine.[93]

Benzonitrile and *o*-tolunitrile have been reduced to the corresponding amines in 72 per cent and 88 per cent yields, respectively.[90] Mandelonitrile gave only a 48 per cent yield of the corresponding amine probably because of the precipitation of intermediate products made insoluble by the bifunctionality of the intermediate.

Other metal hydrides such as sodium borohydride can also be used. One of the features of this reduction is that the metal hydrides have no effect on carbon-carbon unsaturation and consequently unsaturated nitriles are reduced smoothly and in high yields to give the corresponding unsaturated amines.

Brown and Subba Rao[94] report that nitriles are readily reduced to amines with a mixture of sodium borohydride and aluminum chloride in ethylene glycol. Amides and nitro groups are not affected by this reagent.

In the laboratory this represents one of the very best reactions for the preparation of amines but it is of little use commercially. Nystrom and Brown[90] recommend that the reduction of nitriles be carried out under an atmosphere of nitrogen because the intermediate products seem to be oxygen-sensitive.

The catalytic hydrogenation of nitriles has been a very important method for the production of amines. These hydrogenations usually take place in the liquid phase in the presence of a nickel catalyst. In the laboratory, platinum or palladium may be used since the hydrogenations can be accomplished at much lower temperatures and pressures.

A mixture of primary and secondary amines is usually obtained in which much greater quantities of secondary amines are obtained than when the reduction is carried out with sodium and an alcohol. Adkins[36,46] proposes that the secondary amines are formed from primary amines by the loss of ammonia.

$$2RNH_2 \longrightarrow R_2NH + NH_3$$

They can also be formed during the hydrogenation by addition of a molecule of primary amine to the intermediate imine and loss of ammonia by further hydrogenation.

$$RCN + H_2 \longrightarrow RCH{=}NH$$

$$RCH_2NH_2 + RCH{=}NH \longrightarrow \underset{\underset{NH_2}{|}}{RCH}{-}NHCH_2R$$

$$\underset{\underset{NH_2}{|}}{RCH}{-}NHCH_2R + H_2 \longrightarrow RCH_2NH{-}CH_2R + NH_3$$

Inasmuch as ammonia is a by-product of the formation of secondary amines it is not surprising that adding it to the system inhibits production of secondary amines.[36] Schwoegler and Adkins hydrogenated butyronitrile and capronitrile in the presence of ammonia at 125° C using Raney nickel as a catalyst and obtained a 90–95 per cent yield of primary and only about 5 per cent of secondary amines. The preparation of high molecular weight amines from nitriles under rather high partial pressures of ammonia has been described.[95]

Conversion to secondary amines can be entirely suppressed by hydrogenating the nitrile in acetic anhydride which acetylates the primary amine as fast as formed and prevents further reaction with the intermediate imine.[96] Platinum catalysts must be used in this reaction.

In contrast to these procedures, the conversion to secondary amines is favored if the hydrogenation of the nitrile is effected at 200–250° C and the gaseous phase is periodically vented to prevent the build up of ammonia in the system.[97]

Unsaturated nitriles can be hydrogenated to unsaturated amines at 140–240° C and 100–1000 psi in the presence of a copper-chromium oxide catalyst. The catalyst preferably consists of 40–65 per cent CuO, 60–35 per cent Cr_2O_3 with a small amount of barium oxide as a stabilizer.[98]

Unsaturated amines can also be obtained by the reduction of unsaturated nitriles with sodium and an alcohol. A convenient method for the preparation of the unsaturated nitriles involves the reaction of sodium cyanide with the appropriate unsaturated halide. Thus 1-chloro-3-pentene is treated with potassium cyanide in ethylene glycol to give an 80 per cent yield of $CH_3CH=CHCH_2CH_2CN$ which is subsequently reduced with sodium and alcohol to give $CH_3CH=CHCH_2CH_2NH_2$. The alkyl halide may be obtained from the corresponding alcohol.[99]

In the commercial hydrogenation of higher molecular weight nitriles to a mixture of primary and secondary amines, a temperature of 150°C, a pressure of 200 psi, and a Raney nickel catalyst are used. Yields of about 85 per cent of primary amines may be obtained with the remainder being a mixture of secondary and tertiary amines. The tendency for the formation of higher alkylated products increases with temperature but decreases with increasing chain length. With nitriles having 12 or more carbon atoms, little or no tertiary amine is formed even at high temperatures.

Nitriles of fatty acids such as lauric, myristic, palmitic and stearic acids have been hydrogenated to primary amines at 120–135°C in the presence of a catalyst consisting of 25 per cent nickel on Kieselguhr.[100]

It has been reported that in the hydrogenation of high molecular weight nitriles (lauronitrile), the presence of basic substances such as ammonia, sodium hydroxide, methylamine or aniline materially decreases the yield of secondary amine.[101,102]

Renfrew and Warner[103] report that the yield of primary stearylamine can be increased to at least 90 per cent by hydrogenation of stearonitrile using a Raney nickel catalyst in the presence of ammonia and anhydrous ethanol (up to 10 per cent by weight of the nitrile). The hydrogenation is carried out at 130–155°C under a pressure of 220 psi.

Swendloff[104] reports that dinitriles can be partially hydrogenated to aminonitriles. Thus 108 g of adiponitrile and 31 g of Raney nickel, 178 g of methylal and 158 g of anhydrous liquid ammonia were charged in an autoclave and pressured with hydrogen to 1000 psi at 100°C. The hydrogenation was complete in 4 minutes to give an 84 per cent yield of 6-aminocapronitrile. Similarly a 66 per cent yield of 7-aminoheptanonitrile was obtained from pimelonitrile.

One of the most important commercial applications of the hydrogenation of nitriles to amines is the preparation of hexamethylenediamine from adipic acid by the following sequence of reactions:

$$HOOC(CH_2)_4COOH \xrightarrow[-H_2O]{NH_3, \text{ heat}} H_2NCO(CH_2)_4CONH_2 \xrightarrow[H_2O]{\text{heat}} NC(CH_2)_4CN \xrightarrow[Ni]{H_2}$$

$$H_2N(CH_2)_6NH_2$$

The reaction of adipic acid with ammonia gives the ammonium salt which is dehydrated first to the amide then to the nitrile. In practice neither the ammonium salt nor the amide is isolated.

A patent to Montecatini Chemical Co.[105] describes the preparation of hexamethylenediamine from a C_4 hydrocarbon stream containing about 16 per cent butadiene and 30 per cent isobutylene.

The isobutylene is first removed by absorption in 60 per cent sulfuric acid. The residual stream is then chlorinated at 220°C to give a mixture of 60 per cent dichlorobutenes and dichlorobutanes, 38 per cent monochlorobutenes and 2 per cent tetrachlorobutanes. The chlorinated hydrocarbons were next treated with HCN to form 1,4-dicyanobutene (from the dichlorobutenes) which is finally hydrogenated to give hexamethylenediamines. The dichlorobutanes do not react with hydrogen cyanide under the specified conditions but are removed by distillation and pyrolyzed at 600°C to give butadiene.

Adiponitrile may be hydrogenated to hexamethylenediamine in the liquid phase at 115–140°C and at 1200–2600 psi in the presence of a cobalt catalyst.[106]

In the continuous hydrogenation of adiponitrile to hexamethylenediamine a conversion of 80 per cent or better can be achieved in the presence of a nickel catalyst, if the catalyst chamber is sufficiently long. With an active catalyst and a high ratio of catalyst to dinitrile, the hydrogenation may be accomplished at temperatures as low as 80°C under a pressure of 50 atmospheres.

A decrease in the temperature to 60°C and in the pressure to 20 atmospheres results in decreased conversion to the diamine. An increase in temperature and pressure favors side reactions and increases the rate of deactivation of the catalyst.

The addition of as little as 0.24 per cent sodium hydroxide to the dinitrile decreases the yield of diamine and increases the yield of hexamethyleneimine.[107] Vanyushina *et al.*[108] investigated the hydrogenation of adiponitrile to hexamethylenediamine and report that the best selectivity and yield was obtained using a catalyst of cobalt on alumina. The reaction was carried out continuously in the liquid phase. Optimum conditions reported are: temperature 100°C, ratio of nitrile to hydrogen of 1:20 and of nitrile to ammonia 1:8.

Another method for the formation of diamines involves the addition of an amine to acrylonitrile and the subsequent hydrogenation of the amino nitrile. Thus methylamine adds to acrylonitrile to give $CH_3NHCH_2CH_2CN$ in 71 per cent yield. Hydrogenation in alcohol solution saturated with ammonia at 120°C and 2500 psi gives $CH_3NHCH_2CH_2CH_2NH_2$ in about 70 per cent yield.

Benkeser[110] reduced nitriles such as benzo- and benzylnitrile with lithium and methyl- or ethylamine. Thus benzonitrile gave methylaminocyclohexane in 47 per cent yield together with considerable quantities of tar. Benzylnitrile gave a mixture of β-(1-cyclohexenyl)-ethylamine (I) (51 per cent) and β-cyclohexylethylamine (II).

$$
\begin{array}{cc}
\underset{H_2C}{\overset{CH_2}{\diagup}}\ C - CH_2CH_2NH_2 & \underset{H_2C}{\overset{CH_2}{\diagup}}\ CHCH_2CH_2NH_2 \\
\end{array}
$$

I II

Reduction of Amides. Amides may be hydrogenated catalytically to a mixture of primary and secondary amines in much the same way as are nitriles except that considerably higher temperatures and pressures are required. In general, temperatures of 250–265°C and pressures of 200–300 atmospheres are required. Nickel, copper or copper chromite catalysts are usually used and hydrogenations are carried out in solvents such as dioxane.

Sabatier and Mailhe[111] hydrogenated propionamide to propylamine in the presence of nickel at 230°C.

The hydrogenation of lauramide and enanthamide at 175–250°C under pressures of 250 atmospheres in the presence of a copper-chromium oxide catalyst gives a 40–70 per cent yield of primary and a 25–50 per cent yield of secondary amines.[112]

Ueno[113] hydrogenated amides in the presence of a catalyst consisting of a mixture of zinc and chromium oxides to give a mixture of primary and secondary amines and some alcohol. Thus the hydrogenation of palmitamide ($C_{15}H_{31}CONH_2$) at 315–330°C and a pressure of 200 atmospheres gives dipalmitylamine ($C_{16}H_{33})_2NH$ together with palmitylamine ($C_{16}H_{33}NH_2$) and some palmityl alcohol. The yield of secondary amine increases with pressure up to 240 atmospheres. At pressures below 190 atmospheres the production of alcohol is favored and in the presence of ammonia (partial pressure 20–30 atmospheres) the yield of primary amine is increased with no appreciable change in the amount of secondary amine produced. The best yield of the secondary amine is about 40 per cent.

N-mono- and disubstituted amides give secondary and tertiary amines.[114]

Amides are also reduced to amines with lithium aluminum hydride in ether solution. Thus triethylamine has been obtained from N,N-diethylacetamide in 50 per cent yield and ethyl-n-propylamine from N-ethylpropionamide in 53 per cent yield.[115–118]

Amides have been reduced electrolytically to amines.[119,120]

The reduction of amides is of importance for the preparation of amines from N-substituted amides. For unsubstituted amides the best procedure would be dehydration to the corresponding nitrile followed by reduction using methods previously described.

Reduction of Nitroparaffins. This method is very important in the preparation of aromatic amines but finds only limited application in the production of aliphatic amines partly as a result of limited availability of the nitroparaffins and partly because the same amines can be made more economically by other methods. The method is of considerable importance in the preparation of amino alcohols and other substituted amines from corresponding nitro compounds. The preparation of these compounds will be described later.

The two best methods for the reduction of nitroparaffins are catalytic hydrogenation in the presence of Raney nickel or other catalyst and the reaction of a metal, such as iron, and hydrochloric acid.[121]

When iron and hydrochloric acid are employed in the reduction of nitroparaffins using an excess of acid (1.5 moles per mole nitroparaffin) the amines are obtained in better than 95 per cent yield. Sufficient hydrochloric acid must be present to keep the reaction mixture acidic throughout the reduction. If the medium becomes basic, the yield is materially decreased.

The nitro group is more readily hydrogenated than is a carbon-carbon double bond but nitroölefins can be converted to saturated amines in the presence of Raney nickel at slightly elevated temperatures and pressure.[122]

Nightingale and Tweedie[123] have hydrogenated unsaturated alicyclic nitro compounds to amines in the presence of Raney nickel and found that the nitro group is more readily reduced than the olefinic double bond. Thus at room temperature and 300 atmospheres 4-nitro-5-phenylcyclohexene was reduced to 6-phenyl-3-cyclohexenylamine in excellent yield. At 75°C and 200 atmospheres, only 2-phenylcyclohexylamine was obtained. At 50°C a mixture of both compounds were formed.

The yield of aminoparaffins by the hydrogenation of nitroparaffins can be improved if the hydrogenation is stopped when only partially complete and hydrochloric acid is added to convert the amine to a salt so that the unreacted nitroparaffin can be recovered and recycled. The free amine can be recovered by making the distillation residue alkaline by the addition of sodium hydroxide.

The process for the hydrogenation of nitroparaffins may be carried out in the presence of water-soluble diluents such as methyl or ethyl alcohol, or by hydrogenation in absence of a diluent. This method is usually preferred. The reduction product is treated with hydrochloric acid to adjust the pH to about 4, the unreacted nitroparaffin and hydrocarbon sometimes present are removed by steam distillation and the amine precipitated by the addition of sodium hydroxide.

Thus a C_{12} mononitroparaffin was hydrogenated in methanol at 100 atmospheres and 130°C. The methanol was removed by distillation. The product contained 18 per cent primary amine and 82 per cent nitroparaffin. Hydrogen chloride gas was introduced and unreacted nitroparaffin removed by steam distillation. Sodium hydroxide was added to cause a separation of an amine fraction which contained 76 per cent primary C_{12} aminoparaffins.

Kornblum and Fishbein[124] investigated the hydrogenation of optically active nitroparaffins in order to obtain information concerning the mechanism of the reaction. When optically active 2-nitrooctane is reduced by iron powder and acetic acid, optically active 2-aminooctane was obtained with very little racemization. They found that this reduction was 82 per cent stereospecific. The same reduction carried out with lithium aluminum hydride or catalytic reduction with a platinum catalyst gave complete racemization. The racemization resulted from salt formation between the nitroparaffin and the free amine formed. Salts of nitroparaffins racemize very quickly. This was substantiated by adding a few drops of 2-aminooctane to optically active 2-nitrooctane in alchol solution to effect racemization very quickly. When 2-nitrooctane was hydrogenated with a platinum catalyst in glacial acetic acid the reaction was greater than 72 per cent stereospecific.

It was postulated that lithium aluminum hydride causes racemization through salt formation with nitro compounds before reduction. If the solution remained acidic, tautomerism of the nitroparaffin was inhibited and therefore no racemization occurred.

Miscellaneous Reactions for the Preparation of Amines. Hexamethyl-enetetramine reacts with alkyl halides in chloroform or alcohol solutions to form quaternary ammonium salts which are readily converted to primary amines when heated.

$$RX + (CH_2)_6N_4 \longrightarrow (CH_2)_6N_4RX \xrightarrow[\text{heat}]{\text{HCl}} RNH_3Cl + NH_4Cl$$

The reaction proceeds very well with alkyl bromides or iodides but not very well with chlorides. Primary alkyl halides give yields ranging from 40–85 per cent but secondary and tertiary alkyl halides cannot be used successfully.

A well-known laboratory procedure for the preparation of primary amines is the Hoffman degradation of amides. In this procedure the amide is treated with sodium hydroxide and bromine, forming an isocyanate, which is rarely isolated but under the conditions of the experiment it is hydrolyzed to a primary amine and sodium carbonate.

$$RCONH_2 + Br_2 + 2NaOH \longrightarrow RNCO + 2NaBr + 2H_2O$$

$$RNCO + 2NaOH \longrightarrow RNH_2 + Na_2CO_3$$

The amine obtained contains one less carbon atom than the amide from which it is prepared. The reaction is usually carried out by dissolving the amide in a very slight excess of cold hypobromite solution followed by rapid heating. If the amine is steam volatile the reaction mixture is steam distilled as soon as the amide is added to the hypobromite solution.

The method has been used for the preparation of aliphatic, aromatic, aryl-aliphatic and heterocyclic amines and in general represents a good laboratory procedure. Yields for aliphatic amines containing not more than 8 carbon atoms are good, but with increasing molecular weight yields are decreased because of the formation of the corresponding nitriles and acyl aryl ureas.[125,126,127]

The low yields of amines can be accounted for by the fact that the isocyanates react rapidly with the intermediate haloamide salts to give salts of the alkyl acyl ureas.

$$RCONH_2 \xrightarrow[-HBr]{Br_2} RCONBr^- \xrightarrow{RNCO} RNCO-NBr-COR^- \xrightarrow[OBr]{H_2O} RNHCO-NHCOR$$

To obtain better yields with the higher molecular weight compounds, the amides are treated with bromine and sodium methoxide to form urethanes which are subsequently hydrolyzed.[128]

$$RCONH_2 + Br_2 + 2NaOCH_3 \rightarrow RNHCO_2CH_3 + 2NaBr + CH_3OH$$

These alkyl acyl ureas can be converted to amines but are also readily oxidized, by the hypobromite, to nitriles.

Lauramide when treated with aqueous hypobromite gives N-undecyl-N'-laurylurea as the major product[129] but when treated with sodium methoxide and bromine a 90 per cent yield of methylundecylcarbamate is obtained which may be converted almost quantitatively to undecylamine.

$$C_{11}H_{23}CONH_2 \xrightarrow[Br_2]{CH_3ONa} C_{11}H_{23}NHCO_2CH_3 \xrightarrow[H_2O]{OH^-} C_{11}H_{23}NH_2$$

Diamides having 6 or more carbon atoms are converted to diamines by treatment with aqueous alkaline hypobromite or hypochlorite. Thus adipamide is converted to 1,4-butanediamine.[130] Glutaramide on the other hand is converted to dihydrouracil which is apparently formed from the reaction leading to the alkyl acyl urea. α,β-Unsaturated amides are converted to urethanes in good yield with sodium methoxide and chlorine but the urethanes are hydrolyzed to aldehydes so that unsaturated amines cannot be successfully prepared by this method.

Isocyanates are readily hydrolyzed to amines as evidenced by the Hofmann degradation of amides in which they are intermediates. The method is not very practical, however, because one of the best procedures for the preparation of isocyanates involves the reaction of phosgene with amines. Substituted ureas also give amines on hydrolysis. Thus *tert*-butylamine has been obtained in 78 per cent yield by the alkaline hydrolysis of *tert*-butyl urea.[131]

Isothiocyanates and urethanes also give amines on hydrolysis but these compounds are not very available.

From an historical standpoint the Gabriel synthesis is one of the most important methods for the exclusive preparation of primary amines but it is not extensively used today. The method involves the conversion of phthalimide to the potassium salt, alkylation of the salt with an alkyl halide and hydrolysis of the resulting N-alkyl phthalimide.

The alkyl phthalimides were originally prepared by heating phthalimide, potassium carbonate and the organic halide in a nonpolar solvent for 2–24 hours at 100–150°C.[132]

In recent years a polar solvent such as dimethylformamide has been used and the reaction is complete in 10 minutes.[133]

Tertiary alkyl halides lose hydrogen chloride to form olefins in this re-action but *t*-alkylphthalimides can be prepared from *t*-alkylureas and phthalic anhydride at 200–240°C.[134]

The hydrolysis of the alkyl phthalimides can be carried out by refluxing in aqueous alkali or acid. Another procedure which gives improved yield involves the treatment of the N-alkylphthalimide with hydrazine hydrate. This procedure can be illustrated for the preparation of *tert*-butylamine.

Primary fatty amines have been prepared successfully by means of the Gabriel synthesis.[135] Thus cetylphthalimide is prepared from cetyl bromide and potassium phthalimide. This compound is then refluxed with hydrazine hydrate for about an hour and hydrochloric acid added to give cetyl amine. In a similar manner oleylamine is prepared from oleyl bromide and potassium phthalimide.

Secondary amines can be obtained by the reduction of Schiff's bases pre-pared from primary amines and aldehydes. The Schiff's bases are very read-ily hydrolyzed and are difficult to isolate. However, in conversion to secondary amines it is seldom necessary to isolate the pure compounds.

Unsymmetrical secondary amines have been prepared by the reduction of Schiff's bases with lithium aluminum hydride in ether solution. Thus propylbutylamine has been prepared in 79 per cent yield; butylisopropyl-amine in 71 per cent yield and isopropylisobutylamine in 71 per cent yield from the appropriate aldimines.[136]

It should be recognized that the reduction of Schiff's bases is equiva-lent to the reductive alkylation of aldehydes and ketones except that the reaction is carried out in two steps.

Substituted diamines are prepared by the hydrogenation of Schiff's bases made from a diamine and an aldehyde. Thus ethylenediamine with benzal-dehyde gives $C_6H_5CH{=}NCH_2CH_2N{=}CHC_6H_5$ which may be hydro-genated in methyl alcohol at 78–80°C and 135 atmospheres in the presence of Raney nickel to give $C_6H_5CH_2NHCH_2CH_2NHCH_2C_6H_5$.[137]

Southwood[138] effected the same reduction using sodium and a mixture of methyl and isopropyl alcohol. The N,N'-dibenzylethylenediamine was re-covered as the sulfate.

Alicyclic amines can frequently be prepared by the hydrogenation of the corresponding aryl amine. Cyclohexylamine is obtained by the continuous hydrogenation of aniline in the presence of a ruthenium catalyst at 220°C under a pressure of 500 psi. Yields are about 82 per cent.[139]

An older commercial method for the preparation of cyclohexylamine from aniline has been described by Carswell and Morrill.[140] Dicyclohexylamine is formed by the condensation of 2 molecules of cyclohexylamine, and N-phenylcyclohexylamine by the condensation of 1 molecule of cyclohexylamine with 1 of aniline.

$$2C_6H_{11}NH_2 \longrightarrow (C_6H_{11})_2NH + NH_3$$
$$C_6H_{11}NH_2 + C_6H_5NH_2 \longrightarrow C_6H_{11}NHC_6H_5 + NH_3$$

The direct synthesis of amines has been accomplished by passing a mixture of 31 per cent carbon monoxide, 61 per cent hydrogen, and 8 per cent ammonia over a promoted iron catalyst at 210°C and 200 atmospheres. The liquid product obtained, contains amines formed in 8 per cent yield. Increasing the ammonia concentration to 30 per cent increased the yield of amines to about 50 per cent. Increasing the reaction time also increases the yield of amines. The product contained a wide variety of amines boiling from 48° at 4 mm to 150° at 10 mm pressure. The amines are largely primary with smaller amounts of secondary and tertiary amines.[141]

Reppe[142] also described a process for obtaining amines from olefins, carbon monoxide and ammonia. Thus 15.6 per cent aqueous ammonia and iron pentacarbonyl are treated in an autoclave at 120–135°C with a 2:1 ethylene-carbon monoxide mixture under 180–200 atmospheres to give a product containing n-$C_3H_7NH_2$, $(C_3H_7)_2NH$ and $(C_3H_7)_3N$ in a ratio of 2:2:1. Using methylamine in place of ammonia gives $C_3H_7NHCH_3$ and $(C_3H_7)_2NCH_3$ in a ratio of 4.5:1.

Substituted amines are prepared from olefins, water and substituted ammonium formate at 80–160°C under pressure with metal carbonyls or methyl carbonyl hydrides as catalysts. Thus a stainless steel autoclave was charged with aqueous dimethylamine and neutralized with formic acid. Iron pentacarbonyl was added; the air was replaced with nitrogen and a mixture of ethylene and carbon monoxide (mole ratio 1:2) introduced at a temperature of 130°C. A mixture of $(CH_3)_2NC_3H_7$ and $CH_3N(C_3H_7)_2$ was obtained.[143]

When carbon monoxide under high pressure was passed into a mixture of butene, dimethylamine and iron pentacarbonyl, it is readily absorbed but no pentylamine was formed as long as the iron pentacarbonyl was not decomposed. At lower pressures the carbonyl was decomposed to ferrous carbonate and pentylamines were readily formed in an amount not exceeding twice the ferrous carbonate formed.[144] This supports the proposal of Reppe that the reaction proceeds according to the equation.

$$Fe(CO)_5 + 2C_4H_8 + 2(CH_3)_2NH + 2H_2O \longrightarrow$$
$$2C_5H_{11}N(CH_3)_2 + FeCO_3 + 2CO_2$$

The gaseous carbon monoxide apparently does not participate in the reaction and the absorbed CO is used up in the formation of dimethyl-formamide.

Amines have been obtained from olefins by reaction with carbon monoxide and hydrogen at elevated temperatures and pressures and the subsequent hydrogenation of the product in the presence of ammonia or a primary amine.[145] Thus butylene was heated under a pressure of 120 atmospheres with synthesis gas $(CO + H_2)$ in the presence of a cobalt-manganese oxide-iron on pumice catalyst. The mixture was cooled, a methanolic solution of ammonia added and the mixture hydrogenated at 170° C and 200 atmospheres. Amylamine was obtained in about 40 per cent yield in addition to a considerable fraction containing a mixture of amines.

The intermediate formed from a Grignard reagent and a nitrile may be reduced to an amine by lithium aluminum hydride. To illustrate the reaction, propionitrile was added to phenylmagnesium bromide in ether and refluxed for 2 hours. Lithium aluminum hydride in tetrahydrofuran was then introduced and the mixture refluxed for an additional 18 hours. The complex thus formed was decomposed with water to give an 80 per cent yield of 1-phenyl-1-aminopropane.

Phenylmagnesium bromide reacts with propionitrile to give an intermediate imine which when reduced with lithium aluminum hydride gives 1-phenyl-1-aminopropane. 2-amino-1-phenylbutane, 3-aminopentane and 1,2-diphenylethylamine[146] were prepared in a similar manner.

Ethylenediamine can be converted to monoacylated or monoalkylated products with very little reaction occurring on the second nitrogen. Thus ethylenediamine (70 per cent aqueous solution) and ethyl acetate react on standing at room temperature for several days to give $H_2N-CH_2CH_2-NH-COCH_3$ in 60 per cent yield.

Reaction of ethylenediamine with methyl iodide in alcoholic potassium hydroxide gives $CH_3NHCH_2CH_2NH_2$ in 80 per cent yield.[147]

Urethanes have been successfully reduced by lithium aluminum hydride in ether to give excellent yields of secondary amines. In contrast with the reduction of amides which are frequently cleaved to give the original amine, no cleavage products are obtained.

As an example, N-methyl-N-phenylurethane was added to an ether solution of lithium aluminum hydride to give a product which when hydrolyzed gave dimethylaniline in 96 per cent yield.[148]

Propargylamine has been prepared in 50 per cent yield from $C_6H_5SO_3$-$CH_2C\equiv CH$ and hexamethylenetetramine.[149] The propargyl phenylsulfonate can be made in excellent yield by the action of phenylsulfonyl chloride on propargyl alcohol.

$$HC\equiv C-CH_2OH + C_6H_5SO_2Cl \longrightarrow C_6H_5SO_3CH_2C\equiv CH + HCl$$

Hexamethylenetetramine forms, in almost quantitative yield, an addition compound with the propargylsulfonyl ester which is decomposed with dilute hydrochloric acid to give the propargylamine.

Olin and Deger[150] report that secondary amines such as diamylamines or secondary-cyclohexylamines can be converted back into the corresponding primary amine by passing the secondary amine and ammonia over a catalyst consisting of manganese oxide supported on activated carbon.

Tetrasubstituted diamines have been prepared according to the following scheme:[151]

$$HOCH_2CH_2OH + C_6H_5SO_2Cl \longrightarrow C_6H_5OSO_2-CH_2CH_2-OSO_2C_6H_5 \xrightarrow{2R_2NH}$$
$$R_2N-CH_2CH_2-NR_2 + 2C_6H_5OSO_2H$$

The secondary amine is heated with the glycol disulfonate at 50–150° C.

Reactions of Amines

Salt Formation. Amines are bases and consequently react with acids to form salts which resemble ammonium salts and which, for the most part, are soluble in water. This property can frequently be used to separate amines from other materials. Thus amines may be extracted from a mixture of water-insoluble compounds by extraction with dilute hydrochloric acid. Conversely amines, such as the ethanolamines, are used to extract acid gases such as carbon dioxide, hydrogen sulfide or sulfur dioxide from waste gases. The salt decomposes on heating and permits the recovery of the acid gas.

Ammonium nitrites such as diisopropylammonium nitrite or dicyclohexylammonium nitrite are excellent vapor-phase corrosion inhibitors.

Amines form salts with carboxylic acids which are readily dehydrated to amides on heating to high temperatures, preferably in the presence of a dehydrating agent such as phosphorus pentoxide.

$$RCOONH_3R' \longrightarrow RCONHR' + H_2O$$

Direct condensation of ethylenediamine with fatty acids at 200° C gives imidazolines and diamides but no monoamides.

$$RCOOH + H_2NCH_2CH_2NH_2 \longrightarrow R-C \underset{NH}{\overset{N}{\lessgtr}} \overset{CH_2}{\underset{CH_2}{|}} +$$

$$RCONHCH_2CH_2NHCOR$$

Dehydration catalysts may be used to lower the reaction temperature.

Ammonolysis of monoesters with diamines gives a mixture of mono- and diamides. This reaction is very slow but may be catalyzed with sodamide under anhydrous conditions.[152]

2-Benzylimadazole hydrochloride is the chief product obtained when ethylenediamine reacts with phenylacetic acid.[153]

$$C_6H_5CH_2COOH + H_2NCH_2CH_2NH_2 \longrightarrow C_6H_5CH_2-C \underset{NH}{\overset{N}{\lessgtr}} \overset{CH_2}{\underset{CH_2}{|}} + 2H_2O$$

The ethylenediamine and phenylacetic acid were added to concentrated hydrochloric acid and heated for 2 hours at 240° C. On the addition of water a small amount of N,N'-di(phenylacetyl)ethylenediamine precipitated. The filtrate was concentrated and cooled to yield 2-benzylimidazole hydrochloride.

The salts of high molecular weight fatty amines and organic acids are used as cationic detergents and surface-active agents. An example of such a product is octadecylammonium acetate, $[CH_3(CH_2)_{17}NH_3]^+[OCOCH_3]^-$, which in addition to being a very excellent surface-active agent is also effective as a bactericide.

Acylation and Sulfonylation. Primary and secondary amines react with acid halides and acid anhydrides to form N-substituted amides.

$$RNH_2 + (CH_3CO)_2O \longrightarrow CH_3-CO-NHR + CH_3COOH$$

$$R_2NH + (CH_3CO)_2O \longrightarrow CH_3-CO-NR_2 + CH_3COOH$$

$$2RNH_2 + R'COCl \longrightarrow R'CONR_2 + RNH_3Cl$$

Tertiary amines have no hydrogen attached to the nitrogen atom and consequently cannot undergo this reaction. The primary amine has two active hydrogen atoms and might be expected to react with two molecules of anhydride or acyl halide. The second hydrogen is much less reactive than the first so that this replacement rarely occurs, even under rather drastic conditions. In contrast with the amine which is basic, the amide is neutral or in some cases has acidic properties. This arises as a result of the un-shared pair of electrons on the nitrogen being placed under great restraint by the presence of the electronegative acyl group which makes this electron pair less available for the formation of a coordinate bond with a proton or an atom having only a sextet of electrons.

Amines react with acid chlorides in much the same way as with anhydrides. Inasmuch as the acid chlorides are usually more readily prepared than the corresponding anhydrides, this reaction is probably more widely used. An excess of amine is desirable to react with the hydrogen chloride formed in the reaction. Benzoyl chloride is frequently used to prepare solid derivatives of primary or secondary amines.

$$C_6H_5COCl + 2RNH_2 \longrightarrow C_6H_5CONHR + RNH_3Cl$$

$$C_6H_5COCl + 2R_2NH \longrightarrow C_6H_5CONR_2 + R_2NH_2Cl$$

Formyl chloride does not exist but formyl fluoride can be obtained. It reacts with amines to give compounds of the type RNHCHO. The reaction is carried out by adding formyl fluoride to the appropriate amine in absolute ether at ice-salt temperatures and permitting the temperature to rise slowly to 18° C.[154] The yields reported for the various compounds prepared are: 81 per cent CH_3CH_2NHCHO, 84 per cent $(CH_3CH_2)_2NCHO$, 81 per cent C_6H_5NHCHO and 94 per cent $(C_6H_5)_2NCHO$.

The reaction with benzenesulfonyl chloride has been used as a means of classification and of separation of amines. Primary and secondary amines react with benzenesulfonyl chloride to give sulfonamides which are not readily soluble in ether. The reactions are carried out in the presence of aqueous sodium hydroxide.

$$RNH_2 + C_6H_5SO_2Cl \xrightarrow{\text{NaOH}} C_6H_5SO_2NHR + NaCl + H_2O$$

$$R_2NH + C_6H_5SO_2Cl + NaOH \longrightarrow C_6H_5SO_2NR_2 + NaCl + H_2O$$

The tertiary amine does not react and can be removed by ether extraction.

The sulfonamide prepared from the primary amine has a hydrogen attached to the nitrogen which is acidic and forms a salt with the sodium hydroxide.

$$C_6H_5SO_2NHR + NaOH \longrightarrow [C_6H_5SO_2\overset{\ominus}{N}R]\ Na^+ + H_2O$$

Consequently this sulfonamide will be found in the aqueous layer.

Inasmuch as there is no hydrogen attached to the nitrogen of the sulfonamide prepared from the secondary amine, no salt formation can occur and consequently the sulfonamide will be found in the organic layer immiscible with water.

After separation of the sulfonamides, the amines may be recovered by acid hydrolysis.

The reaction with benzenesulfonyl chloride, usually called the Hinsberg reaction, is particularly useful in distinguishing among primary, secondary and tertiary amines because the reaction in each case is quite different.

One interesting application of the Hinsberg reaction involves the alkylation of the sodium salt of the sulfonamide, made from the primary amine with dimethyl sulfate or other convenient alkylating agent, and the subsequent hydrolysis of the amide to give a secondary amine.

$$RNH_2 \xrightarrow[NaOH]{C_6H_5SO_2Cl} [C_6H_5SO_2\overset{\ominus}{N}-R]\ Na^+ \xrightarrow{(CH_3)_2SO_4}$$

$$C_6H_5SO_2-\underset{\underset{CH_3}{|}}{N}-R \xrightarrow[H^+]{H_2O} C_6H_5SO_3H + RNHCH_3$$

Reactions with Nitrous Acid. Nitrous acid reacts with primary amines with the liberation of nitrogen and the formation of alcohols.

$$RNH_2 + HONO \longrightarrow ROH + N_2 + H_2O$$

Although the nitrogen is liberated quantitatively the yields of alcohols are very poor. Where alcohols are formed, rearrangement of the alkyl chain is common. The reaction possible proceeds as follows:

$$RNH_2 + HONO \longrightarrow R-\overset{\overset{\displaystyle H}{|}}{N}-N=O \longrightarrow R-N=N-OH \longrightarrow ROH + N_2$$

The yield of alcohol is improved if the reaction is carried out at a pH of about 3, but considerable dehydration to olefins will also occur.

Rearrangement is more likely to occur at higher pH. Thus *n*-propylamine gives isopropyl alcohol, propylene, and a trace of *n*-propyl alcohol. No methyl alcohol is obtained by the reaction of nitrous acid on methylamine.

The action of nitrous acid (sodium nitrite and hydrochloric acid) on *n*-butylamine gives *n*-butyl alcohol (13.2 per cent), butene (36.5 per cent), *n*-butyl chloride (5.2 per cent), *sec*-butyl chloride (2.8 per cent), and higher boiling materials (7.6 per cent).[11]

Although the deamination of amines to alcohols with nitrous acid is not very successful because of the low yields of alcohols produced, it can be successfully accomplished to give an ester by the following series of reactions.

$$RNH_2 \longrightarrow RNH{-}COR' \longrightarrow R{-}\overset{\displaystyle NO}{\underset{|}{N}}{-}COR' \longrightarrow RO{-}COR' + N_2$$

The reaction is considered to proceed through a rearrangement of the N-alkyl-N-nitrosamide to give a diazoester which loses nitrogen. Two competing reactions occur; one gives the ester and nitrogen, the other gives an acid, an olefin and nitrogen.[155]

$$RCH_2CH_2{-}\overset{\displaystyle N{=}O}{\underset{|}{N}}{-}COR' \longrightarrow RCH_2CH_2{-}N{=}N{-}OCOR'$$

$$N_2 + R'COOH + RCH{=}CH_2 \qquad\qquad N_2 + RCH_2CH_2OCOR'$$

Secondary amines react with nitrous acid to give nitrosamines.

$$R_2NH + HONO \longrightarrow R_2N{-}NO + H_2O$$

These compounds are usually oily yellow liquids which are sparingly soluble in water. They may be hydrolyzed back to the amine by boiling in dilute hydrochloric acid.

Tertiary amines have no active hydrogen atoms and consequently do not react with nitrous acid except to form salts.

The nature of the highly reactive intermediates formed during the reaction of aliphatic amines with nitrous acid have been investigated.[156] A carbonium ion mechanism is consistent with the reaction products which have been identified by infrared analysis. Isobutylamine and nitrous acid gave *iso-*, *sec-*, and *t*-butyl alcohols and 1-butene, *cis-* and *trans*-2-butene and isobutylene but no *n*-butyl alcohol. *t*-Butylamine gave *t*-butyl alcohol and isobutylene but no rearranged products. *Sec*-Butylamine gave *sec*-butyl alcohol, 1-butene and *cis-* and *trans*-2-butene. Quantitatively it was observed that a free carbonium ion mechanism did not account for the observed ratio of elimination to substitution products.

When thiocyanate ions were added to the reaction mixture, thiocyanates and isothiocyanates were obtained as initial products in addition to alcohols and olefins. This is consistent with a carbonium ion mechanism. Isobutylamine and nitrous acid gave *iso-*, *sec-* and *t*-butyl thiocyanates and isothiocyanates; *t*-butylamine gives *t*-butylthiocyanate and isothiocyanate; and *sec*-butylamine gives *sec*-butylthiocyanate and isothiocyanate.

Reaction with Aldehydes. Primary amines react with aldehydes to form aldimines or Schiff's bases.

$$RNH_2 + CH_3CH_2CHO \longrightarrow CH_3CH_2CH{=}NR + H_2O$$

These compounds are weak bases in that they form salts by coordination of the unshared electron pair on the nitrogen with a proton. They are, however, much weaker bases than ammonia and form salts only with strong acids. Schiff's bases are readily hydrolyzed to the aldehyde and the amine so that they are quite difficult to isolate. Isolation is further complicated by the tendency to polymerize to complex products. Reduction of Schiff's bases give secondary amines.

The polymerization of Schiff's bases is of the aldol type. Ethylidenethylamine, $(CH_3CH_2N{=}CHCH_3)$, treated with sodium in liquid ammonia produced a product which on reduction gave 1,3-di-(ethylimino)-butane in 60 per cent yield.

n-Butylidene-*n*-butylamine may be converted to 2-ethyl-2-hexenylbutylamine by merely heating at 140–150 for 3 hours.[157]

$$2C_3H_7CH{=}NC_4H_9 \longrightarrow \left[\begin{array}{c} C_2H_5{-}CH{-}CH{=}NC_4H_9 \\ | \\ C_4H_9NHCH{-}C_3H_7 \end{array} \right] \longrightarrow$$

$$C_2H_5{-}\underset{\underset{CH{-}C_3H_7}{\|}}{C}{-}CH{=}N{-}C_4H_9 + C_4H_9NH_2$$

The purely aliphatic aldimines containing 5 to 10 carbon atoms can be obtained in 50–80 per cent yield but because of their instability should be used as soon as possible after distillation. Aldimines from substituted benzaldehydes and alkyl or arylamines are very much more stable.

The formation of Schiff's bases with ketones is much more difficult and can only be accomplished with alkyl aryl ketones such as acetophenone at temperatures of 160–180° C in the presence of a zinc chloride-aryl amine salt. The reaction is of little use with alkyl amines.

The rate of reaction between piperonal and primary amines cannot be correlated with the basicity of the amines. However, a linear relationship exists between the log K and the free energies of dissociation of the corresponding addition compounds $RNH_2 \cdot B(CH_3)_3$. This indicates that structural effects play a significant rate in the reaction.[159]

Alkanolamines may also form Schiff's bases with aldehydes. Thus ethanolamine added dropwise to a stirred mixture of *p*-nitrobenzaldehyde and water at 80–90° C gave $4\text{-}O_2N{-}C_6H_4CH{=}NCH_2CH_2OH$ in about 90 per cent yield. *Ortho*- and *meta*-nitrobenzaldehydes behaved similarly.[158]

Terephthalaldehyde reacts with diamines to give polymeric Schiff's bases:[160]

$$H_2N(CH_2)_nNH_2 + OHC—C_6H_4—CHO \longrightarrow$$

$$H_2N(CH_2)_n(N=CH—C_6H_4—CH=N(CH_2)_n)_m—N=CH—C_6H_4—CHO$$

Schiff's bases react with Grignard reagents as indicated in the following example

$$C_6H_5CH=NR + R'MgBr \longrightarrow C_6H_5—\underset{\underset{R'}{|}}{C}H—NR$$

The reaction is quite general and is effective with hydroxy- and alkoxy-substituted benzaldehydes, with a wide variety of Grignard reagents and primary or secondary aliphatic amines.

With higher Grignard reagents and especially with large alkyl groups on the nitrogen atom it is necessary to use an excess of the Grignard reagent. Yields of product vary from about 30–75 per cent and are quite sensitive to structure.

In addition to the addition product indicated above a certain amount of dimer

$$RNH—\underset{\underset{C_6H_5}{|}}{C}H—\underset{\underset{C_6H_5}{|}}{C}H—NHR$$

is also obtained. The formation of the dimer increases with the length of the alkyl group (R) and the amount of branching in R' of the Grignard reagent.

The Schiff's base is refluxed in dry ether with the Grignard reagent and the reaction mixture subsequently treated with sodium hydroxide and ice.[161]

The following results were reported.

R	R'	X	% Dimer	% Add'n Product
CH_3	CH_3	I	none	72
CH_3	C_2H_5	I	trace	67
CH_3	C_3H_7	Br	2.0	59

Ammonia or amines add to the carbon-carbon double bond of α,β-unsaturated aldehydes or ketones. Under some conditions the carbonyl group also undergoes reductive alkylation.[162] Robinson and Olin affected the reaction in the presence of a hydrogenation catalyst at 75–175° C and 600–1800 psi. Thus a solution of crotonaldehyde in methanol was added to anhydrous ammonia containing a small amount of Raney nickel at 150°C under an atmosphere of hydrogen at a total pressure of 1000–1600 psi to give a mixture of CH_3—$CHNH_2$—$CH_2CH_2NH_2$ and $CH_3CH_2CH_2$-CH_2NH_2.

Methyl vinyl ketone was treated with aqueous methylamine (31 per cent) at 20–30°C for 1.5 hours and distilled to give a fraction boiling between 80° and 120°C at 10 mm pressure. This fraction partially dissolved in ether. The ether-soluble fraction yielded white crystals which melted at 85°C. The ether-insoluble portion melted at 130°C. These compounds were found to be isomers of 1,4-dimethyl-3-acetyl-4-hydroxypiperidine.[163]

Acrolein reacts at 5–10°C with excess isopropylamine in the presence of anhydrous K_2CO_3 to form N,N-diisopropyl-1,3-propenediamine in 50 per cent yield. The isopropylamine adds to the double bond as well as to the carbonyl group. The resulting amino alcohol is subsequently dehydrated to the product isolated.[164,165]

$$(i\text{-}C_3H_7)_2NH + CH_2{=}CH{-}CHO \longrightarrow$$
$$(i\text{-}C_3H_7)_2NCH_2CH_2CHOH{-}N(i\text{-}C_3H_7)_2 \longrightarrow$$
$$(i\text{-}C_3H_7)_2N{-}CH_2CH{=}CH{-}N(i\text{-}C_3H_7)_2 + H_2O$$

Hydrogenation of the propenediamines gave 1,3-propanediamines.

When the propenediamines were heated with other amines one or both of the amine components of the propenediamine were replaced by the added amine.[166] Either one or both of the amine groups may be replaced depending, in part, on the extent of substitution on the nitrogen of the substituting amine and of the amine groups of the propenediamine. With alkylamines, amine exchange is rapid if the substituting amine is of lower order than the amine group of the propenediamine. Substitution of the second amino group is slow with amine groups of the same order and rapid with amino groups of higher order than the substituting group. Thus N,N'-diisopropyl-1,3-propenediamine reacts with 1,3-dimethylbutylamine to give N-(1,3-dimethylbutyl)-N'-isopropyl-1,3-propenediamine and a small amount of the disubstituted product.

Secondary aliphatic amines also react with α,β-unsaturated aldehydes to give unsaturated diamines. Thus acrolein reacts with dimethylamine to give $(CH_3)_2N{-}CH_2CH{=}CH{-}N(CH_3)_2$. All water must be carefully removed from the reaction and this can be accomplished by adding a large quantity of anhydrous potassium carbonate. The temperature must be held within rather narrow limits. Below −10°C the reaction does not take place and above 20°C large amounts of resinous products are formed.

The reaction products, usually oily liquids, darken quickly in air and decompose on heating so that many cannot be distilled, even at very low pressures. These compounds are readily hydrolyzed when shaken with water with the formation of the original aldehyde. Both amino groups are removed but not at the same time. The amino group next to the double bond is removed first.

Careful hydrogenation gives the diamine.

Aldehydes investigated include acrolein, crotonaldehyde and cinnamaldehyde. The amines used were dimethylamine and piperidine.[167]

Oxidation. Amines are readily oxidized with the initial attack occurring on the nitrogen atom. In most cases it is difficult to isolate useful products from the oxidation of primary or secondary amines but tertiary amines react with hydrogen peroxide to give amine oxides, $R_3N{\rightarrow}O$, or the corresponding hydrated product $R_3N(OH)_2$. Thus trimethylamine reacts with aqueous hydrogen peroxide to give a hydrate (m.p. 98° C) which on warming in a vacuum yields the anhydrous amine oxide (m.p. 208° C). Inasmuch as nitrogen can exhibit a maximum covalence of four, the hydrate is a quaternary ammonium hydroxide in which the fifth valence is ionic.

$$\left[\begin{array}{c} CH_3 \\ | \\ CH_3-N-OH \\ | \\ CH_3 \end{array} \right]^+ \quad OH^-$$

This structure is supported by the properties of the compound. The bond between the nitrogen and oxygen in the amine oxide is a coordinate one in which both electrons are furnished by the nitrogen. It may be represented by

$$R_3N{\rightarrow}O \quad \text{or} \quad \overset{(+)\ (-)}{R_3N:\overset{..}{\underset{..}{O}}:}$$

The oxidation of halogenated tertiary amines gives the corresponding N-oxides. Thus N,N,N′N′-tetrakis(β-chloroethyl)trimethylenediamine in ether solution was oxidized with peracetic acid at temperatures below 30° C to give N,N,N′N′-tetrakis(β-chloroethyl)trimethylenediamine-N,N′-dioxide.[168]

$$(ClCH_2CH_2)_2NCH_2CH_2CH_2N(CH_2CH_2Cl)_2 + CH_3CO-OOH \longrightarrow$$

$$(ClCH_2CH_2)_2\underset{\underset{O}{\downarrow}}{N}CH_2CH_2CH_2\underset{\underset{O}{\downarrow}}{N}(CH_2CH_2Cl)_2 + CH_3COOH$$

Allylmethylaniline oxide and allylethylaniline oxide rearrange on heating with aqueous sodium hydroxide to give O-allyl-N-alkyl-N-phenylhydroxylamines.

$$CH_2\!=\!CH\!-\!CH_2\!-\!\underset{\underset{CH_3}{|}}{\overset{\overset{C_6H_5}{|}}{N}}\!\rightarrow\!O \;\longrightarrow\; C_6H_5\!-\!\underset{\underset{CH_3}{|}}{N}\!-\!O\!-\!CH_2CH\!=\!CH_2$$

Benzylmethylaniline oxide behaves similarly. The role of sodium hydroxide is apparently to free the amine oxide from its salts.

Allyldimethylamine oxide and allyldiethylamine oxide do not rearrange on heating with sodium hydroxide.[169] The amine oxides were recovered unchanged or were converted in small amounts to dimethyl- or diethyl-amine.

It has been suggested that the difference in reaction is related to the greater tendency for the allylalkylamine oxides to form hydrates. This hydration would be expected to reduce the activity of the unshared electron pairs of the amine oxide oxygen. Cope and Towles[170] found that if the allyldimethylamine oxide solution (prepared by the action of 10 per cent hydrogen peroxide on the tertiary amine) was concentrated to a thick syrup and heated to 105–110°C for one-half hour rearrangement to the corresponding hydroxylamine resulted in yields of about 50 per cent. The excess hydrogen peroxide had to be removed by decomposition in the presence of platinum foil.

This was found to be a general method for the rearrangement of allyl-alkylamine oxides.

N,N-dimethyl-(α-phenylethyl)-amine oxide does not rearrange to give trialkylhydroxylamines (RR'N—OR'') but instead is converted to styrene and N,N-dimethylhydroxylamine.[171]

$$CH_3\!-\!\underset{\underset{C_6H_5}{|}}{CH}\!-\!\underset{\underset{CH_3}{|}}{\overset{\overset{CH_3}{|}}{N}}\!\rightarrow\!O \;\longrightarrow\; C_6H_5CH\!=\!CH_2 + (CH_3)_2NOH$$

In an earlier paper Mamlock and Wolffenstein[172] reported that tri-*n*-propylamine oxide decomposes on heating to give propylene and N,N-di-*n*-propylhydroxylamine but this report was not given much attention.

This represents a good method for preparation of olefins from some amine oxides but the reaction is not too general.

The vapor-phase oxidation of triethylamine at 200°C gives ethylamine, diethylamine and acetaldehyde as the major products. At higher temperatures the oxidation becomes autocatalytic and the yield of acetaldehyde decreases rapidly. The effects at lower temperatures are explained by the inhibiting action toward oxidation exerted by the amines.[173]

Amines can be oxidized to nitriles by passing a mixture of the amine, air and steam over a silver catalyst at temperatures of 450–600°C. This method has been used for the preparation of acrylonitrile and methacrylonitrile from the corresponding unsaturated amines.

$$CH_2=CH-CH_2NH_2 + O_2 \longrightarrow CH_2=CHCN + 2H_2O$$

The catalyst consists of a thin layer of silver deposited on porous silicon carbide. Approximately 1.2 moles of oxygen, in the form of air, is used per mole of amine and 6–12 pounds of steam per mole of amine is used as a diluent. A contact time of 0.02 second is sufficient to effect complete conversion of the amine, and yields of nitrile as high as 90 per cent, based on the amine, have been reported.[174]

Florentine[175] reports that the action of ozone on a primary aliphatic or aromatic amine in an inert solvent at temperatures below 50°C gives acids. Thus *n*-decylamine treated with ozone in the absence of a solvent gives a 27 per cent yield of decanoic acid and a nitrogen-containing residue presumably derived from decanal. Ozonolysis of *n*-decylamine in methanol gives a 52 per cent yield of decanoic acid.

Reactions with Olefin Oxides. Primary and secondary amines react with ethylene oxide to give ethanolamines.

$$R_2NH + \underset{\underset{O}{\diagdown\diagup}}{CH_2-CH_2} \longrightarrow R_2N-CH_2CH_2-OH$$

$$RNH_2 + \underset{\underset{O}{\diagdown\diagup}}{CH_2-CH_2} \longrightarrow RNH-CH_2CH_2OH$$

The alkanolamines formed from a primary amine still have a hydrogen atom attached to the nitrogen so that further reaction can occur to give a dialkanolamine.

$$RNH-CH_2CH_2OH + \underset{\underset{O}{\diagdown\diagup}}{CH_2-CH_2} \longrightarrow RN(CH_2CH_2OH)_2$$

Although the lower molecular weight olefin oxides do not react with anhydrous ammonia at ordinary temperatures and pressures, they will react readily with anhydrous mono- and dialkanolamines to form trialkanolamines. Ethylene oxide reacts with monoethanolamine at temperatures of 30°C. Triethanolamine is obtained in 80 per cent yield.[176] Triethanolamine is converted to N-(2-hydroxyethyl) morpholine in the presence of cation exchange resins (polystyrenesulfonic acids).[177]

$$
\begin{array}{c}
\text{HO} \\
\text{HO}
\end{array}
\Big\rangle
\begin{array}{c}
\diagup CH_2\!-\!CH_2 \diagdown \\
\qquad\qquad N\!-\!CH_2CH_2OH \\
\diagdown CH_2\!-\!CH_2 \diagup
\end{array}
\longrightarrow
\;\;O
\begin{array}{c}
\diagup CH_2\!-\!CH_2 \diagdown \\
\qquad\qquad N\!-\!CH_2CH_2OH \\
\diagdown CH_2\!-\!CH_2 \diagup
\end{array}
$$

Ethanolamine and ethylene oxide will react in the absence of a solvent to give diethanolamine.[178] Thus ethylene oxide and ethanolamine in a mole ratio of 6.85:1 were passed through a reactor immersed in boiling water at a rate sufficient to give a residence time of 95 seconds. The pressure was held at 30–40 atmospheres to maintain a liquid phase. The product contained 79 per cent unreacted ethanolamine, 19 per cent diethanol- and 2 per cent triethanolamine.

The formation of dialkanolamines may take place in one step at temperatures of 80–275°C under sufficient pressure to maintain a liquid phase, in the presence of water or alcohol as a solvent. The reaction is dependent on the amount of water or alcohol used. Thus ethylene oxide was added to a 20 per cent solution of methylamine in water (mole ratio of amine to oxide 1:2) and the solution passed continuously through a reactor immersed in boiling water. A reaction time of 33 seconds gave a 95 per cent yield of methyldiethanolamine $(HOCH_2CH_2)_2NCH_3$.[179]

In a similar manner, diethylamine and propylene oxide in methanol solution gave a 96 per cent yield of $CH_3CH(OH)CH_2N(CH_2CH_3)_2$; equimolar amounts of laurylamine and ethylene oxide in methanol gave $HOCH_2\text{-}CH_2NHC_{12}H_{25}$.

The reactions are acid- or base-catalyzed and frequently are carried out in the presence of a base other than the amine itself. Thus lauryl- or stearylamine treated with ethylene oxide at 110–230°C in the presence of a base gave N,N-bis(β-hydroxyethyl)alkylamine $C_{12}H_{25}N(CH_2CH_2OH)_2$. Catalysts investigated in order of decreasing activity are sodium, potassium hydroxide, sodium hydroxide, potassium carbonate and sodium carbonate.[180]

The rate of condensation of stearylamine with ethylene oxide increases with temperature between 110 and 230°C with optimum temperatures being 150–190°C. Noncatalytic condensation yielded mainly the dihydroxyethyltertiaryamines. With strong alkali catalysts the distribution of products was more scattered than with the weaker ones.[181] Pure dry diethylamine does not react with ethylene oxide. However, a 75 per cent yield of β-diethylaminoethyl alcohol is obtained when ethylene oxide is passed into diethylamine in methanol at 45–60°C.[182]

Long, Hascher and Moore[183] treated a lower molecular weight olefin oxide with an anhydrous alkanolamine to give polyalkanolamines. Thus liquid ethylene oxide added to anhydrous monoethanolamine at 10°C gives a product containing 90.6 per cent triethanolamine, 2.4 per cent diethanolamine and 6.7 per cent higher boiling products.

In addition to the amino hydrogens, the hydroxyl hydrogens of the alkanolamines formed will react further with olefins oxides. Polyoxyethylene-alkylamines may be prepared by condensing lauryl or stearylamine with ethylene oxide in the absence of a catalyst or in the presence of sodium or potassium hydroxides or carbonates. Optimum temperatures are 150–190°C. In the absence of a catalyst the chief product is N,N-bis(2-hydroxyethyl)laurylamine.

Compounds of the type

$$C_{12}H_{25}N \begin{cases} C_2H_4OH \\ C_2H_4-(OC_2H_4)_n-OH \end{cases}$$

were also obtained.[181]

With olefin oxides other than ethylene oxide, two isomers may result. Thus with propylene oxide the reaction may proceed as follows:

$$CH_3-CH \overset{\displaystyle \diagup}{\underset{\displaystyle O}{\diagdown}} CH_2 + RNH_2 \rightarrow CH_3CH-CH_2NHR \text{ or } CH_3-CH-CH_2OH$$
$$\qquad\qquad\qquad\qquad\qquad\quad OH \qquad\qquad\qquad\qquad NHR$$

The addition of butadiene monoxide to excess aqueous solutions of various amines and permitting the mixture to stand for 8–10 hours gives unsaturated amino alcohols. Thus methylamine and butadiene monoxide gives

$$CH_2{=}CH-CH-CH_2NHCH_3$$
$$\qquad\qquad OH$$

in 65 per cent yield.[184]

Isoprene oxide also reacts with ammonia and amines to give unsaturated amino alcohols. The OH group in each case is attached to the tertiary carbon atom. The isoprene oxide was treated with excess aqueous solution of the amine at room temperature and the mixture permitted to stand for 1 or 2 days. Yields of product are 60–70 per cent. Some of the products are shown below:[185]

Amine	Product
ammonia	$CH_2{=}CH-C(CH_3)-CH_2NH_2$ $\qquad\qquad OH$
methylamine	$CH_2{=}CH-C(CH_3)-CH_2NHCH_3$ $\qquad\qquad OH$

ethylamine
$$CH_2=CH-\underset{\underset{OH}{|}}{C}(CH_3)-CH_2NHCH_2CH_3$$

dimethylamine
$$CH_2=CH-\underset{\underset{OH}{|}}{C}(CH_3)-CH_2-N(CH_3)_2$$

dibutylamine
$$CH_2=CH-C(OH)(CH_3)-CH_2-N(C_4H_9)_2$$

Olefin oxides such as ethylene, propylene, or styrene oxides have been re-acted with substituted trimethylenediamines such as $C_{12}H_{25}NHCH_2CH_2-CH_2NH_2$ to give products of the type

$$C_{12}H_{25}-\underset{\underset{CH_2CH_2OH}{|}}{N}-CH_2CH_2CH_2N(CH_2CH_2OH)_2$$

The reaction is effected in an autoclave at 100°C and is complete in about 5 hours. The products are useful as wetting agents, emulsifiers and cor-rosion inhibitors.[186]

The diethanolamines may be chlorinated with thionyl chloride in boiling benzene to give a product belonging to a group of compounds referred to as nitrogen mustards because of the similarity in structure and biological activity to mustard gas ($ClCH_2CH_2-S-CH_2CH_2Cl$)

$$R-N\underset{CH_2CH_2OH}{\overset{CH_2CH_2OH}{<}} + SOCl_2 \rightarrow R-N\underset{CH_2CH_2Cl}{\overset{CH_2CH_2Cl}{<}}$$

The toxicity of the nitrogen mustards is believed to be due to reaction with tissue protein.

$$RN(CH_2CH_2Cl)_2 + 2RCH(NH_2)COOH \rightarrow RN(CH_2CH_2NH-CHR-COOH)_2$$

The nitrogen mustards are finding limited use in medicine in the treatment of cancer.

In an entirely different type of reaction, Malinovskii and Baranov[187] passed a mixture of 3 moles of ethylene oxide to 1 mole of ammonia over a magnesium oxide catalyst at 400–410°C to give a mixture of ethylene glycol cyclic acetal, pyrrole, and acetaldehydeammonia products. Picoline, collidine and pyridine are obtained when alumina is added. Zinc oxide did not promote the formation of heterocyclics.

Epichlorohydrin reacts with aqueous diethylamine (33 per cent) to give $(C_2H_5)_2N-CH_2CH(OH)-CH_2Cl$ (55 per cent yield) $(C_2H_5)_2N-CH_2-CH-CH_2$ (6–8 per cent yield) and $(C_2H_5)_2N-(CH_2)_2-CH_2OH$.[188]

The Mannich Reaction. Ammonia, primary, and secondary amines react with formaldehyde and a compound having at least one reactive hydrogen with the introduction of a $-CH_2NR_2$ group where either or both of the R groups may be hydrogen. The amine is usually used as the alkyl ammonium chloride. Thus with alkyl aryl ketones;

$$C_6H_5-CO-CH_3 + HCHO + R_2NH_2Cl \rightarrow C_6H_5COCH_2CH_2NHR_2Cl + H_2O$$

$$C_6H_5-CO-CH_3 + 2HCHO + 2R_2NH_2Cl \rightarrow$$

$$C_6H_5-CO-CH(CH_2NHR_2Cl)_2 + 2H_2O$$

With a primary amine the product is the salt of a secondary amine.

$$C_6H_5-CO-CH_3 + HCHO + RNH_3Cl \rightarrow$$

$$C_6H_5-CO-CH_2CH_2NH_2RCl + H_2O$$

Inasmuch as there is an active hydrogen attached to the nitrogen, the reaction may go further.

$$C_6H_5-CO-CH_3 + HCHO + C_6H_5CO-CH_2CH_2NH_2RCl \rightarrow$$

$$(C_6H_5COCH_2CH_2)_2NHRCl + H_2O$$

Frequently the products formed can react further to form a cyclic compound. Thus with acetone

$$2\ CH_3-CO-CH_3 + 2\ HCHO + CH_3NH_2 \longrightarrow$$

Acetophenone, formaldehyde and methylammonium chloride react to give a mixture of C_6H_5CO—$CH_2CH_2NHCH_3$ and $(C_6H_5COCH_2CH_2)_2$-NCH_3. The latter compound is partially converted to 1-methyl-3-benzoyl-4-hydroxy-4-phenylpiperidine by the treatment with sodium hydroxide during the isolation procedure.[189]

Ammonia would be expected to give a primary amine but further reaction usually occurs to give a secondary or tertiary amine. The reaction is most frequently carried out with dialkylamines, such as piperidine and morpholine, and with alkylarylamines such as methylaniline. Compounds such as methylaniline do not react readily.

Active hydrogen compounds which take part in the reaction include:

1. Ketones such as acetone, methyl ethyl ketone, cyclohexanone, acetophenone, alpha-hydrindone, antipyrine, etc.

2. Aldehydes having alpha-hydrogen atoms.

3. Acids and esters such as cyanoacetic acid, benzoylacetic acid, pyruvic acid, acetoacetic acid, malonic acid and the corresponding esters.

$$RCH(CO_2H)_2 + HCHO + (CH_3)_2NH \longrightarrow \underset{\underset{\displaystyle COOH}{|}}{\overset{\overset{\displaystyle COOH}{|}}{R-C-CH_2N(CH_3)_2}} + H_2O$$

4. With phenols such as phenol, o-, m-, and p-cresol, 2- and 4-methoxyphenol, beta-naphthol, 8-hydroxyquinoline, thiophenol, etc. The reaction occurs in the *ortho* or *para* positions to the hydroxyl group.

5. With alkynes, such as phenylacetylene and some substituted phenylacetylenes.

$$C_6H_5C\equiv CH + HCHO + (CH_3)_2NH \longrightarrow C_6H_5-C\equiv C-CH_2N(CH_3)_2$$

6. With nitroparaffins.

The Mannich reaction may be carried out using aqueous formaldehyde in the absence of an organic solvent or with paraformaldehyde in alcohol, excess ketone or other reactant, or in other organic solvents. The reactants are usually refluxed for several hours. The yields of products are usually very good. The Mannich reaction has been discussed by'Blicke.[190] A few reactions reported in recent years are of interest and illustrate the versatility of the reaction.

Aliphatic amines having long chain (12 or more carbon atoms) alkyl groups undergo the Mannich reaction with formaldehyde and low molecular weight aldehydes which contain alpha-hydrogen atoms in much the same way as do the lower alkylamines. The products are obtained in good yield in every case except those involving primary fatty amines and acetaldehyde. In these cases mixtures are obtained which are almost impossible to separate.[191]

Alpha-Methylstyrene and beta-pinene condense with formaldehyde and secondary amines in acetic acid-sulfuric acid solution according to the following reaction.

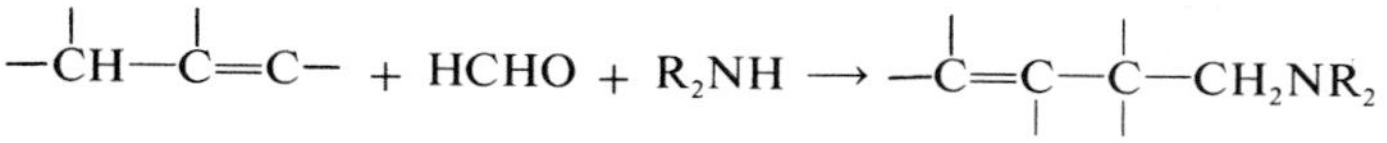

$$-\overset{|}{C}H-\overset{|}{C}=C- \ + \ HCHO \ + \ R_2NH \ \longrightarrow \ -\overset{|}{C}=C-\overset{|}{\underset{|}{C}}-CH_2NR_2$$

to give

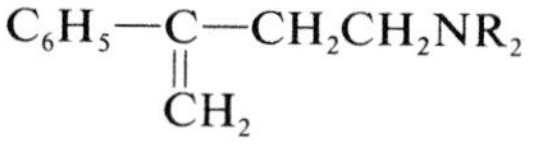

$$C_6H_5-\overset{}{\underset{\overset{\|}{CH_2}}{C}}-CH_2CH_2NR_2$$

and

$$CH_2CH_2NR_2$$

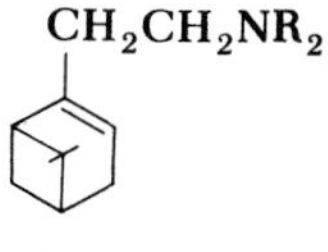

Anethole under similar conditions gave

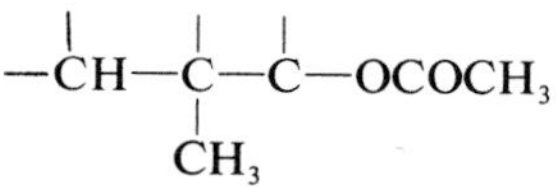

$$-\overset{|}{C}H-\overset{|}{\underset{\overset{|}{CH_3}}{C}}-\overset{|}{C}-OCOCH_3$$

Styrene and cyclohexene did not react.

The reaction is similar to the Prins reaction and possibly proceeds according to the following mechanism.[192]

$$HCHO + R_2NH \rightleftarrows R_2NHCH_2OH \overset{H+}{\rightleftarrows} R_2NHCH_2^{\oplus} + H_2O$$

Alexander and Underhill[193] investigated the Mannich reaction with ethylmalonic acid and made the following observations.

1. In acid solution the reaction of ethylmalonic acid, formaldehyde and dimethylamine follows third-order kinetics, first-order in each of the three components.

2. The rate of reaction shows a critical dependance on pH, passing through a maximum at about pH of 3.8.

3. Under the conditions of the experiment, no reaction takes place between ethylmalonic acid and formaldehyde.

4. Smooth, third-order curves are obtained only if the amine and formaldehyde are mixed and allowed to stand for 12 hours before adding the ethylmalonic acid, but if the formaldehyde and dimethylamine are replaced by dimethylaminomethanol, the reagents may all be mixed at once.

These investigators proposed the following mechanism for the reaction.

$$HCHO + (CH_3)_2NH \rightleftarrows (CH_3)_2NCH_2OH \qquad (1)$$
$$I$$

$$(CH_3)_2NCH_2OH + HA \rightleftarrows (CH_3)_2\overset{\delta+}{N}CH_2-\overset{H}{\underset{|}{O}}-HA \qquad (2)$$
$$II$$

$$III \qquad\qquad (3)$$

$$(CH_3)_2\overset{\delta^+}{N}CH_2-O-HA + \underset{\underset{C_2H_5}{|}}{C}=C\overset{\overset{\oplus}{OH}}{\underset{OH}{\diagup}} \longrightarrow$$

$$\overset{II}{} \qquad\qquad \overset{III}{}$$

$$(CH_3)_2NCH_2-\underset{\underset{C_2H_5}{|}}{\overset{\overset{COOH}{|}}{C}}-C\overset{\overset{\oplus}{OH}}{\underset{OH}{\diagup}} + H_2O + A^- \qquad (4)$$

$$\overset{IV}{}$$

$$(CH_3)_2NCH_2-\underset{\underset{C_2H_5}{|}}{\overset{\overset{COOH}{|}}{C}}-\overset{\oplus}{C}\overset{OH}{\underset{OH}{\diagup}} + A^- \longrightarrow$$

$$(CH_3)_2NCH_2-\underset{\underset{C_2H_5}{|}}{\overset{\overset{COOH}{|}}{C}}-C\overset{O}{\underset{OH}{\diagup}} + HA \qquad (5)$$

Thus the reaction is considered to be initiated by the reversible addition of dimethylamine to formaldehyde to give dimethylaminoethanol (I). The acid (HA) forms a hydrogen bonded complex (II) which places a partial positive charge on the methylene carbon. This complex then reacts with the enol form (III) of ethylmalonic acid to give IV, water and the conjugate base A^-. The conjugate base then extracts a proton to give the final product.

Schmidle and Mansfield[194] reacted alpha-methylstyrene with formaldehyde and dimethylamine in acetic acid to give.

$$C_6H_5-\underset{\underset{CH_2}{\|}}{C}-CH_2CH_2-N(CH_3)_2$$

Other amines such as diethylamine, morpholine and methylbenzylamine reacted similarly to give the unsaturated tertiary amines in 30 to 60 per cent yields.

Terpenes such as alpha-pinene, beta-pinene, camphene and *d*-limonene behave similarly. beta-Pinene and dimethylamine give a 65 per cent yield of product but yields with the other terpenes are 20–30 per cent.

Cresols and chlorophenols condense with formaldehyde and dimethylamine or diethylamine, morpholine or piperidene *ortho* to the phenolic OH group. The products formed from dimethylamine or morpholine are soluble in 5 per cent sodium hydroxide at room temperature but the products from diethylamine or piperidine are generally insoluble.[195]

Furfurylamines may be prepared from 2-methylfuran by means of the Mannich reaction.

$$H_3C \text{(furan)} + HCHO + RNH_2 \longrightarrow H_3C \text{(furan)} CH_2NHR + H_2O$$

As an example of the reaction procedure, 2-methylfuran was added to a solution of ethylammonium chloride in 37 per cent aqueous formaldehyde at 30°C. The temperature was permitted to rise as the reaction proceeded. After neutralization of the reaction mixture with sodium hydroxide and extraction with ether, a 26 per cent yield of 2-methyl-5-ethylaminomethyl-furan was obtained. The following compounds were obtained in the yields indicated.[196]

$$H_3C \text{(furan)} CH_2R$$

R	Yield %	R	Yield %
—NHCH$_2$CH$_3$	25.9	—N(CH$_3$)$_2$	64.7
—NH(CH$_2$)$_3$CH$_3$	21.0	—NHCH(CH$_3$)$_2$	22.2
—NH(CH$_2$)$_7$CH$_3$	31.6	—NHCH$_2$CH$_2$OH	42.2
—NH(CH$_2$)$_{11}$CH$_3$	15.0	—NC$_4$H$_8$O morpholine	78.5
—NH(CH$_2$)$_{17}$CH$_3$	33.6	—NC$_5$H$_{10}$ piperidine	77.6

Secondary aliphatic amines react with formaldehyde and primary or secondary nitroparaffins to give nitroamines. The amine and formaldehyde may react directly with the nitroparaffin,

$$R_2NH + HCHO + (CH_3)_2CHNO_2 \rightarrow R_2NCH_2—C(CH_3)_2NO_2 + H_2O$$

or the amine may be added directly to the nitroalcohol or glycol.

$$2R_2NH + CH_3—C(NO_2)(CH_2OH)_2 \rightarrow R_2NCH_2—\underset{\underset{NO_2}{|}}{\overset{\overset{CH_3}{|}}{C}}—CH_2NR_2 + 2H_2O$$

In the first procedure, aqueous formaldehyde (36 per cent), was added to aqueous dimethylamine at temperatures of 18–25°C. The 2-nitro-propane was then added at one time and the reaction mixture permitted to come to room temperature. The nitroamine was obtained in 72 per cent yield.

In the second procedure a mixture of the nitroalcohol (or glycol) formed by the reaction of formaldehyde with the nitroparaffin and the amine was allowed to stand for about 24 hours. The nitroamine was separated and distilled under vacuum. Yields were about the same by the two methods.[197,198]

Senkus also reported that N-hydroxymethylalkylamines obtained from primary alkylamines and formaldehyde react with secondary nitroparaffins to give nitroamines.

$$R'NHCH_2OH + R_2CHNO_2 \rightarrow R'NHCH_2-C(R)_2-NO_2 + H_2O$$

With primary nitroparaffins, nitrodiamines are obtained.

$$2R'NHCH_2OH + RCH_2NO_2 \rightarrow R'NHCH_2-\underset{\underset{NO_2}{|}}{CR}-CH_2NHR' + 2H_2O$$

The same compounds can also be obtained by reaction of the primary amines with a nitroalcohol.

$$R'NH_2 + HOCH_2-CR_2-NO_2 \rightarrow R'NHCH_2-CR_2-NO_2 + H_2O$$

The reactions were carried out near room temperatures and required about 3 days to obtain maximum yields which in most cases were 60–90 per cent.

N-Hydroxymethylisopropylamine (from isopropylamine and formaldehyde) reacts with 2-nitropropane at room temperature to give N-(2-nitroisobutyl)-isopropylamine in 76 per cent yield.

$$(CH_3)_2CHNH_2 + HCHO \rightarrow (CH_3)_2CHNHCH_2OH \xrightarrow{(CH_3)_2CHNO_2}$$

$$(CH_3)_2CH-NH-CH_2-\underset{\underset{NO_2}{|}}{\overset{\overset{CH_3}{|}}{C}}-CH_3$$

Aqueous formaldehyde (36 per cent) was added to isopropylamine at 20°C and then 2-nitropropane was added and the mixture stirred for several hours. Substitution of nitroethane for 2-nitropropane gave 2-nitro-2-methyl-1,3-diisopropylaminopropane in 71 per cent conversion.

Nitration. Nitramines may be prepared by the treatment of the nitrate salt of the amine in acetic acid with concentrated nitric acid in the presence of zinc chloride. The mixture is permitted to stand at room temperature for 2 hours and then warmed one hour at 40°C. Water is added to the reaction mixture which was neutralized with sodium carbonate and the nitramine extracted with ether.

In this way the nitramine, $(C_4H_9)_2N \cdot NO_2$, prepared from dibutylamine was obtained in 39 per cent yield.

The nitramines are of interest as explosives.[199]

Acetone cyanohydrin nitrate has been found to be an effective reagent for the nitration of amines under alkaline conditions. In this way primary and secondary amines are converted to the corresponding nitramines.

Acetone cyanohydrin nitrate is obtained by the nitration of acetone cyanohydrin with fuming nitric acid in acetic anhydride. Yields of 65–75 per cent are obtained. It is a colorless liquid which can be distilled readily under reduced pressure and is relatively stable.

With this reagent primary and secondary amines are nitrated directly under alkaline conditions.

$$R_2NH + CH_3-\underset{\underset{ONO_2}{|}}{C(CN)}-CH_3 \longrightarrow R_2NNO_2 + CH_3COCH_3 + HCN$$

Yields of nitramine with secondary amines were 55–80 per cent and the yields obtained with primary amines were a little lower (50–60 per cent) as shown in Table 1–5.

TABLE 1–5. NITRAMINES MADE WITH ACETONECYANOHYDRIN NITRATE

Nitramine	Yield (%)	B.P. (°C)
Dimethyl-	76	57–58 (m.p.)
Dimethyl-	60	50–52 0.2 mm
Di-*n*-propyl-	42	90–92 8 mm
Di-*n*-butyl-	54	69–70 0.1 mm
Diisobutyl-	60	79–80 (m.p.)
Mononitropiperazine-	55	127–128 (m.p.)
Nitromorpholine-	81	51–53 (m.p.)
n-Propyl-	50	52–56 0.1 mm
n-Butyl-	52	79–81 0.5 mm

Secondary amines may serve as their own solvent but acetonitrile and tetrahydrofuran may also be used. In general the amine was used in 5:1 excess and heated at 80° for 4 hours with the nitrate ester. The reactivity of primary amines was greatly affected by choice of solvent. Solvents such as acetonitrile and tetrahydrofuran were most successful when a 3:1 excess of amine was used.

The reagent is not successful with aromatic amines or aliphatic amines in which there is a branching of the chain on the α-carbon atom.[202]

Amines can be converted to nitrosamines and nitroamines by reaction with nitrogen tetroxide in a suitable solvent. Thus a solution of nitrogen tetroxide in methylene chloride is added at –80 to –50°C to an excess of the amine in an appropriate solvent. Precautions must be taken to exclude oxygen, water and carbon dioxide from the reaction flask. Some products obtained are shown in Table 1–6.

TABLE 1–6. REACTIONS OF DIETHYLAMINE WITH NITROGEN TETROXIDE

Reactant	Temp. (°C)	Solvent	Products	Yield* (%)
$(C_2H_5)_2NH$	0	CH_2Cl_2	$(C_2H_5)_2N-NO$	98
			$(C_2H_5)_2NH_2{}^+NO_3{}^-$	95
$(C_2H_5)_2NH$	–80	CH_2Cl_2	$(C_2H_5)_2N-NO_2$	97
			$(C_2H_5)_2NH_2{}^+NO_2{}^-$	100
$(C_2H_5)_2NH$	–80	ether	$(C_2H_5)_2N-NO$	39
			$(C_2H_5)_2NH_2{}^+NO_3{}^-$	40
			$(C_2H_5)_2N-NO_2$	59
			$(C_2H_5)_2NH_2{}^+NO_2{}^-$	59

*based on nitrogen tetroxide (tautomeric mixture)

The nitrogen tetroxide behaves as if it were a mixture of two isomers.

The reaction with the amine may proceed in two ways depending upon whether I or II is the reactive species.[200]

Nitration of secondary amines has also been accomplished with nitrogen pentoxide made by the action of trifluoroacetic acid on anhydrous nitric acid.[201] Nitrogen pentoxide was added to diisopropylamine in carbon tetrachloride at –30°C and the temperature permitted to rise to 0°C. The diisopropylnitramine was recovered by washing the organic layer with 10 per cent hydrochloric acid. The yield was 91 per cent.

Reactions with Nitrous Acid. Nitrous acid reacts with secondary amines to give nitrosamines

$$R_2NH + HONO \longrightarrow R_2N-NO + H_2O$$

Nitrosamines have somewhat the same properties as esters or acetylated amines and as such may be hydrolyzed to the starting amine. They are usually yellow oils. Another and probably better reagent for the preparation of nitrosamines is the nitric oxide-boron trifluoride complex. The reaction is carried out near $0°C$.

$$R_2NH + ONBF_4 \longrightarrow R_2N—NO + BF_3 + HF$$

Some common nitrosamines made in this way are shown in Table 1–7.[203]

TABLE 1–7. SOME COMMON NITROSAMINES

Amine	Nitrosamine	Yield	B.P. (°C)	
$(C_2H_5)_2NH$	$(C_2H_5)_2N—NO$	88	175	
$C_6H_5NHC_2H_5$	$C_2H_5—N—NO$ $\quad\quad\vert$ $\quad\quad C_6H_5$	80	130	20 mm
$C_6H_5CH_2NHCH_3$	$C_6H_5CH_2—N—NO$ $\quad\quad\quad\quad\vert$ $\quad\quad\quad\quad CH_3$	86	158	26 mm
Piperidine	$(CH_2)_5N—NO$	88	215	

Nitrosamines of the type $R_2N—NO$ are obtained by liquid or vapor phase reaction of the corresponding amine with a mixture of NO_2 and NO. Thus a mixture of NO_2, NO and diethylamine was passed through a pyrex tube packed with Raschig rings at $140°C$ to give a 90 per cent yield of diethylnitrosamine, $(C_2H_5)_2NNO$.

The reaction with high boiling amines can be carried out in the liquid phase by passing the $NO—NO_2$ mixture through the liquid amine at $100°C$. The nitrosamines $C_6H_5N(C_2H_5)NO$ and $(C_6H_5)_2NNO$ were prepared in this way.

The primary amines react with nitrous acid with the liberation of nitrogen and the formation of alcohols. The reaction probably proceeds in a similar manner to that observed with secondary amines but the corresponding nitrosamine has a hydrogen attached to one of the nitrogen atoms which probably migrates to the oxygen followed by a loss of nitrogen.

$$RNH_2 + HONO \longrightarrow [RNH—NO] \longrightarrow [R\!=\!\!N—NOH] \longrightarrow ROH + N_2$$

Although nitrogen is evolved quantitatively, the yields of alcohols are poor.

If the pH is low (*ca.* 3) during the treatment with nitrous acid, the amine may be converted to the corresponding alcohol. Secondary and tertiary alcohols are appreciably dehydrated to olefins. At higher pH considerable rearrangement occurs. Thus *n*-propylamine gives isopropyl alcohol, propylene and a little *n*-propyl alcohol. Methylamine gives no methanol even though nitrogen is liberated quantitatively.

Tertiary amines having no hydrogen attached to the nitrogen do not react with nitrous acid except to form salts.

When a mixture of amines is treated with nitrous acid the primary amines are destroyed by conversion to alcohols, the secondary amine forms a neutral nitrosamine and the tertiary amine does not react and so may be removed by the extraction of an ether solution with an inorganic acid. The remaining fraction may be hydrolyzed with acid to regenerate the secondary amine from its nitroso derivative.

Addition to Unsaturated Compounds. The addition of amines to unsaturated compounds such as acrolein and mesityl oxide has already been described. In a similar manner amines add to unsaturated esters. Thus benzylamine adds across the double bond of ethyl acrylate on standing for 24 hours at room temperature to give an 87 per cent yield of $C_6H_5CH_2$-$NHCH_2CH_2COOC_2H_5$. When 2 moles of ethyl acrylate to 1 mole of benzyl amine is used the product is $C_6H_5CH_2N(CH_2CH_2COOC_2H_5)_2$ obtained in 84 per cent yield.[204]

Amines add to acetylene and some acetylenic ketones. Thus methylamine reacts with phenyl ethynyl ketone.

$$C_6H_5CO-C{\equiv}CH + CH_3NH_2 \longrightarrow C_6H_5-CO-CH{=}CHNHCH_3$$

Other amines such as dimethylamine, diethylamine, piperidine, aniline and diphenylamine behave similarly. Yields are 36–97 per cent.[205]

Trimethylammonium chloride in ethyl alcohol is made alkaline with trimethylamine, the solution is cooled and $C_6H_5CO-C{\equiv}CH$ added at 25–30°. After 0.5 hour the solution is diluted with ether to give a precipitate of the quaternary ammonium chloride, $C_6H_5-CO-CH{=}CH-N-(CH_3)_3Cl$, in 88 per cent yield.

In a similar manner pyridine gives an 87 per cent yield of (2-benzoyl-vinyl)pyridinium chloride.

Aqueous solutions of quaternary salts treated with alkali rapidly liberate tertiary amines.[206]

To diethylamine containing cuprous chloride in a nitrogen atmosphere at 50 psi was added acetylene until the total pressure was 200 psi and the mixture was heated for 39 hours at 80–100°C. The product, $(C_2H_5)_2$-$N-CH(CH_3)-C{\equiv}CH$, was obtained in 63 per cent yield.[207]

Amines also react with acetylene in a Mannich-type reaction. Thus dimethylamine as a 50 per cent aqueous solution, 30 per cent aqueous formaldehyde and acetic acid were added to a steel autoclave containing about 5 per cent copper acetate. Acetylene and nitrogen (mole ratio 2:1) were introduced at a pressure of 15 atmospheres and the mixture heated at 35–40°C until acetylene was no longer absorbed. After neutralization $(CH_3)_2NCH_2C{\equiv}CH$ was obtained together with a relatively small amount of $(CH_3)_2NCH_2C{\equiv}CCH_2N(CH_3)_2$.[208]

Under certain conditions amines or ammonia can be made to add to olefins. As an example the reaction is carried out under pressure in the presence of an alkaline catalyst. If sodium is added to a benzene solution of isobutylene and ammonia and the mixture is heated for 1 hour at 250–265° under a pressure of 650–700 atmospheres, *tert*-butylamine is obtained in 8 per cent conversion.

Sodium added to a benzene solution of hexamethylenediamine and ethylene and the mixture heated 200 minutes at 225–245°C under a pressure of 400–650 atmospheres gives N-monoethylhexamethylenediamine. The addition of ethylamine to the reaction mixture materially improved the conversion.[209]

Amines also add to olefins in the presence of peroxides. The hydrogen on the α-carbon atom of the amine adds to the double bond. Thus 1-octene reacts with piperidine at 120°C under a pressure of 25 psi of nitrogen in the presence of di-*tert*-butyl peroxide to give 2-octylpiperidine and a small amount of a dioctyl piperidine.[210]

Amines react with fluorinated olefins. Rigby and Schoeder[211] reported the reaction of primary and secondary amines with polyfluoroethylenes in the presence of borax. Sufficient borax must be used to provide the water necessary for the reaction.

$$CClF{=}CF_2 + HNR_2 \longrightarrow CHClF{-}CF_2NR_2 \xrightarrow{H_2O} CHClFCONR_2$$

Pruett *et al.*[212] reported the reaction of primary and secondary amines with chlorotrifluoroethylene and with hexafluorocyclobutene. With primary aliphatic amines, products were imino- or imido-type compounds, whereas secondary amines gave substituted tertiary amines.

$$n\text{-}C_4H_9NH_2 + CClF{=}CF_2 \longrightarrow CHClF{-}CF{=}NC_4H_9 \longrightarrow$$

$$CHClF{-}C\begin{smallmatrix}\diagup NC_4H_9\\ \diagdown NHC_4H_9\end{smallmatrix}$$

$$\begin{array}{c} RN{=}C{-}\!-\!-C{=}NR \\ \mid\qquad\mid \\ F\,CH{-}CF_2 \end{array}$$

$$\begin{array}{c} FC{=}CF \\ \mid\quad\mid \\ F_2C{-}CF_2 \end{array}\quad\xrightarrow{\;RNH_2\;}\quad$$

$$\xrightarrow{\;R_2NH\;}\quad \begin{array}{c} FC{=}CNR_2 \\ \mid\quad\mid \\ F_2C{-}CF_2 \end{array}$$

Tertiary amines react with hexafluorocyclobutene to produce a reactive quaternary ammonium salt which readily undergoes hydrolytic cleavage to give trialkyl-(3,3-difluoro-2,4-dioxocyclobutyl)ammonium betaines.

The reaction probably proceeds as follows:

$$R_3N + \begin{matrix} FC=CF \\ | \quad | \\ F_2C-CF_2 \end{matrix} \longrightarrow \left[\begin{matrix} R_3N^+-C=CF \\ | \quad | \\ F_2C-CF_2 \end{matrix} \right] F^- \xrightarrow{H_2O}$$

$$\left[\begin{matrix} R_3N^+-C=C-OH \\ | \qquad | \\ F_2C \quad CF_2 \end{matrix} \right] F^- \longrightarrow \left[\begin{matrix} R_3N^+-CH-C=O \\ | \qquad | \\ F_2C——CF_2 \end{matrix} \right] F^- \longrightarrow$$

$$\left[\begin{matrix} R_3N^+-C-C=O \\ || \quad | \\ FC-CF_2 \end{matrix} \right] F^- \xrightarrow{H_2O} \left[\begin{matrix} R_3N^+-C-C=O \\ || \quad | \\ HO-C-CF_2 \end{matrix} \right] F^- \longrightarrow$$

$$\begin{matrix} R_3N^+-C=C-O^- \\ | \qquad | \\ O=C-CF_2 \end{matrix}$$

Miscellaneous Reactions. Salts of chlorinated aliphatic amines may be converted into unsaturated amines by heating above their melting points (160–230° C). Thus chlorinated hexylammonium chlorides heated to 180–230° C while a current of nitrogen is passed through the mixture to remove the hydrogen chloride as formed gave a product containing 90 per cent dehydrochlorinated material. When clay (tonsil) was used as a catalyst the yield was increased to 92 per cent.[213]

Dehydrogenation of amines can be accomplished in the presence of a palladium catalyst. Passing 2-aminoheptane over palladium deposited on asbestos at 325° C resulted in dehydrogenation but no ammonia was formed. Hydrolysis of the product gave methyl amyl ketone indicating that the dehydrogenation produced a ketimine. A nickel on alumina catalyst at 220° C was even more effective as a catalyst but a platinum catalyst caused both dehydrogenation and deamination.[214]

Acetoacetamides may be prepared from diketene and primary amines. Diketene was added dropwise to a solution of aniline in toluene at 20–70° C to give acetoacetanilide. Water can also be used as a solvent to prepare a variety of acetoacetamides in yields of 30–70 per cent.[215]

Propiolactone and amines react to give hydroxyamides and β-amino acids.[216]

Two competing reactions occur.

$$\begin{matrix} CH_2-CH_2 \\ | \qquad | \\ O——C=O \end{matrix} + R_2NH \longrightarrow HOCH_2CH_2CONR_2 \quad \text{or} \quad R_2NCH_2CH_2COOH$$

The ratio of products varies with the amine, solvent and order of addition of the reagents. Dimethylamine added to an ethereal solution of propiolactone gives mostly the amino acid but diethylamine under the same conditions gives largely the amide.

In acetonitrile, NH_3, dimethyl-, ethyl-, and dodecylamines give chiefly the amino acids while methyl-, diethyl-, and propylamine give the amides with little or no isolable amino acid. In general aromatic and cyclohexylamines give amino acids more consistently than alkylamines but reaction is slower and with some amines takes place only on heating.

The choice of solvent is important. Water and ammonia gives mostly hydracrylamide. Acetonitrile gives excellent yields of β-alanine.

With few exceptions water is the best solvent for amide formation and acetonitrile is best for the formation of amino acids.

The reactions are almost quantitative but it is difficult to separate the amide from the amino acid.

Tertiary amines react with propiolactone to form betaines which have salt lake properties and are quite hygroscopic, probably because of hydrate formation.

$$R_3N + \begin{matrix} CH_2-CH_2 \\ | \quad\quad | \\ O-\!\!-\!\!-C=O \end{matrix} \longrightarrow R_3N^+CH_2CH_2COO^-$$

Amines or ammonia react with esters to give amides. The reaction is most important with ammonia but may also occur with amines.

$$RCOOC_2H_5 + CH_3NH_2 \longrightarrow RCONHCH_3 + C_2H_5OH$$

The three classes of amines may be differentiated by reaction with diethyl oxalate. Tertiary amines do not react; primary amines give crystalline diamides $(CONHR)_2$ and secondary amines give oily monoamides $(H_5C_2\text{-}OCOCONR_2)$. The mono- and diamides are readily hydrolyzed to the corresponding amines so that this may serve as a means of separation. High molecular weight primary amines give only the monoamides and so may be mistaken for secondary amines.

Methyl caprylate and ethylenediamine heated to 200° C in an autoclave gave $C_7H_{15}CONHCH_2CH_2NH_2$ which when distilled under reduced pressure gave 2-heptylimidazoline.[217]

Heating a fatty acid with 2-aminopyridine at 200–210° C for 4 hours gave a 50–70 per cent yield of 2-acylaminopyridine.

The condensation of 1,2-diamines with 1,3-diketones gives seven member heterocyclic compounds containing two nitrogen atoms, (1,4-diazacyclo-heptatrienes).[218] Thus o-phenylenediamine and acetylacetone at a pH of 4.8 gives the diazepine.

The reaction of *trans*-1,2-diaminocyclopentane with acetylacetone gives either of two products depending largely on the pH at which the condensation occurs.[219] At a pH of about 6–9 the main product is

At a pH of 2–6 essentially the only product is

Halogenated amines can be formed by the action of hypohalites. In these compounds the halogen is positive.

$$RNH_2 + NaOCl \longrightarrow RNHCl + NaOH$$

$$RNH_2 + 2NaOCl \longrightarrow RNCl_2 + 2NaOH$$

$$R_2NH + NaOCl \longrightarrow R_2NCl + NaOH$$

Primary or secondary amines react with phosgene to give alkyl ureas.

$$2RNH_2 + COCl_2 \longrightarrow RNH-CO-NHR + 2HCl$$

Ureas can also be prepared by the reaction of amines with isocyanates.

$$RNCO + RNH_2 \longrightarrow RNH-CO-NHR$$

Reaction with carbon disulfide gives thioureas

$$2RNH_2 + CS_2 \longrightarrow RNH-CS-NHR + H_2S$$

Primary amines react with chloroform in the presence of sodium hydroxide to give isonitriles.

$$RNH_2 + CHCl_3 + 2NaOH \longrightarrow RNC + 2NaCl + 3H_2O$$

The isonitriles have very foul odors and the formation of these serves as a qualitative test for primary amines.

Kinman and Muths[220] found that aminoaldehydes will react with Grignard reagents to give amino alcohols. They report the preparation of 3-diethylamino-2-pentanol and 3-piperidino-2-pentanol from the appropriate aminoaldehydes.

The aminoaldehydes were prepared by reaction of halogenated acetals with amines to give aminoacetals which were hydrolyzed to the free aminoaldehydes or could be reacted directly with the Grignard reagent. The reaction was much slower than when the free aminoaldehyde was used.

Primary alkylamines heated with ammonia in the presence of a catalyst are converted to secondary amines by loss of ammonia.

$$2RNH_2 \longrightarrow R_2NH + NH_3$$

This is comparable to the dehydration of alcohols to form ethers.[221] In the presence of some catalysts considerable decomposition of the primary amine to olefins occurs but this can be largely averted by using a catalyst consisting of alumina which has been activated with acids such as hydrochloric acid. Although ammonia is a product of the reaction, the addition of 0.1–5 moles per mole of amine inhibits the decomposition of the amine to the olefin.

Thus liquid butylamine (100 cc per liter of catalyst per hour) is mixed with ammonia in a mole ratio of 2:1 and passed over the catalyst at 350°C and a total pressure of 20 kg per sq cm. From each 100 moles of butylamine charged there was obtained 34 moles of dibutylamine, 3 moles butylene and ammonia, 3 moles of other products and 60 moles of unreacted *n*-butylamine which could be recycled.

Reaction with Halogen Compounds. The alkylation of amines with alkyl halides has already been discussed as a method for the preparation of secondary and tertiary amines. In addition to these reactions, a few others involving halogen derivatives are of considerable interest.

Ethylenediamine reacts with chlorobenzene when heated with 30 per cent aqueous sodium hydroxide for 25 hours at 240–250°C to give C_6H_5-

$NHCH_2CH_2NH_2$. None of the N,N'-diphenylethylenediamine was reported.[222]

Primary or secondary amines react with β-chloropropionitrile in refluxing alcohol to give β-aminopropionitriles in good yields. With tertiary aliphatic amines, dehydrochlorination results. The reaction with primary or secondary amines may proceed through direct amination or by dehydrochlorination followed by cyanoethylation.

Ethylenediamine may be alkylated with higher molecular weight alkyl chlorides such. as octyl chloride by refluxing a solution of the two in ethanol. N-octylethylenediamine is obtained in 84 per cent yield.[223]

N-substituted ethylenediamines are prepared by reaction with chloronitrobenzenes in the presence of a cupric chloride catalyst. Thus o-Cl—C_6H_4—NO_2 was added to ethylenediamine containing cupric chloride and the mixture refluxed until solidification occurred. N,N'-bis-(o-nitrophenyl)-ethylenediamine was obtained in 30 per cent yield.[224]

The reaction of aromatic amines depends largely on the structure of the amine. Aniline caused dehydrochlorination almost exclusively.[225]

Hexamethylenetetramine and benzyl chloride refluxed for 1.5 hours in dilute aqueous ammonia and the product heated with a small amount of 40 per cent formaldehyde gives an oily residue from which $(C_6H_5CH_2N=CH_2)_2$ may be isolated. This compound is identical to the one obtained from benzylamine and formaldehyde. Some benzylammonium chloride was obtained as a by-product.[226]

Phenacyl halides react with diamines to give the corresponding N,N'-diphenacyldiamines which may be reduced to secondary amino alcohols.[227]

$$2C_6H_5COCH_2Br + H_2NCH_2CH_2NH_2 \xrightarrow[C_2H_5OH]{K_2CO_3}$$

$$C_6H_5COCH_2NHCH_2CH_2NHCH_2COC_6H_5 \xrightarrow[Pd]{H_2}$$

$$C_6H_5CH(OH)CH_2NHCH_2CH_2NHCH_2CHOH—C_6H_5$$

The reaction of α-bromo-α,β-unsaturated esters with primary or secondary amines was investigated by Mouren, Chavin and Petit.[228] The reaction was found to involve not only the replacement of the halogen but also addition to the carbon-carbon double bond to give a diamino ester.

$$R—CH=CBr—COOR + 2R_2NH \rightarrow \underset{\underset{NR_2}{|}}{R—CH}—\underset{\underset{NR_2}{|}}{CH}—COOR + HBr$$

The reaction between α-bromoethyl cinnamate and a secondary amine gives an α,β-diaminoethyl cinnamate. Heating α-bromoethyl cinnamate and morpholine at 60°C for 24 hours yield α,β-dimorpholinophenethyl propionate. Piperidine gives a mixture of two isomeric α,β-dipiperidino-phenethyl propionates.

In general, reactions of α-bromoethyl cinnamate with primary amines are quite slow (24 hours to 1 month) and give derivatives of ethylenimine. Thus ethylamine gives 1-ethyl-2-phenyl-3-carbethoxyethylenimine.

One or more chlorine atoms in silicon tetrachloride can be replaced with *tert*-butylamino groups. This reaction is accomplished by adding tertiary butylamine to an ether solution of silicon tetrachloride. The product is $(CH_3)_3CNHSiCl_3$.[229]

Quaternary Ammonium Compounds. Alkyl halides react with tertiary amines to form quaternary ammonium salts.

$$R_3N + RX \longrightarrow R_4N^+X^-$$

The ease of reaction varies greatly with the halogen and with the amine. Reaction may occur by simply mixing the reagents or the mixture may require heating for several hours under pressure. The addition of 10 per cent aqueous sodium carbonate frequently favors the reaction. Quaternary ammonium salt formation is favored by the use of polar solvents.

Among the halides, the iodides are more reactive than the bromides which in turn are more reactive than the chlorides.

To illustrate the effect of different alkyl groups on the reactivity, trimethylamine and methyl chloride react with the evolution of heat while trimethylamine and ethyl chloride do not react even when heated under a pressure of 50 atmospheres.[230]

The quaternary ammonium salts are all crystalline materials, soluble in water and superficially resemble ammonium salts. One quaternary salt can be converted into another by using a suitably prepared anion exchange resin. Thus a quaternary ammonium iodide can be prepared by passing a solution of the corresponding chloride over an anion exchange resin pretreated with sodium or potassium iodide. Similarly a quaternary ammonium nitrate or sulfate can be prepared from an anion exchange resin pretreated with sodium nitrate or sulfate.

Quaternary ammonium hydroxides may be prepared by passing an aqueous solution of the corresponding salt over an anion exchange resin in the hydroxide form. The resulting solution is evaporated to dryness at low temperatures to isolate the hydroxide. Quaternary ammonium hydroxides are strong bases comparable to sodium and potassium hydroxides except that they are decomposed by heat to give tertiary amines, alcohols or olefins. The quaternary hydroxides may be cast into pellets or sticks in the same way as sodium or potassium hydroxide.

An alternative method for the preparation of quaternary ammonium hydroxides involves the treatment of the corresponding halides with moist silver oxide. The halide ion is precipitated as the silver halide leaving the solution of the quaternary hydroxide which can be isolated by evaporation of the water.

The following serve to illustrate the preparation of quaternary ammonium compounds.

Quaternary ammonium chlorides are obtained by heating a tertiary aliphatic amine with an alkyl chloride under pressure at 100° C in the presence of at least 20 per cent of water. Thus a mixture of 1-chlorododecane, triethylamine and water was agitated for 24 hours at 155° C to give a 64 per cent conversion to dodecyltriethylammonium chloride.[231]

Quaternary ammonium hydroxides decompose on heating. Thus tetramethylammonium hydroxide decomposes to give trimethylamine and methyl alcohol.

$$(CH_3)_4N^+OH^- \longrightarrow (CH_3)_3N + CH_3OH$$

If one of the alkyl groups is larger than methyl an olefin is obtained.

$$RCH_2CH_2-N(CH_3)_3{}^+ \; OH^- \longrightarrow RCH{=}CH_2 + (CH_3)_3N + H_2O$$

This is the basis for the exhaustive methylation reaction developed by Hofmann. It is a very useful reaction for the conversion of amines to olefins of known structure.

n-Butylamine can be converted into 1-butene by the following sequence of reactions.

$$CH_3CH_2CH_2CH_2NH_2 \xrightarrow{CH_3I} CH_3CH_2CH_2N(CH_3)_3{}^+ \; I^- \xrightarrow{Ag_2O}$$

$$CH_3CH_2CH_2CH_2N(CH_3)_3{}^+ \; OH^- \xrightarrow{heat} CH_3CH_2CH{=}CH_2 + (CH_3)_3N + H_2O$$

Dienes may be obtained from heterocyclic amines. Thus pyrrolidine is converted into butadiene.

The method has also been used in the preparation of cyclobutene. Cyclobutane carboxylic acid, prepared from malonic ester and 1,3-dibromopropane, is converted to the amide then to cyclobutylamine by means of the Hoffman degradation. Cyclobutylamine is then treated with methyl iodide and with silver oxide to give trimethylcyclobutylammonium hydroxide which on heating forms cyclobutene.

$$\begin{array}{c} CH_2\!-\!CH_2\!-\!NH_2 \\ | \qquad\quad | \\ CH_2\!-\!CH_2 \end{array} \xrightarrow[\text{2. Ag}_2\text{O}]{\text{1. CH}_3\text{I}} \begin{array}{c} CH_2\!-\!CH_2\!-\!N(CH_3)_3{}^+\,OH^- \\ | \qquad\quad | \\ CH_2\!-\!CH_2 \end{array} \xrightarrow{\text{heat}}$$

$$\begin{array}{c} CH_2\!-\!CH \\ | \qquad\; \| \\ CH_2\!-\!CH \end{array} + (CH_3)_3N + H_2O$$

Aqueous trimethylamine and a mixture of nitrogen and acetylene under a total pressure of 150 psi, heated at 60° C for 6 hours gave $CH_2\!=\!CH\!-\!\overset{+}{N}(CH_3)_3OH^-$. This vinyltrimethylammonium hydroxide was neutralized with hydrochloric acid and evaporated to dryness at 40° C under 15-mm pressure to give vinyltrimethylammonium chloride.[232]

Treating trimethylamine with methanol and carbon dioxide at 200–210° C and a pressure of 85–95 atmospheres gives tetramethylammonium carbonate, $[(CH_3)_4N]_2CO_3$.

Several quaternary ammonium compounds having molecular weights of 250–400 are used commercially as textile finishing agents, as germicides and disinfectants, and as ore flotation agents. Some of these compounds can be prepared from alkylbenzenes such as dodecylbenzene by the following sequence of reactions.

$$C_{12}H_{25}\!-\!C_6H_5 + HCHO + HCl \xrightarrow{ZnCl_2} C_{12}H_{25}\!-\!C_6H_4\!-\!CH_2Cl \xrightarrow{(CH_3)_3N}$$

$$[C_{12}H_{25}\!-\!C_6H_4\!-\!CH_2N^+(CH_3)_3]Cl^-$$

This compound, N-dodecylbenzene-N,N,N-trimethylammonium chloride, has been found to be an effective algaecide.[234]

Trimethylamine was added to a solution of allyl chloroacetate in dimethylacetamide solution at 0–10° C to give $[(CH_3)_3N^+CH_2COOCH_2\text{-}CH\!=\!CH_2]Cl^-$.[235]

Bis-(2-hydroxyethyl)dodecylamine made from the reaction of 2 moles of ethylene oxide with 1 mole of dodecylamine at 150–170° C, heated on the steam bath with benzyl chloride and then let stand at room temperature for several days gave benzyl-bis-(2-hydroxyethyl)-dodecylammonium chloride. This compound is useful as a disinfectant.[236]

Methyl iodide and $p\text{-}(CH_3)_2N\!-\!C_6H_4\!-\!SO_2NH_2$ refluxed in methanol gives $[(CH_3)_3N^+\!-\!C_6H_4\!-\!SO_2NH_2]I^-$.[237]

Acetylenic ethers (C_2H_5O—C≡CH) react with tertiary aliphatic amines and water to give (α-alkoxyvinyl)trialkylammonium hydroxides which may be converted to halide salts [CH_2=C(OC_2H_5)$\overset{+}{N}$(CH_3)$_3$]I^-.[238]

Quaternary ammonium compounds with curare-like activity are prepared from diamines. Methyl iodide added slowly to a solution of m-H_2N—C_6H_4—NH—$COCH_2N$(CH_3)$_2$ in acetone at temperatures of 10–40°C gives an 83 per cent yield of [m-H_2N—C_6H_4—$NHCOCH_2$-$\overset{+}{N}$(CH_3)$_3$]I^-.[239]

Quaternary ammonium salts containing one long chain alkyl radical and three short-chain radicals are effective as germicides. In the alkyl-trimethylammonium bromide series, cetyltrimethylammonium bromide shows the maximum antibacteriacidal activity. The anion present had little or no effect on the germicidal activity. Substitution of N-benzyl, N-butyl, or N-ethyl for the N-methyl groups also had no effect upon the germicidal activity.[240]

1-Dimethylamino-2-butene was chlorinated in concentrated hydrochloric acid to give a 70 per cent yield of 1-dimethylamino-2,3-dichlorobutane. The quaternary salt made from methyl iodide when heated to 110°C with concentrated potassium hydroxide gave pure trimethylamine and vinyl acetylene.[241]

$$(CH_3)_2N—CH_2CH=CHCH_3 \xrightarrow{Cl_2} (CH_3)_2NCH_2CHCl—CHCl—CH_3 \xrightarrow{CH_3I}$$

$$[(CH_3)_3N^+—CH_2CHCl—CHCl—CH_3]I^- \xrightarrow[KOH]{110°C}$$

$$(CH_3)_3N + CH_2=CH—C≡CH$$

Utilization of Amines

Aliphatic amines play a very important role among organic compounds and are used in a variety of ways. It would be very difficult to list every application of amines and amine salts but a few of the more significant applications will be described.

Corrosion Inhibitors. Many amines are effective corrosion inhibitors and are used for a variety of purposes. Aliphatic amines are effective in inhibiting the corrosion of iron by dilute sulfuric acid.[242] Tertiary amines are most effective and in general the longer chain length up to about five carbon atoms, the greater is the inhibiting power.

The corrosion of aluminum by hydrochloric acid is inhibited by ethyl-, propyl-, and butylamines.

Atmospheric corrosion may be prevented by a thin film of a material containing a primary-, secondary- or *tert*-amine phosphate having at least one alkyl group of not less than eight carbon atoms.[243] Amine phosphates are also used to inhibit corrosion caused by hydraulic fluids.

The mechanism of the inhibition of corrosion is not completely understood but it has been shown that amines inhibit the corrosion of iron in acid solution by forming ammonium ions which are adsorbed on the surface preventing iron ions from leaving the surface to be replaced by hydrogen ions. It is necessary only to have a monomolecular layer of cations in order to inhibit the corrosion. It has been shown that for monoaliphatic amines, the longer the hydrocarbon chain the more effective is the inhibition. Increasing the number of substituent radicals of the amine also increases the inhibiting properties.

Although in general low molecular weight aliphatic amines are not very good corrosion inhibitors, n-tributylamine, n-diamylamine and n-triamylamines are excellent inhibitors. As small an amount of n-tributylamine as 0.66 per cent in normal sulfuric acid reduces the corrosion rate of iron by 97 per cent. Similarly 0.34 per cent of n-diamylamine reduces the corrosion by 98 per cent and 0.13 per cent triamylamine reduces the corrosion by 99 per cent.[242]

Aryl and alkylamines are used to inhibit the oxidation of lubricants. Steward et al.[244] have patented phenyl-1-naphthylaminetetraethylenepentamine, triisopropylamine, diethanolamine and dipropylenetriamine for this purpose. They claim that a combination of an aryl and an alkylamine is particularly effective.

The amine salts of weak inorganic acids have been found to be effective vapor phase inhibitors. The use of such volatile rust inhibitors makes possible the protection of steel equipment without the necessity for covering with an oil or grease which is difficult to remove. The equipment need only be wrapped in paper and a small amount of the inhibitor placed inside the package. Alternatively the paper used in wrapping steel equipment may be impregnated with the inhibitor.

In 1944 while searching for an effective vapor-phase inhibitor, diisopropylammonium nitrite was tested and found to be most satisfactory. Subsequent work indicated that dicyclohexylammonium nitrite was even more effective because it is less volatile and less soluble in water. Other alkylammonium nitrites are used. Petit and Estalella[245] report that ferrous metals wrapped in paper impregnated with dicyclohexylammonium nitrite or triethanolammonium nitrite were protected against corrosion produced by air saturated with water vapor at 22°C.

The commercial method for the preparation of dicyclohexylamine involves the hydrogenation of aniline to give cyclohexylamine which is subsequently converted to dicyclohexylamine by heat.[140]

$$C_6H_5NH_2 + 3H_2 \longrightarrow C_6H_{11}NH_2$$

$$2C_6H_{11}NH_2 \longrightarrow (C_6H_{11})_2NH + NH_3$$

Antioxidants. Some amines are effective antioxidants and polymerization inhibitors. Thus isopropyl amine has been found to be very effective for stabilizing vinylidine chloride against oxidation and polymerization[246] and a small amount of dibutylamine or tributylamine prevents the polymerization of liquid tetrafluoroethylene for six months at room temperature. Tributylamine inhibits the polymerization of gaseous tetrafluoroethylene at 200 psi.[247]

The addition of ethylamine to the air in which rubber products are stored inhibits the degradative oxidation.[248] N,N-dialkylpiperazines are used to stabilize cyclized rubber against oxidation.

Vulcanization Accelerators. Large quantities of amines are used in the preparation of rubber vulcanization accelerators. Secondary amines are used in the preparation of thiuram sulfides (R_2N—CS—SS—CS—NR_2) and metallic dialkyldithiocarbonates (R_2NCS_2Na).

Other vulcanization accelerators are prepared from aldehydes and amine salts of higher fatty acids.

Certain sulfonamides, used as accelerators, are prepared by oxidatively condensing 2-mercaptothiazole with an oxidizing agent and a primary amine.[249]

Primary aliphatic amines may be reacted with formaldehyde and hydrogen cyanide to give N-(cyanomethyl)-alkylamines which are further treated with carbon disulfide and sodium hydroxide, followed by reaction with zinc sulfate to give zinc cyanomethylalkyldithiocarbamates.[250]

Secondary amines form salts with 2,6-dimercaptobenzo-(1,2,4,5)-bisthiazole which are useful vulcanization accelerators.[251]

Dibutylammonium oleate is used as a vulcanization accelerator activator.[252]

Plasticizers. Amine salts of organic acids are used as plasticizers for Neoprene.[253]

Phosphated castor oil neutralized with ammonia or an amine has been reported as useful as a plasticizer for natural or synthetic rubber.[254]

Condensation products of ketones and amines are used as softeners for natural or synthetic unvulcanized rubber.[255]

N,N-alkylarylcyclohexylamines have been suggested as plasticizers for cellulose esters, phenolic, vinyl and alkyd resins. N-p-toluenesulfonylcyclohexylamine is marketed under the trade name of "Santicizer 1-H."

Pharmaceuticals. The applications of aliphatic amines in the preparation of pharmaceuticals are far too numerous for all of them to be mentioned here. The naturally occurring alkaloids are all nitrogen bases although few of them involve aliphatic amino groups.

A large number of biologically active materials are substituted aliphatic amines. The very important local anesthetic novocaine p-H_2N—C_6H_4—$COOCH_2CH_2N(C_2H_5)_2$ is prepared by the following sequence of reactions:

$$p\text{-}O_2N\text{—}C_6H_4\text{—}COOH \xrightarrow{PCl_5} p\text{-}O_2N\text{—}C_6H_4\text{—}COCl \xrightarrow{-HOCH_2CH_2N(C_2H_5)_2}$$

$$p\text{-}O_2N\text{—}C_6H_4\text{—}COOCH_2CH_2N(C_2H_5)_2 \longrightarrow$$

$$p\text{-}H_2N\text{—}CH_4\text{—}COOCH_2CH_2N(C_2H_5)_2$$

Ephedrine, $C_6H_5CH(OH)CH(CH_3)NHCH_3$, used in the treatment of asthma and hay fever, is believed to be made by the plant from phenylalanine.

Benzedrine, $C_6H_5CH_2CH(CH_3)NH_2$ has similar activity.

Quaternary ammonium hydroxides such as choline, (2-hydroxyethyl)-trimethylammonium hydroxide and acetyl choline are essential in the metabolism of carbohydrates and in the transportation of fats through the body.

Diethylaminoethanol (from diethylamine and ethylene oxide) is used in the preparation of chloroquine, an antimalarial. di-n-Propylamine is used in the preparation of Benemide, an adjunct to penicillin therapy which markedly increases penicillin tissue and blood levels.

Amines are used in the preparation of penicillin frequently as the penicillin salts.

Antihistamine compounds of the type $(C_6H_5)_2CHO(CH_2)_nNRR'$ where n is 2 to 6 and R and R' are alkyl groups containing not more than four carbon atoms are prepared by the action of $(C_6H_5)_2CHBr$ with the appropriate dialkylamino alcohol in the presence of sodium carbonate.[256]

Ethylamine and β-cyclohexylethyl bromide react to give ethyl-di-(β-cyclohexylethyl) amine which is an effective antispasmodic.[257]

The aliphatic amines also have germicidal activity which increases with the size of the alkyl group and reaches a maximum with n-heptylamine.[258]

Detergents and Surface-Active Agents. As with the lower molecular weight amines, the fatty amines (C_8—C_{18}) react with mineral acids to form salts. The alkylammonium salts containing 8 or fewer carbon atoms are very soluble in water but the solubility decreases with increasing size of the alkyl group so that stearylamine is only sparingly soluble. The salts of unsaturated amines are more soluble than the corresponding saturated ammonium salts.

The fatty amines form salts with acids such as sulfuric or phosphoric acids but these are considerably less soluble in water than the corresponding chlorides. The best method for the preparation of these water-insoluble ammonium salts involves a treatment of a water soluble salt of the amine, such as the acetate, with the anion of the salt to be prepared.

$$2CH_3COONH_3R + H_3PO_4 \longrightarrow (RNH_3)_2HPO_4 + 2CH_3COOH$$

In this way sulfates, phosphates, silicates, etc., can be prepared.

Because of the water insolubility of these amine salts a method has been devised for the waterproofing of surfaces which involves the formation of the insoluble ammonium salts *in situ.*

The surface is first treated with a water-soluble alkylammonium chloride or acetate and then with a solution containing the desired anion.

The primary alkylammonium acetates formed from the amine and acetic acid are all water-soluble and are also appreciably soluble in organic solvents. When the alkyl group contains 12 to 18 carbon atoms the acetates are surface-active and make excellent detergents.

Quaternary ammonium salts are very excellent cationic detergents and are very widely used. Thus quaternary ammonium salts such as $RN(CH_3)_3Cl$ or $R_2N(CH_3)_2Cl$, where R is an alkyl group containing 12 to 18 carbon atoms, are obtained by the action of methyl chloride on the appropriate amine. Commercially these alkylamines are made from fats. The fats are hydrolyzed to give acids which are converted to ammonium salts and heated to give the corresponding amides and nitriles. Hydrogenation of the nitriles give the desired amines. Inasmuch as a mixture of amines is obtained, the resulting quaternary ammonium salts are mixtures in which the R groups may be saturated or unsaturated and contain 12 to 18 carbon atoms.

These quaternary ammonium compounds are good detergents and at the same time are excellent chemical sterilizers having phenol coefficients at 37°C of 200 to 450 against *S Aureus* and 150 to 350 against *E Coli.* At most dilutions the solutions are practically odorless and are essentially nonvolatile so that the salts are not lost from solution.

Quaternary ammonium compounds made from ethylene oxide and primary-, secondary-, or tertiary alkanolamine salts are useful as textile assistants.[259,260]

The ethanolamines made from ethylene oxide and ammonia form salts with organic acids whose water solutions are essentially netural. These ethanolamine soaps therefore have no harsh effect upon the skin and are widely used in cosmetics.

Dehydration of diethanolamine gives morpholine which together with fatty acids is used as an emulsifying agent for self-polishing waxes.

Dehydrohalogenation Catalysts. Tetrachloroethane is dehydrohalogenated to trichloroethylene at 150–200°C in the presence of triethylammonium chloride or tetraethylammonium chloride.[261,262]

High molecular weight acid halides are dehydrohalogenated to ketenes by tertiary amines.[263]

Tertiary amines have been used successfully for the dehydrohalogenation of β-chloro-N-alkylamides to the corresponding acrylamides. Thus $ClCH_2CH_2CON(CH_3)_2$ may be treated with triethylamine for one hour at 130–140°C to give $CH_2{=}CHCON(CH_3)_2$.[264]

In addition to dehydrohalogenation catalysts, tertiary amines are used as catalysts for many reactions which are base catalyzed such as aldol, Knoevenagel and Perkin condensations.

Metal-Amine Reductions. Lower molecular weight alkylamines have been used as solvents for metal-amine reductions. Benkeser[265] reported that aromatic rings are reduced to monoolefins by lithium in ethylamine. Attempts to replace ethylamine by higher primary amines were unsuccessful because lithium becomes progressively less soluble with increasing length of the carbon chain. Ethylenediamine being difunctional has excellent solvent properties for lithium and permits working at higher temperatures. Reductions are carried out at or near reflux temperatures.

Acetophenone is reduced to the corresponding alcohol 1-(1-cyclohexenyl)ethanol) in 65 per cent yield by lithium in methylamine.

$$\langle\!\!\!\!\!\!\!\bigcirc\!\!\!\!\!\!\!\rangle - CO - CH_3 \quad \xrightarrow[CH_3NH_2]{Li} \quad \langle\!\!\!\!\!\!\!\bigcirc\!\!\!\!\!\!\!\rangle - CHOH - CH_3$$

Benzonitrile is reduced to cyclohexanemethylamine in 47 per cent yield with lithium in ethylamine.

$$\langle\!\!\!\!\!\!\!\bigcirc\!\!\!\!\!\!\!\rangle - CN \quad \xrightarrow[CH_3NH_2]{Li} \quad \begin{array}{c} H_2C \diagup CH_2 \diagdown CH \diagup CH_2NH_2 \\ | \qquad\qquad | \\ H_2C \diagdown CH_2 \diagup CH_2 \end{array}$$

and phenylacetonitrile gave a mixture of β-(1-cyclohexenyl)-ethylamine (51 per cent) and β-cyclohexylethylamine

$$\langle\!\!\!\!\!\!\!\bigcirc\!\!\!\!\!\!\!\rangle - CH_2CN \quad \xrightarrow[C_2H_5NH_2]{Li} \quad \begin{array}{c} H_2C \diagup CH_2 \diagdown C \diagup CH_2CH_2NH_2 \\ | \qquad\qquad || \\ H_2C \diagdown CH_2 \diagup CH \end{array} \quad +$$

$$\begin{array}{c} H_2C \diagup CH_2 \diagdown CH \diagup CH_2CH_2NH_2 \\ | \qquad\qquad | \\ H_2C \diagdown CH_2 \diagup CH_2 \end{array}$$

Benzonitrile was the only case observed where a monoolefin was not the major product.[266]

Lithium in ethylenediamine is also an excellent reducing system.[267] Aromatic rings were reduced to cyclomonoolefins and cycloparaffins. Phenols were reduced to cyclic alcohols, ethers are cleaved, acetylenic compounds are reduced whether or not the triple bond is terminal or internal and olefins with internal double bonds are reduced to paraffins. Lithium-ethylenediamine seems to be the most powerful and the least selective of all the metal-amine systems investigated thus far. In carrying out the reduction, the substrate in ethylenediamine is heated to 90–100°C and treated portionwise with lithium wire. The rate of addition is controlled by the hydrogen evolution and the persistence of the blue color. The usual time required is about 1.5–2.0 hours. The mixture is kept under total reflux then cooled and water added slowly to dissolve the solids. The organic layer is washed with dilute hydrochloric acid, then with saturated salt solution after which it is dried and distilled.

Some of the results reported by Reggel, Friedel and Wender are shown in Table 1-8.

TABLE 1-8. REDUCTION BY LITHIUM IN ETHYLENEDIAMINE

Compound	Product	Per cent yield
Phenanthrene	Decahydro- and dodecahydrophenanthrene	90
Benzene	Cyclohexene	51
Benzyl Alcohol	Hexahydrobenzyl alcohol	38.5
Phenol	Cyclohexanone and cyclohexanol	50.0
1-Heptene	Heptane	41

Individual Amines. One of the most important uses for monomethylamine is in the preparation of surface-active agents of the amide-type (Igepon T made by the General Aniline and Film Company). This compound is made by first passing ethylene oxide into 30 per cent aqueous sodium bisulfite at 70°C to form sodium isothioante which is then reacted with an excess of methyl amine at 280°C and a pressure of 200 atmospheres.

$$NaHSO_3 + CH_2\!-\!CH_2 \longrightarrow HOCH_2CH_2SO_3Na$$
$$\backslash O \diagup$$

$$HOCH_2CH_2SO_3Na + CH_3NH_2 \longrightarrow CH_3NHCH_2CH_2SO_3Na + H_2O$$

This compound (the sodium salt of methyl taurine) is then treated in aqueous solution with oleyl chloride.

$$C_{17}H_{33}COCl + CH_3NHCH_2CH_2SO_3Na \longrightarrow C_{17}H_{33}CO\!-\!N\!-\!CH_2CH_2SO_3Na$$
$$\phantom{C_{17}H_{33}COCl + CH_3NHCH_2CH_2SO_3Na \longrightarrow C_{17}H_{33}CO-N-CH}\underset{\textstyle CH_3}{|}$$

Igepon T

An alternate procedure for the preparation of methyl taurine involves the reaction of sodium sulfite with ethylene dichloride to give the sodium salt of β-chloroethylsulfite which is then reacted with methylamine. More than a million pounds of monomethylamine was converted into Igepon T and related compounds in 1954.

Monomethylamine is also used in the preparation of photographic developers ("Eglon," "Metol") and drugs (adrenaline, cocaine, synthetic caffeine, etc.).

Dimethylamine is used largely in the preparation of herbicides, fungicides, rubber vulcanization accelerators, etc. Dimethylformamide which is an important solvent for acrylonitrile polymers and copolymers is made by du Pont and by Rohm & Haas from methylformate and dimethylamine.

$$HCOOCH_3 + (CH_3)_2NH \longrightarrow HCON(CH_3)_2 + CH_3OH$$

About 14 million pounds of dimethylamine are used annually.

Trimethylamine is used in the preparation of choline, a supplement in animal feeds. Choline chloride is made by mixing 0.4 mole of ethylene chlorohydrin with 130 ml of 25 per cent aqueous trimethylamine at room temperature and permitting the mixture to stand for about 22 hours after which it is heated at 55–65°C for about 1 hour. The water and unreacted material are removed by low pressure distillation to give a 98 per cent yield of product.

$$HOCH_2CH_2Cl + (CH_3)_3N \longrightarrow [HOCH_2CH_2 \overset{+}{-} N(CH_3)_3]Cl^-$$

This accounts for 3 million pounds of trimethylamine.[268]

The ethylamines are used in the preparation of drugs such as novocaine and some antimalarials.

Disopropylamine in the form of its nitrite salt is an excellent vapor-phase inhibitor.

Mono- and dibutylamine soaps are used in the formation of oil-water emulsions. Both mono- and dibutylamines are intermediates in the formation of dyes, rubber chemicals, flotation agents, corrosion inhibitors, etc.

Ethylenediamine is made by the action of ammonia on ethylene dichloride. Other polyamines such as diethylenetriamine, triethylenetetramine and tetraethylenepentamine are obtained as by-products. These amines are used in the preparation of soaps, vulcanization accelerators, dyes, wetting agents, electroplating additives, etc.

Ethylenediamine is used in the preparation of the sequestering agent ethylenediaminetetracetic acid.

Polyamines are used in formulations for the emulsion polymerization of butadiene and styrene for the preparation of "cold rubber." In the presence of ferrous ions, the polyamines accelerate the reduction of the peroxides. A mixture of 80 per cent diethylenetriamine and 20 per cent trimethylenetetramine is most effective.[269]

Amines such as octadecylamine, dilaurylamine, 1-(3-ethylpentyl)-4-ethyloctylamine and N-benzyl-1-(3-ethylpentyl)-4-ethyloctylamine are used in the solvent extraction of uranium oxide from ore-leach liquors.[270]

REFERENCES

1. Brown, H. C., and Johannesen, R. B., *J. Am. Chem. Soc.*, **75**, 16 (1953).
2. Brown, H. C., Bartholomay, H., Jr., and Taylor, M. D., *J. Am. Chem. Soc.*, **66**, 435 (1944).
3. Brown, H. C., and Gerstein, M., *J. Am. Chem. Soc.*, **72**, 2926 (1950).
4. Brown, H. C., and Taylor, M. D., *J. Am. Chem. Soc.*, **69**, 1332 (1947).
5. Brown, H. C., and Barbaras, G. K., *J. Am. Chem. Soc.*, **75**, 6 (1953).
6. Brown, H. C., and Sujishi, S., *J. Am. Chem. Soc.*, **70**, 2878 (1948).
7. Brown, H. C., *J. Am. Chem. Soc.*, **69**, 1137 (1947).
8. Brown, H. C., *J. Am. Chem. Soc.*, **67**, 374, 378 (1945).
9. Lambert, J. D., and Strong, E. D. T., *Proc. Roy. Soc. London*, **A200**, 566 (1950).
10. Farbenfabriken Bayer A. G., British Patent 735,779 (Aug. 31, 1955).
11. Whitmore, F. C., and Langlois, D. P., *J. Am. Chem. Soc.*, **54**, 3441 (1932).
12. Westphal, O., and Jerchel, D., *Ber.*, **73**, 1002 (1940).
13. Braun, J. v., *Ber.*, **70**, 979 (1937).
14. Shreve, R. N., and Rothenberger, L. W., *Ind. Eng. Chem.*, **29**, 1361 (1937).
15. Shreve, R. N., and Burtsfield, D. R., *Ind. Eng. Chem.*, **33**, 219 (1941).
16. I. G. Farbenindustrie, A. G., German Patent 648,088 (July 21, 1937).
17. Nekrasova, V. A., and Shuikin, N. I., *Izvest. Akad. Nauk. S.S.S.R., Otdel. Khim. Nauk*, **1952**, 495.
18. Kenyon, R. C., Inskeep, G. C. Gillette, L., and Price, J. F., *Ind. Eng. Chem.*, **42**, 2388 (1950).
19. Schulte, K. E., and Goes, M., *Arch Pharm.*, **290**, 118 (1957).
20. Galat, A., and Elion, G., *J. Am. Chem. Soc.*, **61**, 3585 (1939).
21. Marszak-Fleury, A., *Compt. rend.*, **241**, 808 (1955).
22. Williams, R., Jr., Willner, J. R., and Schaeffer, J., *Chem. Eng. News*, p. 3982 (Sept. 19, 1955).
23. Uchida, H., and Ichinokawa, H., Japan Patent 1623 (May 9, 1952).
24. Davies, P. *et al.*, U. S. Patent 2,609,394 (Sept. 2, 1952).
25. Goshorn, R. H., U. S. Patent 2,349,222 (May 16, 1944).
26. Hindley, F., and Fisher, J. W., U. S. Patent 2,782,237 (Feb. 19, 1957).
27. Krishnamurthy, U. A., and Rai, M. R. A., *J. Indian Inst. Sci.*, **39**, 138 (1957).
28. Kozlov, N. S., and Akhmetshima, L., *Doklady Akad. Nauk. S.S.S.R.*, **85**, 91 (1952).
29. Popov, M. A., and Shuiken, N. I., *Izvest Akad. Nauk. S.S.S.R., Otdel. Khim. Nauk.*, **1955**, 308.
30. Yano, K. *et al.*, Japan Patent 180,950 (Nov. 16, 1949).
31. Whitehead, W. W., British Patent 649,980 (Feb. 7, 1951).
32. Smeykal, K., German Patent 637,731 (Nov. 3, 1936).

33. Arnold, H. R., U. S. Patent 2,078,922 (May 4, 1957).
34. Davies, P., Reynolds, P. W., Coats, R. R., and Taylor, W. C., U. S. Patent 2,609,394 (Sept. 2, 1952).
35. Schreyer, R. C., U. S. Patent 2,754,330 (July 10, 1956).
36. Schwoegler, E. J., and Adkins, H., *J. Am. Chem. Soc.,* **61,** 3499 (1939).
37. Metayer, M., and Xyong, Ng. D., *Bull. Soc. Chim France,* **1954,** 615.
38. Emerson, W. S., and Uraneck, C. A., *J. Am. Chem. Soc.,* **63,** 749 (1941).
39. Winans, C. F., *J. Am. Chem. Soc.,* **61,** 3566 (1939).
40. Haskelberg, L., *J. Am. Chem. Soc.,* **70,** 2811 (1948).
41. Ruhrchemie, A. G., British Patent 728,702 (April 27, 1955).
42. Skita, A., Kiel, F., Havemann, H., *Ber.,* **66,** 1400 (1933).
43. Adkins, H., "Reactions of Hydrogen," University of Wisconsin Press, 1937.
44. Emerson, W. S., Neumann, F. W., and Moundres, T. P., *J. Am. Chem. Soc.,* **63,** 972 (1941).
45. Meissner, F., Schwiedessen, E., and Othmer, D. F., *Ind. Eng. Chem.,* **46,** 724 (1954).
46. Winans, C. F., and Adkins, H., *J. Am. Chem. Soc.,* **55,** 2051 (1933).
47. Brimer, M. R. *et al.,* U. S. Patent 2,518,659 (Aug. 15, 1950).
48. Mignonac, G., *Compt. rend.,* **172,** 223 (1921).
49. Olin, J. F., and Schwoegler, E. J., U. S. Patent 2,278,372.
50. Norton, D. G., Haney, V. E., Davis, F. C., Mitchesl, L. I., and Ballard, S. A., *J. Org. Chem.,* **19,** 1054 (1954).
51. Covert, L. W., U. S. Patent 2,160,058 (May 30, 1939).
52. E. I. du Pont de Nemours, British Patent 713,344, Aug. 11, 1954.
53. Popov, M. A., and Shuiken, N. I., *Doklady Akad. Nauk. S.S.S.R.,* **101,** 273 (1956).
54. Joffe, I. S., U.S.S.R. Patent 102,701 (May 25, 1956).
55. Leuckart *et al., Ber.,* **18,** 2341 (1885); **19,** 2128 (1886); **20,** 104 (1887); **22,** 1409, 1851 (1889).
56. Ingersoll, A. W. *et al., J. Am. Chem. Soc.,* **58,** 1808 (1936).
57. Novelli, A., *J. Am. Chem. Soc.,* **61,** 520 (1939).
58. Sommelet and Ferrand, *Bull. soc. chim. France,* [4], **35,** 446 (1924).
59. Clarke, H. T., Gillespie, H. B., and Weisshaus, S. Z., *J. Am. Chem. Soc.,* **55,** 4571 (1933).
60. Kirby, J. E., U. S. Patent 2,366,534 (Jan. 2, 1945).
61. Eschweiler, W., *Ber.,* **38,** 880 (1905).
62. Decker, H., and Becker, P., *Ber.,* **45,** 2404 (1912).
63. Buck, J. S., and Baltzly, R., *J. Am. Chem. Soc.,* **62,** 161 (1940); **63,** 1964 (1941); **64,** 2263 (1942).
64. Wallach *et al., Ber.,* **34,** 54 (1905).
65. Rohrmann, E., and Shonle, H. A., *J. Am. Chem. Soc.,* **66,** 1516 (1944).
66. Blicke, F. F., and Zienty, F. B., *J. Am. Chem. Soc.,* **61,** 93 (1939).
67. Ingersoll, A. W., Org. Syntheses Coll Vol. 2, 503 (1943).
68. Crossley, F. S., and Moore, M. L., *J. Org. Chem.,* **9,** 529 (1944).
69. Johns, I. B., and Burch, J. M., *J. Am. Chem. Soc.,* **60,** 919 (1938).
70. Moore, M. L. in "Organic Reactions," Vol. V, p. 301, New York, John Wiley & Sons, Inc., 1949.

71. Bunnett, J. F., and Marks, J. L., *J. Am. Chem. Soc.,* **71,** 1587 (1949).
72. Bunnett, J. F., Marks, J. L., and Moe, H., *J. Am. Chem. Soc.,* **75,** 985 (1953).
73. Mousseron, M., Jacquise, R., Zagdoun, R., *Bull. soc. chim. France,* **1953,** 974.
74. Kost, A. N., and Grandbert, I. I., *Zhur. Obschei, Khim.,* **25,** 1432 (1955).
75. Rikasheva, A. F., and Miklukhin, C. A., *Zhur. Obschei. Khim.,* **26,** 2133 (1956).
76. Staple, E., and Wagner, E. C., *J. Org. Chem.,* **14,** 559 (1949).
77. Campbell, K. N., *et al., J. Am. Chem. Soc.,* **68,** 1556 (1946).
78. Adkins, H., and Billica, H. R., *J. Am. Chem. Soc.,* **70,** 695 (1948).
79. Hass, H. B., Susie, A. G., and Heider, R., *J. Org. Chem.,* **15,** 8 (1950).
80. Iffland, D. C., and Yen, T. F., *J. Am. chem. Soc.,* **76,** 4180 (1954).
81. Kametoni, T., and Nomura, Y., *J. Pharm. Soc. Japan,* **74,** 413 (1954).
82. Reeve, W., and Christian, J., *J. Am. Chem. Soc.,* **78,** 860 (1956)
83. Lycan, W. H., Puntambeker, S. V., and Marvel, C. S., Org. Syntheses Coll. Vol. II, 318 (1943).
84. Burger, A., and Bennet, W. B., *J. Am. Chem. Soc.,* **72,** 5414 (1950).
85. Basolo, F., Murmann, P. K., and Chen, Y. T., *J. Am. Chem. Soc.,* **75,** 1478 (1953).
86. Krafft, F., and Moye, A., *Ber.,* **22,** 811 (1889).
87. Harwood, J., U. S. Patent 2,122,644 (July 5, 1938).
88. Sakakibara, S., Fusiwara, B., and Konori, S., *J. Chem. Soc. Japan Ind., Chem. Sect.,* **54,** 594 (1951).
89. Finholt, A. E., *et al., J. Am. Chem. Soc.,* **69,** 1199 (1947).
90. Nystrom, R. F., and Brown, W. G., *J. Am. Chem. Soc.,* **70,** 3738 (1948).
91. Amundson, C. H., and Nelson, L. S., *J. Am. Chem. Soc.,* **73,** 242 (1951).
92. Mousseron, M., *et al., Bull soc. chim. France,* **1952,** 1042.
93. Compaigne, E. E., and Jacoby, F., *El Cristil (Puerto Rico),* **7,** 19 (1953).
94. Brown, H. C., and Subba Rao, B. C. S., *J. Am. Chem. Soc.,* **77,** 3164 (1955).
95. Schmidt, W., U. S. Patent 2,160,578.
96. Carothers, W. H., and Jones, G. A., *J. Am. Chem. Soc.,* **47,** 3051 (1925).
97. Young, H. P., U. S. patent 2,355,356 (Aug. 8, 1944).
98. Armour and Company, British Patent 773,432 (April 24, 1957).
99. Prohé, O., and Cottin, H., *Compt. rend.,* **245,** 1140 (1957).
100. Komori, S. *et al., Oil Chemist Soc. Japan,* **3,** 261 (1954).
101. Sakakabara, S., Takashima, S., and Komori, S., *J. Chem. Soc. Japan,* **56,** 497 (1953).
102. Young, H. P., Jr., and Christensen, C. W., U. S. Patent 2,287,219 (June 23, 1942).
103. Renfrew, M. M., and Warner, D. E., U. S. Patent 2,690,456 (Sept. 28, 1954).
104. Swendloff, J., U. S. Patent 2,762,835 (July 11, 1956).
105. Costabello, D., and Mugno, M. E., Italian Patent 538,058 (Feb. 3, 1956).
106. Horak, B. W., U. S. Patent 2,166,152 (July 18, 1939).
107. Freidlin, L. K., Balandin, A. A., Rudneva, K. G., and Sladkova, T. A., *Izvest. Akad. Nauk. S.S.S.R. Otdel. Khim. Nauk.,* **1957,** 166.
108. Vanyushina, V. S., Vilesova, M. S., and Chistyakova, G. A., *Khim. Prom.,* **1958,** 205; *Chem. Abs.,* **53,** 1111 (1959).
109. Tarbell, D. S., Shakespeare, N., Claus, C. J., and Bunnett, J. F., *J. Am. Chem. Soc.,* **68,** 1217 (1946).

110. Benkeser, R. A., *et al., J. Am. Chem. Soc.,* **77,** 6042 (1955).
111. Sabatier, P., and Mailhe, A., *Ann. Chim.,* [8] **16,** 70 (1909).
112. Adkins, H., and Wojcik, B., *J. Am. Chem. Soc.,* **56,** 247 (1934).
113. Ueno, S., Komori, S., and Morikava, H., *J. Soc. Chem. Ind. Japan, Supp. Binding,* **45,** 214 (1942).
114. Adkins, H., and Wojcik, B., *J. Am. Chem. Soc.,* **56,** 2419 (1934).
115. Tarbell, D. S., and Noble, P., Jr., *J. Am. Chem. Soc.,* **72,** 2657 (1950).
116. Uffer, A., and Schlitter, E., *Helv. Chim. Acta,* **31,** 1397 (1948).
117. Brown, W. G., "Organic Reactions," Vol. 6, p. 469, New York, John Wiley & Sons, Inc., 1951.
118. Ciba Ltd., Swiss Patent 273,953 (June 1, 1951).
119. Gavrilow, *et al., Bull soc. chim. France,* [5] **12,** 773 (1945).
120. Swann, H., in "Techniques of Organic Chemistry," Vol. I, p. 143, New York, Interscience Publishers.
121. Johnson, K., and Degering, Ed. F., *J. Am. Chem. Soc.,* **61,** 3194 (1939).
122. Badische Aniline and Soda Fabrick, German Patent 848,197 (Sept. 1, 1952).
123. Nightingale, D., and Tweedie, V., *J. Am. Chem. Soc.,* **66,** 1968 (1944).
124. Kornblum, N., and Fishbein, L., *J. Am. Chem. Soc.,* **77,** 6266 (1955).
125. Hofmann, A. W., *Ber.,* **15,** 762 (1882).
126. Whitmore, F. C., and Thorpe, R. S., *J. Am. Chem. Soc.,* **63,** 1118 (1941).
127. Whitmore, F. C., and Homeyer, A. H., *J. Am. Chem. Soc.,* **54,** 3435 (1932).
128. Hass, H. B., Susie, A. G., and Heider, R. L., *J. Org. Chem.,* **15,** 8 (1950).
129. Ehestadt, Dessertation Freibert 1B, 1886.
130. Braun, J. V., and Jostes, F., *Ber.,* **59,** 1091 (1926).
131. Pearson, D. E., Baxter, J. F., and Carter, K. N., "Organic Syntheses," Vol. 29, p. 21, New York, John Wiley & Sons, Inc., 1949.
132. Ing, H. R., and Manske, R. H. F., *J. Chem. Soc.,* **1926,** 2348.
133. Sheehan, J. C., and Bolhofer, W. A., *J. Am. Chem. Soc.,* **72,** 2786 (1950).
134. Smith, L. I., and Emerson, O. H., "Organic Syntheses," Vol. 29, p. 18, New York, John Wiley & Sons, Inc., 1949.
135. Wagner Jauregg T., Arnold, H., and Rauen, H., *Ber.,* **74B,** 1372 (1941).
136. Sommers, A. H., and Aaland, S. E., *J. Org. Chem.,* **21,** 484 (1956).
137. Nikoforva, Russian Patent 104,111 (Oct. 25, 1956).
138. Southwood, J., U. S. Patent 2,772,312 (Nov. 27, 1956).
139. Illich, G. M., Jr., and Robinson, R. M., U. S. Patent 2,822,392 (Feb. 4, 1958).
140. Carswell, T. S., and Morrill, H. L., *Ind. Eng. Chem.,* **29,** 1247 (1937).
141. Bashkirov, A. N., Kagan, Yu. B., and Kliger, G. A., *Doklady Akad. Nauk. S.S.S.R.,* **109,** 774 (1956).
142. Reppe, W., German Patent 839,800 (May 26, 1956).
143. Reppe, W., Kutepow, N. V., and Heintseler, M., German Patent 909,937 (April 29, 1954).
144. Uchida, H., and Bando, K., *Report Gov't. Chem. Ind. Research Inst. Tokyo,* **49,** 473 (1954).
145. Schuster, C., and Hartman, A., German Patent 848,653 (Sept. 8, 1956).
146. Pohland, A., U. S. Patent 2,772,311 (Nov. 27, 1956).
147. Aspinall, S. R., *J. Am. Chem. Soc.,* **63,** 852 (1941).

148. Dannley, R. L., Lukin, M., and Shapiro, J., *J. Org. Chem.*, **20**, 92 (1955).
149. Marszak, I., and Marszak-Fleury, A., *Compt. rend.*, **241**, 704 (1955).
150. Olin, J. F., and Deger, T. E., U. S. Patent 2,192,523 (Mar. 5, 1940).
151. Reynolds, D. D., and Laakso, T. M., U. S. Patent 2,716,134 (Aug. 23, 1955).
152. Naudet, M., Baldy, J., and Desnuelle, P., *Bull. soc. chim. France*, **1954**, 1167.
153. Tadeusz, T. *Acta Polon. Pharm.*, **13**, 453 (1956).
154. Olah, C., and Kuhn, I., *Ber.*, **89**, 2211 (1956).
155. White, E. H., *J. Am. Chem. Soc.*, **77**, 6011, 6014 (1955).
156. Cannell, L. G., Ph.D. Thesis, Penn State Univ. 1956, *Dissertation Abstracts*, **16**, 1325 (1956).
157. Emerson, W. S., Hess, S. W., and Uhle, F. C., *J. Am. Chem. Soc.*, **63**, 872 (1941).
158. Businelli, M., *Il Farmace (Pavia) Ed. Sci.*, **10**, 127 (1955).
159. Hill, R. L., and Crowell, T. I., *J. Am. Chem. Soc.*, **78**, 2284 (1956).
160. Krossig, H., Greber, G., *Makromol. Chem.*, **17**, 131 (1956).
161. Thies, A., and Schoenenberger, H., *Arch Pharm.*, **26**, 408 (1956).
162. Robinson, C. N., Jr., and Olin, J. F., U. S. Patent 2,452,602 (Nov. 2, 1948).
163. Murata, N., and Arac, H. J., *Chem. Soc. Japan Ind. Chem. Sect.*, **57**, 578 (1954).
164. Ballard, S. A., *et al.*, British Patent 633,056 (May 9, 1951).
165. Finch, *et al.*, British Patent 658,422 (Oct. 10, 1951).
166. Finch, H. D., Peterson, E. A., and Ballard, S. A., *J. Am. Chem. Soc.*, **74**, 2016 (1952).
167. Mannich, C., Handke, K., and Rogh, K., *Ber.*, **68B**, 2112 (1936).
168. Yoshitomi Drug Co., British Patent 761,001 (Nov. 7, 1956).
169. Meisenheimer, J., Greeske, H., and Willmersdorf, A., *Ber.*, **55**, 513 (1922).
170. Cope, A. C., and Towle, P. H., *J. Am. Chem. Soc.*, **71**, 3423 (1949).
171. Cope, A. C., Foster, T. T., and Towle, P. H., *J. Am. Chem. Soc.*, **71**, 3929 (1949).
172. Mamlock, L., and Wolffenstein, R., *Ber.*, **33**, 149 (1900).
173. Cullis, C. F., and Waddington, D. J., *Proc. Roy. Soc.*, **A244**, 110 (1958).
174. Peters, L. M. *et al.*, *Ind. Eng. Chem.*, **40**, 2044 (1948).
175. Florentine, F. P., Jr., U. S. patent 2,793,221 (May 21, 1957).
176. Huscher, M. E., Long, M. W., Jr., and Moore, J. C., British Patent 704,226 (Feb. 17, 1954).
177. Swistak, E., Mastagli, P., and Zafiriades, Z., *Compt. rend.*, **237**, 1713 (1953).
178. Lowe, A. J., and Butler, D., British Patent 763,932 (Dec. 19, 1956).
179. Lowe, A. J., Butler, D., and Meade, E. M., British Patent 763,434 (Dec. 12, 1956).
180. Sakakibara, S., Fujiwara, A., and Konari, S., *Kôgyô Kaguku Zasshi*, **59**, 1149 (1956).
181. Konori, S., Sakakibara, S., Fujiwara, A., *Technol. Reports Osaka University*, **6**, 387 (1956).
182. Horne, W. H., and Shriner, R. L., *J. Am. Chem. Soc.*, **54**, 2925 (1932).
183. Long, M. W., Jr., Hascher, M. E., and Moore, J. C., U. S. Patent 2,602,819 (July 8, 1952).

184. Petrov, A. A., and Al'bitskaya, V. M., *Zhur. Obschei. Khim.*, **26**, 1907 (1956).
185. Al'bitskaya, V. M., and Petrov, A. A., *Zhur. Obschei. Khim.*, **28**, 901 (1958).
186. Gaar, F. S., and Reck, R. A., U. S. patent 2,759,021 (Aug. 14, 1956).
187. Malinovskii, M. S., and Baranov, S. N., *Zhur. Priklad. Khim.*, **25**, 410 (1952).
188. Rothstein, R., and Binovic, K., *Compt. rend.*, **236**, 1050 (1953).
189. Platie, J. T., *J. Org. Chem.*, **14**, 543 (1949).
190. Blicke, F. F., "Organic Reactions," Vol. I, p. 303, New York, John Wiley & Sons, Inc., 1942.
191. Eilar, K. R., and Moe, O. A., *J. Am. Chem. Soc.*, **65**, 3841 (1953).
192. Hennion, G. F., Price, C. C., and Wolff, V. C., Jr., *J. Am. Chem. Soc.*, **77**, 4633 (1955).
193. Alexander, E. R., and Underhill, E. J., *J. Am. Chem. Soc.*, **71**, 4014 (1949).
194. Schmidle, C. J., and Mansfield, R. C., *J. Am. Chem. Soc.*, **77**, 4636 (1955).
195. Julia, M., and Tchernoff, G., *Bull. soc. chim. France*, **1955**, 830.
196. Holdren, R. F., and Hixon, R. M., *J. Am. Chem. Soc.*, **68**, 1198 (1946).
197. Senkus, M., *J. Am. Chem. Soc.*, **68**, 10 (1946).
198. Johnson, H. G., *J. Am. Chem. Soc.*, **68**, 12 (1946).
199. Wright, G. F., and Chute, W. J., Canadian Patent 479,928 (Jan. 1, 1952).
200. White, E. H., and Feldman, W. R., *J. Am. Chem. Soc.*, **79**, 5832 (1951).
201. Emmons, W. D., Pagano, A. S., and Stevens, T. E., *J. Org. Chem.*, **23**, 311 (1958).
202. Emmons, W. D., and Freeman, J. P., *J. Am. Chem. Soc.*, **77**, 4387 (1955).
203. Olák, G., Moszkó, L., Kuhn, I., and Szelke, M., *Chem. Ber.*, **89**, 2374 (1956).
204. Stork, G., and McElvain, S. M., *J. Am. Chem. Soc.*, **69**, 971 (1947).
205. Hirao, I., *Chem. Soc. J. (Japan) Ind. Chem. Sect.*, **57**, 62 (1954).
206. Cavallito, C. J., *J. Am. Chem. Soc.*, **77**, 4159 (1955).
207. Gardiner, C., Kerrigan, V., Rose, J. V., and Weedon, B. C. L., *J. Chem. Soc.*, **1949**, 780.
208. Reppe, W., *Ann.*, **596**, 12 (1955).
209. E. I. du Pont de Nemours, British Patent 617,347 (Feb. 4, 1949).
210. Urry, W. H., Joveland, O. O., and Stacy, F. W., *J. Am. Chem. Soc.*, **74**, 6155 (1952).
211. Rigby, G. W., and Schoeder, H. E., U. S. Patent 2,409,315 (1946).
212. Pruett, R. L. *et al.*, *J. Am. Chem. Soc.*, **72**, 646 (1952).
213. Ruhrchemie, A. G., British Patent 734, 535 (Aug. 3, 1955).
214. Balandin, H. A., and Vasyuninie, N. A., *Doklady Akad. Nauk. S.S.S.R.*, **103**, 831 (1955).
215. Isoshima, T., Ann. rept. Shionoge Research Lab No. 5, 47 (1955).
216. Gresham, T. L. *et al.*, *J. Am. Chem. Soc.*, **73**, 3168 (1951).
217. Takase, S., *J. Chem. Soc. Japan Pure Chem. Section*, **74**, 59 (1953).
218. Haley, C. A. C., and Maitland, P., *J. Chem. Soc.*, **1951**, 3155.
219. Lloyd, D., and Marshall, D. R., *J. Chem. Soc.*, **1956**, 2597.
220. Kinman, A., and Muths, R., *Compt. rend.*, **239**, 1807 (1954).
221. N. V. de Batasfasche Pet. Maatshcappij, Dutch Patent 65,644 (May 15, 1950).
222. Ciba Ltd., Swiss Patent 306,942 (July 16, 1955).
223. Linsker, F., and Evans, R. L., *J. Am. Chem. Soc.*, **67**, 1581 (1945).

224. Linsker, F., and Evans, R. L., *J. Org. Chem.,* **10,** 283 (1945).
225. Heinimger, S. A., *J. Org. Chem.,* **22,** 701 (1957).
226. Graymore, J., *J. Chem. Soc.,* **1947,** 1116.
227. Niederl, J. B., and Rao, D. S., *J. Org. Chem.,* **14,** 27 (1949).
228. Mouren, H., Chevin, P., and Petit, L., *Bull. soc. chim. France,* **1955,** 1573.
229. Breeder, J. H., and Waterman, H. I., U. S. Patent 2,807,635 (Sept. 24, 1957).
230. Vincent, and Chappius, *Compt. rend.,* **102,** 436 (1886).
231. Buurman, A., German Patent 756,185 (May 19, 1952).
232. Gardiner, C., Kerrigan, U., Rose, J. D., and Weedon, B. C. L., *J. Chem. Soc.,* **1949,** 789.
233. Reppe, W., and Magin, A., German Patent 845,515 (July 31, 1952).
234. Darragh, J. L., and Stayner, R. D., *Ind. Eng. Chem.,* **46,** 254 (1954).
235. Ringwald, E. L., and Ham, G. E., U. S. Patent 2,616,922 (Nov. 4, 1952).
236. Ciba, Ltd., Swiss Patent 306,648 (July 1, 1955).
237. Kato, S., Tsuji, T., and Toyashima, S., Japan 2480 (1957) April 22, 1957.
238. Arens, J. F., Bouman, J. G., and Koerts, D. H., *Rec. trav. chim.,* **74,** 1040 (1955).
239. Henkel et Cie GmbH, British Patent 771,875 (April 3, 1957).
240. Shelton, R. S., *et al., J. Am. Chem. Soc.,* **68,** 753 (1946).
241. Babayan, A. T., Grigoryan, A. A., and Grigoryan, A. N., *Zhur. Obschei. Khim.* **27,** 1827 (1956).
242. Mann, C. A., Lauer, B. E., and Huttin, C. T., *Ind. Eng. Chem.,* **28,** 159 (1936).
243. Goebel, M. T. J., and Walker, I. F., British Patent 562,586 (July 7, 1944).
244. Stewart, W. T., Goldschmidt, A., and Harle, O. L., U. S. Patent 2,687,377 (Aug. 24, 1954).
245. Petit, M., Estalella, F., *Rev. cienc. ap.,* **12,** 293 (1958).
246. Kirkbride, F. W., British Patent 627,930 (Aug. 18, 1949).
247. Hanford, W. E., U. S. Patent 2,407,419 (Sept. 10, 1946).
248. Wolk, I. L., U. S. Patent 2,363,717 (Nov. 28, 1944).
249. Adams, R., "Organic Reactions," Vol. I, New York, John Wiley & Sons, Inc., 1942.
250. Harmon, M. W., U. S. Patent 2,372,895 (April 3, 1945).
251. Dolt, M. L., and Sayre, R. E., U. S. Patent 2,518,670 (Aug. 15, 1950).
252. Williams, I., and Neal, A. M., U. S. Patent 1,940,280 (Dec. 19, 1934).
253. Braz, G. I., and Skorodumov, V. A., *Doklady Akad. Nauk. S.S.S.R.,* **59,** 489 (1948).
254. Omansky, M., U. S. Patent 2,388,618 (Nov. 6, 1945).
255. Throdahl, M. C., U. S. Patent 2,381,526 (Aug. 7, 1945).
256. Rieveschl, G., Jr., U. S. Patent 2,421,714 (June 3, 1947).
257. Blicke, F. F., and Monroe, E., *J. Am. Chem. Soc.,* **61,** 91 (1939).
258. Morgan, G. T., and Cooper, E. A., Orig. Com. 8th Intern. Congr. Appl. Chem., **19,** 243.
259. I. G. Farbenindustrie, A. G., British Patent 460,146 (Jan. 18, 1937).
260. Ulrich, H., and Ploetz, E., U. S. Patent 2,137,314 (Nov. 22, 1939).
261. Vining, W. H., U. S. Patent 2,361,072 (Oct. 24, 1944).
262. E. I. du Pont de Nemours & Co., British Patent 565,494 (Nov. 14, 1944).

263. Hueter, R., U. S. Patent 2,383,863 (Aug. 28, 1945).
264. Ciba Ltd., British Patent 746,747 (Mar. 21, 1956).
265. Benkesser, R. A., Robinson, R. E., Saure, D. M., and Thomas, H., *J. Am. Chem. Soc.,* **76,** 631 (1954).
266. Benkesser, R. A., *et al., J. Am. Chem. Soc.,* **77,** 6042 (1955).
267. Reggel, L., Friedel, R. A., and Wender, I., *J. Org. Chem.,* **22,** 891 (1957).
268. Klein, H. C., U. S. Patent 2,623,901 (Dec. 30, 1952).
269. Embree, W. H., Spolsky, R., and Williams, L., *Ind. Eng. Chem.,* **43,** 2553 (1951).
270. Coleman, C. F., Brown, K. B., Moore, J. G., and Crouse, D. J., *Ind. Eng. Chem.,* **50,** 1756 (1958).

2. ARYLAMINES

When an amino group is attached to a benzene ring, many of the properties are changed. Thus aryl amines are much weaker bases than the alkylamines and this can be accounted for on the basis of resonance. It is possible to write three different electronic structures for aniline in which the unshared pair of electrons on the nitrogen is shifted so as to form a double bond with the adjacent carbon atom and an unshared pair of electrons is found on each *ortho-* and the *para-*positions of the ring.

Since this electron pair, which is responsible for the amino group being a proton acceptor, is effectively smeared out over the benzene ring, especially in the *ortho-* and *para* positions, it is not as readily available for coordination with a proton as is the electron pair of an alkylamino nitrogen.

It follows that any electronegative group substituted on a benzene ring would facilitate the withdrawal of the electron pair from the nitrogen and into the ring and so should decrease the basic strength still more. This is especially true of the nitro group which, when in a position *ortho-* or *para-* to the amino group, is capable of resonance with it and the benzene ring.

The magnitude of the effect of a nitro group on the basic strength of an amino group is shown in Table 2–1.

The nitro group in the *meta* position lowers the basic strength of the amino group very much but still has much less effect than if it were in the *ortho-* or *para-*position.

83

TABLE 2-1. THE BASIC STRENGTHS OF SOME ARYLAMINES

Amine	Formula	pKb
Aniline	$C_6H_5NH_2$	9.30
Methylaniline	$C_6H_5NHCH_3$	9.60
Dimethylaniline	$C_6H_5N(CH_3)_2$	9.62
o-Toluidine	$o\text{-}CH_3\text{—}C_6H_4\text{—}NH_2$	9.47
m-Toluidine	$m\text{-}CH_3\text{—}C_6H_4\text{—}NH_2$	9.30
o-Nitroaniline	$o\text{-}O_2N\text{—}C_6H_4\text{—}NH_2$	13.82
m-Nitroaniline	$m\text{-}O_2N\text{—}C_6H_4\text{—}NH_2$	11.40
p-Nitroaniline	$p\text{-}O_2N\text{—}C_6H_4\text{—}NH_2$	12.00
o-Chloroaniline	$o\text{-}Cl\text{—}C_6H_4\text{—}NH_2$	12.05
m-Chloroaniline	$m\text{-}Cl\text{—}C_6H_4\text{—}NH_2$	10.40
p-Chloroaniline	$p\text{-}Cl\text{—}C_6H_4\text{—}NH_2$	12.00

Two phenyl groups attached to a nitrogen atom as in diphenylamine give a compound possessing no basic properties and in fact the hydrogen attached to the nitrogen atom can be replaced by metals indicating that it is somewhat acidic.

Arylamines undergo reactions of two types, e.g., those involving the amino group and those involving the benzene ring. The amino group, because of the unshared electron pair on the nitrogen, is a source of electrons for electrophilic attack on the ring, especially at the *ortho-* and *para-*positions. The amino group consequently activates the ring so that substitution reactions are made much easier than on benzene itself.

If substitution reactions are carried out in acid solution the electron pair is tied up through formation of an anilinium ion which is electron attracting and results in electron withdrawal from the ring resulting in decreased activity towards substitution. Under these conditions, substitution occurs with considerable difficulty at the *meta*-position.

The parent member of the family of arylamines is aniline, first obtained in 1826 by the destructive distillation of indigo and in 1834 it was isolated from coal tar. It is now made almost exclusively by the reduction of nitrobenzene. Other arylamines can be prepared from substituted nitrobenzenes or by alkylation of the amino group.

Preparation of Arylamines

Reduction of Aromatic Nitro Compounds. The reduction of aromatic nitro compounds can be accomplished in a number of ways. One of the most common involves the use of metal-acid systems. Tin and hydrochloric acid are frequently used in the laboratory. The nitro compound is mixed with the finely divided metal and concentrated hydrochloric acid is added gently. The temperature is controlled to permit a smooth but not too vigorous reaction. All nitro groups in di- and polynitro compounds are re-duced.

Stannous chloride is also capable of reducing nitro groups so that in most cases the final products are the amine and stannic chloride

$$2C_6H_5NO_2 + 3Sn + 12HCl \longrightarrow 2C_6H_5NH_2 + 3SnCl_4 + 4H_2O$$

Acetic acid may be added to increase the solubility of the nitro compound.

The reduction of nitro compounds with tin and hydrochloric acid some-times results in partial chlorination of the benzene ring. The chlorine enters the *ortho-* or *para-*positions with respect to the amino group.[1] When *p*-nitrophenetole is reduced by this method without cooling, 3-chloro-*p*-phe-netidine is formed as the main product.

Aromatic nitro compounds can be reduced to the corresponding amines with zinc and hydrochloric acid in alcohol solution but again chlorina-tion of the ring frequently occurs.

Zinc dust and sodium or potassium hydroxide in alcohol is also an ef-fective reducing system for the preparation of some amines. The method is particularly useful for the reduction of nitro compounds which are soluble in alcoholic sodium hydroxide solutions and for nitro compounds which are unstable in the presence of acids.[2,3]

One of the most important methods for the reduction of aromatic nitro compounds to amines uses iron turnings and an acid. As carried out the reaction actually involves the reducing system iron and water with only sufficient acid added to promote the reaction. As little as 1/40 the amount of hydrochloric acid needed to form the theoretical amount of ferric chloride is adequate to get a satisfactory reaction. The iron is precipitated as a sludge largely in the form of iron oxide.

$$4C_6H_5NO_2 + 9Fe + 4H_2O \xrightarrow{HCl} 4C_6H_5NH_2 + 3Fe_3O_4$$

Nearly all nitro groups may be reduced in this way, even those resisting reduction by other methods.

Nitrobenzene is reduced to aniline in this way in 86 per cent yield; *o*-nitrotoluene to *o*-toluidine in 73 per cent yield; 4-nitrobiphenyl to 4-amino-biphenyl in 93 per cent yield, and *α*-nitronaphthalene to *α*-naphthylamine in 96 per cent yield.[4]

Nitro compounds can be reduced to amines with alcoholic ammonium sulfide. The reaction is generally carried out by dissolving the nitro com-pound in alcoholic ammonia and passing a stream of hydrogen sulfide into the solution. In some cases the reaction will occur at room temperature. More frequently the reaction is carried out at elevated temperatures under pressure. If the reaction is accomplished at sufficiently low temperatures, hydroxylamines may be the primary products.

This procedure finds special utility in the reduction of di- or polynitro compounds. If the reaction is effected at the lowest possible temperature only one of the nitro groups is reduced to the amine.

Selective reduction of 2,4,6-trinitrotoluene is accomplished by treatment in an ethyl acetate solution with ammonium acetate and aqueous sodium bisulfide. The pH is maintained at 7.5–8.5 by periodic addition of hydrochloric acid. The temperature is held at 60–70°C. 2,6-Dinitro-4-aminotoluene is obtained in 50 per cent yield and 2,4-diamino-6-nitrotoluene in 40 per cent yield.[5]

Di- and polynitro compounds are reduced quite rapidly but mononitro compounds only slowly. This accounts for the selectivity obtained.

Sodium hydrogen sulfide and sodium sulfide have a greater reducing power than ammonium sulfide and have the advantage that no free sulfur separates out during the reaction.[6]

Sodium sulfide, Na_2S, and sodium hydrosulfite, $Na_2S_2O_4$, have also been used for the reduction of aromatic nitro compounds. Sodium hydrosulfite successfully reduces the nitro group in nitrophenols. *Ortho-* and *meta*-nitrobenzaldehydes have been reduced to the corresponding aminobenzaldehydes.[7]

Catalytic hydrogenation of aromatic nitro compounds may be carried out in an alcohol solution at temperatures of 25–100°C and a pressure of 30 atmospheres, in the presence of Raney nickel.[8] With a platinum oxide catalyst the reduction will take place at room temperature a pressure[9] of and 1 to 2 atmospheres.

Copper may also be used as a catalyst at temperatures of 300–400°C. Nitrobenzene is hydrogenated to aniline in quantitative yields in the presence of a catalyst consisting of nickel sulfide deposited upon activated alumina. The nitrobenzene vapors and three times the theoretical amount of hydrogen are passed at 300°C over the catalyst at a rate of 300 g of nitrobenzene per liter of catalyst per hour. The catalyst operates for 1600 hours without any substantial decline in activity.[10]

Still other catalysts have been used successfully. Aromatic nitro compounds such as the nitroxylenes may be hydrogenated continuously by passing them together with water and hydrogen over a catalyst consisting of a sulfide of molybdenum, tungsten or chromium.[11] The reaction temperature should be controlled within narrow limits; in the reaction zone the temperatures should be between 170 and 230°C.

p-Xylidene is obtained quantitatively by passing a mixture of the vapors of 2,5-dimethylnitrobenzene (1 volume) and *p*-xylidene (4 volumes) together with a three-fold excess of hydrogen over a tungsten sulfide catalyst at 205°C at 500 psi.[12]

Souders[13] prepared xylidines by continuous liquid-phase hydrogenation of nitroxylenes. Temperatures of 190–200°C were used and 6.5–12 moles of water per mole of nitroxylene was introduced together with sufficient hydrogen to maintain the pressure at 100 psi.

The continuous liquid-phase hydrogenation of 2,4- and 2,6-dinitro-toluene in methanol in the presence of Raney nickel catalyst at low temperatures gives the corresponding tolylenediamines in 99 per cent yield. These diamines are useful intermediates in the preparation of tolylene diisocyanates.[14]

Other reducing agents for the reduction of aromatic nitro compounds to aryl amines include aluminum amalgam in aqueous alcohol,[15,16,17,18] and ferrous sulfate with sodium, potassium or ammonium hydroxide.

Ammonolysis of Aryl Halides. Halogen atoms attached directly to a benzene ring are quite unreactive. In this way they resemble vinyl halides. Consequently the preparation of arylamines by the reaction of aryl halides and ammonia is much more difficult than when alkyl halides are used for the preparation of alkylamines.

With aryl halides, primary amines are formed almost exclusively. High pressures and temperatures and a copper catalyst are required.[19,20] Aniline is made from chlorobenzene by reaction with ammonia in the presence of copper oxide.[21] The reaction is carried out at 190–230°C. The product contains aniline (90 per cent yield), phenol (5 per cent yield) and small amounts of diphenylamine. The mole ratio of ammonia to chlorobenzene should be at least 5:1.

Halogen atoms may be activated by electronegative substituents, such as the nitro group, in a position *ortho-* or *para-* to the halogen. *Ortho-* or *para*-Nitrochlorobenzene reacts with ammonia at moderate temperatures in the absence of a catalyst to give nitroanilines. *meta*-Nitrobenzene will not react in the absence of copper catalyst. 2,4-Dinitrochlorobenzene reacts with ammonia at reflux temperatures to give 2,4-dinitroaniline.

Ammonolysis of Phenols. Phenol may be converted to aniline by heating with zinc chloride and ammonia at 300–350°C.[22]

Naphthols may be converted to naphthylamines by treatment with ammonia and sodium bisulfite. Reaction temperatures of 90–150°C are required and pressure is usually necessary. The yields of amines are high.[23,24] This reaction, known as the Bucherer reaction, is applicable to naphthols, hydroxyquinolines, and resorcinol.[25]

The reaction is reversible and may also be used to convert a naphthylamine to the corresponding naphthol.

Miscellaneous Methods. Azo and hydrazo compounds are reduced to arylamines.

$$C_6H_5{-}NHNH{-}C_6H_5 + 2(H) \longrightarrow 2C_6H_5NH_2$$

$$C_6H_5-N{=}N-C_6H_5 + 4(H) \longrightarrow 2C_6H_5NH_2$$

Successful reducing agents for the reduction of azo compounds include tin and alcoholic hydrogen chloride,[26] alkali polysulfides,[27] hydrogen sulfide,[28] and sodium hydrosulfite.[29]

Azo compounds can also be hydrogenated to amines in the presence of palladium or platinum catalysts.

Amino groups have been introduced into a phenol by coupling with a diazonium salt and reduction of the resulting azo compound with sodium hydrosulfite.[30] Thus phenol may be coupled with diazotized sulfanilic acid and the resulting azo compounds reduced to *p*-aminophenol.

$$HO-C_6H_4-N{=}N-C_6H_4-SO_3Na \xrightarrow{Na_2S_2O_4}$$

$$HO-C_6H_4-NH_2 + H_2NC_6H_4SO_3Na$$

In this manner 1-amino-2-naphthol and 4-amino-1-naphthol have been prepared in 85 and 75 per cent yields.

Aromatic nitriles can be reduced to the corresponding amines by reducing agents as has been described for the preparation of aliphatic amines.

Isophthalonitrile, Raney cobalt, ammonia and a small amount of water heated with hydrogen to 240°F under 1500 psi until no further absorption of hydrogen occurs gives a 90 per cent yield of *m*-xylylenediamine. *ortho*- and *para*-Xylylenediamine are prepared similarly.[31]

Certain aromatic compounds can be converted to amines by direct amination with hydroxylamine. Thus 1-nitronaphthalene when treated with hydroxylamine in methanolic potassium hydroxide yields 4-nitro-1-naphthylamine in 60 per cent yield.[32]

A process for the direct amination of benzene to aniline has been described.[33] Benzene is vaporized and mixed with ammonia (mole ratio 2:1) and passed at 90°C and a pressure of 1 atmosphere through a silent electric discharge. Conversions of ammonia to aniline are about 15–20 per cent per pass.

Arylamines such as *p*-tolylamine, *p*-methoxybenzylamine and *α*-naphthylmethylamine have been prepared by an interesting procedure consisting of: (1) chloromethylation, (2) condensation of the chloromethyl group with urea, and (3) decomposition of the condensation product with alkali.[34]

Thus a mixture of anisole, paraformaldehyde and concentrated hydrochloric acid was agitated for 4 hours at temperatures of 8–10°C to give p-chloromethylanisole. This compound was refluxed with urea in water and steam-distilled. The residue was dried and dispersed in water and the mixture let stand 12–16 hours until crystals appeared. The crystals were anisylurea formed in 75 per cent yield.

Hydrolysis of the anisylurea was effected in aqueous sodium hydroxide to give p-methoxybenzylamine in 91 per cent yield. Cuprous chloride possessed catalytic activity in the formation of the substituted urea.

Aromatic acids can be converted to arylamines by treatment with hydroxylamine and polyphosphoric acid.[35] The reaction mixture is heated usually at 150–170°C until a rapid evolution of carbon dioxide begins, which usually takes 5–10 minutes. The method is less applicable than the Curtius and Hoffmann reactions but has the advantage of simplicity and rapidity. As examples 1- and 2-naphthoic acids have been converted to the corresponding naphthylamines in 80 per cent yield. m- and p-Toluic acids give the corresponding toluidines in 72–76 per cent yield and bromobenzoic acids give bromoanilines in 43–56 per cent yields.

Some ketones can be converted to the corresponding amines by treatment with 2 moles of hydroxylamine. In this case the first step involves a Beckman rearrangement of the ketoxime to an amide which is further transformed into an amine.

$$R_2-CO \rightarrow R_2-C=NOH \rightarrow R-CO-NHR \rightarrow RCH_2NHR$$

Diphenylamine is prepared by passing aniline vapor over a suitable catalyst at temperatures of 350–450°C. The catalyst may consist of copper, nickel, iron or zinc chlorides supported on alumina or alumina-silica.[36,37]

Triphenylamine is prepared by dissolving potassium in hot aniline and adding bromobenzene. It may also be prepared by refluxing diphenylamine, iodobenzene and potassium carbonate in nitrobenzene. Triphenylamine is obtained in 82–85 per cent yield.

$$2(C_6H_5)_2NH + 2C_6H_5I + K_2CO_3 \rightarrow 2(C_6H_5)_3N + 2KI + H_2O + CO_2$$

Preparation of Alkylarylamines

Secondary and tertiary amines in which one of the groups is aryl are important intermediates and are usually made by the alkylation of the arylamine. This may be accomplished with alcohols, alkyl halides and esters of sulfuric and phosphoric acids.

Reaction of Amines with Alkyl Halides. The reaction of alkylamines with alkyl halides is a very good method for the preparation of secondary or tertiary alkylamines but the method is not nearly as effective for the preparation of alkylarylamines. Alkylation of arylamines can be accomplished using alkyl bromides but chlorides are not sufficiently reactive.

As an example of the procedure, ethylaniline may be prepared by heating a mixture of ethyl bromide and aniline at reflux temperatures for several hours.

A mixture of secondary and tertiary amines is usually obtained and in order to suppress the formation of tertiary amine a large excess of arylamine is used. In the synthesis of N-phenylbenzylamine, a 96 per cent yield of the secondary amine is obtained if the mole ratio of aniline to benzyl chloride is at least 4:1.[38]

An interesting application of this reaction has been reported by Dickey[39] for the introduction of trifluoroethyl groups onto the nitrogen atom of aniline. The alkylations have been accomplished by heating aniline and the fluoroalkyl halide in an autoclave for several hours as 250–255°C.

$$C_6H_5NH_2 + CF_3CH_2Br \longrightarrow C_6H_5NHCH_2CF_3 + HBr$$

The temperature required varies considerably with the type of fluoroalkyl halide used. Temperatures much above 250°C frequently lead to decomposition. Yields are approximately 50 per cent.

The N-fluoroalkylanilines in turn may be treated with an olefin oxide such as ethylene oxide to give N-fluoroalkyl-N-hydroxyalkylanilines which have proved to be valuable coupling constituents for a series of gas- and light-fast azo dyes for cellulose acetate. The reaction of the fluoroalkylaniline with ethylene oxide is rather difficult and requires temperatures of 200°C for up to 18 hours. Yields are approximately 60 per cent.

The procedure for the preparation of arylamines from aniline and alkyl halides may be reversed so that a mono- or dialkylamine may be reacted with an aryl halide. Inasmuch as a halogen attached to the benzene ring is very unreactive, a copper salt is necessary to serve as a catalyst. As an example methylaniline is prepared from methylamine and chlorobenzene at elevated temperatures and pressures. The best conditions for this reaction are a temperature of 215°C, a cuprous chloride catalyst and a mole ratio of methylamine to chlorobenzene of 5:1. The pressure under these conditions is about 1000 psi.[40]

Reactions of Amines with Alcohols. The commercial processes for the preparation of alkylarylamines involve the reaction of aniline salts with alcohols at temperatures of about 200°C. Aniline and an alcohol may be heated with a small amount of iodine in an autoclave at 220–230°C for 10 hours. Mono- and dialkylanilines are obtained in 60–90 per cent yield.[41]

N-Methylaniline is obtained by heating a mixture of aniline, methanol and concentrated sulfuric acid in an autoclave for 10 hours at 195–200°C. Best yields are obtained using aniline, methanol and sulfuric acid in a mole ratio of 1:1.25:0.1.[42]

Secondary amines are produced almost exclusively when an aromatic amine is reacted with an alcohol in a hydrogen atmosphere and in the presence of a catalyst consisting of 2–20 per cent copper on alumina promoted with an oxide of calcium, zinc, chromium, magnesium, manganese or iron. Thus aniline, methanol and hydrogen in a molar ratio of 1:1.5:2.5 were passed for 125 hours over a catalyst (4.6 per cent copper, 9.0 per cent zinc, as the oxide, on alumina) at 250°C and a pressure of 1 atmosphere, to give a product consisting of 96 per cent N-methylaniline.[43]

Raney nickel has been found to be a suitable catalyst for the alkylation of aromatic amines with alcohols. Compared with acid catalyzed alkylations, Raney nickel favors the formation of secondary amines. The alkylations are carried out either under atmospheric pressure in which the water of reaction is removed as fast as formed or by heating a mixture of the amine, alcohol and catalyst in an autoclave. Yields of secondary amines ranged from 28–72 per cent.

Thus a mixture of aniline, ethyl alcohol and Raney nickel (about 1 per cent) were heated in a stainless steel autoclave for 6 hours at 220°C. Ethylaniline and diethylaniline were formed in a ratio of about 5:1.

When a mixture of benzene and ethyl alcohol is added dropwise to aniline at 150°C, removing the water as formed, ethylaniline is obtained in 65 per cent yield.

Refluxing a mixture of aniline and n-propyl alcohol for 6 hours in the presence of a U. O. P. nickel catalyst gives N-propylaniline in 80 per cent yield.[44]

Other alcohols such as n-butyl alcohol behave similarly.[45]

Rice and Kohn[46] also report the effective use of Raney nickel to catalyze the alkylation of aniline with alcohols. As an example, aniline, Raney nickel and propyl alcohol were refluxed for 16 hours to give an 82 per cent yield of N-propylaniline. Benzidine when alkylated with ethyl alcohol gave a 63 per cent yield of N,N'-diethylbenzidine. The amount of Raney nickel preferred is 1 to 4 parts by weight per part of primary amino group present in the alkylarylamine.

In the industrial preparation of dimethylaniline, 110 parts of methanol, 100 parts of aniline, and 10 parts of concentrated sulfuric acid are heated in an autoclave for 6 hours at 205° C. Conversions of 99 per cent are obtained. Above 230° C side reactions become noticeable.[47]

An arylamine treated with benzyl alcohol in the presence of an anhydrous alkali hydroxide, with continuous removal of water as formed, gives arylbenzylamines in good yield. Thus aniline and benzyl alcohol heated with anhydrous potassium hydroxide at 250° C gives N-benzylaniline.[48]

Aromatic amines have been alkylated with dialkyl ethers.[49] The vapors of the amine and the dialkyl ether are diluted with 5–50 volumes of an inert gas and passed over a pure alumina catalyst at 200–260°C. A mixture of alkyl and dialkylamines is obtained from the lower molecular weight ethers such as dimethyl, diethyl and dipropyl ethers.

Phenols may sometimes be used in place of the alcohols. Thus Cook[50] describes the preparation of secondary arylamines such as dinaphthylamine from β-naphthylamine and β-naphthol in the presence of β-naphthalenesulfonic acid at temperatures of 210–270° C.

N-tertiary-alkylated aryl secondary diamines are prepared from an aryldiamine and a tertiary alcohol having fewer than eight carbon atoms in the presence of a catalyst such as iodine or a hydrohalogen acid. Thus p-phenylenediamine and *tert*-butyl alcohol were heated for 5 hours at 180° C to give $p\text{-}C_6H_4[NHC(CH_3)_3]_2$.

Reductive Alkylation. Alkylarylamines can also be prepared by reductive alkylation of an amine and a carbonyl compound.

Methylanilines can be obtained by reaction between aniline and formaldehyde followed by hydrogenation of the resulting aldimine. One such procedure is described in a Swiss patent issued to Ciba Ltd.[51]

The reaction is carried out in a basic medium provided by the presence of a tertiary amine. Thus aniline was added during 15 minutes to aqueous formaldehyde containing a small amount of triethylamine and stirred for an additional 10 minutes. The organic layer was removed, dissolved in methanol containing triethylamine and hydrogenated over a nickel-kieselguhr catalyst at 60–85° C and a pressure of 10 atmospheres. The product after removal of triethylamine, methanol and water contained 90 per cent methylaniline, 5 per cent dimethylaniline, and 5 per cent unreacted aniline.

Nitroanilines can be methylated with formaldehyde in formic acid.[52] Thus a 30 per cent formalin solution was added to a warm solution of p-nitroaniline and the mixture heated on the steam bath to give a 67 per cent yield of p-nitrodimethylaniline.

Aromatic nitro compounds as well as arylamines are reductively alkylated by reaction with a ketone and hydrogen in the presence of a hydrogenation catalyst. p-Nitroaniline, methyl ethyl ketone and hydrogen passed over a catalyst consisting of chromic oxide, copper oxide and barium oxide at 160° C and a pressure of 8 atmospheres gives p-$C_6H_4[NHCH(CH_3)$-$CH_2CH_3]_2$.[53]

The reaction may also be carried out at a temperature of 160° C in the presence of a platinum on alumina catalyst using a mole ratio of p-nitro-aniline to methyl ethyl ketone of 1:8 and under a hydrogen pressure of 100 atmospheres. A 94 per cent yield of p-$C_6H_4[NHCH(CH_3)CH_2CH_3]_2$ was obtained. No p-H_2N—C_6H_4—$NHCH(CH_3)CH_2CH_3$ or p-H_2N—C_6H_4—NH_2 were formed.

The catalyst must be pretreated by heating with hydrogen at temperatures above 300° C in order to obtain best yields of the dialkylated diamines. When the catalyst was not pretreated a 43 per cent yield of the dialkylated diamine was obtained together with a 38 per cent yield of p-H_2N—C_6H_4—$NHCH(CH_3)CH_2CH_3$ and a 17 per cent yield of p-phenylenediamine.[54]

Similarly a solution of nitrobenzene and butyraldehyde in acetic acid may be hydrogenated in the presence of a platinum oxide catalyst to give di-butylaniline in 69 per cent yield. Substitution of trimethylammonium chloride and Raney nickel for acetic acid and platinum oxide gives dibutylaniline in 63 per cent yield.[55] Diethylaniline, di-n-propylaniline and dimethylaniline are obtained in 70, 34, and 92 per cent yields respectively. Nitrobenzene and acetone gives N-isopropylaniline in 53 per cent yield.

Reductive amination of benzophenone, using the Leuckart method with diphenylurea and formic acid, gives a mixture of approximately equal amounts of *ortho*- and *para*-H_2N—C_6H_4—$CH(C_6H_5)_2$. In a similar manner benzophenone and C_6H_5NHCHO gives a mixture of the same compounds. Obviously a rearrangement has occurred. It was proposed that C_6H_5N-$(CHO)CH(C_6H_5)_2$ was an intermediate and this was confirmed by substituting $C_6H_5NHCH(C_6H_5)_2$ for benzophenone and again the same mixture of compounds was obtained.[56]

The hydrogenation of azo compounds in the presence of an aldehyde and sodium acetate using a Raney nickel catalyst gives secondary amines. Thus hydrogenation of a mixture of azobenzene and butyraldehyde in alcohol solution in the presence of Raney nickel and sodium acetate gives N-butylaniline in 71 per cent yield. Similarly $C_6H_5NHC_7H_{15}$ and C_6H_5-$NHCH_2C_6H_5$ are obtained in 74 and 79 per cent yields, respectively. The reaction probably involves hydrogenation to the hydrazine which condenses with the aldehyde, which in turn undergoes further hydrogenation to the secondary amine.[57]

An interesting modification of the reductive alkylation of arylamines has been described.[58] The amine is heated with an aromatic alcohol in the presence of potassium hydroxide and a small amount of the corresponding aldehyde. During the reaction the alcohol furnishes the hydrogen for the

reduction of the intermediate aldimine and is itself converted to the aldehyde for further reaction with the amine. Thus aniline is heated with benzyl
alcohol in the presence of potassium hydroxide with removal of the water
as formed. The reaction is accelerated by the addition of small amounts of
benzaldehyde. The reaction proceeds according to the following scheme:

$$C_6H_5NH_2 + C_6H_5CHO \leftrightarrows C_6H_5N{=}CHC_6H_5 + H_2O$$

$$C_6H_5N{=}CHC_6H_5 + C_6H_5CH_2OH \longrightarrow C_6H_5NHCH_2C_6H_5 + C_6H_5CHO$$

Alkylation with Sulfates and Phosphates. Hunig[59] developed a process
for the methylation of aromatic amines under conditions in which phenolic
groups are not affected. The methylation is accomplished with dimethyl
sulfate in the presence of sodium bicarbonate; in this manner p-toluidine
was converted to N,N-dimethyl-p-toluidine in 95 per cent yield at 50–60° C
in the presence of sodium carbonate, sodium sulfate and a little water. The
reaction was carried out until carbon dioxide was no longer evolved.

p-Methyldimethylaniline, o-methyldimethylaniline, p-chlorodimethylaniline and p-hydroxydimethylaniline were obtained from the corresponding substituted aniline in 75–95 per cent yields.[60]

Aniline and nuclear-substituted anilines can be alkylated with esters of
phosphoric acid.

$$3C_6H_5NH_2 + 2(RO)_3PO \longrightarrow 3C_6H_5NR_2 + 2H_3PO_4$$

The reaction proceeds to completion with the formation of dialkylated
anilines. No monoalkylated product is formed. The yields range from 53–
95 per cent.

In comparable cases diethylanilines are usually obtained in better yields
than the dimethylanilines. This can probably be related to the fact that reactions with triethyl phosphate are less vigorous than with trimethyl phosphate. In alkylations with trimethyl phosphate, a very vigorous reaction
occurs as reflux temperatures are approached and after the reaction subsides two layers are invariably present. With triethyl phosphate, refluxing
begins smoothly and the two layers appear only after 30–90 minutes.
Methyl and ethyl alcohols are found in the condensed vapors indicating
the existence of a competing reaction involving cleavage of the alkyl phosphate between the oxygen and phosphorus atom. The reactions are carried
out by refluxing equimolar amounts of amine and trialkyl phosphate.

Refluxing a mixture of arylamine and an alkyl phosphate (R_3PO_4) gives
N-alkylarylamines. Thus aniline heated with trimethylphosphate gives dimethyl aniline in 78 per cent yield. Similarly diethylaniline, dipropylani-
line and dibutylaniline are obtained in 99, 78 and 79 per cent yields,
respectively.[61,62]

The acid chlorides of dialkyl phosphates $(RO)_2POCl$ react with aniline to give $(RO)_2PONHC_6H_5$ which when heated gives N-alkylanilines in 93–95 per cent yields.[63]

Arylpropylamines have been prepared by the reaction of allyl chloride with benzene in the presence of ferric chloride to give 2-chloro-1-phenyl-propane. The reaction has been extended to the preparation of other aryl-chloropropanes in 14–53 per cent yield.

The arylchloropropanes are treated with alcoholic ammonia to give 20–50 per cent yields of arylpropylamines. Some of the arylchloropropanes react successfully with alcoholic methylamine to give 24–62 per cent yields of N-methylarylpropylamines.[64]

Reactions of Aromatic Amines

The reactions of aromatic amines differ from those of aliphatic amines in two important respects. The aromatic amines are much weaker bases and the amino group has an activating effect on reactions involving the benzene ring. Many of the reactions are very similar to those observed with aliphatic amines and these will be discussed only briefly. More attention will be given to those reactions which are different from those of the alkylamines.

Salt Formation. Most arylamines form salts and are therefore soluble in dilute acids such as hydrochloric and sulfuric acids. Arylammonium chlorides are best prepared by adding dry hydrogen chloride to an ether solution of the amine. The salt is precipitated and may be recovered readily by simple filtration. Arylamines are such weak bases, however, that the salts are extensively hydrolyzed in water solutions. Salts of higher molecular weight amines such as the naphthylamines are only slightly soluble in water.

Negatively substituted amines such as the nitroanilines and diphenyl-amine are such weak bases that they do not form salts.

Amines form salts with picric acid which are useful for identification purposes.

Acylation. Arylamines react with acid anhydrides or acid chlorides to form amides. The compounds made from aniline are called anilides and are crystalline solids frequently used for identification of the acids.

$$C_6H_5NH_2 + (CH_3CO)_2O \longrightarrow CH_3CONHC_6H_5 + CH_3COOH$$

Acetanilide is an important analgesic and antipyretic.

Benzenesulfonyl chloride reacts with aryl and arylalkylamines to form sulfonamides in much the same manner as with primary and secondary alkylamines.

$$C_6H_5SO_2Cl + C_6H_5NH_2 \longrightarrow C_6H_5SO_2NHC_6H_5 + HCl$$

Gluzman[65] investigated the reaction of solid aromatic and heterocyclic amines with solid acylating agents such as maleic, succinic and phthalic anhydrides and sulfonyl chlorides. The reagents were ground in a mortar and in some cases heated to a definite temperature in order to promote the reaction. Glutzman presents evidence to show that reaction occurs without formation of a liquid phase. Reactions were carried out at temperatures considerably below those required for the formation of an eutectic.

Acetylation of α- and β-naphthylamines is accomplished with ketene to give the corresponding N-acetylnaphthylamine. The reaction is accomplished by introducing ketene into a toluene solution of the naphthylamine. Yields are 85–90 per cent.[66]

Oxanilide, C_6H_5NH—CO—CO—NHC_6H_5, is prepared in 90 per cent yield by the reaction of oxalic acid with aniline at 125–135°C in the presence of an inert solvent capable of removing the water of reaction as an azeotrope. Alternatively one of the reactants can be heated to 100–110°C and the second added slowly as the temperature is raised to 125–135°C. The product crystallizes on cooling.[67]

The condensation of primary or secondary aryl amines with hydroxy fatty acids in the presence of an anion exchange resin such as Amberlite IRA-400 and Amberlite XR-81 can be accomplished. Thus a mixture of p-aminophenol, lactic acid and the ion exchange resin in toluene is refluxed and the water removed azeotropically to give N-lactyl-p-aminophenol.[68]

When citric acid is heated with an excess of aniline at 124°C for 3 hours, an 88 per cent yield of the trianilide is obtained. At 140–150°C a mixture of the trianilide and the anil-anilide of citric acid is obtained. The anil-anilide is converted to the α,γ, dianalide in 92 per cent yield by boiling with dilute ammonia.

Similar compounds are made from aconitic acid. The anil-anilide of aconitic acid has the structure[69]

o-Phenylenediamine reacts with acids to give benzamidazoles

Reaction with Aldehydes—Formation of Schiff's Bases. Arylamines react with aldehydes in much the same way as do primary alkylamines except that the resulting aldimines are somewhat more stable and more resistant to hydrolysis so that they can be isolated with greater ease. Reduction by any standard method gives secondary amines. Schiff's bases from arylamines and aliphatic aldehydes are readily polymerized to crystalline compounds which seem to be trimers or dimers.

Aniline reacts with benzaldehyde to form benzalaniline in about 85 per cent yield. It is isolated as a yellow solid which melts at 56°C. Hydrogenation of this Schiff's base gives benzylphenylamine.

Aniline reacts with propargyl aldehyde in benzene solution at room temperature to give the enolic form of malonylaldehyde anil.[70]

$$C_6H_5NH_2 + HC{\equiv}CH-CHO \rightarrow C_6H_5N{=}CH-CH{=}CHOH$$

The formation of Schiff's bases is a reversible reaction which is very well illustrated by the work of Porai-Koshits and Renizov.[71]

An interesting example of the formation of Schiff's bases from *o*-phenylenediamine and dialdehydes or diketones is the reaction with glyoxal to give quinoxoline.

α-Diketones react similarly to form quinoxoline derivatives.

The amine component of the Schiff's base may be replaced by reaction with a second amine. Thus reaction of $C_6H_5CH{=}N-C_6H_4-NO_2$ with $p\text{-}CH_3O-C_6H_4-NH_2$ results in the displacement of the *p*-nitroaniline by the more basic amine.

$$C_6H_5CH{=}N{-}C_6H_4NO_2 + p\text{-}CH_3O{-}C_6H_4{-}NH_2 \rightleftarrows$$
$$C_6H_5CH{=}N{-}C_6H_4{-}OCH_3 + O_2N{-}C_6H_4{-}NH_2$$

The reaction proceeds much more slowly in completely anhydrous solutions. The reaction can be run without a solvent in a sealed tube at 120–130°C or in toluene, benzene or carbon tetrachloride. The reaction is reversible and the position of equilibrium depends upon the relative basicities and structural features of the two amines.

Oxidation. Primary and secondary aromatic amines are very sensitive to oxidation and darken quite rapidly on exposure to air. Solid amines are somewhat less sensitive to oxidation than are liquids.

With suitable oxidizing agents aniline is converted into many products such as azobenzene, azoxybenzene, benzoquinone, and aniline black. The initial oxidative attack apparently involves an extraction of a hydrogen attached to the nitrogen to give an unstable free radical which may dimerize, or be further oxidized.

$$C_6H_5NH_2 + O_2 \longrightarrow C_6H_5NH. + (HO_2..?)$$

Peracetic acid oxidizes aniline to nitrosobenzene.[72] Peracetic acid is also reported to be effective in oxidizing arylamines to the corresponding nitrobenzene. Anhydrous solutions of peracetic acid were prepared from acetic anhydride and 90 per cent hydrogen peroxide at ice-bath temperatures. After the exothermic formation of peracetic acid had occurred the aromatic amine was oxidized in the boiling solution. The presence of small amounts of hydrogen peroxide and diacetyl peroxide does not interfere.[73] Yields of nitrobenzenes formed from a number of aromatic amines are shown in Table 2–2.

TABLE 2–2. OXIDATION OR ARYLAMINES TO NITROBENZENES

Amine	Yield of Nitrobenzene (%)
Aniline	83
p-Toluidine	72
o-Toluidine	70
p-Anisidine	82
o-Anisidine	70
p-Chloroaniline	62

In some cases, traces of highly colored impurities (possibly azoxybenzenes) are found, but these can be readily removed by adsorption on silica gel.

The method seems applicable to at least some aliphatic amines. Thus *t*-octylamine was converted to the corresponding nitrooctane in 87 per cent yields; *sec*-butylamine was converted to 2-nitrobutane in 65 per cent yield and *n*-hexylamine to 1-nitrohexane in 33 per cent yield.

Aniline treated with alkaline permanganate gives azobenzene.

$$2C_6H_5NH_2 \longrightarrow C_6H_5-N=N-C_6H_5$$

p-Toluidine is oxidized in a similar manner to the corresponding azo compound.[74] Terent'ev and Mogilyanskii[75] found that aniline, *p*-toluidine and *p*-aminoanisole could be readily oxidized at room temperature to the corresponding azo compounds in good yields. The oxidation is achieved with oxygen or air in pyridine containing cuprous chloride. The yields with the above three amines were 88, 95 and 70 per cent, respectively. *m*-Nitroaniline gives a 25 per cent yield of azo compound but the *p*-isomer and anthranilic acid fail to give any azo compound. 1-Aminonaphthalenes give mainly tars but 2-aminonaphthalenes give mainly dinaphthazine and binaphthyl. Aliphatic amines are not oxidized in this manner. Pyridine seems to be a specific solvent for the reaction although 2-picoline may be used. When sodium hypochlorite is used as the oxidizing agent *p*-aminophenol is obtained together with azobenzene and other products.

$$C_6H_5NH_2 + NaOCl \longrightarrow p\text{-}HO-C_6H_4-NH_2 + NaCl$$

Further oxidation gives quinones.

Lead tetraacetate also has been found to be an effective oxidizing agent for converting aromatic amines to symmetrical azo compounds.[76] Yields of azo compounds amount to 25–40 per cent. The reaction is postulated to proceed by a free radical mechanism. As an example 4,4'-dibromoazobenzene has been prepared by adding finely powdered lead tetraacetate to a benzene solution of *p*-bromoaniline.

Aniline is oxidized by permonophosphoric acid or a mixture of peracetic and phosphoric acid to give *p*-aminophenol and $(p\text{-}H_2N-C_6H_4)H_2PO_4$. Similarly 2-naphthylamine gives 2-amino-1-naphthol and 2-naphthyl dihydrogen phosphate. N,N-Dimethyl-2-naphthylamine gives the corresponding N-oxide.[77]

Direct oxidation of aniline gives benzoquinone. The oxidation can be carried out with chromic acid or manganese dioxide and sulfuric acid.

$$\text{aniline} + 2MnO_2 + 3H_2SO_4 \longrightarrow \text{benzoquinone} + 2MnSO_4 + 2H_2O + NH_4HSO_4$$

Primary aromatic amines react with potassium nitrodisulfonate, $ON(SO_3K)_2$, to form red quinoneimines. If the *p*-position to the amino group is occupied by an alkyl or alkoxy group, substituted quinone anils are formed. A water-methanol solution of aniline is treated with aqueous potassium nitrodisulfonate buffered with potassium dihydrogen phosphate. After 3 hours a 34 per cent yield of red-violet fluorescent needles of 2-amino-5-anilino-1,4-benzoquinone- (1 or 4 anil) and a 49 per cent yield of 2,5-dianilino-1,4-benzoquinonemonoimine[78] are obtained.

Dialkylanilines may be oxidized by manganese dioxide to give aryl sub-stituted formamides.[79] Thus when one part of dimethylaniline was stirred for 15 hours at 20°C with 50 parts of manganese dioxide in chloroform, an 80 per cent yield of N,N-phenylmethylformamide was obtained. Di-ethylaniline gave a 65 per cent yield of N-phenylformamide and a 60 per cent yield of acetaldehyde.

In the oxidation of dimethylaniline by nitric acid-sodium nitrite so-lutions, tetramethylbenzidine is first formed which is then oxidized to a quinonoid salt. The oxidation is characterized by an induction period and is autocatalytic. As the nitrous acid concentration is increased, *p*-nitroso-dimethylaniline nitrate is formed which is slowly converted to 2,4-dinitro-dimethylaniline.[80]

o-Phenylenediamine is oxidized by ferric chloride to give diaminophena-zines.

Reaction with Olefin Oxides. Olefin oxides react with primary or sec-ondary arylamines in much the same way as with alkylamines. Aniline re-acts with ethylene oxide in the presence of a base to give N-(2-hydroxy-ethyl)aniline ($C_6H_5NHCH_2CH_2OH$) and N,N-bis(2-hydroxyethyl)-aniline $[C_6H_5N(CH_2CH_2OH)_2]$. Reaction with methylaniline gives N-methyl-N-(2-hydroxyethyl)aniline ($C_6H_5N(CH_3)CH_2CH_2OH$).

Formaldehyde reacts with $C_6H_5N(CH_2CH_2OH)_2$ in aqueous alcohol in the presence of an acid catalyst to give $(HOCH_2CH_2)_2N-C_6H_4-CH_2-C_6H_4-N(CH_2CH_2OH)_2$ in better than 90 per cent yield.[81]

2-Aminofluorene gives a monosubstituted hydroxyethyl compound when heated with ethylene oxide at temperatures of 90–150°C for 16 hours.

p-Styrylaniline (*p*-$H_2N-C_6H_4-CH=CH-C_6H_5$) gives a monosub-stituted product *p*-$HOCH_2CH_2NH-C_6H_4-CH=CH-C_6H_5$ at 90°C and a disubstituted product at 150°C.

p-Chloroaniline gives a disubstituted hydroxyethyl product at 150°C but *o*-toluidine gives only the monosubstituted product under the same conditions.

β-Naphthylamine, N-ethylaniline and *o*-chloroaniline have been converted to the monosubstituted N-hydroxyethyl derivatives.[82]

With excess ethylene oxide compounds of the type $C_6H_5N(CH_3)CH_2$-CH_2—O—CH_2CH_2—O—H are formed.

Sulfonation. An arylamine such as aniline forms a salt with concentrated sulfuric acid which when heated to 180°C for several hours rearranges to sulfanilic acid.

$$C_6H_5NH_2 + H_2SO_4 \longrightarrow C_6H_5NH_3HSO_4 \xrightarrow{180°C} p\text{-}H_2N\text{—}C_6H_4\text{—}SO_3H + H_2O$$

The reaction proceeds by the initial loss of water from the sulfate to form phenylsulfamic acid, $C_6H_5NHSO_3H$, which then rearranges. On cautious heating the sulfonic acid group migrates to the *ortho*-position giving orthanilic acid which further rearranges to 180°C to sulfanilic acid.

Sulfur trioxide reacts with primary or secondary arylamines to give sulfamic acids.

$$C_6H_5NH_2 + SO_3 \longrightarrow C_6H_5NHSO_3H$$

The reaction is not always quantitative and this failure to obtain quantitative yields has been explained by the reversibility of the reaction.[83] When pyridine and the sulfamic acid prepared from 2,4-dinitroaniline are heated for one hour and the reaction mixture poured into aqueous sodium hydroxide and filtered, the filtrate gives a red color with aqueous phenylammonium chloride. This color is characteristic of the pyridine-SO_3 complex. The color does not form when the sulfamic acid is absent or is replaced with 2,4-dinitroaniline. It is also demonstrated that the sulfamic acid group can be transferred to aniline. The SO_3 group behaves qualitatively like hydrogen ion in its distribution between amines.

Reactions with Phosgene. Aniline reacts readily with phosgene to give diphenylurea.

$$2C_6H_5NH_2 + ClCOCl \longrightarrow C_6H_5NH\text{—}CO\text{—}NHC_6H_5 + 2HCl$$

Phenylurea can be obtained together with the symmetrical diphenylurea by refluxing a mixture of an aqueous solution of phenylammonium chloride and urea.

$$C_6H_5NH_3Cl + H_2N\text{—}CO\text{—}NH_2 \longrightarrow C_6H_5NHCONH_2 + (C_6H_5NH)_2CO$$

$$\phantom{C_6H_5NH_3Cl + H_2N\text{—}CO\text{—}NH_2 \longrightarrow}\quad \text{55 per cent}\qquad\quad \text{40 per cent}$$

The diphenylurea separates out from the hot solution and the phenylurea is obtained on cooling.

Reaction of equimolar amounts of arylamine and phosgene in a solvent such as ethyl acetate gives a phenylcarbamyl chloride which on distillation loses hydrogen chloride and gives an isocyanate.

$$C_6H_5NH_2 + COCl_2 \longrightarrow C_6H_5NHCOCl \overset{heat}{\longrightarrow} C_6H_5NCO + HCl$$

Over-all yields are about 90 per cent.

The isocyanates react with amines to give ureas and this procedure permits the formation of unsymmetrical ureas.

$$C_6H_5NCO + p\text{-}CH_3\text{---}C_6H_4\text{---}NH_2 \longrightarrow p\text{-}CH_3\text{---}C_6H_4\text{---}NH\text{---}CO\text{---}NHC_6H_5$$

Carbonyl sulfide reacts with aniline in the presence of hydrogen peroxide to give diphenylurea.[84] Thus benzylamine, cumene hydroperoxide and methanol were placed in a flask and carbonyl sulfide added at a pressure of 5 psi. The reaction mixture was held at 5°C for 96 hours. Dibenzylurea precipitated out of the mixture as the reaction proceeded and was recrystallized from benzene. Yields are in excess of 90 per cent.

When acetylene is passed into a mixture of α-naphthylamine and mercuric chloride in alcohol, 2-methyl-7,8-benzoquinoline is obtained.[89]

Diphenylthiourea is obtained by heating aniline and carbon disulfide in alcohol in the presence of powdered potassium hydroxide which serves as a catalyst. The yields are about 80 per cent.

$$2C_6H_5NH_2 + CS_2 \longrightarrow (C_6H_5NH)_2CS + H_2S$$

Diphenylthiourea heated with concentrated hydrochloric acid is converted to phenylisothiocyanate.

$$(C_6H_5NH)_2CS + HCl \longrightarrow C_6H_5NCS + C_6H_5NH_3Cl$$

Formation of Quaternary Ammonium Salts. Dialkylarylamines react with alkyl iodides or bromides to form quaternary ammonium salts.

$$C_6H_5N(CH_3)_2 + CH_3I \longrightarrow C_6H_5\overset{(+)}{N}(CH_3)_3I^-$$

The reaction is not very successful with aryl iodides or when the arylamine is sterically hindered by substituents in both *ortho*-positions.

The quaternary ammonium halides can be converted to the corresponding hydroxides by treatment with moist silver oxide or suitable ion exchange resins. Phenyltrimethylammonium hydroxide is a strong base which on heating is decomposed to methyl alcohol and dimethylaniline.

Long chain N-alkyl-*p*-phenylenediamines can be converted to quaternary ammonium salts by treatment with an alkyl halide. Thus N-decyl-*p*-phenylenediamine is treated with methyl iodide in 20 per cent sodium hydroxide in a sealed tube at 120–130°C to give a quantitative yield of CH_3-$(CH_2)_9NH$—C_6H_4—$\overset{(+)}{N}(CH_3)_3I^-$.[85]

Reactions with Acetylene. Aromatic amines can be condensed with acetylene in the presence of suitable catalysts. Thus dry acetylene is passed for 20 hours into an ethanol solution of *p*-chloroaniline in the presence of mercuric chloride to give 6-chloroquinaldine in 30 per cent yield.[86]

Acetylene is introduced, over a period of 4 hours at a rate of 15 liters per hour, into dimethylaniline. Aluminum chloride is added simultaneously. After the addition of the acetylene is complete, the mixture is quenched with water, treated with sodium hydroxide, and steam distilled to give $[p\text{-}(CH_3)_2$—N—$C_6H_4]_2CHCH_3$ in 34 per cent yield.[87]

The addition of acetylene to an ethanol solution of *o*-toluidine and benzaldehyde in the presence of mercuric chloride gives 8-methyl-2-phenylquinoline in 15 per cent yield.

The condensation of aniline, benzaldehyde and acetylene at reflux temperature in the presence of mercuric chloride or cupric chloride gives 2-phenylquinoline. The reaction probably proceeds as follows:[88]

When acetylene is passed into a mixture of α-naphthylamine and mercuric chloride in alcohol, 2-methyl-7,8-benzoquinoline is obtained.[89]

Replacement of an Amino Group with Bromine. An amino group of an arylamine can be replaced by bromine by treating with hydrogen bromide and nitrogen trioxide in acetic acid. As an example, 0.1 mole of the amine is dissolved in 125 ml of acetic acid and 50 ml of 40 per cent hydrobromic acid is added at 5–10°C until a permanent dark color appears. The solution is then heated slowly until a brisk evolution of nitrogen occurs (usually 40–50°C) and finally at reflux temperature for a few minutes. The reaction mixture is poured into a 20 per cent sodium hydroxide solution to obtain the corresponding aryl bromide.

The reaction probably proceeds by the following route.

$$RNH_3Br + N_2O_3 \longrightarrow RN_2Br \longrightarrow RBr + N_2$$

In this way *o*-chlorobromobenzene is obtained from *o*-chloroaniline in 85 per cent yield. The *meta*- derivative is obtained in 46 and the *para*-isomer in 77 per cent yield. Yields of other arylbromides are of the same order.[90]

Mannich Reaction. Arylamines may participate in the Mannich reaction but are much less frequently used than are aliphatic amines. As an example, aromatic amines react with formaldehyde and primary or secondary nitroparaffins but in contrast to the reactions with alkylamines, basic catalysts are required. Again two methods of synthesis may be used. The first involves a reaction of the amine, formaldehyde and the nitroparaffin and the second a reaction of the amine with a nitroalcohol. Secondary aromatic amines do not undergo the reaction unless one of the group is alkyl.

Yields vary quite appreciably with structure but in most cases are between 60 and 95 per cent. Quaternary ammonium hydroxides are usually used as catalysts.[91]

Miscellaneous Reactions. Amines react with four-membered ring lactones such as β-butyrolactone to give either N-substituted-β-amino acids or N-substituted-β-hydroxy acid amides, depending upon the conditions of the reaction.[92]

In the reaction between aniline and β-butyrolactone, water is the most useful solvent for the preparation of β-N-phenylaminobutyric acid and the yield decreases in the order acetonitrile, benzene, diethyl ether when these compounds are used as solvents. When the reaction is carried out in benzene the dropwise addition of aniline to the lactone gives twice the yield of the amino acid as can be obtained by the reverse procedure.

β,β'-dichlorodiethyl ether was reacted with methyl-, ethyl-, *n*-butyl- and isoamylanilines with the hope of preparing phenylalkylaminoethyl-β-chloroethyl ethers. Instead of the expected product N-phenylmorpholines were obtained in each case together with the appropriate alkyl chloride and hydrogen chloride. The reaction was accomplished by refluxing β,β'-dichlorodiethyl ether and the alkylaniline for 2 to 4 hours. It is proposed that the reaction proceeds through the formation of a quaternary ammonium chloride which loses alkyl chloride to give the N-phenylmorpholine.

$$C_6H_5NHC_2H_5 + ClCH_2CH_2OCH_2CH_2Cl \longrightarrow \left[C_6H_5-\overset{\overset{C_2H_5}{|}\oplus}{\underset{|}{N}}-CH_2CH_2OCH_2CH_2Cl \right] Cl^-$$

$$\xrightarrow{-HCl} C_6H_5-\overset{\overset{H_5C_2}{|}\oplus}{NH}\underset{Cl^-}{\overset{CH_2CH_2}{\underset{CH_2CH_2}{<}}}O \xrightarrow{-C_2H_5Cl} C_6H_5-N\overset{CH_2CH_2}{\underset{CH_2CH_2}{<}}O$$

Methyl- and ethylanilines give approximately the same yields, *n*-butyl- and isoamylanilines give smaller yields of N-phenylmorpholine. No olefin is formed.[93]

Aniline and ethylene chlorohydrin heated 4–6 hours at 90–100°C gives an 80 per cent yield of N-β-hydroxyethylaniline, $C_6H_5NHCH_2CH_2OH$.[94] The addition of sodium carbonate or calcium oxide does not improve the yield.

Aniline and styrene heated in a sealed tube at 200–240°C for 6 hours gives a 75 per cent yield of o-(α-phenylethyl)aniline, o-$H_2N-C_6H_4-CH(CH_3)-C_6H_5$.[95]

N-(α-phenylethyl)aniline was present after 1 hour but not after 6 indicating that it was formed first and then rearranged to the o-alkylaniline.

Secondary aromatic amines react with alkyl vinyl ethers in the presence of acids to give N-arylquinaldinium salts.[96] Thus to diphenylamine in xylene concentrated hydrochloric acid was added to form the salt of the amine which precipitated out. *n*-Butyl vinyl ether was then added slowly with considerable evolution of heat after which the mixture was refluxed for 2 hours, water and potassium chlorate introduced to give a 30 per cent yield of N-phenylquinaldinium perchlorate.

Reactions of Nitrous Acid. Tertiary aliphatic amines do not react with nitrous acid except to form salts. However, with tertiary arylamines such as dimethylaniline, nitrous acid attacks the ring to give nitroso compounds.

$$(CH_3)_2N-C_6H_5 + HONO \longrightarrow p\text{-}(CH_3)_2N-C_6H_4-NO + H_2O$$

The reaction is usually carried out at 5–10°C using sodium nitrite and hydrochloric acid as the source of the nitrous acid. *p*-Nitrosodimethylaniline is obtained in 80–90 per cent yield and is isolated as the hydrochloride.

p-Nitrosodimethylaniline is hydrolyzed by hot alkali to *p*-nitrosophenol.

$$p\text{-}(CH_3)_2N\text{—}C_6H_4\text{—}NO + NaOH \longrightarrow p\text{-}NaO\text{—}C_6H_4\text{—}NO \xrightarrow{H^+}$$
$$p\text{-}HO\text{—}C_6H_4\text{—}NO$$

It may be reduced by tin and HCl to N,N-dimethyl-*p*-phenylenediamine,

$$p\text{-}(CH_3)_2N\text{—}C_6H_4\text{—}NO \xrightarrow[HCl]{Sn} p\text{-}(CH_3)_2N\text{—}C_6H_4\text{—}NH_2$$

and oxidized with potassium permangante to *p*-nitrodimethylaniline.

$$p\text{-}(CH_3)_2\text{—}C_6H_4\text{—}NO \xrightarrow{KMnO_4} p\text{-}(CH_3)_2N\text{—}C_6H_4\text{—}NO_2$$

Aliphatic secondary amines react with nitrous acid to give N-nitroso-amines. Alkylarylamines such as methylaniline behave similarly. Thus N-nitroso-N-methylaniline is obtained in about 90 per cent yield by treating N-methylaniline with aqueous sodium nitrite and hydrochloric acid at about 10°C.

$$C_6H_5\text{—}NHCH_3 + HONO \longrightarrow C_6H_5\text{—}N\underset{NO}{\overset{CH_3}{<}}$$

N-Nitroso-N-methylaniline in acetic acid solution may be nitrated in the *ortho*- or *para*-position by nitrous acid. Reduction with zinc dust in dilute acetic acid gives α-methylphenylhydrazine.

$$C_6H_5\text{—}N\underset{CH_3}{\overset{NO}{<}} \longrightarrow \underset{CH_3}{\overset{C_6H_5}{>}}N\text{—}NH_2$$

With a more powerful reducing agent such as zinc and hydrochloric or sulfuric acid, methylaniline is obtained.

$$C_6H_5\text{—}N\underset{CH_3}{\overset{NO}{<}} \longrightarrow C_6H_5NHCH_3 + NH_3$$

N-Nitroso-N-methylaniline rearranges under the influence of hydrochloric acid to give p-nitroso-N-methylaniline.

$$C_6H_5-N\begin{matrix}NO\\ \\CH_3\end{matrix} \xrightarrow{HCl} p\text{-}ON-C_6H_4-NHCH_3$$

The rearrangement is accomplished by adding concentrated hydrochloric acid to an alcoholic solution of the N-nitroso-N-methylaniline.

Nitrous acid reacts with primary alkylamines to give a mixture of alcohol, olefins, nitrogen etc. With primary arylamines the reaction is much more selective at temperatures near 0°C. Addition of aqueous sodium nitrite at 0°C to a solution of the amine in dilute hydrochloric acid gives a diazonium salt.

$$C_6H_5NH_2 + NaNO_2 + 2HCl \longrightarrow C_6H_5-\overset{+}{N}\equiv N\ Cl^- + NaCl + 2H_2O$$

Except in a few special cases the diazonium salts cannot be isolated but in spite of this they are very important chemical intermediates in the preparation of dyes, and for replacement of the amino group on the benzene ring by atoms or other groups. The chemistry of the diazonium salts will be discussed in Chapter 4.

Adding the diazonium salt solution to hot dilute sulfuric acid results in hydrolysis and the formation of phenol.

$$C_6H_5N_2Cl + HOH \xrightarrow{H_2SO_4} C_6H_5OH + HCl + N_2$$

The reaction of nitrous acid with primary aliphatic amines may proceed by very much the same mechanism except that the intermediate diazonium salt is not nearly as stable.

The yields of diazonium salts are fair but side reactions always occur.

Klaasens and Schoot[97] report that side reactions occurring during diazotization can be minimized if the diazotization is carried out in an aqueous solvent containing 20–75 per cent of a ketone such as acetone. Temperatures of 20–35°C can be used successfully if the reaction time is decreased. As an example nitrous gases were introduced gradually into a solution of 50 ml of acetone or methyl ethyl ketone, 100 ml of water and 20 ml nitric acid (d 1.4) and 150 g of 3-methyl-4-hydroxy-5-aminosulfonic acid at a temperature of 20°C. About 130 g of the yellow diazonium compound crystallized out.

The diazotization of certain negatively substituted aromatic amines is facilitated by dissolving the amine in diacetone alcohol containing a non-ionic despersing agent and pouring the mixture into an aqueous acid.

Thus 2-nitro-4-chloroaniline, dissolved in diacetone alcohol containing Triton X-100, was poured, with stirring, into ice and water containing about 5 per cent hydrochloric acid. An aqueous solution of sodium nitrite was then added at a temperature of 5–10°C to give a tar-free solution of the diazonium compound. o-Nitroaniline and 2,5-dichloroaniline were diazotized in the same way.[98]

Aliphatic primary amines do not react with nitrous acid at a pH below 3. Thus methylamine, ethylamine, n-propylamine, benzylamine and cyclohexylamine are not attacked by nitrous acid below this pH. On the other hand, aromatic amines are readily diazotized at pH less than 3. This information together with the fact that hypophosphorous acid smoothly replaces a diazonium group by hydrogen makes it possible to effect a transformation such as:

$$p\text{-}H_2N\text{—}C_6H_4\text{—}CH_2NH_2 \longrightarrow C_6H_5CH_2NH_2$$

The hypophosphorous acid being a strong acid is used not only as the reducing agent but also as the source of required acidity. The diamine is dissolved in hypophosphorous acid, sodium nitrite is introduced at 0–5°C and the mixture allowed to come to room temperature. The only diamine which fails to undergo selective deamination is o-aminobenzylamine. Instead of benzylamine, benzyl alcohol is obtained.[99] Nitrous acid reacts with o-phenylediamine to give benzotriazole.

Halogenation. Halogenation of aniline in aqueous solution proceeds so rapidly than only 2,4,6-trichloro- or 2,4,6-tribromoaniline is obtained. The three halogen atoms decrease the basicity of the amino group so that salt formation with the liberated hydrohalogen acid does not occur in aqueous solution.

Actually trichloro- or tribromoaniline is formed even when the halogen is added to an aqueous solution of the aniline salt. This is a consequence of the fact that the arylamine salts are considerably hydrolyzed in aqueous solution.

If the halogenation is effected in concentrated sulfuric acid solution, the reaction rate is slow and the halogen enters the *meta*-position. In sulfuric acid the anilinium ion ($C_6H_5NH_3^+$) is formed. The $-NH_3^+$ attached to the benzene ring is electron attracting and therefore deactivates the ring, particularly in the *ortho* and *para*-positions so that *meta*-substitution occurs.

Halogenation can be accomplished in the *ortho*- and *para*-positions by protecting the amino group by acetylation and halogenating the resulting acetanilide. When the halogenation is complete the amino group may be recovered by hydrolysis in dilute acid.

$$C_6H_5NH_2 \longrightarrow C_6H_5NHCOCH_3 \overset{Br_2}{\longrightarrow} \textit{o-} \text{ or } \textit{p-Br}-C_6H_4-NH-COCH_3$$

$$\textit{p-Br}-C_6H_4-NHCOCH_3 + HOH \overset{H^+}{\longrightarrow} \textit{p-Br}-C_6H_4-NH_2 + CH_3COOH$$

One interesting method of bromination which probably has only limited application has been described of Fletcher and Namkung.[100] These investigators brominated aminofluorenes in dimethyl sulfoxide with *tert*-butyl bromide. Thus 2-aminofluorenone reacted with *tert*-butyl bromide in dimethylsulfoxide at 105°C to give a 75 per cent yield of 2-amino-3-bromofluorenone. 2-Aminofluorene gave a 45 per cent yield of 3-bromo-2-aminofluorene and 30 per cent of a crude isomer, probably 1-bromo-2-aminofluorene.

Nitration. The nitration of arylamines with nitric acid alone is not satisfactory because the amines are too sensitive to oxidation by the acid. Dissolving the amine in concentrated sulfuric acid stabilizes it toward oxidation but results in the formation of the phenylammonium salt.

Whereas the amino group activates the benzene ring for further substitution, the NH_3^+ group deactivates the ring and directs the substituent to the *meta*-position. Nitration of an arylamine in concentrated sulfuric acid is therefore quite difficult and leads to *meta*-substitution.

ortho- and *para*-Nitroanilines can be obtained by protecting the amino group by acetylation and nitrating the acetanilide with sulfuric and nitric acids. When the nitration is complete, the acetanilide is hydrolyzed back to the amine.

$$C_6H_5NHCOCH_3 + HONO_2 \longrightarrow \textit{o-} \text{ and } \textit{p-O}_2N-C_6H_4-NHCOCH_3 \longrightarrow$$

$$\textit{o-} \text{ and } \textit{p-O}_2N-C_6H_4-NH_2 + CH_3COOH.$$

This reaction yields almost exclusively the *p*-isomer. If the *ortho*-isomer is desired, it is possible to block the *p*-position with a sulfonic acid group which may be removed by hydrolysis in 60 per cent sulfuric acid. *o*-Nitroaniline may be prepared by the following sequence of reactions.

The very diminished basicity of *o*- and *p*-nitroanilines makes it possible to hydrolyze the amino group to a phenol with sodium hydroxide.

$$o\text{-}O_2N\text{—}C_6H_4\text{—}NH_2 + NaOH \longrightarrow o\text{-}O_2N\text{—}C_6H_4\text{—}ONa \xrightarrow{H^+}$$

$$o\text{-}O_2N\text{—}C_6H_4\text{—}OH$$

Dimethylaniline is nitrated with fuming nitric acid to give 2,4,6-N-tetranitromethylaniline, a very powerful explosive known as tetryl. The reaction proceeds in two stages. The first occurs at 45°C giving 2,4-dinitrodimethylaniline and the second requires a temperature of 65°C and gives the tetranitro product.[101]

The first stage is catalyzed by nitrous acid, probably because of the production of nitronium ions from nitrogen tetroxide.

$$N_2O_4 \rightleftarrows NO_2^+ + NO_2^-$$

The second stage is likewise catalyzed by nitrous acid but for a different reason. Nitrous acid has been found to be a powerful demethylating agent and so helps in the removal of one of the N-methyl groups.

Hydrogenation. The benzene ring in arylamines can be readily hydrogenated at 140–160°C and pressures of 100–150 kg/sq cm in the presence of Raney nickel if the amino group is attached directly to the ring or on a carbon atom alpha to the benzene ring. Hydrogenation may also occur readily if a tertiary amino group is present on a β-carbon atom. When a primary or secondary amino group is on a carbon atom beta to the ring or further remote, the hydrogenation must be carried out at higher temperatures, resulting in considerable cracking. Thus N-methylcyclohexyl-amine has been prepared from methylaniline and N-ethylcyclohexylamine from ethylaniline.[102]

Metayer[102] further reports that the presence of an amino or hydroxyl group on the ring favors reduction. An amino group on a carbon atom alpha to the ring also aids in the reduction of the amine. Hydrogenation of the ring is facilitated by a dimethylamino group beta to the ring. Groups beyond the β-carbon atom have no effect on the hydrogenation of the ring.

Ring Alkylation. Several methods have been proposed for the introduction of an alkyl group into the benzene ring of arylamines.

Arylamines may be alkylated on the benzene ring with olefins at temperatures of 200–400°C and pressures of 50–300 atmospheres in the presence of aluminum.[103] Thus 300 g of aniline, 7.5 g of granulated aluminum, and 0.3 g of mercuric chloride were heated for 3 hours at 200°C in an autoclave in the absence of air. The hydrogen evolved was vented and the temperature raised to 300°C. Ethylene was introduced at a pressure of 170 atmospheres. In 6 hours 2 moles of ethylene per mole of aniline was absorbed. The product, 2,6-diethylaniline, was obtained in about 80 per cent yield. 2-Ethyl-*m*-toluidine and 2,6-dimethyl-*m*-toluidine were obtained in the same way.

The nuclear alkylation of aromatic amines with olefins catalyzed by aluminum chloride is not very successful but the alkylation of primary or secondary arylamines catalyzed by aluminum anilides proceeds very satisfactorily. Only the *ortho*-alkylated amines are obtained. The catalyst is formed by heating a mixture of the amine and aluminum turnings to 150°C under a nitrogen atmosphere. The alkylations were carried out at 200–330°C under 500–800 psi.

The reactivity of the olefins decreases in the order $CH_2{=}CH_2 > CH_2{=}CHR > RCH{=}CHR$.

The olefin becomes attached to the ring in a manner which gives the maximum amount of branching, and N-alkylanilines are more reactive than the corresponding primary arylamines.[104]

Stroh *et al.*[105] report that the catalytic activity of aluminum anilide is enhanced by the presence of a Friedel-Craft catalyst such as aluminum chloride. The reactivity of olefins decreases in the order ethylene > propylene > isobutylene > butylenes.

Aromatic amines can be alkylated on the benzene ring by alkyllithium compounds. Gilman and Spatz[106] found that the alkylation occurs on the carbon atom alpha to the nitrogen but in some cases steric hindrance may give rise to exceptions.

REFERENCES

1. Beilstein, A., and Kuhlberg, *Ann.*, 156, **81** (1870).
2. Hinsber, O., and Konig, F., *Ber.*, **28**, 1597 (1895).
3. Wislicenus, W., and Elvert, H., *Ber.*, **41**, 4131 (1908).
4. Hazlet, S. E., and Dornfeld, C. A., *J. Am. Chem. Soc.*, **66**, 1781 (1944).
5. Lowe, E. W., U. S. Patent 2,669,584 (Feb. 16, 1954).
6. Brand, K., *J. Prakt. Chem.*, [2] **74**, 449 (1906).
7. Bertheim, A., *Ber.*, **44**, 3095 (1911).
8. Adkins, H., "Reactions of Hydrogen," University of Wisconsin Press, Madison, Wisconsin, 1937.
9. Adams, R., Cohen, F. H., and Rees, O. W., *J. Am. Chem. Soc.*, **49**, 1093 (1927).
10. Allied Chemical and Dye Corp., British Patent (Nov. 17, 1954).
11. Standard Oil Development Co., British Patent 602,880 (June 4, 1958).
12. Standard Oil Development Co., British Patent 599,252 (Mar. 9, 1948).
13. Souders, M., Jr., U. S. Patent 2,458,214 (June 4, 1948).
14. Farbenfabriken Bayer A. G., British Patent 768,111 (Feb. 13, 1957).
15. Morgan and Harrison, *J. Soc. Chem. Ind. (London)*, **60**, 120T (1941).
16. Friedman, O. M., *et al.*, *J. Am. Chem. Soc.*, **71**, 3012 (1949).
17. Binz, A., and v. Schickh, O., *Ber.*, **68**, 320 (1935).
18. Gilsdorf, R. T., and Nord, F. F., *J. Org. Chem.*, **15**, 807 (1950).
19. Wisansky, W. R., and Ansbacher, S., *Org. Syntheses*, Vol. 28, John Wiley & Sons, New York, 1948, p. 46.
20. Groggins, P. H., and Stirton, A. J., *Ind. Eng. Chem.*, **28**, 1051 (1936); **29**, 1353 (1937).
21. Vorozhtov, N. N., Jr., and Kobelev, V. A., *J. Gen. Chem. USSR*, **4**, 310 (1934).
22. Calm, A., *Ber.*, **16**, 2812 (1883).
23. Bucherer, H. T., *J. Prakt. Chem.*, [2], **69**, 49 (1904).
24. Fuchs, W., *et al.*, *Ber.*, **52**, 2281 (1919); **53**, 886 (1920); **55**, 658 (1922).
25. Warashtzow, N. N., and Kogan, J. M., *Ber.*, **65**, 142 (1932).
26. Michaelis, A., and Bressel, H., *Ann.*, **407**, 275 (1914).
27. Cobenzyl, A., *Chem. Ztg.*, **37**, 299 (1913); **39**, 859 (1915).
28. Weil, H., Traum, M., and Marcel, S., *Ber.*, **55**, 2671 (1922).
29. Grandmougin, E., *J. Prakt. Chem.*, [2], **76**, 124 (1907).
30. Fieser, L. F., *Org. Syntheses Coll.* Vol. II, pp. 35, 39, New York, John Wiley & Sons, Inc., 1943.
31. Heaton, C. D., U. S. Patent 2,773,902 (Dec. 11, 1956).
32. Price, C. C., and Voong, S. T., Org. Syntheses, Vol. 28, p. 80, New York, John Wiley & Sons, Inc., 1948.
33. Thomas, C. L., U. S. Patent 2,749,297, 2,749,298 (June 15, 1956).
34. Kreton, A. E., and Chertok, E. R., *Ukrain. Khim. Zhur.*, **20**, 293 (1954).
35. Snyder, H. R., Elston, C. T., and Kellorn, E. B., *J. Chem. Soc.*, **75**, 2014 (1953).

36. Ohta, N., and Kagani, K., Repts. of Govt. *Chem. Ind. Research Inst. Tokyo,* **49,** 193 (1954).
37. Weight, D., and Wilde, B. E., British Patent 738,986 (Oct. 26, 1955).
38. Willson, F. G., and Wheeler, T. S., Org. Syntheses Coll, Vol. I, p. 102, New York, John Wiley & Sons, Inc., 1941.
39. Dickey, J. B., *et al., Ind. Eng. Chem.,* **46,** 2213 (1954).
40. Hughes, E. C., Veatch, F., and Elersich, V., *Ind. Eng. Chem.,* **42,** 787 (1950).
41. Knoevenagel, E., *J. Prakt. Chem.,* [2[, **89,** 30 (1913).
42. Pilc, A., and Rybacki, L., *Przemysl Chem.,* **8,** 529 (1952).
43. Deahl, T. J., Stross, F. H., and Taylor, M. D., U. S. Patent 2,580,284 (Dec. 25, 1951).
44. Corson, B. B., and Dressler, H., *J. Org. Chem.,* **21,** 474 (1956).
45. Hornya, S., and Cerny, O., *Chem. Listy,* **50,** 381 (1956).
46. Rice, R. G., and Kohn, E. J., U. S. Patent 2,813,124 (Nov. 2, 1957).
47. Shreve, R. N., Vriens, G. N., and Vogel, D. A., *Ind. Eng. Chem.,* **42,** 791 (1950).
48. Sprinzak, Y., British Patent 726,545 (Mar. 23, 1955).
49. Haarer, E., and Rotler, E., German Patent 922,347 (Jan. 13, 1955).
50. Cook, E. W., U. S. Patent 2,165,747 (July 11, 1939).
51. Ciba Ltd., Swiss Patent 310,827 (Jan. 14, 1956).
52. Bogoslovskii, B. M., *Zhur. Obschei. Khim.,* **24,** 922 (1954).
53. Universal Oil Products Co., British Patent 774,345 (May 8, 1957).
54. Rosewald, R. H., and Haatson, J. R., British Patent 753,740 (Aug. 1, 1956).
55. Emerson, W. S., and Uraneck, C. A., *J. Am. Chem. Soc.,* **63,** 749 (1941).
56. Horu, Z., Saki, T., and Tamura, Y., *Pharm. Bull. (Tokyo),* **5,** 132 (1957).
57. Emerson, W. S., Reed, S. K., and Merner, R. R., *J. Am. Chem. Soc.,* **63,** 751 (1941).
58. Sprinzak, Y., *J. Am. Chem. Soc.,* **78,** 3207 (1958).
59. Hunig, S., *Ber.,* **85,** 1056 (1952).
60. Stuhmer, W., and Kaupmann, W., *Arch. Pharm.,* **285,** 120 (1952).
61. Billman, J. H., Radike, A., and Mundy, B. W., *J. Am. Chem. Soc.,* **64,** 2977 (1942).
62. Thomas, D. G., Billman, J. H., and Davis, C. E., *J. Am. Chem. Soc.,* **68,** 895 (1946).
63. Gerrard, W., and Jeacock, G. J., *Chem. and Ind.,* **1954,** 1538.
64. Patrick, T. M., McBee, E. T., and Hass, H. B., *J. Am. Chem. Soc.,* **68,** 1009 (1946).
65. Gluzman, M., Kh Uchenye Zapiski Kharikoo Univ. *54, Trudy Khim. Fak i Nauch—Issle Dovatel Inst Khim.,* No. 12, 333 (1954).
66. Svetkin, Yu V., *Uchenye Zapiski Kishenev Univ.,* **14,** 67 (1954).
67. Schenck, L. M., U. S. Patent 2,739,983 (Mar. 27, 1956).
68. Zienty, M. F., U. S. Patent 2,824,883 (Feb. 25, 1958).
69. Leulier, A., Cifr, A., and Drevon, B., *Bull. soc. chim. France,* **1954,** 1091.
70. Postobskii, I. Ya, Matevosyan, R. C., and Sheinker, Yu. N., *Zhur. Obschei. Khim.,* **26,** 1443 (1956).
71. Porai-Koshits, B. A., and Renizow, A. L., *Sbornik Statei Obschie Khim.,* **2,** 1570 (1953).

72. D'ans, U., and Kneip, A., *Ber.,* **48,** 1144 (1913).
73. Emmons, W. D., *J. Am. Chem. Soc.,* **79,** 5528 (1957).
74. Green, A. G., *Ber.,* **26,** 2772 (1893).
75. Terent'ev, A. P., and Mogilyanskii, Yu. O., *Doklady Akad. Nauk. S.S.S.R.,* **103,** 91 (1955).
76. Baer, E., and Tosoni, A. L., *J. Am. Chem. Soc.,* **78,** 2857 (1956).
77. Boyland, E., and Manson, D., *J. Chem. Soc.,* **1957,** 4689.
78. Tauber, H. J., and Jellinek, G., *Chem. Ber.,* **87,** 1841 (1954).
79. Henbest, H. E., and Thomas, A., *Chem. and Ind.,* **1956,** 1097.
80. Lang, F. M., and Magdalena, T., *Bull. soc. chim. France,* **1954,** 1043.
81. Petrov, K. D., and Tal'hovskii, G. B., *Zhur Obschei Khim.,* **25,** 120; *J. Gen. Chem. (USSR),* **25,** 105 (1955).
82. Yar'ev Yu. K., Novitskii, K. Yu, Liberov, L. G., and Katsenko, R. D., *Vestnick Moskov Gosudarst Univ.,* **1953,** No. 6, 129.
83. Lantz, R. L., and Obellianne, P. M., *Compt. rend.,* **238,** 2243 (1954).
84. Baischii, F., Franz, R. A., and Horwitz, L., *J. Org. Chem.,* **21,** 1546 (1956).
85. Morita, S., Japan Patent 1373 (1955); Feb. 28, 1955.
86. Kozlov, N. S., and Kostromina, O. E., *Zhur. Obschei Khim.,* **23,** 929 (1953).
87. Gar'kovets, T. G., and Tsukervanik, I. P., *Zhur. Obschei Khim.,* **26,** 1656 (1956).
88. Kozlov, n. S., *J. Gen. Chem. USSR,* **8,** 413 (1938).
89. Kozlov, N. S., *J. Gen. Chem. USSR,* **8,** 419 (1938).
90. Newman, M. S., and Fones, W. S., *J. Am. Chem. Soc.,* **69,** 1221 (1947).
91. Johnson, H. G., *J. Am. Chem. Soc.,* **68,** 14 (1958).
92. Iwakura, Y., Nagakubo, K., Aoki, J., and Yamada, A., *Nippon Kagaku Zasshi,* **75,** 315 (1954).
93. Brill, H. C., Webb, C. N., Halbedel, H. S., *J. Am. Chem. Soc.,* **63,** 971 (1941).
94. Yamamoto, S., and Ikegami, H., *Science and Ind. (Japan),* **30,** 17 (1956).
95. Hart, H., and Kosak, J. R., *J. Org. Chem.,* **22,** 1752 (1957).
96. Pilyugin, G. T., and Opanasenko, E. P., *Zhur. Obschei Khim.,* **27,** 1015 (1957).
97. Klaasens, K. H., and Schoot, C. J., Dutch Patent 69,026 (Dec. 15, 1951).
98. Chase, H. M., and Carpening, A. L., U. S. Patent 2,825,724 (Mar. 4, 1958).
99. Kornblum, N., and Iffland, D. C., *J. Am. Chem. Soc.,* **71,** 2137 (1949).
100. Fletcher, T. L., and Namkung, M., *Chem. and Ind. London,* **1957,** 660.
101. Clarkson, C. E., Holden, I. G., and Malkin, T., *J. Chem. Soc.,* **1950,** 1556.
102. Mayater, M., *Bull. Soc. chim. France,* **1952,** 276.
103. Stroh, R., Ebersberger, J., and Haberland, H., U. S. Patent 2,762,845 (Sept. 11, 1956).
104. Ecke, G. G., Napolitano, J. P., Filbey, A. H., Kolka, A. J., *J. Org. Chem.,* **22,** 639 (1957).
105. Stroh, R., Ebersberger, J., and Haberland, H., and Hahn, W., *Angew Chem.,* **69,** 124 (1957).
106. Gilman, H., and Spatz, S. M., *J. Org. Chem.,* **17,** 860 (1952).

3. HETEROCYCLIC AMINES

Many heterocyclic amines are found in nature and many are physiologically active. They differ widely in basic strength dependant upon the structure of the molecule. Saturated heterocyclic amines are strong bases resembling aliphatic amines. Unsaturated cyclic amines which may be stabilized by resonance, e.g., pyrrole, pyridine, and quinoline are weak bases resembling aromatic amines.

The most important naturally occuring heterocyclic amines are the alkaloids found in many plants. However we will not attempt to discuss the chemistry of the alkaloids in this book because these compounds are described in much detail elsewhere. In this chapter an attempt will be made to discuss the chemistry of a number of the simpler ring systems in order to illustrate some of the more important type reactions.

Ethylenimine

Ethylenimine is the nitrogen analog of ethylene oxide. It is very toxic and is a very strong vesicant. It is also quite unstable especially in the presence of acids, which cause spontaneous polymerization with the liberation of a great deal of heat. Ethylenimine, therefore, must be handled with a great deal of caution and respect.

Preparation of Ethylenimine. Ethylenimine was first synthesized by Gabriel[1,2] who treated β-bromoethylammonium bromide with concentrated potassium hydroxide. Gabriel and Stelzner believed that they had prepared vinylamine but it was left to Markwald[3] to show that the structure was that of the cyclic imine.

$$\text{BrCH}_2\text{CH}_2\text{NH}_2 \longrightarrow \underset{\displaystyle \diagdown \text{NH} \diagup}{\text{CH}_2-\text{CH}_2} + \text{HBr}$$

A more convenient method of synthesis is described by Wenker.[4] Ethanolamine with sulfuric acid gives the inner salt, $H_3\overset{+}{N}-CH_2CH_2OSO_3^-$ which when distilled in the presence of a strong base gives ethylenimine. Yields are about 35 per cent.[5]

Jones[6] prepared a number of ethylenimine homologous using Winkler's method with the results shown in Table 3–1.

Ethylenimine was prepared in Germany by a three-step process which is also recommended by Braz.[7]

TABLE 3–1. ETHYLENIMINES FROM ETHANOLAMINES

Ethanolamine	Imine	Yield %
$HOCH_2CH_2NH_2$	Ethylenimine	32
$HOCH(CH_3)CH_2NH_2$	2-Methylethylenimine	65
$HOCH_2CH(C_2H_5)NH_2$	2-Ethylethylenimine	46
$HOCH(CH_3)CH(CH_3)NH_2$	2,3-Dimethylethylenimine	47
$HOCH_2C(CH_3)_2NH_2$	2,2-Dimethylethylenimine	68
$HOCH(C_3H_7)C(CH_3)_2NH_2$	2,2-Dimethyl-3-*n*-propyl-ethylenimine	57

1. Ethanolamine was converted into ethanolammonium chloride with dry hydrogen chloride at temperatures below 30°C.

2. This salt was treated with thionyl chloride to give first a sulfite ester-chloride then chloroethylammonium chloride by loss of sulfur dioxide. Thionyl chloride was added at 20°C after which the temperature was raised to 30°C to drive off the sulfur dioxide.

$$Cl^- H_3\overset{+}{N}—CH_2CH_2OH + SOCl_2 \rightarrow Cl^- H_3\overset{+}{N}CH_2CH_2OSOCl + HCl$$

$$Cl^- H_3\overset{+}{N}CH_2CH_2OSOCl \rightarrow Cl^- H_3\overset{+}{N}CH_2CH_2Cl + SO_2$$

3. Chloroethylammonium chloride was treated with 30 per cent sodium hydroxide.

$$Cl^- H_3\overset{+}{N}CH_2CH_2Cl + 2NaOH \rightarrow \underset{\diagdown NH \diagup}{CH_2—CH_2} + 2NaCl + 2H_2O$$

A modification of the sulfuric acid process of Winkler was also used. To a solution of monoethanolamine in *o*-dichlorobenzene is added concentrated sulfuric acid at room temperature to form the salt. After standing for 2 hours the temperature is raised to 80–90°C to remove the water of reaction as a water-dichlorobenzene azeotrope.

The salt is insoluble in dichlorobenzene and separates out as the reaction proceeds. Conversion to ethylenimine is accomplished by heating the salt with 50 per cent sodium hydroxide.

Substituted ethylenimines may be prepared by several methods. Thus 2-phenylethylenimine has been prepared by the Gabriel method by treating β-phenyl-β-chloroethylamine with silver oxide.[8]

$$H_2N—CH_2—CHCl—C_6H_5 \overset{-HCl}{\longrightarrow} \underset{\diagdown NH \diagup}{CH_2—CH—C_6H_5}$$

Similarly 2,3-diphenylethylenimine is made by the action of a base on α-amino-β-chlorodibenzyl.[9]

$$C_6H_5-\underset{\underset{Cl}{|}}{CH}-\underset{\underset{NH_2}{|}}{CH}-C_6H_5 \xrightarrow{NaOH} C_6H_5-CH-\underset{NH}{\overset{}{\underset{\diagdown}{CH}}}-C_6H_5$$

This compound may exist in optically active forms.

$$
\begin{array}{cc}
\underset{C_6H_5}{\overset{H}{\underset{|}{\overset{|}{C}}}}\text{---}\underset{H}{\overset{C_6H_5}{\underset{|}{\overset{|}{C}}}} & \underset{H}{\overset{C_6H_5}{\underset{|}{\overset{|}{C}}}}\text{---}\underset{H}{\overset{C_6H_5}{\underset{|}{\overset{|}{C}}}} \\
\end{array}
$$

The optically active (*trans*) form is made from 1-iso-α-amino-β-chloro-dibenzyl and the optically inactive (*cis*) form from 1-α-amino-β-chloro-dibenzyl.

Reaction of a ketoxime with a Grignard reagent gives a satisfactory yield of a substituted ethylenimine.[10]

$$C_6H_5-\underset{\underset{NOH}{||}}{C}-CH_3 + C_2H_5MgBr \longrightarrow C_6H_5-\underset{\underset{BrMg-N-OH}{|}}{\overset{\overset{C_2H_5}{|}}{C}}-CH_3 \longrightarrow$$

$$C_6H_5-\underset{NH}{\overset{\overset{C_2H_5}{|}}{\underset{\diagdown}{C}}}\text{---}CH_2$$

The method has general applicability.

N-substituted ethylenimines may be prepared by treatment of the N-alkyl-β-chloroethylamines with silver oxide.

$$CH_3-NH-CH_2CH_2Cl \xrightarrow{Ag_2O} CH_3-N\underset{CH_2}{\overset{CH_2}{\diagset}}$$

Tertiary chloroethylamines may be converted into quaternary ethylenimmonium compounds.[11,12]

$$CH_3-N\underset{CH_2CH_2Cl}{\overset{CH_2CH_2Cl}{\diagset}} \longrightarrow CH_3-\underset{\underset{CH_2CH_2Cl}{|}}{\overset{+}{N}}\underset{CH_2}{\overset{CH_2}{\diagset}} \quad Cl^-$$

Reactions of Ethylenimines. Ethylenimine undergoes many of the reactions of secondary amines. Benzenesulfonyl chloride and benzoyl chloride react to give the corresponding amides.

$$C_6H_5-SO_2-N \underset{CH_2}{\overset{CH_2}{<}} \quad \text{and} \quad C_6H_5-CO-N \underset{CH_2}{\overset{CH_2}{<}}$$

Phenylisocyanate and phenylisothiocyanate give the corresponding ureas and thioureas.

$$C_6H_5-NHCO-N \underset{CH_2}{\overset{CH_2}{<}} \quad \text{and} \quad C_6H_5-NHCS-N \underset{CH_2}{\overset{CH_2}{<}}$$

The latter compound is converted to 2-anilino-4,5-thiazoline.[2]

$$\begin{array}{c} CH_2-N \\ | \qquad\quad \diagdown \\ CH_2-S \diagup \end{array} C-NH-C_6H_5$$

1-Lithiumethylenimine made from ethylenimine and methyllithium can be used to introduce the ethylenimine ring into an aromatic ring.[13]

The ethylenimine ring may also be introduced into the quinoline ring by reaction of 2-chloroquinoline with 1-lithiumethylenimine.

$$\text{(quinoline)}-Cl + Li-N \underset{CH_2}{\overset{CH_2}{<}} \longrightarrow \text{(quinoline)}-N \underset{CH_2}{\overset{CH_2}{<}}$$

Ethylenimine derivatives will add to activated double bonds as in acrylonitrile.

$$\underset{H_2C}{\overset{H_2C}{>}}NH + CH_2{=}CH-CN \longrightarrow \underset{H_2C}{\overset{H_2C}{>}}N-CH_2CH_2CN$$

Hydrohalogen acids promote an opening of the ethylenimine ring and the formation of a β-chloroethylamine.[14]

$$\underset{CH_3-HC}{\overset{H_2C}{>}}NH + 2HCl \longrightarrow CH_3-\underset{\underset{|}{CH_2Cl}}{\overset{}{CH}}-NH_3Cl$$

Many ethylenimine derivatives are dimerized to form piperazines in the presence of acids.[15]

$$\underset{H_2C}{\overset{H_2C}{\diagdown}}NCH_3 \xrightarrow{H^+} CH_3-N\underset{CH_2-CH_2}{\overset{CH_2-CH_2}{\diagdown}}N-CH_3$$

The ethylenimine ring is sensitive to hydrolysis and in aqueous solution the ring is opened to give an ethanolamine.

$$\underset{H_2C}{\overset{H_2C}{\diagdown}}NH + H_2O \longrightarrow HOCH_2CH_2NH_2$$

The hydrolysis occurs in acid solution and is especially rapid in neutral or alkaline solutions.

The hydrolysis of 2,2-dimethylethylenimine in hydrochloric acid gives $(CH_3)_2C(NH_2)CH_2Cl$ and $(CH_3)_2C(OH)CH_2NH_2$ in varying ratios depending on the temperature and concentration of the hydrochloric acid.[16]

Ethylenimines react with alkylamines in the presence of aluminum chloride to give substituted ethylenediamines.[17,18]

$$\underset{H_2C}{\overset{H_2C}{\diagdown}}NH + HNR_2 \longrightarrow H_2NCH_2CH_2NR_2$$

Gabriel showed that ethylenimine reacts with sulfurous acid to give taurine.

$$\underset{H_2C}{\overset{H_2C}{\diagdown}}NH + H_2SO_3 \longrightarrow H_2NCH_2CH_2SO_3H$$

Carbon disulfide reacts rapidly to form 2-mercaptothiazolines.

$$\begin{array}{c} H_2C-N \\ | \quad\quad\quad C-SH \\ H_2C-S \end{array}$$

Catalytic hydrogenation opens the ring to give ethylamine.[19,20]

Ethylenimine reacts with starch to give aminoethyl ethers.[21]

Triethylenemelamine is prepared by adding an aqueous solution of ethylenimine and potassium carbonate to cyanuric chloride at 0–5°C.[22]

Ethylenimine containing about 1 per cent sodium metal may be added to styrene at 45°C to give N-phenethylethylenimine in 90 per cent yield.[23]

The 2-ethylamino group can be introduced directly into benzene or other aromatic compounds by reaction with ethylenimine in the presence of aluminum chloride.[24] Thus ethylenimine is added to anhydrous benzene containing aluminum chloride and the mixture heated in a sealed tube at 120–130°C for 8 hours. The reaction mixture is then poured over ice, the product ($C_6H_5CH_2CH_2NH_2$) extracted with ether and recovered by distillation. The yield is 60 per cent. At 170–180°C the yield is 70–80 per cent.

Ethylenimine polymerizes very readily and with the evolution of large amounts of heat. Even carbon dioxide is sufficiently acidic to initiate the polymerization. Because of the very great evolution of heat the polymerization is difficult to control and often occurs spontaneously. In Germany the polymerization was accomplished by adding 0.1 per cent of carbon dioxide to the monomer as it distilled out from the reaction mixture.

Jones[25] claims that the polymer of ethylenimine is a linear poly-secondary amine of 25–100 ethylenimine units.

$$
\begin{array}{c}
H_2C \\
\quad \diagdown \\
\quad\quad N-(CH_2CH_2NH)_n-CH_2CH_2NH_2 \\
\quad \diagup \\
H_2C
\end{array}
$$

Polyethylenimine has several specialized uses, probably the most important of which is improving the wet strength of paper. For this purpose the polymer is added to the paper pulp which is processed in the conventional manner.

Textile fibers may be given the characteristic dyeing properties of wool by copolymerizing ethylenimine and aromatic diisocyanates.[26]

Azetidine and Derivatives

The four-membered heterocyclic amine is not widely known and is of relatively little importance. This arises from the fact that it is difficult to prepare in reasonable yield and that the four-membered ring is not found in nature except in a few alkaloids.

The completely saturated four-membered ring containing one nitrogen is called azetidine or trimethylenimine. It is prepared in a manner similar to that used for the synthesis of ethylenimine, e.g., by dehydrohalogenation of gamma-haloalkylamines.[27,28]

$$
BrCH_2CH_2CH_2NHR \xrightarrow{KOH}
\begin{array}{c}
H_2C-N-R \\
\;|\quad\quad| \\
H_2C-CH_2
\end{array}
$$

If the amino group is primary the yields are very poor. The yields of substituted azetidines may be as high as 80 per cent. Thus 1,2-dimethyl-4-isobutylazetidine is obtained from the corresponding gamma-bromoalkylamine by treatment with 30 per cent potassium hydroxide.

$$(CH_3)_2CHCH_2\!-\!\underset{\underset{NHCH_3}{|}}{CH}\!-\!CH_2\!-\!\underset{\underset{Br}{|}}{CH}\!-\!CH_3 \xrightarrow{KOH} (CH_3)_2CHCH_2\!-\!\underset{\underset{CH_3-N}{|}}{CH}\!-\!\underset{\underset{CH-CH_3}{|}}{CH_2}$$

Similarly, 1,3,3-trimethylazetidine is prepared in 80 per cent yield.[29]

$$CH_3NH\!-\!CH_2\!-\!C(CH_3)_2\!-\!CH_2Br \rightarrow \begin{array}{c} H_2C\!-\!N\!-\!CH_3 \\ |\quad\ | \\ (H_3C)_2C\!-\!CH_2 \end{array}$$

If a choice of starting material can be made, best results are obtained when the amino group is secondary and the halogen is primary.

Azetidine may also be prepared by the pyrolysis of trimethylenediamonium chloride.

$$H_2C\!\!\begin{array}{c}\diagup CH_2NH_3Cl \\ \diagdown CH_2NH_3Cl \end{array} \xrightarrow[\text{dist'n}]{\text{dry}} \begin{array}{c} H_2C\!-\!NH \\ |\quad\ | \\ H_2C\!-\!CH_2 \end{array} + NH_4Cl + HCl$$

The yields are very low, being in the order of 5–10 per cent. β-picoline is the major product.[30]

1,3-Dibromopropane reacts with toluene sulfonamide in the presence of a base to give sulfonazetidide which may be reduced with sodium and an alcohol to give the free imine.[31,32]

$$H_2C\!\!\begin{array}{c}\diagup CH_2Br \\ \diagdown CH_2Br \end{array} + H_2NSO_2C_6H_4CH_3 \xrightarrow{NaOH} \begin{array}{c} H_2C\!-\!N\!-\!SO_2C_6H_4CH_3 \\ |\quad\ | \\ H_2C\!-\!CH_2 \end{array} \xrightarrow[C_5H_{11}OH]{Na}$$

$$\begin{array}{c} H_2C\!-\!NH \\ |\quad\ | \\ H_2C\!-\!CH_2 \end{array} + C_6H_5CH_3 + H_2S$$

Reactions of Azetidine. The azetidines behave very much like typical secondary or tertiary amines. They are, for the most part, liquids having amine-like odors and form salts with acids.

The reactions have not been extensively studied so that only a few will be described here.

Azetidine reacts with formaldehyde at room temperature to give an N-hydroxymethyl derivative which undergoes further condensation to give 1,1-methylenebisazetidine.[33,34]

$$
\begin{array}{c}
\text{H C--NH} \\
\text{|~~~~~|} \\
\text{H}_2\text{C--CH}_2
\end{array}
\ +\ \text{HCHO} \longrightarrow
\begin{array}{c}
\text{H}_2\text{C--N--CH}_2\text{OH} \\
\text{|~~~~~~~|} \\
\text{H}_2\text{C--CH}_2
\end{array}
\longrightarrow
\begin{array}{c}
\text{H}_2\text{C--N--CH}_2\text{--N--CH}_2 \\
\text{|~~~~|~~~~~~~~~~|~~~~~|} \\
\text{H}_2\text{C--CH}_2~~~~\text{H}_2\text{C--CH}_2
\end{array}
$$

At temperatures of 110–115°C an isomeric alcohol is obtained.

$$
\begin{array}{c}
\text{H}_2\text{C--NH} \\
\text{|~~~~~~|} \\
\text{H}_2\text{C--CH--CH}_2\text{OH}
\end{array}
$$

Concentrated acids such as hydrochloric acid open up the ring to give a gamma-chloroamine.[35]

$$
\begin{array}{c}
\text{H}_2\text{C--NH} \\
\text{|~~~~~|} \\
\text{H}_2\text{C--CH}_2
\end{array}
\ +\ \text{HCl} \longrightarrow \text{ClCH}_2\text{CH}_2\text{CH}_2\text{NH}_2
$$

Dilute acids catalyze the hydrolysis to amino alcohols.

A quaternary azetidinium chloride may be prepared by heating N-γ-bromopropylpiperidine.[36]

$$
\text{BrCH}_2\text{CH}_2\text{CH}_2\text{--N}
\begin{array}{c}
\diagup\text{CH}_2\text{CH}_2\diagdown \\
~~~~~~~~~~~~~~~~~~~\text{CH}_2 \\
\diagdown\text{CH}_2\text{CH}_2\diagup
\end{array}
\xrightarrow{100°}
\left[
\text{H}_2\text{C}
\begin{array}{c}
\diagup\text{CH}_2\diagdown~~~~\diagup\text{CH}_2\text{CH}_2\diagdown \\
~~~~~~~~~~\overset{+}{\text{N}}~~~~~~~~~~~~~~~~\text{CH}_2 \\
\diagdown\text{CH}_2\diagup~~~~\diagdown\text{CH}_2\text{CH}_2\diagup
\end{array}
\right]
\text{Br}^-
$$

An azetidinium iodide may be formed by treating γ-chloroalkyldimethyl-amine with methyl iodide.

$$
\text{ClCH}_2\text{CH}_2\text{--CH--N(CH}_3)_2 \ +\ \text{CH}_3\text{I} \longrightarrow
\left[
\begin{array}{c}
\text{H}_3\text{C--CH--}\overset{+}{\text{N}}\text{(CH}_3)_2 \\
\text{|~~~~~~|} \\
\text{H}_2\text{C----CH}_2
\end{array}
\right]
\text{I}^- \ +\ \text{CH}_3\text{Cl}
$$

with CH_3 below the first CH.

The quaternary iodide may be converted to the quaternary hydroxide with silver oxide. These compounds are strong bases which decompose on heating to N,N-dimethyl-γ-hydroxypropylamines.

Other derivatives of the azetidines are known, such as the 2-azetidinones (β-lactams).

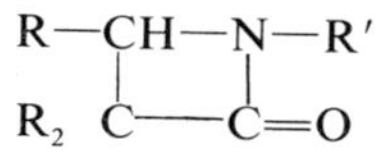

$$R-CH-N-R'$$
$$R_2 C - C = O$$

2,4-azetidinediones (Malonimides)

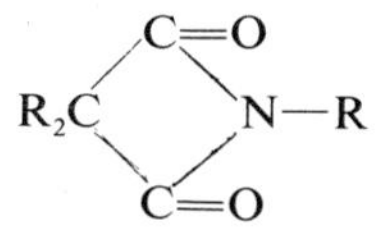

$$
\begin{array}{c}
C=O\\
R_2CN-R\\
C=O
\end{array}
$$

and the azetes

$$
\begin{array}{c}
HC=N\\
HC=CH
\end{array}
$$

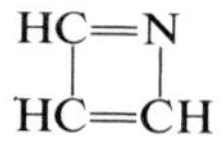

None of these compounds are of much practical importance.

Pyrrole

The most important five-membered heterocyclic amine is pyrrole, first recognized in 1834 in products obtained by the dry distillation of proteins.[37]

It is probably obtained from glutamic acid which is converted to pyrrolidone-α-carboxylic acid on heating.[38] Further heating with calcium hydroxide gives pyrrole.

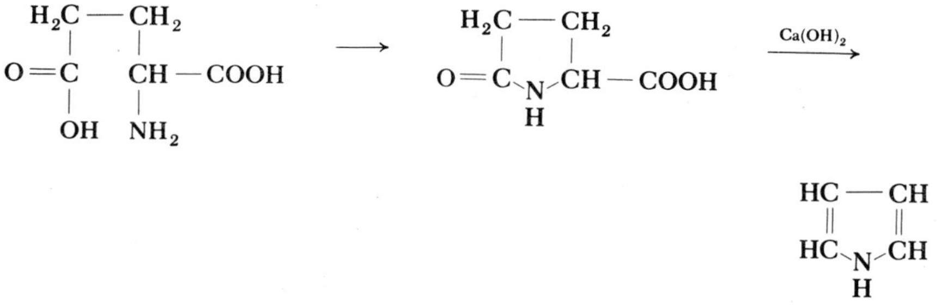

$$
\begin{array}{ccc}
H_2C - CH_2 & & H_2C - CH_2\\
| \quad\quad | & \longrightarrow & | \quad\quad |\\
O=C \quad CH-COOH & & O=C_{\diagdown N \diagup}CH-COOH\\
| \quad\quad | & & H\\
OH \quad NH_2 & &
\end{array}
$$

$$\xrightarrow{\text{Ca(OH)}_2}$$

$$
\begin{array}{c}
HC - CH\\
\| \quad\quad \|\\
HC_{\diagdown N \diagup}CH\\
H
\end{array}
$$

Pyrrole has also been isolated from bone oil and coal tar.

The preferred laboratory method of preparation involves heating ammonium mucate.[39] The reaction probably proceeds through the formation of a dienol.

$$
\begin{array}{c}
\text{HOHC} - \text{CHOH} \\
| \quad\quad | \\
\text{H}_4\text{NOOC} - \text{HC} \quad \text{CH} - \text{COONH}_4 \qquad \xrightarrow{-\text{H}_2\text{O}} \\
| \quad\quad | \\
\text{OH} \; \text{HO}
\end{array}
$$

$$
\begin{array}{c}
\text{HC} - \text{CH} \\
\| \quad \| \\
\text{H}_4\text{NOOC} - \text{C} \quad \text{C} - \text{COONH}_4 \qquad \longrightarrow \\
| \quad\quad | \\
\text{OH} \; \text{HO}
\end{array}
\qquad
\begin{array}{c}
\text{HC} - \text{CH} \\
\| \quad \| \\
\text{HC}_{\diagdown\text{N}\diagup}\text{CH} \\
\text{H}
\end{array}
+
\begin{array}{c}
\text{HC} - \text{CH} \\
\| \quad \| \\
\text{HC}_{\diagdown\text{N}\diagup}\text{C} - \text{CONH}_2 \\
\text{H}
\end{array}
$$

Saccharic acid obtained by the oxidation of sucrose or starch with nitric acid may be converted to the ammonium salt, mixed with glycerol and heated to 175–200° to give pyrrole in about 45 per cent yield.[40]

Pyrrole is also prepared by the distillation of succinimide in the presence of zinc dust.

Reppe[41] prepared pyrrole from 1,4-butynediol and ammonia.

$$
\text{HOCH}_2 - \text{C} \equiv \text{C} - \text{CH}_2\text{OH} \; + \; \text{NH}_3 \qquad \longrightarrow
\qquad
\begin{array}{c}
\text{HC} - \text{CH} \\
\| \quad \| \\
\text{HC}_{\diagdown\text{N}\diagup}\text{CH} \\
\text{H}
\end{array}
$$

The butynediol is made from acetylene and formaldehyde.

1,4-Butynediol and aniline passed over alumina at 300°C give 1-phenyl-pyrrole in about 30 per cent yield.[42]

Pyrrole has recently become available from the reaction of furan with ammonia.

$$
\begin{array}{c}
\text{HC} - \text{CH} \\
\| \quad \| \\
\text{HC}_{\diagdown\text{O}\diagup}\text{CH}
\end{array}
+ \; \text{NH}_3 \qquad \longrightarrow
\qquad
\begin{array}{c}
\text{HC} - \text{CH} \\
\| \quad \| \\
\text{HC}_{\diagdown\text{N}\diagup}\text{CH} \\
\text{H}
\end{array}
+ \; \text{H}_2\text{O}
$$

The reaction is carried out in the vapor phase at 480–490°C using steam as a diluent in the presence of an alumina catalyst. Yields range from 60–80 per cent.[43]

Pyrrole has long been of interest because the ring system is an integral part of hemin and chlorophyl. It is only now becoming of interest as an industrial chemical.

Pyrrole is a weak base because the unshared electron pair of the nitrogen is tied up through over-all reasonance stabilization of the ring. Five resonance structures for pyrrole are possible and the actual structure is a hybrid of them all.

$$
\begin{array}{cccccc}
HC\!-\!CH & HC\!=\!CH & HC\!=\!CH & \overset{(-)}{HC}\!-\!CH & \overset{(-)}{HC}\!-\!CH \\
HC_{\diagdown N\diagup}CH & HC_{\diagdown \underset{(-)}{N}\diagup}CH & HC_{\diagdown \underset{(-)}{N}\diagup}CH & HC_{\diagdown N\diagup}CH & HC_{\diagdown N\diagup}CH \\
H & H & H & H & H \\
 & (+) & (+) & (+) & (+)
\end{array}
$$

All bonds possess some double bond character so that substitution rather than addition reactions would be expected. Pyrrole is such a weak base that the hydrogen attached to the nitrogen atom is readily replaced by metals.

Preparation of Derivatives of Pyrrole. Pyrrole derivatives can be prepared by the reaction of α-amino ketones with a ketone having an active methylene group such as ethyl acetoacetate.[44]

$$
\begin{array}{c}
CH_3\!-\!C\!=\!O \\
C_2H_5OOC^{\diagup CH}\diagdown_{NH_2}
\end{array}
+
\begin{array}{c}
H_2C\!-\!COOC_2H_5 \\
O\!=\!C\diagdown_{CH_3}
\end{array}
\longrightarrow
$$

$$
\begin{array}{c}
H_3C\!-\!C\!-\!C\!-\!COOC_2H_5 \\
H_5C_2OOC^{\diagdown}C_{\diagdown N\diagup}C\diagdown CH_3 \\
H
\end{array}
$$

N-substituted pyrroles can be made by treatment of succindialdehyde with amines[43,45] or by reaction of furan with amines.

Triebs and Neumays[46] prepared pyrrole derivatives by heating α,α-dibromoadiponitriles and amines such as aniline in methanol in a sealed tube at 150–160°C for 4 hours. Thus N-phenylpyrrole was prepared in 20 per cent yield. Substituting benzylamine for aniline gave N-benzylpyrrole in 40 per cent yield. The α,α'-dibromoadiponitrile is prepared by (1) heating adipic acid with thionyl chloride to form the acid chloride; (2) adding bromine to the reaction mixture to obtain α-bromination; (3) addition of ammonia to form α,α'-dibromoadipodiamide; (4) dehydration to the dinitrile by heating with more thionyl chloride.

Treibs and Hitzler[47] prepared N-phenylpyrrole by heating a mixture of 1,2,3,4-tetrabromobutane and excess aniline for a few hours at 150–160°C. The yield was about 10 per cent. Similarly benzylamine gave a 26 per cent yield of N-benzylpyrrole and methylamine gave a very small yield of N-methylpyrrole.

When sodium hydrosulfite ($Na_2S_2O_4$) is used as the reducing agent in the Knorr synthesis the reaction can be carried out at room temperature.[48] Thus ethyl acetoacetate in acetic acid is treated with a concentrated aqueous sodium nitrite solution at 20°C. After the reaction is complete the solution is neutralized with sodium hydroxide to give an 85 per cent yield of 2,4-dimethyl-3,5-dicarbethoxypyrrole. The reaction proceeds by formation of the intermediate isonitroso compound which reacts with more ethyl acetoacetate.

In reactions involving two different compounds, one of them is converted to the isonitroso compound and the second carbonyl compound is added. Thus an equimolar mixture of isonitrosoacetone and ethyl acetoacetate in water is treated with sodium hydrosulfite at room temperature to give a 75 per cent yield of 2,4-dimethyl-3-carbethoxypyrrole.

Similarly isonitrosoethyl acetoacetate reacts with acetylacetone to give 2,4-dimethyl-3-acetyl-5-carbethoxypyrrole.

Reactions of Pyrrole and its Derivatives. *Salt Formation.* Pyrrole is a very weak base. It dissolves only slightly in dilute acids and is resinified by concentrated acids. In many ways it resembles phenol. It forms salts with alkali metals by replacement of a proton on the nitrogen.

$$\begin{array}{c} HC \!-\! CH \\ \| \quad\quad \| \\ HC_{\diagdown N \diagup} CH \\ (-)\ \ K^+ \end{array}$$

Alkylation. Alkylation of pyrroles can be accomplished with sodium alkoxides in an autoclave at temperatures of 200–220°C.[49]

The α-position is more reactive than the β-position. Potassium pyrrole treated with alkyl iodides give N-alkylpyrroles.

Pyrrolepotassium reacts with allyl bromide to give 2-allylpyrrole.[50]

Hydrogenation gives 2-propylpyrrole.

Halogenation. Chlorination of pyrrole is readily accomplished and sulfuryl chloride is most frequently used for this purpose.[51] Bromination is usually carried out with elemental bromine and iodination with the triodide ion. Iodination is so rapid that only the tetraiodide is obtained when pyrrole is treated with triodide ion.[52] In this respect pyrrole resembles phenol.

Substituted pyrroles are readily brominated.

If the hydrogen and carbethoxy groups are interchanged an abnormal bromination results.

Bromination at low temperatures gives the normal 5-bromo derivative.[53,54]

2,4-Dimethyl-3-ethylpyrrole is so reactive that the mononuclear bromide has not been isolated.

In some cases bromine displaces substituents on the pyrrole ring.

Pyrrole, in benzene solution, treated with bromine and lead thiocyanate gives α,α-dithiocyanopyrrole.[55]

Introduction of Aldehyde Groups. Pyrrole undergoes the Reimer-Tiemann reaction to introduce an aldehyde group in the 2-position. The yields are however very low.[56]

Alkylated pyrroles may be converted into aldehydes by means of the Gatterman reaction.[57]

Potassium pyrrole undergoes ring enlargement when treated with chloroform to give 3-chloropyridine. 2,5-Dimethylpyrrole treated with chloroform and KOH gives a mixture of the corresponding aldehyde and 3-chloro-2,5-dimethylpyridine.

The reaction proceeds through the formation of a dichloromethylpyrroline.

which rearranges to the chloropyridine.

Pyrrole-2-carboxylic acid can be prepared by adding pyrrole to aqueous potassium carbonate and adding carbon dioxide at 900 psi and heating at 100°C. The acid is obtained by acidification of the salt.[58]

Methyl groups may be introduced into the pyrrole nucleus by reduction of Mannich bases. Treibs and Zinsmeister[59] refluxed 2,4-dimethyl-5-carbethoxypyrrole in alcohol with diethylamine and 40 per cent aqueous formaldehyde to give almost a quantitative yield of 2,4-dimethyl-3-diethylaminomethyl-5-carbethoxypyrrole which was hydrogenated at 150–160°C and a pressure of 100 atmospheres in the presence of Raney nickel to give an 88 per cent yield of 2,3,4-trimethyl-5-carbethoxypyrrole.

Bachman and Heisy[60] condensed pyrrole and formaldehyde with piperidine and morpholine to form 2-(N-substituted aminoethyl)-pyrroles. Herz,

Dittmer and Cristol[61] successfully used primary amines in the condensation with formaldehyde and pyrrole to obtain 2-methylaminomethyl and 2-ethylaminomethyl pyrroles in 15 and 27 per cent yields.

Burke and Hammer[62] reacted pyrrole with equimolar proportions of formaldehyde and cyclohexylamonium chloride at room temperature to give 2-cyclohexylaminomethylpyrrole hydrochloride in 66 per cent yield. No monomeric products were formed when this compound reacted further with formaldehyde or when pyrrole, formaldehyde and cyclohexylammonium chloride were condensed directly in a molar ratio of 1:2:1.

In attempts to avoid side reactions, substituted pyrroles were used. 3-Carbethoxy-2,4-dimethylpyrrole, formaldehyde and cyclohexylamine (mole ratio 1:2:1) reacted with the introduction of a heterocyclic ring forming 6-carbethoxy-2-cyclohexyl-2,3-dihydro-5,7-dimethyl-1H-imidazo[1,4-a] pyrrole in 66 per cent yield.

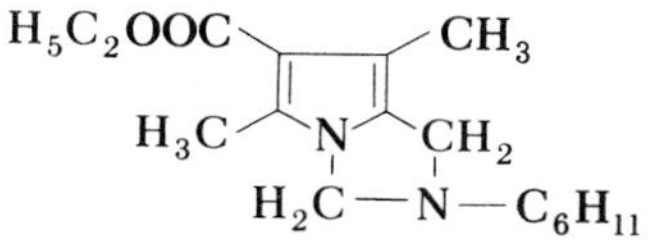

$$H_5C_2OOC \quad CH_3$$
$$H_3C \quad N \quad CH_2$$
$$H_2C-N-C_6H_{11}$$

Equimolar amounts of reagents gave 4-carbethoxy-2-cyclohexylaminomethyl-3,5-dimethylpyrrole.

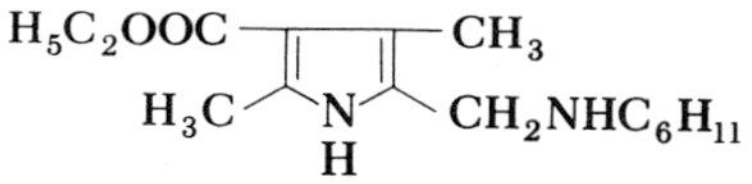

$$H_5C_2OOC \quad CH_3$$
$$H_3C \quad N \quad CH_2NHC_6H_{11}$$
$$H$$

Pyrroles react with formaldehyde under slightly acidic conditions to give dipyrrylmethanes.[63]

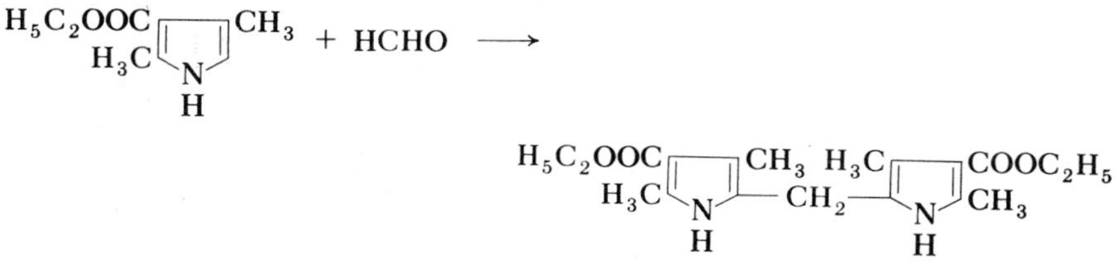

$$H_5C_2OOC \quad CH_3$$
$$H_3C \quad N \quad + \; HCHO \longrightarrow$$
$$H$$

$$H_5C_2OOC \quad CH_3 \quad H_3C \quad COOC_2H_5$$
$$H_3C \quad N \quad CH_2 \quad N \quad CH_3$$
$$H \qquad\qquad H$$

Structures of this type in which pyrrole rings are joined by methylene or —CH= groups are found in nature particularly in porphyrins, chlorophyl and hemin.

It is beyond the scope of this book to discuss these compounds but excellent reviews are available.[64]

Hydrogenated Pyrroles

The reduction of pyrrole with hydrogen iodide gives Δ^3-pyrroline and pyrrolidine.

$$\underset{\substack{|\\N\\H}}{\boxed{}} \quad \xrightarrow[\text{red P}]{\text{HI}} \quad \underset{\substack{|\\H_2C \diagdown N \diagup CH_2 \\ H}}{HC = CH} \quad \longrightarrow \quad \underset{\substack{|\\H_2C \diagdown N \diagup CH_2 \\ H}}{H_2C - CH_2}$$

The Δ^2-pyrroline which might be expected is not obtained.[65]

When $CH_3COCH_2CH_2CH_2OH$ and ammonia are passed over a palladium on alumina catalyst at 450°C 2-methyl-2-pyrroline is obtained in 5 per cent yield together with 10 per cent of 2-methylpyrrolidine and 20 per cent 2-methylpyrrole.[65] The keto alcohol $CH_3COCH_2CH_2CH(CH_3)OH$ gave similar results with a 22–30 per cent yield of dimethylpyrroline.

Pyrrolidines may be prepared by the reduction of pyrrole with phosphorus and hydrogen iodide[67] or by catalytic hydrogenation.[68] Pyrrolidines have also been prepared by the electrolytic reduction of succinimide.[69]

Yur'ev[42] has prepared pyrrolidine by passing 1,4-butanediol and ammonia over an activated alumina catalyst at temperatures of 325°C. Yields were about 68 per cent.

With a 1:1 mixture of 1,4-butanediol and aniline an 88 per cent yield of 1-phenylpyrrolidine may be obtained.

Pyrrolidone is prepared by heating butyrolactone and ammonia for 8 hours in an autoclave at 230°C under 20–40 atmospheres pressure.[70] The yield of α-pyrrolidone is about 89 per cent.

$$\underset{\substack{|\quad\;\; |\\H_2C \diagdown O \diagup C=O}}{H_2C - CH_2} \;+\; NH_3 \quad \longrightarrow \quad \underset{\substack{|\quad\;\; |\\H_2C \diagdown N \diagup C=O\\H}}{H_2C - CH_2} \;+\; H_2O$$

N-Phenylpyrrolidone is obtained by passing an equimolar mixture of 1,4-butanediol and aniline over an aluminosilicate catalyst at 300°C.[71]

α-Pyrrolidone treated with potassium hydroxide to form the potassium salt then with acetylene diluted 2 to 1 with nitrogen at 140–160°C under 200 psi gives vinyl pyrrolidone in about 90 per cent yield.

$$\underset{\substack{|\quad\;\; |\\H_2C \diagdown N \diagup C=O\\K}}{H_2C - CH_2} \quad \xrightarrow{HC \equiv CH} \quad \underset{\substack{|\quad\;\; |\\H_2C \diagdown N \diagup C=O\\|\\CH=CH_2}}{H_2C - CH_2}$$

Vinylpyrrolidone is readily polymerized to give a material useful as a blood plasma extender and is used to an appreciable extent as a copolymer in the preparation of synthetic plastics and fibers.

Pyrazole

The pyrazole ring system consists of a five-membered doubly unsaturated ring containing two adjacent nitrogen atoms. The first compound having this ring system to be synthesized was 1-phenyl-3-methyl-5-pyrazolone. It was prepared by Knorr in 1883[72] from ethyl acetoacetate and phenylhydrazine.

Pyrazoles are made from 1,3-diketones and hydrazines. N-Phenylpyrazoles have been extensively investigated because of the availability of phenylhydrazine.

$$CH_3-CO-CH_2-COCH_3 \ + \ C_6H_5NHNH_2 \ \longrightarrow$$

Similarly pyrazolones are obtained from β-ketoesters and hydrazines.

Cyanoacetic acid hydrazide, $NCCH_2CONHNH_2$, reacts with 1,3-diketones in acidic media to give pyrazole derivatives. In the presence of basic catalysts in alcohol, N-aminopyridinones are formed. Thus cyanoacetic acid hydrazide in dilute hydrochloric acid is treated with acetylacetone in ethanol to give 1-cyanoacetyl-3,5-dimethylpyrazole. In boiling alcohol containing diethylamine, 1-amino-2,4-dimethyl-5-cyano-6-pyridinone is obtained.[73]

Another procedure involves the action of hydrazine on α,β-unsaturated ketones. An acetylenic ketone is required to give a pyrazole. Ethylenic ketones give dihydropyrazoles.

$$CH_3-C \equiv C-CO-CH_3 \ + \ H_2NNH_2 \ \longrightarrow$$

Pyrazolines (dihydropyrazoles) can be obtained by the reaction of diazomethane on α,β-unsaturated esters.[74]

$$C_2H_5-OCOCH=CH-COOC_2H_5 \ + \ CH_2N \ \longrightarrow$$

$$C_2H_5OCO-CH-CH-COOC_2H_5 \ \longrightarrow \ C_2H_5OCO-CH-C-COOC_2H_5$$

Properties and Reactions of Pyrazole. Pyrazole is a colorless crystalline solid which melts at 70°C and boils at 187°C. It has a pyridinelike odor.

Pyrazole is a very weak base. It forms salts with hydrochloric, sulfuric and nitric acids but these are completely hydrolyzed in water solution. As in pyrrole, the hydrogen on the nitrogen may be replaced by alkali metals.

Alkyl pyrazoles exist as tautomers.

Alkylation of substituted pyrazoles with methyl iodide or other alkylating agents occurs very readily on either nitrogen atom to give a mixture of isomers in which the ratio of isomers is determined by the basicity of the medium, the amount of moisture and the alkylating agent used.[75]

N-Substituted pyrazoles react readily with alkyl halides to give pyrazolium salts. Electrophilic substitutions occur primarily at the 4-position. The ease of substitution lies somewhere between the ease of substituting benzene and phenol or pyrrole. N-Phenylpyrazole is substituted on the 4-position but reaction does not occur in the benzene ring.

1-Arylpyrazoles are readily reduced with sodium and an alcohol to pyrazoline. The pyrazole ring is very stable towards oxidizing agents so that alkyl side chains can be selectively attacked. A methyl group in the 4-position is attacked more readily than one in the 3- or 5-position.

Pyrazolones

5-Pyrazolones are probably the most important of the compounds containing the pyrazole ring. As mentioned previously they may be obtained by treating β-keto esters with hydrazines. The pyrazolones have been of considerable importance in the fields of dyes and drugs.

1-Phenyl-3-methyl-5-pyrazolone couples with diazonium salts to give a series of well known pyrazolone dyes.

A large number of such dyes are known.

Imidazole

Imidazole, sometimes called glyoxaline, is a doubly unsaturated five-membered heterocyclic compound having nitrogen atoms in the 1 and 3-positions.

Imidazole was first prepared in 1858[76] by the reaction of ammonia with glyoxal but it was not until about 24 years later that the structure was proved to be

$$
\begin{array}{c}
\text{H} \\
\text{HC} \overset{\text{N}}{\diagup} \diagdown \text{CH} \\
\parallel \qquad \parallel \\
\text{HC} \!-\!\!-\!\! \text{N}
\end{array}
$$

Because of tautomerism, the 4- and 5-positions are equivalent. A substituent in the 4- or 5-position therefore, is referred to as being in the 4(5)- or 5(4)-position.

Alkylation of 4(5)-methylimidazole gives a mixture of 1,4- and 1,5-disubstituted imidazoles.[77]

Preparation of Imidazoles. Modifications of the original method for making imidazole are still used. Thus α,β-diketones react with ammonia or an amine and an aldehyde.

$$
\begin{array}{c}
\text{CH}_3 \!-\! \text{C} \!=\! \text{O} \\
\vert \\
\text{CH}_3 \!-\! \text{C} \!=\! \text{O}
\end{array}
+ \ 2\text{NH}_3 \ + \ \text{RCHO} \ \longrightarrow \
\begin{array}{c}
\qquad\qquad \text{N} \\
\text{CH}_3 \!-\! \text{C} \!-\! \text{H} \diagdown \\
\parallel \qquad\qquad \text{C} \!-\! \text{R} \\
\text{CH}_3 \!-\! \text{C} \!-\! \text{N} \diagup
\end{array}
$$

In a method developed by Weidenhagen[78] an acyloin and an aldehyde are heated in 25 per cent aqueous ammonia containing an equimolar amount of cupric acetate. This method gives good yields of imidazoles.

$$
\begin{array}{c}
\text{R} \!-\! \text{CH} \!-\! \text{OH} \\
\vert \\
\text{R} \!-\! \text{C} \!=\! \text{O}
\end{array}
\ \xrightarrow{\text{Cu}^{++}} \
\begin{array}{c}
\text{R} \!-\! \text{C} \!=\! \text{O} \\
\vert \\
\text{R} \!-\! \text{C} \!=\! \text{O}
\end{array}
+ \ \text{NH}_3 \ + \ \text{RCHO} \ \longrightarrow
$$

$$
\begin{array}{c}
\qquad\qquad\quad \text{Cu} \\
\text{R} \!-\! \text{C} \!-\! \text{N} \diagup \\
\parallel \qquad\qquad \text{C} \!-\! \text{R} \\
\text{R} \!-\! \text{C} \!-\! \text{N} \diagup
\end{array}
\ \xrightarrow{\text{H}_2\text{S}} \
\begin{array}{c}
\qquad\qquad \text{N} \\
\text{R} \!-\! \text{C} \!-\! \text{H} \diagdown \\
\parallel \qquad\qquad \text{C} \!-\! \text{R} \\
\text{R} \!-\! \text{C} \!-\! \text{N} \diagup
\end{array}
$$

Several other more elegant syntheses are available for the preparation of imidazole derivatives but they will not be discussed here.

A number of imidazoles possess biological activity. 4(5)-Methylimidazole shows hypertensive activity.[79] N-Substituted-4-aminomethylimidazoles cause vasoconstriction and increase the blood pressure.[80] One of the most biologically active derivatives of imidazole is histamine, 4(5)-(β-amino-ethyl)imidazole.

Imidazolines (4,5-dihydroimidazoles) are prepared from acids and 1,2-diamines. Imidazoline itself is made from formic acid and ethylenediamine.[81] Several other methods of synthesis have been reported.

The 1,2-dialkylimidazoles in which the alkyl group contains 1 to 14 carbon atoms have been reported to have bacteriostatic activity[82] as well as anesthetic activity.[83] Some imidazolines are vasodilators, others are vasoconstricters and there is little correlation between structure and the effect on the circulatory system.

2-Amino substituted imidazolines are reported to be good rubber vulcanization accelerators.[84]

Pyridine

Pyridine is a heterocyclic tertiary amine having six atoms in the ring. In structure pyridine resembles benzene and is resonance-stabilized in much the same way. Five valence bond structures may be drawn for pyridine, two of which are analogous to the Kekule structures for benzene and three in which there is a charge separation.

This means that all bonds have some double and some single bond character, as in benzene, so that substitution rather than addition reactions occur. It is also indicated that pyridine should be vulnerable to nucleophilic attack at the 2-, 4-, and 6-positions.

Pyridine has been obtained almost entirely from coal tar. However, in recent years, pyridine and pyridine derivatives have been obtained from aldehydes and ammonia. Thus paraldehyde and concentrated aqueous ammonia containing about 12 per cent acetic acid were heated to 220°C and 760 psi to give 2-methyl-5-ethylpyridine and 2-methylpyridine.[85] Synthetic pyridine is now commercially available.

Metallic fluorides are effective catalysts for the conversion of acetaldehyde and ammonia to pyridine derivatives.[86] Paraldehyde and ammonia (mole ratio 1:8) together with a little water and KHF_2 were charged into a stainless steel bomb which is purged with nitrogen and then heated to 490–500°F for 3 hours to give a 70 per cent yield of 2-methyl-5-

ethylpyridine. Sodium and potassium fluorides are not effective catalysts unless activated by hydrogen fluoride.

In another example paraldehyde, aqueous ammonia and a metal fluoride were heated under a nitrogen atmosphere at 490–500°F under pressure to give picolines and 2-methyl-5-ethylpyridine. When no catalyst was used a 56 per cent yield of 2-methyl-3-ethylpyridine was obtained. The yield with antimony fluoride was 77 per cent, with cupric fluoride 72 per cent, and with bismuth or zinc fluorides 71 per cent. Crotonaldehyde may also be used as the carbonyl compound.[87]

2-Methyl-5-ethylpyridine is prepared from paraldehyde and an ammonium salt such as ammonium acetate in water at 200°C for 5 hours under a pressure of about 20 atmospheres.[88] The yield of the dialkylpyridine is about 65 per cent.

In another process paraldehyde and ammonia are vaporized, preheated and passed into a reactor containing a catalyst consisting of 82 per cent silica gel, 15 per cent alumina, and 3 per cent thoria heated to 450°C. The reaction product is stripped of ammonia, extracted with benzene and distilled to give 34 per cent α-picoline, 32 per cent γ-picoline, 10 per cent 2-methyl-5-ethylpyridine, and 3 per cent 4-methyl-3-ethylpyridine.[89]

The vapor phase reaction of aqueous formaldehyde (40 per cent) with acetaldehyde and ammonia at 360°C in the presence of a catalyst gives a 49 per cent optimum yield of pyridine and picolines. A three-fold excess of ammonia is used and the total feed rate is 1.18 grams per hour per gram of catalyst. Catalysts found to be effective are activated silica-alumina (15 per cent Al_2O_3), activated boron phosphate, gel-type silica-alumina (90 per cent SiO_2) and crystalline type silica-alumina.[90]

Bradshaw, Parkes and Ford[91] obtained a mixture of pyridine and 3-picoline by reacting formaldehyde, acetaldehyde and ammonia at temperatures of 200–400°C in the presence of a catalyst. Thus formaldehyde (32 per cent aqueous) and acetaldehyde were preheated to 325°C, mixed with ammonia (mole ratio 1:2:3) and passed over fuller's earth to give a 22 per cent yield of pyridine based on the acetaldehyde.

If the initial concentration of formaldehyde is doubled, the yield of pyridine is increased to 28 per cent and 3-picoline is obtained as a by-product.

Allyl alcohol reacts with ammonia (mole ratio 1:5) in the presence of a copper on alumina catalyst to give β-picoline in about 20 per cent yield.[92]

Ethylene oxide and ammonia (mole ratio 3:1) passed over alumina at 400–450°C gives a 15–20 per cent yield of pyridine.[93]

A commercial process for the preparation of pyridine and 3-picoline consists of passing acetylene, ammonia and methyl alcohol through a reactor in contact with a fluidized catalyst. These three gases in a mole ratio of acetylene:ammonia:methyl alcohol of 1:1:3 are passed through a reactor at 425°C together with fluidized alumina impregnated with 10 per cent zinc fluoride.[94] Conversions of 16 per cent to pyridine and 25 per cent to 3-picoline are obtained and a small amount of 2-picoline is also formed. No 4-picoline is obtained.

Pyridine and 3-picoline are prepared either batchwise or continuously by the reaction of acetylene or acetaldehyde with ammonia and formaldehyde hemiacetal (from methanol and formaldehyde) in the vapor phase at 400–455°C over a catalyst such as alumina, silica or fuller's earth.[95] The catalyst may be fluidized and passed together with the reactants through a reactor heated to 500°C.

2,4,6-Trimethylpyridine in high purity is obtained by the reaction of acetone and ammonia at 400–500°C at atmospheric pressure in the presence of a silica-alumina catalyst.[96]

γ-Picoline can be prepared by adding β-methylglutaricaldehyde to a boiling solution of ferrous ammonium sulfate. β-Methylglutaraldehyde is obtained by the hydrolysis of 2-methoxy-4-methyl-2,3-dihydropyran.[97]

Ethyl vinyl ether and anhydrous ammonia heated to 220°C in a stirred autoclave under a pressure of 230 atmospheres in the presence of a copper phosphate catalyst gives a product which consists largely of 2-methyl-5-ethylpyridine.[98]

Pyridine and pyridine derivatives are obtained by passing a 2-alkoxy-3,4-dihydro-2H-pyran, ammonia, steam and hydrogen over a catalyst at 275°C. The catalyst consists of copper and chromium oxides on alumina.[99]

Pyridine compounds can be obtained by heating pyrones in the presence of ammonia.[100] Thus γ-pyrone is converted to γ-pyridone which exists in tautomeric equilibrium with 4-hydroxypyridine.

A similar reaction gives α-pyridone.

As has been mentioned previously, pyrrole treated with chloroform undergoes a ring enlargement with the formation of 3-chloropyridine. Similar ring enlargements occur with benzal chloride, and bromoform. The thermal decomposition of some N-substituted pyrroles give pyridine derivatives. Thus N-benzylpyrrole gives 3-phenylpyridine.

Nitriles react with dienes at moderately high temperatures to form pyridine derivatives.[101] Thus phenylpyridine is prepared from butadiene and benzonitrile. The over-all reaction involves cyclization and dehydro-genation.

$$
\begin{array}{c} \ce{HC}{\overset{\displaystyle CH_2}{\Big\|}} \\ | \\ \ce{HC}{\underset{\displaystyle CH_2}{\Big\backslash}} \end{array} \;+\; \begin{array}{c} C_6H_5 \\ | \\ C \\ \| \\ N \end{array} \;\longrightarrow\; \left[\underset{N}{\bigcirc}\!\!-C_6H_5 \right] \;\longrightarrow\; \underset{N}{\bigcirc}\!\!-C_6H_5 \;+\; H_2
$$

A continuous process has been reported by Janz, McCulloch and Timpani[102] in which the butadiene and benzonitrile were passed over a catalyst consisting of chromic oxide (4 per cent) on alumina at temperatures of 400°C. Yields of 60 per cent of phenylpyridine based on the benzonitrile were obtained. About one-half of the butadiene was converted to polymer. Other effective catalysts consisted of vanadium or molybdenum oxide on alumina.

A mixture of trifluoroacetonitrile and ethylene in a mole ratio of 1:7 passed continuously through a reactor at 475°C at such a rate as to have a contact time of 43 seconds gives a 13 per cent conversion to 2-trifluoro-methylpyridine.

Similarly cyanamide $(CN)_2$ and ethylene in a mole ratio of 1:2 with a contact time of 82 seconds gives a 47 per cent conversion of cyanamide to 2-cyanopyridine.[103]

Alkylpyridines are dealkylated to pyridine by passing them in the vapor phase at elevated temperatures together with hydrogen over a hydrogena-tion catalyst such as nickel, cobalt or copper molybdates.[104]

Reactions of Pyridine. *Nitration.* The nitration of pyridine is very diffi-cult as might be expected from its electronic structure. Resonance in pyridine places a positive charge on the carbon atoms in the 2-, 4-, and 6-positions. Nitration proceeds by an electrophilic attack by the NO_2^+ ion and the positive charge on the ring would make this attack more difficult especially in the 2-, 4-, and 6-positions. Any reaction which does occur takes place at the 3-position.

Benzene is nitrated with a mixture of sulfuric and nitric acids at tem-peratures as low as 40°C. Pyridine requires a mixture of potassium nitrate and fuming sulfuric acid at a temperature of 300°C.

It follows that other electrophilic reactions such as sulfonation, bromina-tion and Friedel-Crafts proceed only with great difficulty. No Friedel-Crafts reaction involving pyridine has been reported.

Bromination. The bromination of pyridine can be accomplished at 300°C. The products are 3-bromo- and 3,5-dibromopyridine. At 500°C bromination gives 2-bromo- and 2,6-dibromopyridines. At this temperature the reaction undoubtedly proceeds by a free radical mechanism resulting from the thermal dissociation of bromine molecules into bromine atoms.

The presence of cuprous bromide favors bromination in the 2-position even at lower temperatures.[105,106,107]

Vapor phase chlorination of pyridine at 270°C gives 2-chloropyridine (46 per cent yield) and some 2,6-dichloropyridine. The 3-isomer is not obtained.

The best method for the preparation of 3-chloropyridine is by the reaction of pyrrole and chloroform previously described. A mixture of these two compounds is diluted with nitrogen and passed through a pyrex glass tube at 550°C.[108] 3-Chloropyridine is obtained in 33 per cent yield.

Shermer[109] reports the chlorination of pyridine in the vapor phase at 325–355°C to give 2-chloropyridine in 77 per cent yield. Steam is used as a diluent to moderate the reaction. The mole ratio of chlorine to pyridine to steam may be varied widely.

Chlorination of picolines does not give nuclear chlorination products. Chlorination occurs on the methyl groups with all of the hydrogens being replaced by chlorine. McBee, Hass and Hodnett[110] chlorinated 2,6-dimethylpyridine at 50°C for 3 hours, then at 150°C for 2 hours and finally at 180°C for 6 hours to give 2,6-di-(trichloromethyl)pyridine in 38 per cent yield. 2-Picoline gave the following compounds in addition to 2-trichloromethylpyridine.

With a strongly *ortho- para*-orienting group on the pyridine ring, bromination of the pyridine ring occurs quite rapidly. Thus bromination of 2-aminopyridine at 20°C in ethyl alcohol gives a 46 per cent yield of 2-amino-5-bromopyridine. The dibromide 2-amino-3,5-dibromopyridine is also obtained.

The chlorination of 3-aminopyridine is much more difficult to control but with hydrogen chloride and hydrogen peroxide at 70–80°C an 88 per cent yield of 2-chloro-3-aminopyridine is obtained.[111]

Amination. Pyridine reacts readily with sodium amide to give 2-aminopyridine.[112,113] This reaction proceeds by a nucleophilic attack by the NH_2^- ion at the positions of lowest electron density.

Further reaction gives 2,6-diaminopyridine.

2-Bromopyridine heated with aqueous ammonia at 200°C for 10 hours gives a 70 per cent yield of 2-aminopyridine. 3-Bromopyridine will not react with ammonia unless a catalyst is used. With aqueous ammonia at 200°C in the presence of copper sulfate, an 80 per cent yield of 3-amino-pyridine is obtained after 30 hours.[114]

When pyridine derivatives having carbethoxy or cyano groups in the 3- and 5-positions are treated with lithium aluminum hydride, the pyridine ring is attacked before the substituent groups are reduced. However, when these groups are in the 2-, 4-, and 6-positions, the substituents are pref-erentially reduced.[115]

Other Nucleophilic Reactions. Alkyl groups may be introduced onto the pyridine ring at the 2- and 4-positions. Butyllithium and pyridine at 100°C gives 2-butylpyridine and phenyllithium gives 2-phenylpyridine in ether solution at room temperature.[116] A Grignard reagent, e.g., phenyl-magnesium chloride and pyridine at a temperature of 150°C gives 2-, and 2,6-diphenylpyridine.

Reduction. Pyridine is readily reduced to piperidine by a variety of methods such as reaction with sodium and alcohol, hydrogenation in the presence of a nickel catalyst, and electrolytic reduction. Partial reduction of pyridines has not been possible but some pyridine-carboxylic acids have been reduced to the corresponding dihydropyridine-carboxylic acids with aluminum amalgam in moist ether.[117]

Reduction of pyridine with hydriodic acid causes cleavage of the ring with the formation of pentane and ammonia. Cleavage of the ring occurs to some extent during the catalytic hydrogenation of pyridines at tem-peratures above 150°C.

Alkali Metals. The alkali metals react with pyridine to give N-metal derivatives of partially hydrogenated bipyridyls. On hydrolysis, tetrahydro-bipyridyls are obtained which are readily oxidized even by the oxygen of the air to give bipyridyls.

The reaction is carried out by adding sodium to dry pyridine at room temperature.

Reactions Involving the Nitrogen. Pyridine is a weak base ($K_b = 2.3 \times 10^{-4}$) and a tertiary amine which undergoes most of the typical reactions of tertiary amines.

Pyridine forms salts with strong acids which are far more stable than those of tertiary aliphatic amines. Pyridinium chloride may be distilled without decomposition.

Pyridine is extensively used as a basic catalyst, frequently as the acetate, in aldol condensations, epimerization of sugars, etc., as a reagent for dehydrohalogenation and as a proton acceptor in the halogenation of alcohols with thionyl chloride, phosphorus halides, etc.

Quaternary ammonium salts are prepared by the reaction of pyridine with alkyl halides.

$$C_5H_5N + CH_3I \longrightarrow [C_5H_5NCH_3]^+I^-$$

These pyridinium salts are crystalline solids and are very soluble in water. They are quite stable and in most cases have well-defined melting points. Heating to 300°C in a sealed tube results in ring alkylation.

Pyridinium halides may be converted to the corresponding quaternary pyridinium hydroxides by treatment with moist silver oxide. The pyridinium hydroxides are obtained as syrups on evaporation of water solutions but they have not been isolated in solid form.

N-Alkylpyridinium hydroxides (alkaline solutions of N-alkylpyridinium halides) are oxidized to N-alkyl-2-pyridones with potassium ferricyanide.

If an alkyl group is present in the 2-position, the addition of a base or silver oxide causes the elimination of water to give a compound which may be considered as a Schiff's base formed from 2-pyridone.

These compounds are frequently referred to as anhydro bases.

Arylmethylpyridinium halides useful as germicides are prepared by the chloromethylation of aromatic hydrocarbons and the subsequent reaction with pyridine.[118] The chloromethylation of dodecylbenzene is accomplished by adding tin tetrachloride, chloromethyl ether and carbon disulfide at 0°C and after 1 hour permitting the temperature to rise to room temperature. The p-$C_{12}H_{25}$—C_6H_4—CH_2Cl which is obtained by extraction with petroleum ether, is dried and let stand with pyridine to give p-dodecylbenzylpyridinium chloride.

Shelton *et al.*[119] prepared a number of N-alkylated quaternary ammonium salts of pyridine, piperidine and morpholine for testing as germicides. The most effective were cetylpyridinium and cetylpiperidinium salts.

Miscellaneous Addition Reactions. Pyridine readily forms addition products with halogens.[120] Bromine water added to aqueous pyridine forms an addition compound ($C_5H_5N \cdot Br_2$) which separates as a red crystalline precipitate. The addition compound is also formed in carbon tetrachloride. The dibromide is capable of forming a hydrobromide indicating that the electron pair on the nitrogen is still available for salt formation.

Other halogens including fluorine form addition compounds of this type.

Sulfur dioxide reacts with pyridine to give a complex, C_5H_5N—SO_2.[121] and with picolines to give $2(\alpha$-$CH_3C_5H_4N) \cdot 3SO_2$ and α-$CH_3C_5H_4$-$N \cdot 2SO_2$.

The addition product $C_5H_5N \cdot SO_3$ and one from chlorosulfonic acid $C_5H_5NSO_3Cl$ are mild sulfating agents capable of sulfating a phenolic OH group without attack on the ring.[122,123]

$$C_6H_5OH + C_5H_5NSO_3HCl \longrightarrow C_6H_5OSO_3H + C_5H_5N \cdot HCl$$

Reactions of Pyridine Derivatives. *Halopyridines.* Halogen atoms in the 2- or 4-positions of pyridine are very reactive, comparable to those in *ortho*- and *para*-halonitrobenzenes. Thus these chlorine atoms are readily hydrolyzed, replaced by amine groups, etc. Hydrolysis will occur at 170°C in the presence of potassium hydroxide. 3-Chloropyridine will not react under these conditions.

2-Bromopyridine readily reacts with amines to give amino-pyridines.[124]

The greater reactivity of halogens in the 2- and 4-positions can be ascribed to the partial positive charge on these two carbon atoms as a result of resonance in the pyridine molecule.

Hydroxypyridines. 2-Hydroxypyridine reacts as if it exists in two tautomeric forms.

Thus phosphorus oxychloride gives 2-chloropyridine, diazomethane gives 2-methoxypyridine and methyl iodide gives N-methyl-2-pyridone. The existence of the tautomeric forms is confirmed by ultraviolet absorption spectra.

2-Hydroxypyridine is amphoteric in that it forms salts with strong bases involving the phenolic OH group and pyridinium salts with acids. 4-Hydroxypyridine exists in neutral solution largely as the zwitterion.

Aminopyridines. Tautomerism is also observed with 2- and 4-aminopyridines.

Methyl iodide in the presence of sodium amide gives 2-methylaminopyridine while in the presence of silver oxide N-methyl-2-pyridonimine is formed.

Picolines (Methylpyridines). The hydrogen on the methyl groups of 2- and 4-methylpyridine are particularly active as might be expected from the resonance structures which place a positive charge on the 2-, 4-, and 6-carbon atoms. By analogy this is comparable to methyl ketones

in which the methyl hydrogens participate in aldol condensations etc.[125]

The reaction is carried out in the presence of potassium persulfate to give a 70 per cent yield of the ethanol derivative and a 15 per cent yield of the vinylpyridine.[126]

2-Picoline and formaldehyde (37 per cent aqueous) are charged into a steel bomb together with a small amount of BF_3 and heated for 3 hours at 312–322°F. The product distilled after the addition of a little *tert*-butyl catechol gives about 27 per cent 2-vinylpyridine, 17 per cent of the mono-methylol derivative and a residue consisting largely of polyvinylpyridine.[127]

2-Picoline reacts with sodium amide or with phenyllithium to form metalic derivatives

The resulting alkali metal salts react with alkyl halides, carbon dioxide, benzoyl chloride, etc., in the expected manner.

The alkylpyridines resemble pyridine quite closely with expected variations in properties as the number of the alkyl groups is increased. The alpha-isomer in each case has the lowest boiling point with the beta- and gamma-isomers boiling quite close together.

The monomethylpyridines are called picolines, the dimethyl derivatives are called lutidines and the trimethylcompounds are collidines.

The picolines are somewhat stronger bases than is pyridine as a result of the electron-releasing tendencies of the methyl group.

The three picolines are available from coal tar and may be used for the preparation of higher derivatives. Thus 2-picoline reacts with sodium amide and *n*-butyl chloride to give 2-amylpyridine in about 60 per cent yield.

Further reaction with sodium amide and *n*-butyl chloride gives

2,3-Lutidine introduced rapidly into a solution of sodium amide in liquid ammonia and methyl iodide added gives a 60 per cent conversion to 2-ethyl-3-methylpyridine.[130]

The lithium derivatives of 2-picoline react with aldehydes in very much the same way as do Grignard reagents.

2,4-Dimethyl-6-(β-hydroxyethyl)pyridine and the corresponding 6-vinyl compound are obtained by reaction of formaldehyde with 2,4,6-collidine.[131]

Alkanol pyridines are prepared by treating a dispersion of finely divided sodium amide in liquid ammonia to form a picolylsodium; adding ethylene oxide to form a sodium derivative of a pyridinepropanol and recovering the pyridinepropanol by hydrolysis.[132]

Some alkylpyridines may be dealkylated by treatment with water at high temperatures. Thus 2-methylpyridine and water vapor (mole ratio 1:22) passed over a nickel on alumina catalyst at 415°C gives a mixture of pyridine, carbon dioxide, carbon monoxide, hydrogen and methane. The yield of pyridine is as much as 50 per cent.[133]

2,2'-Bipyridyls are formed by heating pyridine to 300–500°C in the presence of ferric chloride.[134,135]

When anhydrous pyridine is warmed with sodium in the absence of a solvent 4,4'-bipyridyl and 2,2'-bipyridyl are formed in a ratio of 3:1 together with a small amount of the 3,4'-isomer.[136]

Vinylpyridines are obtained by the dehydrogenation of ethyl pyridines in much the same way that styrene is made from ethylbenzene. 2-Methyl-5-vinylpyridine is prepared from 2-methyl-5-ethylpyridine by vapor phase dehydrogenation at temperatures of 500–800°C in the presence of a vanadium pentoxide on silica catalyst.[137]

Such dehydrogenations are also accomplished in the presence of catalysts containing tungsten, or cerium.[138] Thus ethylpyridine is vaporized, mixed with about one-half its volume of carbon dioxide, heated to 450°C and the mixture passed over a cerium oxide catalyst at 700°C. The yield of vinyl pyridine is about 90 per cent.

Alkenylpyridines are prepared by catalytic dehydrogenation of the corresponding alkylpyridines at 1000–1300°F in the presence of an inert diluent and a catalyst composed of Fe_2O_3, Cr_2O_3, and KOH.[139] Thus, 2-methyl-5-ethylpyridine is dehydrogenated over a catalyst consisting of 93 per cent Fe_2O_3, 5 per cent Cr_2O_3 and 2 per cent KOH. The dialkylpyridine is mixed with steam at 400–600°F, heated to 1100°F and passed over the catalyst to give a 77 per cent yield of 2-methyl-5-vinylpyridine.

Vinylpyridines are also prepared by treatment of picolines with formaldehyde.

Vinylpyridines are very interesting compounds in that they are readily polymerized and the double bond is sufficiently reactive so that active hydrogen compounds can be made to add.

Vinylpyridine is usualy copolymerized with other monomers in the preparation of plastics and elastomers. The presence of relatively small amounts of vinylpyridine in a polymer improves the dyeing properties and other characteristics.

Oil-resistant elastomers may be made by quaternizing a copolymer of butadiene and 2-methyl-5-vinylpyridine. The ratio of butadiene to 2-methyl-5-vinylpyridine used is about 3:1. The quaternization is accomplished by reacting an alkyl halide, such as methyl iodide, with the polymer at ambient temperatures.[140]

Ketones undergo a Michael condensation with vinylpyridine at reflux temperatures in the presence of metallic sodium. In the case of methyl ethyl ketone condensation occurs on the methylene group to give

$$\text{[pyridine ring]} - CH_2CH_2 - \underset{\underset{CH_3}{|}}{CH} - CO - CH_3$$

With methyl isobutyl ketone condensation occurs on the α-methyl group.[141] Quaternary ammonium hydroxides such as Triton B have also been found to be effective catalysts.[142]

Reich and Levine[143] condensed a number of secondary amines with 2-vinylpyridine to give compounds of the type

$$\text{[pyridine ring]} - CH_2CH_2NR_2$$

Pyrrole and 2,5-dimethylpyrrole are sufficiently weak bases that no reaction occurs unless a sodium metal catalyst is used. Yields of products vary from 40 to 85 per cent.

Aniline and 2-vinylpyridine refluxed for 8 hours in a mixture of glacial acetic acid and absolute methanol give 2-(2-anilinoethyl)-pyridine. Secondary aliphatic amines give similar products in acetic acid solution or in the absence of a solvent.

Phillips[144] heated 4-vinylpyridine and pyrrolidine for two hours at 100°C and obtained 4-(2-pyrrolidinoethyl)-pyridine.

Other active hydrogen compounds add across the double bond in a similar manner. The reaction does not proceed quite as readily as does cyanoethylation reactions with acrylonitrile.

Hydroxypyridines or Piperidones. 3-Hydroxypyridine, which cannot tautomerize to a pyridone, behaves very much like a phenol. It gives a color with ferric chloride; is methylated and acetylated to give the corresponding methoxy and acetoxy derivatives, and reacts with formaldehyde to give 2-hydroxymethyl-3-hydroxypyridine.[145]

3-Hydroxypyridine may be nitrated in mixed nitric and sulfuric acids and sulfonated with concentrated sulfuric acid to give the corresponding 2-nitro- and 2-sulfonic acid derivatives.

The 2- and 4-hydroxypyridines do not behave as much like phenols. Only a pale red color is obtained with ferric chloride. Nitration of 2-hydroxypyridine at temperatures below 40°C gives 2-hydroxy-3-nitropyridine and a much smaller amount of 2-hydroxy-5-nitropyridine.[146]

2-Hydroxypyridine treated with methyl iodide gives primarily N-methyl-2-pyridone rather than the 2-methoxypyridine as would be expected if it behaved as a phenol.[147] With diazomethane in neutral solution however, the product is 2-methoxy pyridine.[148] The 4-hydroxypyridine, although it has been studied much less, apparently behaves similarly.

Aminopyridines. The most direct method for the preparation of aminopyridines involves the attack on the pyridine molecule by sodium amide.[112] Sodium amide is added to a solution of pyridine in xylene at reflux temperatures until there is no longer any evolution of hydrogen. After hydrolysis of the resulting intermediate; 2-aminopyridine is obtained in about 50 per cent yield.

In addition to 2-aminopyridine, 2,6-diaminopyridine and 2,4,6-triaminopyridine are obtained and these may become the major products if the reaction is carried out at 170°C in dimethylaniline as the solvent. Alkylaminopyridines may be obtained by treating pyridine halides with amines.

Nitration of 2-aminopyridines may occur quite readily if the 3-position is free. The nitro group enters the 3- or the 3- and 5-positions.

2-Aminopyridine dissolved in concentrated sulfuric acid and treated with a 1:1 mixture of nitric and sulfuric acids at temperatures below 20°C gives pyridylnitramine. If the mixture is warmed cautiously to 35–40°C and poured onto ice a mixture of 2-amino-3-nitropyridine and 2-amino-5-nitropyridine is obtained. 2-Aminopicolines can also be nitrated in a similar manner.[149]

3-(Methylamino)pyridine reacts with nitric acid to give 3-nitro(methylamino)pyridine in about 38 per cent yield but the aminopyridine is so readily attacked by oxidizing agents that the reaction has not been studied very much.[150]

Halogenation occurs in the 3- and 5-positions. In obtaining the mono-halogenated derivative it is desirable to protect the amino group by acetylation.

Benzyl or anisyl alcohol will condense with aminopyridines in xylene in the presence of potassium hydroxide. Thus p-CH_3O—C_6H_4—CH_2OH and 2-aminopyridine in xylene are refluxed for 2 hours in the presence of a small amount of potassium hydroxide to give 2-(p-methoxy-benzylamino)-pyridine in 80 per cent yield.[151]

2-Amino-4-ethylpyridine is brominated by heating with bromine in 20 per cent sulfuric acid for 4 hours and letting the mixture stand overnight at 0°C. 2-Amino-3,5-dibromo-4-ethylpyridine is obtained in 65 per cent yield.[152]

The reaction of 2-aminopyridine with anhydrides of unsaturated acids gives the monoamide of the acid.

The reactions may be carried out by refluxing in anhydrous benzene.

Refluxing 2-pyridylsuccinamide with acetic anhydride gives 2-pyridyl succinimide.[153]

3-Aminopyridine behaves as a typical aromatic amine and may be diazotized in the same way as aniline. 2-Aminopyridine may also be diazotized but special conditions must be used.

Pyridine Carboxylic Acids. Pyridine carboxylic acids may be obtained in a variety of ways only a few of which will be discussed.

Many carboxylic acids are obtained by ring closure from suitable starting materials.

The pyridine ring is very resistant to oxidation so that monocarboxylic acids are obtained by oxidation of picolines.[154]

The oxidation of α-picoline with alkaline permanganate gives picolinic acid in 50 per cent yield. β-Picoline gives nicotinic acid in 60 per cent yield[155,156] and γ-picoline gives isonicotinic acid in 65 per cent yield.[157,158,159]

4-Ethylpyridine is oxidized to isonicotinic acid by nitric acid (d 1.43) and sulfuric acid (3 times the weight of the nitric acid) containing copper sulfate and cupric chloride. The nitric acid is introduced in three portions. One-half is introduced dropwise at 200–270°C, then after distilling out the spent acid two-thirds of the remaining acid is introduced at 180°C and the remainder at 150°C. Isonicotinic acid is obtained in 75 per cent yield.[160]

In the air oxidation of pyridine homologs to nicotinic acid and isonicotinic acids the presence of phosphoric acid increases the yield. β-Picoline is oxidized to nicotinic acid in 50–60 per cent yield at 230°C and a pressure of 35–40 atmospheres in the presence of an equivalent amount of 10 per cent phosphoric acid. Under the same conditions γ-picoline is converted to isonicotinic acid in 93 per cent yield.

Alkylpyridines may be oxidized with air over a vanadium pentoxide-silica gel catalyst at temperatures below 350°C. The presence of steam is advantageous. Thus an 85 per cent yield of nicotinic acid is obtained when air is first passed through 2-methyl-5-ethylpyridine and water at 480°C and then over the catalyst at 265°C. Similarly β-picoline gives 50 per cent yields of nicotinic acid and gamma-picoline gives an 80 per cent yield of isonicotinic acid.[161]

Alkyl pyridines are oxidized to carboxylic acids with selenium dioxide. The oxidation is accomplished by adding selenium dioxide in small portions to the boiling alkylpyridine. The mixture is boiled for 30 minutes after the vigorous reaction has subsided. In this way 2-methyl-5-ethylpyridine gives 5-ethyl-2-pyridinecarboxylic acid in 58 per cent yield. Better yields are obtained if the reaction is carried out in a bomb at 110–120°C.

Ethylpyridines and their corresponding N-oxides can be oxidized with chromic acid in 50 per cent yields. The ease of oxidation decreases in the order 3-ethyl-, 4-ethyl, and 2-ethylpyridine.[162]

Nicotinic acid may be obtained by the oxidation of nicotine and is obtained commercially by the oxidation of quinoline and the decarboxylation of the resulting quinolinic acid.

The latter reaction indicates that (1) the pyridine ring is more resistant to oxidation than is the benzene ring and (2) decarboxylation occurs more readily at the 2- than at the 3-position.

Stepwise decarboxylation of 2,3,4-pyridinetricarboxylic acid may be effected.

Pyridinecarboxylic acids behave normally. They can be esterified, converted to acid chlorides, salts, amides, etc., in the usual ways.

When pyridine derivatives with $-COOC_2H_5$ or $-CN$ groups at the 3- and 5-positions are treated with lithium aluminum hydride in ether the ring system is first attacked but when the 2-, 4-, and 6-positions are substituted the functional groups are reduced.

The reduction of diethyl-2,6-lutidine-3,5-dicarboxylate gives a 40 per cent yield of ethyl-3-hydroxymethyl-2,6-lutidine-5-carboxylate. When the mixture is refluxed for 2 hours a 65 per cent yield of 3,5-bis(hydroxymethyl)-2,6-lutidine is obtained.[163]

Cyanopyridines. Cyanopyridines have been prepared by the action of ammonia and oxygen on a picoline.[164] Thus an air stream containing 1.6 per cent by volume of β-picoline and 3 per cent ammonia was passed through a reactor containing vanadium pentoxide at 350°C. The contact time was held at 5.5 seconds. 3-Cyanopyridine was obtained in 82 per cent yield. Comparable results were obtained with α- and γ-picolines.

Denton and Bishop[165] obtained pyridine nitriles by treating 2- or 4-methylpyridine with ammonia in the presence of molybdenum oxide. Thus 4-picoline and ammonia (mole ratio 1:2) are passed over a catalyst consisting of 10 per cent MoO_3 on alumina at 540°C. Conversions are about 1.5 per cent per pass.

Aldehydes and Ketones. Aldehydes of pyridine are not readily available but 2-pyridine aldehyde can be obtained by the oxidation of 2-picoline with selenium dioxide.[166] Other less direct methods are available. The 2-pyridinealdehyde undergoes normal reactions of aldehydes having no α-hydrogen atoms. Thus it undergoes a benzoin condensation in the presence of cyanide ion to give pyridoin. Pyridine-4-aldehyde undergoes the Cannizzaro reaction and pyridine 3-aldehyde condenses with malonic acid in a typical Knoevenagel reaction.

2-Pyridinealdehyde and *n*-butylamine heated to 70°C gives the expected imine in 90 per cent yield. Reduction with Raney nickel in acetic acid gives

$$\text{（pyridine ring）}-CH_2NHC_4H_9$$

Reduction with sodium in ethanol gave the corresponding piperidyl derivative.[167]

Pyridyl ketones can be obtained from esters of pyridinecarboxylic acids by means of a Claisen condensation.[168,169,170]

$$\text{（pyridine ring）}-COOC_2H_5 \ + \ CH_3COOC_2H_5 \ \xrightarrow{NaOC_2H_5}$$

$$\text{（pyridine ring）}-CO-CH_2COOC_2H_5 \ \xrightarrow[\text{2) } H/\text{heat}]{\text{1) NaOH}} \ \text{（pyridine ring）}-COCH_3$$

Picolyllithium may also be treated with an acid chloride to give a ketone

$$\text{（pyridine ring）}-CH_2Li \ + \ C_6H_5COCl \ \longrightarrow \ \text{（pyridine ring）}-CH_2-CO-C_6H_5$$

Picoline may be condensed with a nitrile in the presence of sodium amide to give an intermediate which is converted to a ketone on hydrolysis

$$\text{（pyridine ring with } CH_3\text{）} \ + \ C_6H_5CN \ \xrightarrow[\text{2) } H_2O]{\text{1) } NaNH_2} \ \text{（pyridine ring with } CH_2-CO-C_6H_5\text{）}$$

The pyridyl ketones, for the most part, undergo typical ketone reactions.

Pyridine-1-Oxide

Pyridine-1-oxide is playing an increasingly important role as an intermediate in the preparation of pyridine derivatives. Whereas electrophilic substitution reactions on the pyridine ring are quite difficult, conversion to pyridine-1-oxide facilitates such substitutions and when the reaction is complete, the oxygen is easily removed.

Pyridine-1-oxide has recently become commercially available so that interest in the compound has greatly increased. A large number of papers are appearing each year describing reactions of the compound.

Pyridine-1-oxide is prepared most frequently by heating pyridine in glacial acetic acid at 70–80°C with 30 per cent hydrogen peroxide. The acid is neutralized and the oxide recovered by distillation.[171,172,173] Large scale reactions have yielded pyridine oxides in 80–90 per cent yields. Other acids such as formic, tartaric, succinic and even sulfuric acid have been used with 20–30 per cent hydrogen peroxide to give the desired pyridine-N-oxides.

Pyridine derivatives may also be converted to the corresponding N-oxides in this manner. These derivatives include alkyl and aryl pyridines,[174–179] acyl pyridines,[180,181] carboxylic acids, esters and amides.[181]

Pyridine oxides can also be obtained by the action of a per-acid on pyridine or its derivatives.[173,184–192] Peracetic, perbenzoic, and monoperphthalic acids have been used most frequently.

In some cases substituents on the pyridine ring will be oxidized or otherwise altered in the process. For example ethyl (2-pyridyl)-acetate treated with acetic acid and hydrogen peroxide gives picolinic acid-N-oxide,[193] and nicotinonitrile treated with acetic acid and hydrogen peroxide yields nicotinamide-1-oxide.[183]

It is very difficult to prepare the N-oxides of 2-amino- and 2-nitropyridines. 2-Nitropyridine undergoes no reaction with hydrogen peroxide and acetic or sulfuric acids. 2-Aminopyridine is not affected by peracetic acid[184] but if the acetate salt is first made and reacted with peracetic acid, an N-oxide is obtained which gives 2-aminopyridine-1-oxide on hydrolysis.

The formation of pyridine-1-oxide is also affected by steric hindrance. Thus 2,6-diphenylpyridine is converted to the corresponding 1-oxide in only 5 per cent yield.[185]

Reactions of Pyridine-1-oxides. *Nitration.* Using a mixture of nitric and sulfuric acid, pyridine-1-oxide is nitrated exclusively in the 4-position.[172,179,183,194,195,196] 3,5-Diethoxypyridine-1-oxide gives the 2,6-dinitro derivative.[197] Usually if the 4-position is occupied, nitration is difficult but 4-hydroxypyridine-1-oxide can be nitrated to give the 3-nitro derivative.[196]

Acetic acid-nitric acid mixtures convert 4-hydroxypyridine-1-oxide to 3,5-dinitro-4-hydroxypyridine-1-oxide at high temperatures and 3-nitro-4-hydroxypyridine-1-oxide at low temperatures.[198]

The mononitration of a number of pyridine-1-oxides was investigated by Hands and Katritzky.[199] 2-, and 4-Phenylpyridine-1-oxides give significantly greater proportions of the *m*-nitro compounds than the parent compound. 2-Phenylpyridine-1-oxide is nitrated 10 to 100 times faster than 2-phenylpyridine.

Halogenation. Pyridine-1-oxide yields 2- and 4-chloropyridines when chlorinated with phosphorus oxychloride,[200] sulfuryl chloride,[201] or phosphorus pentachloride.[202] It is noted that these reagents not only chlorinate the ring but also remove the oxygen. Phosphorus trichloride only removes the oxygen.

2-Methylpyridine-1-oxide with phosphorus oxychloride gives 2-methyl-3-chloropyridine and α-chloropicoline[203] and 2,6-dimethylpyridine-1-oxide gives 2,6-dimethyl-4-chloropyridine and 2,6-dimethyl-3,4-dichloropyridine.[204]

In some cases alkoxy and nitro groups may be replaced during chlorination. Thus 4-ethoxypyridine-1-oxide with phosphorus oxychloride gives a mixture of 2-chloro-4-ethoxypyridine and 2,4-dichloropyridine.[205] 4-Nitropyridine-1-oxide with phosphorus oxychloride gives a mixture of 4-chloropyridine and 2,4-dichloropyridine.

Sulfonation and Tosylation. Pyridine-1-oxide with fuming sulfuric acid and mercuric sulfate at 240°C yields 3-pyridyl-1-oxide sulfonic acid.[206] Toluene sulfonyl chloride at 200°C yields 3-pyridyl-*p*-toluene sulfonate.[202]

Miscellaneous Reactions. Pyridine-1-oxide reacts with a Grignard reagent such as phenyl magnesium bromide to give 2-phenylpyridine.[207] Reaction with sodium and ammonia at room temperature gives 4,4'-bipyridyl.[208]

Pyridine-1-oxide reacts with acetic or benzoic anhydrides to give 2-pyridone after hydrolysis.[209,210]

Sodium added to pyridine-1-oxide hydrochloride in liquid ammonia at –40°C and the ammonia evaporated, gives 4,4'-bipyridyl in low yield. 4-Nitropyridine-1-oxide yields only starting material because it is insoluble in liquid ammonia.[211]

Deoxygenation. Many reagents cause the deoxygenation of pyridine-1-oxides in addition to the desired reaction. Thus chlorination results in the formation of chloropyridines rather than chlorinated N-oxides. Other reagents cause only deoxygenation and these will be discussed here.

The nitrogen-oxygen bond is strongly resistant to reduction in that it is not reduced by aqueous sulfur dioxide and does not release iodine from potassium iodide solutions.[196,212]

Many derivatives of pyridine-1-oxide are deoxygenated with iron and acetic acid at 100°C. Halogen, alkoxy, amino and alkyl substituents remain unaffected but the nitro group is reduced to amino.[172,183,197,213,214]

Catalytic hydrogenation over palladium on carbon catalyst in hydrochloric or acetic acid causes not only the deoxygenation of the N-oxide group but also the reduction of the nitro group to the amine.[174,189,215-218] If an alcoholic or water solution is used, the nitro group is reduced but no deoxygenation takes place.[174,186,218] Katritzky and Monro[219] have deoxygenated about 25 derivatives of pyridine-1-oxide using a palladium on carbon catalyst. They observed that a substituent in the 2-position hinders but does not inhibit deoxygenation.

The use of phosphorus trichloride to deoxygenate pyridine-N-oxides without chlorination of the ring has already been mentioned. Other reagents capable of deoxygenating the pyridine-N-oxides without further reaction include stannous chloride,[220] copper or zinc at 200°C,[221] sodium borohydride and aluminum chloride,[222] sulfur and ammonia at 100°C.[223]

Piperidine

Piperidine, $C_5H_{11}N$, is a completely saturated 6-membered heterocyclic amine which bears the same relationship to pyridine that cyclohexane does to benzene.

In contrast with pyridine, piperidine is a strong base comparable to aliphatic secondary amines. Piperidine and its derivatives are prepared by the reduction of the corresponding pyridines. In the early work, sodium and alcohol were used as the reducing agents but currently piperidines are obtained almost entirely by catalytic hydrogenation. Piperidine itself is obtained by the catalytic hydrogenation of pyridine at 170–200°C in the presence of a nickel catalyst.[224] Pyridine homologs are hydrogenated in the same way. At temperatures much above 200°C pyridine undergoes cleavage of the ring with the formation of amylamine, pentane and ammonia. Successful hydrogenation of pyridine and its homologs can be accomplished at temperatures below 200°C.

In general, pyridine derivatives are more easily reduced to piperidines than is pyridine itself and substituents in the 2-positions are especially effective in increasing the ease of reduction.

Platinum oxide is also an effective hydrogenation catalyst. When it is used, hydrogenations can be carried out at room temperature under pressures of 2–3 atmospheres.[225]

Piperidine has been prepared by heating pentamethylenediamine at 300–500°C in the presence of a catalyst consisting of silica gel, alumina-silica or boron phosphate. Thus pentamethylenediamine is vaporized, diluted with nitrogen and passed over a pellitized catalyst at 400°C.[226] A 62 per cent yield of piperidine is obtained.

The reactions of piperidine are those of a typical secondary amine. Thus it may be acetylated with acetyl chloride or acetic anhydride, reacted with nitrous acid to give the stable N-nitrosopiperidine and reacted with phosgene to give the dipiperidyl urea.

Piperidine is dehydrogenated to pyridine in about 95 per cent yield by passing it together with hydrogen at 200–500°C over a platinum or palladium catalyst supported on silica. At least 7 moles of hydrogen for each mole of piperidine should be used.[227]

Piperidine and ethylene at 125°C and under a pressure of 30–40 psi in the presence of ditertiarybutyl peroxide react to give 2-ethylpiperidine. A similar reaction with propylene gave *d,l*-coniine.[228]

Piperidine is frequently used as a catalyst in aldol and Knoevenagel reactions and in other cases where a weak base is effective. Piperidine acetate is more effective than piperidine itself in catalyzing Knoevenagel reactions.

Pyrazine

Pyrazine is a six-membered heterocyclic aromatic amine having nitrogen atoms in the 1- and 4-positions

In many of its reactions it resembles pyridine.

The first systematic investigation of pyrazines was made by Gutneckt[229] and Treadwell[230] who discovered that the reduction of a monooxime of an α,β-diketone gave a pyrazine rather than the expected amino ketone.

The formation of a pyrazine from an α-aminoketone requires the loss of water as well as of hydrogen and it was found by Gabriel and Pinkus[231] that higher yields of pyrazines were obtained by carrying out the condensations in the presence of oxidizing agents.

Pyrazines have not been found in nature to any appreciable extent and until very recently have not been of much importance. About 1940 however, it was reported that hydrazides of pyrazinemonocarboxylic acid were effective as analeptics and that pyrazinecarboxylic acids have value in the treatment of pellegra. In 1954 sulfapyrazine was introduced as one of the more effective sulfa drugs. The result has been a renewal of interest in pyrazine chemistry.

Synthesis of Pyrazines. One of the most effective methods for the preparation of pyrazine has been heating the acetal of iminodiacetaldehyde with hydrochloric acid to form a dihydroxymorpholine which when treated with hydroxylamine gives pyrazine.[232]

Commercial methods of preparation include (1) dehydrogenation of piperazine over certain metal oxides or dehydrogenation catalysts such as copper chromite or palladium;[233] (2) passing vapors of hydroxyethylethyl-enediamine or diethylenetriamine over a nickel on alumina catalyst at 400°C—yields are about 50 per cent. Alkyl or aryl pyrazines are usually made by ring closure reactions.

Reactions of Pyrazine. Pyrazine is a weaker base than pyridine. It usu-ally behaves as a monoacidic base but may form diacidic salts under an-hydrous conditions. The dihydrochlorides, dihydrobromides and sulfates of certain aryl-substituted pyrazines have been obtained in non-aqueous media.[235,236]

Quaternary salts are formed much less readily than with pyridines.

Oxidation. Pyrazine is more readily oxidized than is pyridine as evi-denced by the fact that it decolorizes alkaline permanganate in the cold. Pyrazinecarboxylic acids can be obtained by the oxidation of alkyl side chains but yields are poor. Quinoxaline is oxidized to pyrazine-2,3-dicar-boxylic acid

in good yield indicating that the pyrazine ring is somewhat more resistant to oxidation than is the benzene ring.[237,238]

Alkylpyrazines form mono- and di-N-oxides.[239]

Reduction. Pyrazines are reduced to the corresponding piperazines with sodium and an alcohol or by catalytic hydrogenation.[240]

Substitution and Addition Reactions. As with pyridine, pyrazine does not readily undergo ring substitution by electrophilic reagents. A hydroxyl group activates the ring toward electrophilic attack so that nitration will occur.

Pyrazine may be converted to 2-aminopyrazine with sodium amide in about 65 per cent yield.[241] This represents an attack by a nucleophilic reagent.

Methylpyrazines react with aromatic aldehydes to give compounds of the type

Formaldehyde condenses on heating with 2-methylpyrazine to give 2-(β-hydroxyethyl)pyrazine which is converted to 2-vinylpyrazine on heating with potassium hydroxide.[242]

Hydroxylpyrazines behave very much like phenol. They are soluble in aqueous sodium hydroxide and react with acetic anhydride or benzoyl chloride. 3,6-Dimethyl-3-hydroxypyrazine couples with diazonium compounds in alkaline solution.

Piperazine

Piperazine is the nitrogen analog of dioxane and behaves very much as an aliphatic secondary diamine.

Piperazine and its derivatives are of some importance in pharmacology and piperazine is potentially of great interest as a chemical intermediate if a more economical route can be found for its preparation.

Synthesis of Piperazine. Piperazine is made by the cyclodehydration of 2-hydroxyethylamine.[243] The salts of this amine are heated at 230–240°C in the presence of iron, aluminum or magnesium halides.

Similarly N-(2-hydroxyethyl)ethylenediamine is dehydrated to piperazine by heating with Raney nickel, alumina, silica gel or copper chromite[242,244]

Piperazine can also be obtained by the dimerization of ethylenimine.

Reactions. Piperazine is a typical secondary amine and as such can be alkylated on the nitrogen atoms by treatment with alkyl halides. Quaternary salts may also be formed.

Piperazine reacts with aldehydes to give polymers of the type[245]

Piperazine adds to activated double bonds as in α,β-unsaturated esters and ketones to give, N,N'-disubstituted piperazines[246]

Reaction with organic acids give salts which on heating are dehydrated to amides. If dibasic acids are used polyamides should be obtained.

Piperazine is converted to pyrazine in about 70 per cent yield by passing the vapors over a catalyst consisting of cobalt, nickel, copper or iron at 375–425°C. The metal or the corresponding oxide is usually supported on alumina. The contact time is about 4 seconds.[247]

2,5-Diketopiperazines. 2,5-Diketopiperazines are obtained from the cyclodehydration of α-amino acids.

$$2R-CH \begin{array}{c} COOH \\ NH_2 \end{array} \longrightarrow \begin{array}{c} R-CH \diagup NH \diagdown C=O \\ | \qquad\qquad | \\ O=C \diagdown NH \diagup CH \diagdown R \end{array}$$

These compounds are amides. The first 2,5-diketopiperazine was the one obtained from leucine and was isolated in 1849 from protein hydrolyzates.[248] Many 2,5-diketopiperazines have been obtained by the partial hydrolysis of proteins.

The best procedure for the preparation of these compounds involves heating the dry amino acid in glycerol or ethylene glycol.[249] These compounds are of importance primarily because of their relationship to amino acids.

Pyridazene

The pyridazines
have been less thoroughly studied than the other diazine ring systems. Pyridazine is a relatively stable compound having aromatic properties but is very resistant to substitution reactions involving electrophilic attack.

Pyridazines are obtained from unsaturated 1,4-diketones by reaction with hydrazine.[250,251]

$$\begin{array}{c} HC \diagup CO-C_6H_5 \\ || \\ HC \diagdown CO-C_6H_5 \end{array} + \begin{array}{c} H_2N \\ H_2N \end{array} \longrightarrow \begin{array}{c} C_6H_5 \\ | \\ C \\ HC \diagup \diagdown N \\ || \qquad | \\ HC \diagdown \diagup N \\ C \\ | \\ C_6H_5 \end{array}$$

Pyridazine has been made from the acetal of maleic dialdehyde and hydrazine without actually isolating the dialdehyde.[252]

The reaction proceeds very readily with cis isomers but trans isomers frequently fail to react.

A few other methods have been used with varying success.

Pyridazines are weak monoacidic bases having high boiling points. They behave in many respects like pyridine. The reactions of pyridazines have not been studied very much. The pyridazines are somewhat unstable towards heat and show a tendency to darken on exposure to air. Methyl groups α- to one of the nitrogen atoms condense with aromatic aldehydes.[253,254,255]

Reduction with sodium and an alcohol opens the ring to give 1,4-diaminobutane in low yield.[256]

Aminopyridazines have been investigated as therapeutic agents particularly as the sulfanilamido compounds.

Pyrimidines

Pyrimidine is sometimes referred to as *m*-diazine.

The ring system has been known for a long time and is found in nucleic acids, vitamins, coenzymes and purines and in synthetic drugs such as the barbiturates.

Synthesis of Pyrimidines. Pyrimidine itself is not well known but has been prepared by the reduction of di- and tri-chloropyrimidines.[257,258]

One of the more important syntheses of pyrimidine derivatives involves the reaction between esters of malonic acid and urea in the presence of sodium ethoxide. Thus diethyl malonate and urea give barbituric acid.

The barbituric acid exists in tautomeric forms one of which is a trihydroxypyrimidine. When mono- and dialkylmalonic esters are used, barbiturates are obtained.

β-Ketoesters may also be condensed with urea to give pyrimidine derivatives. A great number of variations of this type of reaction is observed.

Propionitrile reacts with potassium hydroxide in liquid ammonia to give 2,4-diethyl-5-methyl-6-aminopyrimidine, propionamide and dipropionitrile.[259]

The pyrimidine ring is stabilized by resonance in much the same way as is pyridine. The properties of pyrimidine should therefore be quite similar to those of pyridine. The electron density is low on carbon atoms 2-, 4-, and 6- so that electrophilic attack would be very difficult at these positions. Electrophilic attack should be much easier at the 5-position but should still be much more difficult than with benzene. Nucleophilic reagents should attack at the 2-, 4-, and 6-positions. Thus an amino group may be introduced into the 2- and 4-positions of 6-methylpyrimidine by reaction with sodium amide.[260] The amino group is not introduced at the 5-position in this way.

Alkyl groups in the 2-, 4- and 6-positions are activated in the same way as the methyl group in 2-picoline. Thus benzaldehyde in the presence of zinc chloride gives styrylpyrimidines.[261]

That the methyl group in the 5-position is less highly activated is illustrated by the oxidation of 4,5-dimethylpyrimidine to give 5-methyl-pyrimidine-4-carboxylic acid.[262]

Most of the derivatives which are easily prepared have substituents in the 2-, 4-, and/or 6-positions.

Groups can be introduced directly into the 5-position by electrophilic substitution. As would be expected from the resonance structures the carbon atom in the 5-position is much more vulnerable to electrophilic attack and undergoes substitution reactions of the type observed with benzene. Thus pyrimidine and its derivatives are halogenated by chlorine or bromine in water,[263] chloroform,[264] or acetic acid.[265] In each case the halogen substitutes at the 5-position.

Direct nitration of pyrimidine with concentrated nitric or a mixture of nitric and sulfuric acids is very common with substitution occuring at the 5-carbon atom.

Quaternary ammonium compounds can be prepared from pyrimidine derivatives. Thus a mixture of 2-chloro-4,6-dimethylpyrimidine and trimethylamine in benzene was held at room temperature for seven days to give 2-trimethylamino-4,6-dimethylpyrimidium chloride in 80 per cent yield.[266]

Morpholine

Morpholine is prepared almost exclusively by the dehydration of diethanolamine with sulfuric acid or other dehydrating agent

$$\text{HN}\underset{CH_2-CH_2}{\overset{CH_2-CH_2}{\Big\langle}}\begin{matrix}OH\\OH\end{matrix} \longrightarrow \text{NH}\underset{CH_2-CH_2}{\overset{CH_2-CH_2}{\Big\langle}}O$$

Morpholine is also prepared by the reaction of β,β'-dichlorodiethyl ether with ammonia. The reaction is accomplished using anhydrous ammonia in benzene solution at 50°C under a total pressure of 1500 psi.[267] The yield of morpholine is about 80 per cent.

Substituted morpholines are obtained by heating a diethanolamine in the vapor phase with dehydration catalysts such as alumina activated with thoria at 280–350°C. Thus diethanolaniline is passed through a tube containing an Al_2O_3/ThO_2 (5 per cent ThO_2) catalyst at 300–310°C to give N-phenylmorpholine.[268]

Substituted morpholines can be obtained similarly by cyclization of substituted diethanolamines in the cold with sulfuric acid. Thus HOCH-$(C_6H_5)CH_2$—NH—CH_2CH_2OH mixed with concentrated sulfuric acid and left overnight, then poured over ice and neutralized with sodium hydroxide gives an 83 per cent yield of 2-phenylmorpholine.[269]

Morpholine (b.p. 129°C) is a moderately strong base, miscible with water in all proportions. The vapor pressure from water solutions is much the same as that of water itself so that evaporation of such solutions maintains a constant alkalinity. Morpholines reacts with aldehydes and hydrogen cyanide to give morpholine substituted nitriles. Thus acetaldehyde (1 mole) and 1 mole sodium bisulfite in water were warmed to 60°C then cooled and stirred with 1 mole of morpholine. After 2–3 hours 1 mole of sodium cyanide in water was added with vigorous stirring. After permitting the reaction mixture to sit overnight a 76 per cent yield of α-morpholinopropionitrile was obtained.[270]

Morpholine forms emulsifying agents with fatty acids which are used in the formation of water-resistant waxes and polishes. Morpholine is particularly successful for this purpose because of its moderate volatility, which is much the same as water, and the ease with which it leaves the amine-fatty acid reaction product. The morpholine gradually evaporates along with the water from the film of polish and as it does so, the film is rendered impervious to subsequent re-emulsification by water.

Morpholine is also used as a corrosion inhibitor, in the preparation of rubber vulcanization inhibitors, etc.

Quinoline and Quinoline Derivatives

Quinoline is found in coal tar and was isolated from this source in crude form as early as 1834.[271] A number of alkyl quinolines have been isolated from coal tar fractions boiling from 265–310°C.[272]

Quinoline and a number of alkyl quinolines have also been isolated from California petroleum.[273]

The quinoline ring system is present in a large number of alkaloids.

The best method of obtaining quinoline and quinoline derivatives is synthesis from less complex substances. Many methods for preparing quinoline derivatives are available but only a few illustrative procedures will be described here. A comprehensive review of the chemistry of quinoline has been prepared by Elderfield.[274]

The Skraup Synthesis. In 1880 Skraup[275] heated an aromatic amine, glycerol and an oxidizing agent with sulfuric acid to form a quinoline. The glycerol is presumable dehydrated to acrolein which reacts with the amine having substituents on no more than one of the carbon atoms *ortho* to the amino group

$$\underset{\underset{OH}{|}}{CH_2}-\underset{\underset{OH}{|}}{CH}-\underset{\underset{OH}{|}}{CH_2} \longrightarrow CH_2{=}CH{-}CHO + 2H_2O$$

A dihydroquinoline is formed which must be oxidized to the corresponding quinoline. Skraup found that nitrobenzene was a very satisfactory oxidizing agent for this purpose.

The Skraup synthesis is very general and can be used to prepare a large number of quinolines substituted on the benzene ring, provided that the substituent groups can survive the rather harsh treatment involved in heating with strong acids.

The Doebner-v. Miller Synthesis. The Doebner-v. Miller synthesis is somewhat more general than the Skraup synthesis. In 1881 ethylene glycol was substituted for glycerol to give quinaldine and on the assumption that ethylene glycol was converted to acetaldehyde, aniline and paraldehyde were heated with sulfuric acid and again quinaldine was obtained.[276]

The acetaldehyde is undoubtedly first converted to crotonaldehyde. Mills, Harris and Lambourne[277] reported that yields were improved by adding a little zinc chloride to the reaction mixture.

$$\text{(aniline)} + 2CH_3CHO \longrightarrow \text{(quinoline)} - CH_3$$

The reaction is applicable to almost any aromatic amine and the aldehyde may be any α,β-unsaturated aldehyde. Any aldehyde or mixture of aldehydes which will condense to give such a substituted acrolein can be used. Beyer[278] substituted a methyl ketone for one of the aldehydes to give a 2,4-disubstituted quinoline.

The Friedlander Synthesis. Friedlander prepared quinoline by condensing o-aminobenzaldehyde with acetaldehyde in the presence of sodium hydroxide. The reaction involves the formation of a Schiff's base followed by ring closure involving the loss of water from the carbonyl group and the α-hydrogen of the acetaldehyde portion.

$$\text{(o-aminobenzaldehyde)} + CH_3CHO \xrightarrow{\text{NaOH}} \text{(intermediate)} \longrightarrow \text{(quinoline)}$$

This method has rather wide applicability, limited by the availability of the starting materials. In some cases the reaction occurs without a catalyst. In other cases piperidine has been very effective in promoting the condensation.[279,280]

Ketones usually give better yields than aldehydes when sodium hydroxide is used as the condensing agent.

The method is of particular importance for the preparation of quinoline substituted in the 3-position.

v. Niementowski[281] substituted anthranilic acid for o-aminobenzaldehyde in a Friedlander synthesis and obtained hydroxyquinolines.

$$\text{(anthranilic acid)} + \begin{array}{c} H_2C-R \\ | \\ O{=}C-R' \end{array} \longrightarrow \text{(4-hydroxyquinoline)}$$

Fuson and Burness[282] obtained 2-phenyl-4-hydroxyquinoline by condensing ethyl anthranilate with the diethyl ketal of acetophenone.

$$\text{(ethyl anthranilate)} + \begin{array}{c} C_6H_5-C(OC_2H_5)_2 \\ | \\ CH_3 \end{array} \longrightarrow \text{(2-phenyl-4-hydroxyquinoline)}$$

Ethyl acetate undergoes a Claisen condensation with ethyl anthranilate to give a product which gives 2,4-dihydroxyquinoline on ring closure.[283]

Quinoline can be obtained in about 40 per cent yield by heating *o*-toluidine with glyoxal in the presence of sodium hydroxide.[284] The reaction has quite limited applicability.

Quinoline derivatives are sometimes prepared by ring expansion methods. Thus indanone oxime undergoes a Beckmann rearrangement in the presence of phosphorus pentachloride to give 2-hydroxyquinoline.[285]

and 2-methylindole heated with methyl iodide gives 1,3-dimethyl-1,2-dihydroquinoline

A few miscellaneous methods for the preparation of quinoline and quinoline derivatives are of interest.

Passage of acetylene for 20 hours into a solution of aniline and *p*-tolualdehyde in anhydrous ethyl alcohol containing mercuric chloride as a catalyst gives a 15 per cent yield of 2-(*p*-methylphenyl)quinoline.[286]

2,4-Dimethylquinoline is formed when acetylene is passed into a mixture of aniline, acetone and mercuric chloride. The toluidines give the corresponding trimethylquinolines.

Under these reaction conditions acetone does not react with acetylene. The intermediate is probably the ethylidene base $C_6H_5N=CHCH_3$ which condenses with acetone and cyclizes to the quinoline derivative.[287] Cuprous bromide is also an effective catalyst for the reaction.

N-Phenylacetamide with formaldehyde and methyl ethyl ketone gives an 18 per cent yield of 3,4-dimethylquinoline. Acetyl-*p*-toluidine and methyl ethyl ketone gives a 21 per cent yield of 3,4,8-trimethyl quinoline.[288]

Quinaldine is obtained in 50 per cent yield by heating a mixture of aniline, butyl vinyl ether, nitrobenzene and concentrated HCl for 30 minutes on a steam bath.[289]

2,2,4-Trimethyl-1,2-dihydroquinoline has been prepared from acetone and aniline in the presence of benzene sulfonic acid.[290]

Pure 1,2-dihydroquinoline is prepared by the reduction of quinoline in liquid ammonia.[291] Thus quinoline in absolute ethanol is added to liquid ammonia at 65°C and heated under a nitrogen atmosphere with metallic sodium. The ammonia is evaporated and the product isolated by extraction with ether. The yield is 84 per cent.

Reaction of Quinoline Derivatives. As in the case of 2- and 4-methyl-pyridines, 2-methylquinoline (quinaldine) has appreciably different properties from 4-methylquinoline (lepidine).

Quinaldine reacts with benzaldehyde in the presence of zinc chloride and hydrogen chloride or acetic anhydride to give 2-styrylquinoline.[292,293]

The reaction is general and nearly all aldehydes can be used.

Acetic anhydride is a somewhat better condensing agent than is zinc chloride.[294] Methylquinolines undergo aldol condensation with aldehydes in the presence of bases and a methyl group in the 2-position is more reactive than one in the 4-position. Kaslow and Stayner[294] condensed benzaldehyde with 2,4-dimethylquinoline in the presence of only a trace of alkali to give exclusively 2-styryl-4-methylquinoline.

Quinaldine in the presence of an equivalent of sodium amide undergoes Michael additions.[295] Thus benzalacetophenone reacts as follows

Lepidine probably does not react in this way. In addition to a Michael addition ethyl cinnamate undergoes a Claisen condensation.

The hydrogen atoms of the methyl groups of both lepidine and quinaldine can be replaced by bromine or chlorine. Halogenation can best be accomplished in acetic acid solution buffered with sodium acetate.[296] 2-Tribromomethyl- and 2-trichloromethylquinoline can be obtained from quinaldine in almost quantitative yields. Hydrolysis of either the trichloro- or tribromomethylquinolines give almost quantitative yields of quinaldinic acid.

Alkyl substituents on the pyridine ring of quinoline can be oxidized to carboxyl groups, usually in poor yield. With 2,4-dimethylquinoline the methyl group in the 4-position is most readily attacked so that oxidation with chromic acid gives aniluvitoninic acid.[297]

Oxidation of quinaldine with permanganate results in rupture of the pyridine ring and the formation of N-acetylanthranilic acid.[298]

Alkyl groups on the benzene ring are oxidized to carbonyl and carboxyl groups with potassium dichromate and sulfuric acid.

Alkyl groups on the benzene ring are most readily oxidized than are those on the pyridine ring.

Quinoline heated with dry potassium hydroxide gives fair yields of 2-hydroxyquinoline.[299]

2-Hydroxyquinoline may also be prepared by treating quinoline with hypochlorous acid.[300]

3-Hydroxyquinoline and 5-hydroxyquinoline can be prepared by the diazotization of the corresponding aminoquinolines.

8-Hydroxyquinoline is prepared either by diazotization of 8-aminoquinoline or by fusion of 8-quinoline sulfonic acid with sodium hydroxide.

2- and 4-Hydroxyquinolines behave as if they are tautomeric mixtures with ketonic forms.

The compounds having the OH group in the 3-position or on the benzene ring behave as true phenols. These compounds undergo the Reimer-Tiemann reaction and others characteristics of phenols.

Certain 4-hydroxyquinolines are prepared from aniline and appropriate β-ketonitriles by a reaction of aniline with acyltolunitrile and the cyclization of the resulting amide. Thus 2-methyl-3-phenyl-4-hydroxyquinoline is made by the following sequence of reactions.

The formation of the anil occurs in acetic acid and ring closure is effected with polyphosphoric acid. The over-all yield is about 50 per cent. A 39 per cent yield can be obtained in one step using polyphosphoric acid.

In a similar manner 2,3-diphenyl-4-hydroxyquinoline is obtained in 87 per cent yield.[301]

7,8-Dihydroxyquinoline is prepared by heating 8-hydroxyquinoline with potassium hydroxide at 240–250°C.[302]

6-Methoxyquinoline has been prepared by adding a mixture of 26 g anisidine, 25 m of 90 per cent sulfuric acid and 120 g glycerol gradually through a reflux condenser to 22 g nitroanisole preheated to 170°C. The mixture is refluxed 4.5–5 hours, cooled to 70°C and diluted with water to give a 64 per cent yield of 6-methoxyquinoline.[303]

Aminoquinolines are prepared in a number of ways. 2-Aminoquinoline is most readily prepared by the direct introduction of an amino group with sodium amide in an inert solvent.[304]

Brooks and Rudner[305] prepared 2-aminoquinoline in 40 per cent yield by passing chloramine through quinoline at room temperature.

Yields are about 25 per cent.

Better yields are obtained by treating quinoline with potassium amide in liquid ammonia in the presence of potassium nitrate or mercury.[306] Small amounts of 4-aminoquinoline are produced at the same time.

Amino groups have been introduced into the 2- or 4-positions by means of the Hoffman degradation starting with the corresponding acid or amide.[307]

3-Aminoquinoline is most readily prepared by replacement of the bromine in 3-bromoquinoline with ammonia in the presence of copper sulfate.

Yields are about 73 per cent.[308,309]

Introduction of an amino group into the benzene ring can usually be accomplished by the reduction of the corresponding nitro compound.

A number of quinoline derivatives are important therapeutic agents. These include quinine and the cinchona alkaloids, quinicrine, chloroquine, camoquine and pamaquine. These compounds are all important antimalarials.

Quinoline is converted to N-formyl-1,2,3,4-tetrahydroquinoline by refluxing with anhydrous formic acid and sodium formate for 21 hours. The yield of product is 85 per cent. The reduction can also be accomplished with formamide and formic acid but the yields are not as high.[310]

Isoquinoline

The chemistry of isoquinoline is quite similar to that of quinoline. The isoquinoline ring system is of interest because it is found in many naturally occurring alkaloids.

Iosquinoline derivatives are obtained by ring closure procedures which usually give a dihydro- or tetrahydroisoquinoline which may be dehydrogenated. Thus treatment of N-benzoylphenethylamine with phosphorus pentoxide, phosphorus oxychloride or phosphorus pentachloride gives 1-phenyl-3,4-dihydroquinoline which may be dehydrogenated to 1-phenyl-isoquinoline.[311,312,313]

The preparation of tetrahydroisoquinolines from phenethylamines and acetals has been accomplished.[314]

Decker and Becker[315] modified the procedure by first preparing the imine from the phenethylamine and the aldehyde, then cyclizing the imine to the tetrahydroisoquinoline by heating with hydrochloric acid.

Isoquinoline has been prepared from benzaldehyde and aminoacetal to form an iminoacetal which is cyclized with sulfuric acid.[316]

Reactions of Isoquinolines. The hydrogenation of isoquinoline is more difficult than the hydrogenation of quinoline,[317] and it is possible to reduce substituent groups without affecting either ring. Thus a vinyl group in the 1-position is easily reduced to ethyl,[318,319,320] a carbonyl group is reduced to the corresponding carbinol,[321,322] and a nitro group is reduced to the amine. Halogens on the ring may be replaced by hydrogen without further hydrogenation of the isoquinoline nucleus.

Isoquinoline may, however, by hydrogenated to the decahydroisoquinoline in acetic acid solution containing a little hydrochloric acid in the presence of a platinum catalyst. Isoquinoline is converted to 1,2-dihydroisoquinoline with lithium aluminum hydride in boiling ether.[323] Dehydrogenation to isoquinoline may be accomplished by oxidation with tetra-chloro-o-benzoquinone. Hydrogenation of dihydroquinoline in the presence of a platinum oxide catalyst gives tetrahydroisoquinoline.

The pyridine ring is attacked first. 5,6,7,8-Tetrahydroisoquinoline is prepared by dehydrogenation of decahydroisoquinoline. The 1,2,3,4-tetrahydroisoquinoline is made only by ring closure procedures as previously described.[324]

Dehydrogenation of hydroisoquinolines can be accomplished with iodine or mercuric acetate.[325,326] Other oxidizing agents which may be used include potassium permanganate, nitric acid and bromine.

Dehydrogenation can be accomplished by heating in the presence of a catalyst such as palladium on asbestos.[327]

Isoquinoline is resistant to attack by electrophilic reagents. Electrophilic substitution is most likely to occur in the 5- and 8-positions and is least likely to occur in the 3- and 1-positions.

Nucleophilic substitution occurs quite frequently in the 1- and 3-position, especially when certain substituents are present on the nucleus.

Isoquinoline is sulfonated somewhat easier than is quinoline.[328] Isoquinoline can be sulfonated with 40 per cent oleum at ordinary temperatures largely in the 5-position. At 180–200°C using concentrated sulfuric acid isoquinoline-5-sulfonic acid is the chief product. Increasing the temperature to 300°C causes the formation of isomeric isoquinoline sulfonic acids.[329,330]

Nitration gives 5-nitroisoquinoline[331] together with a small amount of 8-nitroisoquinolines. 3-Methylisoquinoline and 1-chloroisoquinoline are both nitrated in the 5-position.[332,333,334]

Nucleophilic substitution occurs at the 1-position. Sodium amide reacts with isoquinoline to give 1-aminoisoquinoline.[335] The reaction is most readily accomplished with sodium amide in liquid ammonia.

Hydroxylation is accomplished when isoquinoline is heated with potassium hydroxide.[336,337]

Nucleophilic attack by hydroxyl ion occurs at the 1-position and the intermediate rearranges with the loss of a hydride ion to isocarbostyril.

Grignard reagents may be used to introduce an alkyl or aryl group into the 1-position. Thus 1-ethylisoquinoline is prepared by treating isoquinoline with ethyl magnesium bromide in ether at 150–160°C. The hydrogen in the 1-position is lost as hydrogen gas or in hydrogenation of some other part of the molecule.[338]

Other metalo organic compounds such as alkyl lithium will also introduce alkyl groups into the 1-position.

Isoquinoline-N-oxide has been obtained by treating an acetic acid solution of coal tar bases with 25 per cent hydrogen peroxide and heating at 80–90°C for 12 hours. The reaction mixture is neutralized with sodium carbonate and extracted with chloroform.[339]

REFERENCES

1. Gabriel, S., *Ber.,* **21,** 1049 (1888).
2. Gabriel, S., and Stelzner, R., *Ber.,* **28,** 2929 (1895).
3. Markwald, W., *Ber.,* **33,** 764 (1900).
4. Wenker, H., *J. Am. Chem. Soc.,* **57,** 2328 (1935).
5. Allen, C. F. H., Spangler, F. W., and Webster, E. R., "Organic Syntheses," Vol. 30, p. 38, New York, John Wiley & Sons, Inc., 1950.
6. Jones, G. D., *J. Org. Chem.,* **9,** 484 (1944).
7. Braz, G. I., *Zhur. Obschei Khim.,* **25,** 763, *J. Gen. Chem. U.S.S.R.,* **25,** 731 (1955).
8. Wolfheim, F., *Ber.,* **47,** 1450 (1914).
9. Weissberger, A., and Bach, H., *Ber.,* **64,** 1095 (1931).
10. Campbell, K. N., *et al., J. Org. Chem.,* **8,** 103 (1943).
11. Golumbic, D., Fruton, J. S., and Bergmann, M., *J. Org. Chem.,* **11,** 518 (1946).
12. Ford-Moore, A. H., Lidstone, A. G., and Waters, W. A., *J. Chem. Soc.,* **1946,** 819.
13. Gilman, H., *et al., J. Am. Chem. Soc.,* **67,** 2106 (1945).
14. Gabriel, S., and Ohle, H., *Ber.,* **50,** 804 (1917).
15. Knorr, L., *Ber.,* **37,** 3507 (1904).
16. Schatz, V. B., and Clapp, L. B., *J. Am. Chem. Soc.,* **77,** 5113 (1955).
17. Coleman, G. H., and Collin, J. E., *J. Am. Chem. Soc.,* **68,** 2006 (1946).
18. Hicks, Z. A., and Coleman, G. H., *Proc. Iowa Acad. Sciences,* **53,** 207 (1946).
19. Karabinos, J. V., and Serijan, K. T., *J. Am. Chem. Soc.,* **67,** 1856 (1945).
20. Campbell, K. N., Sommers, A. H., and Campbell, B. K., *J. Am. Chem. Soc.,* **68,** 140 (1946).
21. Kerr, R. W., and Neukom, H., *Starke,* **4,** 255 (1952).
22. Weystrach, V. P., and Kaiser, D. W., U. S. Patent 2,520,619 (Aug. 29, 1950).
23. Erlenbach, M., and Sieglitz, A., British Patent 692,368 (June 3, 1953).
24. Braz, G. I., *Doklady Akad. Nauk. U.S.S.R.,* **87,** 589 (1952).
25. Jones, G. D., *et al., J. Org. Chem.,* **9,** 125 (1944).

26. I. G. Farbenind. A. G., French Patent 840,709 (May 3, 1939).
27. Gabriel, S., and Weiner, J., *Ber.,* **21,** 2676 (1888).
28. Ruzika, L., Salomen, G., and Meyer, K. E., *Helv. Chim. Acta,* **20,** 109 (1937).
29. Mannich, C., and Baumgarten, G., *Ber.,* **70,** 210 (1937).
30. Ladenberg, A., and Sieber, J., *Ber.,* **23,** 2727 (1890).
31. Marckwald, W., and van Droste-Huelshoff, A. F., *Ber.,* **31,** 3264 (1898).
32. Howard, C. C., and Marckwald, W., *Ber.,* **32,** 2032 (1899).
33. Yanbikar, Ya. M., *J. Gen. Chem. USSR,* **8,** 1470 (1938).
34. Gibson, G. M., *et al., J. Chem. Soc.,* **1942,** 163.
35. Potokhin, *J. Russ Chem. Soc.,* **59,** 761 (1927).
36. Gabriel, S., and Stelzner, R., *Ber.,* **29,** 210 (1937).
37. Runge, *Ann. Physik.,* **31,** 67 (1834).
38. Menozzi, A., and Appiani, G., *Gazz. chim. ital.,* **24,** I 373 (1894).
39. Gilman, H., "Organic Syntheses," Coll. Vol. I, 2nd Ed., p. 473, New York, John Wiley & Sons, Inc., 1941.
40. Fujita, H., Masshima, T., and Hakihawa, Y', *J. Soc. Chem. Ind., Japan,* **41,** 63 (1938).
41. Reppe, W., *et al.,* German Patent 701,825 (Dec. 24, 1940).
42. Yur'ev Yu K, *et al., Vestnick Moskov. Univ. 6 No. 2 Ser. Fiz. Mat. i Estestven. Nauk. No. 1,* **37** (1951).
43. Bornder, C. A., U. S. Patent 2,600,289 (June 10, 1952).
44. Knorr, L., *Ann.,* **236,** 318 (1886).
45. Harries, *Ber.,* **34,** 1488 (1901).
46. Treibs, A., and Neumays, F., *Chem. Ber.,* **90,** 76 (1957).
47. Treibs, A., and Hitzler, O., *Chem. Ber.,* **90,** 787 (1957).
48. Treibs, A., Schmidt, R., and Zinsmeister, R., *Chem. Ber.,* **90,** 79 (1957).
49. Fischer, H., and Bartholomäus, E., *Z. Physiol. Chem.,* **77,** 189 (1911); *ibid,* **80,** 6 (1912).
50. Cantor, P. A., and Vanderwerf, C. A., *J. Am. Chem. Soc.,* **80,** 970 (1958).
51. Nef, J. U., *Ann.,* **318,** 140 (1901).
52. Fischer, H., and Ernst, P., *Ann.,* **447,** 147 (1926).
53. Fischer, H., and Baumler, R., *Ann.,* **468,** 58 (1929).
54. Corwin, A. H., and Viohl, P., *J. Am. Chem. Soc.,* **66,** 1143 (1944).
55. Soderbach, E., *Acta Chim. Scand.,* **8,** 1851 (1954).
56. Bamberger, E., and Djierdjian, G., *Ber.,* **33,** 536 (1900).
57. Fischer, H., and Zerweck, W., *Ber.,* **55,** 1942 (1922).
58. Smissman, E. E., Graber, M. B., and Winzler, R. J., *J. Am. Pharm. Assoc.,* **45,** 509 (1956).
59. Treibs, A., and Zinsmeister, T., *Chem. Ber.,* **90,** 87 (1957).
60. Bachman, G. B., and Heisy, L. N., *J. Am. Chem. Soc.,* **68,** 2496 (1946).
61. Herz, W., Dittmer, K., Cristol, S. J., *J. Am. Chem. Soc.,* **69,** 1698 (1941).
62. Burke, W., and Hammer, G. N., *J. Am. Chem. Soc.,* **76,** 1294 (1954).
63. Colocicchi, *Gazz. chim. ital.,* **42,** I, 10 (1912).
64. Elderfield, R. C., "Heterocyclic Compounds," Vol. I, New York, John Wiley & Sons, Inc., 1950.
65. Ciamician, G. L., and Dennstedt, M., *Ber.,* **16,** 1536 (1883).

66. Terent, ev A. P., Volodina, M. A., Podlesova, N. L., and Golubeva, N. E., *Doklady Akad. Nauk. USSR*, **114**, 1036 (1957).
67. Ciamician, G., and Magnaghi, P., *Ber.*, **18**, 2079 (1885).
68. Andrews, L. H., and McElvain, S. M., *J. Am. Chem. Soc.*, **51**, 887 (1929).
69. Späth, E., and Breusch, F., *Monatsh.*, **50**, 349 (1928).
70. Copenhaver, J. W., and Bigelow, M. H., "Acetylene and Carbon Monoxide Chemistry," p. 163, New York, Reinhold Publishing Co., 1947.
71. Yuur'ev, Yu. K., *et al.*, *Zhur. Priklad. Khim.*, **28**, 781 (1955).
72. Knorr, L., *Ber.*, **16**, 2597 (1883).
73. Reid, W., and Meyer, A., *Chem. Ber.*, **90**, 3841 (1957).
74. Buchner, E., *et al.*, *Ann.*, **273**, 214 (1893).
75. V. Auwers, K., and Breyhan, Th., *J. Prakt. Chem.*, [2], **143**, 259 (1935).
76. Debus, *Ann.*, **107**, 204 (1858).
77. Pyman, F. L., *J. Chem. Soc.*, **97**, 1814 (1910).
78. Weidenhagen, R., Hermann, R., and Wegner, H., *Ber.*, **70**, 570 (1937).
79. Loeper, M., Mougeot, A., and Aubertot, V., *Compt. rend. soc. biol.*, **116**, 33 (1934).
80. Supniewski, J. V., *Compt. rend. soc. biol.*, **98**, 1229 (1928).
81. Soc. pour l'Ind. Chim. Ã Bâle, British Patent 514,411 (Nov. 7, 1939).
82. Kyrides, L. P., U. S. Patent 2,392,326 (Jan. 8, 1946).
83. Scholz, C. R., *Ind. Eng. Chem.*, **37**, 120 (1945).
84. Kränzlein, Cr., and Ochwat, P., U. S. Patent 1,912,849 (June 6, 1933).
85. Celanese Corp. of America, British Patent 749,718 (May 30, 1956).
86. Mahan, J. E., U. S. Patent 2,703,804 (Mar. 8, 1955).
87. Mahan, J. E., U. S. Patent 2,775,596 (Dec. 25, 1956).
88. Bamford, W. R., U. S. Patent 2,769,007 (Oct. 30, 1956).
89. Aries, R. S., U. S. Patent 2,698,849 (Jan. 4, 1955).
90. Levy, S. L., and Othmer, D. F., *Ind. Eng. Chem.*, **47**, 789 (1955).
91. Bradshaw, P. L., Parkes, D. W., and Ford, I. A. M., British Patent 742,643 (Dec. 30, 1955).
92. Hoog, H., and Engel, W. F., U. S. Patents 2,603,645 (July 15, 1952); 2,605,264 (July 29, 1952).
93. Malinovski, M. S., *Ukrain. Khim. Zhur.*, **16**, No. 3, 351 (1950).
94. Cislak, F. E., and Wheeler, W. R., U. S. Patent 2,744,904 (May 8, 1956).
95. Cislak, F. E., and Wheeler, W. R., U. S. Patent 2,807,618 (Sept. 24, 1957).
96. Zellner, R. J., U. S. Patent 2,796,421 (June 18, 1957).
97. Badische Anilin and Soda Fabrik Akt Ges. British Patent 726,378 (Mar. 12, 1955).
98. Krzikalla, H., German Patent 896,648 (Nov. 12, 1953).
99. Young, F. G., U. S. Patent 2,741,618 (Apr. 10, 1956).
100. Fuson, R. C., *Chem. Revs.*, **16**, 1 (1935).
101. Hawkins, P. J., and Janz, G. J., *J. Chem. Soc.*, **1949**, 1479, 1485.
102. Janz, G. J., McCulloch, W. J. D., Timpani, E. F., *Ind. Eng. Chem.*, **45**, 1343 (1953).
103. Jarvie, J. M. S., Fitzgerald, W. E., and Janz, G. J., *J. Am. Chem. Soc.*, **78**, 978 (1956).

104. Milner, D. W., Clapham, P., British Patent 739,088 (Oct. 26, 1956).
105. Wibaut, J. P., *et al., Rec. trav. chim.,* **64,** 55 (1945).
106. Hertog, H. J. den, and Wibaut, J. P., *Rec. trav. chim.,* **51,** 940 (1952).
107. Wibaut, J. P., and Bickel, A. F., *Rec. trav. chim.,* **58,** 994 (1939).
108. Rice, H. L., and Londergan, T. E., *J. Am. Chem. Soc.,* **77,** 4678 (1955).
109. Shermer, D. A., U. S. Patent 2,820,791 (Jan. 21, 1958).
110. McBee, E. T., Hass, H. B., and Hodnett, E. M., *Ind. Eng. Chem.,* **39,** 389 (1947).
111. Schickh, O. V., Binz, A., and Schultz, A., *Ber.,* **69,** 2593 (1936).
112. Chichibabin, A. E., and Scheide, O. A. J., *Russ. Phys. Chem. Soc.,* **46,** 1216 (1914).
113. Leffler, M. T., "Organic Reactions," Vol. I, Ch. 4, New York, John Wiley & Sons, Inc.
114. den Hertog, H. J., and Wibaut, J. P., *Rec. trav. chim.,* **55,** 122 (1936).
115. Bohlmann, F., and Bohlmann, M., *Chem. Ber.,* **86,** 1419 (1953).
116. Ingold, C. K., *Ann. Reports Progress Chem. (Chem. Soc. London),* **23,** 129 (1926).
117. Mumm, O., and Beth, W., *Ber.,* **54,** 1592 (1921).
118. Harris, B. R., U. S. Patent 2,678,316 (May 11, 1954).
119. Shelton, R. S., *et al., J. Am. Chem. Soc.,* **68,** 757 (1946).
120. Williams, D. M., *J. Chem. Soc.,* **1931,** 2783.
121. Hoffman, K. R., and Van der Werf, C. A., *J. Am. Chem. Soc.,* **68,** 997 (1946).
122. Reitz, H. C., *et al., J. Am. Chem. Soc.,* **68,** 1031 (1946).
123. Baumgarten, P., *et al., Z. Physiol. Chem.,* **209,** 145 (1932).
124. Whitmore, F. C., Goldsmith, D. P. J., and Mosher, H. S., Rytina, A. W., *J. Am. Chem. Soc.,* **67,** 393 (1945).
125. Doering, W. E., and Weil, R. A. N., *J. Am. Chem. Soc.,* **69,** 2461 (1947).
126. Frank, R. L., *et al., J. Am. Chem. Soc.,* **68,** 1368 (1946).
127. Mahan, J. E., U. S. Patent 2,698,848 (Jan. 4, 1955).
128. Chichibabin, A. E., German Patent 676,114 (May 26, 1939); *Bull. soc. chim. France,* [5], **3,** 1607 (1936).
129. Knight, G. A., and Shaw, B. D., *J. Chem. Soc.,* **1938,** 682.
130. Lochte, H. L., and Cheavers, T. H., *J. Am. Chem. Soc.,* **79,** 1667 (1957).
131. Melichor, F., *Ber.,* **88,** 1208 (1955).
132. Cislak, F. F., U. S. Patent 2,789,982 (Apr. 23, 1957).
133. Balandin, A. A., Sovalova, L. I., and Slovokhotova, T. A., *Doklady Akad. Nauk. USSR,* **110,** 79 (1956).
134. Hein, F., and Schwedler, H., *Ber.,* **68,** 681 (1935).
135. Morgan, G. T., and Burstall, F. H., *J. Chem. Soc.,* **1932,** 20.
136. Schulenberg, German Patent 588,641 (Nov. 13, 1933).
137. Cislak, F. E., U. S. Patent 2,716,119 (Aug. 23, 1955).
138. Cislak, F. E., U. S. Patent 2,716,118 (Aug. 23, 1955).
139. Mahan, J. E., U. S. Patent 2,769,811 (Jan. 6, 1956).
140. Pritchard, J. E., and Opheim, M. H., *Ind. Eng. Chem.,* **46,** 2242 (1954).
141. Levine, R., and Wilt, M. H., *J. Am. Chem. Soc.,* **74,** 342 (1952).
142. Levine, R., and Wilt, M. H., *J. Am. Chem. Soc.,* **75,** 1368 (1953).

143. Reich, H. E., and Levine, R., *J. Am. Chem. Soc.,* **77,** 4913 (1955).
144. Phillips, A. P., *J. Am. Chem. Soc.,* **78,** 4441 (1956).
145. Urbánski, T., *J. Chem. Soc.,* **1946,** 1104.
146. Chichibabin, A. E., and Shapiro, S. A., *J. Russ. Phys. Chem. Soc.,* **53,** 233 (1921).
147. Räth, C., *Ann.,* **489,** 108 (1931).
148. Meyer, *Monatsh.,* **26,** 1311 (1905).
149. Pino, L. N., and Zehring, W. S., *J. Am. Chem. Soc.,* **77,** 3154 (1955).
150. Plazek, E., Marcinków, A., and Stammer, C., *Roczniki Chem.,* **15,** 365 (1935).
151. Hirao, I., and Hayashi, M., *J. Pharm. Soc. Japan,* **74,** 853 (1954).
152. Halverson, K., *Arkiv. Kemi,* **7,** 225 (1954).
153. Schmid, L., and Mann, H., *Monatsh.,* **85,** 864 (1954).
154. Singer, A. W., and McElvain, S. M., "Organic Syntheses," Vol. 20, p. 79, New York, John Wiley & Sons, Inc., 1940.
155. Kaufman, J. G., *J. Am. Chem. Soc.,* **67,** 497 (1945).
156. Kulka, M., *J. Am. Chem. Soc.,* **68,** 2472 (1946).
157. Koelsch, C. F., *J. Am. Chem. Soc.,* **65,** 2565 (1943).
158. Burrus, H. O., and Powell, G., *J. Am. Chem. Soc.,* **67,** 1468 (1945).
159. Leis, D. G., and Curran, B. C., *J. Am. Chem. Soc.,* **67,** 79 (1945).
160. Leni, M., and Georgiev, A., *Formatsiya (Sofia),* **1955,** No. 3, p. 27.
161. Wettstein, W., U. S. Patent 2,845,428 (July 29, 1958); Jerchel, D., Bauer, E., and Hippchin, H., *Chem. Ber.,* **88,** 156 (1955).
162. Sugimoto, N., Kugila, H., and Tonaka, T., *J. Pharm. Soc. Japan,* **76,** 1309 (1956).
163. Bohlmann, F., and Bohlmann, M., *Ber.,* **86,** 1419 (1953).
164. Hadey, D. J., and Wood, B., British Patent 777,746 (June 26, 1957).
165. Denton, W. I., and Bishop, R. B., U. S. Patent 2,582,123 (Apr. 8, 1952).
166. Henze, M., *Ber.,* **67,** 750 (1934).
167. Profft, E., *Chem. Tech. (Berlin),* **6,** 484 (1951).
168. Koelsch, C. F., *J. Org. Chem.,* **10,** 34 (1945).
169. Burres, H. O., and Powell, G., *J. Am. Chem. Soc.,* **67,** 1468 (1945).
170. Kolloff, H. G., and Hunter, J. W., *J. Am. Chem. Soc.,* **63,** 490 (1941).
171. Hertog, H. J., *Rec. trav. chim.,* **70,** 581 (1951).
172. Katritzky, A. R., Randell, E. W., and Sutton, L. E., *J. Chem. Soc.,* **1957,** 1769.
173. Mosher, H. S., Turner, L., Carlsmith, A., "Organic Syntheses, Vol. 33, p. 79, New York, John Wiley & Sons, Inc., 1953.
174. Berson, J. A., and Cohen, T., *J. Org. Chem.,* **20,** 1461 (1955).
175. Boekelheide, V., and Linn, W. J., *J. Am. Chem. Soc.,* **76,** 1286 (1954).
176. Hardegger, E., and Nikles, E., *Helv. Chim. Acta,* **39,** 505 (1956), *ibid,* **40,** 1016 (1957).
177. Kata, T., *J. Pharm. Soc. Japan,* **75,** 1233 (1955).
178. Lee, T. B., and Swan, G. A., *J. Chem. Soc.,* **1956,** 771.
179. Taylor, E. C., Jr., and Crovetti, A. J., "Organic Syntheses," Vol. 36, p. 53, New York, John Wiley & Sons, Inc., 1956.
180. Kano, S., *J. Pharm. Soc. Japan,* **73,** 120 (1953); *ibid,* **75,** 1233 (1955).
181. Katritzky, A. R., *J. Chem. Soc.,* **1956,** 2404.

182. Clemo, G. R., and Koenig, H., *J. Chem. Soc.,* **1949,** 2231.
183. Taylor, E. C., Jr., and Crovetti, A. J., *J. Org. Chem.,* **19,** 1633 (1954).
184. Adams, R., and Mayano, S., *J. Am. Chem. Soc.,* **76,** 2785 (1954).
185. Adams, R., and Reifschneider, W., *J. Am. Chem. Soc.,* **79,** 2236 (1957).
186. Brown, E. V., *J. Am. Chem. Soc.,* **79,** 3565 (1957).
187. Childress, S. J., and Scudi, J. V., *J. Org. Chem.,* **23,** 67 (1958).
188. Gardner, T. S., Wenis, E., and Lee, J., *J. Org. Chem.,* **22,** 984 (1957).
189. Herz, W., and Tsai, L., *J. Am. Chem. Soc.,* **76,** 4184 (1954).
190. Katritzky, A. R., and Gardner, J. N., *J. Chem. Soc.,* **1958,** 2192.
191. Katritzky, A. R., and Hands, A. R., *J. Chem. Soc.,* **1958,** 2195.
192. Katritzky, A. R., *et al., J. Chem. Soc.,* **1958,** 2182.
193. Adams, R., and Mayano, S., *J. Am. Chem. Soc.,* **76,** 3168 (1954).
194. Itai, T., *J. Pharm. Soc. Japan,* **75,** 292 (1955).
195. Ishikawa, M. J., *Pharm. Soc. Japan,* **65,** 6 (1945).
196. Ochaia, E., *J. Org. Chem.,* **18,** 534 (1953).
197. Hertog, H. J., den Henkens, C. H., and Dilz, K., *Rec. trav. chim.,* **72,** 296 (1953).
198. Hayashi, E., *J. Pharm. Soc. Japan,* **70,** 142 (1950).
199. Hands, A. R., and Katritzky, A. R., *J. Chem. Soc.,* **1958,** 3719.
200. Culvenor, C. C., Reys, J., *Pure and Appl. Chem.,* **3,** 83 (1953).
201. Katritzky, A. R., *Quarterly Revs.,* **10,** 395 (1956).
202. Murakami, M., and Matsumura, E., *J. Chem. Soc. Japan,* **70,** 393 (1949).
203. Kato, T., *J. Pharm. Soc. Japan,* **75,** 1239 (1955).
204. Kato, T., *J. Pharm. Soc. Japan,* **75,** 1236 (1955).
205. Itai, T., *J. Pharm. Soc. Japan,* **65,** 70 (1945).
206. Mosher, M. S., and Welch, F. J., *J. Am. Chem. Soc.,* **77,** 2902 (1956).
207. Ochiai, E., and Arima, K., *J. Pharm. Soc. Japan,* **69,** 51 (1949).
208. Tokuyama, M., *J. Pharm. Soc. Japan,* **74,** 1404 (1954).
209. Katada, M., *J. Pharm. Soc. Japan,* **67,** 41 (1946).
210. Iobayashi, G., and Furukawa, S., *Pharm. Bull.,* **1,** 347 (1953).
211. Ishakawa, A. M., and Takuyama, K., *Ann Rept Shionogi Research Lab.,* **1953,** 37.
212. Ochiai, E., Ishidawa, M., and Katade, M., *J. Pharm. Soc. Japan,* **63,** 307 (1943).
213. Amera, M., and Hertog, H. J., *Rec. trav. chim.,* **77,** 340 (1958).
214. Murray, J. G., and Hauser, C. R., *J. Org. Chem.,* **19,** 2008 (1954).
215. Itai, T., and Ogura, H., and Kamiya, S., *J. Pharm. Soc. Japan,* **75,** 292 (1955).
216. Ochiai, E., and Suzuki, I., *J. Pharm. Soc. Japan,* **67,** 158 (1947).
217. Taylor, E. C., Jr., Crovetti, A. J., and Boyer, N. E., *J. Am. Chem. Soc.,* **79,** 3549 (1957).
218. Kato, T., Hamaguchi, F., and Oiwa, T., *Pharm. Bull.,* **4,** 178 (1956).
219. Katritzky, A. R., and Monro, A. M., *J. Chem. Soc.,* **1958,** 1263.
220. Newbold, G. T., and Spring, F. S., *J. Chem. Soc.,* **1949,** 2133.
221. Katada, M., *J. Pharm. Soc. Japan,* **67,** 53 (1947).
222. Brown, H. S., and Subba Rao, B. O., *J. Am. Chem. Soc.,* **77,** 3164 (1955); *ibid,* **78,** 2582 (1956).

223. Takada, K., and Tokuyama, K., *J. Pharm. Soc. Japan,* **75,** 620 (1955).
224. Adkins, H., "Reactions of Hydrogen with Organic Compounds," p. 66, University of Wisconsin Press, 1947.
225. Hamilton, T. S., and Adams, R., *J. Am. Chem. Soc.,* **50,** 2260 (1928).
226. Silverstone, G. A., British Patent 755,534 (Aug. 22, 1956).
227. Horrobin, S., and Young, R. J., British Patents 744,928 (Feb. 15, 1956); 745,400 (Feb. 22, 1956).
228. Urry, W. H., U. S. Patent 2,772,271 (Nov. 27, 1956).
229. Gutneckt, H., *Ber.,* **12,** 2291 (1879).
230. Treadwell, F. P., *Ber.,* **14,** 1461, 2158 (1881).
231. Gabriel, S., and Pinkus, G., *Ber.,* **26,** 2197 (1893).
232. Wolff, L., and Marburg, R., *Ann.,* **363,** 176,217 (1908).
233. Dixon, J. K., U. S. Patent 2,400,398; 2,474,781; 2,474,782 (June 28, 1949).
234. Pfann, H. F., and Dixon, J. K., U. S. Patent 2,414,522.
235. Stoehr, C., *J. Prakt. Chem.,* [2], **47,** 439 (1893).
236. Tutin, F., and Caton, F. W., *J. Chem. Soc.,* **97,** 2524 (1910).
237. Krems, I., and Spoerri, P. C., *Chem. Revs.,* **40,** 279 (1947).
238. Jones, R. G., and McLaughlin, K. C., "Organic Syntheses," Vol. 30, p. 86, New York, John Wiley & Sons, Inc., 1950.
239. Newbold, G. T., and Spring, F. S., *J. Chem. Soc.,* **1947,** 1183.
240. Godchot, M., and Mousseron, M., *Compt. rend.,* **190,** 798 (1930).
241. Shreve, R. N., and Berg, L., *J. Am. Chem. Soc.,* **69,** 2116 (1947).
242. Kitchen, L. J., and Hanson, E. S., *J. Am. Chem. Soc.,* **73,** 1838 (1951).
243. Société Des Usines Chimiques Rhone-Poulenc, British Patent 595,430, December 4, 1947.
244. Kitchen, L. J., and Pollard, C. B., *J. Am. Chem. Soc.,* **69,** 854 (1947).
245. Forsee, W. T., Jr., and Pollard, C. B., *J. Am. Chem. Soc.,* **57,** 2363 (1935).
246. Pollard, C. B., *et al.,* *J. Am. Chem. Soc.,* **57,** 199 (1935); **58,** 1980 (1936); **59,** 1719, 2006 (1935).
247. Dixon, J. K., U. S. Patent 2,580,221 (Dec. 25, 1951).
248. Bopp, *Ann.,* **69,** 28 (1848).
249. Sannié, C., *Bull. soc. chim. France,* **9,** 487 (1942).
250. Paal, C., and Schulze, H., *Ber.,* **33,** 3784 (1900); **35,** 168 (1902).
251. Lutz, R. E., and King, S. M., *J. Org. Chem.,* **17,** 1519 (1952).
252. Wohl, A., and Bernreuther, E., *Ann.,* **481,** 1 (1930).
253. Borsche, W., and Klein, A., *Ann.,* **548,** 74 (1941).
254. Jones, R. G., Kornfeld, E. C., and McLaughlin, K. C., *J. Am. Chem. Soc.,* **72,** 3539 (1950).
255. Mizzoni, R. H., and Spoerri, P. E., *J. Am. Chem. Soc.,* **76,** 2201 (1954).
256. Marquis, R., *Compt. rend.,* **136,** 369 (1903).
257. Gabriel, S., *Ber.,* **33,** 3666 (1900).
258. Lythgoe, B., and Rayner, L. S., *J. Chem. Soc.,* **1951,** 2323.
259. Takeda, K., and Tokuyama, I., *J. Pharm. Soc. Japan,* **76,** 77 (1956).
260. Ochiai, E., and Karii, M., *J. Pharm. Soc. Japan,* **59,** 18 (1939).
261. Gabriel, S., and Colman, J., *Ber.,* **36,** 3379 (1903).
262. Schlenker, J., *Ber.,* **34,** 2812 (1901).

263. English, J. P., *et al.*, *J. Am. Chem. Soc.*, **68**, 453, 1039 (1946).
264. Hepner, B., and Frenkenberg, S., *J. Prakt. Chem.*, **134**, 249 (1932).
265. Johnson, T. B., and Ambelang, J. C., *J. Am. Chem. Soc.*, **60**, 2941 (1938).
266. Klotzer, W., *Monatsh*, **87**, 131 (1956).
267. Campbell, A. W., U. S. Patent 2,034,427 (1936).
268. Weiss, E., German Patent 844,006 (July 14, 1952).
269. Boehringer, A., *et al.*, British Patent 773,780 (May 1, 1957).
270. Malen, Ch., and Boissier, J. R., *Bull. soc. chim. France*, **1956**, 923.
271. Runge, *Ann. Physik.*, [2], **31**, 65 (1834).
272. Kruber, O., and Rappen, L., *Chem. Ber.*, **81**, 483 (1948).
273. Schenck, L. M., and Bailey, J. R., *J. Am. Chem. Soc.*, **63**, 1365 (1941).
274. Elderfield, R. C., "Heterocyclic Compounds," Vol. 4, New York, John Wiley & Sons, Inc., 1952.
275. Skraup, H., *Ber.*, **13**, 2086 (1880); **15**, 897 (1882).
276. Doebner, O., v. Miller, W., *Ber.*, **14**, 2812 (1881).
277. Mills, W. H., Harris, J. E. G., and Lambourne, H., *J. Chem. Soc.*, **119**, 1294 (1921).
278. Beyer, C., *J. Prakt. Chem.*, [2], **33**, 393 (1886); *Ber.*, **20**, 1767 (1887).
279. Stark, O., *Ber.*, **40**, 3425 (1907).
280. Stark, O., and Hoffmann, F., *Ber.*, **42**, 715 (1909).
281. v. Niementowski, S. T., *Ber.*, **27**, 1394 (1894).
282. Fuson, R. C., and Burness, D. M., *J. Am. Chem. Soc.*, **68**, 1270 (1946).
283. Erdmann, H., *Ber.*, **32**, 3570 (1899).
284. Kulish, *Monatsh.*, **15**, 276 (1894).
285. Kipping, F. S., *J. Chem. Soc.*, **65**, 489 (1894).
286. Kozlov, N. S., and Panova, N. I., *Zhur. Obschei Khim.*, **24**, 317 (1954).
287. Kozlov, N. S., *J. Gen. Chem. USSR*, **7**, 1860 (1937).
288. Ardashev, B. I., and Tertov, B. A., *Zhur. Obschei Khim.*, **26**, 895 (1954).
289. Parai-Koshits, B. A., *et al.*, *Zhur. Obschei Khim.*, **24**, 895 (1954).
290. Wilde, B. E., British Patent 764,957 (Jan. 2, 1957).
291. Huckel, W., and Hagedorn, L., *Chem. Ber.*, **90**, 752 (1957).
292. Hamer, F. M., *J. Chem. Soc.*, **123**, 246 (1923).
293. Henze, *Ber.*, **70B**, 1270 (1937).
294. Kaslow, C. E., and Stayner, R. D., *J. Am. Chem. Soc.*, **67**, 1716 (1945).
295. Weiss, M. J., and Hausser, C. R., *J. Am. Chem. Soc.*, **71**, 2026 (1949).
296. Hammick, D. L., *J. Chem. Soc.*, **123**, 2882 (1923).
297. Beyer, C., *J. Prakt. Chem.*, [2], **33**, 410 (1886).
298. Bergstrom, F. W., *J. Am. Chem. Soc.*, **53**, 3027 (1931).
299. Chichibabin, A. E., *Ber.*, **56**, 1883 (1923).
300. Erlenmeyer, E., and Rosenhek, J., *Ber.*, **18**, 3295 (1885).
301. Hauser, C. R., and Murray, J. G., *J. Am. Chem. Soc.*, **77**, 2851 (1955).
302. Ohla, T., Mori, Y., and Koike, K., *Chem. and Ind. (London)*, **1957**, 1241.
303. Ardeshiv, B. O., and Minkin, V. I., *Zhur. Priklad Khim.*, **30**, 1877 (1957).
304. Chichibabin, A. E., and Zatzepina, E. V., *J. Russ. Phys. Chem. Soc.*, **50**, 553 (1920).
305. Brooks, M. E., and Rudner, B., *J. Am. Chem. Soc.*, **78**, 2339 (1956).

306. Bergstrom, F. W., *J. Am. Chem. Soc.*, **56**, 1748 (1934); *J. Org. Chem.*, **2**, 411 (1937).
307. Renshaw, R. R., and Friedman, H. L., *J. Am. Chem. Soc.*, **61**, 3320 (1939).
308. Kuhn, R., and Westphal, O., *Ber.*, **73**, 1107 (1940).
309. Clemo, G. R., and Swan, G. A., *J. Chem. Soc.*, **1945**, 867.
310. Kost, A. N., and Yudin, L. G., *Zhur. Obschei Khim.*, **25**, 1947 (1955).
311. Bischler, A., and Napieralski, B., *Ber.*, **26**, 1903 (1893).
312. Spath, E., Berger, F., and Kuntara, W., *Ber.*, **63**, 134 (1930).
313. Decker, H., *et al.*, *Ann.*, **395**, 299 (1913).
314. Pictet, A., and Spengler, T., *Ber.*, **44**, 2030 (1911).
315. Decker, H., and Becker, P., *Ann.*, **395**, 342 (1913).
316. Poneranz., *Monatsh.*, **15**, 299 (1894).
317. Cavallito, C. S., and Haskell, T. H., *J. Am. Chem. Soc.*, **66**, 1166 (1944).
318. Spath, E., and Kruta, E., *Ber.*, **62**, 1024 (1929).
319. Haworth, R. D., and Perkin, W. H., *J. Chem. Soc.*, **127**, 1453 (1925).
320. Spath, E., and Polgar, N., *Ber.*, **59**, 2787 (1926).
321. Buck, J. S., Perkin, W. H., and Stevens, T. S., *J. Chem. Soc.*, **127**, 1462 (1925).
322. Noller, C. R., and Azima, M., *J. Am. Chem. Soc.*, **72**, 17 (1950).
323. Jackman, L. M., and Packham, D. I., *Chem. and Ind.*, **1955**, 360.
324. Witkop, B., *J. Am. Chem. Soc.*, **70**, 2617 (1948).
325. Spath, E., and Meinhard, T., *Ber.*, **75**, 400 (1942).
326. Haworth, R. D., *et al.*, *J. Chem. Soc.*, **125**, 1675 (1924).
327. v. Braun, J., Bayer, O., and Cassel, L., *Ber.*, **60**, 2602 (1927).
328. Weissgerber, R., *Ber.*, **47**, 3175 (1914).
329. Claus, A., and Raps, G., *J. Prakt. Chem.*, [2], **45**, 241 (1892).
330. Claus, A., and Seelemann, A., *J. Prakt. Chem.*, [2], **52**, 1 (1895).
331. Le Fevre, C. G., and Le Fevre, R. J. W., *J. Chem. Soc.*, **1935**, 1470.
332. Bergstrom, F. W., and Paterson, R. E., *J. Org. Chem.*, **10**, 479 (1945).
333. Robinson, R. A., *J. Am. Chem. Soc.*, **69**, 1939 (1947).
334. Elpern, B., and Hamilton, C. S., *J. Am. Chem. Soc.*, **68**, 1436 (1946).
335. Leffler, M. T., "Organic Reactions," Vol. I, p. 91, New York, John Wiley & Sons, Inc., 1942.
336. Chichibabin, A. E., and Kursanova, A. I., *Chem. Abs.*, **25**, 2727 (1931).
337. Wibaut, J. P., and Haaijman, P. W., *Rec. trav. chim.*, **62**, 466 (1943).
338. Bergström, F. W., and McAllister, S. H., *J. Am. Chem. Soc.*, **52**, 2845 (1903).
339. Ochiai, E., and Ikehara, M., Japan Patent 3326 ('54) June 9, 1954.

4. HYDRAZINES, AZO COMPOUNDS, DIAZONIUM SALTS, AND OXIMES

HYDRAZINES

Hydrazine, in addition to being a strong base, is a powerful reducing agent. It reacts with alkyl halides to form hydrazines in much the same way as ammonia reacts to form amines.

Preparation of Hydrazines

Hydrazine is formed by first reacting equimolar quantities of sodium hypochlorite and ammonia in alkaline solution to give chloramine (NH_2Cl) which further reacts with ammonia at elevated temperatures. It has been postulated that the reaction proceeds through the intermediate $NHCl^-$ ion.

The synthesis of hydrazine proceeds in two steps.

$$NH_3 + NaOCl \longrightarrow NaOH + NH_2Cl$$

$$NH_3 + NH_2Cl + NaOH \longrightarrow H_2NNH_2 + NaCl + H_2O$$

A side reaction occurs, however, which leads to the decomposition of hydrazine

$$2NH_2Cl + H_2NNH_2 \longrightarrow N_2 + 2NH_4Cl$$

This reaction is catalyzed by dissolved copper, and in order to obtain satisfactory yields of hydrazine, some type of metal deactivator must be added. Gelatin or glue is commonly used for this purpose but other substances capable of forming copper complexes are also used. These include amino acids and simple peptides.[1]

When amines are reacted with chloramine, N-alkyl-hydrazines are obtained. The yield of these N-substituted hydrazines depend on (a) the mole ratio of amine to chloramine, (b) the addition of a metal deactivator such as gelatin, (c) the presence of a permanent base such as sodium hydroxide, and (d) the temperature of the reaction.

The preparation of alkylhydrazines in maximum yields requires a smaller ratio of amine to chloramine than the ratio of ammonia to chloramine used in the preparation of hydrazine and the reaction temperature is ap-

179

preciably lower. Yields of ethylhydrazine of 60 per cent are obtained with a 5:1 molar ratio of methylamine to chloramine in the presence of small amounts of gelatin.[2,3] Alkylhydrazines have been prepared in excellent yield by the action of chloramine, made by the gas phase reaction of chlorine and ammonia, on anhydrous primary or secondary amines.[4]

N,N'-disubstituted hydrazines are prepared from chloramine and a suitable secondary amine. If the amine is water-soluble, such as dimethyl- or diethylamine, the reaction takes place quite rapidly in the cold. If the amine is not particularly water soluble, the mixture must be agitated for about 30 minutes.[5]

Chloramine reacts with a variety of tertiary amines to form the 1,1,1-trisubstituted hydrazonium chlorides.

$$(CH_3)_3N + NH_2Cl \longrightarrow (CH_3)_3NNH_2{}^+Cl^-$$

Omietanski[5] has prepared a series of 1,1,1-trisubstituted hydrazinium hexafluorophosphates using this technique.

Monoalkylhydrazines in which the alkyl group contains six or more carbon atoms can be made by the alkylation of anhydrous hydrazine with an alkyl halide.[6,7] A large excess of hydrazine and temperatures of 100–120°C favor monoalkylation. Yields of monoalkylhydrazines vary from 26 per cent for hexylhydrazine to 60 per cent for the cetyl derivative.[8]

Alkylation with lower molecular weight alkyl halides gives di-, tri-, and tetrasubstituted hydrazines,[9] but ethylhydrazine has been prepared in 32 per cent yield by the alkylation of hydrazine with ethyl sulfate.[10]

Monosubstituted hydrazines are prepared by indirect methods. Thus methylhydrazine is prepared by condensing hydrazine with benzaldehyde, treating the resulting hydrazone with dimethyl sulfate and hydrolyzing the methyl derivative.[11]

$$C_6H_5CHO + H_2NNH_2 \longrightarrow C_6H_5CH{=}NNH_2 + H_2O$$

$$C_6H_5CH{=}NNH_2 + (CH_3)_2SO_4 \longrightarrow C_6H_5CH{=}NNHCH_3 + CH_3HSO_4$$

$$C_6H_5CH{=}NNHCH_3 + H_2O \longrightarrow H_2NNHCH_3 + C_6H_5CHO$$

Alternatively an N-alkylurea may be treated with a hypochlorite to give the corresponding hydrazine

$$RNHCONH_2 + NaOCl \longrightarrow RNHNH_2 + CO_2 + NaCl$$

Aryl halogens, if activated by nitro groups, will react with hydrazine.[12] Thus 2,4-dinitrophenylhydrazine is made in 85 per cent yield from 2,4-dinitrochlorobenzene.

Aryldiazonium salts may be reduced with sodium sulfite to give arylhydrazines. Thus phenylhydrazine is obtained from benzenediazonium chloride in 84 per cent yield.[13]

$$C_6H_5N_2Cl \xrightarrow{Na_2SO_3} C_6H_5NHNH_2 \cdot HCl$$

In the laboratory, aryl hydrazines are most readily obtained by the reduction of diazonium salts with atannous chloride and hydrochloric acid at temperatures below 0°C.[14,15,16,17]

$$C_6H_5N_2Cl + 2SnCl_2 + 4HCl \longrightarrow C_6H_5NHNH_3^+Cl^- + 2SnCl_4$$

This reduction can be accomplished with zinc dust and acetic acid. Electrolytic reduction has also been successful.[18,19]

N-Alkylated aromatic hydrazines can be obtained by the reaction of alkyl bromides with aryl hydrazines.[20,21]

Symmetrical diarylhydrazines can be prepared by the reduction of azo compounds which in turn are obtained by the selective reduction of nitro compounds. The over-all reduction can be accomplished with zinc dust and alkali or by electrolytic methods.[22,23]

$$2C_6H_5NO_2 \xrightarrow{(H)} C_6H_5NHNHC_6H_5$$

The yields vary from 50 to 95 per cent depending on the structure of the nitro compound.

Kabayashi[24] obtained aromatic hydrazo compounds by reducing a dispersion of an aromatic nitro compound in xylene and water at 90°C with 0.3 per cent sodium amalgam. Thus a 90 per cent yield of $C_6H_5NHNHC_6H_5$ can be obtained from nitrobenzene in 2 hours. Nitroso-, azoxy- and azo compounds give the same products.

Hydrazine is capable of reducing aromatic nitro compounds to the corresponding hydrazo compounds in the presence of a suitable catalyst. Thus Pietra and Marco[25] reduced aromatic nitro compounds to hydrazo compounds by hydrazine in the presence of a 5 per cent ruthenium on carbon catalyst in 5 per cent potassium hydroxide. Thus nitrobenzene gave hydrazobenzene ($C_6H_5NHNHC_6H_5$) in 80 per cent yield and o- and p-nitrotoluenes gave the corresponding hydrazo compounds in 61 and 70 per cent yields. A palladium on carbon catalyst tends to cause the reaction to proceed with the formation of amines. Only amines can be isolated from the reduction of *o*-nitrobenzoic acid or *o*- and *p*-nitroanaline.

Hydrazine in the presence of Raney nickel will also reduce azo to hydrazo compounds in good yield.[26]

Aromatic nitro compounds such as *o*-nitroanisole or *o*-chloronitrobenzene are reduced to hydrazines in alkaline solution with ferrosilicon containing 10–15 per cent silicon.[27]

$$o\text{-CH}_3\text{O}-\text{C}_6\text{H}_4-\text{NO}_2 \xrightarrow[\text{NaOH}]{\text{Fe/Si}} o\text{-CH}_3\text{O}-\text{C}_6\text{H}_4-\text{NHNH}-\text{C}_6\text{H}_4-\text{OCH}_3\text{-}o$$

Nitroanisole is added to 13–18 per cent aqueous sodium hydroxide containing calcium hydroxide and ferrosilicon and heated for 2–6 hours at 100°C. The hydrazines are obtained in 40–90 per cent yield.

Nitrosamines may be reduced with zinc and acetic acid to unsymmetrical disubstituted hydrazines

$$(\text{CH}_3)_2\text{NNO} \xrightarrow{\text{(H)}} (\text{CH}_3)_2\text{NNH}_2$$

Unsymmetrical dimethylhydrazine is prepared in this way in 73 per cent yield.[28] unsym-Dimethylhydrazine has also been prepared by Hovitz[29] by passing dimethylnitrosamine and aqueous sodium hydroxide through a column packed with aluminum granules. A yield of dimethylhydrazine of 42 per cent was obtained after three passes through the column.

Unsymmetrical disubstituted hydrazines, $RRNNH_2$, can be prepared from the corresponding nitrosamines by the following reducing agents: (a) lithium aluminum hydride in ether, (b) sodium in alcohol, (c) sodium in liquid ammonia in the presence of substances such as alcohols which act like acids in ammonia. The following unsymmetrical hydrazines, (R_2NNH_2) have been prepared where R is C_2H_5, iso-C_3H_7, n-C_4H_9, n-C_5H_{11}. The dimethyl and diethyl derivatives are very soluble in water but the di-n-propyl and diisopropylhydrazines are only partially soluble.

The reduction of diisobutylnitroamine in isopropyl alcohol with sodium at 60°C gives unsym-diisobutyl-hydrazine in 50 per cent yield. unsym-n-Butylhydrazine is obtained similarly in 42 per cent yield. Morpholino-hydrazine is prepared in 60–70 per cent yield from nitrosomorpholine by reduction with lithium aluminum hydride.[30]

As an example of the formation of dialkylnitrosoamines, di-n-amylnitrosamine is prepared by converting diamylamine to the hydrochloride, warming to 70°C and allowing it to react with a suspension of sodium nitrite in water.[31] The over-all procedure is therefore the conversion of a secondary amine to the hydrazine.

Hydrazinium Salts

Alkylation of a hydrazine always occurs on the more basic of the two nitrogen atoms, and since the presence of an alkyl group increases the basicity of the hydrazine molecule, further alkylation is favored.

With low molecular weight substituents, further alkylation occurs to give hydrazinium salts of the type $H_2NN(CH_3)_3{}^+X^-$.[32,33] Quaternization is favored at temperatures below about 110°C. Steric hindrance with larger alkyl halides decreases the probability of the formation of quaternary compounds.

The hydrazinium salts are similar to tetraalkylammonium salts except that they are not quite as stable. They may be converted to hydrazinium hydroxides by the action of moist silver oxide but these compounds are not readily isolated. Hydrolysis of hydrazinium hydroxides at low temperatures gives the hydrazine and an alcohol. At high temperatures decomposition occurs to give a mixture of compounds including nitrogen and ammonia.

Properties of Hydrazines

Phenylhydrazine is stabilized by the addition of 3 per cent hexamethylenetetramine. Phenylhydrazine stabilized in this manner has a solidification point of 19.3°C, is stable at 25–35°C for more than six months and is not affected by metals.[34]

Alkylhydrazines are strong bases and are very difficult to separate from water. They reduce Fehling's solution and Tollen's reagent. Methyl- and ethylhydrazine have boiling points which are lower than that of hydrazine itself.[35]

The unsymmetrical dialkylhydrazines are also strong bases. They react quantitatively with alkyl chlorides to form water-soluble hydrazinium salts.

Trialkyl hydrazines are very weak bases. Triethyl- and tripropylhydrazine are soluble in concentrated mineral acids but higher homologs are practically insoluble.[9,32]

Reactions of Hydrazines

The utilization of hydrazine as a reducing agent in the formation of hydrazones has been mentioned. Hydrazine in the presence of a palladium catalyst can be used to reduce some other unsaturated compounds. The reaction proceeds with the evolution of the calculated amount of nitrogen and it is suggested that a direct exchange of hydrogen occurs at the catalyst surface. Thus maleic acid is converted to succinic acid in 95 per cent yield by adding hydrazine hydrate to an alkaline solution of the acid containing catalytic amounts of palladium on charcoal. The hydrogenation is complete in about 20 minutes at 100°C.[36]

Elaidic and ricinoleic acids have been converted to stearic acid and 12-hydroxystearic acid, respectively, in 90 per cent yield by the action of hydrazine hydrate in ethanol at 50°C for 8 hours.

The reaction of hydrazine with alkyl and aryl halides has already been described. Hydrazine reacts with other halogen-containing compounds. Thus β,β'-dichlorodiethyl ether refluxed in ethanol with hydrazine hydrate for 2.5 hours gives 4-aminomorpholine. Refluxing the ether with hydrazine sulfate in water containing sodium hydroxide for 15 hours gives 4-amino-morpholine and 5–10 per cent di-4-morpholinyl.[38]

2-Chloropyridine and 2-chloroquinoline react with hydrazine at reflux temperatures to give the corresponding 2-hydrazine derivatives.[39]

In a similar manner α-chloro and α-bromo acids are converted to α-hydrazino acids. Esters of α-bromo malonic acid are reduced to the corresponding malonic esters with the elimination of nitrogen and hydrogen bromide.[40]

$$BrCH(COOC_2H_5)_2 + H_2NNH_2 \longrightarrow H_2C(COOC_2H_5)_2 + N_2 + HBr$$

N-Chlorosuccinimide is also reduced with hydrazine to succinimide with the elimination of hydrogen chloride.

Olefin oxides react with hydrazine to give hydroxyalkylhydrazines. Thus ethylene oxide gives hydroxyethylhydrazine, $HOCH_2CH_2NHNH_2$, or dihydroxyethylhydrazine, $(HOCH_2CH_2)_2NNH_2$.[41,42] Gever[43] has prepared 1-hydrazino-2-propanol, 1-hydrazino-2-butanol, 1-hydrazino-2-hexanol and 3-hydrazino-2-butanol from the corresponding olefin oxides.

Hydrazine alcohols can also be obtained from hydrazine hydrate and chlorohydrins. When 1-chloro-2-propanol and hydrazine were heated in the presence of sodium hydroxide at 95–100°C, 1-hydrazino-2-propanol was obtained exclusively. However under the same conditions 2-chloro-1-propanol also gave only 1-hydrazino-2-propanol indicating that the reaction probably proceeded through the epoxide. At 28°C, with no sodium hydroxide present, both isomers were obtained suggesting that in addition to intermediate epoxide formation, some direct substitution occurred.

Alkyl hydrazines are oxidized with ferric, cobaltic, manganic or ceric ions to the corresponding hydrocarbon with formation of nitrogen and water. Thus cyclohexylhydrazine is converted to cyclohexane with potassium ferricyanide.[44]

$$C_6H_{11}NHNH_2 \xrightarrow{(O)} C_6H_{12} + N_2 + H_2O$$

Oxidation of unsymmetrically disubstituted hydrazines gives symmetrical tetrazenes.

$$2R_2NNH_2 \longrightarrow R_2N-N=N-NR_2$$

The best oxidizing agent is reported to be azodicarboxylic ester which is reduced to the hydrazo ester. These tetrazenes are converted, by loss of nitrogen at 120–140°C into tetrasubstituted hydrazines.[8]

Symmetrically disubstituted hydrazines are oxidized in good yield to the corresponding azo compound. Thus diheptylhydrazine is oxidized with mercuric oxide to azoheptane in 80 per cent yield.[45,46] Air or iodine may also be used as oxodizing agents.

Hydrazine condenses with most aldehydes in the cold to form aldehyde hydrazones which react more rapidly with aldehydes than does hydrazine itself so that further reaction occurs to give the corresponding azine.

$$RCHO + H_2NNH_2 \longrightarrow RCH=NNH_2 \xrightarrow{RCHO} RCH=N-N=CHR$$

The azine can also be obtained from the hydrazone

$$2RCH=NNH_2 \longrightarrow RCH=N-N=CHR + H_2NNH_2$$

This reaction is reversible. Similar reactions occur with ketones except that the azines are much more difficult to prepare.[8,37]

Oxidation of hydrazones of both aldehydes and ketones occurs very readily to give diazo compounds. Thus oxidation of benzophenone hydrazone with mercuric oxide in cold petroleum ether gives a 90 per cent yield of diazophenyl methane, $(C_6H_5)_2CN_2$.[47]

The double bond in hydrazones is surprisingly difficult to reduce but catalytic hydrogenation or reduction with sodium amalgam in acetic acid gives a mixture of amines.[48]

$$C_6H_5NHN=CHCH_3 + 2H_2 \xrightarrow{Ni} C_6H_5NH_2 + CH_3CH_2NH_2$$

Nitrogen is eliminated from many hydrazones with or without the aid of a catalyst to give the corresponding hydrocarbon. Catalysts most frequently used are solid potassium hydroxide[44,45] and sodium ethoxide.[49,50,51] This reaction is frequently used to convert aliphatic, aromatic, or alicyclic ketones to the corresponding hydrocarbons.

The phenylhydrazone of methyl ethyl ketone heated in the presence of a cation exchange resin (hydrogen form) gives α,β-dimethylindole.[52] A yield of 75–80 per cent is obtained in anhydrous ethanol in 2.5 to 3.5 hours.

HYDRAZIDES

Hydrazides are formed in much the same way as amides. Methyl or ethyl esters are treated with 85 per cent hydrazine.

$$RCOOCH_3 + H_2NNH_2 \longrightarrow RCONHNH_2 + CH_3OH$$

The reactions usually take place at room temperature but some times it is necessary to heat on a water bath. In some cases, in order to insure solubility, it is necessary to use an organic solvent.

Acid chlorides can be used in place of esters but in general the results are not as satisfactory. However in some cases, where the ester is particularly unreactive, it is necessary to use the acid chloride.

Acid anhydrides frequently give cyclic hydrazides.

Amides may also react with hydrazine but the reactions are much more difficult than with esters. Yields of hydrazides from amides of greater than 70 per cent have been reported.[53] This reaction is also reversible.

Hydrazides can be obtained by heating the fused hydrazine salts of organic acids but the method is not used very often.[54,55]

Aryl substituted hydrazides can be obtained by the action of the free hydrazine with acids.[56]

$$C_6H_5NHNH_2 + RCOOH \longrightarrow RCONHNHC_6H_5 + H_2O$$

Many acids, particularly acids obtained from sugars, react so readily that it is only necessary to heat them with an aqueous solution of the hydrazinc acetate.

Acid anhydrides react with hydrazo compounds ($C_6H_5NHNHC_6H_5$) to give a diacylated product.[57,58]

Hydrazides have been suggested as suitable derivatives for the identification of acids. Isonicotinic acid hydrazide (isoniazid) has been reported to have therapeutic activity in the treatment of tuberculosis.

A compound made by the reaction of isonicotinoyl hydrazide and cinnamaldehyde (1-isonicotinoyl-2-cinnamylidene hydrazine) is also reported to be an effective therapeutic agent for the treatment of tuberculosis.[59]

Carboxylic acid hydrazides are cleaved by Raney nickel to give amides and ammonia. Thus an ethanol solution of the hydrazide is refluxed for several hours with a relatively large amount of moist Raney nickel.[60] The amides are obtained in 60–80 per cent yield.

Some primary hydrazides, when heated, form diacyl hydrazides with loss of hydrazine.[8,61] In many cases water is eliminated and N-aminotriazoles are obtained.

$$2RCONHNH_2 \longrightarrow R-C\underset{\displaystyle \underset{NH_2}{\overset{|}{N}}}{\overset{\displaystyle \overset{N=N}{}}{\diamond}}C-R + 2H_2O$$

Consequently it is very difficult to purify hydrazides by distillation.

Hydrazides react readily with aldehydes and ketones to form hydrazidehydrazones, $R-CO-NH-N=CHR'$.

Hydrazides containing a quaternary ammonium group in the acid part of the molecule, e.g., trimethylacethydrazide hydrochloride or acethydrazide pyridinium chloride, are known as Girard's reagents. These compounds form water-soluble derivatives of ketones and have been of special importance in the isolation of natural hormones containing the carbonyl group.[64] The ketone can be recovered by hydrolysis.

$$(CH_3)_3N(Cl)-CH_2CONHNH_2 + R_2CO \longrightarrow$$

$$(CH_3)_3N(Cl)CH_2CONHN=CR_2 + H_2O$$

Hydrazides react with nitrous acid in the cold to give acid azides.

$$RCONHNH_2 + HNO_2 \longrightarrow RCON_3 + H_2O$$

Decomposition of the azides give isocyanates.

$$RCON_3 \longrightarrow RNCO + N_2$$

Alkaline hydrolysis of the isocyanate gives an amine having one fewer carbon atom than the starting acid.[65] The reaction serves as an effective method for the preparation of isocyanates and for decreasing the length of the carbon chain.

Semicarbazides

Semicarbazide is obtained by the action of hydrazine hydrate with urea in amyl alcohol solution.[66]

$$H_2NCONH_2 + H_2NNH_2 \longrightarrow H_2NNHCONH_2 + NH_3$$

Semicarbazide can also be prepared from potassium cyanate and hydrazine hydrochloride. Hydrazine cyanate is first formed which isomerizes to the semicarbazide.

$$KCNO + H_2NNH_3{}^+Cl^- \longrightarrow H_2NNH_3{}^+CNO^- + KCl$$

$$H_2NNH_3{}^+CNO^- \longrightarrow H_2NCONHNH_2$$

The reaction takes place at room temperature.[67] Thiosemicarbazide is prepared in a similar manner, starting with potassium thiocyanate.

Alkyl or aryl isocyanates react with hydrazine to give 4-substituted semicarbizides.[37]

$$RNCO + H_2NNH_2 \longrightarrow H_2NNHCONHR$$

Semicarbazide has the properties of a hydrazide and in some cases it behaves as a hydrazine. Aqueous solutions of semicarbazide are neutral but the compound forms salts with strong acids. It reduces Fehling's solution and Tollen's reagent.

Semicarbazides react very much like hydrazines with halogen compounds, esters, aldehydes and ketones. Semicarbazones formed from aldehydes and ketones are useful for identification purposes.

Semicarbazide reacts with nitrous acid to give an azide which is cyclized to tetrazole.[37]

$$H_2NCONHNH_2 + HNO_2 \longrightarrow H_2NCON_3 + 2H_2O$$

$$H_2NCON_3 \longrightarrow HO-C{\overset{\nearrow NH-N}{\underset{\searrow N-N}{}}}\Vert$$

Aromatic amines form symmetrical diaryl ureas. A 4-substituted semicarbazide is formed as an intermediate.[68,69]

$$C_6H_5NH_2 + H_2NNHCONH_2 \xrightarrow{-NH_3} H_2NNHCONHC_6H_5 \rightarrow$$

$$C_6H_5NHCONHC_6H_5 + H_2NNH_2$$

beta-Keto esters form pyrazolone derivatives with semicarbazide.[70,71] Thus ethyl acetoacetate gives methylpyrazolone.

$$CH_3-COCH_2-COOC_2H_5 + H_2NNHCONH_2 \rightarrow$$

Semicarbazones are reduced by sodium amalgam to substituted carbazides.

$$R_2C=NNHCONH_2 \rightarrow R_2CHNHNHCONH_2$$

Aromatic amines react to give 4-substituted semicarbazones which can be hydrolyzed to the corresponding carbazides.[72]

$$R_2C=NNHCONH_2 + C_6H_5NH_2 \rightarrow R_2C=NNHCONHC_6H_5 + NH_3$$

$$R_2C=NNHCONHC_6H_5 + H_2O \rightarrow R_2CO + H_2NNHCONHC_6H_5$$

The reaction is also effective with primary and secondary alkyl amines.[73]

HYDRAZOBENZENES

The preparation of hydrazobenzene has been described previously. The most important method is the selective reduction of aromatic nitro compounds.

Hydrazobenzenes do not form salts with acids but the imino hydrogen atoms can be replaced by metals. Vigorous reduction gives amines and mild oxidizing agents such as air or ferric chloride give the corresponding azo compounds.

Heating hydrazobenzenes causes a disproportionation into an azo compound and an amine.[74]

$$2C_6H_5NHNHC_6H_5 \longrightarrow C_6H_5N{=}N{-}C_6H_5 + 2C_6H_5NH_2$$

This disproportionation may occur even at room temperature if given sufficient time.

Tetraarylhydrazines are crystalline solids which can be kept for some time in the dark but decompose quite rapidly in solution to give free radicals.[75,76]

$$(C_6H_5)_2N{-}N(C_6H_5)_2 \rightleftarrows 2(C_6H_5)_2N \cdot$$

Mineral acids such as hydrochloric acid cause a rearrangement to give diaminobiphenyls. Thus hydrazobenzene gives benzidine and the rearrangement is usually referred to as the benzidine rearrangement.

$$C_6H_5NHNHC_6H_5 + 2HCl \longrightarrow Cl^-H_3N^+{-}C_6H_4{-}C_6H_4{-}NH_3^+Cl^- \xrightarrow{OH^-}$$

$$H_2N{-}C_6H_4{-}C_6H_4{-}NH_2$$

If the *para* position in the ring is blocked, the product is an aminodiphenylamine (Semidine rearrangement).

If both *para* positions are blocked, rearrangement may occur at the *ortho* position. This is particularly true if the rearrangement is promoted by stannous chloride and hydrochloric acid.

Yamada, Chibata, and Tsurui[77] found that in many cases ion exchange resins were superior catalysts to sulfuric or hydrochloric acid in the rearrangement of substituted hydrazobenzenes.

AZOXY COMPOUNDS

Aromatic azoxy compounds are prepared by the reduction of aromatic nitro compounds. Sodium or potassium alkoxides in alcohol solution are usually used as the reducing agents.[78,79]

$$4C_6H_5NO_2 + 3CH_3ONa \longrightarrow 2C_6H_5NO{=}NC_6H_5 + 3HCOONa + H_2O$$

At low temperatures, aldehydes rather than acid salts are obtained. Ethoxides are somewhat more reactive than methoxides. The reduction probably proceeds through intermediate nitroso compounds and hydroxylamines which condense to form the azoxy compound

$$C_6H_5NO + HONHC_6H_5 \longrightarrow C_6H_5NO{=}NC_6H_5 + H_2O$$

Substituents on the ring, such as methyl or hydroxyl, decrease the rate of reaction while carboxyl groups increase the rate.[80]

In many cases, alcoholic sodium hydroxide can be used to reduce nitro to azoxy compounds. The reaction takes place at reflux temperatures.[57,81] Alkaline solutions of sodium arsenate are also effective reducing agents.[82,83,84]

$$4C_6H_5NO_2 + 6Na_3AsO_3 \longrightarrow 2C_6H_5NO{=}NC_6H_5 + 6Na_3AsO_4$$

Other reducing agents which have been used include alkaline sodium stannite,[85] zinc dust and alcoholic sodium hydroxide,[86] ferrous sulfate and sodium hydroxide[87] and lithium aluminum hydride in ether solution.[88]

Azoxy compounds are for the most part crystalline solids and cannot be distilled without decomposition. They are not attacked by bases or dilute acids and are resistant to oxidation unless a hydroxyl or amino group is present on the benzene ring. Many azoxy compounds have been separated into optical isomers.[89] When heated with iron filings, reduction to the corresponding azo compound is accomplished.[90]

When azoxy compounds are heated in concentrated sulfuric acid, rearrangement occurs to give hydroxy azo compounds (Wallach transformation.[91,92,93,94,95]

$$C_6H_5NO{=}NC_6H_5 \longrightarrow HOC_6H_4{-}N{=}N{-}C_6H_5$$

AZO COMPOUNDS

As previously described, azo compounds are obtained by heating azoxy compounds with iron filings. Azo compounds can also be obtained by direct reduction of aromatic nitro compounds with zinc dust and alcoholic sodium hydroxide.[96,97] Small amounts of hydrazo compounds are also formed. Commercially, iron and aqueous sodium hydroxide are used. The reaction is not satisfactory for nitro compounds having substituents on the benzene ring.

Other reducing agents, which may be used for the preparation of azo compounds from aromatic nitro compounds, include sodium stannite,[85] sodium amalgam and stannous oxide, sodium arsenite,[98] and lithium aluminum hydride.[88,99]

Azo compounds can be made by the oxidation of hydrazobenzenes and by the oxidation of primary amines.[100,101] Aromatic hydrazines may be oxidized to azo compounds with air in the presence of sodium hydroxide or by sodium hypobromite.[22] Azomethane ($CH_3N{=}NCH_3$) has been prepared in 70 per cent yield by the oxidation of sym-dimethylhydrazine with cupric chloride.[102]

Suitable oxidizing agents for the oxidation of amines include per-acids, potassium permanganate, potassium ferricyanide in alkaline solution and sodium hypochlorite.

$$2(CH_3)_3C_6H_2NH_2 \xrightarrow{(O)} (CH_3)_3C_6H_2{-}N{=}N{-}C_6H_2(CH_3)_3$$

Aromatic azo compounds are obtained by the reaction of aromatic amines with nitro compounds in the presence of powdered sodium or potassium hydroxides at 180–200°C.[103]

Azo nitriles, useful as polymerization catalysts, are prepared by treating a ketone with a β-hydroxyalkylhydrazine to give a hydrazone which, in the presence of a cyanide, forms a hydrazonitrile. Thus equimolar amounts of 2-hydroxyethylhydrazine and methyl isobutyl ketone are heated for 90 minutes at 50–52°C and then permitted to stand at room temperature for 16 hours. The hydrazone is recovered by distillation and after cooling to 0°C, excess hydrogen cyanide is added to give the hydrazonitrile which is then treated with chlorine for 90 minutes at 0°C in acetic acid-ethylene dichloride solution. After neutralization with sodium bisulfite, 2-(2'-hydroxyethylazo)-2,4-dimethylvaleronitrile is obtained in 40 per cent yield.[104]

Aliphatic azo compounds suitable as polymerization initiators have been prepared by Anderson.[105] Thus $NC{-}C(CH_3)_2{-}CN$ may be converted to $H_2N{-}C(CH_3)_2{-}CN$ by the action of sodium hypochlorite in a water-ice mixture. After 8–10 minutes the azo compound, which precipitates as formed, is removed by filtration, washed with water and dried in vacuo.

2,2'-Azoisobutane, $(CH_3)_3C{-}N{=}N{-}C(CH_3)_3$, is obtained from *tert.*-butylamine by bromination with potassium hypobromite and treating the resulting N-bromo-*tert*-butylamine with silver oxide.

$$(CH_3)_3CNH_2 + KOBr \longrightarrow (CH_3)_3CNHBr + KOH$$

$$2(CH_3)_3CNHBr \xrightarrow{Ag_2O} (CH_3)_3C{-}N{=}N{-}C(CH_3)_3$$

The 2,2'-azoisobutane undergoes thermal decomposition to give tertiary-butyl free radicals.[106]

$$(CH_3)_3C-N=N-C(CH_3)_3 \rightarrow 2(CH_3)_3C. + N_2$$

Aromatic azo compounds can also be prepared by the reaction of nitroso compounds with amines.

$$C_6H_5NO + C_6H_5NH_2 \rightarrow C_6H_5-N=N-C_6H_5$$

Thus aniline condenses with nitrosobenzene in acetic acid to give quantitative yields of azobenzene.[107]

In a similar manner nitrosobenzene has been condensed with *o*-methoxyaniline,[108] *p*-aminobenzoic acid,[109] and *m*-nitroaniline[110] to form the corresponding azobenzenes.

o-Nitrosonitrobenzene (o-ON—C_6H_4—NO_2) and *m*-nitroaniline in acetic acid at 15–20°C for 16 hours gives a 77 per cent yield of 2,3'-dinitroazobenzene. *ortho*- and *para*-Nitroanilines do not behave similarly.[111]

Azo compounds exist in *cis* and *trans* forms. The *trans* may be changed to the *cis* form by irradiation.

Aromatic azo compounds are very stable and can be nitrated, brominated or sulfonated without decomposition.

Reducing agents give hydrazobenzenes and amines.

Benzene reacts with azobenzene in the presence of aluminum chloride to give 4-aminobiphenyl

$$C_6H_5-N=N-C_6H_5 + 2C_6H_6 \rightarrow 2C_6H_5C_6H_4NH_2$$

This reaction must be carried out at low temperatures and permits the introduction of a $-C_6H_4NH_2$ group into a benzene ring.

Diazomethane

Diazomethane, CH_2N_2, is a yellow highly toxic gas which is very explosive in the vapor state. Ether solutions can be handled safely at room temperature or below with a reasonable amount of caution.

An ethereal solution of diazomethane can be prepared at 0°C from N-nitrosomethylurea and the solution can be used without purification.[112] The preparation may be carried out as follows: To a mixture of ether and 40 per cent aqueous potassium hydroxide is added N-nitrosomethyl urea in small portions. The diazomethane remains in the ether solution which can be separated and after drying is used as needed. Solutions of diazomethane in benzene can be prepared similarly.

Diazomethane can also be prepared by the decomposition of N-nitroso-methylurethane with sodium alkoxides.[113] Diazomethane made in this way usually must be purified by distillation.

A very convenient method for the preparation of diazomethane from *p*-tolylsulfonylmethylnitrosamide has been described.[114] The method has the advantage that the nitrosoamide can be prepared and stored indefinitely until diazomethane is needed and can then be obtained by a simple hydrolysis.

Diazomethane is formed from *p*-toluenesulfonyl chloride by this method in three steps.

1. The sulfonyl chloride is converted to the sulfonylmethylamide by reaction with methylamine.

$$p\text{-}CH_3\text{---}C_6H_4\text{---}SO_2Cl + CH_3NH_2 \longrightarrow p\text{-}CH_3\text{---}C_6H_4\text{---}SO_2NHCH_3$$

2. The methylsulfonamide reacts with nitrous acid to give *p*-tolylsulfonylmethylnitrosoamide.

$$p\text{-}CH_3C_6H_4SO_2NHCH_3 + HONO \longrightarrow p\text{-}CH_3C_6H_4SO_2N(NO)CH_3$$

The nitrosoamide is a very stable nontoxic compound which can be kept for years at room temperature in a dark bottle without decomposition.

3. The nitrosoamide is hydrolyzed with either aqueous or alcoholic sodium hydroxide. Distillation gives an ethereal solution of diazomethane in 80–90 per cent yield.

An anhydrous ethereal solution of nitrosyl chloride reacts with an excess of methylamine at –80°C to give diazomethane.[115]

Reactions of Diazomethane. Diazomethane is an excellent methylating agent for acids, converting the acids into the corresponding methyl esters.

$$RCOOH + CH_2N_2 \longrightarrow RCOOCH_3 + N_2$$

These reactions take place smoothly at low temperatures and the reaction is usually complete in less than one minute. Phenols react much less readily and alcohols are not attacked. Water reacts very easily with the formation of methanol and nitrogen.[116] Aliphatic amino and imino groups do not react with diazomethane but aryl amines are frequently monomethylated.

If a carbon atom has attached to it three strongly electronegative groups and a hydrogen atom, diazomethane can convert the hydrogen to a methyl group.

The rate of methylation with diazomethane depends upon the acidity of the groups being methylated so that carboxyl groups can be selectively methylated in the presence of phenolic hydroxyl groups or alcohols.

The mechanism for the reaction of diazomethane with active hydrogen compounds is believed to involve:

1. The formation of a proton bridge between the active hydrogen compound and diazomethane:

$$R—COOH + CH_2N_2 \longrightarrow R—COOH\text{--}CH_2—N_2$$

2. Elimination of nitrogen

$$R—COOH\text{--}CH_2—N_2 \longrightarrow RCOOH—CH_2 + N_2$$

3. Rearrangement of the resulting radical

$$R—COOH—CH_2 \longrightarrow R—COOCH_3$$

In many cases aldehydes are converted into methyl ketones[117,118] by the action of diazomethane. In other cases an aldehyde containing an additional methylene group is obtained. If the carbonyl group is adjacent to a strongly electronegative group such as —CCl$_3$, or —COOR, an epoxide is formed. All three products can be obtained through a common intermediate.

Diazomethane adds to some carbon-carbon double bonds to give pyrazoline derivatives. Thus ethylene and diazomethane give pyrazoline.[119]

This reaction is not too general but is more common with diazoacetic ester. However, diazomethane adds to butadiene in the 1,2-position; the presence of an electronegative group such as CO or COOR increases the ease of addition.

Diazomethane can be used to convert an acid to its next higher homolog by way of the acid chloride.[120] This reaction, called the Arndt-Eistart reaction, is carried out in three steps:

1. The acid is converted to an acid chloride.
2. The acid chloride reacts with diazomethane to give a diazoketone

$$RCOCl + 2CH_2N_2 \longrightarrow RCO-CH_2N_2 + CH_3Cl + N_2$$

3. The diazoketone reacts with water in the presence of colloidal silver, platinum or copper.

$$R-CO-CH_2N_2 \xrightarrow{-N_2} [RCO-CH<] \xrightarrow{\sim R} [RCH=C=O] \xrightarrow{H_2O} RCH_2COOH$$

Loss of nitrogen gives an intermediate which undergoes rearrangement to a ketene and the acid is formed by addition of water. Over-all yields range from 50–80 per cent.

The diazoketones are formed at low temperatures and isolated by evaporation of the solvent at temperatures of 20–30°C. The rearrangement is effected using silver oxide in dioxane at temperatures of 60–70°C.

The method is of special importance in working in the field of steroids and other complex molecules.

The diazoketones react with other active hydrogen compounds. Thus alcohols give esters, and amines or ammonia give amides.

$$RCOCH_2N_2 + R'OH \longrightarrow RCH_2COOR' + N_2$$

$$RCOCH_2N_2 + NH_3 \longrightarrow RCH_2CONH_2 + N_2$$

$$RCOCH_2N_2 + R'NH_2 \longrightarrow RCH_2CONHR' + N_2$$

Mercury halides react with diazomethane with the formation of a halomethylmercuric halide. Thus when a cold solution of mercuric chloride in diethyl ether is treated with one equivalent of diazomethane, chloromethyl mercuric chloride is obtained in quantitative yield.[121]

$$HgCl_2 + CH_2N_2 \longrightarrow ClCH_2HgCl + N_2$$

If two equivalents of diazomethane are used, bis(chloromethyl)mercury is obtained.

$$HgCl_2 + 2CH_2N_2 \longrightarrow (ClCH_2)_2Hg + 2N_2$$

When alcohol is used as a solvent in place of ether, the mercuric chloride is reduced to metallic mercury.[122]

p-Tolylmercuric chloride is apparently converted to p-tolyl(chloromethyl) mercury on heating with diazomethane in ether solution but this compound rapidly disproportionates to give di-p-tolylmercury which precipitates and bis(chloromethyl)mercury which remains in solution.

$$p\text{-}CH_3C_6H_4HgCl + CH_2N_2 \longrightarrow p\text{-}CH_3C_6H_4HgCH_2Cl + N_2$$

$$2p\text{-}CH_3C_6H_4HgCH_2Cl \longrightarrow (p\text{-}CH_3C_6H_4)_2Hg + (ClCH_2)_2Hg$$

Diazomethane, with a large excess of phenylmagnesium bromide, gives benzylphenylhydrazine, probably, by the following sequence of reactions.[123]

$$CH_2N_2 + C_6H_5MgBr \longrightarrow CH_2\!=\!N\!-\!N\!\!\begin{array}{c} C_6H_5 \\[2pt] \diagup\diagdown \\[-2pt] MgBr \end{array} \xrightarrow{C_6H_5MgBr}$$

$$\underset{\underset{MgBr}{|}}{C_6H_5CH_2\!-\!N}\!\!-\!\!\!\underset{\underset{MgBr}{|}}{N\!-\!C_6H_5} \xrightarrow{2H_2O} C_6H_5CH_2NHNHC_6H_5 + 2Mg(OH)Br$$

Diazomethane can be decomposed in the presence of certain boron compounds to give a high molecular weight polymethylene. Diazomethane is decomposed with copper or copper salts to give polyethylidene. Polymerization of diazoethane using a gold chloride catalyst gives a crystalline solid, melting at 195–200°C which appears to have a skeleton chain of carbon atoms of a regular steric arrangement.[124,125]

Ethyl diazoacetate ($N_2CH_2COOC_2H_5$) treated with hydroxylamine in aqueous pyridine at 40°C for several days gives a mixture of hydroxamic acids. One of the products identified is $HONH\!-\!CH_2\!-\!COOC_2H_5$.

Ethyl diazoacetate reacts with concentrated aqueous ammonia at 60–70°C in 10 hours to give $H_2NCH_2CONH_2$, H_2NCH_2COOH, HOOCCH $(NH_2)CH_2COOH$ and peptides of the latter two. Ethyl glycine is not obtained.[126]

ARYLDIAZONIUM SALTS

Primary arylamines react with nitrous acid to form diazonium salts. These salts have the structure $C_6H_5\!-\!\overset{+}{N}\!\!\equiv\!\!N\ Cl^-$ in acid solution, but as the pH is increased the quaternary ammonium hydroxide which might be expected to form undergoes an electronic rearrangement to give a diazo hydroxide which is amphoteric and consequently forms diazotate salts with strong bases. An equilibrium among three forms therefore exists which is dependent upon pH

$$C_6H_5-\overset{+}{N}\equiv N \ Cl^- \underset{HCl}{\overset{NaOH}{\rightleftharpoons}} C_6H_5-N=N-OH \underset{HCl}{\overset{NaOH}{\rightleftharpoons}} C_6H_5-N=N-O^-Na^+$$

The diazohydroxide exists as *cis* and *trans* isomers

$$\begin{array}{ccc} C_6H_5-N & & C_6H_5-N \\ \| & \text{and} & \| \\ N-OH & & HO-N \\ \textit{trans} & & \textit{cis} \end{array}$$

Diazonium salts are prepared essentially by two methods. If the primary arylamine is soluble in dilute acids, the solution of the amine salt is treated with aqueous sodium nitrite at temperatures near 0°C. If the amine contains acid groups, the procedure is usually reversed in that a solution of the amine in aqueous sodium hydroxide containing the required amount of sodium nitrite is added to the acid.

Solid diazo compounds can frequently be prepared by treating a solution or suspension of the amine salt in an inert solvent with amyl nitrite or nitrosyl chloride. The diazo compound precipitates from solution as formed.

In the direct method for the diazotization of amines, sodium nitrite is added rapidly to a cooled solution of the amine salt in water. If the amine salt is not completely soluble a suspension is prepared by dissolving the amine salt in hot water and cooling the solution rapidly.[127] In general about 2.5 times the theoretical amount of acid required to form the amine salt is used. Excess nitrous acid must be removed by the addition of urea or sulfamic acid.[128]

The optimum temperature for diazotization is 0–5°C for simple amines and *meta*-halogenated amines and 10–22°C for benzidine, naphthylamines, or *ortho*- or *para*-halogenated amines. In some cases higher temperatures are used. Thus temperatures of 35–40°C may be used with *meta*- and *para*-nitroaniline, *ortho*- and *para*-chloroaniline and *ortho*-anisidine. *o*-Nitroaniline has been diazotized at 58°C.[129]

This method is satisfactory for the diazotization of amines that dissolve readily in dilute hydrochloric acid, or sulfonated anilines which are also soluble in dilute acid.

With amines of equal basicity the reaction proceeds most rapidly with compounds having *ortho*-substituents and is slowest for those having *meta*-substituents. Electronegative substituents tend to increase the rate of diazotization. The diazotization rate increases with the concentration of hydrochloric acid in the range 0.05 N and 4 N.[130]

Schmid[131] found that maximum diazotization rates for the reaction of nitrous acid with aromatic amines were obtained by using excess acid; about 3.5 to 6.5 moles per liter of solution in the case of hydrochloric acid and 6 to 9 moles per liter with sulfuric acid.

Diazotization in the presence of hydrobromic acid proceeds at about four times the rate observed with hydrochloric acid but sulfuric and nitric acids slow down the reaction.

In the method in which the amine, having an acid group, and sodium nitrite in aqueous sodium hydroxide are added to a solution of the appropriate acid, diazotization occurs immediately and the diazonium salt separates as a solid. Compounds diazotized in this way include sulfonic acids, aminobenzoic acids, anilinedisulfonic acids and naphthylaminesulfonic acids.

Weakly basic amines which are insoluble in dilute acids may be diazotized in concentrated sulfuric or phosphoric acids.[132,133,134] Nitrosylsulfuric acid which is the active diazotization agent is formed in solution by adding sodium nitrite or a concentrated aqueous solution of the salt to the sulfuric acid and after the reaction is complete, the mixture is poured onto ice.[135,136]

Arylamines may be diazotized by heating the amine salts with amyl nitrite in alcohol, glacial acetic acid or dioxane. The diazonium salt is precipitated by the addition of ether.[137,138,139] This method permits the isolation of dry diazonium salts.

When two or more amino groups are present on the benzene ring, diazotization of all of them is often very difficult. m-Phenylenediamine can be tetrazotized in glacial acetic acid with nitrosylsulfuric acid.[140,141] If activating substituents are present in the m-phenylenediamine molecule, tetrazotization may be accomplished in the normal way. The presence of a negative substituent frequently prevents diazotization of both amine groups in a diamine but the second group may be diazotized after coupling has occurred through the first one. A maximum of three diazo groups can exist on a benzene ring.[142,143]

The diazonium group can be introduced directly into the aromatic nucleus by reaction of the compound with excess nitrous acid and hydrochloric or other strong acid. Two reactions are involved; a nitroso compound is first formed which subsequently reacts with more nitrous acid and the hydrohalogen acid to give the diazonium salt. Except for phenols and tertiary amines the nitroso compound cannot be isolated.

Aromatic diazonium salts are inherently unstable.[144] In many cases decomposition occurs in water at temperatures above 5°C. Decomposition is promoted by light. The dry salts explode with violence when heated or when struck, but many form stable complexes with salts of alkaline earth and related metals, particularly with zinc salts.

An excess of nitrous acid decreases the stability of the diazo compound and metal ions such as iron or copper greatly accelerate the decomposition. In general the more basic the amine, the more unstable is the diazonium salt. The presence of negative substituents such as halogen, alkoxyl or nitro groups increases the stability.[145,146,147]

Diazonium salts which give essentially neutral water solutions are formed with all strong inorganic acids. The diazohydroxides are strong bases which can be titrated to a methyl orange end point. The free bases however, are not sufficiently stable to permit isolation in pure form. The metal salts of the diazohydroxides (sodium or potassium diazotates) can be isolated by salting out with an excess of strong base.[148,149]

Reactions of Diazonium Compounds

Diazonium halides are converted to diazocyanides by addition of an aqueous solution of an alkali cyanide to an acid solution of the diazonium salt.[150,151]

The diazocyanides exist as *cis* and *trans* isomers indicating their existence as $C_6H_5-N=N-CN$. The *cis* form is obtained in the cold and is gradually converted to the *trans* form when warmed. This isomerization occurs quite rapidly in alcohol solution.

Metal sulfites in neutral or slightly alkaline solution form diazosulfonates ($C_6H_5N_2SO_3Na$). The sulfite must be in slight excess and the solution should be as concentrated as possible.

Aryldiazonium salts react with primary and secondary arylamines to form diazoamines.

$$C_6H_5N_2Cl + C_6H_5NH_2 \longrightarrow C_6H_5-N=N-NHC_6H_5 + HCl$$

The reaction is accomplished by mixing an aqueous solution of the diazonium salt with an aqueous solution of the arylammonium chloride and adding sodium acetate to increase the pH. The same result may be obtained if one equivalent of sodium nitrite is added to a solution containing two equivalents of amine and one of acid.[152,153]

Primary aliphatic amines react with two molecules of aryldiazonium chloride to form bisdiazo compounds.[154] The formation of the monodiazo compound can be successfully accomplished by carrying out the reaction in water solution in the presence of ether. The monodiazo compound is extracted into the ether layer as fast as formed and so is not available for further reaction with the diazonium chloride which is ether insoluble. Bis-diazo compounds are formed with primary arylamines.

The diazoamino compounds in aqueous solutions are converted into the starting amine and diazonium compound when acidified.

Diazoamino compounds undergo slow molecular rearrangement to aminoazo compounds in the presence of arylammonium chlorides

$$C_6H_5-N=N-NHC_6H_5 \xrightarrow{C_6H_5NH_3Cl} C_6H_5-N=N-C_6H_4-NH_2(para)$$

Aromatic diazonium salts may be reduced to hydrazines with zinc dust and hydrochloric acid. Diazoamino compounds are reduced to hydrazines by zinc dust and acetic acid in alcohol solution[155]

$$C_6H_5-N=N-NHC_6H_5 \rightarrow C_6H_5NHNH_2 + C_6H_5NH_2$$

Aryldiazonium chlorides are converted into the corresponding hydro-carbons by heating with an alcohol.[156,157]

$$C_6H_5N_2Cl + C_2H_5OH \rightarrow C_6H_6 + N_2 + HCl + CH_3CHO$$

The alcohol serves as a gentle reducing agent and is itself oxidized to an aldehyde.

The reduction step in the conversion of the diazonium salt to the hydro-carbon with methanol is improved by irradiation of the mixture with ultra-violet light. Thus *p*-chlorobenzenediazonium chloride in ice-cooled methanol was irradiated with ultraviolet light in a nitrogen atmosphere until the evolution of nitrogen ceased. The methanol was removed by distillation and the residue steam distilled. Chlorobenzene was obtained in 60 per cent yield from an ether extract of the distillate.[158] Finely divided copper, cuprous oxide and zinc oxide have been used as promoters for the reaction but in some cases they may have an adverse effect.[159]

A competing reaction involves the formation of an ether[160]

$$C_6H_5N_2Cl + C_2H_5OH \rightarrow C_6H_5-O-C_2H_5 + N_2 + HCl$$

The tendency toward ether formation decreases with increase in molecular weight of the alcohol but is quite significant in the case of methanol. Polyhydric alcohols give ethers almost exclusively.[160,161]

The thermal decomposition of benzenediazonium chloride or benzene-diazonium fluoborate in methanol gives a 93 per cent yield of anisole under acidic conditions. In the presence of sodium acetate as a buffer, some anisole is formed, but the main product is benzene. A very small amount of biphenyl is also obtained.[162]

In general, electronegative substituents favor the replacement of the diazonium group with hydrogen. The effect is most marked with substituents in the *ortho*-position and least with *para*-substituents.[163,164]

A very effective method for the reduction of diazonium salts to hydrocarbons involves reaction with alkaline formaldehyde. The method cannot be used with diazonium compounds having halogen atoms substituted in the *ortho*- or *para*-positions or with other substituents which are attacked by strong bases. The procedure is considerably better with diazonium compounds having electropositive substituents than the one using ethyl alcohol as the reducing agent. Yields of reduction products from alkoxy- or aryloxy derivatives range from 50–75 per cent. *m*-Methylphenyldiazonium chloride is reduced to toluene in 80 per cent yield.[165]

Replacement of a diazonium group with hydrogen can also be accomplished with cuprous oxide in methanol,[166] stannous chloride,[167] alkaline sodium stannite,[168] and alkaline sodium sulfide.[169]

A diazonium group can be replaced with a hydroxyl group by the action of a dilute acid.

$$C_6H_5N_2Cl + HOH \xrightarrow{H_2SO_4} C_6H_5OH + N_2 + HCl$$

The reaction is usually accomplished by adding the cold solution of the diazonium salt to a hot solution of dilute sulfuric acid and removing the phenol as fast as formed by steam distillation. Amino and other electronegative groups interfere with the reaction.

Aromatic sulfides and disulfides are formed by heating diazonium salts in alcohol solutions of sodium or potassium sulfide[170,171] or by reactions with sodium mercaptides.[172,173]

$$C_6H_5N_2Cl + NaSC_6H_5 \longrightarrow (C_6H_5)_2S + NaCl + N_2$$

Busch and Schulz[173] prepared aryl alkyl sulfides by adding a cold solution of the alkali metal xanthate to a cold solution of the diazonium salt.

$$C_6H_5N_2Cl + C_2H_5OCSSK \longrightarrow C_6H_5SCSOC_2H_5 + N_2 + KCl$$

The aromatic xanthate is converted to the aryl mercaptan by treatment with a base.[174,175,176]

$$C_6H_5SCSOC_2H_5 + NaOH \longrightarrow C_6H_5SNa + C_2H_5OH + COS$$

and to an aryl alkyl sulfide by heating

$$C_6H_5SCSOC_2H_5 \rightarrow C_6H_5SC_2H_5 + COS$$

The replacement of a diazonium group by halogen may be accomplished by boiling the diazonium halide with a concentrated solution of the hydrogen halide.[177] In actual practice only the iodides are prepared in satisfactory yields by this method.

The first satisfactory method for the preparation of aryl chlorides from diazonium chlorides was reported by Sandmeyer.[178] The method was investigated by a large number of workers.[179,180,181,182,183,184]

Sandmeyer found that cuprous chloride had a catalytic effect on the decomposition of diazonium chlorides. The reaction involves the addition of the cold diazonium chloride solution to a solution of cuprous chloride in concentrated hydrochloric acid at such a rate that a rapid evolution of nitrogen occurs. A one-half molecular proportion of cuprous chloride is required for best results.

The same procedure can be used for the preparation of aryl bromides using cuprous bromide and hydrobromic acid.

It is possible to prepare an aryl bromide from the corresponding diazonium chloride or sulfate.[183]

The decomposition of a diazonium halide to the corresponding aryl halide is catalyzed by copper powder.[185,186]

The most satisfactory procedure for the preparation of aryl fluorides involves the thermal decomposition of diazonium fluoborates.[187,188]

$$C_6H_5N_2BF_4 \rightarrow C_6H_5F + BF_3 + N_2$$

The reaction may be carried out by diazotizing the aryl amine in the presence of fluoboric acid, HBF_4, and heating the resulting fluoborate with copper powder.[189] Another procedure involves the conversion of the diazonium chloride with fluoboric acid to an insoluble fluoborate which is isolated and thermally decomposed.[190]

The replacement of a diazonium group by cyanide is readily accomplished by the action of cuprous cyanide. With this method, *ortho-* and *para-*tolunitriles are prepared in 65–70 per cent yield.[191] The diazonium group may also be replaced by a cyano group by heating a solution of the diazonium salt with cuprous cyanide and sodium or potassium cyanide.[178,192] The pH must be maintained at a value slightly more than 7 by the addition of sodium bicarbonate to prevent the escape of hydrogen cyanide. The temperature is usually held below 50°C.

$$C_6H_5N_2Cl + KCN \cdot CuCN \longrightarrow C_6H_5CN + KCl + CuCN + N_2$$

In an alternate procedure the diazonium chloride is treated with an alkali metal cyanide in the presence of finely divided copper.[185,193]

Conversion of a diazonium salt to a sulfonic acid can be accomplished by passing sulfur dioxide into a solution of a diazonium sulfate and heating in the presence of copper powder. As an alternate procedure the diazonium sulfate may be treated with an alcoholic solution of sulfur dioxide and sodium bisulfite followed by decomposition of the diazonium compound with copper powder.[185,194]

Replacement by a nitro group was accomplished by Sandmeyer by adding freshly precipitated cuprous oxide to a solution of the diazonium nitrite containing excess nitrous acid.[192,195]

Aromatic diazonium salts decompose to form nitro compounds in the presence of excess sodium nitrite and copper powder. *Ortho-* and *para-*dinitrobenzenes have been prepared by this method from the diazonium sulfates in about 75 per cent yield.[196]

Sometimes the diazonium fluoborate is first prepared and treated with sodium nitrite in the presence of copper powder

$$C_6H_5N_2BF_4 + NaNO_2 \xrightarrow{Cu} C_6H_5NO_2 + N_2 + NaBF_4$$

p-Dinitrobenzene has been obtained from *p*-nitroaniline in 82 per cent yield in this way.[197]

Diazonium salts react with some unsaturated compounds by addition accompanied by loss of nitrogen. Thus diazonium chlorides react with methyl vinyl ketone in aqueous acetone in the presence of cuprous chloride and hydrochloric acid. Benzenediazonium chloride and methyl vinyl ketone give $C_6H_5CH_2CHCl$—CO—CH_3 in 18 per cent yield. *p*-Nitrophenyldiazonium chloride gives *p*-O_2N—C_6H_4—CH_2CHCl—$COCH_3$ in 41 per cent yield.[198]

Benzenediazonium chloride adds at 5°C to acrylonitrile in acetone containing cuprous chloride and sodium acetate. The reaction is stopped, after evolution of nitrogen has ceased, to give a 35 per cent yield of chlorobenzene and a 43 per cent yield of $C_6H_5CH_2CHCl$—CN.

Acrylonitrile and *p*-nitrobenzenediazonium chloride give a 96 per cent yield of *p*-O_2N—C_6H_4—CH_2CHCl—CN. Chlorides of tin, cobalt, manganese, nickel, cadmium, zinc and aluminum do not catalyze the reaction.[199]

The reaction of a diazonium salt at the double bond of a vinyl ether is illustrated by the following procedure. The diazonium salt of *p*-nitroaniline in hydrochloric acid is neutralized to congo red with sodium acetate and treated with ethyl vinyl ether in an ice bath. After standing over night a precipitate of glyoxal-*p*-nitrophenylhydrazone (85 per cent yield) is obtained. Refluxing with hydrogen chloride in methanol for one hour produces the corresponding osazone. Methyl- and butyl vinyl ether give the same products in 91 per cent yield.[200]

The addition of diazomethane to cooled solutions of some diazonium salts in methanol results in the formation of hydrazine derivatives. Thus the following reaction occurs with *p*-nitrobenzenediazonium chloride

$$p\text{-}O_2N\text{---}C_6H_4\text{---}N_2Cl + CH_2N_2 \longrightarrow p\text{-}O_2N\text{---}C_6H_4\text{---}NH\text{---}N\text{==}CHCl + N_2$$

Yields are about 95 per cent.

If the diazonium salt is added to an excess of diazomethane more than one mole of diazomethane reacts but the structure of the product has not been determined.[201]

Diazonium salts react with formaldoxime in aqueous solution at a pH of 5.5–6.0 in the presence of a cupric sulfate-sodium sulfite catalyst to give aldehydes

$$C_6H_5N_2Cl + H_2C\text{==}NOH \longrightarrow C_6H_5\text{---}CH\text{==}NOH \xrightarrow[H^+]{H_2O} C_6H_5CHO$$

Yields of aldehydes range from about 30 to 60 per cent as indicated in Table 4–1. If oximes of other aldehydes are used, ketones are formed. This represents a convenient method for making aromatic aldehydes and some ketones from aromatic amines.[202]

TABLE 4–1. YIELDS OF ALDEHYDES AND KETONES FROM DIAZONIUM SALTS.

	Yield %		Yield %
Benzaldehyde	40	*p*-Anisaldehyde	42
o-Tolualdehyde	46	*o*-Chloroacetophenone	43
o-Chlorobenzaldehyde	52	*p*-Chloroacetophenone	30
p-Chlorobenzaldehyde	60	*m*-Chloroacetophenone	40
o-Nitrobenzaldehyde	33		

Diazonium compounds are capable of reaction with a number of substituted aromatic hydrocarbons without loss of nitrogen. Thus benzenediazonium chloride reacts with phenol to give an azo compound.

$$C_6H_5N_2Cl + C_6H_5OH \longrightarrow p\text{-}HOC_6H_4\text{---}N\text{==}N\text{---}C_6H_5 + HCl$$

This reaction is referred to as coupling. The products are all colored and if suitable auxochrome groups are present they may be used as dyes.

Coupling reactions of this type are very dependant upon the pH and in most cases will occur only near the neutral point. The presence of electronegative substituents on the diazotized amine increases the ability of the diazonium compound to undergo coupling reactions and permits coupling to occur in more acid solutions.

The types of compounds which readily undergo coupling reactions with diazonium salts are (1) phenols and naphthols, (2) aromatic amines, (3) naphthylamine- and aminonaphthol sulfonic acids, (4) compounds containing reactive methylene groups. In addition, phenol ethers and some hydrocarbons may react under very exceptional conditions.

The active coupling agent is the diazohydroxide rather than the diazonium salt.[203] Therefore the pH must be adjusted so that a sufficient concentration of the diazohydroxide is present to make coupling occur. Aromatic amines undergo coupling in the pH range of 3.5–7.0 and phenols from pH 5.0–9.0. This is the pH region in which diazonium compounds are least stable so that a competition exists between decomposition and coupling.

As the number of electronegative substituents is increased, coupling reactions will take place under more acid conditions indicating that such groups displace the equilibrium towards higher concentrations of the diazohydroxides.

Coupling reactions with phenols occur largely at the *para* position although small amounts of the *ortho* compounds are usually formed also. If the *para* position is blocked, reaction occurs exclusively at the *ortho* position. Negative substituents on the phenol or naphthol molecule increases the difficulty of coupling. Thus salicylic acid or 4-nitro-β-naphthol are coupled only with difficulty and frequently such substituents prevent any coupling. Electron releasing groups increase the rate of coupling. Thus resorcinol is more readily coupled than is phenol, and three diazonium groups may be introduced. Phenolic compounds may be arranged in order of increasing ease of coupling as follows: salicylic acid, phenol, catechol, β-naphthol, resorcinol, α-naphthol, phloroglucinol. Of these β-naphthol is probably of greatest importance in the preparation of insoluble azo pigments.

β-Naphthol couples only in the 1-position whereas α-naphthol couples at both the 2- and 4-positions.

Diazotized *p*-aminostyrene and alkaline solutions of α-naphthol gives $p\text{-}CH_2{=}CH\text{--}C_6H_4\text{--}N{=}N\text{--}C_{10}H_6OH$. Similarly the same diazonium salt and α-naphthylamine gives $p\text{-}CH_2{=}CH\text{--}C_6H_4\text{--}N{=}N\text{--}C_{10}H_6NH_2$. Coupling occurs largely on the 4-position of α-naphthol. Diazonium salts of *p*-aminostyrene polymers have also been coupled with α-naphthol and α-naphthylamine.[204] Martynoff has also coupled diazotized *p*-aminostyrene and its polymer with phenol and dimethylaniline to give

$$p\text{-}CH_2\!=\!CH\!-\!C_6H_4\!-\!N\!=\!N\!-\!C_6H_4OH\text{-}p \text{ and}$$

$$p\text{-}CH_2\!=\!CHC_6H_4\!-\!N\!=\!N\!-\!C_6H_4\!-\!N(CH_3)_2$$

The products made from the polymers of *p*-aminostyrene were non-crystalline dyes that precipitated from all solvents.

Examples of azo dyes made by coupling a diazonium compound with a phenol are given in Table 4–2.

TABLE 4–2. SOME ACID AZO DYES

Name	Structure	Amine	Phenol
Orange II		Sulfanilic acid	β-Naphthol
Fast Red A		Naphthionic acid	β-Naphthol
Chrome Yellow 2G		*m*-Nitro aniline	Salicylic acid

An interesting application of the coupling of diazonium compounds with phenols is in a photocopying process which takes advantage of the fact that diazonium salts are decomposed by light and that coupling with a phenol will not occur under acid conditions. In this process a paper is coated with a stabilized diazonium salt and phloroglucinol at a pH sufficiently low so that coupling will not occur. If a drawing is placed on top of this paper and exposed to light, the diazonium salt is decomposed wherever the light hits the paper. The paper is developed by exposure to ammonia vapors which increases the pH and permits coupling to occur on all unexposed areas to give a positive reproduction of the drawing.

Aromatic amines couple with diazo compounds in much the same way as phenols except that they are not as reactive. Arylamines couple in the *para* position or, when this position is blocked, attack sometimes occurs at the *ortho* carbon atom. In contrast with phenols, coupling at the *ortho* position is much more difficult. β-Naphthylamine, however, is quite easily coupled in the 1-position.

Electron releasing substituents in the *meta* position to the amino group increase the ease of coupling. Thus *m*-toluidine and *p*-xylidine couple very readily in the position *para* to the amino group. Also *meta*-diamines couple more readily than monoamines. N-Alkyl- or N-arylanilines are very reactive. Both dimethylaniline and diphenylamine couple more readily than aniline.[205]

When two amino groups are present on the benzene ring it is difficult to diazotize both of them, but under special conditions this may be accomplished in some cases. It has not been possible to introduce more than two groups onto the benzene ring.[142] *o*-Diamines react to give triazines, probably through an intermediate mono-diazo compound.[206,207]

p-Diamines are more apt to undergo tetrazotization, especially by nitrosylsulfuric acid.[208]

Negatively substituted *m*-diamines are tetrazotized by normal procedures for diazotization.

Diamines such as benzidine containing only one amino group for each benzene ring are readily tetrazotized and are the parent compounds for a series of tetrazo dyes.

TABLE 4-3. SOME COMMON BASIC DIAZO DYES

Name	Structure	Diazotized Amine	Coupled with
Aniline Yellow		Aniline	Aniline
Butter Yellow		Aniline	Dimethyl-aniline
Chrysoidine		Aniline	*m*-phenylene-diamine

Coupling occurs with a number of heterocyclic compounds. For example, Binks and Ridd[209] investigated the reaction of diazonium ions with excess indole in dilute aqueous solution. They interpret the kinetics of the reaction as indicating that two competing reactions occur; a normal azo coupling and an autocatalytic side reaction that removes diazonium ions but does not form the azo compounds. Over the pH range of 4–6, the substitution probably occurs directly into the neutral indole molecule and not by previous formation of the conjugate base. No deuterium isotope effect was observed. The product, 3-(p-nitrophenylazo)indole, is formed in almost quantitative yield over the pH range 4–6.

As early as 1876 V. Meyer[210] reported that benzenediazo hydroxide reacted with ethylaceto acetate in alkaline solution. Other active methylene compounds such as diethylmalonate,[211] acetylacetone,[212] acetonedicarboxylic acid,[213] and cyclic β-diketones,[124] also react.

There is some question concerning the structure of the product but it is probably a tautomeric mixture of two forms.

$$CH_3\!-\!CO\!-\!\underset{\underset{N=N-C_6H_5}{|}}{CH}\!-\!COOC_2H_5 \;\rightleftharpoons\; CH_3\!-\!CO\!-\!\underset{\underset{N-NH-C_6H_5}{\|}}{C}\!-\!COOC_2H_5$$

The product obtained by the coupling of benzenediazo hydroxide with diethyl malonate is identical with the phenylhydrazone of mesoxalic ester.[215]

Nitroparaffins couple with diazo compounds on the α-carbon atom in slightly alkaline solution to give hydrazones.

A few phenol ethers couple with negatively substituted diazonium compounds such as p-nitrobenzenediazonium chloride. Coupling is accomplished in acetic acid with ethers of resorcinol or phloroglucinol. Coupling with anisole and phenetole will take place with 2,4-dinitrobenzenediazonium salts.[217] Coupling of phenol ethers is always accompanied by partial or complete removal of the alkyl group of the ether.

Hydrocarbons such as butadiene and isoprene couple with negatively substituted diazonium compounds in acetic acid or alcohol.[218] Unstable hydrazo compounds are obtained by reduction of the diazo compounds which are the immediate products of the reaction.

OXIMES

The most common procedure for the preparation of oximes involves the reaction of hydroxylamine salts with aldehydes or ketones in the presence of a base. Thus heptaldehyde is added to a cold aqueous solution of hydroxylammonium chloride and an aqueous solution of sodium carbonate is added at such a rate as to keep the reaction temperature below 45°C. The oxime is obtained by low pressure distillation and is purified by re-crystallization.[219]

Benzophenone oxime is prepared in a similar manner except that alcohol is added to improve the solubility of the ketone.

In some cases, sodium hydroxylamine disulfonate, $HON(SO_3Na)_2$, is first formed from sodium bisulfite and sodium nitrite and this reagent is used in preparing the oxime. The reagent is not isolated. Thus cyclo-hexanone oxime is prepared by adding the ketone to an aqueous solution containing sodium nitrite and sodium bisulfite. The mixture is heated to 75°C then cooled slowly to room temperature and permitted to stand for 48 hours. The oxime is recovered by ether extraction from a neutral so-lution.[220]

Oximes of ketones having large hydrocarbon groups (polynuclear ke-tone derivatives) are sometimes prepared in the presence of pyridine.[221]

Compounds having active methylene groups react with nitrous acid to form oximino derivatives. Ethyl nitrite is frequently used as the nitrosating agent. Methyl ethyl ketone is converted to biacetylmonoxime in 60 per cent yield[222]

$$CH_3-CO-CH_2CH_3 + CH_3CH_2ONO \longrightarrow$$

$$CH_3CO-C(=NOH)-CH_3 + C_2H_5OH$$

Similarly propiophenone is converted to isonitrosopropiophenone in 68 per cent yield.[223]

Pyruvic aldoxime can be obtained from acetone through the nitroso de-rivative.

$$CH_3COCH_3 + HONO \longrightarrow CH_3COCH_2N(OH)_2 \longrightarrow CH_3COCH=NOH$$

It may also be prepared by a continuous process from acetone and methyl nitrite. The time and temperature of the reaction play a critical role in the conversion. At 60–65°C, a residence time of 20–30 seconds can be used. At 45–50°C, 8–10 minutes are required.[224]

Oximes can also be prepared by the partial reduction of nitro com-pounds. Such reductions can be accomplished with zinc dust and acetic acid but the yields are not good because of the simultaneous production of amines.

Satisfactory results can be obtained by the reduction of salts of pri-mary or secondary nitroparaffins with hydrogen sulfide in an acid medium at a pH of 2–4.[225] The introduction of hydrogen sulfide into a mixture of nitrocyclohexane and piperidine at 60°C gives cyclohexanone in 98 per cent yield. Similarly, acetonoxime is prepared in 75 per cent yield from 2-nitropropane and cyclohexylamine.[226]

Nitroethane in 10 per cent sodium hydroxide is added to a sulfuric acid solution (pH of 3) and hydrogen sulfide simultaneously introduced over a period of about 3 hours. Cyclohexanone oxime is obtained from nitro-cyclohexane in the same way.

In a similar process an alcohol is used as the reducing agent.[227] The sodium salt of nitrocyclohexane and methanol are added to a suspension of ammonium chloride in methanol and stirred for 1.5 hours at 50°C. The pH is maintained at 3 by the addition of hydrochloric acid. Cyclohexanone oxime is obtained in 70 per cent yield.

Aldehydes, such as formaldehyde or benzaldehyde have also been used to reduce nitro compounds to oximes.[228]

The reduction of nitro compounds to oximes is also reported using zinc dust and methanol. A salt of a primary or secondary nitroparaffin is suspended in an organic solvent and a suspension of zinc dust in methanol is added at 25°C. The pH is maintained at 3 until the reaction is complete. Simultaneous reduction to the corresponding amine occurs at the same time.

Aliphatic and alicyclic nitro compounds are reduced to the corresponding oximes by catalytic hydrogenation in the presence of basic nitrogen compounds such as ammonia, ethyl-, propyl-, or butylamines. Effective catalysts consist of copper, silver or platinum metals or oxides. Thus platinum oxide is suspended in a mixture of nitrocyclohexane and cyclohexylamine (1:1 by weight) and hydrogen added at 70°C and a pressure of 100 atmospheres. The principal product is cyclohexanone oxime but in addition small amounts of cyclohexanol and cyclohexanone are obtained. Most of the cyclohexylamine is consumed.[229]

From a commercial point of view, cyclohexanone oxime is probably the most important of the oximes because it is an intermediate in the preparation of caprolactam used in the production of Nylon 6.

Reactions of Oximes

With a very few exceptions, oximes are crystalline solids useful in the identification of aldehydes and ketones. Oximes of aldehydes or unsymmetrical ketones exhibit stereoisomerism and may exist in syn and anti forms.

$$
\begin{array}{cc}
\text{R}-\text{C}-\text{R}' & \text{R}-\text{C}-\text{R}' \\
\| & \| \\
\text{N}-\text{OH} & \text{HO}-\text{N}
\end{array}
$$

This type of isomerism is always observed in aromatic unsymmetrical ketoximes but isomers of aliphatic or aryl alkyl ketoximes usually are not isolatable.

Oximes may be acylated by treatment with acid chlorides

$$RR'C{=}NOH + CH_3COCl \xrightarrow{\text{NaOH}} RR'C{=}NOCOCH_3$$

In the presence of sufficient quantities of base, the original configuration of the oxime is not changed.[230]

Acylation of aldoximes occurs only under very mild conditions. The *anti* form of aldoximes lose water when treated with dehydrating agents to form nitriles.

$$\begin{array}{c} R{-}\!\!\!-\overset{\displaystyle C}{\underset{\displaystyle N}{\|}}{-}H \\ HO{-}N \end{array} \longrightarrow RCN + H_2O$$

Basic hydrolysis of acylated *anti* forms also give a nitrile but *syn* forms hydrolyze to the oxime.

Isocyanates react with oximes to give carbamic acid derivatives.

$$C_6H_5CH{=}NOH + C_6H_5NCO \longrightarrow C_6H_5CH{=}N{-}O{-}CO{-}NHC_6H_5$$

Alkylation of oximes can be accomplished with alkyl sulfates in the presence of sodium hydroxide. Alkylation occurs either on the oxygen or the nitrogen.

$$RR'C{=}NOH + (CH_3)_2SO_4 + NaOH \longrightarrow$$

$$RR'C{=}N(CH_3)O \text{ and } RR'C{=}NOCH_3$$

The N-methylated product is obtained exclusively by treating acetaldoxime with methyl iodide. Both products are obtained with alkyl iodides in the presence of sodium alkoxides.[231]

Aldoximes in cold alcohol in the presence of Raney nickel are hydrogenated to a mixture of primary, secondary, and probably some tertiary amines. Ketoximes in alcohol are readily hydrogenated at 70°C under a pressure of 50 atmospheres to give primary amines in 80–95 per cent yields.[232] Heptanaldoxime is hydrogenated by agitation with hydrogen in the presence of Raney nickel, in alcohol at 15°C and atmospheric pressure to give 64 per cent of *n*-heptylamine and 15 per cent diheptylamine.

Oximes treated with phosphorus pentachloride in ether solution rearrange to amides. This reaction is referred to as the Beckmann rearrangement.

$$C_6H_5-\underset{\underset{NOH}{\|}}{C}-C_6H_5 \xrightarrow[\text{ether}]{PCl_5} C_6H_5-CO-NHC_6H_5$$

If the two groups are different, two amides might be expected, however, only one is obtained from each of the stereoisomers. It has been shown that an *anti* shift occurs and that the reaction proceeds as follows:

$$C_6H_5-\underset{N-OH}{C}-C_6H_4CH_3 \longrightarrow CH_3C_6H_4-\underset{NHC_6H_5}{C}=O$$

The other stereoisomer would give $C_6H_5-CO-NHC_6H_4CH_3$.

The Beckmann rearrangement will also take place by heating the oxime with sulfuric acid. Alicyclic ketoximes undergo a Beckmann rearrangement involving ring expansion. Thus cyclohexanone oxime is converted into caprolactam.

This is accomplished by heating in 75–100 per cent sulfuric acid at 60–120°C.[233] Yields are about 85 per cent.

The Beckmann rearrangement of oximes can be effected by using liquid hydrogen fluoride. The corresponding amides or lactams are obtained in 30–74 per cent yields.[234]

Moller *et al.*[235] rearranged cyclohexanone oxime to caprolactam in hydrogen fluoride at elevated temperatures and pressures. The hydrogen fluoride may be almost completely recovered and recycled. Sulfur dioxide or fluorinated hydrocarbons may be used as diluents. Thus a solution of cyclohexanone oxime in four times its volume of hydrogen fluoride, heated to 80–100°C for 2 hours was converted to the lactam in 95 per cent yields. At this temperature hydrogen fluoride is released and condensed and the product is obtained from the neutralized residue by extraction with chloroform.

Donaruma[236] obtained caprolactam from water-soluble salts of nitrocyclohexane in a single reaction. The potassium salt of nitrocyclohexane, sodium nitrite and hydrazine sulfate were mixed with water and the solution added to concentrated hydrochloric acid and warmed at 35–50°C for 1 hour. After neutralization, the products were isolated by extraction with chloroform.

Davydov[237] reports that a boric acid-alumina catalyst is effective for the conversion of cyclohexanone oxime to caprolactam. Polyphosphoric acid has been reported to be an effective catalyst for the rearrangement of aldoximes.[238]

References

1. Sanftner, R. W., Jones, M. M., and Audrieth, L. F., *Ind. Eng. Chem.,* **47,** 1203 (1955).
2. Diamond, L. H., Ph.D. Thesis, Univ. of Ill., 1954. *Dissertation Abstr.,* **15,** 33 (1955).
3. Diamond, L. H., and Audrieth, L. F., *J. Am. Chem. Soc.,* **77,** 3131 (1955).
4. Omietanski, G. M., *Dissertation Abstr.,* **16,** 1379 (1956).
5. Rowe, R. A., and Audrieth, L. F., *J. Am. Chem. Soc.,* **78,** 563 (1956).
6. Smith, I. I., and Howard, K. L., "Organic Syntheses," Vol. 24, p. 53, New York, John Wiley & Sons, Inc., 1944.
7. Barber, H. J., and Wragg, W. R., *J. Chem. Soc.,* **1948,** 1458.
8. Sidgwick, N. V., "Organic Chemistry of Nitrogen," Oxford, Clarendon Press, 1949.
9. Westphal, C., *Ber.,* **74,** 759 (1941).
10. Brown, R. D., and Kearly, R. A., *J. Am. Chem. Soc.,* **72,** 2762 (1950).
11. Thiele, J., *Ann.,* **376,** 239 (1910).
12. Allen, C. F. H., "Organic Syntheses," Collective Volume II, p. 228, New York, John Wiley & Sons, Inc., 1943.
13. Coleman, G. H., "Organic Syntheses," Collective Volume I, p. 442, New York, John Wiley & Sons, Inc., 1941.
14. Meyer, V., and Lecco, M. T., *Ber.,* **16,** 2976 (1883).
15. Bischler, A., *Ber.,* **22,** 2801 (1889).
16. Mohlau, R., *Ber.,* **45,** 2233, 2244 (1912).
17. Angeli, A., and Jolles, Z., *Ber.,* **62,** 2099 (1929).
18. Fichter, F., and Willi, E., *Helv. Chim. Acta,* **17,** 1416 (1934).
19. Cook, E. W., and France, W. G., *J. Am. Chem. Soc.,* **56,** 2225 (1934).
20. Fischer, E., *Ber.,* **17,** 2844 (1884).
21. Paal, C., and Bodewig, A., *Ber.,* **25,** 2896 (1892).
22. Gattermann, L., and Wieland, H., "Laboratory Methods of Organic Chemistry," p. 183, New York, The Macmillan Co., 1935.
23. McKee, R. H., and Gerapostolou, B. G., *Trans. Electrochem. Soc.,* **71,** 289 (1949).
24. Kabayashi, S., Japan Patent 6875 ('54), (Oct. 23, 1954).

25. Pietra, S., and Marco, R., *Ann. Chim. (Rome)*, **48**, 299 (1958).
26. Stafford, W. H., Los, M., and Thomson, N., *Chemistry & Industry (London)*, **1956**, 1277.
27. Ikda, H., and Konishi, K., *J. Chem. Soc. Japan, Ind. Chem. Sect.*, **57**, 47 (1954).
28. Hatt, H. H., "Organic Syntheses," Collective Volume II, p. 208, New York, John Wiley & Sons, Inc., 1943.
29. Hovitz, D., U. S. Patent 2,802,031 (Aug. 6, 1957).
30. Zimmer, H., Audrieth, L. F., and Zimmer, M., *Chem. Ber.*, **89**, 1116 (1956).
31. Zimmer, H., Audrieth, L. F., Zimmer, M., and Rowe, R. A., *J. Am. Chem. Soc.*, **71**, 790 (1955).
32. Westphal, C., *Ber.*, **74**, 1365 (1941).
33. Harrier, C., and Haga, T., *Ber.*, **31**, 56 (1898).
34. Baker, R., and Fuchs, H. G., U. S. Patent 2,701,815 (Feb. 8, 1955).
35. Wieland, H., "Die Hydrazine," p. 16, Stuttgart, F. Enke, 1913.
36. Pietra, S., *Ann. Chim. (Rome)*, **46**, 477 (1956).
37. Aylward, F., and Rao, C. V. N., *J. Appl. Chem. (London)*, **6**, 559 (1956).
38. Farrar, W. V., *J. Chem. Soc.*, **1956**, 782.
39. Fargher, R. G., and Furness, R., *J. Chem. Soc.*, **1915**, 688.
40. Hirst, E. L., and Macbeth, A. K., *J. Chem. Soc.*, **1922**, 904, 2169.
41. Benoit, G., *Bull. soc. chim. France*, **6**, 708 (1939).
42. Soc. pour l'ind. chim. à Bâle, British Patent 559,516 (Feb. 23, 1944); U. S. Patent 2,371,133 (Mar. 13, 1945).
43. Gever, G., *J. Am. Chem. Soc.*, **76**, 1283 (1959).
44. Kizhner, N., and Byelov, S., *J. Russ. Phys. Chem. Soc.*, **43**, 577.
45. Baker, B. R., *J. Am. Chem. Soc.*, **65**, 1572 (1943).
46. Foldi, A., and Foder, G., *Ber.*, **74**, 589 (1941).
47. Staudinger, H., Anthes, E., and Pfenninger, F., *Ber.*, **49**, 1832 (1916).
48. Winans, C. F., *J. Am. Chem. Soc.*, **55**, 2051 (1933).
49. Knorr, L., and Hess, K., *Ber.*, **44**, 2758, 2765 (1911).
50. Staudinger, H., and Kupfer, O., *Ber.*, **45**, 501 (1912).
51. Wolff, L., *Ann.*, **394**, 86 (1912).
52. Suzuki, N., and Sato, Y., *Nagoya Shiritsu Daigaku Kyoyobu Kiya*, **1**, 35 (1955).
53. Galat, A., and Elion, G., *J. Am. Chem. Soc.*, **65**, 1566 (1943).
54. Semishin, V. I., *J. Gen. Chem. (U.S.S.R.)*, **13**, 632 (1943).
55. Curtius, T., *J. Prakt. Chem.*, **50**, 275 (1894).
56. Jarosky, S., *Monatsh.*, **31**, 951 (1910).
57. Schmidt, and Schultz, *Ann.*, **207**, 327 (1881).
58. Stern, D., *Ber.*, **17**, 380 (1884).
59. Roche Products Ltd., British Patent 734,100 (July 27, 1955).
60. Ainsworth, C., *J. Am. Chem. Soc.*, **76**, 5774 (1954).
61. Curtius, T., *Ber.*, **23**, 3023, 3029 (1890).
62. Stolle, R., *J. Prakt. Chem.*, **68**, 464 (1903).
63. Silberrad, O., *J. Chem. Soc.*, **77**, 1190 (1900).
64. Gilman, H., "An Advanced Treatise on Organic Chemistry," 2nd Edition, Vol. 2, p. 1470, 1511, New York, John Wiley & Sons, Inc., 1943.

65. Smith, P. A., "Organic Reactions," Vol. 3, p. 337–449, New York, John Wiley & Sons, Inc., 1946.
66. Mistry, S. M., and Guha, P. C., *J. Indian Chem. Soc.*, **7**, 793 (1930).
67. Baker, E. M., and Gilbert, E. C., *J. Am. Chem. Soc.*, **64**, 2777 (1942).
68. Mazourewitch, H., *Bull. soc. chim.*, **35**, 1183 (1924).
69. Nacurewiez, M., *Roczniki Chem.*, **4**, 295 (1924).
70. De, S. C., *J. Indian Chem. Soc.*, **3**, 30 (1926).
71. De, S. C., and Dutt, N. C., *J. Indian Chem. Soc.*, **5**, 459 (1928).
72. Borsche, W., *et al.*, *Ber.*, **34**, 4297, 4299 (1901); **37**, 3177 (1904); **38**, 831 (1905).
73. Wilson, F. J., and Crawford, A. B., *J. Chem. Soc.*, **1925**, 799.
74. Steiglitz, J., and Curme, G. O., *Ber.*, **46**, 911 (1913).
75. Wieland, H., *Ann.*, **381**, 212 (1911).
76. Wieland, H., and Lecher, H., *Ann.*, **392**, 156 (1912).
77. Yamada, S., Chibata, I., and Tsurui, R., *Pharm. Bull. (Japan)*, **2**, 59 (1954).
78. Bruhl, J. W., *Ber.*, **37**, 2076 (1904).
79. Antener, I., *Helv. Chim. Acta*, **21**, 812 (1938).
80. Goldschmidt, H., *et al.*, *Z. Physik. Chem.*, **48**, 435 (1905); **56**, 1, 385 (1906); **71**, 437 (1910).
81. Reissert, A., *Ber.*, **42**, 1364 (1909).
82. Vorlander, D., *Ber.*, **39**, 803 (1906).
83. Meyer, R., and Wesche, H., *Ber.*, **50**, 449 (1917).
84. Bigelow, H. E., *Trans. Roy. Soc. Can., Sect. III*, **23**, 119 (1929).
85. Evans, I., and Fry, H. S., *J. Am. Chem. Soc.*, **26**, 1161 (1904).
86. Bigelow, H. E., and Robinson, D. B., "Organic Syntheses," Vol. 22, p. 28, New York, John Wiley & Sons, Inc., 1942.
87. Alway, F. S., and Bonner, W. O., *J. Am. Chem. Soc.*, **27**, 1107 (1905).
88. Nystrom, R. F., and Brown, W. G., *J. Am. Chem. Soc.*, **70**, 3738 (1948).
89. Müller, E., *Ann.*, **495**, 132 (1932).
90. Urey, H. C., and Lavin, G. I., *J. Am. Chem. Soc.*, **51**, 3286 (1929).
91. Wallach, O., and Belli, L., *Ber.*, **13**, 525 (1880).
92. Wallach, O., and Kiepenheuer, L., *Ber.*, **14**, 2617 (1881).
93. Angeli, A., *Gazz. chim. ital.*, **46**, II, 82 (1916).
94. Cumming, W. M., and Ferrier, G. S., *J. Chem. Soc.*, **127**, 2374 (1925).
95. Gore, P. H., and Hughes, G. K., *Australian J. Sci. Research, Ser. A*, **4**, 185 (1951).
96. Schultz, G., *Ber.*, **17**, 473, 475, 476 (1884).
97. Noelting, E., and Stricker, Th., *Ber.*, **21**, 3139 (1888).
98. Kirpal, A., *Ber.*, **67**, 70 (1934).
99. Gaylor, N. G., and Snyder, J. A., *Rec. trav. chim.*, **72**, 1007 (1953).
100. Fischer, O., and Trost, J., *Ber.*, **26**, 3083 (1893).
101. Prileschajew, N., *Ber.*, **42**, 4811 (1909).
102. Jahn, J., *J. Am. Chem. Soc.*, **59**, 1761 (1937).
103. Martynoff, M., *Bull. soc. chim. France*, **18**, 214 (1951).
104. Hyson, A. M., and Schreyer, R. C., U. S. Patent 2,778,818 (Jan. 22, 1957).
105. Anderson, U. S. Patent 2,716,405 (June 21, 1955).
106. Farenhorst, E., and Kooijman, E. C., *Rec. trav. chim.*, **72**, 993 (1953).

107. Mills, C., *J. Chem. Soc.,* **67**, 928 (1895).
108. Bamberger, E., *Ber.,* **33**, 3188 (1900).
109. Anspon, H. D., "Organic Syntheses," Vol. 25, p. 86, New York, John Wiley & Sons, Inc., 1945.
110. Ruggli, P., and Wüst, W., *Helv. Chim. Acta,* **28**, 781 (1945).
111. Amorosa, M., and Cesaroni, M. R., *Gazz. chim. ital.,* **83**, 853 (1953).
112. Arndt, F., "Organic Syntheses," Vol. 15, p. 4, New York, John Wiley & Sons, Inc., 1935.
113. Hartman, W. W., and Phillips, R., "Organic Syntheses," Vol. 13, p. 84, New York, John Wiley & Sons, Inc., 1933.
114. Boer, T. J. de, and Backer, H. J., *Rec. trav. chim.,* **73**, 229 (1954).
115. Müller, E., and Rundel, W., *Chem. Ber.,* **91**, 466 (1958).
116. Schmidt, O. T., and Zeisen, H., *Ber.,* **67**, 2120 (1934).
117. Schlotterbeck, F., *Ber.,* **40**, 479 (1907).
118. Meyer, H., *Monatsh.,* **26**, 1300 (1905).
119. Pechmann, H. v., *Ber.,* **31**, 2950 (1898).
120. Bachmann, W. E., and Struve, W. S., "Organic Reactions," Vol. 1, p. 38, New York, John Wiley & Sons, Inc., 1942.
121. Hellerman, L., and Newman, M. S., *J. Am. Chem. Soc.,* **54**, 2859 (1932).
122. Merrwein, H., and Hinz, G., *Ann.,* **484**, 11 (1930).
123. Coleman, G. J., Gilman, H., Adams, C. A., and Pratt, P. E., *J. Org. Chem.,* **3**, 99 (1938).
124. Bawn, C. E. H., and Ledwith, A., *Chemistry & Industry (London),* **1957**, 1180.
125. Saini, G., Campi, E., and Parodi, S., *Gazz. chim. ital.,* **87**, 342 (1957).
126. Wieland, T., and Piel, H., *Chem. Ber.,* **89**, 2408 (1956).
127. Gomberg, M., and Bachmann, W. E., "Organic Syntheses," Collective Volume I, p. 113, New York, John Wiley & Sons, Inc., 1941.
128. Grimmel, H. W., and Morgan, J. F., *J. Am. Chem. Soc.,* **70**, 1750 (1948).
129. Yamamoto, E., *J. Soc. Chem. Ind., Japan, Suppl.,* **36**, 593 (1933); **38**, 275B (1935).
130. Ueno, S., and Suzuki, T., *J. Soc. Chem. Ind., Japan, Suppl.,* **36**, 615 (1933).
131. Schmid, H. S., Austrian Patent 191,399 (Aug. 26, 1957).
132. Claus, Ad, *et al., Ann.,* **266**, 224 (1891).
133. Jacobson, P., *Ann.,* **367**, 345 (1909).
134. Gattermann, L., *Ann.,* **393**, 132 (1912).
135. Schoutissen, H. A. J., *J. Am. Chem. Soc.,* **55**, 4531 (1933); *Rec. trav. chim.,* **54**, 97 (1935).
136. DeMilt, C., and Van Zandt, G., *J. Am. Chem. Soc.,* **58**, 2044 (1936).
137. Griess, P., *J. Chem. Soc.,* **3**, 299 (1865).
138. Knoevenagel, E., *Ber.,* **23**, 2994 (1890).
139. Smith, W., and Waring, C. E., *J. Am. Chem. Soc.,* **64**, 469 (1942).
140. Misslin, E., *Helv. Chim. Acta,* **3**, 638 (1920).
141. Sakelaries, E., *Ber.,* **56**, 2536 (1923).
142. Morgan, G. T., and Davies, G. R., *J. Chem. Soc.,* **123**, 228 (1923).
143. Hein, Fr., and Wagner, Fr., *Ber.,* **68**, 858 (1935).
144. Hirsch, R., *Ber.,* **24**, 324 (1891).

145. Silberstein, *J. Prakt. Chem.,* **27,** 105 (1883).
146. Hantzsch, A., *Ber.,* **28,** 685 (1895).
147. Cain, J. L., and Norman, G. M., *J. Chem. Soc.,* **89,** 19 (1906).
148. Griess, A., *Ann.,* **137,** 54 (1866).
149. Wohl, A., *Ber.,* **25,** 3633 (1892).
150. Hantzsch, A., *et al., Ber.,* **28,** 666 (1895).
151. Wolff, L., *Ann.,* **394,** 41 (1912).
152. Staedel, W., and Bauer, H,, *Ber.,* **19,** 1953 (1886).
153. Pechmann, H. v., and Frobenius, L., *Ber.,* **27,** 703 (1894).
154. Goldschmidt, H., and Badl, V., *Ber.,* **22,** 933 (1889).
155. Fischer, *Ann.,* **190,** 77 (1877).
156. Griess, P., *Ann.,* **137,** 67 (1866).
157. Remsen, I., *Ber.,* **18,** 65 (1885).
158. Hormer, L., and Stohr, H., German Patent 898,298 (Nov. 30, 1953).
159. Ruggli, P., and Staub, A., *Helv. Chim. Acta,* **20,** 50 (1937).
160. Hantzsch, A., and Jochem, E., *Ber.,* **34,** 3337 (1901).
161. Hantzsch, A., *et al., Ber.,* **36,** 2061 (1903).
162. Detar, D. F., and Turetzky, M. N., *J. Am. Chem. Soc.,* **77,** 1745 (1955).
163. Hodgson, H. H., and Turner, H. S., *J. Chem. Soc.,* **1942,** 748.
164. Huisgen, R., and Nakaten, H., *Ann.,* **573,** 181 (1951).
165. Brewster, R. Q., and Poje, J. A., *J. Am. Chem. Soc.,* **61,** 2418 (1939).
166. Hodgson, H. H., and Birtwell, S., *J. Chem. Soc.,* **1943,** 433.
167. Culmann, and Gasiorowski, *J. Prakt. Chem.,* [2], **40,** 97 (1889).
168. Hantzsch, A., *Ber.,* **36,** 2065 (1903).
169. Zitscher, A., U. S. Patent 2,040,587 (May 12, 1936).
170. Klason, P., *Ber.,* **20,** 350 (1887).
171. Ziegler, J. H., *Ber.,* **23,** 2471 (1890).
172. Leuckart, *Ber.,* **21,** 565 (1888); *J. Prakt. Chem.,* [2], **41,** 179 (1890).
173. Busch, M., and Schulz, K., *J. Prakt. Chem.,* [2], **150,** 173 (1938).
174. Tarbell, D. S., and Fukushima, D. K., "Organic Syntheses," Vol. 27, p. 81, New York, John Wiley & Sons, Inc., 1947.
175. Schwarzenbach, G., and Egli, J., *Helv. Chim. Acta,* **17,** 1177 (1934).
176. Wilson, H. F., and Tarbell, D. S., *J. Am. Chem. Soc.,* **72,** 5200 (1950).
177. Gries, P., *Ann.,* **113,** 335 (1860); *Ber.,* **18,** 961 (1885).
178. Sandmeyer, T., *Ber.,* **17,** 1633, 2650 (1884); **23,** 1880 (1890).
179. Erdmann, H., *Ann.,* **272,** 141 (1893).
180. Hantzsch, A., and Blagden, J. W., *Ber.,* **33,** 2544 (1900).
181. Noyes, A. A., and Chow, M., *J. Am. Chem. Soc.,* **40,** 745 (1918).
182. Hodgson, H. H., *et al., J. Chem. Soc.,* **1941,** 770.
183. Hodgson, H. H., *Chem. Rev.,* **40,** 251 (1947).
184. Lewis, E. S., and Hinds, W. H., *J. Am. Chem. Soc.,* **74,** 304 (1952).
185. Gattermann, L., *Ber.,* **23,** 1218 (1890); **25,** 1091 (1890).
186. Marvel, C. S., and McElvain, S. M., "Organic Syntheses," Collective Volume I, p. 170, New York, John Wiley & Sons, Inc., 1941.
187. Balz, G., and Schiemann, G., *Ber.,* **60,** 1186 (1927).
188. Schiemann, G., *et al., Ann.,* **487,** 270 (1931); *Ber.,* **69,** 960 (1936).

189. Starkey, E. B., *J. Am. Chem. Soc.,* **59,** 1479 (1931); "Organic Syntheses," Vol. 19, p. 40, New York, John Wiley & Sons, Inc., 1939.
190. Roe, A., "Organic Reactions," Vol. 5, p. 193, New York, John Wiley & Sons, Inc., 1949.
191. Clarke, H. T., and Read, R. R., "Organic Syntheses," Collective Volume I, p. 514, New York, John Wiley & Sons, Inc., 1941.
192. Sandmeyer, T., *Ber.,* **18,** 1496 (1885); **20,** 1495 (1887).
193. Waters, W. A., *J. Chem. Soc.,* **1939,** 864.
194. Gattermann, L., *Ber.,* **32,** 1136 (1899).
195. Meisenheimer, J., *et al., Ber.,* **36,** 4157 (1903); **39,** 2529 (1906).
196. Hodgson, H. H., Haworth, F., and Ward, E. R., *J. Chem. Soc.,* **1948,** 1512.
197. Starkey, E. B., "Organic Syntheses," Collective Volume II, p. 225, New York, John Wiley & Sons, Inc., 1943.
198. Malinowski, S., *Roczniki Chem.,* **29,** 37 (1955).
199. Dombrovski, A. V., Terent'ev, A. P., and Yurkevich, A. M., *Zhur. Obshchei Khim.,* **26,** 3214 (1956).
200. Terent'ev, A. P., and Zagorevskii, V. A., *Zhur. Obshchei Khim.,* **26,** 200 (1956).
201. Huisigen, R., and Koch, H. J., *Naturwissenschaften,* **41,** 16 (1954).
202. Beech, W. F., *J. Chem. Soc.,* **1954,** 1297.
203. Goldschmidt, H., *Ber.,* **28,** 2020 (1895).
204. Martynoff, M., *Compt. rend.,* **240,** 540 (1955); **239,** 1512 (1954).
205. Levi, G. R., and Faldino, M., *Gazz. chim. ital.,* **54,** 818 (1924).
206. Ladenburg, A., *Ber.,* **9,** 221 (1876).
207. Hoffmann, L., *J. Prakt. Chem.,* [2[, **44,** 190 (1899).
208. Hantzsch, A., and Borghaus, H., *Ber.,* **30,** 93 (1897).
209. Binks, J. H., and Ridd, J. H., *J. Chem. Soc.,* **1957,** 2398.
210. Meyer, V., *Ber.,* **9,** 384 (1876).
211. Meyer, V., *Ber.,* **11,** 1417 (1878).
212. Bulöw, C., and Schlotterbeck, F., *Ber.,* **35,** 2187 (1902).
213. Pechmann, H. v., and Hennisch, *Ber.,* **24,** 3255 (1884).
214. Sen, H. K., and Gosh, S. K., *J. Indian Chem. Soc.,* **4,** 477 (1927).
215. Beyer, C., and Claisen, L., *Ber.,* **21,** 1697 (1888).
216. Meyer, K. H., and Lenhardt, S., *Ann.,* **398,** 74 (1913).
217. Meyer, K. H., Irschick, A., and Schlösser, H., *Ber.,* **47,** 1741 (1914).
218. Meyer, K. H., *Ber.,* **52,** 1468 (1919).
219. Bousquet, E. W., "Organic Syntheses," Collective Volume II, p. 313, New York, John Wiley & Sons, Inc., 1943.
220. Eck, J. C., and Marvel, C. S., "Organic Syntheses," Collective Volume II, p. 76, New York, John Wiley & Sons, Inc., 1943.
221. Bachmann, W. E., and Boatner, C. H., *J. Am. Chem. Soc.,* **58,** 2097 (1936).
222. Semon, W. L., and Damerell, V. R., *J. Am. Chem. Soc.,* **46,** 1290 (1924).
223. Hartung, W. H., and Crossley, F., "Organic Syntheses," Collective Volume II, p. 363, New York, John Wiley & Sons, Inc., 1943.
224. Langsdorf, W. P., Jr., and Naylor, M. A., U. S. Patent 2,709,709 (May 31, 1955).

225. Welz, H., German Patent 825,544 (Dec. 20, 1951).
226. Directie van de Staatsmijnen in Limburg, Dutch Patent 72,867 (July 15, 1953).
227. Welz, H., and Weise, J., German Patent 837,692 (May 2, 1952).
228. Welz, H., German Patent 837,691 (May 2, 1952).
229. Weise, J., Welz, H., Schuckmann, G. v., and Danziger, H., German Patent 916,948 (Aug. 23, 1954).
230. Vermillion, G., *et al., J. Org. Chem.,* **5,** 68, 75, (1940).
231. Dunstan, W. R., and Goulding, E., *J. Chem. Soc.,* **71,** 573 (1897); **79,** 628 (1901).
232. Paul, R., *Bull. soc. chim.,* [5], **4,** 1121 (1937).
233. Wagner, G. M., and O'Hara, J. B., U. S. Patent 2,797,216 (June 25, 1957).
234. Hudlicky, M., Czechoslovakia Patent 85,971 (Oct. 15, 1956).
235. Möller, F., Bayer, O., and Wilims, H., German Patent 924,866 (Mar. 10, 1955).
236. Donaruma, L. G., U. S. Patent, 2,763,644 (Sept. 18, 1956).
237. Davydov, V., *Chem. Tech. (Berlin),* **7,** 647 (1955).
238. Horning, E. C., and Stronberg, V. L., *J. Am. Chem. Soc.,* **74,** 5151 (1952).

5. NITRILES, AMIDES AND AMINO ACIDS

NITRILES

Nitriles are organic cyanides and as such contain a carbon-nitrogen triple bond. The π electrons of the triple bond are highly polarizable and because of the difference in electronegativity between carbon and nitrogen, the bond is highly polarized and the nitriles have large dipole moments. This is reflected in the boiling points which are all much higher than would be expected on the basis of molecular weight.

The nitriles containing up to 13 carbon atoms are liquids having rather pleasant ethereal odors and are only slightly toxic. Acetonitrile is completely miscible with water but the solubility decreases very rapidly with increasing molecular weight.

One of the most common methods for the preparation of nitriles involves the reaction of alkyl halides with alkali metal cyanides. Primary alkyl halides give nitriles in very good yield.[1,2] Secondary alkyl halides give much poorer yields, usually about 30 per cent, and tertiary halides do not react. There is considerable difference in the reactivity of the alkyl halides with the reactivity increasing in the order chlorides, bromides and iodides. In commercial procedures the chlorides are usually used for economic reasons. The addition of sodium iodide frequently has a favorable catalytic effect on the reactivity of the chlorides.

Allyl-type chlorides are especially reactive. Thus benzyl chloride is rapidly converted into benzyl cyanide in 85–90 per cent yield.

Although the formation of nitriles from alkyl halides involves a nucleophilic attack by a cyanide ion, different results are frequently obtained with potassium and sodium cyanides. With cetyl bromide and similar alkyl halides, potassium cyanide is more effective.

ω,ω'-Dichloroparaffins react with sodium cyanide in stages so that it is possible to obtain either the ω-chloronitrile or the dinitrile. Thus 1,5-dichlorohexane refluxed in an ethanol-water solution of sodium cyanide resulted in a 37 per cent conversion to 7-chloroheptanonitrile. The yield is about 90 per cent and no sebaconitrile is formed.

Low boiling nitriles cannot be made from alkyl halides and sodium cyanide in aqueous alcohol because of the difficulty in isolating the products. Other solvents such as ethylene glycol which dissolves appreciable amounts of sodium cyanide can be used successfully. Valeronitrile is formed in 90 per cent yield by refluxing n-butyl bromide with sodium cyanide in ethylene glycol for 1 hour. The best yield reported using an aqueous alcohol solvent is 80 per cent after 25–30 hours at reflux temperatures.

Not only does the use of ethylene glycol permit an easier separation of products but it also permits the use of higher temperatures.[3]

1,4-Dichlorobutane in ethanol-water solution gives a 45 per cent conversion to 5-chlorovaleronitrile; 1,7-dichloroheptane gives a 33 per cent conversion to 8-chlorooctanonitrile and 1,10-dichlorodecane gives a 37 per cent conversion to 11-chloroundecanonitrile.[4]

In some cases, cuprous cyanide can be used in the preparation of nitriles where alkali cyanides are not successful.[5] The reaction with cuprous cyanide is carried out at 150–250°C with, or without, an organic base such as pyridine being present. The reaction is autocatalytic and may be catalyzed by the addition of small amounts of the nitrile and copper sulfate.[6,7]

The preparation of unsaturated nitriles can be accomplished most effectively by using dry powdered cuprous cyanide. Alcoholic solutions of alkali cyanides frequently cause isomerization and alcoholysis of the double bond but this is less likely to occur with cuprous cyanide.[8] With cuprous cyanide, allyl cyanide is obtained from allyl chloride in 84 per cent yield.[9] With higher allylic chlorides rearrangement occurs even with cuprous cyanide. Thus 1-chloro-2-butene and 3-chloro-1-butene give the same mixture of isomeric nitriles (mole ratio 9:1).[10]

In a similar manner isomerization occurs when sorbyl chloride reacts with potassium cyanide.[11]

$$CH_3CH{=}CHCH{=}CHCH_2Cl + KCN \longrightarrow$$

$$CH_3CH(CN)CH{=}CHCH{=}CH_2 + KCl$$

With few exceptions, vinyl chlorides are unreactive.

Aromatic nitriles are prepared by passing an aromatic halogen compound, in the vapor phase, together with hydrogen cyanide diluted with hydrogen or other inert gas over a catalyst consisting of silver or a silver-copper alloy. The temperature depends on the nature of the halogen compound and the catalyst.[12] Willett and Pailthorp[13] used a catalyst consisting of nickel on alumina. Molten p-dichlorobenzene and hydrogen cyanide are introduced into a reactor containing a catalyst consisting of 14 per cent nickel, as nickel oxide, on alumina at a temperature of 550–580°C. p-Phthalonitrile is obtained in 84 per cent yield together with only 1 per cent of p-chlorobenzonitrile.

Alpha-keto nitriles can be prepared by treating acyl halides with dry cuprous cyanide

$$2ArCOBr + Cu_2(CN)_2 \longrightarrow 2Ar-CO-CN + Cu_2Br_2$$

Yields range from 60 to 85 per cent.[14,15,16] In some cases arylsulfonates can be substituted for aryl halides.

$$ArSO_3Na + NaCN \longrightarrow ArCN + Na_2SO_3$$

The reaction procedure involves fusion of a mixture of the salts and yields are usually low. The method has, however, been quite successful in the preparation of naphthonitriles,[17,18] and cyanopyridines.[19,20]

Methyl sulfate may be converted into acetonitrile in good yield but yields with ethyl sulfate are not satisfactory.

The preparation of aryl nitriles from the corresponding diazonium salts has been described previously (Chapter 4) and represents a convenient laboratory method of synthesis.

A very important method for the preparation of nitriles involves the dehydration of amides.

$$RCONH_2 \longrightarrow RCN + H_2O$$

Dehydrating agents such as phosphorus pentoxide, phosphorus oxychloride and thionyl chloride may be used or the reaction may be accomplished at high temperatures in the presence of alumina.

Isobutyronitrile has been prepared in 86 per cent yield by heating a dry intimate mixture of the powdered amide and phosphorus pentoxide at temperatures of 100–220°C and distilling off the product as fast as formed.[21] Thionyl chloride is usually used for the dehydration of high molecular weight amides because the by-products are gases thus permitting easier purification of the nitrile.[22]

Phthalonitrile is obtained in 50–95 per cent yield by the dehydration of phthalamide with phosphorus oxychloride, thionyl chloride or phosphorus pentachloride at 60–70°C. Dehydration with acetic anhydride gives a maximum yield of 78 per cent. If the dehydration is carried out with acetic anhydride in chlorobenzene, with the removal of the acetic acid as formed, a 100 per cent yield of nitrile is obtained.[23] Hull[24] dehydrated amides to nitriles by passing the amide vapors at 400–500°C through a reactor filled with alumina pellets containing 20 per cent phosphoric acid.

Fatty acids are frequently converted to nitriles in one operation. This is accomplished by heating the acid with dry ammonia at high temperatures. The ammonium salt first formed is converted to the amide then to the nitrile by loss of water in yields of 80–85 per cent.[25,26] Armour and Company has used this procedure for the preparation of nitriles from fatty acids such as stearic, oleic, or palmitic acids.[27] The vapor-phase conversion of acids to nitriles has been reported at 350–450°C in the presence of barium phosphate. This method has been used to make adiponitrile from adipic acid.

Nitriles of fatty acids are prepared commercially by means of a combined liquid-vapor phase process.[28,29] The acid is treated with ammonia in the liquid phase to form a mixture of fatty acids, amides and nitriles. This mixture is vaporized and passed over an alumina catalyst at 200–300°C.

Titanium oxide gel has been found to act as a promoter for a silica gel catalyst in the preparation of nitriles from acids and ammonia.[30] Glacial acetic acid is vaporized at 150°C and the vapor passed through a quartz tube containing promoted silica gel. A stream of anhydrous ammonia, preheated to 550°C, is simultaneously introduced into the tube. The effluent gases contain acetonitrile, ammonia and water. Conversions range from 45–75 per cent dependent upon the promoter used; best results are obtained with titanium dioxide. Other additives investigated include methyl borate, phosphorus oxychloride, triethylsilicoacetate and ferric oxide. Volatile additives inhibit the reaction. Yields are all within 85–95 per cent.

Acids containing 8–20 carbon atoms react with ammonia in the presence of a dehydration catalyst such as activated alumina or silica gel in the liquid phase at temperatures of 200–300°C.[31] Toland[32] obtained nitriles by heating a thermally stable acid, ammonium salt or amide with ammonium sulfate or diammonium hydrogen phosphate to 200–400°C. Thus heating isophthalic acid with diammonium hydrogen phosphate for 40 minutes at 340–370°C gives a 95 per cent yield of isophthalonitrile. A fluidized activated alumina catalyst was used by Kircher[33] to prepare nitriles from fatty acids and ammonia. Temperatures of 360–370°C were required.

Niederhauser[34] converted fatty acids to the corresponding nitriles by heating with ammonia in the liquid phase to 250–290°C in the presence of a cobalt soap. The presence of about 0.4 per cent cobalt oleate or cobalt naphthenate increases the rate of conversion of oleic acid to oleonitrile about 3 or 4 times. In the presence of these cobalt salts a quantitative conversion is obtained in 6 hours. In the absence of cobalt salts only a 75 per cent conversion is obtained in the same time under the same conditions.

An interesting process for the preparation of unsaturated dinitriles is reported by Frank and Nobis.[35] The process involves the following steps:

1. Butadiene is treated with a dispersion of sodium in an inert hydrocarbon to give s-disodiumbutadiene dimer (mixed disodiumoctadienes).

2. These disodium derivatives are carbonated and after acidification give a mixture of dibasic, 10 carbon atom unsaturated acids.

3. The acids are treated with ammonia at high temperatures to give dinitriles. The acids are converted to the ammonium salts which are dehydrated to amides and nitriles.

Diethyl isophthalate added dropwise down a vertically packed tube filled with silica gel at 450°C through which a stream of nitrogen is passing gives isophthalonitrile. The product is removed from the bottom of the reactor in 61 per cent yield.[36]

Alcohols can be converted into the corresponding nitriles by passing a mixture of the alcohol and ammonia over a zinc sulfide catalyst at 400–460°C.[37] Yields of about 60 per cent are obtained. A catalyst consisting of a mixture of nickel sulfide and tungsten sulfide is effective. Thus *n*-heptyl alcohol and ammonia are passed over a zinc sulfide catalyst to give heptanonitrile in 60 per cent yield. The same nitrile is obtained in 52 per cent yield from heptanal.[38]

Nitriles are prepared by the reaction of alcohols with excess ammonia in the presence of oxides of thorium, molybdenum or aluminum. Much higher yields (80–90 per cent) of nitriles have been reported using a catalyst consisting of iron or iron oxides usually supported on kieselguhr or ceramics. This catalyst may be promoted by the presence of 1–5 per cent of copper and 30 per cent of silica.

Hexanal and ammonia passed downward through a reactor packed with a catalyst consisting of 100 parts of iron and 1.5 parts of potassium oxide at a temperature of 400°C gives capronitrile in 80 per cent yield.

Ethyl or isoamyl alcohols are converted to the corresponding nitriles by passing with ammonia over a catalyst consisting of 10 per cent molybdenum oxide on alumina. Acetonitrile begins to form at 350°C and the yield from ethyl alcohol reaches a maximum of 23 per cent at 487°C. At temperatures below 400°C, ethyl alcohol gives some pyridine. The mole ratio of alcohol to ammonia used is about 1:2.

Isoamyl alcohol gives isovaleronitrile at temperatures of 319–510°C with maximum yield of 18 per cent. With increasing temperature more low molecular weight nitriles are formed.[39]

Benzonitrile is prepared by passing benzyl alcohol and ammonia into a reaction vessel containing molybdenum oxide at 240°C. Benzonitrile is removed continuously from a packed column at a head temperature of 160°C. The yield is 96 per cent based on the benzyl alcohol.[40]

Allyl alcohols react with hydrogen cyanide to give unsaturated nitriles in the presence of copper salts and ammonium or alkaline earth salts. Allyl alcohol and anhydrous hydrogen cyanide together with cuprous and ammonium chloride are heated in a steel bomb at 90–100°C to give $CH_2=CHCH_2CN$ in 65 per cent yield.[41] Allylic type halides can be used in place of the alcohols.

Ammonia reacts with a tertiary olefin oxide such as isobutylene oxide at 600–1000°F at pressures up to 100 psi in the presence of a mixed dehydration-dehydrogenation catalyst to give aliphatic nitriles. Thus isobutylene oxide and ammonia (mole ratio 1:3) were passed over the catalyst at temperatures of 730–820°F and at atmospheric pressure with a reaction time of 1.5 seconds.[42] Isobutyronitrile is obtained in 37 per cent conversion.

Molybdenum and chromium oxides are good catalysts for the reaction of olefin oxides with ammonia.[43] Temperatures of 500–625°C and ammonia-to-olefin oxide ratios of at least 3:1 are desirable. Isobutylene oxide and ammonia in a mole ratio of 5:1.18 react at 497°C to produce isobutyronitrile in 80 per cent yields. Chromium oxide is used as the catalyst. Molybdenum oxide catalysts tend to promote the formation of unsaturated nitriles at the lower temperatures.

Unsaturated nitriles may be obtained by heating a mixture of a saturated nitrile and an olefin oxide to 300–800°F in the presence of an alumina or silica catalyst. Thus acetonitrile is preheated to 600°F in the presence of an alumina catalyst and ethylene oxide is introduced at a rate of 0.5 volume of liquid per hour per volume of catalyst until 1 mole of ethylene oxide has been added for each mole of acetonitrile charged. The reaction product is a mixture of allyl cyanide, crotononitrile and methacrylonitrile.[44]

Nitriles can be prepared by the action of ammonia on hydrocarbons. Thus nitriles are formed by passing olefins over silica catalysts at temperatures of 300–350°C and pressures of about 3000 psi. As an example, Mahan and Turk[45,46] prepared acetonitrile as the principal product when saturated hydrocarbons and ammonia were passed over the catalyst at 570°C with a contact time of about 1.3 seconds, to give for example a 6–10 mole per cent conversion of propane to acetonitrile.

Denton and Bishop[47] developed a process for making acetonitrile from C_2 to C_5 hydrocarbons and ammonia at 500°C and atmospheric pressure in the presence of a catalyst consisting of molybdenum oxide (10 per cent) on alumina, with a reaction time of 10–15 seconds. Conversions of 10–40 per cent and yields of 60 per cent nitrile were obtained. Although paraffin hydrocarbons are converted to nitriles, unsaturated hydrocarbons are somewhat more satisfactory starting materials. Best yields are obtained using an excess of the hydrocarbon and relatively long residence times.

When propylene is used as the hydrocarbon, the reaction proceeds as follows:

$$CH_3CH{=}CH_2 + NH_3 \longrightarrow CH_3CH_2CN + 2H_2$$

$$CH_3CH_2CN + H_2 \longrightarrow CH_3CN + CH_4$$

That this is the mechanism for the reaction is supported by the fact that 5–10 per cent of propionitrile is always obtained together with acetonitrile and that under mild conditions, such as using a nickel catalyst at 350°C, and moderate pressures, the propionitrile is the major product.

The second reaction is supported by the fact that by charging propionitrile and ammonia, instead of propylene and ammonia, at 525°C with a 1.2 second residence time and a ratio of 2 moles of ammonia to 1 of nitrile, approximately 20 per cent of the propionitrile is converted to acetonitrile, 30 per cent was recovered unchanged and the remainder was converted to gas, polymers and coke.

Hydrocarbons containing seven or more carbon atoms are converted to aromatic nitriles as well as to acetonitrile.

Paushkin and Osipova[48] prepared acetonitrile in 44 per cent yield by passing *n*-pentane and ammonia (mole ratio 1:2) over a catalyst consisting of 10 per cent molybdenum oxide on alumina at 520°C.

Olefins such as ethylene, propylene and isobutylene may be converted to acetonitrile by heating with ammonia in the presence of a catalyst consisting of molybdenum and aluminum oxides.[49] The yields vary with the olefin used but amount to 16.7 per cent with ethylene, 33.5 per cent with propylene and 29.9 per cent with isobutylene. Pretreating the catalyst by heating in a stream of hydrogen for 2 hours results in a marked increase in yield. Addition of small amounts of oxygen decreases the rate of competing reactions, thus increasing the yield of acetonitrile. Other catalysts found to be effective include the oxides of tungsten, vanadium, uranium and chromium.

Caldwell and Chapman[50] reacted olefins with ammonia at 900°C in the presence of molybdenum trioxide on alumina to give acetonitrile. Ammonia and propylene in a mole ratio of 3:1 gave a 32 per cent conversion to acetonitrile. At 985°C ethylene and ammonia (mole ratio 1:2) gave a 25 per cent conversion, ammonia and butadiene in a mole ratio of 2:1 gave only a 4 per cent conversion to acetonitrile but when the mole ratio was 6:1 a 16 per cent conversion was obtained.

Acetonitrile may also be obtained in about 78 per cent yield by passing an approximately equimolar mixture of acetylene and ammonia over a zinc chromite catalyst at temperatures of 400–420°C.[51]

Reaction of cyanogen with ethylene gives succinonitrile. The reaction is accomplished by passing a mixture of the gases over a nichrome wire coil at about 800°C.[52] In a similar manner propylene gives $NCCH(CH_3)CH_2-CN$.

Aromatic nitriles may be prepared by the reaction of hydrocarbons and ammonia in the presence of a catalyst at temperatures of 524-552°C. Toluene is converted to benzonitrile at 538°C and atmospheric pressure in the presence of a catalyst consisting of molybdenum oxide on alumina. Xylene gives a mixture of mono- and di-nitriles

In cases where a methyl and a higher alkyl side chain are present, the methyl group is preferentially attacked. Ethylbenzene is converted to benzonitrile and methane.

$$C_6H_5CH_2CH_3 + NH_3 \longrightarrow C_6H_5CN + CH_4$$

Methylnaphthalenes are converted to the corresponding nitriles. Conversions of toluene to benzonitrile are 5–10 per cent and ultimate yields are 60–85 per cent.[53] Trimethylbenzenes may also be converted to nitriles.

Hydrogen cyanide and benzonitrile (mole ratio of 4:1) passed over a dehydrogenation catalyst such as platinum oxide at 900–950°C gives a mixture of phthalonitriles in 60 per cent yield.[54] The phthalonitrile mixture contains 10 per cent *ortho-*, 55 per cent *meta-* and 35 per cent of the *para*-isomer.

Toland[55] prepared nitriles by heating an anhydrous mixture of sulfur, ammonia and an alkylbenzene under pressure at 400–700°F. Thus *p*-xylene, sulfur and ammonia (mole ratio 10:4.27:7) heated for 50 minutes at 600°F gave a 27 per cent conversion of the *p*-xylene to a product which contained 60 per cent p-$CH_3C_6H_4CN$. Other examples include the conversion of cumene to $C_6H_5CH(CH_3)CN$ in 28 per cent yield, *p*-toluonitrile to teraphthalonitrile, p-NC—C_6H_4—CN, in 73 per cent yield. 3-Cyanopyridine is obtained in 15 per cent yield from 3-methylpyridine.

Cosby and Erchak[56] prepared benzonitrile from toluene in 75 per cent yield by oxidizing toluene with air in the vapor phase in the presence of ammonia. A preheated mixture consisting of 2 parts of ammonia, 1 part of toluene and 75 parts of air was passed at 50°C over a supported catalyst containing 11.4 per cent vanadium pentoxide, 2.9 per cent molybdenum trioxide and 0.034 per cent phosphorus pentoxide.

Saturated nitriles may be converted to unsaturated nitriles by molecular oxygen. The oxidation is facilitated by the addition of 0.2–0.5 per cent of a halogen. Thus isobutyronitrile is oxidized to methacrylonitrile with conversions of 32 per cent.[57] Over-all yields of unsaturated nitriles of about 86 per cent are obtained.

Schulze and Mahan[58] patented a method for making unsaturated nitriles from conjugated diolefins and hydrogen cyanide. Thus a mixture of butadiene and hydrogen cyanide (mole ratio about 2:1), in acetonitrile as a diluent, is passed over a solid, porous, cuprous chloride catalyst at 100–350°F under a pressure of 100–700 psi. A conversion to pentenenitrile of about 36 per cent is achieved.

Mahan[59] found that aldehydes having secondary or tertiary carbon atoms could be converted to nitriles by reaction with ammonia. Thus isobutyraldehyde and ammonia (mole ratio 1:5) were preheated to 670°F and passed over a catalyst consisting of 15 per cent copper on activated alumina. With a contact time of 1.0–1.5 seconds a conversion to isobutyronitrile of 25 per cent per pass was obtained. In a similar manner conversions of benzaldehyde to benzonitrile of 46 per cent per pass were obtained.

Boron trifluoride causes a dehydration-hydrolysis of an amide to give a nitrile and an acid.[60]

$$2RCONH_2 \xrightarrow[CH_3COOH]{BF_3} RCN + RCOOH + NH_3$$

Aldoximes may be dehydrated to nitriles by heating in acetic anhydride.[61,62] With arylaldoximes, yields vary from 80–90 per cent.

Nitriles having α-hydrogen atoms can be alkylated with an alkyl halide in an inert solvent in the presence of sodium amide.[63,64]

$$CH_3CN + RCl + NaNH_2 \longrightarrow RCH_2CN + NaCl + NH_3$$

Suitable solvents for the reaction include ether, benzene, toluene and liquid ammonia. Mono-, di-, or trialkylated products may be obtained. Bromides are more satisfactory than chlorides and yields of 60–80 per cent are obtained.

Acetonitrile has been alkylated by diphenylmethyl bromide in the presence of freshly precipitated silver sulfate.[65] The reactants are warmed in benzene, filtered and the benzene solution washed with water to give the intermediate $CH_3\overset{(+)}{-}C=N-CH(C_6H_5)_2$ which under the conditions of the experiment forms the amide $CH_3CONHCH(C_6H_5)_2$.

Aromatic nitriles have been prepared by heating aromatic hydrocarbons and cuprous cyanide above 175°C. Benzonitrile is formed from benzene and cuprous cyanide at 330°C.[66]

Ethyl cyanoacetate has a very reactive methylene group and behaves very much like ethyl acetoacetate. It may be alkylated very readily by procedures used with ethyl acetoacetate or diethyl malonate. Esters of the type $NC-CHR-COOC_2H_5$ and $NC-CRR'-COOC_2H_5$ may be obtained by adding an alkyl halide to a solution of ethyl cyanoacetate in alcohol containing sodium ethoxide.

Ethyl cyanoacetate also undergoes Knoevenagel reactions with carbonyl compounds to give unsaturated cyanoethyl esters.

$$NC-CH_2-COOC_2H_5 + RCHO \xrightarrow{base} NC-\underset{\underset{CHR}{\|}}{C}-COOC_2H_5$$

This type of reaction will also take place with cyanoacetic acid and the product on decarboxylation gives an unsaturated nitrile.[67]

$$RCH{=}C(CN){-}COOH \rightarrow RCH{=}CHCN + CO_2$$

α,β-Unsaturated aldehydes, heated with ammonia and air in the presence of suitable catalysts, give unsaturated nitriles. When acrolein, ammonia, steam and air are passed at 440°C over a catalyst consisting of ferric molybdate on silica gel, a 34 per cent yield of acrylonitrile is obtained. When ammonium molybdate pellets activated by heating 5 hours at 400°C are used as the catalyst, an 82 per cent conversion is obtained. When oxygen is excluded no conversion to nitrile occurs.

Methylacrylonitrile is obtained similarly and tetrahydrobenzaldehyde is converted to a mixture of tetrahydrobenzonitrile and benzaldehyde.[68]

Hydrogen cyanide adds to carbonyl compounds to give cyanohydrins

$$RCHO + HCN \rightleftharpoons RCH(OH)CN$$

The reaction is reversible. A favorable equilibrium is obtained from aliphatic and alicyclic aldehydes and ketones but arylalkyl ketones such as acetophenone react only to a small extent and diaryl ketones not at all.[69] The reaction may be accomplished by adding liquid hydrogen cyanide to the carbonyl compound in the presence of a basic catalyst.[70,71]

An alternate procedure involves first converting the carbonyl compound to the sodium bisulfite addition product followed by treatment with sodium cyanide.

$$(CH_3)_2CO + NaHSO_3 \rightarrow (CH_3)_2C(OH)SO_3Na \xrightarrow{NaCN}$$
$$(CH_3)_2C(OH)CN + Na_2SO_3$$

This procedure is usually prefered. Acetone cyanohydrin is obtained in this way in 78 per cent yield.[72]

Acetone cyanohydrin has been prepared by the following procedure: An equimolar amount of sulfur dioxide is dissolved in acetone and the solution added dropwise to an aqueous solution of sodium cyanide and acetone at temperatures below 25°C. The mixture is stirred for about 1 hour until the solution becomes alkaline. The cyanohydrin which has precipitated is removed by filtration. Acetone cyanohydrin is thus formed in 95 per cent yield.[73]

Anion exchange resins in the cyanide form (e.g., the CN⁻ salt of "Dowex 2") are found to be excellent catalysts for the conversion of ketones to cyanohydrins with hydrogen cyanide. The reaction may be carried out continuously by passing a mixture of acetone and hydrogen cyanide (mole ratio 5:1) at 25°C through a reactor packed with the resin The cyanohydrin is obtained in 99 per cent yield.

Hydroxyacetonitrile ($HOCH_2CN$) has been prepared by adding sufficient sodium hydroxide to aqueous formaldehyde (40 per cent) to adjust the pH to 8–9. Hydrogen cyanide is added at a temperature of 10°C, the pH adjusted to 5 with hydrochloric acid and the mixture distilled.[74]

Reaction of an orthoester with hydrogen cyanide gives an alkoxy nitrile of the type $RC(OR)_2CN$. Thus trimethyl orthoformate reacts with hydrogen cyanide at 150°C to give dimethoxyacetonitrile.[75]

$$HC(OCH_3)_3 + HCN \longrightarrow (CH_3O)_2CHCN + CH_3OH$$

α-(N-Alkylamino)-nitriles have been prepared by the reaction of amines, carbonyl compounds and hydrogen cyanide. Anhydrous hydrogen cyanide may be added as a liquid, to the imine, formed from the amine and the carbonyl compound, or the amine may be added to the cyanohydrin formed from the carbonyl compound and hydrogen cyanide.

α-N-Methylaminoisobutyronitrile has been prepared by bubbling methylamine into acetone cyanohydrin at temperatures of 23–32°C and the mixture refrigerated and permitted to stand overnight. The product was obtained in 93 per cent yield.

α-Allylaminoacetonitrile has been prepared by adding commercial formalin to aqueous allylamine at temperatures of 15–20°C and then introducing hydrogen cyanide at 20°C.[76] The reaction is complete in 3 hours and the product isolated in 67 per cent yield.

Aqueous dimethylamine is treated with 37 per cent formaldehyde at 25°C and then with sodium cyanide. After 15 hours a 73–83 per cent yield of dimethylaminocyanamide is obtained. Hydrogenation over Raney nickel at 70°C and 1000 psi gives a 47 per cent yield of $(CH_3)_2NCH_2$-CH_2NH_2.[77]

One of the more important nitriles from an industrial point of view is acrylonitrile, because of its importance as a chemical intermediate in the preparation of synthetic fibers ("Orlon," "Dynel") and one form of synthetic rubber (NBR) which is particularly resistant to attack by oils. Acrylonitrile is prepared in several ways, of which two are of most importance. The oldest method involves the dehydration of ethylene cyanohydrin made by the reaction of hydrogen cyanide with ethylene oxide

$$CH_2\!\!-\!\!-\!\!CH_2 + HCN \longrightarrow HOCH_2CH_2CN$$
$$\diagdown O \diagup$$

$$HOCH_2CH_2CN \longrightarrow CH_2\!=\!CH\!-\!CN + H_2O$$

The reaction between ethylene oxide and hydrogen cyanide is carried out in a vertical reactor provided with cooling coils to dissipate the heat of reaction.[78] The reaction is catalyzed by bases and a suitable medium for the reaction consists of about 200 parts of water, 8 parts of diethylamine and 5 parts of 50 per cent sodium hydroxide which is introduced into the column. Ethylene oxide is added near the bottom of the column and an equimolar amount of liquid hydrogen cyanide is added above the surface of the liquid. The dimethylamine serves as a catalyst for the reaction.

The reaction is started at 55°C and the reactants are added at such a rate that will maintain this temperature. When 6 to 7 volumes of ethylene oxide are used per volume of water initially present, about 10 hours are required. The temperature is then raised to 60°C where it is held for several more hours to complete the reaction. The alkaline mixture is neutralized and the product separated by distillation.

Several catalysts are effective in promoting the dehydration of ethylene cyanohydrin but magnesium carbonate is most commonly used. The process can be made semicontinuous in the liquid phase. Ethylene cyanohydrin and magnesium carbonate in the approximate ratio of 12:1 are added to a cast iron reactor and heated to 200°C. Acrylonitrile and water are taken overhead. Ethylene cyanohydrin is continuously added to the reaction vessel at the same rate as that at which the product is removed.

Sekino[79] obtained acrylonitrile in 85 per cent yield by heating ethylene cyanohydrin rapidly to 100-230°C in the liquid phase in the presence of sodium carbonate.

The second method for the preparation of acrylonitrile involves the direct addition of hydrogen cyanide to acetylene

$$HCN + HC{\equiv}CH \longrightarrow CH_2{=}CH{-}CN$$

This appears to be the better method and is being adopted in all new plants being built. The reaction may be carried out in solution or in the vapor phase.

The reaction is effected in the liquid phase using a catalyst consisting of an aqueous solution of equimolar quantities of ammonium chloride and cuprous chloride. The control of the pH of the catalyst solution is very important.

The reaction is carried out in a rubber or acid-brick lined reactor. The catalyst solution is charged to the vessel and acetylene is continuously added through a number of orifices near the bottom. Liquid hydrogen cyanide is added at a point somewhat higher in the reactor. About 10 moles of acetylene are used for each mole of hydrogen cyanide. The operating temperatures are about 80-90°C which requires that a pressure of about 15 psi be used. The acrylonitrile is removed by washing with water and is recovered by distillation. The yields of acrylonitrile are about 80–85 per cent based on acetylene and 90–95 per cent based on hydrogen cyanide.

Keller[80] passed acetylene diluted with nitrogen through a water solution of cuprous chloride, potassium chloride and sodium chloride at 90°C and added the required amount of hydrogen cyanide to give acrylonitrile in 90 per cent yield.

Kastner, Zobel and Kurtz[81] prepared acrylonitrile by passing acetylene and hydrogen cyanide at 80°C through a solution of ammonium chloride and cuprous chloride in formamide. Methylammonium chloride can be used in place of ammonium chloride.

Substantially pure acrylonitrile can be obtained by the direct addition of hydrogen cyanide to acetylene in formamide containing anhydrous cuprous bromide as a catalyst. Acetamide, pyrrolidone or the corresponding N-substituted amides may also be used as solvents.

In the vapor phase, acrylonitrile is prepared by passing acetylene and hydrogen cyanide (mole ratio 1:2) at 550–600°C over a catalyst consisting of 3–15 per cent of an alkali metal hydroxide, cyanide or carbonate on a porous carbon support.[83] The conversion of hydrogen cyanide to acrylonitrile is about 66 per cent with a yield of 82 per cent.

In one process for making acrylonitrile, acetylene and hydrogen cyanide vapor together with steam are passed over a solid catalyst consisting essentially of cuprous chloride deposited on a support such as silica.[84] Reaction temperatures are 170–180°C.

A continuous process for the production of acrylonitrile has been described in which acetylene and hydrogen cyanide are passed in the vapor phase at temperatures of 550–600°C into a reactor through which moves a solid catalyst of activated carbon counter current to the reacting gases.[85] The velocity of the reaction gases is more than 500 times the velocity of the catalyst and slightly below the velocity necessary to fluidize the catalyst.

Acrylonitrile can be prepared from hydrogen cyanide and an acetylene-containing gas stream, such as one made by the partial combustion of natural gas. The gases are introduced into a water solution of ammonium chloride, cuprous chloride and salts of rare earth metals such as cerium or lanthanum. A gas stream containing 7.2 per cent acetylene, 55.6 per cent hydrogen, 27 per cent carbon monoxide, 3.8 per cent carbon dioxide and small amounts of methane and nitrogen is introduced together with hydrogen cyanide into the bottom of a reactor filled with the catalyst solution.[86] The gases other than acetylene, are not absorbed. The presence of ceric chloride in the solution enables the catalyst to be used for about 350 hours. In the absence of cerium the catalyst life is about 48 hours.

Acrylonitrile has also been prepared by passing a mixture of 9.2 parts of oxygen, 1.3 parts of ammonia and 1 part of acrolein over a molybdic oxide catalyst at 405°C with a residence time of 2.7 seconds.[87] The yield of acrylonitrile based on the acrolein varies from 66 to 71 per cent.

Hadley[88] prepared α,β-unsaturated nitriles by reaction of α,β-unsaturated aldehydes with ammonia and oxygen at 330–500°C in the presence of a molybdenum oxide-alumina catalyst.

The Standard Oil Co. of Ohio has developed a new process for the preparation of acrylonitrile which has not been fully described but involves the direct reaction between propylene and ammonia at high temperatures in the presence of a catalyst.

Adiponitrile is another very important nitrile used as an intermediate in the preparation of Nylon 66. It can be hydrolyzed to adipic acid, but of greater importance is its hydrogenation to hexamethylenediamine. Adiponitrile has been prepared from adipic acid by heating with ammonia as previously described. It is also made from 1,4-dichlorobutane by way of furfural, furan, tetrahydrofuran and from 1,4-dichloro-2-butene by way of butadiene and chlorine.

Adiponitrile is formed in a continuous process by passing 1,4-dichlorobutane and 20 per cent sodium cyanide together with preformed adiponitrile through a reactor under pressure at 95–120°C at a rate so that the reaction time is about 0.5 hour.[89] A two phase product results and adiponitrile is recovered from the organic layer by distillation.

Crane[90] reports that the yield of adiponitrile prepared by the reaction of 1,4-dichlorobutane with sodium cyanide is increased by the addition of calcium chloride to the reaction system. Excess adiponitrile is used as a solvent and the reaction temperature is maintained at about 140°C. The yield of adiponitrile reported was 88 per cent.

In another process for the continuous conversion of 1,4-dichlorobutane to adiponitrile, a mixture of the two compounds together with a 15–40 per cent aqueous solution of sodium cyanide is passed into a reactor at 140°C with continuous removal of the sodium chloride formed.[91] The adiponitrile recycled serves as a solvent for the dichloride. The amount of water in the reactor is maintained at 1–8 per cent. Other nitriles such as butyronitrile or benzonitrile may be used as solvents.

The most recent method for the preparation of adiponitrile uses butadiene as a starting material, and the first step involves chlorination to give a mixture of 1,4-dichloro-2-butene and 3,4-dichloro-1-butene. The vapor phase chlorination of butadiene at temperatures of 50–75°C gives a mixture of these dichlorides in 78 per cent yield.[92] It has been shown that both dichlorides give the same nitrile ($NCCH_2CH{=}CHCH_2CN$) on treatment with hydrogen cyanide.

The formation of the dinitrile has been described by Farlow.[93] The initial feed to the reactor consists of 2000 parts of water, 15 parts of cuprous chloride, 3 parts of copper powder, 3.6 parts of concentrated hydrochloric acid, and 6.9 parts of potassium chloride. The mixture is heated to 80°C and 525 parts of powdered calcium carbonate is introduced along with an additional 1000 parts of water. The temperature is then raised to 95°C and a mixture of 625 parts of dichlorobutenes and 308 parts of liquid hydrogen cyanide is added over a 2-hour period. The calcium carbonate serves as a hydrogen chloride acceptor to remove it from solution.

At the end of the reaction period, the liquid product is cooled to 60°C and a small amount of chloroform is added to prevent the precipitation of the dicyanobutene. After further cooling, the organic material is extracted with a suitable organic solvent and the dicyanobutene is recovered by crystallization.

The 1,4-dicyanobutene is hydrogenated to adiponitrile at 200–350°C under a pressure of hydrogen of 0.5 to 5 atmospheres and in the presence of a palladium on coconut charcoal catalyst.[94]

AZONITRILES

Azonitriles are of considerable interest as sources of free radicals. Azobisisobutyronitrile $(CH_3)_2C(CN)-N=N-C(CN)(CH_3)_2$ is used as a polymerization catalyst.

Azodinitriles are prepared by condensing a ketone, an alkali metal cyanide and hydrazine, and dehydrogenating with a halogen.[95] As an example, sodium cyanide is added to aqueous hydrazine sulfate and acetone is added dropwise at 25–30°C. The mixture is agitated overnight at room temperature to give hydrazodi(isobutyronitrile). This compound is suspended in ice water and chlorine introduced with agitation below 15°C. Azodi(isobutyronitrile) is obtained in 90 per cent yield.

The hydrazonitriles may also be made from cyanohydrins.

$$C_6H_5NHNH_2 + (CH_3)_2C(OH)CN \longrightarrow C_6H_5NHNHC(CH_3)_2CN + H_2O$$

The reaction is carried out in ether solution in a pressure bottle at room temperatures for 8 days.

The oxidation of the hydrazine is accomplished by shaking a chloroform solution of the hydrazine with 15 per cent potassium bromide saturated with bromine at temperatures near 0°C.[96]

Reactions of Nitriles

Hydrolysis. Nitriles may be hydrolyzed by either strong bases or strong acids to give amides or acids.

$$RCN + H_2O + NaOH \longrightarrow RCOONa + NH_3$$

$$RCN + 2H_2O + H_2SO_4 \longrightarrow RCOOH + NH_4HSO_4$$

The reaction proceeds through the formation of the amide but in most cases the amide is difficult to isolate

$$RCN + H_2O \longrightarrow RCONH_2 \xrightarrow{H_2O} RCOOH + NH_3$$

Alkaline hydrolysis is probably most frequently employed with aliphatic nitriles. Usually 20–40 per cent sodium hydroxide is used and the progress of the reaction can be followed by the liberation of ammonia. With such a procedure, valeric acid has been obtained from valeronitrile in 81 per cent yield,[97,98] and isocaproic acid from the nitrile in 82 per cent yield. Water-alcohol solutions of sodium or potassium hydroxides are sometimes used to improve the solubility of the nitrile.

Acid hydrolysis is employed more frequently with aromatic and aryl substituted aliphatic nitriles. Sulfuric acid is used in 20–70 per cent concentration and hydrochloric acid in 20 per cent concentration.

Phenylacetonitrile has been hydrolyzed to phenylacetic acid with sulfuric acid in 78 per cent yield[99] and o- and m-toluic acids have been obtained from the corresponding nitriles in 96 per cent yields.[100,101] Acetic acid is sometimes added to increase the solubility of the nitrile. *Ortho* substituents tend to interfere with the hydrolysis of aromatic nitriles.

A number of dinitriles have been hydrolyzed to dibasic acids by refluxing with concentrated hydrochloric acid. Thus glutaric and suberic acids are obtained from the corresponding dinitriles in about 90 per cent yield.[102,103]

Acid hydrolysis of the lower molecular weight unsaturated nitriles proceeds without appreciable migration of the double bond. Allyl cyanide is hydrolyzed to vinylacetic acid with concentrated hydrochloric acid in about 80 per cent yield.[104] Alkaline hydrolysis of higher molecular weight α,β-unsaturated nitriles gives a mixture of α,β- and β,γ,unsaturated acids.[105]

Although the hydrolysis of nitriles to acids proceeds very well it is difficult to stop the reaction at the intermediate amide stage. Aliphatic amides are in general more easily hydrolyzed than the corresponding nitriles so that the isolation of aliphatic amides is particularly difficult. Aryl amides can be more readily isolated from the hydrolysis products of the corresponding nitriles.

A few nitriles can be converted to amides by treatment with cold concentrated acids. Thus arylacetonitriles are hydrolyzed to the corresponding amides by vigorous agitation with cold concentrated hydrochloric acid.[106]

Travagli[107] has recently reported that mercuric oxide has catalytic activity for the hydrolysis of nitriles to amides but has no effect on the hydrolysis of amides.

Hydrogen peroxide reacts with both aliphatic and aromatic nitriles in alkaline solution at 50°C to give amides in 50–95 per cent yields

$$2RCN + 2H_2O_2 \longrightarrow 2RCONH_2 + O_2$$

The hydrogen peroxide is used in 3–30 per cent concentrations.[108,109] The reaction is not exothermic and its progress may be followed by the evolution of oxygen.

Galat[110] hydrolyzed nicotinonitrile to the amide in the presence of an anion exchange resin ("Amberlite IRA-400") which is a quaternary ammonium hydroxide derivative of polystyrene. He obtained nicotinamide in 90 per cent yield. If hydrolysis to the acid has occurred the resin would have become inactivated very quickly and this was not found to be the case. Pierce[111] extended the work of Galat and found that the method was not satisfactory for the hydrolysis of aliphatic nitriles but aromatic nitriles were hydrolyzed very readily to the corresponding amides with no evidence obtained for the formation of acids.

The reactions were carried out at reflux temperatures with an alcohol-water solution of the nitrile in the presence of a strongly basic anion exchange resin. Benzonitrile, toluonitriles, chloro- and nitro-substituted benzonitriles were hydrolyzed to the corresponding amides in conversions of 40–80 per cent.

Reactions with Alcohols. Alcohols react with nitriles in anhydrous ether in the presence of hydrogen chloride to give imino ethers

$$RCN + R'OH \xrightarrow{HCl} R-\underset{\underset{NH}{\|}}{C}-OR'$$

These imino ethers are readily hydrolyzed to esters,[112,113,114] and react with ammonia to give amidines.

$$RC(OR'){=}NH \cdot HCl \xrightarrow{NH_3} RC(NH_2){=}NH \cdot HCl + R'OH$$

N-Substituted amidines are obtained when amines are substituted for ammonia.[115,116,117]

Nitriles are converted directly to esters when heated with an alcohol containing sulfuric or hydrochloric acid.[118] Some water must be present to effect hydrolysis of the intermediate imino ether.

$$RCH_2CN + R'OH + H_2SO_4 \longrightarrow RCH_2(OR'){=}NH \cdot HSO_4 \xrightarrow{H_2O}$$

$$RCH_2COOR' + NH_4HSO_4$$

Aliphatic,[119] aromatic,[120,121] and heterocyclic[122,123] nitriles are all converted to esters in this way. Monosubstituted malonic esters are readily prepared from α-cyano esters by this procedure.

Cyanohydrins are readily converted to unsaturated esters by heating in an aqueous alcohol solution in the presence of sulfuric acid. Dehydration accompanies the preparation of the ester. Thus acetone cyanohydrin is converted to methylmethacrylate by heating in methanol containing sulfuric acid.

$$\underset{\underset{CH_3}{|}}{\overset{\overset{OH}{|}}{CH_3-C-CN}} + CH_3OH \xrightarrow{H_2SO_4} \underset{\underset{CH_3}{|}}{CH_2{=}C-COOCH_3} + NH_3 + H_2O$$

Reactions with Amines. Ammonia or ammonium chloride add to nitriles only with considerable difficulty[116] but the reaction can be accomplished in the presence of a Lewis Acid such as aluminum chloride.[124]

$$RCN + NH_3 \xrightarrow{AlCl_3} RC(NH_2){=}NH$$

Potassium derivatives of amidines may be formed by the action of potassium amide on a nitrile[125]

$$RCN + KNH_2 \longrightarrow RC({=}NH)NHK$$

Some nitriles add amines or their hydrochlorides to form N-substituted amidines in yields of 13–86 per cent.[116]

A special case of amidine formation involves the addition of ammonia to cyanamide to form guanidines. Thus alkylammonium chlorides react with cyanamide to form N-substituted guanidines[126]

$$H_2NCN + RNH_2Cl \longrightarrow \underset{\underset{NH}{\|}}{H_2N-C-NH_2RCl}$$

The reaction is general for aliphatic, arylaliphatic, and some arylamines.

Guanidine itself is obtained by heating an alcoholic solution of cyanamide and ammonium chloride.

Although nitriles ordinarily do not react with amines, activation of the group by a second nitrile or an ester group permits reaction to occur. Thus methyl cyanoacetate reacts with aqueous benzylamine at reflux temperatures to give a 92 per cent yield of the N,N'-dibenzylamide. Cyanoacetamide gives the same product in 95 per cent yield.

Sterically hindered primary amines do not react with the nitrile but give instead the corresponding salt of the cyanoalkanoic acid.[127]

Ammonia may add to unsaturated nitriles to give aminonitriles. Thus ammonia in methanol adds to the double bond of allyl cyanide at 150°C in an autoclave to give β-aminobutyronitrile.[128] In a similar manner, piperidine gives β-piperidinobutyronitrile.

Ammonia and amines add very readily to acrylonitrile but these reactions will be discussed later in this chapter.

Halogenation. Aliphatic nitriles are not easily chlorinated and usually require a catalyst for an effective reaction. Where halogenation does occur, the attack is on the carbon atom alpha to the nitrile group. Chlorination can be accomplished in the vapor phase at temperatures of 200–400°C, in the presence of catalysts such as copper or zinc chloride impregnated on carbon.[129]

Acetonitrile may be converted to trichloroacetonitrile by saturating it with HCl and chlorinating at 50–80°C until the density of the mixture is 1.19.[130] Chlorination requires 25–40 hours. Propionitrile has been chlorinated in the absence of a catalyst. Isobutyronitrile has been chlorinated in the presence of direct sunlight at 45–65°C to give α-chloroisobutyronitrile.[131] In a similar manner, benzonitrile gives hexachlorobenzonitrile but the reaction is quite slow.[132]

Grignard Reagents. Nitriles normally react with Grignard reagents to form ketimine salts which are readily hydrolyzed to ketones. The procedure is most effective for high molecular weight aliphatic and for aromatic nitriles.

$$RCN + R'MgX \longrightarrow \underset{\underset{R'}{|}}{R-C}=N-MgX \xrightarrow{H_2O} R-CO-R'$$

In some cases satisfactory results are obtained from low molecular weight aliphatic nitriles and aromatic Grignard reagents.[133,134,135]

Low yields have been attributed to a competing reaction involving an abstraction of a hydrogen atom alpha to the nitrile group by the Grignard reagent.[136]

$$RCH_2CN + R'MgX \longrightarrow R'H + (RCHCN)MgX$$

Ketones obtained from fatty acid nitriles and high molecular weight Grignard reagents are usually contaminated with hydrocarbons.[137,138] Separation is made easy by decanting the ether solution, which contains the hydrocarbon, from the ketimine salt before hydrolysis.

Nitriles containing relatively unreactive halogen atoms have been converted to halo ketones. Thus a methylmagnesium halide reacts with *o*-bromophenyl cyanide to give *o*-bromoacetophenone in 80 per cent yield.[139]

A hydroxy ketone has been prepared by the reaction of a benzyl Grignard reagent with the cyanohydrin of phenylacetaldehyde. Keto ethers have also been prepared by means of a Grignard reaction starting with cyano ethers.

Reduction. The reduction of nitriles to amines has been discussed elsewhere (Chapter 1) but the preparation of other products will be described here.

Partial reduction of nitriles with hydrazine hydrate at temperatures of 35–55°C in the presence of Raney nickel gives a hydrazone which may be hydrolyzed to an aldehyde. The reaction can be expressed by the equation.

$$2RCN + 3H_2NNH_2 \longrightarrow 2RCH{=}NNH_2 + 2NH_3 + N_2$$

The reaction probably proceeds by the initial formation of $RC({=}NH){-}NHNH_2$ and is largely restricted to aromatic nitriles.

Electrophilic substituents such as $-NO_2$ and $-COOH$ inhibit the reaction. As a general procedure the nitrile is heated for 18 hours at 55°C with three parts of Raney nickel.[140] Yields of about 70 per cent are obtained in most cases.

Nitriles are reduced to aldimines with ethereal solutions of stannous chloride and hydrogen chloride.[141] The aldimines may subsequently be hydrolyzed to aldehydes.

The reaction, as usually carried out, is nonhomogeneous involving two liquid phases. A homogeneous reagent may be prepared by adding acetyl chloride to stannous chloride dihydrate in ether. Extra hydrogen chloride is formed by adding acetyl chloride and water in equal amounts.

The first step in the reaction is probably the formation of the nitrilium salt from the nitrile and chlorostannous acid

$$RCN + H_2SnCl_4 \longrightarrow [R{-}C{\equiv}NH]^+ HSnCl_4^-$$

The concentration of chlorostannous acid must depend upon the concentration of all three reactants, and this has been observed.

For aliphatic nitriles the reagent used contains four moles of hydrogen chloride for each mole of stannous chloride. The reaction is too slow with smaller concentrations. Reaction with acetonitrile, propionitrile, butyronitrile, isobutyronitrile, and trimethylacetonitrile indicated that the structure of the nitrile has little effect upon the rate. With acetonitrile, the precipitation of the aldimine-stannic chloride complex occurs after 25 hours and markedly accelerates the reaction. Such a precipitation is a major factor in driving the reaction to completion.

In reactions with aromatic nitriles, an *ortho-* or *para*-methyl or chloro group markedly increases the reaction rate. The acceleration caused by precipitation of the aldimine salt again increases the reaction rate.

The lower aliphatic nitriles give only poor to moderate yields of product but the yield from normal nitriles increases with chain length. Chain branching in the α-position lowers the yield.[142]

Knight and Zook[143] claim that lauronitrile is not reduced with stannous chloride to give the corresponding aldehyde. Instead the N,N'-alkylidine-bisacylamide $(C_{11}H_{22}CONH)_2CHC_{11}H_{23}$ is obtained. This compound can be hydrolyzed to lauraldehyde, ammonia and lauric acid. If the reaction is carried out in the presence of phenylhydrazine, the hydrazone of the aldehyde is obtained.

The reaction probably proceeds according to the following scheme:

$$[RCH{=}NH_2]^+Cl^- \xrightarrow{R'CN} \left[\underset{(+)}{R'C}{=}N{-}\underset{NH_2}{CHR}\right] Cl^- \xrightarrow[HCl]{R'CN}$$

$$[\underset{(+)}{R'C}{=}NCHR{-}N{=}\underset{(+)}{CR'}]2Cl^- \xrightarrow{H_2O} (R'CONH)_2CHR + 2HCl$$

Aldehydes may be obtained from fatty acid nitriles by reduction with lithium aluminum hydride in tetrahydrofuran. Thus stearonitrile gives a 25 per cent yield of octadecanal in 48 hours at $-60°C$.[144]

Nitriles may also be reduced to aldehydes in tetrahydrofuran by $NaHAl(OC_2H_5)_3$ prepared from sodium hydride and aluminum ethoxide.[145] The reaction is complete after 1–2 hours at room temperature. The aldehydes are recovered by solvent extraction or by steam distillation. Thus benzaldehyde is obtained from benzonitrile in 92 per cent yield and *o*-methylbenzaldehyde from *o*-methylbenzonitrile in 88 per cent yield. Aliphatic nitriles are converted to aldehydes in 25–30 per cent yield.

Hydrogenation of benzonitrile over a nickel-copper-kiesulguhr catalyst at 200–400°C results in the cleavage of the $C{\equiv}N$ bond with the formation of toluene and ammonia. The optimum temperature is 250°C to give toluene in 87 per cent yield. Above 250°C the CN group is eliminated from benzoniitrile with the formation of benzene and methylamine and at 370°C conversion to benzene is 40 per cent. Under similar conditions benzylamine gives more toluene and less benzene than does the benzonitrile. It is believed that the cleavage to toluene and ammonia takes place through the intermediate benzylamine and that direct elimination of the nitrile group is the main route to benzene.[146]

Watanabe[147] investigated the hydrogenation of *p*- and *o*-aminobenzonitriles. *p*-Aminobenzonitrile gives an 80 per cent yield of *p*-aminotoluene. Under the same conditions the ortho isomer is relatively stable, giving only a 9 per cent yield of *o*-aminotoluene. In this case the main reaction involves the elimination of the cyanide group with the formation of aniline. The yield is 52 per cent at 350°C.

Catalytic hydrogenation of *p*-nitrobenzonitrile in the presence of a 6:4 nickel-copper on kieselguhr catalyst gives *p*-toluidine (35–39 per cent yield) and *p*-aminobenzonitrile (16–35 per cent yield). Higher temperatures favor the formation of *p*-aminobenzonitrile. Optimum temperatures for the formation of *p*-toluidine are 280–300°C. Above 300°C aniline is obtained in about 14 per cent yield.[148]

m-Nitrobenzonitrile under similar conditions gives *m*-toluidine, *m*-aminobenzonitrile and aniline. At a temperature of 350°C the yield of aniline is 45 per cent. Maximum yields of *m*-toluidine (55 per cent) are obtained at 250°C and of *m*-aminobenzonitrile (27 per cent) at 300°C.

Similar products are obtained with *o*-nitrobenzonitrile. The maximum yield of aniline (64 per cent) is obtained at 330°C. *o*-Toluidine is obtained in 17 per cent yield at 300°C and *o*-aminobenzonitrile in 20 per cent yield at 300°C.

The presence of an amino group tends to favor the elimination of cyano groups and other side reactions. The nearer the amino group is to the nitrile, the greater is the interference.

Selective hydrogenation can sometimes be effected with dinitriles. Thus adiponitrile is hydrogenated in benzene solution in the presence of Raney nickel to give an 81 per cent yield of ε-aminocapronitrile.[149] A temperature of 120°C and a pressure of 175 atmospheres are required.

Monoaminonitriles are prepared by the hydrogenation of dinitriles in the presence of a nickel catalyst and anhydrous ammonia.[150] Thus adiponitrile is hydrogenated in methylal solution in the presence of Raney nickel and anhydrous ammonia at 100°C and pressures of 700–1000 psi. The products obtained are in part dependent upon the amount of hydrogen absorbed and the reaction is not continued until all of the dinitrile is consumed. Yields of 84 per cent of ε-aminocapronitrile have been obtained. The remainder of the product is hexamethylene diamine.

Catalytic hydrogenation of glutaronitrile at 170°C and under a pressure of 3800 psi in the presence of a cobalt on kieselguhr catalyst and anhydrous ammonia gives piperidine and some 1,5-pentanediamine which can be further converted to piperidine by pyrolysis.[151] A Raney nickel catalyst gives yields of about 83 per cent.

Biggs and Bishop[152] report that methylamine is a good solvent in which to hydrogenate dinitriles and may be used alone or in conjunction with liquid ammonia.

Miscellaneous Reactions. The α-hydrogens of nitriles can be exchanged quite easily for deuterium by refluxing the nitrile with deuterium oxide in the presence of a base. Thus refluxing acetonitrile with calcium deuteroxide in heavy water produced 93 per cent CD_3CN. Similarly propionitrile is converted to CH_3CD_2CN. These deuterated nitriles can be hydrolysed to the corresponding acids in the presence of mineral acid catalyst without loss of deuterium.[153]

The oxidation of saturated nitriles containing 3 to 5 carbon atoms at temperatures of 300–800°C in the presence of metal catalysts gives unsaturated nitriles having the same number of carbon atoms. Satisfactory catalysts include, silver, copper, gold and the platinum metals.

Air or oxygen is mixed with the preheated nitrile and passed over the catalyst at such a rate as to give residence times of 0.001–2.0 seconds. In this manner methacrylonitrile is obtained from isobutyronitrile.[154] Because of thermal cracking a small amount of acrylonitrile is also formed.

In the presence of sodium amide, nitriles having α-hydrogens may undergo two different types of reaction. One involves the addition of the amide ion to form an amidine

$$RCH_2CN + NaNH_2 \longrightarrow \underset{\underset{NH_2}{|}}{RCH{=}NH} \quad \text{or} \quad \underset{\underset{NH^-Na^+}{|}}{RCH{=}NH}$$

The second involves the removal of an α-hydrogen to form a nitrile anion which is the reactive intermediate in carbon-carbon condensations such as acylation or alkylation

$$RCH_2{-}C{\equiv}N + NaNH_2 \longrightarrow R{-}CH{=}C{=}N^-Na^+ + NH_3$$

Phenylacetonitrile forms the nitrile ion exclusively but acetonitrile and especially the higher aliphatic nitriles may form the amidine as well as the nitrile ion.

Nitriles can be acylated with esters to form β-keto nitriles with sodium amide.[155]

$$C_6H_5CH_2CN \xrightarrow[\text{ether}]{\text{NaNH}_2} \overset{(-)}{C_6H_5CH-CN} \xrightarrow{\text{RCOOCH}_3}$$
$$Na^+$$

$$\underset{\overset{|}{COR}}{C_6H_5-CH-CN} \xrightarrow{\text{NaNH}_2} \underset{\overset{|}{COR}}{\overset{Na^{(+)}}{\underset{}{C_6H_5-C-CN}}}$$

The yields are considerably better with phenylacetonitrile (68 per cent α-acetylphenylacetonitrile) than are observed with aliphatic nitriles (propionylacetonitrile, 40 per cent). Sodium amide gives higher yields of products than are obtained with sodium ethoxide.

A similar method can be employed using sodium amide in liquid ammonia. The reaction is carried out by adding a solution of the nitrile in ether to sodium amide in liquid ammonia followed after 5 minutes by the rapid addition of the ester in ether. The yields of ketonitriles are 55–95 per cent.

Nitriles having only one α-hydrogen react with sodium amide to form amidines. The addition of benzoyl chloride to an ether solution of sodium amide and isobutyronitrile gives an N-acylated amide.[156]

$$(CH_3)_2CHCN \xrightarrow{\text{NaNH}_2} \underset{\overset{|}{NH_2}}{(CH_3)_2CH-C=N-Na} \xrightarrow{C_6H_5COCl}$$

$$\underset{\overset{||}{NH}}{(CH_3)_2CH-C-NHCOC_6H_5} \xrightarrow{H_2O} (CH_3)_2CHCONHCOC_6H_5$$

Malononitrile is dimerized by reaction with alkali alkoxides.[157] Thus malononitrile added to a methanol solution containing 4 per cent sodium methoxide at 45°C gives a tautomeric mixture of

$$(NC)_2CH-C(=NH)-CH_2CN \text{ and } (NC)_2C=C(NH_2)-CH_2CN$$

Only 5 minutes are required to complete the reaction.

Acetonitrile can participate in a Diels-Alder type reaction in which the carbon-nitrogen triple bond is involved. The reaction of acetonitrile with butadiene, isoprene and 2-methyl-1,3-pentadiene at 400°C in the presence of alumina yields 2-methylpyridine, 2,4-dimethylpyridine and 2,4,6-trimethylpyridine. The relative reactivity of the above dienes is found to be 1:6:8, respectively. Contact times of about four seconds give conversions of about eight per cent of the value predicted for the reaction equilibrium. The reaction is considered to proceed by the following mechanism.

$$
\begin{array}{c}
\underset{HC}{\overset{\displaystyle CH_2}{\diagup}} \\
\underset{HC}{\overset{|}{}} \\
\underset{CH_2}{\diagdown}
\end{array}
\;+\;
\underset{N}{\overset{\displaystyle}{/\!/}}C-CH_3
\;\longrightarrow\;
\overset{\displaystyle}{\bigcirc}\!\!\underset{N}{}\diagdown CH_3
\;+\; H_2
$$

Hydrogen cyanide and nitriles react with butadiene to give pyridine or pyridine derivatives. A mixture of the nitrile and butadiene is passed over an alumina or chromia-alumina catalyst at 400°C to give pyridine compounds in 30–60 per cent yields.[158] Reaction times of about 4 seconds are desirable. Some of the products obtained are shown in Table 5–1.

TABLE 5–1. DIELS ALDER ADDUCTS OF BUTADIENES WITH NITRILES

Nitrile	Butadiene	Isoprene
C_6H_5CN	2-Phenylpyridine	2-Phenyl-4-methylpyridine 2-Phenyl-5-methylpyridine
CH_3CN	2-Methylpyridine	2,4-Dimethylpyridine 2,5-Dimethylpyridine
NC—CN	2-Cyanopyridine	2-Cyano-4-methylpyridine 2-Cyano-5-methylpyridine
HCN	Pyridine	

Nitriles react with formaldehyde in acidic media (mole ratio 2:1) to yield methylenebisamides.[159] Magat has described the reaction of dinitriles with formaldehyde to form polyamides.[160]

Polymerization does not occur if the dinitrile contains basic centers because in the strongly acidic media a proton can attach itself to the basic nitrogen atom thus imparting an over all positive charge to the dinitrile. This confirms the postulated mechanism which involves the initial attack by a methylolcarbonium ion ($^+CH_2OH$) formed by the addition of a proton to formaldehyde.

The polymer formed from succinonitrile and formaldehyde is a solid which darkens at about 200°C and decomposes at 300°C.

Acetylation of cyanohydrins is best accomplished with ketene according to Yates.[161] Thus the cyanohydrin of acetaldehyde is converted to α-cyanoethyl acetate, $CH_3COOCH(CN)CH_3$, in 99 per cent yield in 2 hours in the presence of about 0.1 per cent sodium hydroxide. In the absence of the sodium hydroxide a 70 per cent yield was obtained after 4.5 hours. The ester can be readily pyrolyzed to unsaturated nitriles and this method for the preparation of unsaturated nitriles frequently is more satisfactory than the dehydration of cyanohydrins.

Nitriles react with unsaturated acids in the presence of concentrated sulfuric acid by addition of the corresponding amide across the double bond.[162] Thus acetonitrile reacts with oleic acid in 95 per cent sulfuric acid to give

$$CH_3(CH_2)_7CHCH_2(CH_2)_7COOH \text{ and } CH_3(CH_2)_7CH_2CH(CH_2)_7COOH$$
$$|$$
$$H_3CCONH \qquad\qquad\qquad H_3CCO-NH$$

Benzonitrile adds to the carbon-nitrogen double bond of imines, Schiff's bases and some hydrazones. Slow evaporation of an ether solution of $(C_6H_5)_2C=NH$ and benzonitrile gives a 97 per cent yield of $(C_6H_5)_2$-$\underset{\underset{CN}{|}}{C}NHC_6H_5$. Treating $(C_6H_5)_2C=NH$ with anhydrous HCN in benzene and distilling the benzene gives $(C_6H_5)_2C(NH_2)CN$ in 82 per cent yield.[163]

Nitriles can be made to form cyclic trimers under very high pressures.[164] Thus acetonitrile, propionitrile, n-butyronitrile and benzonitrile form triazines at 60–150°C under a pressure of 7000–8500 atmospheres. Even nitriles having no alpha hydrogens react in this way.

Nitriles undergo aldol-like condensations in the presence of sodium amide.[165] Thus acetonitrile reacts with butyronitrile to give β-amino-β-n-propylglutaronitrile.

$$n\text{-}C_3H_7CN + 2CH_3CN \xrightarrow{\text{NaNH}_2} n\text{-}C_3H_7-C(NH_2)-(CH_2CN)_2$$

Acrylonitrile

From an industrial point of view, acrylonitrile is one of the most important nitriles. It is prepared, as previously described, by the dehydration of ethylene cyanohydrin and by the addition of hydrogen cyanide to acetylene.

Acrylonitrile is a very versatile compound exhibiting reactions of the nitrile group and of the double bond. In addition to the usual reagents which add to the carbon-carbon double bond, the cyanoethyl group is introduced into a wide variety of compounds containing active hydrogen atoms. This is a special case of addition referred to as cyanoethylation.

Reactions of the Nitrile Group. Acrylonitrile is converted to acrylamide by treatment with 85 per cent sulfuric acid. The acrylamide is freed from the amide sulfate thus formed, with a base.[166]

$$CH_2=CHCN + H_2SO_4 + H_2O \rightarrow CH_2=CHCONH_2 \cdot H_2SO_4 \xrightarrow{\text{CaO}}$$

$$CH_2=CHCONH_2 + CaSO_4 + H_2O$$

The acrylamide sulfate reacts with alcohols to form acrylic acid esters.

$$CH_2{=}CHCONH_2 \cdot H_2SO_4 + CH_3OH \rightarrow CH_2{=}CHCOOCH_3 + NH_4HSO_4$$

Acrylonitrile is readily hydrolyzed to acrylic acid in the presence of either strong acids or strong bases.[167,168]

N-Substituted amides can be obtained by the action of acrylonitrile with an olefin in the presence of aqueous sulfuric acid. Thus 2-methyl-2-butene gives N-*tert*-amyl acrylamide

$$CH_2{=}CHCN + (CH_3)_2C{=}CHCH_3 + H_2O \xrightarrow{H_2SO_4}$$

$$CH_2{=}CH{-}CONH{-}\underset{\underset{C_2H_5}{|}}{C}{-}(CH_3)_2$$

Formaldehyde in 85 per cent sulfuric acid gives methylenediacrylamide.[169]

$$2CH_2{=}CHCN + HCHO + H_2O \rightarrow (CH_2{=}CHCONH)_2CH_2$$

Reactions of the Double Bond. Acrylonitrile readily participates as a dienophile in the Diels Alder reaction. Thus with butadiene, 1,2,5,6-tetrahydrobenzonitrile is formed.[170,171]

With piperylene it is possible to form two pairs of *cis-trans* isomers

The major product is the *cis-ortho* isomer.

Diels Alder reactions have been carried out with a large number of dienes including chloroprene,[170] cyclopentadiene,[173] isoprene,[174] and myrcene.[175]

The Diels Alder reactions with acrylonitrile require reaction times of 5–24 hours at temperatures of 100–150°C.

Acrylonitrile reacts with some unsaturated compounds to form cyclobutane derivatives. Thus prolonged heating with tetrafluoroethylene at 150°C gives 2,2,3,3-tetrafluorocyclobutanecarbonitrile.[176,177,178]

$$CH_2\!\!=\!\!CHCN + CF_2\!\!=\!\!CF_2 \longrightarrow \begin{array}{c} CH_2\!-\!CF_2 \\ | \qquad | \\ CH\ -\!CF_2 \\ | \\ CN \end{array}$$

At 190–300°C under pressure, acrylonitrile dimerizes to a mixture of the *cis*- and *trans*- forms of 1,2-dyclobutanedicarbonitrile.[179]

$$2CH_2\!\!=\!\!CHCN \longrightarrow \begin{array}{c} CH_2\!-\!CH\!-\!CN \\ | \qquad\qquad | \\ CH_2\!-\!CH\!-\!CN \end{array}$$

Hydrogenation of acrylonitrile in the presence of a copper or nickel catalyst first gives propionitrile then *n*-propylamine.[180,181]

Under alkaline conditions, e.g., with magnesium in anhydrous methanol or with sodium amalgam in water, adiponitrile is formed.[182]

$$2CH_2\!\!=\!\!CHCN + 2CH_3OH + Mg \longrightarrow NC(CH_2)_4CN + (CH_3O)_2Mg$$

When sodium amalgam is used the yield of adiponitrile is 37 per cent.

Halogens add to the double bond of acrylonitrile only with great difficulty. A dilute solution of bromine in carbon tetrachloride does not show any discoloration in 15 minutes and no apparent reaction with chlorine occurs for at least 2 hours.[183]

Chlorine adds to acrylonitrile, in pyridine, quite readily to give α,β-dichloropropionitrile.[184] The same compound can also be made at room temperature by direct chlorination in the presence of ultraviolet light.[185] Chlorination of acrylonitrile in water solution gives α-chloro-β-hydroxy-propionitrile, $HOCH_2CH_2ClCN$.[186,187] α-Chloroacrylonitrile has been obtained by high temperature chlorination in the presence of activated carbon.[188]

Diazonium chlorides add to acrylonitrile at low temperatures with the loss of nitrogen to give α-chloro-β-arylpropionitriles.[189,190,191]

$$CH_2\!\!=\!\!CHCN + C_6H_5N_2{}^+Cl^- \xrightarrow{Cu^+} C_6H_5CH_2CHClCN + N_2$$

Acetone has been reported to be the only effective solvent and cuprous salts are necessary catalysts. A large number of diazotized amines have been investigated with positive results.

Cyanoethylation Reactions. A large number of compounds containing active hydrogen atoms add across the carbon-carbon double bond of acrylonitrile in the presence of a strong base. These compounds include water, alcohols, amines, amides, mercaptans, active methylene compounds such as ethyl cyanoacetate, ketones, nitroparaffins, etc.[192] The reaction proceeds by a nucleophilic attack, rather than the usual electrophilic attack which occurs with most carbon-carbon double bond systems. Thus an alcohol adds in the following manner.

$$ROH + CH_2\!\!=\!\!CHCN \longrightarrow [ROCH_2CHCN]^- H^+ \longrightarrow ROCH_2CH_2CN$$

The role of the base is probably to extract a proton from the alcohol to leave an alkoxide ion which attacks the double bond.

The more common basic catalysts used include alkali metal hydroxides, alkoxides, hydrides and cyanides. In some cases the alkali metals themselves are used as catalysts.

Many of the reactions are highly exothermic and require cooling. Usual reaction temperatures are near room temperature but in some cases may be as high as 100°C.

Most of the reactions with primary and secondary alcohols take place near room temperature. The cyanoethylation of alcohols is an equilibrium reaction with the position of equilibrium being more favorable with primary than with secondary alcohols. Thus 2-propanol gives a lower yield of cyanoethylated product (69 per cent) than does methanol (89 per cent) ethanol (78 per cent) or 1-butanol (86 per cent).

Tertiary alcohols react only with difficulty. *tert*-Butyl alcohol requires temperatures of about 80°C in the presence of 2 per cent sodium hydroxide to form β-(*tert*-butoxy)propionitrile.[195] The reactions of other tertiary alcohols have not been sufficiently investigated.

Other alcohols which have been successfully cyanoethylated include benzyl alcohol,[193] cyclohexanol,[196] menthol[197] and unsaturated alcohols such as allyl alcohol,[195,198] furfuryl alcohol, oleyl alcohol, cinnamyl alcohol, geraniol, linallol and citronellol.

Acrylonitrile reacts with cyclohexanol in the presence of potassium hydroxide at temperatures below 30°C to give $C_6H_{11}OCH_2CH_2CN$ which may be hydrogenated in methanol saturated with ammonia over Raney nickel at 95–105°C and 145 atmospheres pressure to give the corresponding amine.[199]

Glycols usually give di-cyanoethylated products. Thus ethylene glycol gives $NCCH_2CH_2OCH_2CH_2OCH_2CH_2CN$ in 80 per cent yield[200,201] and 1,4-pentanediol gives the dicyanoethylated product in 83 per cent yield. Glycerol gives a tricyanoethylated derivative in 74 per cent yield.

Astle and Etherington[202] report that anion exchange resins of the quaternary ammonium hydroxide type ("Dowex 1") are good catalysts for the cyanoethylation of alcohols and that when a ratio of 2 moles of acrylonitrile to 1 of ethylene glycol is used a 68 per cent yield of monocyano-ethylated product is obtained.

Carbohydrates may also be cyanoethylated and the most important of these reactions occurs with cellulose. Cotton is steeped in aqueous sodium hydroxide then treated with acrylonitrile to give a cyanoethylated cellulose which is rot- and mildew-resistant. This process is finding considerable application in the textile field.

Formaldehyde in aqueous solution behaves as if it were methylene glycol to give a dicyanoethylated product, $NCCH_2CH_2OCH_2OCH_2CH_2CN$.[203]

Cyanohydrins and chlorohydrins are successfully cyanoethylated through the OH groups.

Water reacts with acrylonitrile in the presence of a base to give β,β'-oxy-dipropionitrile.[200,204] This compound has been suggested as a selective solvent for the separation of aromatic hydrocarbons from aliphatic and alicyclic hydrocarbons.

The reactions of acrylonitrile with thiols are analogous to those with alcohols. The reaction takes place at temperatures below 50°C in the presence of a basic catalyst.[205] Alkanethiols give β-cyanoethyl sulfides.

$$RSH + CH_2{=}CHCN \longrightarrow RSCH_2CH_2CN$$

and hydrogen sulfide gives β,β'-thiodipropionitrile $S(CH_2CH_2CN)_2$.

The reaction of acrylonitrile with hydroxyl groups of phenols occurs at temperatures of 120–140°C in the presence of alkali metals or hydroxides, tertiary amines such as pyridine, quinoline or dimethyl aniline, or quaternary ammonium hydroxides ("Triton B").[206] With phenol, a good yield of β-phenoxypropionitrile is obtained.

$$C_6H_5OH + CH_2{=}CHCN \longrightarrow C_6H_5OCH_2CH_2CN$$

Other phenolic compounds behave similarly.

Phenol is cyanoethylated in the presence of anhydrous aluminum chloride and hydrogen chloride to give β-(p-hydroxyphenyl)propionitrile in 72 per cent yield.[207] None of the o-cyanoethylated phenol is obtained, suggesting that steric hindrance is important in the determination of the point of attack.

Alkyl phenols such as nonyl-, decyl-, and octyl-phenols react with acrylonitrile to form β-(alkylphenoxy)-propionitriles.

$$C_{12}H_{25}C_6H_4OH + CH_2{=}CHCN \longrightarrow C_{12}H_{25}C_6H_4OCH_2CH_2CN$$

The reaction is accomplished by heating the alkyl phenol with sodium methoxide and a little sodium to 150°C, adding acrylonitrile and heating at reflux temperatures for 24–48 hours. Hydroquinone is added to inhibit the polymerization of the acrylonitrile.

The products are excellent biological toxicants, liquid dielectrics, lubricants, and plasticizers. β-(Nonylphenoxy)propionitrile is an excellent aquatic herbicide.[208]

Oximes can be cyanoethylated at temperatures of 25–50°C. Thus a solution of acetone oxime or cyclohexanone oxime in dioxane reacts with acrylonitrile in the presence of small amounts of sodium methoxide at 25–35°C to give oximino ethers in 60–90 per cent yield

$$(CH_3)_2C{=}NOH + CH_2{=}CHCN \longrightarrow (CH_3)_2C{=}N{-}O{-}CH_2CH_2CN$$

Acetophenone oxime in benzene containing a small amount of "Triton B" adds to the double bond of acrylonitrile at 40–50°C.[200,209]

Cyanoethylation of ammonia and most amines does not require a catalyst. A primary amine is capable of forming a mono- or di-cyanoethylated and ammonia a tricyanoethylated product. Low temperatures favor monocyanoethylation.[210,211] When anhydrous liquid ammonia and acrylonitrile (mole ratio 5:4) are heated in an autoclave at 90°C for 30 minutes, β-aminopropionitrile is obtained in 12.5 per cent yield and bis-(2-cyanoethyl)-amine in 75 per cent yield.[212]

With a mole ratio of 8:1 and a temperature of 40°C, a 22 per cent yield of monocyanoethylated and a 64 per cent yield of dicyanoethylated product is obtained.

Rapid addition of acrylonitrile below the surface of a large excess of aqueous ammonia at a temperature of 110°C; allowing a short reaction time followed by rapid cooling, gives a 60 per cent yield of β-aminopropionitrile.[213] The tricyanoethylated product does not form readily.

Ammonium acetate and acrylonitrile in aqueous methanol refluxed 20 hours at 68°C gives tris(β-cyanoethyl)-amine in 30 per cent yield.[214]

Methylamine adds to acrylonitrile in the cold to give β-methylaminopropionitrile in 78 per cent yield. At 80°C in a sealed tube the dicyanoethylation becomes the major reaction.[215] Similar results are obtained with other low molecular weight primary amines.

Secondary amines having one long chain and one short chain alkyl group may be prepared by the following steps:

1. Cyanoethylation of a long-chain fatty amine

$$C_{18}H_{37}NH_2 + CH_2{=}CHCN \longrightarrow C_{18}H_{37}NHCH_2CH_2CN$$

2. Alkylation of the amino nitrile with a low molecular weight alkyl halide

$$C_{18}H_{37}NHCH_2CH_2CN + CH_3Cl \rightarrow C_{18}H_{37}N(CH_3)CH_2CH_2CN$$

3. Pyrolysis at 200–275°C for 5–6 hours

$$C_{18}H_{37}N(CH_3)CH_2CH_2CN \rightarrow C_{18}H_{37}NHCH_3 + CH_2{=}CHCN$$

The over-all yield is determined largely by the success of the alkylation step and the reaction is made possible by the reversibility of the cyano-ethylation reaction.

To illustrate the process, dodecylamine is cyanoethylated at 35°C to give 2-cyanoethyldodecylamine which is methylated with methanol and formic acid at temperatures not greater than 65°C. The resulting 2-cyanoethyl-methyldodecylamine is pyrolyzed at 250–275°C to give N-methyldodecyl-amine. The over-all yield is about 80 per cent.

Alkylation with ethylene oxide gives an 80 per cent yield of 2-hydroxy-ethyldodecylamine.

The reactions of piperidine and morpholine with acrylonitrile are exo-thermic and give cyanoethylated products in almost quantitative yields. Diethylamine is somewhat less reactive but gives excellent yield of prod-ucts.[210,217] Whitmore's work indicates that the rate of reaction is primarily dependent upon the size and complexity of the amine and has little relation-ship to the basicity of the amine.

Cupric chloride has been reported to be a highly effective catalyst for the cyanoethylation of aromatic amines. Unlike other catalysts its action is not appreciably affected by the presence of *ortho*- or N-substituents on the amine to be cyanoethylated. Improved yields and shorter reaction times re-sult from its use as a catalyst. With amines melting above 75°C, dioxane is used as a solvent. The reactions are carried out at reflux temperatures, or at 100–110°C, whichever is lower.[218]

Pietra[219] used choline hydrate to promote the cyanoethylation of nitro- or halogen-substituted aryl amines. Thus acrylonitrile and *o*-nitroaniline give a 70 per cent yield of N-2-cyanoethyl-*o*-nitroaniline.

Arylamines can be cyanoethylated by an exchange reaction with $(C_2H_5)_2NCH_2CH_2CN$. The reaction is dependant upon the basic strength of the arylamine and is hindered by *ortho*-substituents and by bulky N-substituents. The yield is also affected by the nature of the amino group displaced. The diethylamino group gives optimum yields.

Instead of preformed $(C_2H_5)_2NCH_2CH_2CN$, a mixture of acrylonitrile and diethylamine may be used. The cyanoethylation reaction is accom-

plished by refluxing the arylammonium chloride or benzene sulfonate with
β-diethylaminopropionitrile at 180°C to give $R-C_6H_4-NHCH_2CH_2CN$
in 70–90 per cent yields.[220]

The reversibility of the cyanoethylation reaction is evidenced by the
fact that cyanoethyldiethanolamine when distilled gives diethanolamine
and a polymer of acrylonitrile[210] and cyanoethylcyclohexylamine gives a
20 per cent yield of cyclohexylamine.

A large variety of amines have been reacted with acrylonitrile. Piperazine gives a dicyanoethylated product.[221]

$$NCCH_2CH_2N \underset{CH_2CH_2}{\overset{CH_2CH_2}{<}} N-CH_2CH_2CN$$

Amides undergo cyanoethylation in the presence of sodium or potassium
hydroxides. Thus formamide gives a mono- or dicyanoethylated product.[192]

$$HCONH_2 + CH_2=CHCN \longrightarrow HCONHCH_2CH_2CN \longrightarrow HCON(CH_2CH_2CN)_2$$

Up to 5 or 6 moles of acrylonitrile have reacted with amides but the structures of these products are not known.

Acetamide when used in excess gives a good yield of β-acetaminopropio-
nitrile.

Imides and lactams are readily cyanoethylated at 90–95°C.

Acrylonitrile reacts with nitroparaffins having α-hydrogen atoms in the
presence of sodium or potassium hydroxide, sodium ethoxide or quaternary ammonium hydroxide ("Triton B"). Equimolar quantities of nitromethane and acrylonitrile in the presence of sodium hydroxide gives mainly
the monocyanoethylated product,[222] $O_2NCH_2CH_2CN$. With excess acrylonitrile, *tris*-(2-cyanoethyl)-nitromethane is the major product together with
small amounts of the mono- and di-cyanoethylated products.[223]

Nitroethane and 1-nitropropane give a mixture of mono- and di-cyanoethylated nitropropanes with the reaction occurring on the carbon atom
alpha to the nitro group.

2-Nitropropane and nitrocyclohexene[222,224] give only monocyano-
ethylated products.

Ketones react in much the same way as nitroparaffins. α-Hydrogen
atoms of the ketones are involved to give mono-, di-, or tri-cyanoethylated
products.

Acetone gives a tricyanoethylated derivative $CH_3COC(CH_2CH_2CN)_3$ in
80 per cent yield in the presence of sodium hydroxide.[225]

Heating chloroform and freshly distilled acrylonitrile and a small
amount of hydroquinone in an autoclave gives $Cl_3CCH_2CH_2CN$ as the

major product together with Cl_2CHCH_2CHCl—CN. Carbon tetrachloride gives predominantly Cl_3CCH_2CHCl—CN.[226]

Methyl ethyl ketone, methyl propyl ketone, etc., are dicyanoethylated on the α-methylene carbon atom. Cyclohexanone and cyclopentanone react with 4 moles of acrylonitrile to get complete reaction on both of the α-carbon atoms.[225,227]

Aryl alkyl ketones react very readily. Acetophenone and its derivatives give tri-cyanoethylated products in good yield.

Aldehydes having α-hydrogen atoms also may be easily cyanoethylated but the reactions are complicated by competing aldol condensations and resinification.

Other compounds having active methylene groups such as malonic and acetoacetic esters may be mono- or di-cyanoethylated. Diethyl malonate is dicyanoethylated in 83 per cent yield in the presence of "Triton B." to give $(NCCH_2CH_2)_2C(COOC_2H_5)_2$.[228]

Polymerization. Acrylonitrile polymerizes rapidly at room temperatures if oxygen, moisture and amines are carefully excluded. The polymerization is rapid, exothermic and usually initiated by peroxide promoters. Polymerization may occur in the vapor or liquid phase or in solution.

Redox catalyst systems are frequently employed for polymerization of acrylonitrile in water solutions.

Acrylonitrile is frequently used as a copolymer with butadiene, vinyl acetate, vinyl chloride, etc. Polyacrylonitrile is a good synthetic fiber but since it is insoluble in ordinary spinning solvents a copolymer with vinyl chloride or vinyl acetate is most frequently used. Copolymers containing 60–80 per cent acrylonitrile are reported to have some advantages over wool. These fibers have good strength and resiliency and are not attacked by moths or mildew.

Acrylonitrile is polymerized readily in the presence of 2 per cent tributylboron and 2 mole per cent boron trifluoride etherate at 70°C. In 2 hours 66.5 per cent polymer is formed in xylene solution. After 6 hours a yield of 82 per cent polymer is obtained. Higher molecular weight polymers are probably formed when dimethylformamide is used as the solvent.[229]

Copolymers with butadiene are speciality synthetic rubbers used primarily because they are inert to the action of oils and greases.

AMIDES

Amides are compounds containing the functional group —$CONH_2$. Dehydration results in the formation of nitriles and hydrolysis gives acids. The properties of the amino group are greatly modified by the presence of the carbonyl oxygen.

Amides are far less basic than amines and this can be readily explained by the resonance concept involving structures of the type

$$R-\overset{\overset{\displaystyle \frown}{\ddot{}}}{\underset{\displaystyle O}{\underset{\|}{C}}}-NH_2 \longleftrightarrow R-\underset{\underset{\displaystyle O_{(-)}}{|}}{C}=\overset{(+)}{N}H_2$$

in which the unshared electron pair on the nitrogen atom is much less available for bonding with a proton than in the amine. That the amides are basic can be demonstrated by the fact that many of them can be titrated in glacial acetic acid with hydrochloric acid. They also behave as weak acids especially in liquid ammonia in which they neutralize metal amides.

$$RCONH_2 + NaNH_2 \overset{NH_3}{\longrightarrow} RCONHNa + NH_3$$

Formamide, like water, has a very high dielectric constant[84] and consequently is of some interest as an ionizing solvent and as a medium for the deposition of metals.

Dimethyl formamide, $HCON(CH_3)_2$, is an excellent solvent for acetylene and for certain high polymers such as polyacrylonitrile. It is also an excellent solvent for the formation of nitriles from alkyl halides and sodium cyanide.[230] The reaction is carried out at reflux temperature.

The amides of the fatty acids are relatively high melting crystalline solids which are only slightly soluble in organic solvents and in water. The high melting points and low solubilities of the amide are a result of molecular association through hydrogen bonding.

Preparation of Amides

Amides are most readily obtained by the action of ammonia or amines on acids or acid derivatives. Ammonia reacts with acids to give ammonium salts which are dehydrated to amides on heating. This dehydration is reversible

$$RCO_2NH_4 \longrightarrow RCONH_2 + H_2O$$

Good yields of amides are obtained by distilling off the water from the reaction mixture as fast as it is formed. Acetamide is prepared in 90 per cent yield by heating ammonium acetate in glacial acetic acid at 110°C.[231] Higher molecular weight aliphatic amines are prepared by passing excess ammonia through the molten acid at 160–210°C.[232,233]

Primary and secondary amines can be substituted for ammonia in the preparation of N-substituted amides. Benzanilide, $C_6H_5CONHC_6H_5$, is obtained in 84 per cent yield by heating a mixture of benzoic acid and aniline to 180–190°C and removing the water together with some aniline as the water is formed in the reaction.[234]

N-Methylformanilide is prepared from formic acid and N-methylaniline by removing the water as formed as a toluene azeotrope.[235]

The dehydration of ammonium salts is of particular interest in the preparation of long-chain fatty acid amides. The reaction may be considered to take place in two steps but in practice only one is involved. Thus palmitamide is prepared by heating the free acid with ammonia at temperatures of 160–200°C.[236] The reaction velocity increases at first with the amount of ammonia but gradually reaches a constant value. Silica gel is reported to be an effective catalyst.

Substituted amides can be prepared by the action of an acid with an amine in the presence of a tetraalkyl pyrophosphite,[237] $(C_2H_5)_2P—O—P(C_2H_5)_2$. Thus when tetraethylpyrophosphite is added to a mixture of salicylic acid and aniline, a reaction starts spontaneously. The mixture is heated for 20 minutes at 95°C after which time aqueous sodium bicarbonate is added to neutralize the solution. Salicylanilide is isolated in 50 per cent yield.

Boric acid has been proposed as a catalyst for the preparation of amides from amines and carboxylic acids.[238] Boric acid reduces the reaction time, the amount of product degradation and improves the color of the product. Thus one mole of $(H_2NCH_2CH_2CH_2)_2NH$ is heated with three moles of stearic acid and 1–2 per cent boric acid and toluene. The toluene serves as a water entrainer. Yields of amides of 95 per cent, as white products, are obtained in 4.5 hours. In the absence of the boric acid 7 hours are required and the product is gray.

Carboxylic acids react with weakly basic amines in the presence of polyphosphoric acid to give the corresponding amides. Yields of amides from benzoic acid and amines increases markedly as the basic strength of the amine decreases. Aliphatic acids behave similarly except that the yields of amides are somewhat lower. Acetic acid and *p*-nitroaniline heated for 20 minutes at 160°C in the presence of polyphosphoric acid give *p*-$O_2N—C_6H_4—NHCOCH_3$ in 67 per cent yield.[239]

Pyrolysis of ammonium salts of dibasic acids containing 4 or 5 carbon atoms gives imides. Thus ammonium succinate on heating gives succinimide in 83 per cent yield.[240]

Amides are also formed by the action of acid anhydrides on ammonia, or amines. This method is most frequently used for the preparation of acyl derivatives of aryl amines. The anhydrides and amines are heated, frequently in the presence of small amounts of sulfuric acid.

Acetic anhydride is used in the acetylation of amino acids. The reaction may occur in aqueous solution at room temperature.

Cyclic anhydrides of dibasic acids react with ammonia or primary amines to form imides. Thus phthalic anhydride and ammonia give phthalimide in 97 per cent yield.[241] N-(2-Pyridyl)-phthalimide is obtained from 2-amino-pyridine and phthalic anhydride.[242]

Acid halides are important intermediate in the formation of amides from acids. The reaction of acid halides with ammonia or amines probably represents the best procedure for preparing amides in the laboratory. Cold concentrated aqueous ammonia reacts with butyryl chloride to give butyramide in 83 per cent yield.[243] The reaction may also be carried out by passing anhydrous ammonia into an etherial solution of the acid halide. Amines may be substituted for ammonia for the preparation of N-substituted amides. A base such as pyridine or sodium hydroxide is usually added to react with the hydrogen chloride as formed.

Secondary amides are formed by the reaction of a primary amide with an acid chloride

$$RCONH_2 + RCOCl \longrightarrow (RCO)_2NH + HCl$$

Distearamide has been recommended as a waterproofing agent for textiles.

Urea can be successfully employed for the preparation of amides. Thus stearic acid and urea are heated at 195°C for 3 hours in the presence of about 1 per cent diammonium hydrogen phosphate to give a 65 per cent yield of stearamide. In the absence of the catalyst the conversion is only 35–40 per cent under the same conditions.[244] Phosphates and molybdates are excellent catalysts for the preparation of amides from fatty acids and urea. Optimum temperatures are 170–230°C with an acid to urea ratio of 1:2.

p-Nitrobenzamide is prepared from *p*-nitrobenzoic acid and urea in 90 per cent yield. In a similar manner *p*-methoxybenzamide is prepared in 66 per cent yield.

Acids mixed with thiourea and heated to 200–210°C are converted to amides. Ammonia and hydrogen sulfide are formed as by-products.[245] Acetic acid is not successfully converted to acetamide but propionic, butyric and isobutyric acids are converted to the corresponding amides in 28–35 per cent yields. Stearamide is obtained from stearic acid in 67 per cent yield, and succinic acid gives succinimide in 27 per cent yield. Best yields of amide are obtained with diphenylacetic acid (75 per cent) and β-phenylpropionic acid (83 per cent).

A very convenient method for the preparation of amides involves the reaction of ammonia or an amine with an ester. Acetamide is made in very good yield by permitting ethyl acetate and concentrated aqueous ammonia to stand for a day or two at room temperature. The reaction is catalyzed by water or other solvents containing hydroxyl groups.[246] Other amides made in this way include chloroacetamide, obtained in 67 per cent yield,[247] and cyanoacetamide obtained in 88 per cent yield.[248] Diethyl malonate is converted to the diamide of malonic acid by heating for two days with 20 per cent aqueous ammonia.[249]

Esters of lactic acid have been converted to α-hydroxyamides with liquid ammonia or amines.[250,251]

N-Substituted acrylamides can be prepared in the vapor phase from acrylic esters and primary or secondary amines. Thus N-dimethylamino-acrylamide, $CH_2=CHCONHCH(CH_3)_2$, may be prepared by passing ethyl acrylate and isopropyl amine over a catalyst at 400°C with a residence time of 2.8 seconds. The catalyst consists of phosphoric acid on alumina.[252]

Amides of trifluoroacetic acid have been prepared by reacting the tertiary butyl ester of the acid with the appropriate amine for 1–4 days at room temperature. Yields range from 60–84 per cent. In this manner the diethylamide, the piperidide and the pyrrolidide of trifluoroacetic acid are obtained. The *tert*-butyl ester of trifluoroacetic acid is prepared by the action of isobutylene on the free acid.[253]

The ammonolysis of natural fats and oils in liquid ammonia gives a mixture of fatty acid amides. The ammonium ion is an acid in the ammonia system in the same way that the hydronium ion is in water. Consequently ammonium salts, such as ammonium chloride, are catalysts for ammonolysis reactions.

Ammonolysis of oils and fats in liquid ammonia containing ammonium chloride proceeds slowly at 25°C but quite rapidly at 165°C. Fatty acid amide mixtures are obtained from olive, cottonseed, corn, soybean, castor and tung oils.[254]

Roe[255] investigated the direct conversion of fats to amides and glycerol by reaction under pressure with liquid ammonia or amines. Essentially quantitative yields of amide are obtained from olive, castor and tobacco seed oils. Anhydrous liquid ammonia gives higher yields than does aqueous ammonia.

Work done with methyl oleate is summarized in Table 5–2.

N-(2-Hydroxyethyl)- and N-(*n*-dodecyl)amides have been obtained from oils using ethanolamine and *n*-dodecylamine. The reaction with ethanolamine is accomplished at reflux temperatures in 15 minutes while *n*-decylamine required heating the reaction mixture for 3 hours at 230°C. Yields of pure amides are for the most part, greater than 90 per cent.

Ammonolysis with diamines takes place to a much higher degree with triglycerides than with monoesters of fatty acids. The rapid ammonolysis of fats may be due to the presence of partially hydrolyzed glycerides

TABLE 5-2. AMMONOLYSIS OF METHYL OLEATE

Ammonia	Temp. (°C)	Time (Hrs)	Conv. to Oleamide (%)
28% aqueous	25	25	0
	100	6	2.5
	150	6	45.
	175	6	50
Anhydrous	25	6	trace
	100	7	8-9
	135	12	62
	165	12	90
	175	12	89
	200	12	83

containing hydroxyl groups which are soluble in the reaction phase. Water, which catalyzes the ammonolysis of mono-esters, has a decided influence with glycerides possibly because of the surface activity of the HCl salt of the mono-amide formed.[256]

Some amides can be prepared successfully by the hydrolysis of nitriles. This method has already been discussed.

Oximes may be made to rearrange to give amides (Beckmann rearrangement). Ketoximes rearrange in the presence of acidic reagents such as sulfuric acid or phosphorus pentachloride. The reaction is of importance only in a limited number of cases. Probably the most important is the conversion of cyclohexanone oxime to ω-caprolactam.

Aldoximes are converted to amides at temperatures of 100–150°C in the presence of Raney nickel.[257] Amides have been obtained from oximes of acetaldehyde, heptaldehyde, benzaldehyde and furfural in yields of 75–95 per cent.

Propionaldehyde and the mono-amide of malonic acid heated in refluxing pyridine containing catalytic amounts of piperidine acetate give a 43 per cent yield of β-ethylacrylamide.[258]

$$CH_3CH_2CHO + HOOCCH_2CONH_2 \xrightarrow{-H_2O} CH_3CH_2CH=\underset{\underset{COOH}{|}}{C}-CONH_2 \xrightarrow{-CO_2}$$

$$CH_3CH_2CH=CHCONH_2$$

Aryl-substituted acetamides are obtained by heating a methyl aryl ketone or a vinyl aromatic hydrocarbon with aqueous ammonium polysulfide under pressure at 160–200°C (Willgerodt reaction).[259]

$$C_6H_5COCH_3 \xrightarrow{(NH_4)_2S_x} C_6H_5CH_2CONH_2$$

$$C_6H_5CH=CH_2 \xrightarrow{(NH_4)_2S_x} C_6H_5CH_2CONH_2$$

p-Hydroxyacetophenone heated with aqueous ammonium polysulfide and isopropyl alcohol in a steel bomb at 150–300°C gives *p*-hydroxyphenylacetamide in good yield. Better yields are obtained when dioxane is used as a solvent.[260,261] A combination of sulfur, aqueous ammonia and pyridine may be used in place of the ammonium polysulfide.[262]

Aromatic compounds containing halo, hydroxyl, alkoxyl, amino or nitro groups have all been utilized in the Willgerodt reaction.

Low yields of products have been obtained from aliphatic aldehydes and ketones, alcohols, olefins and acetylenes.[263,264]

When β-keto esters are hydrolyzed in the presence of ammonium polysulfide, the ketones are converted to amides. Ethyl acetoacetate heated with aqueous ammonia (14.5 molar) and sulfur at 175–185°C in an autoclave under a pressure of 15 kg per sq cm gives propionamide. α-Benzylethylacetoacetate under similar conditions gives γ-phenylbutyramide.[265]

A mixture of sulfur, isobutane and 28 per cent aqueous ammonia heated in a steel bomb at 320–330°C and pressures of 2600–3400 psi gives a 21 per cent yield of $(CH_3)_2CHCONH_2$. Propane treated similarly gives a mixture of acetamide and formamide. If the reaction is carried out under anhydrous conditions, thioamides are formed.[266]

Hydrazides are reduced with Raney nickel and ethanol to amides and ammonia or amines.[267] Thus $C_3H_7CONHNHC_6H_5$ gives a mixture of butyramide and aniline.

Carbon monoxide reacts with primary or secondary amines under about 150 atmospheric pressure in the presence of alcohols and sodium alkoxides to form amides of formic acid. The reaction proceeds in two steps, the first of which is rate determining and involves the formation of an ester

$$CO + ROH \longrightarrow HCO_2R$$

The second step is much faster and involves the reaction of the amine with the ester

$$HCO_2R + (CH_3)_2NH \longrightarrow HCON(CH_3)_2 + ROH$$

The rate of reaction is markedly affected by temperature. This is a representative reaction and requires reaction times of 6–7 hours at 18°C but only ten minutes at 100°C. Methyl, ethyl, propyl or butyl alcohols are equally effective.[268]

Acrylamide is prepared from acetylene, nickel carbonyl and ammonia in the presence of a little acid to liberate carbon monoxide from the carbonyl.

The procedure involves the reaction of acetylene and carbon monoxide (as nickel carbonyl), ammonia or an amine at 25–90°C in the absence of air and in the presence of an inert solvent such as methyl ethyl ketone, toluene, or ethylene dichloride and in the presence of a polymerization inhibitor. The acids used include acrylic acetic or hydrochloric acids. In addition to acrylamide, N-phenyl- and N-butylacrylamides have been prepared.[269]

Ammonia and carbon monoxide treated in a shaking autoclave at 120–130 kg/sq cm at 90°C in the presence of basic catalysts give formamide. The yield of formamide varies with the catalyst used as shown below.[270]

Catalyst	Formamide % Yield
CH_3ONa	88
$HOCH_2CHOHCH_2ONa$	95
$(C_6H_5)_3CONa$	59
$NaNH_2$	43
Na	62

N-Substituted formamides can be prepared by reaction between hydrogen cyanide and an amine.[271] Thus a mixture of hydrogen cyanide and *n*-butylamine was kept for 25 days at 20°C, a small amount of water was added and the mixture kept for another 3 days and at this time a 71 per cent yield of $HCONHC_4H_9$ was obtained. In a similar manner a 22 per cent yield of N,N-diethylformamide was obtained together with a black residue which when hydrolyzed for 13 days gave a 46 per cent yield of $HCON(C_2H_5)_2$. Piperidine and hydrogen cyanide gave a 90 per cent yield of N-formylpiperidine in 34 days.

N-(2-chloroalkyl)amides have been prepared by the interaction of chlorine and an olefin in the presence of a nitrile to give an imide chloride that can be hydrolyzed to the amide. The reaction is applicable to aromatic and aliphatic nitriles and to hydrogen cyanide in combination with such olefins as ethylene, cyclohexene, 1-octene and styrene. Bromine may be used to give N-(2-bromoalkyl)amides.

The reaction proceeds in two steps. The first gives a chloroimide chloride as well as a dichlorohydrocarbon (from the original olefin). The second step involves the hydrolysis of the chloroimide chloride to the amide.[272]

$$RCH{=}CH_2 + Cl_2 \rightarrow [R{-}\overset{+}{C}H{-}CH_2Cl]\,Cl^-$$

$$\overset{+}{R}CHCH_2Cl + R'CN \rightarrow$$

$$R{-}\underset{\underset{(+)}{\overset{|}{N}{=}C{-}R'}}{\overset{|}{C}HCH_2Cl} \xrightarrow{Cl^-} R{-}\underset{\overset{|}{N}{=}C(Cl)R'}{\overset{|}{C}H{-}CH_2Cl} \xrightarrow{H_2O} R{-}\underset{NHCOR'}{\overset{|}{C}HCH_2Cl} + HCl$$

Some of the N-(2-chloroalkyl)amides obtained are shown in Table 5-3.

TABLE 5-3. N-(2-CHLOROALKYL)AMIDES—R'NH—COR

R	Alkene	R	% Yield
CH_3	Styrene	2-Chloro-1-phenylethyl	28
$(CH_3)_3C$	Ethylene	2-Chloroethyl	40
CH_3	Cyclohexene	2-Chlorocyclohexyl	58
$(CH_3)_2COH$	Cyclohexene	2-Chlorocyclohexyl	11
$(CH_3)_3C$	Cyclohexene	2-Chlorocyclohexyl	47
C_6H_5	Ethylene	2-Chloroethyl	24
C_6H_5	Cyclohexene	2-Chlorocyclohexyl	21

Reactions of Amides

Amides may be hydrolyzed to acids by warming with dilute bases or dilute acids. N-Substituted amides are hydrolyzed almost as readily as the unsubstituted compounds. Duffy and Leisten[273] investigated the hydrolysis of amides in concentrated sulfuric acid. They found that the rate of hydrolysis decreases as the concentration of water in the solvent increases, that polar substituents in the acyl group affect the rate, and that *ortho* substituents cause steric acceleration of the hydrolysis.

The results of kinetic studies are consistent with a unimolecular mechanism in which the rapidly formed conjugate acid $R'CONH_2R$ is decomposed to $R'CO^+$ and RNH_2. This slow rate-determining step is followed by the conversion of the amine to its conjugate acid, RNH_3SO_4H, and the acyl ion to the corresponding carboxylic acid

$$RCO^+ + (H_2SO_4)^+OH^- \rightarrow RCOOH + H_3SO_4^+$$

The reaction of a monosubstituted amide with an amine is reversible and is acid catalyzed.

$$R^1CONHR^2 + R^3NH_2 \rightleftharpoons R^1CONHR^3 + R^2NH_2$$

Jaunin[274] showed that the following equilibria exist:

1. $CH_3CONHC_6H_5 + p\text{-}CH_3OC_6H_4NH_2 \rightleftharpoons$

$$p\text{-}CH_3CONHC_6H_4OCH_3 + C_6H_5NH_2$$

2. $CH_3CONHC_6H_5 + p\text{-}CH_3C_6H_4NH_2 \rightleftharpoons$

$$p\text{-}CH_3CONHC_6H_4CH_3 + C_6H_5NH_2$$

3. $CH_3CONHC_6H_5 + p\text{-}HO_2CC_6H_4NH_2 \rightleftharpoons$

$$p\text{-}CH_3CONHC_6H_4CO_2H + C_6H_5NH_2$$

Benzoic acid is a suitable catalyst for the first two reactions and *p*-amino-phenol for the third.

Amides of phthalic acids are hydrolyzed completely to the corresponding acids with 1–4 normal sulfuric acid at 400–500°C in 3–30 minutes.[275]

Amides which resist hydrolysis may be converted to acids by the action of nitrous acid

$$RCONH_2 + HONO \longrightarrow RCOOH + N_2 + H_2O$$

The amide is dissolved in about five times its weight of concentrated sulfuric acid and five equivalents of sodium nitrite are added as a 20 per cent solution. The reaction occurs at about 100°C and is complete in a few minutes.

Amides may be converted to sodium salts by the action of sodium amide in liquid ammonia

$$RCONH_2 + NaNH_2 \longrightarrow RCONHNa + NH_3$$

The hydrogen in imines is more acidic than those in amides so that phthalimide or succinimide may be converted into an alkali metal salt by the action of the hydroxide.

This is the first step in the Gabriel synthesis for the preparation of primary amines or amino acids.

The sodium salts of the amides react with alkyl iodides to give N-alkyl amides.

The dehydration of amides to nitriles has been discussed previously. In addition to the dehydrating agents previously discussed Stephens *et al.*[276] report that primary amides can be dehydrated to the corresponding nitriles by benzoyl or toluenesulfonyl chloride in pyridine at temperatures below 70°C. Yields range from 60–80 per cent.

The dropwise addition of $POCl_3$ to a suspension of an amide in pyridine results in an exothermic reaction and the formation of a nitrile in excellent yield.[277]

The hydrogen atom attached to the nitrogen is replaced by halogens when treated with hypohalous acids.[278] This is particularly true with imides. Thus N-bromo-succinimide is formed by adding bromine to a cold solution of succinimide in potassium hydroxide.

The N-bromosuccinimide separates out from the solution as formed in 97 per cent purity. The bromine atom is considered to be a positive bromine because on hydrolysis it combines with a hydroxyl group to give hypobromous acid.

N-Bromosuccinimide is capable of introducing a bromine atom onto a carbon atom next to a position of unsaturation. Thus 1-butene is converted to 3-bromo-1-butene

and methyl crotonate is converted into methyl-γ-bromocrotonate, $BrCH_2$-$CH{=}CHCOOCH_3$, in 86 per cent yield. The course of the reaction suggests that it proceeds by a free radical mechanism and this is supported by the fact that the reaction is catalyzed by peroxides and light.

Amides are converted to amines, having one less carbon atom, by the action of bromine and sodium hydroxide (Hofmann reaction). This reaction, which has been discussed in chapter one, probably proceeds by way of bromination of the —NH$_2$ group, loss of hydrogen bromide, rearrangement to an isocyanate and hydrolysis to the amine.

$$RCONH_2 \longrightarrow [RCONHBr] \xrightarrow{-HBr} [R-CON<] \longrightarrow RNCO \xrightarrow[NaOH]{H_2O}$$

$$RNH_2 + Na_2CO_3$$

The R group does not become completely free during its migration to the nitrogen in forming the isocyanate. Optical activity, if present, is not destroyed and no inversion occurs.[279,280] The rate determining step seems to be the loss of halogen from the halogenated amide.[281]

Good yields are obtained with amides having six or fewer carbon atoms. With higher molecular weight amides there is considerable competition from the formation of nitriles.

The Hoffmann degradation of polymeric amides is a good method for the preparation of polymeric amines.[282] A butadiene-acrylonitrile rubber has been hydrolyzed to the amide by heating with water at 180°C under pressure. The resulting amide copolymer was treated with bromine and potassium hydroxide in ethanol to give a butadiene-alkylamine copolymer. This material retains the original unsaturation of the rubber and may be vulcanized. The rubber swells readily and can be dispersed in water containing a little sodium hydroxide. The dispersions are unusually stable and are intermediate between a true solution and the usual dispersion of hydrophobic materials in water.

Amides are not readily reduced by chemical reducing agents with the exception of lithium aluminum hydride. This reagent reduces amides, mono- and disubstituted amides to the corresponding primary, secondary or tertiary amines. Thus acetanilide and N-methylacetanilide are reduced to N-ethylaniline (60 per cent yield) and N-methyl-N-ethylaniline (91 per cent yield), respectively.

Benzamide and N-methylbenzamide are not reduced by refluxing with lithium borohydride in tetrahydrofuran. N,N-Dimethylbenzamide however, is completely reduced to give a 33 per cent yield of dimethylbenzylamine and 58 per cent benzyl alcohol.

p-Nitro-N,N-dimethylbenzamide refluxed with lithium borohydride in tetrahydrofuran gives a 41 per cent yield of the azoxybenzene p-(CH$_3$)$_2$-N—COC$_6$H$_4$NO=NC$_6$H$_4$CON(CH$_3$)$_2$-p and 52 per cent of p-nitrobenzyl alcohol.[283]

Amides can be hydrogenated at high temperatures and pressures but a mixture of primary and secondary amines is usually obtained. Thus lauramide is hydrogenated at 250°C and under a pressure of 500 atmospheres in the presence of a copper-chromium catalyst to give approximately equivalent amounts of laurylamine and dilaurylamine. Under the same conditions ammonium laurate gave a 14 per cent yield of mono- and a 79 per cent yield of the diamine.[284]

Guyer, Bieler and Gerliczy[285] report that the hydrogenation of $C_9H_{19}CONH_2$ in the presence of a copper chromite catalyst and in the absence of a solvent at 300°C and under a pressure of 326 atmospheres gives an 8.7 per cent yield of monodecylamine and an 83 per cent yield of didecylamine. When dioxane or ethylbenzene are used as solvents at 275–330°C and under a pressure of 243–331 atmospheres the yield of monodecylamine is 11–18 per cent and of didecylamine 57–78 per cent.

Raney cobalt gives about the same results as Raney nickel except that the temperature can be about 40° lower.

Acetanilide has been hydrogenated to ethylaniline at 225°C and a pressure of 10 atmospheres in the presence of a nickel catalyst.[286]

The hydrogen atoms attached to the nitrogen are sometimes sufficiently reactive to undergo condensations with carbonyl compounds. Thus nitrobenzamide reacts with formaldehyde in basic solution to give N-hydroxymethylnitrobenzamide. In sulfuric acid the corresponding N,N'-methylenebisnitrobenzamide is formed. Nitrobenzamide and dimethyl ammonium chloride gives N,N-dimethylaminomethylnitrobenzamide.[287]

The pyrolysis of amides is accompanied by the evolution of ammonia. It has been proposed that the reaction proceeds through the formation of an imide analogous to the formation of anhydrides from acids.

$$2RCONH_2 \longrightarrow RCO-NH-COR + NH_3$$

The formation of cyclic imides from amides such as phthalimide is well known and the formation of acyclic imides from monoamides occurs in the presence of hydrogen chloride.[288] Furthermore acyclic imides undergo pyrolysis to nitriles and acids.[289] These facts suggest the process by which the pyrolysis of amides to nitriles, carboxylic acids and ammonia occurs. The thermal dehydration of amides to nitriles may consist of three steps:

1. deamination to an imide,
2. pyrolysis of the imide, and
3. ammonolysis of the resulting acid.

Davidson and Newman[290] found that deamination of amides proceeds more readily than dehydration of monocarboxylic acids. The reaction proceeds smoothly at 220°C and the imide can be detected and frequently isolated.

That ammonolysis of acids occurs in the pyrolysis of amides can be demonstrated by adding an equivalent of an unrelated acid to the amide being pyrolyzed. Thus refluxing an equimolar mixture of acetamide and benzoic acid gives a fair yield of benzamide. No ammonia is evolved and acetonitrile and water appear in the distillate.[291]

Amides may be converted to thioamides by the action of phosphorus pentasulfide[292] and by the addition of hydrogen sulfide to nitriles.[293]

Amides can be converted into N-alkyl-N-nitrosamides by several methods:[294]

1. The acidification of an aqueous solution of sodium nitrite and an amide at 0°C.

2. The reaction of a mixture of sodium nitrite, acetic anhydride, acetic acid and the amide at 0°C.

3. The reaction of nitrogen tetroxide with amides in the presence of sodium acetate at 0°C.

$$RCONHR' \xrightarrow{N_2O_4} RCO-N(R')-NO$$

The first method requires about 40 hours and is limited to water-soluble amides. The second method is much faster, requiring about 15 hours and is successful with amides of primary amines and of cyclohexylamine but fails with amides of secondary amines. The third method requires only 10 minutes for complete reaction and is applicable to most types of amides. Better conversions are obtained in the presence of sodium acetate.

Primary amides react with ethylene oxide to give a class of non-ionic surface-active agents made by Armour and Co. and sold under the trade name "Ethomids."[295]

$$C_{17}H_{33}CONH_2 + (x + y)CH_2-CH_2 \longrightarrow C_{17}H_{33}CON \Big\langle {\! (CH_2CH_2O)_xH \atop (CH_2CH_2O)_yH} $$

The properties of these products can be altered widely by changing the amount of ethylene oxide used.

Cyclic imides undergo a Mannich reaction with formaldehyde and ammonia or primary or secondary amines.[296] Thus phthalimide in alcohol is treated with aqueous 33 per cent dimethylamine and 40 per cent aqueous formaldehyde to give dimethylaminomethylphthalimide in 42 per cent yield. Hydroxymethylphthalimide is also found in the reaction product, formed in about 38 per cent yield.

It has been indicated that N-substituted amides are formed by the reaction of an amine with an acid or acid derivative. If the amino and carboxyl groups are in the same molecule, a polyamide may be obtained. Thus 6-aminocaproic acid will react to give a polyamide having the following structure

$$[-NHCH_2CH_2CH_2CH_2CH_2CO-]_n$$

This condensation is actually accomplished using caprolactam to give the well known product "Nylon 6."

Polyamides are prepared from dicarboxylic acids and diamines. Thus adipic acid and hexamethylene diamine react to form a polyamide ("Nylon 66") which is one of the most important of the synthetic fibers.

$$nHOOC(CH_2)_4COOH + nH_2N(CH_2)_6NH_2 \longrightarrow$$

$$[-CO-(CH_2)_4-CONH(CH_2)_6NH-]_n$$

Sulfonamides are derivatives of sulfanilic acid and are prepared by the reaction of ammonia or amines upon the sulfonic acid chloride. The most important of these are the sulfanilamides which have found wide acceptance as chemotherapeutic agents.

These sulfa drugs have the structure

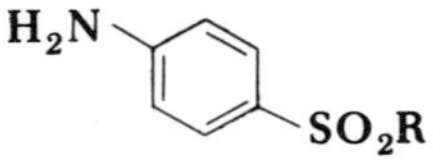

where R is

sulfaquanidine

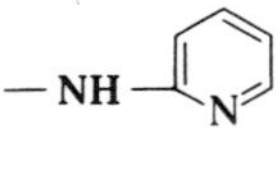

sulfapyridine

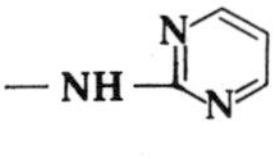

sulfadiazine

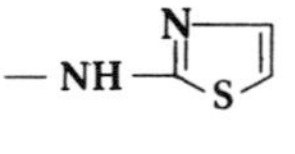

sulfathiazole

AMINO ACIDS

No attempt will be made here to give a complete description of the chemistry of amino acids and their relation to proteins. Comprehensive reviews are found elsewhere. The objective will be to discuss a sufficient number of the more fundamental reactions to understand the chemical nature of these compounds.

Amino acids contain both acid and basic groups and therefore are amphoteric. The molecules exist largely as dipolar ions in which the proton from the carboxyl group has been transferred to the amino group

$$\underset{\underset{\displaystyle NH_2}{|}}{RCH}\!\!-\!\!COOH \rightleftharpoons \underset{\underset{\displaystyle NH_3^+}{|}}{RCHCOO^-}$$

Such a structure, referred to as a zwitterion, is really an internal salt and accounts for the high melting points, the solubility of the acids in water, and the insolubility of amino acids in ether and other organic solvents.

The zwitterion may react with either acids or bases as indicated below:

$$\underset{\underset{\displaystyle NH_3^+}{|}}{RCHCOOH} \underset{OH^-}{\overset{H^+}{\rightleftharpoons}} \underset{\underset{\displaystyle NH_3^+}{|}}{RCHCOO^-} \underset{H^+}{\overset{OH^-}{\rightleftharpoons}} \underset{\underset{\displaystyle NH_2}{|}}{RCHCOO^-} + H_2O$$

At some definite hydrogen ion concentration, the two equilibria would be in balance and the amino acid should exist primarily as a neutral internal dipolar ion.

Methods of Preparation

The most common method for the preparation of amino acids is the hydrolysis of proteins which can be accomplished in acid solution. A large number of amino acids are obtained and it is difficult to separate pure compounds in appreciable quantities.

One of the more important methods for the preparation of amino acids is the reaction of α-halogen acids with ammonia. Yields are not very good but the method is useful in the preparation of alanine from α-bromopropionic acid and valine from α-bromoisovaleric acid. Phenylalanine has been prepared also, using this procedure, from α-bromo-β-phenylpropionic acid.[297] β-Alanine may be prepared by treating β-bromopropionic acid in water solution with hexamethylenetetramine at room temperature, and holding the mixture at this temperature for 15 hours. On addition of alcohol a betaine complex is formed which on refluxing with concentrated hydrochloric acid gives an 85 per cent yield of the β-alanine.[298]

Cheronis and Spitzmueller[299] treated α-bromo acids at 60°C with aqueous ammonia containing ammonium carbonate. The presence of ammonium carbonate permits a large reduction in the amount of aqueous ammonia required.

A modification of the Gabriel synthesis gives better yields of amino acids. This reaction proceeds as follows:

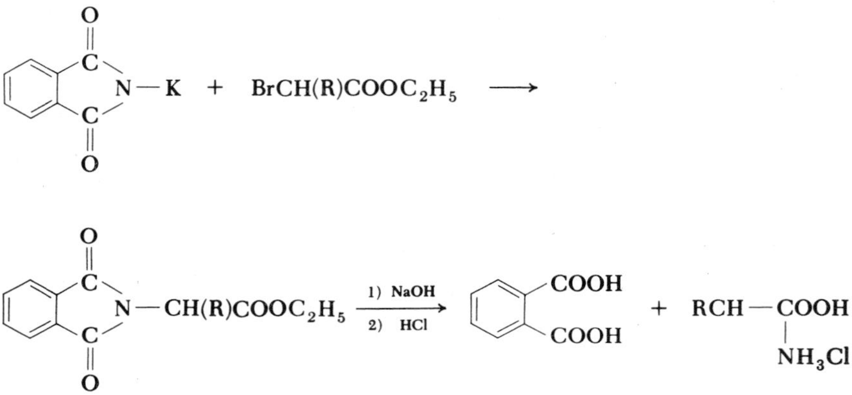

β-Alanine is prepared by heating β-hydroxypropionitrile for 1 hour to 4 weeks at 70–250°C in the presence of 0.5 to 3 per cent aqueous 28 per cent ammonia.[300] Ammonolysis and hydrolysis of the nitrile proceed simultaneously.

One of the oldest methods for the preparation of amino acids was developed by Strecker in 1850[301] and involves the reaction of an aldehyde with hydrogen cyanide and ammonium chloride. The reaction probably proceeds through the formation of the intermediate cyanohydrin

$$RCHO \xrightarrow[\text{NH}_3]{\text{HCN}} RCH(OH)CN \longrightarrow RCH(NH_2)CN \longrightarrow RCH(NH_2)COOH$$

The reaction has rather wide applicability and has been used for the preparation of alanine,[302] isoleucine,[303] phenylalanine[304] and others.

A modification of the Strecker synthesis involves treating an aminonitrile with ammonium carbonate to form a hydantoin which is hydrolyzed readily to an amino acid.

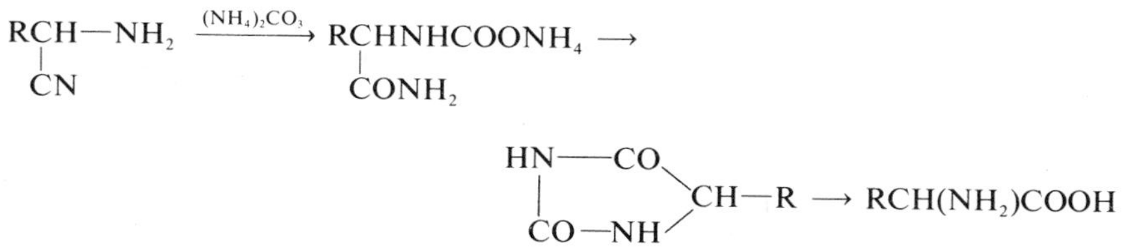

$$RCH-NH_2 \xrightarrow{(NH_4)_2CO_3} RCHNHCOONH_4 \longrightarrow$$
$$\qquad | \qquad\qquad\qquad\qquad\qquad |$$
$$CN \qquad\qquad\qquad\qquad CONH_2$$

$$HN-CO$$
$$\quad| \qquad\qquad CH-R \longrightarrow RCH(NH_2)COOH$$
$$CO-NH$$

Tryptophane is made in good yield by condensing 3-indolecarboxylic acid with hydantoin to give 5-(3-indolylmethylene)hydantoin which is treated with 14–25 per cent by weight of ammonium sulfide in water to give the amino acid.[305]

The malonic ester synthesis can be modified for the preparation of amino acids according to the following scheme:

$$(CH_3)_2CHCH_2Br + NaCH(COOC_2H_5)_2 \longrightarrow (CH_3)_2CHCH_2CH(COOC_2H_5)_2 \longrightarrow$$

$$(CH_3)_2CHCH_2CH(COOH)_2 \longrightarrow (CH_3)_2CHCH_2CBr-(COOH)_2 \longrightarrow$$

$$(CH_3)_2CHCH_2CHBrCOOH \xrightarrow{NH_3} (CH_3)_2CHCH_2CH(NH_2)COOH$$
$$\qquad\qquad\qquad\qquad\qquad\qquad\qquad\qquad\text{leucine}$$

Aromatic aldehydes condense with hydantoin to give intermediates which are hydrolyzed to amino acids.

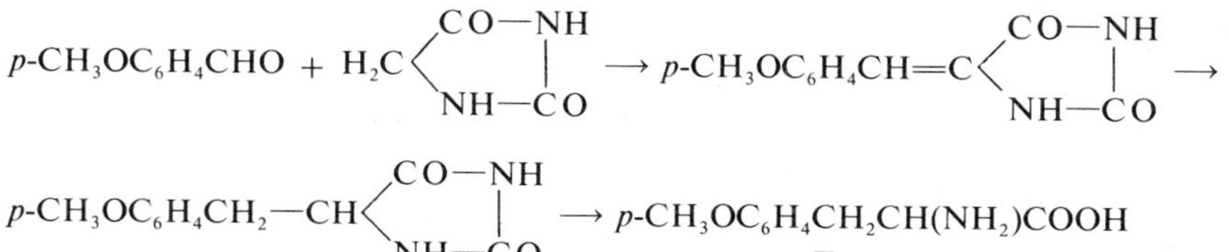

$$p\text{-}CH_3OC_6H_4CHO + H_2C\begin{array}{c}CO-NH\\|\\NH-CO\end{array} \longrightarrow p\text{-}CH_3OC_6H_4CH=C\begin{array}{c}CO-NH\\|\\NH-CO\end{array} \longrightarrow$$

$$p\text{-}CH_3OC_6H_4CH_2-CH\begin{array}{c}CO-NH\\|\\NH-CO\end{array} \longrightarrow p\text{-}CH_3OC_6H_4CH_2CH(NH_2)COOH$$
$$\qquad\qquad\qquad\qquad\qquad\qquad\qquad\qquad\qquad\text{\textit{Tyrosine}}$$

In the synthesis of tyrosine the over-all yields are about 60 per cent. Aliphatic aldehydes do not condense with hydantoin in this way.

ω-Amino acids have been prepared by the ozonolysis of unsaturated amines. Thus oleylamine (made from oleic acid by way of the nitrile) is ozonized in chloroform at 0°C and the ozonide hydrolyzed in dilute hydrochloric acid to give a mixture of $H_2N(CH_2)_3COOH$ and $H_2N(CH_2)_3CHO$ and the corresponding hydrochlorides. The ω-aminoaldehyde is oxidized to the acid with air at 30°C in the presence of manganese stearate.[306]

There has been considerable interest in recent years in the commercial preparation of essential amino acids to be used as food supplements for animals. Among those commercially available are valine, leucine, tryptophane, lysine and methionine. Methionine, a sulfur containing amino acid, is made from acrolein by the indicated method:[307,308,309]

$$CH_2\!=\!CHCHO + CH_3SH \longrightarrow CH_3SCH_2CH_2CHO \xrightarrow{HCN}$$

$$CH_3SCH_2CH_2\underset{\underset{OH}{|}}{CH}\!-\!CN \xrightarrow{NH_3} CH_3SCH_2CH_2\underset{\underset{NH_2}{|}}{CH}\!-\!CN \xrightarrow{H_2O}$$

$$CH_3SCH_2CH_2CH(NH_2)COOH$$
Methionine

Reactions of Amino Acids

Amino acids, existing largely as the zwitterions, do not form esters when heated with alcohols and a little sulfuric acid. This probably means that the alcohol does not react with the zwitterion because if the amino acid is dissolved in anhydrous alcohol and the solution heated after it is first saturated with hydrogen chloride, esterification proceeds smoothly. The hydrochloric acid probably converts the zwitterion into an acid which is subsequently esterified. The ester is obtained as the hydrochloride and must be liberated by treatment with moist silver oxide.

Esterification of amino acids or their derivatives such as hippuric acid may be accomplished in the presence of cation exchange resins such as "Amberlite IR-120."[310]

Amino acids lose carbon dioxide when heated with barium hydroxide. Primary amines are formed.

$$RCH(NH_2)COOH + Ba(OH)_2 \longrightarrow RCH_2NH_2 + BaCO_3 + H_2O$$

Processes similar to this occur during putrefaction of proteins.

α-Amino acids react with nitrous acid to give α-hydroxy acids and nitrogen

$$R\!-\!CH(NH_2)COOH + HONO \longrightarrow RCH(OH)COOH + N_2 + H_2O$$

This does not represent a satisfactory method for the preparation of hydroxy acids but the nitrogen is liberated quantitatively. The reaction does, therefore, serve as a basis for the determination of amino acids, by collecting and measuring the liberated nitrogen, one-half of which comes from the amino acid. The method was developed by van Slyke and is known by his name.

Lithium aluminum hydride has been used to convert amino acids to amino alcohols. The reduction may be carried out in tetrahydrofuran under a nitrogen atmosphere. Thus $C_6H_5CH(NH_2)CH_2COOH$ is converted to 3-amino-3-phenyl-1-propanol in 38 per cent yield.[311]

gamma- and *delta-*Amino acids react internally to form cyclic amides called lactams.

The reaction is analogous to the behavior of *gamma* and *delta* hydroxy acids which form lactones under similar conditions.

α-Amino acids when heated form cyclic dimers known as diketopiperazines.

which may undergo partial hydrolysis to give a linear dimer known as a dipeptide.

$$RCH(NH_2)CO—NH—CH(R)—COOH$$

If several amino acids are condensed to form a linear polymer the compound is called a polypeptide and if the molecular weight becomes sufficiently great it is a protein. The living organism is capable of joining together amino acids in this way by the loss of water but this has not proved to be a satisfactory procedure in the laboratory.

It has been possible to effect the stepwise condensation of a number of amino acids by way of the acid chlorides but since the amino group interferes with the formation of the acid chloride, it must be protected. The usual reagents, acid chlorides or anhydrides, used for protecting the amino group are not satisfactory here because the only method for recovering the amino group is hydrolysis and such procedures would hydrolyze the peptide back into the starting amino acids.

A satisfactory method for the preparation of peptides from amino acids has been developed by Bergmann.[312,313,314,315] and consists of four steps.

1. The amino group is protected by reaction with benzylchloroformate made from benzyl alcohol and phosgene

$$RCHCOOH + C_6H_5CH_2OCOCl \rightarrow C_6H_5CH_2OCONH-CHCOOH$$
$$\underset{NH_2}{|} \qquad\qquad\qquad\qquad\qquad \underset{R}{|}$$

2. Conversion to the acid chloride

$$C_6H_5CH_2OCONHCH(R)COOH \rightarrow C_6H_5CH_2OCONHCH(R)COCl$$

3. Reaction with a second molecule of amino acid

$$C_6H_5CH_2OCONHCH(R)COCl + R'CH(NH_2)COOH \rightarrow$$

$$C_6H_5CH_2OCONHCH(R)CONHCH(R')COOH$$

This compound may be converted into the acid chloride and reacted with a third amino acid, etc.

4. Recovery of the amino group by hydrogenation

$$C_6H_5CH_2OCONHCH(R)CONHCH(R')COOH \xrightarrow[cat]{H_2}$$

$$H_2NCH(R)CONHCH(R')COOH + C_6H_5CH_3 + CO_2$$

Kallonitsch, Gabor and Hajos[316] have used the C_6H_5-CS- group to protect the amino group of an amino acid during a peptide synthesis

$$R-CH-COOH + C_6H_5CSCl \rightarrow R-CH-COOH$$
$$\underset{NH_2}{|} \qquad\qquad\qquad\qquad\qquad \underset{NH-CS-C_6H_5}{|}$$

This group is removed from the peptide by oxidation at $-5°C$ with perbenzoic acid in acetic acid and benzene or a mixture of benzene, tetrahydrofuran and dioxane. The products of oxidation probably represent a type of mixed anhydride of carbamic acids with sulfinic acids. With water, carbon dioxide is liberated and the resulting peptides may be isolated by adsorption on cation exchange resins such as "Dowex 50."

References

1. Fierz-David, H. E., and Kuster, W., *Helv. Chim. Acta,* **22,** 82 (1939).
2. Ruhoff, J. R., "Organic Syntheses," Collective Vol. II, p. 292, New York, John Wiley & Sons, Inc., 1943.
3. Lewis, R. N., and Susi, P. V., *J. Am. Chem. Soc.,* **74,** 840 (1952).
4. Vereinigte Glanzstoff-Fabriken, A. G., British Patent 768,303 (Feb. 13, 1957).
5. Wawzonek, S., and Hsu, H. L., *J. Am. Chem. Soc.,* **68,** 2741 (1946).
6. Koelsch, C. F., and Whitney, A. G., *J. Org. Chem.,* **6,** 795 (1941).
7. Newman, M. S., "Organic Syntheses," Vol. 21, p. 89, New York, John Wiley & Sons, Inc., 1941.
8. Tamele, M., *et al., Ind. Eng. Chem.,* **33,** 115 (1941).
9. Rietz, "Organic Syntheses," Vol. 24, p. 96, New York, John Wiley & Sons, Inc., 1944.
10. Lane, J. F., Fentress, J., and Sherwood, L. T., *J. Am. Chem. Soc.,* **66,** 545 (1944).
11. Reichstein, T., and Trivelli, G., *Helv. Chim. Acta,* **15,** 2541 (1932).
12. Engelhardt, R., and Arledter, H., German Patent 842,045 (June 23, 1952).
13. Willett, A. V., and Pailthorp, J. R., U. S. Patent 2,716,646 (Aug. 30, 1955).
14. Tschelinzeff, W., and Schmidt, W., *Ber.,* **62,** 2210 (1929).
15. Hurd, C. D., Edwards, O. E., and Roach, J. R., *J. Am. Chem. Soc.,* **66,** 2013 (1944).
16. Oakwood, and Weisgerber, "Organic Syntheses," Vol. 24, p. 14, New York, John Wiley & Sons, Inc.
17. Whitmore, F. C., and Fox, A. L., *J. Am. Chem. Soc.,* **51,** 3363 (1929).
18. Colver, C. W., and Noyes, W. A., *J. Am. Chem. Soc.,* **43,** 898 (1921).
19. McElvain, S. M., and Goese, M. A., *J. Am. Chem. Soc.,* **65,** 2233 (1943).
20. Webb, J. L., and Corwin, A. H., *J. Am. Chem. Soc.,* **66,** 1456 (1944).
21. Kent, R. E., and McIlvain, S. M., "Organic Syntheses," Vol. 25, p. 61, New York, John Wiley & Sons, Inc., 1945.
22. Sherk, K. W., and Augur, M. V., and Soffer, M. D., *J. Am. Chem. Soc.,* **67,** 2239 (1945).
23. Koike, E., Okawa, M., and Uchiyama, K., *J. Chem. Soc. Japan, Ind. Chem. Sect.,* **57,** 925 (1954).
24. Hull, D. C., U. S. Patent 2,732,397 (Jan. 24, 1956).
25. Ralston, A. W., Harwood, H. J., and Pool, W. O., *J. Am. Chem. Soc.,* **59,** 986 (1937).
26. Whitmore, F. C., Sutherland, L. H., and Cosby, J. N., *J. Am. Chem. Soc.,* **64,** 1360 (1942).
27. Ralston, A. W., Pool, W. O., and Harwood, J., U. S. Patents 2,033,536; 2,033,537 (Mar. 10, 1935).
28. Kenyon, R. L., Stingley, D. V., and Young, H. P., *Ind. Eng. Chem.,* **42,** 202 (1950).
29. Potts, R. H., and Christensen, C. W., U. S. Patent 2,314,894 (1943).
30. Zemplen, G., and Dory, L., *Acta Chim. Acad. Sci. Hung.,* **14,** 89 (1958).
31. Jansen, J. E., and Roha, M. E., U. S. Patent 2,791,043 (May 28, 1957).

276   *ORGANIC NITROGEN COMPOUNDS*

32. Toland, W. G., Jr., U. S. Patent 2,800,496 (July 23, 1957).
33. Kircher, R., *Bull. soc. chim. France,* **1955,** 455.
34. Niederhauser, W. D., U. S. Patent 2,493,637 (Jan. 3, 1950).
35. Frank, C. E., and Nobis, J. F., U. S. Patent 2,824,118 (Feb. 18, 1958).
36. Hill, A., and Statham, F. X., British Patent 737,409 (Sept. 28, 1955).
37. Max, N., U. S. Patent 2,644,834 (July 7, 1953).
38. Max, N., Dutch Patent 70,867 (Oct. 15, 1952).
39. Paushkin, Ya M., Osipova, L. V., and Khershkovits, N., *Doklady Akad. Nauk. SSSR,* **113,** 832 (1957).
40. McKeever, C. H., U. S. Patent 2,770,641 (Nov. 13, 1956).
41. Kurtz, P., German Patent 857,374 (Nov. 27, 1952).
42. Mahon, J. E., U. S. Patent 2,500,256 (Mar. 14, 1950).
43. Spillane, L. G., and Kayser, W. G., Jr., U. S. Patent 2,557,703 (June 19, 1951).
44. Heinemann, H., U. S. Patent 2,672,477 (Mar. 16, 1954).
45. Mahan, J. E., and Turk, S. D., U. S. Patent 2,642,454 (June 16, 1953).
46. Mahan, J. E., U. S. Patent 2,535,082 (Dec. 26, 1950).
47. Denton, W. J., and Bishop, R. B., *Ind. Eng. Chem.,* **45,** 282 (1953).
48. Paushkin, Ya. M., and Osipova, L. V., *Doklady Akad Nauk SSSR,* **111,** 117 (1956).
49. Plate, A. F., and Vol'pin, M. E., *Izvest. Akad Nauk Azerbaidzhan SSSR,* **1954,** No. 2, 55.
50. Caldwell, H. P., Jr., and Chapman, H. D., U. S. Patent 2,450,637 (Oct. 5, 1948).
51. Mizuhara, K., and Tsuno, G., *Yûki Gôsei Kagaku Kyôkaishi,* **14,** 718 (1956).
52. Ayers, G. W., U. S. Patent 2,780,638 (Feb. 5, 1957).
53. Denton, W. I., Caldwell, H. P., and Chapman, H. D., *Ind. Eng. Chem.,* **42,** 796 (1950).
54. Jennings, N. L., U. S. Patent 2,758,129 (Aug. 7, 1956).
55. Toland, W. G., Jr., U. S. Patent 2,783,266 (Feb. 26, 1957).
56. Cosby, J. N., and Erchak, M., U. S. Patent 2,499,055 (Feb. 28, 1950).
57. Gee, R. E., Jr., and Hagemeyer, H. J., Jr., U. S. Patent 2,734,909 (Feb. 14, 1956).
58. Schulze, W. A., and Mahan, J. E., U. S. Patent 2,464,723 (Mar. 15, 1949).
59. Mahan, J. E., U. S. Patent 2,525,818 (Oct. 17, 1950).
60. Sowa, F. J., and Nieuwland, J. A., *J. Am. Chem. Soc.,* **59,** 1202 (1937).
61. Newman, M. S., and Closson, R. D., *J. Am. Chem. Soc.,* **66,** 1553 (1944).
62. Buck, J. S., and Ide, W. S., "Organic Syntheses," Collective Vol. II, p. 622, New York, John Wiley & Sons, Inc., 1943.
63. Ziegler, K., and Ohlinger, H., *Ann.,* **495,** 84 (1932).
64. Schuerch, C., and Huntress, E. H., *J. Am. Chem. Soc.,* **70,** 2824 (1948).
65. Cast, J., and Stevens, T. S., *J. Chem. Soc.,* **1953,** 4180.
66. Toland, W. G., Jr., U. S. Patent 2,780,637 (Feb. 5, 1957).
67. Letch, R. A., and Linstead, R. P., *J. Chem. Soc.,* **1932,** 443.
68. Bellringer, F. J., Newley, T., and Stanley, H. M., British Patent 709,337 (May 19, 1954).
69. Lapworth, A., and Manske, R. H. F., *J. Chem. Soc.,* **1928,** 2533; **1930,** 1976.
70. Jacobson, R. A., *J. Am. Chem. Soc.,* **68,** 2628 (1946).

71. Hurd, C. D., and Rector, C. H., *J. Org. Chem.*, **10**, 441 (1945).
72. Cox, R. F. B., and Stormont, R. T., "Organic Syntheses," Collective Vol. II, p. 7, New York, John Wiley & Sons, Inc., 1943.
73. Kabaivanov, V., and Mikhailow, M., *Doklady Akad Nauk. SSSR*, **117**, 234 (1957).
74. Fujisaki, N., and Takimoto, T., Japan Patent 7,220 ('54) (Nov. 4, 1954).
75. Erickson, J. G., U. S. Patent 2,519,957 (Aug. 22, 1950).
76. Exner, L. J., Luskin, L. S., and de Benneville, P. L., *J. Am. Chem. Soc.*, **75**, 4841 (1953).
77. Turner, R. A., *J. Am. Chem. Soc.*, **68**, 1607 (1946).
78. Sherwood, P. W., *Petroleum Processing*, **1954**, 384.
79. Sekino, M., *Repts Research Lab Asaki Glass Co.*, **1**, 208 (1951).
80. Keller, R., German Patent 851,494 (Oct. 6, 1952).
81. Kastner, D., Zobel, F., and Kurtz, P., German Patent 850,889 (Sept. 29, 1952).
82. Christopher, G. L., Carpenter, E. L., and Spector, M. L., U. S. Patent 2,798,882 (July 9, 1957).
83. Steadman, T. R., and Baggett, J. F., Jr., U. S. Patent 2,780,639 (Feb. 5, 1957).
84. Kurtz, P., Schneider, H. E., and Muller, H., German Patent 877,302 (May 21, 1953).
85. Deutsche Gold and Silber Scheideanstalt, British Patent 736,111 (Aug. 31, 1955).
86. Eder, D., and Keller, R., German Patent 908,856 (Apr. 12, 1954).
87. Howe, B. K., and Bewley, T., British Patent 719,635 (Dec. 8, 1954).
88. Hadley, D. J., British Patent 744,011 (Jan. 25, 1956).
89. Copelin, H. B., Feldhousen, F. J., Jr., U. S. Patent 2,783,268 (Feb. 26, 1957).
90. Crane, G. B., U. S. Patent 2,715,138 (Aug. 9, 1955).
91. Copelin, H. B., and Feldhousen, F. J., Jr., U. S. Patent 2,786,072 (Mar. 19, 1957).
92. I. G. Farbenindustrie A. G., British Patent 518,697 (Aug. 27, 1939).
93. Farlow, M. S., U. S. Patent 2,518,608 (Aug. 15, 1950).
94. Calkin, W. H., and Welton, D. E., U. S. Patent 2,749,359 (June 5, 1956).
95. Defek, French Patent 1,040,895 (Oct. 19, 1953).
96. Ford, M. C., and Rust, R. A., *J. Chem. Soc.*, **1958**, 1297.
97. King, F. E., *J. Chem. Soc.*, **1935**, 984.
98. Noyes, W. A., *J. Am. Chem. Soc.*, **23**, 393 (1901).
99. Adams, R., and Thal, A. F., "Organic Syntheses," Collective Vol. I, p. 436, New York, John Wiley & Sons, Inc., 1941.
100. Clarke, H. T., and Taylor, E. R., "Organic Syntheses," Collective Vol. II, p. 588, New York, John Wiley & Sons, Inc., 1943.
101. Tomisek, A. J., *et al., J. Am. Chem. Soc.*, **68**, 1587 (1946).
102. Marvel, C. S., and Tuley, W. F., "Organic Syntheses," Collective Vol. I, p. 289, New York, John Wiley & Sons, Inc., 1941.
103. Müller, A., and Bleier, P., *Monatsh.*, **56**, 397 (1930).
104. Reitz, "Organic Syntheses," Vol. 24, p. 96, New York, John Wiley & Sons, Inc., 1944.
105. Osman, E. M., and Cope, A. C., *J. Am. Chem. Soc.*, **66**, 885 (1944).

106. Wenner, G., *J. Org. Chem.*, **15**, 548 (1950).
107. Travagli, G., *Gazz. chim. ital.*, **87**, 673 (1957).
108. Noller, C. R., "Organic Syntheses," Collective Vol. II, p. 586, New York, John Wiley & Sons, Inc., 1943.
109. West, B. L., *J. Am. Chem. Soc.*, **42**, 1662 (1920).
110. Galat, A., *J. Am. Chem. Soc.*, **70**, 3945 (1948).
111. Pierce, J. B., Ph.D. Thesis, Case Institute of Technology, 1958.
112. McElvain, S. M., and Stevens, C. L., *J. Am. Chem. Soc.*, **68**, 1919 (1946).
113. Glichman, S. A., and Cope, A. C., *J. Am. Chem. Soc.*, **67**, 1019 (1945).
114. McIlvain, S. M., and Schroeder, J. P., *J. Am. Chem. Soc.*, **71**, 43 (1949).
115. Dox, A. W., "Organic Syntheses," Collective Vol. I, p. 5, New York, John Wiley & Sons, Inc., 1941.
116. Short, W. F., and Oxley, P., *J. Chem. Soc.*, **1946**, 147, 763; **1949**, 703, 2027.
117. Djerassi, C., and Scholz, C. R., *J. Am. Chem. Soc.*, **69**, 1691 (1947).
118. Rising, M. M., and Zee, T. W., *J. Am. Chem. Soc.*, **50**, 1211 (1928).
119. Adams, R., and Marvel, C. S., *J. Am. Chem. Soc.*, **42**, 310 (1920).
120. Adams, R., and Thal, A. F., "Organic Syntheses," Collective Vol. I, p. 270, New York, John Wiley & Sons, Inc., 1941.
121. Blicke, F. F., and Feldknap, R. F., *J. Am. Chem. Soc.*, **66**, 1087 (1944).
122. Blicke, F. F., and Leonard, N. J., *J. Am. Chem. Soc.*, **68**, 1934 (1946).
123. Jones, R. G., *et al.*, *J. Am. Chem. Soc.*, **70**, 2843 (1948).
124. Oxley, P., and Short, W. F., *J. Chem. Soc.*, **1947**, 1110.
125. Cornell, E. F., *J. Am. Chem. Soc.*, **50**, 3311 (1928).
126. Erlenmeyer, *Ann.*, **146**, 259 (1868).
127. Hurwitz, M. J., Exner, L. J., and de Benneville, P. L., *J. Am. Chem. Soc.*, **77**, 3251 (1955).
128. Kurihara, T., and Ro, K., *J. Pharm. Soc. Japan*, **75**, 1267 (1955).
129. Fister, British Patent 567,289 (1945).
130. Kabish, G., U. S. Patent 2,745,868 (May 15, 1956).
131. Pieroh, K., U. S. Patent 2,174,756 Oct. 3, 1940; Loder, D. J., U. S. Patent 2,175,810 (Oct. 10, 1940).
132. Van der Linden, T., *Rec. trav. chim.*, **53**, 45 (1934).
133. Shriner, R. L., and Turner, T. A., *J. Am. Chem. Soc.*, **52**, 1268 (1930).
134. Hauser, C. R., Humphlett, T. A., and Weiss, M. J., *J. Am. Chem. Soc.*, **70**, 426 (1948).
135. Kumler, W. D., Strait, L. A., and Alpen, E. L., *J. Am. Chem. Soc.*, **72**, 1463 (1950).
136. Hauser, C. R., and Humphlett, W. J., *J. Org. Chem.*, **15**, 359 (1950).
137. Whitmore, F. C., *et al.*, *J. Am. Chem. Soc.*, **67**, 2059 (1945).
138. Sherk, K. W., Augur, M. V., and Soffer, M. D., *J. Am. Chem. Soc.*, **67**, 2239 (1945).
139. Adams, R., Shriner, R. L., and Voorhees, V., "Organic Syntheses," Collective Vol. I, p. 463, New York, John Wiley & Sons, Inc., 1941.
140. Pietra, S., and Trinchira, S., *Gazz. chim. ital.*, **85**, 1705 (1955), *ibid.* **86**, 1045 (1956).
141. Mosettig, E., "Organic Reactions," Vol. VIII, p. 246, New York, John Wiley & Sons, Inc.

142. Turner, L., *J. Chem. Soc.,* **1956,** 1686.
143. Knight, J. A., and Zook, H. D., *J. Am. Chem. Soc.,* **74,** 4560 (1952).
144. Kaufmann, H. P., and Krischner, H., *Fette u Seifen,* **55,** 851 (1953).
145. Hesse, G., and Schrödel, R., *Angew. Chem.,* **68,** 438 (1956).
146. Tanake, M., Watanabe, K., and Hato, K., *Nippon Kagaku Zasshi,* **76,** 1392 (1955).
147. Tanaka, M., Watanabe, K., and Hato, K., *Nippon Kagaku Zasshi,* **77,** 221 (1956).
148. Watanabe, K., *Nippon Kagaku Zasshi,* **76,** 391 (1955).
149. Neinburg, H., and Schwartz, G., German Patent 836,938 (Apr. 17, 1952).
150. Swerdloff, J., U. S. Patent 2,762,835 (Sept. 11, 1956).
151. Silverstone, G. A., U. S. Patent 2,790,804 (Apr. 30, 1957); British Patent 768,257 (Feb. 13, 1957).
152. Biggs, B. S., and Bishop, W. S., *Ind. Eng. Chem.,* **38,** 1084 (1946).
153. Leitch, L. C., *Canadian J. Chem.,* **35,** 345 (1957).
154. Hagemeyer, H. J., Jr., U. S. Patent 2,701,260 (Feb. 1, 1955).
155. Levine, R., and Hauser, C. D., *J. Am. Chem. Soc.,* **68,** 760 (1946).
156. Eby, C. J., and Hauser, C. R., *J. Am. Chem. Soc.,* **79,** 723 (1957).
157. Coenen, M., German Patent 922,531 (Jan. 17, 1955).
158. Janz, G. J., and McCilloch, W. J. H., *J. Am. Chem. Soc.,* **77,** 3014, 3143 (1955).
159. Batt, R. F., and Woodcock, D., *J. Chem. Soc.,* **1948,** 2322.
160. Magat, E. E., *J. Am. Chem. Soc.,* **73,** 1028, 1031 (1951).
161. Yates, W. F., U. S. Patent 2,727,257 (Dec. 6, 1955).
162. Roe, E. T., and Swern, D., *J. Am. Chem. Soc.,* **75,** 5479 (1953).
163. Dornow, A., and Lupfert, S., *Ber.,* **89,** 2718 (1956).
164. Anon., *Ind. Eng. Chem.,* **45,** 15A, (1953).
165. Morris, R. O., U. S. Patent 2,409,061.
166. American Cyanamide Co., British Patent 631,592 (1949).
167. Kaszuba, F. J., *J. Am. Chem. Soc.,* **67,** 1227 (1945).
168. Namiya, M., *J. Soc. Chem. Ind. Japan,* **44,** 860 (1941).
169. Chandler, *et al.,* "Catalyzed Reactions of Nitriles," (presented at 117th Meeting of the American Chemical Society, Philadelphia 1950).
170. Petrov, A. A., and Sopov, N. P., *J. Gen. Chem. USSR,* **17,** 2228 (1947).
171. Pistor, H. J., and Plieninger, H., *Ann.,* **562,** 239 (1949).
172. Meeks, J. S., and Ragsdale, J. W., *J. Am. Chem. Soc.,* **70,** 2502 (1948).
173. Bruson, H. A., *J. Am. Chem. Soc.,* **64,** 2457 (1942).
174. Alder, K., and Vogt, W., *Ann.,* **564,** 109 (1949).
175. Miller, A. A., and Bradley, T. F., U. S. Patent 2,382,803 (Aug. 14, 1945).
176. Barrick, P. L., U. S. Patent 2,642,345 (1949).
177. Barrick, P. L., and Cramer, R. D., U. S. Patent 2,441,128 (May 11, 1948).
178. Coffman, D. D., *et al., J. Am. Chem. Soc.,* **71,** 490 (1949).
179. Coyner, E. C., and Hillman, W. S., *J. Am. Chem. Soc.,* **71,** 324 (1949).
180. Reppe, W., and Hoffmann, U. S. Patent 1,891,055.
181. Winans, C. F., U. S. Patent 2,334,140 (Nov. 9, 1943).
182. Leekley, R. M., U. S. Patent 2,439,308 (Apr. 6, 1948).
183. Heim, G., *Bull. soc. chim. Belg.,* **39,** 458 (1930).

184. Brintzinger, H., and Pfannstiel, K., *Z. Anorg Chem.*, **255**, 325 (1948).
185. Sullivan, D. J., U. S. Patent 2,431,001 (Nov. 18, 1947).
186. D'Ianni, J., U. S. Patent 2,231,360 (Feb. 11, 1941).
187. Tuerck, K. W. H., and Lichtenstein, H. J., U. S. Patent 2,394,644 (Feb. 12, 1946).
188. Long, J. R., U. S. Patent 2,231,363 (Feb. 11, 1941).
189. Brunner, W. H., and Perger, H., *Monatsh.*, **79**, 187 (1949).
190. Koelsch, C. S., *J. Am. Chem. Soc.*, **65**, 57 (1943).
191. Müller, E., *Angew. Chem.*, **61**, 179 (1949).
192. Bruson, H. A., "Organic Reactions," Vol. V, p. 81, New York, John Wiley & Sons, Inc., 1949.
193. Utermohlen, W. P., *J. Am. Chem. Soc.*, **67**, 1505 (1945).
194. Terent'ev, A. P., Kost, A. N., and Berlin, A. M., *Zhur. Obschei Khim.*, **26**, 719 (1956).
195. American Cyanamide Co., British Patent 544,421 (Apr. 13, 1942).
196. I. G. Farbenind. A. G., British Patent 796,001 (Mar. 27, 1936).
197. Bruson, H. A., U. S. Patent 2,280,791 (Apr. 28, 1942).
198. Bruson, H. A., U. S. Patent 2,280,790 (Apr. 28, 1942).
199. Naravov, A. N., and Shvekhgeiner, G. A., *Zhur. Obschei. Khim.*, **24**, 163 (1954).
200. Bruson, H. A., and Riener, T. W., *J. Am. Chem. Soc.*, **65**, 23 (1943).
201. Bruson, H. S., U. S. Patent 2,401,607 (June 4, 1946).
202. Astle, M. J., and Etherington, R., *Ind. Eng. Chem.*, **44**, 2871 (1952).
203. Walker, J. F., U. S. Patent 2,353,671 (July 4, 1944).
204. Bruson, H. A., U. S. Patent 2,382,036 (Aug. 14, 1945).
205. Gershbein, L. L., and Hurd, C. D., *J. Am. Chem. Soc.*, **69**, 241 (1947).
206. Ufer, H., German Patent 670,357 (Jan. 17, 1939).
207. Johnston, H. W., and Gross, F. J., *J. Org. Chem.*, **22**, 124 (1957).
208. Heininger, S. A., U. S. Patent 2,818,422 (Dec. 31, 1957).
209. Bruson, H. A., and Riener, T. W., U. S. Patent 2,352,516 (June 27, 1941).
210. Whitmore, F. C., *et al.*, *J. Am. Chem. Soc.*, **66**, 725 (1944).
211. Wiedmann, O. F., and Montgomery, W. H., *J. Am. Chem. Soc.*, **67**, 1994 (1945).
212. Hoffman, U., and Jacobi, B., U. S. Patent 1,992,615 (Feb. 26, 1935).
213. Ford, J. H., Buc, S. R., and Greiner, J. W., *J. Am. Chem. Soc.*, **69**, 845 (1947).
214. Montgomery, P. D., U. S. Patent 2,816,129 (Dec. 10, 1957).
215. Cook, A. H., and Reed, K. J., *J. Chem. Soc.*, **1945**, 399.
216. Du Brow, P. L., and Harwood, J., U. S. Patent 2,627,526 (Feb. 3, 1953); *J. Org. Chem.*, **17**, 1043 (1952).
217. Pearson, D. E., Jones, W. H., and Cope, A. C., *J. Am. Chem. Soc.*, **68**, 1225 (1946).
218. Heininger, S. A., *J. Org. Chem.*, **22**, 1213 (1957).
219. Pietra, S., *Gazz. chim. ital.*, **86**, 70 (1956).
220. Bates, R. J., *et al.*, *J. Chem. Soc.*, **1956**, 388.
221. Behr, L. C., *et al.*, *J. Am. Chem. Soc.*, **68**, 1296 (1946).
222. Buckley, G. O., and Lowe, A., British Patent 586,099 (Mar. 6, 1947).
223. Bruson, H. A., U. S. Patent 2,361,259 (Oct. 24, 1944).

224. I. G. Farbenind A. G., French Patent 882,077.
225. Wiest, G., and Glaser, H., U. S. Patent 2,403,570 (July 9, 1946).
226. De Malde, M., *Chimica e Industrie (Milan),* **38,** 371 (1956).
227. Bruson, H. A., U. S. Patent 2,287,510 (June 23, 1943).
228. Koelsch, C. F., *J. Am. Chem. Soc.,* **65,** 2458 (1943).
229. Kolesnikov, G. S., and Fedoroba, L. S., *Izvest. Akad. Nauk. SSSR Otdel. Khim. Nauk,* **1957,** 236.
230. Copelin, H. B., U. S. Patent 2,714,137 (Aug. 9, 1955).
231. Coleman, G. H., and Alvarado, A. M., "Organic syntheses," Collective Vol. I, p. 3, New York, John Wiley & Sons, Inc., 1941.
232. Mitchell, J. A., and Reid, E. E., *J. Am. Chem. Soc.,* **53,** 1879 (1931).
233. Ralston, A. W., Hoerr, C. W., and Pool, W. O., *J. Org. Chem.,* **8,** 463 (1943).
234. Webb, C. N., "Organic Syntheses," Collective Vol. I, p. 82, New York, John Wiley & Sons, Inc., 1941.
235. Fieser, L., and Jones, J. E., "Organic Syntheses," Vol. 20, p. 66, New York, John Wiley & Sons, Inc., 1940.
236. Yoshizake, T. Y., *J. Chem. Soc. Japan, Ind. Chem. Sect.,* **54,** 186 (1951).
237. Anderson, G. W., and Young, D. W., U. S. Patent 2,691,010 (Oct. 5, 1954).
238. Cottle, D. L., and Young, D. W., U. S. Patent 2,711,415 (June 21, 1955).
239. Snyder, H. R., and Elston, C. T., *J. Am. Chem. Soc.,* **76,** 3039 (1954).
240. Clarke, H. T., and Behr, L. D., "Organic Syntheses," Collective Vol. II, p. 562, New York, John Wiley & Sons, Inc., 1943.
241. Noyes, W. A., and Porter, P. K., "Organic Syntheses," Collective Vol. I, p. 457, New York, John Wiley & Sons, Inc., 1941.
242. Feist, K., and Schultz, J., *Arch. Pharm.,* **272,** 789 (1934).
243. Kent, R. E., and McIlvain, S. M., "Organic Syntheses," Vol. 25, p. 58, New York, John Wiley & Sons, Inc., 1945.
244. Garbo, P. W., U. S. Patent 2,606,915 (Aug. 12, 1952).
245. Rahman, A., and Faroo, M. O., *Naturwissenschaften,* **40,** 460 (1953).
246. Gordon, M., Miller, J. G., and Day, A. B., *J. Am. Chem. Soc.,* **71,** 1245 (1949).
247. Jacobs, W. A., and Heidelberger, M., "Organic Syntheses," Collective Vol. I, p. 153, New York, John Wiley & Sons, Inc., 1941.
248. Corson, B. B., Scott, R. W., and Voss, C. E., "Organic Syntheses," Collective Vol. I, p. 179, New York, John Wiley & Sons, Inc., 1941.
249. Rohrs, W., and Lang, S., *J. Prakt. Chem.,* **158,** 112 (1941).
250. Audrieth, L. F., and Kleinberg, J., *J. Org. Chem.,* **3,** 312 (1938).
251. Ratchford, W. P., and Fisher, C. H., *J. Org. Chem.,* **15,** 317, 326 (1950).
252. Coover, H. W., Jr., and Shearer, N. H., Jr., U. S. Patent 2,719,165 (Sept. 27, 1955).
253. Joullie, M. M., *J. Am. Chem. Soc.,* **77,** 6662 (1955).
254. Balaty, V. F., Fellinger, L. L., and Audrieth, L. F., *Ind. Eng. Chem.,* **31,** 280 (1939).
255. Roe, E. T., *et al., J. Am. Oil Chemists' Soc.,* **29,** 18 (1952).
256. Nandit, M., Balder, J., and Disnuelle, P., *Bull. soc. chim. France,* **1954,** 1174.
257. Paul, R., *Bull. soc. chim. France,* [5], **4,** 1115 (1937); *Compt. rend.,* **204,** 363 (1937).
258. Sargent, L. J., *J. Org. Chem.,* **21,** 827 (1956).

259. Ott, A. O., Mattano, L. A., and Coleman, G. H., *J. Am. Chem. Soc.,* **68,** 2633 (1946).
260. Gilman, H., and Avakian, S., *J. Am. Chem. Soc.,* **68,** 2104 (1946).
261. Bachmann, W. E., and Cortes, G. D., *J. Am. Chem. Soc.,* **65,** 1332 (1943).
262. De Tar D. F., and Carmack, M., *J. Am. Chem. Soc.,* **68,** 2025, 2029 (1946).
263. King, J. A., and McMillan, F. H., *J. Am. Chem. Soc.,* **68,** 1369 (1946).
264. Cavalieri, L., Pattison, D. B., and Carmack, M., *J. Am. Chem. Soc.,* **67,** 1783 (1945).
265. Ruhrchemie, A. G., British Patent 706,798 (Apr. 7, 1954).
266. Naylor, M. A., Jr., U. S. Patent 2,744,134 (May 1, 1956).
267. Ainsworth, C., *J. Am. Chem. Soc.,* **78,** 1635 (1956).
268. Winteler, H., Bieler, A., and Guyer, A., *Helv. Chim. Acta,* **37,** 2370 (1954).
269. Specht, E. H., Neuman, A., and Neher, H. T., U. S. Patent 2,773,063 (Dec. 4, 1956).
270. Kodama, S., *et al., J. Chem. Soc. Japan, Ind. Chem. Sect.,* **58,** 157 (1955).
271. Erickson, J. G., *J. Org. Chem.,* **20,** 1569 (1955).
272. Cairns, T. L., Graham, P. J., Barrick, P. L., and Schreiber, R. S., *J. Org. Chem.,* **17,** 751 (1952).
273. Duffy, J. A., and Leisten, J. A., *Nature,* **178,** 1242 (1956).
274. Jaunin, R., *Helv. Chim. Acta.,* **35,** 1414 (1952).
275. Wilkes, J. B., U. S. Patent 2,734,078 (Feb. 7, 1956).
276. Stephens, C. R., Beance, E. J., and Pilgrim, F. J., *J. Am. Chem. Soc.,* **77,** 1701 (1955).
277. Delaby, R., Tsatsas, G., and Lusinchi, X., *Compt. rend.,* **242,** 2644 (1956).
278. Hofmann, A. W., *Ber.,* **15,** 407, 752 (1882).
279. Wallis, E. S., and Nagel, S. C., *J. Am. Chem. Soc.,* **53,** 2787 (1931).
280. Wallis, E. S., and Moyer, W. W., *J. Am. Chem. Soc.,* **55,** 2598 (1933).
281. Hauser, C. R., *et al., J. Am. Chem. Soc.,* **59,** 121, 2308 (1937); *ibid.,* **61,** 618 (1939).
282. Zakharob, N. D., and Parlov, S. A., *Zhur. Obschei. Khim.,* **26,** 2290 (1956).
283. Davis, M., *J. Chem. Soc.,* **1956,** 3981.
284. Wojcik, B. H., and Adkins, H., *J. Am. Chem. Soc.,* **56,** 2419 (1934).
285. Guyer, A., Bieler, A., and Gerliczy, G., *Helv. Chim. Acta,* **38,** 1649 (1955).
286. Lazier, W. A., U. S. Patent 1,187,745 (Jan. 23, 1940).
287. Chechelska, B., *Roczniki Chem.,* **30,** 149 (1956).
288. Polya, J. B., and Spotswood, T. M., *Rec. trav. chim.,* **67,** 927 (1948).
289. Hurd, C. D., and Dull, M. F., *J. Am. Chem. Soc.,* **54,** 2432 (1932).
290. Davidson, D., and Newman, P., *J. Am. Chem. Soc.,* **74,** 1515 (1952).
291. Davidson, D., and Kasten, M., *J. Am. Chem. Soc.,* **78,** 1066 (1956).
292. Gatewood, E., and Johnson, T. B., *J. Am. Chem. Soc.,* **48,** 2900 (1926).
293. Olin, J. F., and Johnson, T. B., *Rec. trav. chim.,* **50,** 72 (1931).
294. White, E. H., *J. Am. Chem. Soc.,* **77,** 6008 (1955).
295. Harwood, H. J., *J. Am. Oil Chem. Soc.,* **31,** 559 (1954).
296. Hellman, H., and Loschmann, I., *Chem. Ber.,* **87,** 1684 (1954).
297. Marvel, C. S., "Organic Syntheses," Vol. 21, p. 99, New York, John Wiley & Sons, Inc., 1941.

298. Wender, N. L., *J. Am. Chem. Soc.,* **71,** 375 (1949).
299. Cheronis, N. D., and Spitzmeuller, K. H., *J. Org. Chem.,* **6,** 349 (1941).
300. Boatright, L. G., U. S. Patent 2,734,081 (Feb. 7, 1956).
301. Strecker, *Ann.,* **75,** 27 (1850).
302. Kendall, E. C., and McKenzie, B. F., "Organic Syntheses," Vol. 9, p. 4, New York, John Wiley & Sons, Inc., 1929.
303. Ehrlich, F., *Ber.,* **37,** 1809 (1904).
304. Ehrlenmeyer and Lipp, *Ann.,* **219,** 161, 179 (1883).
305. Livak, J. E., and Murray, M. F., U. S. Patent 2,435,399 (Feb. 3, 1948).
306. Otsuki, H., and Fanabashi, H., Japan Patent 4,117 ('56).
307. Kralovec, R., U. S. Patent 2,504,425 (Apr. 18, 1950).
308. Pierson, E. H., and Tishler, M., U. S. Patent 2,584,496 (Feb. 5, 1952).
309. Bernard, R. A., and Merner, R. R., U. S. patent 2,676,190 (Apr. 20, 1954).
310. Mill, P. J., and Crimmin, W. R. C., *Biochem. et Biophys. Acta,* **23,** 432 (1957).
311. Rodionov, V. M., and Kiseleva, V. V., *Izvest. Akad. Nauk. SSSR Otdel Khim. Nauk.,* **1956,** 575.
312. Bergmann, M., and Zervas, L., *Ber.,* **65,** 1192 (1932).
313. Kenner, G. W., and Stedman, R. J., *J. Chem. Soc.,* **1952,** 2069.
314. Wieland, T., and Schäfer, W., *Ann.,* **576,** 104 (1952).
315. Goldschmidt, S., and Wick, M., *Ann.,* **575,** 217 (1952).
316. Kallonitsch, H., Gabor, V., and Hajos, A., *Nature,* **177,** 841 (1956).

6. ISOCYANATES, UREAS, THIOUREAS

The isocyanates have been known for a long time and the chemistry of the compounds has been investigated quite extensively. Phenyl- and α-naphthylisocyanates have been used in the identification of alcohols and amines because solid derivatives which have characteristic melting points are readily obtained in good yield.

It has been only since World War II that isocyanates have been utilized on a commercial scale.

Preparation of Isocyanates

One of the most important methods for the preparation of isocyanates involves the reaction of primary amines with phosgene. The reaction was discovered by Hentschel[1] in 1884 and modified by later investigators. Gattermann and Schmidt[2] in 1888 reported the preparation of methyl isocyanate in essentially quantitative yield by passing phosgene into molten methylammonium chloride at 250°C. Methylcarbamyl chloride was obtained and decomposed by heating with lime.

$$CH_3NH_3Cl + COCl_2 \longrightarrow CH_3NHCOCl + 2HCl$$

$$2CH_3NHCOCl + 2CaO \longrightarrow 2CH_3NCO + CaCl_2 + Ca(OH)_2$$

More recently the reaction has been carried out in solvents such as toluene[3] and o-dichlorobenzene.[4] Yields are usually 85–95 per cent.

Aromatic isocyanates are prepared by the reaction of an aromatic amine with phosgene in a chlorinated solvent with removal of hydrogen chloride and unreacted phosgene continuously. Thus 2,4-tolylenediamine and phosgene are continuously fed into o-dichlorobenzene at reflux temperatures and hydrogen chloride and phosgene continuously removed from the top of the condenser to give 2,4-tolylenediisocyanate in 87 per cent yield.[5]

Smutz[6] describes a process for making aromatic isocyanates by treating a primary arylamine with phosgene at a temperature below the decomposition temperature of the corresponding aromatic carbamyl chloride and subsequently raising the temperature to drive off hydrogen chloride and form the isocyanate. The reaction is carried out in an inert solvent using an excess of phosgene.

Thus phosgene and tetramethylurea (about 2 per cent of the weight of the phosgene) are added to xylene and the mixture heated to reflux temperature. *p*-Chloroaniline is added slowly at a uniform rate at a temperature not to exceed 60°C. When all of the amine has been added the temperature is increased at a rate of 1°C per minute to decompose the carbamate. *p*-Chlorophenylisocyanate is obtained in 95 per cent yield.

Another procedure for the preparation of isocyanates involves the continuous, separate introduction of phosgene and an amine such as α-naphthylamine in a solvent into a high-speed mixer heated to about 65°C by the heat of reaction. The mixture is then passed into a vertical tube where the temperature is raised to 150°C, the excess phosgene is stripped out with nitrogen and the solvent removed to give 98 per cent pure α-naphthylisocyanate.[7]

Irwin and Swanner[8] describe a similar process. An aromatic amine or its hydrochloride is suspended or dissolved in an inert liquid which has a boiling point higher than that of the isocyanate to be formed. The mixture is heated above the boiling point of the isocyanate, phosgene is introduced and the isocyanate distilled out as fast as formed. Thus 2,4-tolylenediamine in *o*-dichlorobenzene, and phosgene are passed into a chlorinated polyphenyl and the 2,4-tolylenediisocyanate is distilled away from the reaction mixture as fast as it is formed. The yield of diisocyanate is 85–90 per cent.

Slocombe and Saunders[9] describe the preparation of 2,4-tolylenediisocyanate using *o*-dichlorobenzene as a reaction solvent. 2,4-Tolylenediamine is treated with phosgene in the presence of *o*-dichlorobenzene to form a slurry which on further treatment with phosgene gives 2,4-tolylenediisocyanate. The phosgene and hydrogen chloride are removed by blowing the mixture with natural gas and the solvent is removed by distillation to give a black solid. The solid is melted with a mixture of chlorinated terphenyls and the diisocyanates recovered by distillation at 162°C under 5 mm of mercury pressure.

Hartmann[10] prepared isocyanates by heating primary amines, in a suitable solvent, with phosgene in a series of reactors in which the temperature is progressively increased. Thus phosgene is passed at 0°C into a solution of an arylamine in *o*-dichlorobenzene. The product is passed into a second reactor at 60–80°C and into a third at 140°C. The carbamyl chloride formed in the first reactor is dehydrochlorinated to the isocyanate in the second and third reactors.

The preparation of mono-, di-, and polyisocyanates by a continuous liquid phase process has also been described by Slocombe *et al.*[11] Phosgene and the amine in a molar ratio of 1.2:3.2 are reacted in an organic solvent at temperatures of 30–50°C followed by further treatment with phosgene at 130–220°C to give the corresponding isocyanate which is separated by distillation.

A carbonate salt was found to be more effective than the corresponding hydrochloride for the preparation of diisocyanates from hexamethylene diamine.[4]

$$H_2N(CH_2)_6NH_2 + CO_2 \longrightarrow H_3\overset{+}{N}(CH_2)_6NHCO_2^- \xrightarrow{\ 2COCl_2\ }$$

$$OCN(CH_2)_6NCO + 4HCl + CO_2$$

Lower molecular weight diisocyanates cannot be made in this way because of a tendency for intramolecular formation of ureas.

Boron trifluoride is an effective catalyst for the formation of isocyanates from primary amines and phosgene. Thus $(4\text{-}H_2NC_6H_4)_2CH_2$ in toluene is heated with phosgene at 40°C in the presence of BF_3-etherate. The temperature is held between 40 and 92°C for 2 hours while more phosgene is continuously added. The diisocyanate $OCN\text{---}C_6H_4CH_2C_6H_4\text{---}NCO$ is prepared in about 85 per cent yield. Higher operating temperatures lower the yield because of the formation of insoluble polymers.[12]

Vapor-phase reactions are also effective. In Germany the amine and phosgene were passed at temperatures of 180–400°C over a catalyst such as clay impregnated with barium chloride, zinc chloride or sodium bisulfate.[13] Yields of isocyanates as high as 80 per cent have been reported. The method is not satisfactory for the preparation of high-boiling isocyanates and diisocyanates.

Slocombe and Hardy[14] prepared isocyanates in the vapor phase without using a catalyst. The amine vapors and phosgene were heated to 275°C and the reaction mixture cooled. The carbamyl chloride thus formed was isolated and converted to the isocyanate by refluxing in benzene or toluene. Low boiling isocyanates were obtained by treating the carbamyl chloride with a tertiary amine. Yields of isocyanates having nine or fewer carbon atoms were 75–85 per cent.

The isocyanate was formed directly at 275°C but reacted with the hydrogen chloride as the reaction mixture was cooled to give the carbamyl chloride. A small amount of a urea is formed by the reaction between the isocyanate and the amine

$$C_6H_5NCO + C_6H_5NH_2 \longrightarrow C_6H_5NHCONHC_6H_5$$

but this compound may react further with phosgene at 150°C to give the isocyanate[15]

$$C_6H_5NHCONHC_6H_5 + COCl_2 \longrightarrow 2C_6H_5NCO + 2HCl$$

Phenylisocyanate may be prepared by passing aniline diluted with benzene through a reactor where it is mixed with phosgene. At temperatures of 220–300°C the reaction proceeds smoothly. The mole ratio of phosgene to aniline should be about 1.2:1. Phenylisocyanate is produced in 85 per cent yield.[16]

Tertiaryalkyl primary amines react with urea at elevated temperatures to form tertiary-alkylisocyanates.

$$R_3CNH_2 + H_2NCONH_2 \longrightarrow R_3CNHCONH_2 + NH_3$$

$$R_3CNHCONH_2 \xrightleftharpoons{180-250°C} R_3CNCO + NH_3$$

The reaction does not give isocyanates when primary or secondary alkylamines are used, but 1-methylcyclohexylamine gives 1-methylcyclohexylisocyanate in 32 per cent yield.[17]

Isocyanates are prepared by the rearrangement of an acid azide in a neutral solvent (Curtius rearrangement)

$$RCON_3 \xrightarrow{-N_2} [RCON <] \longrightarrow RNCO$$

The acid azides are usually prepared by treating an acid hydrazide with a cold aqueous solution of nitrous acid[18]

$$RCONHNH_2 + HONO \longrightarrow RCON_3 + 2H_2O$$

Another method for the preparation of azides involves the reaction of acid chlorides with sodium azide

$$RCOCl + NaN_3 \longrightarrow RCON_3 + NaCl$$

This method has been satisfactorily demonstrated by Naegeli and his coworkers.[19,20,21]

The azides rearrange to isocyanates in inert solvents such as benzene or chloroform from which the isocyanate may be isolated. In the presence of water or alcohols, further reaction occurs and urethanes or amines are obtained.

Good yields of isocyanates are obtained from both saturated and unsaturated acids by both methods. Methyl isocyanate is obtained in 60–72 per cent yield from acetyl chloride.[22] Undecyl isocyanate is obtained in 86 per cent yield from lauroyl chloride by the sodium azide procedure.[23]

The intermediate hydrazides are formed from low molecular weight esters in good yields, but with higher esters the reaction is much more difficult.

Curtius prepared substituted ethylene diisocyanates from the diazides prepared from succinic hydrazides and nitrous acid.

Isocyanates are intermediates in the Hoffmann degradation of amides to amines but the method is a satisfactory synthesis of isocyanates only in those cases in which hydrolysis to the amine is rather difficult.

Hydroxamic acids rearrange to give isocyanates (Lossen rearrangement) but this method is not frequently used.

Other methods of more or less minor importance include the reaction of

1. an alkyl sulfate with potassium cyanate[22]

$$R_2SO_4 + 2KCNO \longrightarrow 2RNCO + K_2SO_4$$

This may be the best method for the preparation of methyl and ethyl isocyanates.

2. a diazonium chloride with potassium cyanate in the presence of copper powder

$$C_6H_5N_2Cl + KCNO \xrightarrow{Cu} C_6H_5NCO + KCl + N_2$$

3. phosphorus pentoxide or phosphorus pentachloride on urethanes.[24]

Isocyanates are easily prepared by heating the corresponding carbamate in the presence of a metallic oxide or hydroxide

$$RNHCO_2R' \longrightarrow RNCO + R'OH$$

where R is a saturated secondary or tertiary hydrocarbon group and R' is a lower molecular weight alkyl group. Thus heating ethyl-N-*tert*-octyl carbamate with lime at 195–200°C and distilling off the ethyl alcohol as formed gives *tert*-octylisocyanate.[25] Yields are about 70 per cent.

Polyisocyanates are prepared by the reaction of phosgene with a condensation product of aniline and formaldehyde. A mixture of concentrated hydrochloric acid and 37 per cent aqueous formaldehyde is added slowly to aniline at a temperature of 80°C. The solution is then heated 5–6 hours at 90°C, the unreacted aniline removed by steam distillation and the reaction mixture neutralized to give a mixture of di- and polyamines. Conversion to the isocyanate is accomplished with phosgene at low temperatures.[26]

It is possible to write three electronic structure for isocyanates

$$R\!-\!N\!=\!C\!=\!O \leftrightarrow R\!-\!\ddot{N}\!=\!C\!-\!\ddot{O}\!: \leftrightarrow R\!-\!\overset{..}{N}\!-\!C\!=\!\ddot{O}\!:$$
$$\qquad\qquad\qquad (+)\ (-)\qquad\quad (-)\ (+)$$

The resonance theory would therefore predict that the carbon atom of the isocyanate group would bear a positive charge.

Since the reactions of isocyanates involve nucleophilic attack on this carbon atom the presence of an electron-withdrawing substituent on the R group should increase the ease of reaction. It is possible to predict qualitatively the effect of different groups on the reactivity of isocyanates. This order which has been verified by experiment is $O_2NC_6H_4 > C_6H_4NH_2 > p\text{-}CH_3C_6H_4 > p\text{-}CH_3OC_6H_4 >> C_nH_{2n+1}$. It should also follow that an increase in the electron-releasing ability of substituents of the attacking reagent should increase the rate of reaction. The rate of reaction for a number of active hydrogen compounds with isocyanates decreases in the order indicated

$$CH_3NH_2 > C_6H_5NH_2 > CH_3OH > C_6H_5OH > CH_3SH$$

Steric hindrance frequently becomes the major factor in determining the ease of reaction. A substituent *ortho* to either the isocyanate or the amino group interferes with the reaction but an *ortho* substituent to the isocyanate group is most effective.

Reactions of Isocyanates

Amines react with isocyanates to give disubstituted ureas

$$RNCO + R'NH_2 \longrightarrow RNH\!-\!CO\!-\!NHR'$$

Naegeli et al.[28] investigated the effect of nuclear substituents on the reactivity of aryl isocyanates with arylamines. They reported that the activity of the isocyanates decreased in the order

$$2,4\text{-}(NO_2)_2 > 3,5\text{-}(NO_2)_2 > 4\text{-}NO_2 > 3\text{-}NO_2 > 3\text{-}OCH_3 > H > 4\text{-}CH_3 > OCH_3$$

The activity of the substituted amines increased in the same order.
Amides give acylureas

$$RNCO + R'CONH_2 \longrightarrow RNH\!-\!CO\!-\!NH\!-\!COR'$$

and ureas give biurets[29]

$$RNCO + H_2NCONH_2 \longrightarrow RNHCONHCONH_2$$

N-Substituted amides give some rather anomalous reactions as indicated by the following equations[30]

$$C_6H_5CONHCH_3 + C_6H_5NCO \xrightarrow{120°C} C_6H_5CONHC_6H_5$$

$$C_6H_5CONHC_6H_5 + C_6H_5NCO \xrightarrow{200-220°C} C_6H_5-\underset{\underset{N-C_6H_5}{\|}}{C}-NHC_6H_5 + CO_2$$

These reactions are in competition with the formation of the principal product which is of the type

$$R-CON-CONHR''$$
$$\underset{R'}{|}$$

obtained from the amide $RCONHR'$ and the isocyanate $R''NCO$.

Hydroxylamine reacts with two molecules of phenylisocyanate

$$2C_6H_5NCO + H_2NOH \longrightarrow C_6H_5NH-CONH-O-CONHC_6H_5$$

but if a large excess of hydroxylamine is used and the temperature kept low the urea is formed[31]

$$C_6H_5NCO + H_2NOH \longrightarrow C_6H_5NHCONHOH$$

Reaction of an isocyanate with a secondary amine is complete and makes possible a good method of analysis. Stagg[32] has demonstrated that the titration of an isocyanate with di-*n*-butylamine is both reproducible and accurate.

Isocyanates react with water at ordinary temperatures to give disubstituted ureas and carbon dioxide.[33] The reaction probably proceeds as follows:

$$RNCO + H_2O \longrightarrow RNHCOOH \xrightarrow{-CO_2} RNH_2 \xrightarrow{RNCO} RNH-CO-NHR$$

The evolution of carbon dioxide is of importance in the formation of foamed polyureas and polyurethanes.

Isocyanates are hydrolyzed in dilute sodium or potassium hydroxide solutions to give primary amines as the major products.

Alcohols react with isocyanates to give urethanes

$$RNCO + R'OH \longrightarrow RNHCOOR'$$

The reaction is successful with primary, secondary and tertiary alcohols with the exception of triphenylcarbinol.[34,35] At 26°C all primary alcohols react at about the same rate. Secondary alcohols react 0.3 times as fast as primary and tertiary alcohols 0.005 times as fast as primary alcohols. Phenols react successfully in the presence of aluminum chloride.

Tertiary alcohols may be dehydrated by heating with isocyanates.[14]

$$2C_6H_5NCO + (CH_3)_3COH \longrightarrow (CH_3)_2C{=}CH_2 + C_6H_5NHCONHC_6H_5$$

Weak aromatic and aliphatic acids react with isocyanates to form mixed anhydrides

$$C_6H_5NCO + RCOOH \longrightarrow C_6H_5NHCO{-}O{-}COR$$

The anhydrides formed from strong acids such as formic, trichloroacetic or cyanoacetic acid spontaneously decompose to give carbon dioxide and an amide

$$C_6H_5NH{-}CO{-}O{-}COR \longrightarrow CO_2 + C_6H_5NHCOR$$

The more stable mixed anhydrides break down at elevated temperatures to give disubstituted ureas, carboxylic acid anhydrides and carbon dioxide[28,37]

$$2C_6H_5NH{-}CO{-}O{-}COR \longrightarrow C_6H_5NH{-}CO{-}NHC_6H_5 + (RCO)_2O + CO_2$$

Compounds capable of existing in the enol form react with isocyanates. Thus nitromethane, malonic esters, and acetoacetic esters react to give the expected product in the presence of sodium.[38,39]

$$C_6H_5NCO + NaCH(COOC_2H_5)_2 \xrightarrow{H_2O} C_6H_5NHCOCH(COOC_2H_5)_2$$

Aryl and alkyl isocyanates are reduced with lithium aluminum hydride to the corresponding methylamine in good yield.[40,41]

$$RNCO \xrightarrow{LiAlH_4} RNHCH_3$$

Grignard reagents react readily with isocyanates to give N-substituted amides.

Isocyanates give addition products with sodium bisulfite which are more stable than those obtained from aldehydes or ketones.[42] The addition products from aliphatic isocyanates can be recrystallized from water but those prepared from aromatic isocyanates are more sensitive to hydrolysis.

Alkyl sulfonic acids are prepared by treating alkyl isocyanates with fuming sulfuric acid. Ice-cooled 20 per cent oleum is treated dropwise, with stirring, with ethyl isocyanate and the mixture added slowly to anhydrous ether.[43] The precipitate is washed with ether to give $CH_3CH_2NHSO_3H$ in good yield.

Most aromatic isocyanates form dimers in the presence of triethyl phosphine.[44,45]

$$2C_6H_5NCO \longrightarrow C_6H_5-N \underset{CO}{\overset{CO}{<}} \underset{}{>} N-C_6H_5$$

The dimer is also formed by treating phenylisocyanate with pyridine.[46] When pyridine is used as the catalyst it is usually the solvent for the reaction. Alkyl phosphines are more active and are used only in trace amounts.

The dimer of phenylisocyanate has been prepared by the action of excess thionyl chloride on N-phenyl-urethane at room temperature.[47]

The dimerization of isocyanates is an equilibrium reaction. Conversion to dimer is favored by low temperatures and dissociation of isocyanate dimers occurs only at high temperatures. At 175°C the dimer of toluene-2,4-diisocyanate is completely dissociated. The dissociation follows first-order kinetics.

Ethylisocyanate gives a trimer in the presence of triethyl phosphine.[45]

$$3C_2H_5NCO \longrightarrow H_5C_2-N \underset{CO-N}{\overset{CO-N}{<}} \underset{C_2H_5}{\overset{C_2H_5}{<}} CO$$

Other catalysts which will convert either aliphatic or aromatic isocyanates to the corresponding trimers are calcium or potassium acetates,[48] sodium formate, sodium carbonate, sodium methoxide[38] and triethylamine.

Aryl isocyanates are converted into cyclic trimers in olefin oxide solutions in the presence of catalytic amounts of pyridine. Thus phenyl isocyanate in solution in ethylene oxide or epichlorohydrin with a trace of pyridine gives triphenylisocyanurate in high yields. No reaction is obtained in the absence of pyridine.

Cetylpyridinium chloride is also an effective catalyst. A 48 per cent conversion to trimer is obtained in one month in the presence of 2 per cent of this catalyst.

Some trimer is obtained when diphenylyl- or 1- or 2-naphthyl isocyanate in epichlorohydrin is treated with small amounts of pyridine.

The dimeric and trimeric forms of 2,4-tolylene diisocyanate have been prepared[27] but treatment with pyridine in propylene oxide or epichlorohydrin gives a resin. Presumably some of the *ortho-* as well as the *para*-isocyanate groups are involved in the polymerization because the resin appears to be highly cross-linked.[49]

Diisocyanates. Only the diisocyanates are of appreciable commercial interest and these are prepared and react in much the same way as the mono-isocyanates. There is a difference in reactivity between two isocyanate groups on a substituted benzene ring. In toluene-2,4-diisocyanate the group *para* to the methyl group is much more reactive than the one in the *ortho*-position. There is also a considerable difference in the reactivity of the *ortho* NCO group in toluene-2,4- and 2,6-diisocyanates.

Linear polyurethanes prepared from glycols such as 1,4-butanediol and hexamethylene diisocyanate ("Perlon Y") have been found to be interesting synthetic fibers. Molecular weights of 10,000–12,000 are obtained. These fibers have high tensile strength, low water absorption and good electrical properties. Although they have found limited application in Germany they have not been used in this country. The structure of the polyurethan made from ethylene glycol and toluene-2,4-diisocyanate is

Elastomers have been obtained from diisocyanates and polyether glycols or polyester glycols obtained from aliphatic, aromatic or unsaturated compounds, and polyester amides having molecular weights in excess of 1000. Both aromatic and aliphatic diisocyanates have been used. The products range from liquids to solids: some must be molded immediately and others may be stored for some time.

A highly abrasion-resistant synthetic rubber, called "Vulcollan," is made from 2,4-tolylenediisocyanate or 4,4'-diphenylmethanediisocyanate with polyhydroxy compounds such as polyethylene glycols or more particularly polyesters having terminal hydroxyl groups.[50] The preparation of the polymer has been carried out by adding slowly the polyol to the diisocyanate with constant stirring. Following an induction period of 5–10 minutes, an exothermic reaction results and the temperature rises to 80–120°C. After the reaction subsides, heating is continued at 80–100°C for 30 minutes to insure complete reaction. On cooling, the condensation products obtained vary from clear, amber glasses to viscous liquids, being more fluid as the distance between hydroxyl groups is increased.

In some cases solvents such as benzene are used and if the reaction is a very slow one, trace amounts of N-methylmorpholine or other tertiary amine are added to serve as a catalyst. Monoglycerides are used effectively as polyols.

Excellent adhesives are prepared from diisocyanates and polyols such as trimethylolnitromethane, triethylene glycol, dipropylene glycol or monoglycerides.

The diisocyanate-polyol adducts may be cured by allowing them to react with water. In addition to the liberation of carbon dioxide, the amine which is formed reacts with other isocyanate groups to give ureas. Since the amino group and the isocyanate group may be in different chains, considerable cross-linking occurs to make very high molecular weight polymers. Cross-linking may also result from the reaction of an isocyanate group with an active hydrogen of urea or urethan links.

Curing of the raw polymer is accomplished by heating alone or in the presence of added polyisocyanate or active halogen compound. Curing is also accomplished by using unsaturated polymers in the presence of peroxides.[27]

The urethan rubbers contain no unsaturated linkages and consequently cannot be vulcanized by conventional methods. The polyurethanes do have active hydrogen atoms that will react further with diisocyanates to cause cross-linking. The vulcanization can be effected with water, glycols or diamines which cause cross-linking through reaction with residual isocyanate groups, but the most common vulcanization agent is 4,4'-methylenedi-*o*-tolylisocyanate.

Elastomers are formed from diisocyanates and relatively high molecular weight linear low-melting glycols and diamines. Low molecular weight, or highly crystalline, high molecular weight glycols, amine, or carboxylic acids, form plastics useful in coatings, films, and fibers.

As has been mentioned previously, when isocyanates react with water or carboxylic acids, carbon dioxide is evolved. If such a reaction occurs during polymer formation the gas escapes leaving a voluminous, porous structure. Careful control of such a process gives foams with excellent structures. Basic compounds such as amines or alkali phenates catalyze the reaction. Surface-active agents and emulsifiers are added to help control the pore size and the structure of the foam.

The type of foam obtained is dependent on the distances between reactive sites. Thus if a low molecular weight tri-functional polyester reacts with a diisocyanate, these distances are small, and a brittle, rigid foam is obtained. If a high molecular weight linear diol is used the foam is soft and flexible.

In the formation of foams, excess diisocyanate is used and a relatively low molecular weight, very viscous liquid is obtained. Water or an acid is added immediately before curing. The mixture is poured into a reactor and chain extension, cross-linking and foaming all occur at the same time.

The water or acid and the catalyst may be added as a separate step. This permits the condensation reaction between the diisocyanate and the diol to take place in the plant and the foaming operation at a site far removed.

Tolylenediisocyanate or diphenylmethane-4,4'-diisocyanate react with castor oil using various amines, such as diethanolamine or N-ethylmorpholine as curing agents to give surface coatings possessing outstanding chemical resistance.[51]

Mono-, di- and polyisocyanates have been used as cross-linking agents for other polymer systems and the condensation of isocyanates with polymers containing carboxyl or other groups give excellent adhesives for the bonding of rubber to polar substrates and for other applications.

Polyurethane paints and lacquers find increasing application in Western Europe because they form hard, elastic films which are completely resistant to water up to 70°C and heat up to 200°C. The films have excellent resistance to most solvents and to acids and alkalies. The weathering characteristics, adhesion and electrical properties are excellent but being highly toxic, stringent safety measures must be employed when they are used.

UREAS

Urea is the first organic compound to have been prepared from inorganic sources. In 1828 Friedrich Wöhler mixed together ammonium sulfate and potassium cyanate in an attempt to prepare ammonium cyanate and was very much surprised to find that his product was urea.

Urea is obtained by the reaction of ammonia with phosgene

$$COCl_2 + NH_3 \longrightarrow H_2NCOCl \xrightarrow{NH_3} H_2N-CO-NH_2$$

Chloroformic esters also react with ammonia to give urea but the yields are low

$$ClCOOC_2H_5 + 3NH_3 \longrightarrow H_2N-CO-NH_2 + NH_4Cl + C_2H_5OH$$

Substitution of amines for ammonia gives substituted ureas. Cyanamide gives urea on hydrolysis

$$NH_2CN + H_2O \longrightarrow H_2N—CO—NH_2$$

Urea is prepared commercially by the reaction between ammonia and carbon dioxide. These two compounds first react to give ammonium carbamate which is then dehydrated to urea.

$$2NH_3 + CO_2 \longrightarrow H_2NCOONH_4 \longrightarrow H_2N—CO—NH_2 + H_2O$$

The process may be carried out in two steps but ordinarily the entire operation is accomplished in one step.

Although several processes are used for the preparation of urea, they are all similar and the following is representative.[52] Liquid ammonia and liquid carbon dioxide (mole ratio 3:1) are charged to a silver-lined reactor and heated for 2 hours at 190°C under a pressure of 1500–3000 psi to give a product containing about 35 per cent urea, 8 per cent ammonium carbamate, 10 per cent water and 47 per cent unreacted ammonia. The ammonia and any unreacted carbon dioxide are flashed off and the urea recovered by crystallization. Yields are 80–85 per cent. About 60 per cent of the crude product is recovered as crystalline urea and the remainder is used as a liquid fertilizer.

The Montecatini process for the preparation of urea involves heating carbon dioxide with an excess of ammonia and water, amounting to 6–20 per cent of the total charge, at 70–140°C under a pressure of 120–160 atmospheres. The yield of urea amounts to 67.5 per cent based on ammonia and 77 per cent based on carbon dioxide.[53]

Kamlet[54] describes a process for making urea in which carbon dioxide and ammonia are dissolved in a hydrocarbon such as xylene, which is capable of removing water of reaction as an azeotrope below the temperature of decomposition of ammonium carbamate. As the reaction proceeds, a slurry of ammonium carbamate is formed which is heated to 130–210°C under a pressure of 70–300 atmospheres. Unreacted carbon dioxide and ammonia are flashed off and recycled, and urea is obtained in yields of 95–97 per cent.

The Lion Oil Co.[55] patented a process for making urea from carbonyl sulfide and ammonia. The carbonyl sulfide reacts with ammonia in methanol at room temperature to give ammonium thiocarbamate

$$COS + 2NH_3 \longrightarrow H_2N—CS—ONH_4$$

The mixture is then heated for 1 hour at 100°C under a pressure of 172 psi to give an almost quantitative yield of urea.

$$H_2N—CS—ONH_4 \longrightarrow H_2N—CO—NH_2 + H_2S$$

Substituted ureas are prepared by the action of phosgene or ethyl carbonates on amines.

$$COCl_2 + 4RNH_2 \rightarrow RNH{-}CO{-}NHR + 2RNH_3Cl$$

$$(C_2H_5O)_2CO + 2RNH_2 \rightarrow RNH{-}CO{-}NHR + 2C_2H_5OH$$

Unsymmetrical ureas are best prepared from isocyanates and amines.

$$C_6H_5NCO + RNH_2 \rightarrow C_6H_5NH{-}CO{-}NHR$$

Symmetrical dialkylureas are prepared by treating an aqueous solution of a primary aliphatic amine with neutral carbonate esters of alcohols or phenols. Thus finely powdered *o*-cresyl carbonate added to an aqueous solution of methylamine at temperatures of 30–70°C gives N,N'-dimethylurea in almost quantitative yields.[56]

Symmetrical dialkyl- and diarylureas are also prepared by heating urea and a primary amine in the dry state at 160°C or by refluxing an aqueous solution of the alkyl or aryl ammonium chloride with urea.[58,59]

$$2RNH_2 + H_2N{-}CO{-}NH_2 \rightarrow RNH{-}CO{-}NHR + 2NH_3$$

The urea is converted to ammonium cyanate which reacts with the amine to give a monosubstituted urea. This compound in turn is decomposed to an alkylisocyanate which adds a second molecule of amine.

Methylammonium chloride with urea gives a mixture of mono- and disubstituted ureas. Increasing the quantity of urea increases the quantity of monosubstituted urea formed and increasing the temperature favors the formation of the disubstituted urea.

Monoarylureas are converted to symmetrical diarylureas at temperatures near their melting points. The rate and degree of conversion depend on the position and nature of the substituent in the aromatic ring.[60] Symmetrical diarylureas are converted into monoarylureas by heating with urea.

Gilbert and Sorma[61] prepared *sym*-diphenylurea by heating aniline and urea (mole ratio 8:1) at 140–180°C for 1.5 hours with stirring. Neutralization with sodium hydroxide gives a 94 per cent yield of the product. The diphenylurea and dimethylamine (mole ratio 1:5.2) passed through a tube heated to 400°C gives a 71 per cent yield of N-phenyl-N',N'-dimethylurea.

It is possible in some cases to interrupt the reaction with the formation of monosubstituted ureas. Phenylurea has been obtained from urea and aniline in 55 per cent yield.[62]

Diphenylurea is obtained by the reaction of phosgene with aniline in water at 60°C in the presence of sodium acetate or a base such as sodium carbonate which will neutralize the hydrochloric acid formed.[63] The yields are reported to be very high.

Methylamine and carbon dioxide are heated for 1–2 hours at 185°C under a pressure of 150 atmospheres to give N,N'-dimethylurea, CH_3NH—CO—$NHCH_3$, in 70 per cent yield.[64]

The hydrohalide salts of ammonia, amines, hydroxylamines or hydrazines are converted to ureas by passing over an anion exchange resin converted to the cyanate (a quaternary ammonium cyanate, e.g., "Amberlite" IRA-400 cyanate). The resin in the chloride form is washed with sodium cyanate then with distilled water until the eluate is free of chloride. A solution of hydroxylammonium chloride is then passed through a column packed with the resin until a hot spot, which develops as the reaction begins, works its way down the column. The column is then washed with a large excess of water and the resulting solution evaporated to dryness to give H_2N—CO—NHOH in about 55 per cent yield.[65]

Sulfanilylurea is prepared from sulfanilic acid and urea by heating to 100–120°C in triethylene glycol containing potassium hydroxide, until the evolution of ammonia has ceased.[66]

$$p\text{-}H_2N\text{—}C_6H_4SO_2NH_2 + H_2NCONH_2 \xrightarrow{\text{KOH}} p\text{-}H_2NC_6H_4SO_2NHCONH_2 + NH_3$$

Tetrasubstituted ureas are made by refluxing R_2NCOCl with aqueous sodium hydroxide. Thus $(C_2H_5)_2N$—CO—$N(C_2H_5)_2$ is obtained from $(C_2H_5)_2NCOCl$.[67]

Ethylenethiourea is prepared by refluxing aqueous ethylenediamine, adding carbon disulfide dropwise and heating the mixture for 1 hour at 98–100°C. Hydrogen sulfide formed is removed by blowing with air. The product is used as a vulcanizing accelerator for neoprene.[68]

Ethyleneurea (2-imidazolidone) is prepared from ethylenediamine by a two-step process.[69] In the first step solid or gaseous carbon dioxide is added to ethylenediamine in a solvent such as ethyl, isopropyl or butyl alcohol. Ethylenediamine carbamate separates at first as a heavy viscous oil that eventually solidifies.

$$H_2NCH_2CH_2NH_2 + CO_2 \longrightarrow H_3\overset{+}{N}CH_2CH_2COO^-$$

In the second step the carbamate is heated in a bomb to about 200°C for about 4 hours. Pressures of 400–900 psi are used. Best yields of ethyleneurea are obtained when the carbamate is heated in the presence of excess diamine

$$H_3\overset{+}{N}\text{--}CH_2CH_2COO^- \rightarrow \begin{matrix} CH_2\text{--}NH \\ | \qquad\qquad \\ CH_2\text{--}NH \end{matrix}\!\begin{matrix} \\ \diagdown \\ \diagup \end{matrix}\!\!\!C\text{=}O + H_2O$$

A continuous process has been developed in which the over-all yields are as high as 96 per cent.

Sulfuryl chloride reacts with ammonia in an inert solvent to give sulfamide which has some structural similarities to urea[70]

$$Cl\text{--}SO_2\text{--}Cl + 4NH_3 \rightarrow H_2N\text{--}SO_2\text{--}NH_2 + 2NH_4Cl$$

By-products of the reaction are $H_2N\text{--}SO_2\text{--}NH\text{--}SO_2\text{--}NH_2$ and higher homologues. The reaction is carried out by adding liquid ammonia to a solution of sulfuryl chloride in petroleum ether at solid carbon dioxide-chloroform-carbon tetrachloride temperatures. The addition requires 20–40 minutes and sulfamide is recovered in 74–80 per cent yields.

Reactions of Urea

Heating urea to 130–205°C under a pressure of 200 mm of mercury for several hours results in loss of ammonia and the formation of biuret.[71] Yields are about 50 per cent.

$$2H_2N\text{--}CO\text{--}NH_2 \rightarrow H_2N\text{--}CO\text{--}NH\text{--}CO\text{--}NH_2 + NH_3$$

Ammonium phosphomolybdate or vanadate and sodium perborate are good catalysts for the reaction and permit reduction in reaction time to 1 hour or less.

As an alternative procedure, fused urea is stirred at 120–130°C until the mass solidifies. In order to obtain better temperature control, inert diluents such as dimethylformamide, diethanolamine or triethanolamine may be used.[72]

On further heating biuret gives cyanuric acid and other compounds so that urea pyrolysis gives a diversity of products.

Kinoshita[73] investigated the effect of heat on urea in closed and open vessels. At 133°C only biuret is formed and at temperatures of 150–175°C cyanuric acid and biuret are both formed. The rate of decomposition of urea is faster in open than in closed vessels.

Cyanuric acid has been prepared in 99 per cent yield by treating urea with sulfuric acid for 5 hours at 200°C. The ammonium sulfate formed during the reaction is extracted with water.[74]

Cyanuric acid has also been prepared by heating urea or biuret to about 200°C in a phenolic solvent.[75]

Heating urea at 425°C under a pressure of 140–170 kg/cm^2 gives melamine.[76]

$$H_2N-C\underset{\underset{N}{\Vert}}{\overset{N}{\diagup}}\overset{N}{\diagdown}\underset{\underset{C}{\diagup N}}{C}-NH_2$$

$$NH_2$$

in 95 per cent yield. Intermediate pyrolysis products, biuret and cyanuric acid are isolated at temperatures below 250°C.

In another process melamine is obtained continuously by passing urea and anhydrous ammonia through a reactor at 450°C.[77] Ammonia is removed to maintain a pressure of 3500 psi. Melamine is usually prepared by heating cyanamide, H_2NCN, under pressure.

Okada[78] heated a mixture of carbon dioxide and ammonia (mole ratio 1:2) at 140–160°C and a pressure of 120 atmospheres, then at 400°C under a pressure of 430 atmospheres to give a 79 per cent yield of melamine, 1.3 per cent of cyanuric acid, 1.4 per cent ammelide and 8.5 per cent ammeline.

Urea is a weak base and forms salts with strong acids. Urea nitrate is insoluble in water so that the addition of nitric acid permits the isolation of urea from urine.

Hydrolysis of urea to ammonia and carbon dioxide is possible with either aqueous bases of acids. The enzyme *urease*, found in soybeans, effects the same hydrolysis at room temperature.

Nitrous acid and urea react with the liberation of nitrogen

$$H_2N-CO-NH_2 + 2HONO \longrightarrow CO_2 + 2N_2 + 3H_2O$$

Bromine and sodium or potassium hydroxide gives essentially the same products.

$$H_2N-CO-NH_2 + 3NaOBr + 2NaOH \longrightarrow Na_2CO_3 + N_2 + 3NaBr + 3H_2O$$

It has been demonstrated that in this case a Hoffmann rearrangement occurs. The course of the reaction is

$$H_2NCONH_2 \xrightarrow[-HBr]{Br^+} \underset{(+)}{NHCONH_2} \longrightarrow \underset{(+)}{H_2NNH-C=O} \xrightarrow{H_2O}$$

$$H_2NNH_2 + CO_2$$

The hydrazine may be separated as a hydrazone by adding benzaldehyde. At 0°C using only one equivalent of hypohalite, hydrazine is the major product.

Chlorination of urea in water solution gives a mono- or dichloro product in which the chlorine is positive in that it liberates iodine from iodides.

Heating a mixture of urea, sulfur dioxide and ammonia (mole ratio 1:3:9) in an autoclave for 0.5 hour at a temperature of 275°C and a pressure of 200 psi gives guanidine sulfate in good yields. At 300°C a mixture of guanidine sulfamate and guanidine sulfate are obtained.

$$H_2N-CO-NH_2 \xrightarrow[SO_2]{NH_3} H_2N-C(=NH)-NH_2$$

Doubling the amount of urea gives a 44 per cent yield of guanidine, based on urea, as the sulfate only. The remainder of the urea is converted to melamine.[79]

The reaction of a primary amine with urea may lead to the formation of many compounds through a series of reversible reactions but by controlling the ratio of reactants, temperature and time of reaction, one of the products may be favored.[80] A hot, equimolar mixture of primary amines and urea rapidly evolves ammonia to give alkylureas, $RNH-CO-NH_2$. On further heating, evolution of ammonia occurs at a reduced rate to give 1,5-dialkylbiurets, $RNH-CONH-CONHR$, together with 1,3-dialkylureas, $RNH-CO-NHR$. If the mixture of a primary amine and urea is heated for a long time at 200°C, the 1,5-dialkylbiuret disappears, the amount of 1,3-dialkylurea increases and some 1,3-dialkylbiuret, $RNH-CO-NR-CONH_2$, is formed.

By using an excess of urea over primary amine, one increases the amount of 1-alkylbiuret formed. When an excess of amine is used, the yield of 1,3-dialkylurea is increased almost to the exclusion of all other products.

A mixture of octadecylamine, urea and ethylene glycol heated at 130°C yields 1,5-dioctadecylbiuret. Refluxing a mixture of dodecylamine, urea and butyl alcohol yields butyldodecylcarbamate, together with 1,3-dodecylurea.

The reactions are usually carried out without using a solvent or in pyridine solutions.

Ethylene oxide passed into molten urea at 136°C gives β-aminoethyl carbamate;

$$\begin{array}{c} H_2N \diagdown \quad \diagup O \\ \quad C \\ O \diagup \quad \diagdown NH_2 \\ | \qquad\qquad | \\ CH_2 \!\!-\!\!\!-\!\! CH_2 \end{array}$$

with smaller amounts of β-hydroxyethylurea, $HOCH_2CH_2NHCONH_2$, and 2-oxazolidinone are formed

The reaction is believed to proceed by the mechanism in which the ethylene oxide reacts with urea to give the transient intermediate

This intermediate may stabilize itself by a proton transfer from nitrogen to oxygen to form β-hydroxyethylurea or by an intramolecular nucleophilic attack of the negatively charged oxygen on the carbon to form a cyclic intermediate which dissociates into β-aminoethylcarbamate.[81]

Urea reacts with malonic acid esters to give barbiturates. In the presence of sodium ethoxide, diethyl malonate and urea give barbituric acid

With methylene-substituted diethylmalonates a series of barbiturates are obtained. Two of the more important of these are barbital and pheno-barbital

$$(H_5C_2)_2 - C \overset{CO}{\underset{NH}{\diagup}} \qquad \overset{H_5C_2}{\underset{C_6H_5}{\diagdown}} C \overset{CO}{\underset{NH}{\diagup}}$$

Barbital   *Phenobarbital*

The formation of crystalline complexes between urea and straight-chain organic compounds (urea adducts) was first reported by Bengen[82,83] who observed that many types of linear organic molecules containing six or more carbon atoms form adducts with approximately six molecules of urea. He believed that a small amount of a solvent for urea, such as water or alcohol, served as a catalyst for the complex formation.

Zimmerscheid *et al.*[84] found that the number of molecules of urea in the adduct is dependent upon the number of carbon atoms in the linear compound and that branched-chain compounds do not form urea adducts. In some cases, the adducts are formed in the absence of a urea solvent. The decomposition of the adduct may be accomplished by heating, or adding a large amount of the urea solvent. The formation of a typical adduct of a hydrocarbon and urea is described by Zimmerscheid: Urea (90 g, 1.5 moles) and methanol (5 g, 0.15 mole) were added to a solution of *n*-hexadecane (19.2 g, 0.085 mole) in decahydronaphthalene (180 g). The suspension was stirred in a round-bottomed flask for 45 minutes at 25°C. After filtering with suction and washing on the filter three times with 500 ml of iso-pentane, the mass was decomposed in 300 ml of water. The liberated hydrocarbon was taken up in 100 ml of ether and the ether layer was separated. Evaporation of ether and residual isopentane left *n*-hexadecane (18.6 g, 0.02 mole) in a yield of 97 per cent. Further examples are given by Swern.[85]

The following generalizations can be made:

1. Yields of adduct formed in 1 hour decrease at temperatures above and below room temperature.

2. The yield of adduct increases with concentration of urea, at least up to 20 moles, per mole of hydrocarbon.

3. Better yields are obtained at higher *n*-alkane concentrations.

4. Large amounts of methanol or water lower the yield of the recovered hydrocarbon.

5. Washing at temperatures much above 25°C results in considerable decomposition of the adduct.

6. Under comparable conditions, higher molecular weight *n*-alkanes give greater yields of adducts.

7. The number of urea molecules per mole of hydrocarbon required to form the adduct increases with the number of carbon atoms in the hydrocarbon.

Akai and Yada[86] describe the preparation of a cetane-urea adduct by heating a mixture of cetane and benzene in an autoclave with a solution of urea in liquid ammonia at 7–8°C. The ammonia is driven off by heating and the adduct removed from the benzene by filtration.

McAdie and Frost[87] report that the formation of adducts between urea and *n*-octane does not occur in the absence of water vapor but if these adducts are decomposed *in vacuo* the complexes can be formed again in the absence of water.

The rate of adduct formation seems to show a linear dependency on water vapor pressure over the range 8 to 15 mm.

Photomicrographic evidence indicates that not all urea crystals react at once but once initiated the reaction progresses rapidly through the crystal. Methanol and ethanol and perhaps nitromethane and ethylenediamine promote the formation of adducts but much more slowly than water.

In the formation of urea adducts a minimum number of straight-chain carbon atoms is essential. For limited branching, longer straight chains are required to make possible the formation of adducts.

The dissociation constants for the adducts decrease with increasing chain lengths and increases with temperature.

The functional groups exert a strong influence on the heat of formation. The highest heats of formation are found for the fatty acid adducts which accounts for their stability.[88]

The formation of urea adducts is not limited to hydrocarbons and fatty acids. 1-Bromohexane forms a urea adduct but 2-bromooctane does not. With alcohols, however, 2-octanol does form a complex so that a secondary hydroxyl does not interfere as much as a secondary bromine atom.

Bengen reported the formation of urea adducts from straight-chain hydrocarbons, acids, esters, alcohols, aldehydes and ketones. His work was further investigated and extended to other classes of compounds by a number of others.[89–95]

Contrary to earlier reports it has been found possible to form urea complexes of branched-chain and cyclic structures provided that these molecules contain a sufficiently long straight-chain portion.[85] Thus benzene and cyclohexane do not form complexes but 1-phenyloctadecane and 1-cyclohexyleicosane will. Phenyl hexanoate will not form a urea adduct because the straight-chain portion of the molecule is too short but phenyldodecanoate will.

The formation of hydrocarbon-urea adducts has been proposed as a method for the separation of straight chain from branched chain and cyclic hydrocarbons.[96] A mixture of lower molecular weight ketones and water has been found to be a better solvent than either methyl alcohol or water for a continuous extraction process. Methyl isobutyl ketone was found to be very effective. Water has very limited solubility in methyl isobutyl ketone which is a good solvent for the oil. Urea is soluble in water but not in the ketone. The process therefore involves adding a saturated aqueous solution of urea to the oil containing methyl isobutyl ketone. The urea adduct precipitates out and is removed by filtration.

Monoesters of glycerol can be separated from di- and triesters as urea adducts. Thus a commercial product containing 39 per cent monostearin was concentrated to a product containing 86 per cent monoester.[97]

Tall oil containing 40 per cent fatty acids gives urea adducts containing essentially all of the fatty acids, leaving non-adduct forming acids such as the resin acids and a lesser amount of polymerized and oxidized fatty acids.[98]

An x-ray investigation on single crystals indicates that urea in the complex is hexagonal whereas urea itself is tetragonal. The urea molecules in the adduct form a helical pattern around a more or less cylindrical center. The diameter of this helical unit cell varies from 5 to 6 Å. Straight chain hydrocarbons having a cross section of 4.1 Å can fit inside the helix very easily. Hydrocarbons with a single methyl group have a cross section of 5.5 Å so that if the straight-chain portion of the molecule is relatively short, it cannot fit very well into the cylindrical center of the helix but if a sufficiently long unbranched section is present, the methyl group may be dragged in.

Double branching on the same carbon as in 2,2,4-trimethylpentane requires a 6 Å channel, and benzene requires a 5.9 Å channel so that these molecules do not form adducts.

Thiourea also forms adducts with organic molecules[85] but the complexes are not as stable as those made from urea. In contrast with urea, thiourea forms complexes with many branched chain and alicyclic compounds. Thiourea adducts usually are not formed from straight chain, aromatic or terpene hydrocarbons. The molar ratio of thiourea to hydrocarbon is a little lower than the mole ratio of urea to straight-chain hydrocarbons.

The unit cell of thiourea in the complex is rhombahedral and the arrangement of the thiourea molecules is similar to that observed for urea in its adducts. However, the channel size in the thiourea complex is about 8 Å permitting larger molecules to be accommodated.

The most important commercial applications of urea are as a fertilizer and in the production of ureaformaldehyde resins.

In the presence of a base, equimolar quantities of urea and formaldehyde react to give monomethylol urea

$$HCHO + H_2NCONH_2 \longrightarrow HOCH_2NHCONH_2$$

In the presence of excess formaldehyde, dimethylol urea $HOCH_2NHCO-NHCH_2OH$ is formed.[99] Both compounds can be isolated but further condensation occurs to give high molecular weight condensation polymers. Monomethylol urea will give polymers of the type:

$$
\begin{array}{ccc}
-N-CH_2-N-CH_2- \\
| \qquad\qquad | \\
C{=}O \qquad C{=}O \\
| \qquad\qquad | \\
NH_2 \qquad NH_2
\end{array}
$$

Dimethylol urea will condense similarly except that crosslinking will occur to give thermosetting polymers of the type

$$
\begin{array}{c}
-CH_2-N-CH_2- \\
| \\
C{=}O \\
| \\
-N-CH_2-N-CH_2-N-CH_2- \\
| \qquad\qquad\qquad\qquad | \\
O{=}C \qquad\qquad\qquad C{=}O \\
| \qquad\qquad\qquad\qquad | \\
-N-CH_2-N-CH_2-N-CH_2- \\
|
\end{array}
$$

Some investigators believe that the methylolureas lose water to give methyleneureas which can polymerize by addition

$$HOCH_2NH-CO-NHCH_2OH \xrightarrow{-H_2O} H_2C{=}N-CO-N{=}CH_2$$

In any event the structure of the polymer will be the same.

The resins may be modified by addition of alcohols which react with urea, probably as formals, to give structures of the type $ROCH_2NH-CO-NHCH_2OR$ which will undergo further reaction with formaldehyde to give urea-formaldehyde resins. Such modified resins can also be made by condensing urea and formaldehyde in the presence of alkyd resins. These alkyd resins having free hydroxyl groups will undergo the type reactions indicated above.

These resins are particularly useful in surface coatings to give enamel finishes. The polymers have little or no color and can be successfully pigmented to give a surface of any desired color.

Urea-formaldehyde resins are used to a large extent in molded objects. A branched chain linear polymer is compounded with the necessary dyes and fillers, and treated with excess formaldehyde in the presence of inorganic acids or salts to give a tough thermosetting resin.

Very similar resins are made from formaldehyde and melamine; a product made by the trimerization of cyanamide

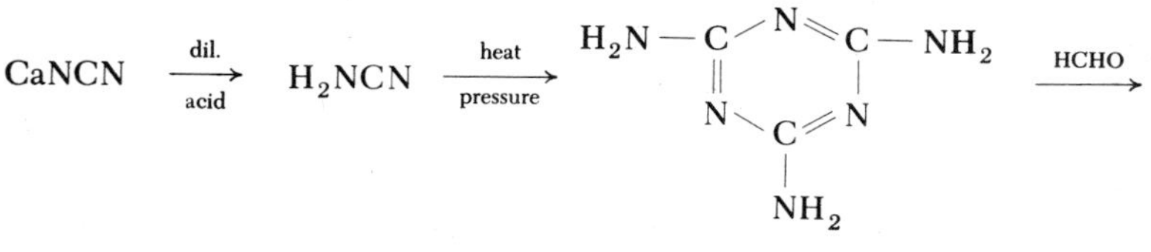

$$CaNCN \xrightarrow[\text{acid}]{\text{dil.}} H_2NCN \xrightarrow[\text{pressure}]{\text{heat}}$$

Melamine

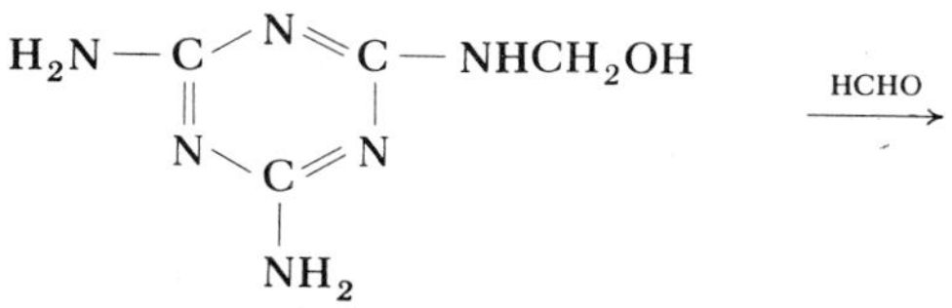

Methylolmalamine

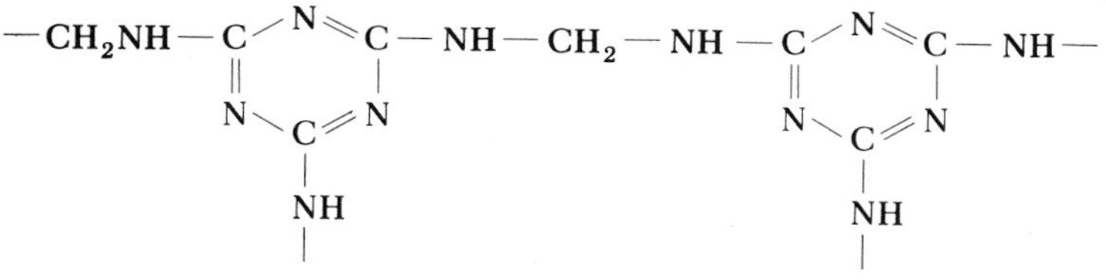

Formaldehyde-Melamine Resin

THIOUREA

Thiourea and its derivatives are of much less importance than is urea. However, thiourea is used in dyes, photographic film, elastomers, plastics and textiles.[100] Thiourea derivatives are used as insecticides, preservatives, rodentocides and pharmaceuticals.

Thiourea is prepared by the rearrangement of ammonium thiocyanate at 170°C. An equilibrium is established consisting of 75 per cent ammonium thiocyanate and 25 per cent thiourea.

$$NH_4SCN \rightleftarrows NH_3 + HN{=}C{=}S \rightleftarrows H_2N{-}CS{-}NH_2$$

Thiourea may also be prepared by treating cyanamide with ammonium sulfide. Because of the hydrolysis of the ammonium sulfide this is equivalent to using hydrogen sulfide

$$H_2NCN + H_2S \longrightarrow H_2N-C(SH)=NH \rightleftarrows H_2N-CS-NH_2$$

Thiourea exists as an equilibrium mixture of tautomers shown above.

Thiourea can be prepared from calcium cyanamide and hydrogen sulfide. An aqueous solution of calcium cyanamide is treated with hydrogen sulfide and the resulting mixture treated at 45–50°C by the addition of sulfuric acid, phosphoric acid or carbon dioxide in the presence of aniline which serves as a catalyst. The pH of the thiourea solution is maintained between 7.5 and 9.5. The yield of thiourea is reported to be about 99 per cent and the product is not contaminated with ammonium sulfate or thiodicyanamide.[101]

Substituted thioureas are made by the reaction of primary amines with carbon disulfide. The reaction probably proceeds as follows:

$$RNH_2 \longrightarrow CS_2 \longrightarrow RNH-CS-SH \tag{1}$$

$$RNHCS-SH + RNH_2 \longrightarrow (RNHCS-S)^- RNH_3{}^+ \tag{2}$$

$$(RNHCS-S)^- RNH_3{}^+ \longrightarrow RNCS + RNH_2 + H_2S \tag{3}$$

$$RNCS + RNH_2 \longrightarrow RNH-CS-NHR \tag{4}$$

Secondary amines do not behave in this way. This is probably due to the fact that the anion $(R_2NCS-)^-$ has no hydrogen attached to the nitrogen and so the salt can not liberate hydrogen sulfide to form the thiocyanate.

The reaction may be modified to prepare monosubstituted thioureas or 1,3,3-trisubstituted thioureas by heating the dithiocarbamic acid with ammonia or a secondary amine

$$RNHCSSH + NH_3 \longrightarrow (RNHCS-S)^- NH_4{}^+ \longrightarrow RNH-CS-NH_2 + H_2S$$

$$RNHCS-SH + R_2'NH \longrightarrow (RNHCS-S)^- R_2'NH_2{}^+ \xrightarrow{\text{heat}} RNHCS-NR_2'$$

The reaction is slow but may be accelerated by the addition of sulfur,[102] hydrogen peroxide,[103] ethanolic or aqueous sodium or potassium hydroxide, pyridine and iodine.[104] The iodine reacts with hydrogen sulfide to give hydrogen iodide and sulfur. The pyridine reacts with the hydrogen iodide.

Another method for the preparation of thiourea involves the reaction of thiophosgene with primary or secondary amines.

$$CSCl_2 + RNH_2 \rightarrow RNCS + 2HCl$$

$$CSCl_2 + 2RNH_2 \rightarrow RNH{-}CS{-}NHR + 2HCl$$

Usually 1 mole of thiophosgene is refluxed with 2 moles of the amine in aqueous solution.[105,106] Chloroform-water[107,108] or acetone-water[109] mixtures may be used as solvents.

On heating, substituted ammonium thiocyanates rearrange to give thioureas.[110] A primary or secondary alkyl or arylammonium chloride is heated for a few hours. 1-Monosubstituted or 1,1-disubstituted compounds are obtained.

$$R_2NH_2Cl + NH_4SCN \rightarrow NH_4Cl + R_2NH_2SCN \xrightarrow{heat} R_2NCSNH_2$$

The reaction may be carried out in either an inert organic solvent[111] or in aqueous solution.[112,113,114]

Substituted thioureas are prepared by heating thiourea with a long-chain fatty amine for 10–15 minutes at 170–180°C. Alternate routes involve reaction of the fatty amine with carbon disulfide in toluene or with a slight excess of an alkyl or aryl isothiocyanate at 25°C.[115]

Thiourea on heating with water at 140°C is converted back into ammonium thiocyanate. Hydrolysis with acids or bases gives ammonia, hydrogen sulfide and carbon dioxide. The oxides of silver, mercury or lead in water at ordinary temperatures give cyanamide.[116]

Careful oxidation with potassium permanganate gives urea

$$H_2NCSNH_2 \xrightarrow{KMnO_4} H_2NCONH_2 + S$$

With hydrogen peroxide a sulfinic acid is formed. This oxidation proceeds through the tautomeric form

$$H_2N{-}C(SH){=}NH \xrightarrow{H_2O_2} H_2N{-}C({=}NH){-}SO_2H$$

Alkyl halides give sulfur-alkylated products

$$H_2NCSNH_2 \rightarrow H_2N{-}C({=}NH){-}SH \xrightarrow{RI} H_2N{-}C({=}NH){-}SR$$

Thiourea shows a marked tendency to react in the —SH form.

Thiourea may be acetylated in toluene with ketene if a very small amount of water is present.[117] No acetylation occurs if the system is completely anhydrous. The product is $CH_3CONH{-}CS{-}NH_2$.

Substituted thioureas, e.g., N,N'-dimethylthiourea and 40 per cent aqueous formaldehyde acidified with hydrochloric acid and allowed to stand for 1 day on a steam bath gives $CH_3NH-CS-N(CH_3)-CH_2N-(CH_3)-CH_2N(CH_3)-CS-NHCH_3$.[118]

Thiourea dioxide, $H_2\overset{+}{N}=C(NH_2)SO_2^-$, is a powerful reducing agent capable of reducing aromatic nitro, azoxy, azo, and hydrazo compounds to amines, quinones to hydroquinones and a number of dyes to their leuco derivatives. The yields are high. The reductions are accomplished by adding the reagent to water, pyridine, dimethyl formamide or mixtures of these solvents in the presence of excess ammonia or sodium hydroxide and warming the mixture to 70°C on the water bath.[119]

Chloroacetaldehyde reacts with thiourea to give 2-aminothiazole

$$ClCH_2CHO \; + \; \overset{H_2N}{\underset{H_2N}{}}C=S \; \longrightarrow \; \overset{HC=N}{\underset{H_2C\diagdown S\diagup C=NH}{|\quad|}} \; \longrightarrow \; \overset{HC-N}{\underset{HC\diagdown S\diagup C-NH_2}{\|\quad\|}}$$

However, chloroacetaldehyde is available as a 40 per cent aqueous solution and attempts to isolate it results in the formation of a polymer. Acetals of chloroacetaldehyde are obtained pure and can be used with equal effectiveness. Astle and Pierce[120] prepared 2-aminothiazole from chloromethyldioxolane, the ethylene glycol acetal of chloroacetaldehyde

$$ClCH_2CH\overset{O-CH_2}{\underset{O-CH_2}{\big\backslash \big /}} \; + \; HN=C(SH)-NH_2 \; \longrightarrow$$

$$\overset{HC-N}{\underset{HC\diagdown S\diagup C-NH_2}{\|\quad\|}} \; + \; HOCH_2CH_2OH$$

Markees, Kellerhals and Erlenmeyer prepared 2-aminothiazole from 1,2-dichlorodiethyl ether and thiourea.[121] This ether hydrolyzes readily to give the hemiacetal of chloroacetaldehyde.

References

1. Hentschel, W., *Ber.,* **17,** 1284 (1884).
2. Gattermann, L., and Schmidt, G., *Ann.,* **244,** 29 (1888).
3. Ziegler, K., *et al., Ann.,* **551,** 80 (1942).
4. De Bell, J. M., Goggin, W. C., and Gloor, W. E., "German Plastics Practice," p. 300, Springfield, Mass., Pub. with permission of the Dept. of Commerce by De Bell and Richardson, 1946.

5. Irwin, C. F., U. S. Patent 2,683,160 (July 6, 1954).
6. Smutz, W. B., U. S. Patent 2,795,597 (June 11, 1957).
7. Farbenfabriken Bayer, A.-G., British Patent 761,590 (Nov. 14, 1956).
8. Irwin, C. F., and Swanner, F. W., U. S. Patent 2,757,183 (July 31, 1956).
9. Slocombe, R. J., and Saunders, J. H., U. S. Patent 2,680,128 (June 1, 1954).
10. Hartmann, E., German Patent 844,896 (Sept. 15, 1952).
11. Slocombe, R. J., Flores, H. W., and Cleveland, J. H., U. S. Patent 2,680,127 (June 1, 1954).
12. Allen, T. C., and Chadwick, D. H., U. S. Patent 2,733,254 (Jan. 31, 1956).
13. Modersohn, "Action of Phosgene on Primary and Secondary Amines in the Gas Phase," PB 707, Washington, D. C., Dept. of Commerce, O.T.S., n.d.
14. Saunders, J. H., and Slocombe, R. J., *Chem. Rev.,* **43,** 203 (1948).
15. Krey, "Production of Phenyl Isocyanate," PB L 58913, Frames 1082–1087, Washington, D. C., Dept. of Commerce, O.T.S., May, 1938.
16. Masuo, F., and Nomachi, T., Japan 425 ('54) (Jan. 29, 1954).
17. Bortnick, N. M., U. S. Patent 2,611,782 (Sept. 23, 1952).
18. Curtius, Th., *Ber.,* **23,** 3023 (1890); *J. Prakt. Chem.,* **50,** 275 (1894).
19. Naegeli, C., Grüntluch, L., and Lendorff, P., *Helv. Chim. Acta,* **12,** 227 (1929).
20. Naegeli, C., and Lendorff, P., *Helv. Chim. Acta,* **12,** 894 (1929).
21. Naegeli, C., and Stefanovich, G., *Helv. Chim. Acta,* **11,** 609 (1928).
22. Slotta, K. H., and Lorenz, L., *Ber.,* **58,** 1320 (1925).
23. Allen, C. F. H., and Bell, A., "Organic Syntheses," Vol. 24, p. 94, New York, John Wiley & Sons, Inc., 1944.
24. Wenker, H., *J. Am. Chem. Soc.,* **58,** 2608 (1936).
25. Bortnick, N. M., U. S. Patent 2,713,591 (July 19, 1955).
26. Seeger, N. V., and Fauser, E. E., U. S. Patent 2,683,730 (July 13, 1954).
27. Arnold, R. G., Nelson, J. A., and Verbanc, J. J., *Chem. Rev.,* **57,** 47 (1957).
28. Naegeli, C., *et al., Helv. Chim. Acta,* **21,** 1100 (1938).
29. Lakra, H., and Dains, F. B., *J. Am. Chem. Soc.,* **51,** 2220 (1929).
30. Wiley, P. F., *J. Am. Chem. Soc.,* **71,** 1310, 3746 (1949).
31. Fischer, E., *Ber.,* **22,** 1930 (1889).
32. Stagg, H. E., *Analyst,* **71,** 557 (1946).
33. Mohr, E., *J. Prakt. Chem.,* [2], **71,** 133 (1905).
34. Gumpert, Fr., *J. Prakt. Chem.,* [2], **31,** 119 (1885); [2], **32,** 278 (1885).
35. Knoevenagel, E., and Schurenberg, A., *Ann.,* **297,** 148 (1897).
36. Davis, T. L., and Farnum, J. M., *J. Am. Chem. Soc.,* **56,** 883 (1934).
37. Naegeli, C., and Tyabji, A., *Helv. Chim. Acta,* **17,** 931 (1934).
38. Michael, A., *Ber.,* **38,** 22 (1905).
39. Dieckmann, W., Hoppe, J., and Stein, R., *Ber.,* **37,** 4627 (1904).
40. Finholt, A. E., Anderson, C. D., Agre, C. L., *J. Org. Chem.,* **18,** 1338 (1953).
41. Ried, W., and Miller, F., *Chem. Ber.,* **85,** 470 (1952).
42. Petersen, S., *Ann.,* **562,** 205 (1949).
43. Breber, T., U. S. Patent 2,785,196 (Mar. 12, 1957).
44. Blair, J. S., and Smith, G. E. P., *J. Am. Chem. Soc.,* **56,** 907 (1934).
45. Hoffmann, A. W., *Ber.,* **3,** 765 (1870); **4,** 246 (1871).
46. Raiford, L. C., and Freyermuth, H. B., *J. Org. Chem.,* **8,** 230 (1943).

47. Warren, W. H., and Wilson, F. E., *Ber.*, **68**, 957 (1935).
48. Hofmann, A. W., *Ber.*, **18**, 765 (1885).
49. Jones, J. I., and Savill, N. G., *J. Chem. Soc.*, **1957**, 4392.
50. Heiss, H. L., *et al., Ind. Eng. Chem.*, **46**, 1498 (1954).
51. Szukiewicz, W., Hull, J. W., Toone, G. C., and Bailey, M. E., Paper presented at the Miami, Florida meeting of the American Chemical Society, April 7–12, 1957.
52. Faith, W. L., Keyes, D. B., and Clark, R. L., "Industrial Chemicals," p. 619, New York, John Wiley & Sons, Inc., 1950.
53. Fauser, G., U. S. Patent 2,777,877 (Jan. 15, 1957).
54. Kamlet, J., U. S. Patent 2,811,553 (Oct. 29, 1957).
55. Franz, R. A., U. S. Patent 2,681,930 (June 22, 1954).
56. Rabald, E., and Voeller, F., German Patent 848,039 (Sept. 1, 1952).
57. Davis, T. L., and Underwood, H. W., *J. Am. Chem. Soc.*, **44**, 2601 (1922).
58. Davis, T. L., and Blanchard, K. C., *J. Am. Chem. Soc.*, **45**, 1817 (1923).
59. Kurzer, F., "Organic Syntheses," Vol. 31, p. 11, New York, John Wiley & Sons, Inc., 1951.
60. Bognár, R., Farkas, I., and Békése, I., *Acta Chim. Acad. Sci. Hung.*, **4**, 355 (1954).
61. Gilbert, E. E., and Sorma, G. J., U. S. Patent 2,729,677 (Jan. 3, 1956).
62. Davis, T. L., and Blanchard, K. C., "Organic Syntheses; Collective Volume I," p. 453, New York, John Wiley & Sons, Inc., 1941.
63. Gehauf, B., and Faber, E. M., U. S. Patent 2,806,062 (Sept. 10, 1957).
64. Badische Anilin- & Soda-Fabrik Akt. -Ges., British Patent 750,549 (June 20, 1956).
65. Graham, P. J., U. S. Patent 2,705,727 (April 5, 1955).
66. Novotny, L., Czechoslovakia Patent 85,828 (July 15, 1956).
67. Schollenberger, C. S., U. S. Patent 2,722,550 (Nov. 1, 1955).
68. Hachitami, S., and Ichiyama, Y., Japan Patent 7514 ('56) Aug. 30, 1956).
69. Mulvaney, J. F., and Evans, R. L., *Ind. Eng. Chem.*, **40**, 393 (1948).
70. Degering, E. F., and Gross, G. C., *Ind. Eng. Chem.*, **35**, 751 (1943).
71. Harmon, J., U. S. Patent 2,145,392 (Jan. 31, 1939).
72. Sonn, A., German Patent 726,290 (Aug. 27, 1942).
73. Kinoshita, H., *Rev. Phys. Chem. Japan*, **25**, 34 (1955).
74. Manello, G., Baroni, A., and Garlando, T., U. S. Patent 2,790,801 (April 30, 1957).
75. Christmann, L. J., U. S. Patent 2,822,363 (Feb. 4, 1958).
76. Kinoshita, H., *Rev. Phys. Chem. Japan*, **23**, 1 (1953).
77. Monsanto Chemical Co., British Patent 735,356 (Aug. 17, 1955).
78. Okada, T., *et al.*, Japan Patent 5319 ('53) (Oct. 16, 1953).
79. Boivin, J. L., *Can. J. Chem.*, **34**, 827 (1956).
80. Erickson, J. G., *J. Am. Chem. Soc.*, **76**, 3977 (1954).
81. Tousignant, W. F., and Baker, A. W., *J. Org. Chem.*, **22**, 166 (1957).
82. Bengen, F., German Patent application O. Z. 12438 (Mar. 18, 1940). Technical Oil Mission Reel 6, Frames 263–270.
83. Bengen, F., and Schlenk, W., *Experientia*, **5**, 200 (1949).

84. Zimmerscheid, W. J., *et al., Ind. Eng. Chem.*, **42**, 1300 (1950).
85. Swern, D. S., *Ind. Eng. Chem.*, **47**, 216 (1955).
86. Akai, Y., and Yada, N., Japan Patent 1367 ('55) (Feb. 28, 1955).
87. McAdie, H. G., and Frost, G. B., *Can. J. Chem.*, **33**, 1275 (1955).
88. Terres, E., and Sur, S. N., *Brennstoff-Chem.*, **38**, 330 (1957).
89. Knight, H. B., *et al., Anal. Chem.*, **24**, 1331 (1952).
90. Linstead, R. P., and Whalley, M., *J. Chem. Soc.*, **1950**, 2987.
91. Newey, H. A., *et al., Ind. Eng. Chem.*, **42**, 2538 (1950).
92. Redlich, O., *et al., J. Am. Chem. Soc.*, **72**, 4153 (1950).
93. Schlenk, H., and Holman, R. G., *J. Am. Chem. Soc.*, **72**, 5001 (1950).
94. Swern, D., and Parker, W. E., *J. Am. Oil Chemists' Soc.*, **29**, 431 (1952).
95. Tiedt, J., and Truter, E. V., *J. Chem. Soc.*, **1952**, 4628.
96. Bailey, W. A., Jr., *et al., Ind. Eng. Chem.*, **43**, 2125 (1951).
97. Aylward, F., and Wood, P. S., *Nature*, **177**, 146 (1956).
98. Matsumato, T., and Tamura, J., *J. Japan Oil Chemists' Soc.*, **4**, 23 (1955).
99. Hodgins, T. S., and Hovey, A. G., *Ind. Eng. Chem.*, **30**, 1021 (1938).
100. Schroeder, D. C., *Chem. Rev.*, **55**, 181 (1955).
101. Landa, S., and Landa, M., Czechoslovakia Patent 84,207 (May 1, 1955).
102. Hugershoff, A., *Chem. Ber.*, **32**, 2245 (1899).
103. Hünig, S., Lehmann, H., and Grimmer, G., *Ann.*, **579**, 77 (1953).
104. Fry, H. S., *J. Am. Chem. Soc.*, **35**, 1539 (1913).
105. Dyson, G. M., *J. Chem. Soc.*, **1934**, 174.
106. Dyson, G. M., and George, H. J., *J. Chem. Soc.*, **125**, 1702 (1924).
107. Dyson, G. M., George, H. J., and Hunter, R. F., *J. Chem. Soc.*, **1927**, 436.
108. Dyson, G. M., and Hunter, R. F., *Rec. trav. chim.*, **45**, 421 (1926).
109. Morley, J. S., and Simpson, J. C. E., *J. Chem. Soc.*, **1952**, 2617.
110. Drozdov, N. S., *J. Gen. Chem. U.S.S.R.*, **12**, 1168 (1931).
111. Schubert, M., and Schütz, K., German Patent 604,639 (Oct. 26, 1934).
112. De Beer, E. J., *et al., J. Pharmacol. Exptl. Therap.*, **57**, 19 (1936).
113. Erlenmeyer, H., and Ueberwasser, H., *Helv. Chim. Acta*, **25**, 515 (1942).
114. Kurzer, F., "Organic Syntheses," Vol. 31, p. 21, New York, John Wiley & Sons, Inc., 1951.
115. Erickson, J. G., *J. Org. Chem.*, **21**, 483 (1956).
116. Volhard, J., *Ber.*, **7**, 277 (1890).
117. Svetkin, Yu. V., and Forostyan, Yu. N., *Zhur. Obshchei Khim.*, **25**, 1966 (1955).
118. Staudinger, H., and Niessen, G., *Makromol. Chem.*, **15**, 75 (1955).
119. Gore, P. H., *Chem. & Ind. (London)*, **1954**, 1355.
120. Astle, M. J., and Pierce, J. B., *J. Org. Chem.*, **20**, 178 (1955); U. S. Patent 2,725,383 (Nov. 29, 1955).
121. Markees, D., Kellerhals, M., and Erlenmeyer, H., *Helv. Chim. Acta*, **30**, 304 (1947).

7. AROMATIC NITRO AND NITROSO COMPOUNDS

AROMATIC NITRO COMPOUNDS

Nitro compounds are among the most important and best known derivatives of the aromatic hydrocarbons. These compounds have been used as intermediates in the preparation of dyes since 1856 when Perkin prepared Mauve and founded the synthetic dye industry.

Aromatic nitro compounds are high boiling materials or crystalline solids. Nitrobenzene boils at 210°C, the dinitrobenzenes at 200–320°C. Nitrobenzene has a melting point of 5.7°C. o-Dinitrobenzene melts at 118°C and the m- and p-isomers at 90°C and 174°C, respectively.

Aromatic hydrocarbons for the most part are easily nitrated but the ease of nitration is greatly affected by substituents on the benzene ring. Thus ortho-para directing groups with the exception of halogen increase the rate of nitration but meta-directing groups decrease the rate of nitration on the ring.

Nitrating Agents

The nitration of aromatic compounds can be accomplished by a number of methods. The most common reagents to be used are nitric acid and mixed nitric and sulfuric acid. Nitric acid used alone tends to cause excessive oxidation of the organic compound which within limits tends to increase as the acid is made more dilute.

Nitric acid is frequently used in acetic acid or acetic anhydride solutions. This permits the nitration to be carried out using only the theoretical amount of nitric acid. In addition to serving as an effective solvent, acetic anhydride serves as a dehydrating agent by reacting with the water as fast as formed. Nitration of acetanilide in acetic anhydride gives predominantly the ortho isomer whereas a nitric-sulfuric acid mixture gives much larger quantities of the para isomer.[1]

The presence of nitrous acid enhances the nitrating power of nitric acid. Thus phenols are readily nitrated with nitric acid containing small amounts of nitrous acid, whereas nitric acid alone, in ether, is ineffective.[2] Nitrous acid must be carefully excluded in the nitration of amines.

Many aromatic compounds which are not nitrated with nitric acid alone may be nitrated readily with mixtures of nitric and concentrated sulfuric acid (mixed acid). The sulfuric acid serves not only as a dehydrating agent but it also increases the concentration of the nitronium ions which are the actual nitrating agents.

In most cases, nitration with mixed acid is more efficient and can be carried out at lower temperatures. In some cases a mixture of nitric and fuming sulfuric acid is used. Thus terephthalic acid may be nitrated with this mixture but is not attacked with ordinary mixed acid.[3]

Mixtures of concentrated sulfuric acid and metal nitrates have also been used successfully as nitrating agents.

Nitrosylsulfuric acid, $HOSO_2NO_2$, is a powerful nitrating agent effective at 20–30°C. The nitrosylsulfuric acid is obtained by passing sulfur dioxide into nitric acid at room temperature until one-half of the theoretically required quantity of the dioxide has been absorbed.[4] The nitric acid solution thus obtained contains about 40–50 per cent nitrosylsulfuric acid and can be used directly as a nitrating agent. This reagent is a more powerful nitrating agent than is mixed acid. Aromatic hydrocarbons are readily nitrated, halogen compounds are converted to *para* derivatives and benzoic acid is nitrated in the *meta* position.

Acetyl nitrate, $CH_3CO-ONO_2$, is a very vigorous nitrating agent and permits nitration in an homogeneous solution. Nitration in the *ortho* position is favored by this reagent. Thus with mixed acid, *o*-nitrotoluene is obtained in about 60 per cent yield.[5] Acetyl nitrate gives the same isomer in 90 per cent yield. Toluene, benzyl chloride and acetanilide are readily nitrated by acetyl nitrate.

The reagent is prepared by adding dinitrogen pentoxide to an equal weight of acetic anhydride and distilling the product under reduced pressure (22°C at 70 mm). Acetyl nitrate is a powerful explosive and must be handled with extreme care.

Nitration has also been accomplished using acetic anhydride and a nitrate of a metal such as copper, iron, cobalt, nickel, mercury, sodium or lithium.[6] Such a mixture acts in much the same manner as acetyl nitrate and gives larger quantities of *o*-nitro derivatives than are obtained with most nitrating agents.

Benzoyl nitrate, $C_6H_5CO-ONO_2$, is sometimes used as a nitrating agent in carbon tetrachloride or chloroform solutions. It gives much the same results as acetyl nitrate and must also be handled with extreme caution.

Mechanism of Nitration

The mechanism for the nitration of the benzene ring, in common with most reactions of aromatic compounds, involves an electrophilic attack on the ring. Melander[7] studied the mechanism of the nitration of toluene and proposed that the addition of the nitronium ion, NO_2^+, is the rate-determining step. This addition is followed by a very rapid ejection of a proton. His views are supported by Gillespie *et al.*[8]

The mechanism for the nitration of aromatic hydrocarbons has been investigated also by Hughes, Ingold and co-workers.[9] They also postulate that the reaction involves an electrophilic attack on the benzene ring by the nitronium ion, the existence of which has been established by cryoscopic measurements. Its formation occurs as follows:

$$2HNO_3 \rightleftarrows H_2NO_3^+ + NO_3^- \qquad \text{(fast)}$$

$$H_2NO_3^+ \longrightarrow NO_2^+ + H_2O \qquad \text{(slow)}$$

The nitration of the benzene ring then involves attack by the nitronium ion

$$ArH + NO_2^+ \longrightarrow \left[Ar \Big\langle {\overset{H}{\underset{NO_2}{}}} \right]^+ \qquad \text{(slow)}$$

$$\left[Ar \Big\langle {\overset{H}{\underset{NO_2}{}}} \right]^+ \longrightarrow ArNO_2 + H^+ \qquad \text{(fast)}$$

In addition to cryoscopic measurements, the existence of the nitronium ion has been proved by Ingold, Goddard and Hughes[10] who prepared several nitronium salts in the pure state and established their ionic structure spectroscopically.

The sulfuric acid in "mixed acid" serves as a dehydrating agent but of greater importance it increases the concentration of the nitronium ions. It has been quite well established that nitric acid behaves as a base towards sulfuric acid and that in concentrated sulfuric acid the following ionization occurs.

$$HONO_2 + 2H_2SO_4 \rightleftarrows NO_2^+ + H_3O^+ + 2HSO_4^-$$

The substituent on the benzene ring plays a very important role on the course of the nitration reaction. If the substituent has a tendency to be a source of electrons for the ring, the nitration is made easier than with the unsubstituted benzene ring and the nitro group is directed towards the *ortho* and *para*-positions. Thus toluene is nitrated much more readily than is benzene. Hydroxy and alkoxy groups are also ring activating and this can be explained by the theory of resonance. The following electronic structures can be drawn for phenol.

The actual structure is therefore a resonance hybrid of all of these and has a negative charge on the *para* and the two *ortho* positions. Since the nitration of the benzene ring involves an electrophilic attack, the reaction is much faster with phenol, particularly in the *ortho* and *para* positions where the electron density is highest.

Halogen substituents must be considered an exception to the rule because being powerfully electron attracting, they tend to deactivate the entire ring. However, at the demand of the attacking reagent, electrons can be supplied more readily at the *ortho* and *para* positions than at the *meta* position. Therefore even though the nitration is much slower than with benzene, the electron density remains somewhat greater at the *ortho* and *para* positions where the major reaction occurs.

Electron attracting groups such as nitro-, carboxyl- and carbonyl, withdraw electrons from the ring making nitration more difficult, particularly at the *ortho* and *para* positions.

Electrophilic groups therefore, attack the *meta* positions but with considerably more difficulty because the electrons even at these positions are much less available than are the electrons around each carbon atom in benzene.

These negatively substituted benzene rings are open to attack by nucleophilic reagents. Such reactions occur in the *ortho* and *para* positions.

In addition to electronic effects, steric effects play a considerable role in the position taken by an entering group. The effect of steric hindrance on the *ortho-para* ratio in many nitrations of alkyl benzenes was investigated by Nelson and Brown.[11] The mononitration of tertiary butyl benzene with mixed acid gives 15.8 per cent *ortho*, 11.5 per cent *meta* and 72.7 per cent *para*-nitro-*tert*.-butylbenzene. In contrast toluene gives 58.8 per cent *ortho*, 4.4 per cent *meta* and 37.1 per cent *para*-nitrotoluene.

Haun and Kobe[12] investigated the nitration of cumene using a 2:1 ratio of 81 per cent sulfuric acid and a 20 per cent excess of nitric acid at 15°C. A 94.5 per cent yield of mononitrocumene was obtained. The product contained 24 per cent of the *ortho* and 76 per cent of the *para* isomer.

Nitration of Hydrocarbons

Benzene. Benzene is nitrated with a mixture of concentrated nitric and sulfuric acids. A typical laboratory procedure calls for using equal volumes of concentrated nitric acid (sp. gr. 1.42) and concentrated sulfuric acid. The mixed acid is added in small portions to the benzene at temperatures near 60°C.

The commercial process is very similar. A mixed acid, consisting of 60–63 per cent sulfuric acid, 32–39 per cent nitric acid and 8 per cent water, is added slowly under the surface of the benzene. The temperature is maintained at 50–55°C. The weight ratio of mixed acid to benzene used is about 2.5:1 and the reaction is complete in 2–4 hours. The temperature is raised to about 90°C toward the end of the reaction period. The spent acid contains 77–85 per cent sulfuric acid, 0–3 per cent nitric acid and water. The yield of nitrobenzene is 95–98 per cent.[13]

Nitrobenzene is prepared by a continuous process by passing benzene and nitric acid over activated clay or diatomaceous earth at 150–350°C and atmospheric pressure.[14]

The presence of a nitro group on a benzene ring makes further nitration more difficult. Consequently it is quite easy to stop the reaction with the formation of the mononitro compound. *m*-Dinitrobenzene is obtained at higher temperatures using a more concentrated nitric acid. *m*-Dinitrobenzene is also prepared by dropping benzene into cooled fuming nitric acid.

ortho and *para*-Dinitrobenzenes are usually obtained from the corresponding diazotized nitroanilines. Because of the deactivating effect of the two nitro groups on the benzene ring, trinitrobenzene is not obtained satisfactorily even by the action of fuming nitric acid.

Trinitrobenzene is best prepared from 2,4,6-trinitrotoluene in two steps. The methyl group of the trinitrotoluene is first oxidized to a carboxyl group with sodium dichromate and sulfuric acid at 45–55°C to give 2,4,6-trinitrobenzoic acid which is subsequently decarboxylated by heating the sodium salt in acetic acid.[15] Yields are about 40 per cent.

The presence of alkyl groups on the benzene ring makes nitration much easier. Thus toluene is nitrated much more readily than benzene. A mixture of *ortho-* and *para-*nitrotoluenes is obtained using a mixed acid consisting of 60 per cent sulfuric acid, 25 per cent nitric acid and 15 per cent water. Cumene is nitrated with a mixture of 1 part by weight of concentrated nitric and 2 parts of concentrated sulfuric acid at 5–10°C to give an 89 per cent yield of *p*-nitrocumene.[16] It is difficult to obtain a mononitrated mesitylene using a mixed acid, but such a product can be obtained using fuming nitric acid in a glacial acetic acid-acetic anhydride solution at 10–15°C.[17]

Dinitrodurene is obtained by treating durene with nitric acid (sp. gr. 1.5) at temperatures below 50°C. The reaction requires only a few minutes.[18]

Hennion[19] reports the nitration of aromatic compounds such as benzene, toluene, nitrobenzene and benzoic acid with a mixture of nitric acid and boron trifluoride. Thomas, Anzilotte and Hennion[20] report that many organic compounds are nitrated quickly and in high yield by using stoichiometric amounts of nitric acid in the presence of boron trifluoride. The amount of boron trifluoride required suggests that it is acting as a dehydrating agent through the formation of a hydrate.

$$RH + HONO_2 + BF_3 \longrightarrow RNO_2 + BF_3 \cdot H_2O$$

In some cases the nitration of polyalkylbenzenes results in the replacement of one of the alkyl groups. Thus the nitration of cymene to give 2-nitro- and 2,6-dinitrocymene also gives appreciable amounts of *p*-nitro- and 2,4-dinitrotoluene, even when the nitration is accomplished at low temperatures.[21,22,23] Kobi and Doumani[22] nitrated cymene at –10°C using a mixture of glacial acetic acid, nitric acid and sulfuric acid and obtained a 90 per cent yield of *p*-nitrotoluene.

Inasmuch as nitric acid is a good oxidizing agent, methyl-*p*-tolyl ketone, *p*-toluic acid, 2-nitro-*p*-toluic acid and 2,6-dinitro-*p*-toluic acid have been reported among the nitration products of *p*-cymene.

The nitration of *p*-diisopropylbenzene gives *p*-nitrocumene in 50 per cent yield.[24,25]

The xylenes are nitrated more readily than toluene. The *ortho*-isomer is less readily nitrated than the *meta* or *para* isomers. The mixed xylenes have been nitrated to give a mononitrated product which on reduction gives xylidines which are useful in increasing the octane rating of aviation fuels.

Kobe and Pritchett[26] nitrated *o*-xylene to give a 90 per cent yield of mononitrated products. Under optimum conditions the product contains 58 per cent 3-nitro-*o*-xylene and 42 per cent 4-nitro-*o*-xylene.

One of the most important nitrated products of an aromatic hydrocarbon is 2,4,6-trinitrotoluene (TNT) which is used extensively as an explosive.

The preparation of trinitrotoluene is usually carried out as a three stage process. The mixed acid for the mononitration stage is a fortified spent acid from the dinitration. It contrains approximately 48 per cent sulfuric acid, 18 per cent nitric acid, 14 per cent nitrosylsulfuric acid, 12 per cent water and 8 per cent nitrotoluenes.

In a like manner, the acid for the dinitration step is a fortified spent acid from the trinitration and consists of approximately 50 per cent sulfuric acid, 20 per cent nitric acid, 12 per cent nitrosylsulfuric acid, 12 per cent nitrotoluenes and 6 per cent water.

The acid for the trinitration step is a fresh mixed acid containing 60 per cent sulfuric acid and 40 per cent nitric acid.

Nitration of aromatic hydrocarbons such as benzene or toluene with nitric acid is made possible by removing the water of reaction as a hydrocarbon-water azeotrope.[27,28]

m-Nitrotoluene, obtained only in small yield by the direct nitration of toluene, can be obtained from the nitration of acetylated *p*-toluidine followed by diazotization of the amino group and removal of the resulting diazonium group by warming with alcohol.

Polystyrene nitrated with a 3 to 1 mixture of nitric and sulfuric acid gives a poly(dinitrostyrene).[29] The nitration is accomplished by adding 1 part of polystyrene rapidly with stirring to 10–15 parts anhydrous mixed acid at –5°C. The temperature is allowed to rise to 20°C and held there for 3 minutes then raised to 50°C and held there for 15 minutes. The mixture is finally poured over ice and the product removed from the spent acid.

The nitration of naphthalene gives a 94 per cent yield of α- and a 6 per cent yield of the β-isomer.[30] The β-isomer is readily removed by recrystallization from alcohol. β-Nitronaphthalene is made from β-naphthylamine by diazotization and replacement of the diazonium group with the nitro group. β-Naphthylamine is made from β-naphthol by way of the Bucherer reaction.

The nitration of naphthalene can be accomplished at approximately room temperature with concentrated nitric acid to give mainly α-nitronaphthalene and a relatively small amount of the β-isomer.[31,32,33]

At higher temperatures 1,5- and 1,8-dinitronaphthalenes are obtained. The use of mixed acids is usually preferred. Thus naphthalene is added to about three times its weight of mixed acid consisting of 1 part of 62 per cent nitric acid and 3 parts of 80 per cent sulfuric acid. Reaction temperatures are held at 50–60°C. The product contains 90–92 per cent α-nitro-naphthalene, 4–5 per cent β-nitronaphthalene and 2–3 per cent dinitro-naphthalenes.[34]

Attempts to effect the direct nitration of anthracene results largely in oxidation to anthraquinone. However, nitration in acetic acid below 30°C using nitric acid (sp. gr. 1.42) followed by addition of concentrated hydro-chloric acid and glacial acetic acid gives 9-nitro-10-chloro-9,10-dihydro-anthracene which when treated with 10 per cent aqueous sodium hydroxide at 60–70°C gives 9-nitroanthracene.[35]

Phenanthrene behaves in much the same way but nitration in acetic an-hydride with nitric acid (sp. gr. 1.45) at room temperature for 1 or 2 hours then at water bath temperatures gives 9-nitrophenanthrene.[36]

Reactions of Aromatic Nitro Compounds

The reduction of aromatic nitro compounds to amines has been dis-cussed previously (Chapter 2). The reduction can be accomplished with a metal and an acid, or with a suitable metal and water. Thus nitrobenzene is reduced to aniline with iron and water with only sufficient acid added to get the reaction started.

One of two or more nitro groups on a benzene ring is selectively reduced with ammonium or sodium sulfides to give nitroamines. Hydrogenation in the presence of copper, nickel or platinum catalysts is also an excellent method for the conversion of a nitro group to an amine.

A few additional examples of the reduction of aromatic nitro compounds will be described here. von Bramer, Magoffin and Clemens[37] reduced aro-matic nitro compounds to amines by passing them together with steam into a reducing medium consisting of a metal and an acid. Reduction takes place the moment of mixing and gives a pure product. As an example, steam at 200°C is passed over molten *p*-nitroaniline and the resulting vapors mixed with iron dust and sulfuric acid in a reactor at 60–90°C. A 96 per cent yield of *p*-phenylenediamine is obtained.

Nitrobenzene and α-nitronaphthalene are reduced by hydrogen sulfide in pyridine at 0°C to give amines and appreciable amounts of azoxy com-pounds. The hydrogen sulfide is oxidized to sulfur. Carrying out the reduc-tion at 0°C materially increases the yield of azoxy compound and in the case of 2,4- and 2,6-dinitrotoluene the azoxy compound is formed in better than 50 per cent yield.

Pyridine plays a specific role in accelerating the condensation reaction between the intermediate nitroso compounds and phenylhydroxylamines.

Reduction of nitrobenzene with hydrogen sulfide in pyridine at 140–150°C and 10 atm. pressure gives aniline in 92 per cent yield.[38]

Nitroaromatic compounds can be hydrogenated to amines continuously at 400–550°F in the presence of a metallic sulfide catalyst activated with hydrogen sulfide.[39]

Aromatic nitro compounds such as nitrobenzene can be hydrogenated in acid media at high temperatures and reduced pressure to give p-hydroxy-amines (p-HOC$_6$H$_4$NH$_2$).[40] p-Aminophenol can be obtained from nitro-benzene in 83 per cent yield together with 17 per cent of aniline. The pre-ferred catalyst is platinum supported on carbon. The presence of quaternary ammonium compounds increases the yield of the p-hydroxy-amine and also increases the rate of hydrogenation.

Hydrazine hydrate reduces nitro compounds to amines very slowly but Balcom and Furst[41] found that the reaction is speeded up with a Raney nickel catalyst. Dewar[42] found palladium on charcoal to be a better catalyst for the reduction of polycyclonitro compounds. Reaction times are for the most part 10 minutes to 1 hour. The reactions are carried out in alcohol solution. Yields with such compounds as 1- and 2-nitronaphthalene, 1-, 2-, and 3-nitrophenanthrene, 3-nitropyrene, 2-nitrochrysene and 3-nitro-perylene are greater than 60 per cent.

Aromatic nitro compounds are reduced to the corresponding amines in good yield by refluxing with hydrazine hydrate in the presence of 5 per cent palladium on carbon catalyst.

Nitrobenzene in ethanol containing three volumes of hydrazine hydrate is heated to 40–50°C. A small amount of palladium on carbon catalyst is added and the mixture refluxed until the evolution of gas stops. The yield of aniline is 95 per cent.[43]

Nitrobenzene is reduced to aniline by refluxing with hydrazine hydrate in ethanol solution in the presence of copper or iron powder. Similarly o-, m-, and p-nitro toluenes are reduced to the corresponding toluidines.[44]

The catalytic hydrogenation of a phenol and a nitrobenzene at 25–50°C in the presence of dilute sulfuric acid and a quaternary ammonium com-pound gives hydroxydiphenylamines. A solution of p-nitroanisole and phenol are added to a ten per cent sulfuric acid solution containing a small amount of C$_{18}$H$_{37}$N(CH$_3$)$_3$$^+Cl^-$. This mixture is hydrogenated in the pres-ence of a platinum on carbon catalyst at 25–30°C and essentially atmos-pheric pressure. The product contains p-(p-methoxyanilino)phenol together with a considerable quantity of phenol and smaller amounts of p-anisidine and p-aminophenol.[45]

Baude, Linstead and Wooldridge[46] found that if a nitro compound is heated for about 17 hours with cyclohexene in a suitable solvent such as ethanol or tetrahydrofuran and in the presence of palladium, a hydrogen transfer from cyclohexene to the nitro compound occurs resulting in the formation of amines. The cyclohexene is dehydrogenated to benzene. Nitro compounds such as p-nitrotoluenes, nitrobenzene, nitrophenols, nitroacetophenones, nitrobenzoic acids and aliphatic nitro compounds such as nitropropane are all reduced to the corresponding amines. The yields are more satisfactory with aromatic nitro compounds.

By proper choice of reducing agent, intermediate products such as azoxy, azo-, and hydrazo compounds are obtained (Chapter 4). Reduction to nitroso and hydroxylamine compounds is also possible.

A nitro group has a deactivating effect towards further substitution on the ring by electrophilic reagents, but has an activating effect upon substituents present. Thus an alkyl group is readily oxidized to give the corresponding nitrobenzoic acid, with 25 per cent nitric acid at temperatures of 150–180°C under a pressure of 275–300 psi.[47]

The same oxidation can be accomplished with sodium dichromate and sulfuric acid at moderate temperatures.[48]

Other alkyl groups may be oxidized in a similar manner. To illustrate the usefulness of such procedures *ortho* or *para*-aminobenzoic acids are prepared by the following sequence of reactions:

1. Toluene is nitrated to give *o*- and *p*-nitrotoluenes.
2. The nitrotoluene is oxidized to the corresponding nitrobenzoic acid.
3. The nitrobenzoic acid is reduced to the amino acid.

One of the nitro groups of trinitrobenzene is removed by the attack of a nucleophilic reagent. Thus reaction with sodium methoxide gives 3,5-dinitroanisole.[49]

The reaction is carried out by refluxing the trinitrobenzene with a methanol solution of sodium methoxide.

The methyl group in some nitro-substituted methyl benzenes is activated sufficiently to undergo condensation reactions in which water is eliminated. Thus in the presence of secondary amines, 2,4-dinitrotoluene reacts with benzaldehyde to give 2,4-dinitrostilbene.[50,51]

Similarly *p*-nitrosodimethylaniline reacts with 2,4-dinitrotoluene to give dinitrobenzylidine-*p*-aminodimethyl aniline.[52,53] Hydrolysis gives 2,4-dinitrobenzaldehyde.

Trinitrotoluene is used as a source of phloroglucinol.[54] The process was developed at the end of World War II as a means of using up the large stock piles of T.N.T. on hand. The phloroglucinol is of great importance in the Ozalid Process for photocopying and in the dyeing of textiles.

The process involves three steps.

1. The oxidation of trinitrotoluene to trinitrobenzoic acid

2. The reduction and simultaneous decarboxylation of trinitrobenzoic acid to 1,3,5-triaminobenzene

3. The hydrolysis of 1,3,5-triaminobenzene to phloroglucinol

The oxidation is carried out by adding solid sodium dichromate to a solution of trinitrotoluene in concentrated sulfuric acid. After about 4 hours at 50–60°C, a large quantity of ice is added and the trinitrobenzoic acid recovered in about 82 per cent yield.

The reduction is accomplished by adding finely divided iron to a solution of the trinitrobenzoic acid in 26°Be hydrochloric acid at 90°C. Decarboxylation occurs at the same time as the reduction. The yields of 1,3,5-triaminobenzene are about 95 per cent.

The hydrolysis of 1,3,5-triaminobenzene is carried out at about 105°C using hydrochloric acid. The reaction requires about 20 hours and a 75 per cent yield of phloroglucinol is obtained.

Nitrophenols. A hydroxyl group on a benzene ring activates the ring so that further substitution is facilitated. Thus phenol is nitrated by 20 per cent nitric acid to give a mixture of *o*- and *p*-nitrophenol. Oxidation is also made easier by the presence of the hydroxyl group so that the reaction is complicated by the formation of oxidation products.

The nitration of phenols with 30 per cent nitric acid at 5–10°C gives an approximately equal mixture of *o*- and *p*-nitrophenol.[55] Better yields are obtained using concentrated nitric acid or mixtures of nitric in acetic acid. Acetic acid favors the formation of the *ortho* isomer. Considerable quantities of tars are obtained but this can be minimized by nitrating in acetic acid solutions at temperatures of –15° to –10°C.[56,57]

The two isomers are easily separated by steam distillation. Both compounds form hydrogen bonds but the geometry of the *ortho*-isomer permits the formation of an intramolecular bond

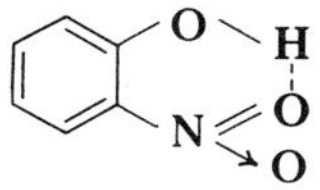

and minimizes the formation of hydrogen bonds with other nitrophenol molecules or with water.

p-Nitrophenol can not form intramolecular hydrogen bonds but instead bonds with other nitrophenol molecules or with hydrogen bonding solvents such as water. The volatility with steam is therefore greatly decreased resulting in the selective removal of the *ortho* isomer from the mixture by steam distillation.

Other properties are affected by the differences in the type of hydrogen bonds formed by the two isomers. some of these are illustrated below

	Nitrophenols	
	Ortho	*Para*
Melting point	45°C	114°C
Solubility in C_6H_6	50. %	0.5%
Solubility in H_2O	1.1%	21.2%

m-Nitrophenol is prepared from *m*-dinitrobenzene by the following steps:
1. Reduction with sodium or ammonium bisulfide to *m*-aminophenol.
2. Diazotization.
3. Hydrolysis of the diazonium salt group with sulfuric acid.[58]

Topchiev, Alaniya and Schnaider[59] nitrated phenol, saturated with boron trifluoride, with 10 per cent nitric acid at 5–20°C. They report that up to 9.4 per cent of the *m*-nitrophenol is formed. If the boron trifluoride is not present the product contains none of the *meta* isomer. In addition to having some directive influence the boron trifluoride tends to increase the total yield of nitrated products. With 20 per cent nitric acid considerable quantities of tars are obtained.

A very interesting procedure for preparing nitrophenols has been described by Conner.[60] Nitrated products of alkyl benzenes, such as nitro-cumene, are oxidized to the corresponding hydroperoxide and the hydro-peroxide on treatment with an acid is decomposed to give the nitrophenol.

The cresols are nitrated even more readily than phenol itself. *p*-Cresol is nitrated in benzene solution with one volume of concentrated nitric acid and one volume of water at 20°C to give *o*-nitro-*p*-cresol in 88 per cent yield.[61]

Probably the best nitration medium for the nitration of cresols is a mixture of nitric and glacial acetic acids. The cresol to be nitrated is dissolved in an equal weight of acetic acid and this solution is added to a mixture of one part concentrated nitric acid and two or three parts of glacial acetic acid. About 1.7 to 2.5 moles of nitric acid per mole of cresol should be used. The temperature of the reaction is held to about –10°C. After completion of the reaction, the mixture is poured onto ice and the solid nitro-cresols removed and purified.[62] For the most part the nitro group enters the molecule *ortho* to the hydroxyl group.

2-Nitroresorcinol may be prepared by disulfonation of resorcinol with 20 per cent fuming sulfuric acid at 90–100°C followed by nitration of the di-sulfonic acid at 10–15°C by adding 0.6 part of 90 per cent nitric acid mixed with three times its weight of concentrated sulfuric acid. When the nitration is complete the sulfonic acid groups are removed by adding six parts of water and distilling with super heated steam.[63] The product is 2-nitroresorcinol.

The introduction of a second nitro group into a phenol molecule is more difficult than the first because of the deactivating effect of the nitro group. Dinitrophenols are sometimes obtained by nitrating sulfonated phenols followed by removal of the sulfonic acid group. Thus phenol may be sulfonated at 130–140°C with twice its weight of concentrated sulfuric acid. This mixture is then treated with seven parts of 30 per cent nitric acid.[64] The sulfonic acid groups are removed by hydrolysis to give dinitrophenols and a small amount of picric acid.

The preferred procedure for the preparation of 2,4-dinitrophenol involves the nitration of chlorobenzene to give 2,4-dinitrochlorobenzene followed by replacement of the chlorine by hydroxyl. This is accomplished by refluxing the 2,4-dinitrochlorobenzene for 24 hours with 10 per cent aqueous sodium carbonate.

The reaction is made possible by two facts: 1. the nitration of chlorobenzene although more difficult than the nitration of phenol is more easily controlled and does not result in the formation of oxidation products. It is not necessary to work at low temperatures or use dilute nitric acid which facilitates the formation of oxidation products. 2. the nitro groups in an *ortho* or *para* relationship to a chlorine atom activates the chlorine, so that it is readily removed by hydrolysis. This is in contrast to the chlorine in chlorobenzene, which is very inactive.

Two nitro groups sufficiently counteract the activating effect of the hydroxyl group so that the introduction of the third nitro group is made possible with nitric acid or mixed acid. The best route to picric acid starts with chlorobenzene and proceeds by way of 2,4-dinitrochlorobenzene and 2,4-dinitrophenol.

An alternate method proceeds by way of phenol- di- and trisulfonic acids. Phenol may be treated with concentrated sulfuric acid to give phenol-2,4-disulfonic acid. The addition of nitric acid to this solution gives picric acid.

The sulfonic acid groups stabilize the molecule and inhibit the formation of oxidation products. Yields as high as 70 per cent are obtained by this method.

Picric acid is an explosive but being a strong acid, it attacks metals with the formation of picrates. Consequently unless a non-metal liner is provided, it deteriorates in the shell casing and can not be used as an explosive. It is not as satisfactory as trinitrotoluene and is not used appreciably at the present time. It was used to some extent during World War I when trinitrotoluene became scarce. Picric acid is a bright yellow compound which has been found to be a direct dye for silk and wool. However, as a dye, it is not very fast and has been largely replaced by other materials. Picric acid has bacteriacidal activity and has been used for the treatment of burns. Even here it has largely been replaced by other preparations.

Bachmann *et al.*[65] obtained 2,4-dinitrophenol by treating benzene with nitric acid in the presence of mercuric nitrate. Thus benzene (50 g) was added at 50°C over a 3.3-hour period to a mixture of 750 ml of 10.65 *m* nitric acid containing 0.37 mole of mercuric nitrate. The mixture was stirred for an additional 2.7 hours at 50°C, then chilled to room temperature and permitted to stand for 12 hours. 2,4-Dinitrophenol was obtained in 68 per cent yield together with 4 per cent picric acid, 8 per cent nitrobenzene and oxidation products such as oxalic acid.

A similar procedure has been used to prepare picric acid. Thus Aristoff *et al.*[66] developed a procedure for preparing picric acid by adding benzene below the surface of a 50 per cent nitric acid solution containing mercuric nitrate and small amounts of manganese and aluminum nitrates. The nitric acid concentration was maintained at 50 per cent by continuous addition of 70 per cent acid. After all the benzene had been added the temperature was permitted to rise to 117°C over a 20-minute period. Large quantities of oxides of nitrogen were evolved. The reaction mixture was then cooled and the picric acid which had crystallized out was removed by filtration. One hundred grams of benzene product 150 grams of picric acid. The reaction required 140–160 g of nitric acid.

Teeters and Mueller[67] patented a process for the preparation of nitrophenols by the oxynitration of benzene or alkylbenzenes with 50 per cent nitric acid containing about 7 per cent mercuric nitrate at 45–55°C. The weight ratio of nitrophenols to nitrobenzene produced is about 9:1.

The nitrophenols are much stronger acids than is phenol. The di- and trinitrophenols form salts with sodium bicarbonate and in this respect resemble carboxylic acids. Picric acid has an ionization constant of 1.6×10^{-1} compared with that for acetic acid of 1.8×10^{-5}. The hydroxyl group in picric acid is not a typical phenolic group. Thus picric acid is converted into picryl chloride (2,4,6-trinitrochlorobenzene) on treatment with phosphorus pentachloride and an acetate.

Kriesky[68] has described a method for the preparation of esters of p-nitrophenol with acids such as acetic, butyric, n-caproic, lauric, stearic and oleic acids. An illustrative esterification describes refluxing a mixture of 13.9 g of p-nitrophenol, 0.12 mole of the acid chloride, 0.12 mole magnesium ribbon, 30 g of benzene and a few crystals of iodine for 1–4 hours.

One of the nitro groups of picric acid can be selectively reduced by treatment with sodium sulfide in 85 per cent alcoholic sodium hydroxide at 65°C.

2,4,6-Trinitroresorcinol, styphnic acid, is prepared by nitrating resorcinol-4,6-disulfonic acid in much the same way as picric acid is obtained from phenol disulfonic acid. The over-all yields are 90–95 per cent.

Styphnic acid is also obtained from m-nitrophenol. On nitration, a tetranitro compound is obtained which has one nitro group in an *ortho-para* relation to the other two and so is readily removed by hydrolysis.

Nitration of phenols or phenol ethers having *ortho* or *para*-secondary or tertiary alkyl substituents frequently results in the replacement of the alkyl group. Thus nitration of the methyl ether of thymol results in the replacement of the isopropyl group and the formation of nitrocresol ethers. Nitration with mixed acids gives a trinitro derivative and even fuming nitric acid at low temperatures gives a dinitro compound.[69]

Halogen atoms of halogenated phenols or phenol ethers may be replaced by nitro groups. Thus 2,4-dibromoanisole treated with nitric acid gives 2-bromo-4-nitroanisole.[70] 2,4,6-Tribromoresorcinol treated with fuming nitric acid gives 2-bromo-4,6-dinitroresorcinol.[71]

The carboxyl group in some phenolic acids is also replaceable by a nitro group. Thus the nitration of anisic acid with 100 per cent nitric acid in sulfuric acid gives three products.[72,73]

Salicylic acid has been nitrated with fuming nitric acid to give picric acid, and 3,5-dibromosalicyclic acid has been nitrated to give 6-bromo-2,4-dinitrophenol.[74] Naphthols are readily nitrated by nitric acid but a more useful procedure for obtaining the desired nitronaphthols involves heating the naphthol sulfonic acids with nitric acid.[75,76] The nitronaphthols find utility as dyes. Thus 2,4-dinitro-1-naphthol, Martius Yellow, is obtained by first dissolving α-naphthol in concentrated sulfuric acid, then adding 100 per cent nitric acid.

Forced sulfonation of α-naphthol followed by nitration gives 1-naphthol-2,4-dinitro-7-sulfonic acid, Naphthol Yellow.

Trinitronaphthol can be obtained from dinitronaphthol by treatment with a large excess of concentrated sulfuric acid followed by nitration with concentrated nitric acid.[77] The reaction is slow, requiring about 10 days for completion.

Nitroaromatic Amines. An amino group substituted on a benzene ring is an activating group which should lead to *ortho-para* substitution. Like the phenols, aromatic amines are easily oxidized so that attack by nitric acid yields largely oxidation products. Oxidation can be eliminated by carrying out the reaction in the presence of a large excess of sulfuric acid but under these conditions the amine is converted to an arylammonium sulfate. The positive charge on the nitrogen resulting from the addition of a proton makes the group strongly electrophilic. Consequently the benzene ring becomes deactivated, the nitration becomes quite difficult and the nitro group enters the *meta* position.

A mixture of *o-* and *p*-nitroaniline is obtained by protecting the amino group of the aniline by acetylating with acetyl chloride or acetic anhydride, nitrating the acetanilide to give a mixture of *o-* and *p*-nitroacetanilides and hydrolyzing the amides to restore the original amino group.

m-Nitroaniline is obtained by partial reduction of *m*-dinitrobenzene with sodium or ammonium bisulfides.

The aniline-boron trifluoride complex, $C_6H_5NH_2 \cdot BF_3$, has been nitrated at 0°C with a mixture of nitric acid (d 1.526) and sulfuric acid (d 1.84). The product is a mixture of 13 per cent *o-*, 20 per cent *p-* and 67 per cent *m*-nitroaniline.[59]

o-Nitroaniline can be made by nitrating the sulfanilic acid followed by removal of the sulfonic acid group by hydrolysis with an approximately equal volume of concentrated sulfuric acid and water.

Dinitro derivatives may be obtained by nitrating the appropriate arylamine, but frequently these compounds are obtained in a somewhat different manner. 2,4-Dinitroaniline is readily prepared from 2,4-dinitrochlorobenzene by treatment with ammonia and ammonium acetate at 170°C.[78] Yields are 68–76 per cent.

2,4,6-Trinitroaniline can be prepared by the nitration of *o-* or *p*-nitroaniline with a mixture of 100 per cent sulfuric acid and potassium nitrate.[79] It can be prepared in better yields by the ammonolysis of 2,4,6-trinitrochlorobenzene.

N-Alkylarylamines, in many cases, can be nitrated directly with a mixture of nitric and sulfuric acids. Dimethylaniline is nitrated by dissolving the amine in concentrated sulfuric acid, with cooling, and adding at 0°C a mixture of one volume of fuming nitric acid in five volumes of sulfuric acid.

The reaction mixture, consisting of approximately equal amounts of o-, p- and m-nitrodimethylanilines separates out.[80]

p-Nitrodimethylaniline is obtained by treating p-nitrobromobenzene with dimethylamine.[81] An aqueous solution of dimethylammonium chloride is added to p-nitrobromobenzene and sodium bicarbonate in pyridine and the mixture is refluxed for 10 hours. The yield is about 95 per cent. o-Nitrodimethylaniline may be prepared in 85 per cent yield in the same way.

3-Nitrodimethylaniline may be further nitrated to give 3,6-dinitrodimethylaniline, and this in turn may give 2,4,6-trinitrodimethylaniline and 2,3,4,6-tetranitrodimethylaniline. The latter compound on boiling with nitric acid gives 2,3,4,6-tetranitrophenylmethylnitramine.[82]

The nitration of dimethylaniline in concentrated sulfuric acid with a large excess of fuming nitric acid at 40–55°C gives the very excellent explosive "tetryl," 2,4,6-trinitrophenylmethylnitramine.[83,84]

The position taken by a nitro group may be influenced by the strength of the sulfuric acid used. Thus p-chlorodimethylaniline nitrated in 97 per cent sulfuric acid gives 3-nitro-4-chlorodimethylaniline. In 70 per cent sulfuric acid the product is almost exclusively 2-nitro-4-chlorodimethylaniline.[85]

Trinitroaniline is obtained by the action of urea on picric acid.

$$\text{(2,4,6-trinitrophenol)} + H_2NCONH_2 \longrightarrow \text{(2,4,6-trinitroaniline)} + NH_3 + CO_2$$

A mixture of picric acid and urea (mole ratio 1:3) is heated at 173°C for 36 hours. The cooled reaction mixture is extracted with acetone, leaving a solid residue of the trinitroaniline. The yield is about 80 per cent.

The carboxyl group in some amino acids is replaced during nitration. Thus the nitration of p-dimethylaminobenzoic acid with a mixture of sulfuric and 60 per cent nitric acid at 5–10°C gives 3-nitro-4-dimethylaminobenzoic acid.[86] At 60–70°C a mixture of compounds is obtained.

$$\text{(p-dimethylaminobenzoic acid)} \longrightarrow \text{(3-nitro-4-N(CH}_3)_2\text{-COOH)} + \text{(NO}_2\text{ ... N(CH}_3)_2) + \text{(NO}_2\text{ ... N(CH}_3)_2)$$

Nitroanilines are useful intermediates in the preparation of a variety of nitro compounds. In most cases the amino group is diazotized and the

diazonium group displaced. Thus *o*-nitrobenzonitrile is prepared by reacting diazotized *o*-nitroaniline with copper sulfate and potassium cyanide
at 90°C.[87] The yield is about 65 per cent.

Similarly *p*-iodonitrobenzene is obtained by treating *p*-nitrobenzene-
diazonium sulfate with potassium iodide.

o-Nitrophenylhydrazine is obtained by the reduction of *o*-nitrobenzene-
diazonium chloride with potassium sulfite at 0–5°C.[88] Yields are about
85 per cent.

Nitroaldehydes. Aldehydes may be nitrated satisfactorily under certain
conditions. The carbonyl group is ring deactivating so that the entering
nitro group is directed to the *meta* position. The oxidation of the aldehyde group is suppressed by using a mixture of nitric and sulfuric acid as
the nitrating agent. Low temperatures are usually required. *m*-Nitrobenz-
aldehyde is obtained together with about 20 per cent of the *ortho* isomer
by the direct nitration of benzaldehyde. The benzaldehyde is added to
mixed acid containing 28–30 per cent nitric acid at 0–5°C. After stirring
for some time, the mixture is poured onto ice. The yield of the *meta* isomer
is about 65 per cent.[89,90] The *ortho* isomer can not be separated in a
pure form.

o-Nitro-*m*-chlorobenzaldehyde may be prepared by adding slowly *m*-
chlorobenzaldehyde to a mixture of nitric acid and 20 times its volume of
sulfuric acid at 0°C. The reaction requires several hours with constant
agitation. The product is isolated by pouring the reaction mixture onto ice
and filtering the solid precipitate.[91]

2,4-Dinitrobenzaldehyde has been obtained by the oxidation of 2,4-dinitrobenzoyl aniline or its sulfonic acid with potassium permanganate or chromic acid.

2,4,6-Trinitrobenzaldehyde is prepared from trinitrotoluene in two steps:[92]

1. *p*-Nitrosodimethylaniline is added to a solution of trinitrotoluene in equal volumes of ethanol and acetone containing sodium carbonate.

2. The resulting 2,4,6-trinitrobenzal-*p*-dimethylaminoaniline is hydrolyzed in concentrated hydrochloric acid at about 100°C.

Alkyl aryl ketones are more resistant to oxidation and so can be somewhat more readily nitrated. *m*-Nitroacetophenone is obtained by dissolving acetophenone in about 2.5 times its weight of concentrated sulfuric acid and nitrating at 0°C with a mixture of concentrated nitric and sulfuric acids.[93]

Nitro Acids. Aromatic acids are nitrated without great difficulty with the nitro group entering the *meta* positions. Benzoic acid is nitrated at 15°C with concentrated sulfuric and nitric acids.[94] *o*-Chlorobenzoic acid is nitrated in the same way to give *o*-chloro-*m*-nitrobenzoic acid.[95]

2,6-Dichlorobenzoic acid, first dissolved in concentrated sulfuric acid then treated with mixed acid at 65–70°C gives 2,6-dichloro-3-nitrobenzoic acid in 94 per cent yield.[96]

3,5-Dinitrobenzoic acid is prepared by nitrating benzoic acid with a mixture of fuming nitric and sulfuric acids.

m-Nitrobenzoic acid is obtained by nitrating the methyl ester of benzoic acid and saponifying the resulting product.

Mono-, di- and trinitrobenzoic acids are obtained by oxidizing the appropriate nitrotoluene. The nitro groups help to stabilize the benzene ring so that the oxidation of the methyl group is easier. *p*-Nitrobenzoic acid has been obtained by the oxidation of *p*-nitrotoluene with sodium dichromate and sulfuric acid.[48]

The oxidation of trinitrotoluene to trinitrobenzoic acid has already been described. The oxidation of 2-nitro-4-chlorotoluene in pyridine with potassium permanganate on a steam bath gives 2-nitro-4-chlorobenzoic acid in 48 per cent yield.[97]

Phthalic anhydride heated for two hours at 100–110°C with a mixture of fuming nitric and sulfuric acids (volume ratio 1:3) gives 3-nitrophthalic acid with a small amount of the 4-isomer.[98] An alternate synthesis involves the oxidation of α-nitronaphthalene.

4-Nitrophthalic acid is obtained in 60–70 per cent yield by nitrating phthalimide with mixed acid followed by hydrolysis of the resulting nitrophthalimide.[99]

Nucleophilic Attack on Aromatic Compounds

The nitro group being highly electronegative promotes the withdrawal of electrons from the benzene ring and more specifically from the *ortho* and *para* positions. This places a positive charge on the *ortho* and *para* positions and it is not surprising that the molecule becomes vulnerable to attack by nucleophilic reagents at these positions. The effect is greater when two nitro groups are present *meta* to each other. Thus *m*-dinitrobenzene is attacked by cyanide ion to give 2,6-dinitrobenzonitrile.[100]

In the reaction, the hydrogen is eliminated as a hydride ion and must be oxidized to give, in this case, potassium hydroxide. Air may be sufficient to effect this oxidation.

Similarly potassium salts of imides attack the ring in a position *ortho* or *para* to the nitro group.[101]

In some halogenated nitrobenzenes the nitro group is eliminated by the attack of a nucleophilic reagent. Thus p-nitrobromobenzene is attacked by cyanide ion to give m-bromobenzonitrile.[102] The reaction involves a nucleophilic attack by the cyanide ion on the carbon *ortho* to the nitro group and proceeds as follows.[103]

Bunnett, McCormack and McKay[104] suggest that the reaction proceeds as follows:

These are representative of a number of nucleophilic reactions which occur with aromatic nitro compounds.

The nitro group activates a vinyl group attached to the ring in the *para*-position so that the double bond is attacked by nucleophilic reagents.[105] Thus diethylamine adds to the double bond of p-nitrostyrene in absolute alcohol to give p-$O_2NC_6H_4CH_2N(C_2H_5)_2$ in 98 per cent yield. Other primary or secondary amines behave similarly.

AROMATIC NITROSO COMPOUNDS

The direct introduction of a nitroso group into the benzene ring can be accomplished only in the case of phenols or tertiary aryl amines. p-Nitrosophenol can be prepared by the action of nitrous acid on phenol in aqueous solution at temperatures of about $-10°C$.[106,107] The nitroso group enters the *para* position.

The same product can be obtained by the action of a hydroxylamine salt on p-benzoquinone indicating that p-nitrosophenol and p-benzoquinone-monoxime exist as a tautomeric mixture of the two compounds.

Dihydric phenols such as resorcinol react with nitrous acid to give dinitroso compounds. Substituted phenols such as phenolcarboxylic acids may also be converted to the nitroso derivatives in this way. α-Naphthol gives a mixture of 2- and 4-nitroso-α-naphthol. β-Naphthol gives only α-nitroso-β-naphthol.

In some cases amyl nitrite may be used as a nitrosating agent. Thus mononitrosoresorcinol is prepared by adding amyl nitrite to a cold solution of potassium hydroxide in alcohol.[108] After 3 or 4 hours the potassium salt of the nitrosoresorcinol precipitates out. The pure compound is obtained by treatment with acid.

The direct introduction of a nitroso group into a nitrogen-substituted dialkylaniline may be accomplished by adding sodium nitrite to an aqueous solution of the amine hydrochloride.[109,110] The nitroso group enters the *para* position. *p*-Nitrosodimethylaniline is obtained in 89 per cent yield.

A substituent in the *ortho* position and the presence of large alkyl groups on the nitrogen interfere with the reaction.[111,112]

Aromatic acids containing a tertiary amino group may be nitrosated with nitrous acid or nitrosyl chloride. Amines which contain an alkyl or alkoxy group in the *meta* position can be converted to *p*-nitrosoarylamines by treatment at room temperature with alcoholic hydrogen chloride.

Nitroso compounds can be prepared in a variety of ways. Nitrosamines prepared from nitrous acid and secondary amines rearrange at room temperature when treated in alcoholic solution with hydrogen chloride or hydrogen bromide.[113,114,115]

The reaction apparently involves the removal of the nitroso group by the halogen acid to form nitrosyl chloride which causes nitrosation on the ring in the *para* position.[116]

The Fischer-Hepp rearrangement is applicable to diaryl, alkyl-, aryl-, α-naphthyl- and alkyl-β-naphthylnitramines. Concentrated hydrochloric acid or a solution of hydrogen chloride in acetic acid will promote the rearrangement in many cases where alcoholic hydrogen chloride fails.[117] Nitrosamines containing a tertiary-N-alkyl group will not undergo the rearrangement. Instead the nitroso group is eliminated.[118]

Treatment of nitrosamines with sulfuric acid results in decomposition with the regeneration of the amine.

A nitroso and a hydroxyl group may be introduced simultaneously into a benzene ring by the reaction of a nitrosyl radical in the presence of an oxidizing agent.[119] The nitrosyl radical is formed either by the reduction of nitrous acid or the oxidation of hydroxylamine. Copper salts are necessary catalysts to stabilize the nitrosyl radical. o-Nitrosophenols are formed. Yields are reported to be low. o-Nitrosophenol is obtained from benzene, hydroxylamine and hydrogen peroxide.

$$\text{C}_6\text{H}_6 + \text{H}_2\text{NOH} + \text{H}_2\text{O}_2 \longrightarrow \text{o-C}_6\text{H}_4(\text{OH})(\text{NO}) + \text{H}_2\text{O}$$

Aromatic amines and hydroxylamines may be oxidized to the corresponding nitroso compounds. Nitrosobenzene is readily obtained by the chromic acid oxidation of β-phenylhydroxylamine which in turn is prepared by the reduction of nitrobenzene with zinc dust and ammonium chloride.[120] The hydroxylamines need not be isolated. Nitroso compounds can also be obtained from hydroxylamines by oxidation with ferric chloride.[121,122]

Aromatic oximes may also be oxidized to nitroso compounds. p-Quinonedioximes are oxidized to the corresponding dinitroso compounds with alkaline potassium ferricyanide.[123]

$$\text{HON}={\text{C}_6\text{H}_2(\text{CH}_3)}={\text{NOH}} \longrightarrow \text{ON}-{\text{C}_6\text{H}_2(\text{CH}_3)}-\text{NO}$$

Aromatic nitro compounds under special conditions are reduced to nitroso compounds: nitronaphthalenes treated with methanolic sodium hydroxide gives the methyl ether of nitrosonaphthalene.[124,125]

In most cases the nitro group is reduced to the corresponding hydroxylamine with zinc dust and ammonium chloride and this compound is then oxidized to the nitroso compound as previously described. This procedure is used for the preparation of nitrosobenzyl alcohols,[128] and nitrosobenzaldehydes[129] from the corresponding nitro compounds.

Reactions of Nitroso Compounds

Aromatic nitroso compounds are white in the crystalline state but are blue in the liquid or vapor state. Solid nitrosobenzenes are dimers which dissociate more or less completely in solution. The solutions are blue, characteristic of the monomer. If substituents are found in both the *ortho* positions, the dissociation is retarded.

Nitrosophenols are tautomeric with quinone monoximes. *p*-Nitrosophenol in ether is found in the quinonemonoxime form to the extent of about 70 per cent.[128] Hydroxylamine reacts with *p*-nitrosophenol to give *p*-benzoquinonedioxime.

Aromatic nitroso compounds react with primary amines to give azo compounds.[129,130]

$$C_6H_5NO + RNH_2 \longrightarrow C_6H_5N{=}N{-}R + H_2O$$

Similarly hydroxylamine in the presence of sodium carbonate gives *syn*-diazo compounds[131]

$$C_6H_5NO + H_2NOH \longrightarrow syn\text{-}C_6H_5{-}N{=}N{-}OH + H_2O$$

Nitroso compounds condense with compounds containing active methylene groups to give azomethines.[132,133,134] As an example *p*-nitrosodimethylaniline reacts with benzyl cyanide

$$p\text{-}(CH_3)_2NC_6H_4NO + C_6H_5CH_2CN \longrightarrow (CH_3)_2NC_6H_4N{=}C(CN)C_6H_5 + H_2O$$

The condensation is usually carried out in alcohol solution in the presence of a basic catalyst such as sodium carbonate, potassium cyanide, pyridine or sodium alkoxides. In some cases the reaction can only be accomplished satisfactorily in absolute alcohol using a sodium alkoxide catalyst.[135]

As another example, 2,4-dinitrotoluene is refluxed with *p*-nitrosodimethylaniline in alcohol solution to give 2,4-dinitrobenzaldehydedimethylaminoanil. Sodium carbonate or some other base is required as a catalyst.

$$2,4\text{-}(O_2N)_2C_6H_3CH_3 + ONC_6H_4N(CH_3)_2 \longrightarrow$$

$$2,4\text{-}(O_2N)_2C_6H_3CH{=}NC_6H_4N(CH_3)_2 + H_2O$$

Nitroso groups are reduced to amines by the action of stannous chloride or sodium sulfide, zinc or iron and hydrochloric acid, or hydrogen and a catalyst. Sodium bisulfite reduces the nitroso group of nitroso phenols with the simultaneous introduction of a sulfonate group.

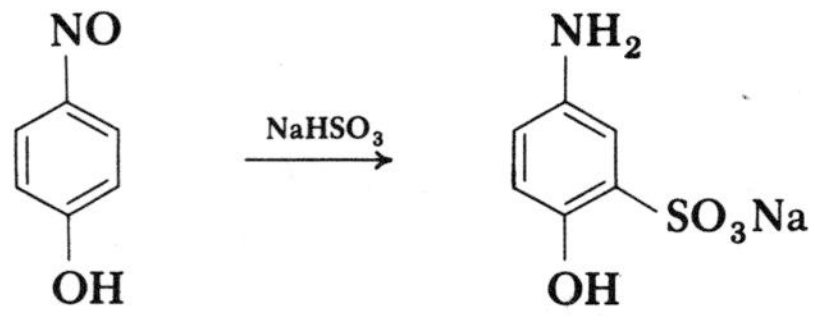

β-Nitroso-α-naphthol gives 1-hydroxy-2-aminonaphthalene-4-sulfonic acid.[136]

Oxidation of nitroso groups with nitric acid and other oxidizing agents gives the corresponding nitro compounds. Nitrosophenols are successfully oxidized with nitric acid or alkaline potassium ferricyanide.[137]

o-Dinitrosobenzene is transformed by copper in hydrochloric acid to give *o*-nitroaniline. The reaction probably proceeds according to the following scheme.[138]

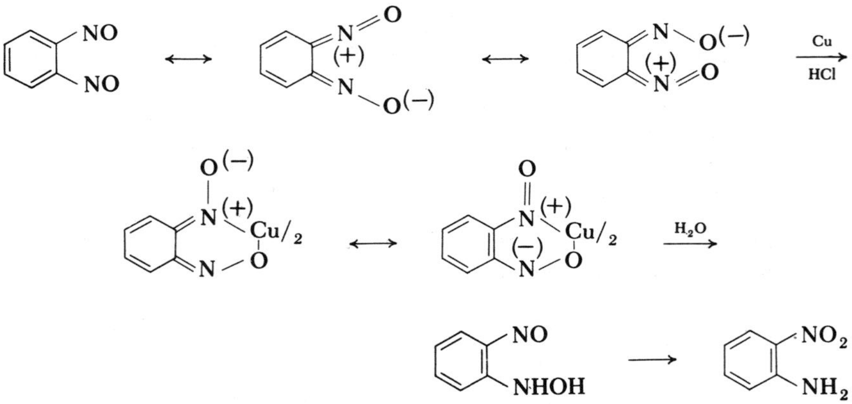

References

1. Witt, O. N., and Uterman, A., *Ber.,* **39,** 3901 (1906).
2. Klemenc, A., and Ekl, E., *Monatsh.,* **39,** 641 (1918).
3. Wegscheider, R., and Faltis, F., *Monatsh.,* **33,** 2 (1912).
4. Varma, P. S., *et al., J. Am. Chem. Soc.,* **47,** 143 (1925); *J. Soc. Chem. Ind. (London),* **7,** 629 (1930).
5. Holleman, A. F., *Ber.,* **39,** 1716 (1906).
6. Menke, J. B., *Rec. trav. chim.,* **44,** 141 (1925).

7. Melander, L., *Nature,* **163,** 599 (1949).
8. Gillespie, R. J., *et al., Nature,* **163,** 599 (1949).
9. Hughes, E. D., Ingold, C. K., and Reed, R. I., *J. Chem. Soc.,* **1950,** 2400.
10. Ingold, C. K., Goddard, D. R., and Hughes, E. P., *J. Chem. Soc.,* **1950,** 2559.
11. Nelson, K. L., and Brown, H. C., *J. Am. Chem. Soc.,* **73,** 5605 (1951).
12. Haun, J. W., and Kobe, J. A., *Ind. Eng. Chem.,* **43,** 2355 (1951).
13. Faith, W. L., Keyes, D. B., and Clarke, R. L., "Industrial Chemicals," p. 438, New York, John Wiley & Sons, Inc., 1956.
14. Yoto, A., Japan Patent 6319 ('56) (July 28, 1956).
15. Clarke, H. T., and Hartman, W. W., "Organic Syntheses," Collective Volume I, p. 541, 543, New York, J. Wiley & Sons, Inc., 1941.
16. Haworth, R. O., and Barker, R. L., *J. Chem. Soc.,* **1939,** 1302.
17. Powell, G., and Johnson, F. R., "Organic Syntheses," Collective Volume II, p. 449, New York, John Wiley & Sons, Inc., 1943.
18. Smith, L. I., "Organic Syntheses," Collective Volume II, p. 254, New York, John Wiley & Sons, Inc., 1943.
19. Hennion, G. F., U. S. Patent 2,314,212 (Mar. 16, 1943).
20. Thomas, R. J., Anzilotti, W. F., and Hennion, G. F., *Ind. Eng. Chem.,* **32,** 408 (1940).
21. Alfthan, J., *Ber.,* **53,** 78 (1920).
22. Kobe, K. A., and Doumani, T. F., *Ind. Eng. Chem.,* **31,** 257 (1939).
23. Wheeler, A. S., and Harris, C. R., *J. Am. Chem. Soc.,* **49,** 2819 (1927).
24. Smith, L. I., and Harris, S. A., *J. Am. Chem. Soc.,* **57,** 1289 (1935).
25. Smith, L. I., and Guss, C. O., *J. Am. Chem. Soc.,* **62,** 2635 (1940).
26. Kobe, R. A., and Pritchett, P. W., *Ind. Eng. Chem.,* **44,** 1398 (1952).
27. Kokatnur, V. R., U. S. Patents 2,435,314, 2,435,544 (Feb. 3, 1948).
28. Othmer, D. F., Jacobs, J. J., Jr., and Levy, J. F., *Ind. Eng. Chem.,* **34,** 286 (1942).
29. Pujo, A. M., Boileau, J., and Lang, F. M., *Mem. poudres,* **35,** 41 (1953).
30. Weiland, A. J., and Gubelmann, I., U. S. Patent 1,836,211 (Dec. 15, 1932).
31. Gossman, Ch., *Ber.,* **29,** 1243, 1521 (1896).
32. Friedlander, P., *Ber.,* **32,** 3531 (1899).
33. Leuchold, *J. Chem. Ind.* (U.S.S.R.) **6,** 805 (1929).
34. Migradichian, V., "Organic Syntheses," p. 1600, New York, John Wiley & Sons, Inc., 1957.
35. Braun, C. E., *et al.,* "Organic Syntheses," Vol. 31, p. 77, New York, John Wiley & Sons, Inc., 1951.
36. Schmidt, J., *Ber.,* **44,** 1494 (1911).
37. Von Bramer, H., Magoffin, J. E., and Clemens, M. L., U. S. Patent 2,578,328 (Dec. 11, 1951).
38. Jozkiewicz, S., and Kuczynskii, H., Zeszyty Nauk. Politech. Wroclaw. No. **4,** Chem. No. 1, 5 (1954).
39. Munday, J. L., U. S. Patent 2,620,356 (Dec. 2, 1952).
40. Spiegler, L., British Patent 713,662 (Aug. 11, 1954).
41. Balcom, D., and Furst, A., *J. Am. Chem. Soc.,* **75,** 4334 (1953).
42. Dewar, M. J. S., and Mole, T., *J. Chem. Soc.,* **1956,** 2556.

43. Pietra, S., *Ann. chim.,* (Rome) **45,** 859 (1955).
44. Kubota, S., Nara, K., and Anishi, S., *J. Pharm. Soc. Japan,* **76,** 801 (1956).
45. Spiegler, L., U. S. Patent 2,780,647 (Feb. 5, 1957).
46. Baude, E. A., Linstead, R. P., and Wooldridge, K. R. H., *J. Chem. Soc.,* **1954,** 3586.
47. Mayurnik, G., U. S. Patent 2,815,373 (Dec. 3, 1957).
48. Kamm, O., and Mathews, A. O., "Organic Syntheses," Collective Volume I, p. 392, New York, John Wiley & Sons, Inc., 1941.
49. Reverdin, F., "Organic Syntheses," Collective Volume I, p. 219, New York, John Wiley & Sons, Inc., 1941.
50. Thiele, J., and Escales, R., *Ber.,* **34,** 2842 (1901).
51. Borsche, *Ann.,* **386,** 351 (1911).
52. Sachs, F., and Kempf, R., *Ber.,* **35,** 1224 (1902).
53. Bennett, G. M., and Pratt, W. L. C., *J. Chem. Soc.,* **1929,** 1466.
54. Kastens, M. L., and Kaplan, J. F., *Ind. Eng. Chem.,* **42,** 402 (1950).
55. Veibel, S., *Ber.,* **63,** 2074 (1930).
56. Blackie, K. G., and Perkin, W. H., *J. Chem. Soc.,* **125,** 307 (1924).
57. Gibson, G. P., *J. Chem. Soc.,* **127,** 42 (1925).
58. Manske, R. H. F., "Organic Syntheses," Collective Volume I, p. 408, New York, John Wiley & Sons, Inc., 1941.
59. Topchiev, A. V., Alaniya, V. P., and Schnaider, G. S., *Doklady Akad. Nauk. S.S.S.R.,* **95,** 89 (1954).
60. Conner, J. C., Jr., U. S. Patent 2,718,530 (Sept. 20, 1955).
61. Schultz, G., *Ber.,* **40,** 4324 (1907).
62. Gibson, G. P., *J. Chem. Soc.,* **123,** 1269 (1923).
63. Kauffmann, H., and de Pay, E., *Ber.,* **37,** 725 (1904).
64. Reverdin, F., and Hayse, *Chem. Ztg.,* **16,** 45 (1892).
65. Bachmann, W. E., Cherneida, J. M., Deno, A. C., and Horning, E. C., *J. Org. Chem.,* **13,** 390 (1948).
66. Aristoff, E. E., *et al., Ind. Eng. Chem.,* **40,** 128 (1948).
67. Teeters, W. O., and Mueller, M. B., U. S. Patent 2,455,322 (Nov. 30, 1948).
68. Kiresky, S., *Acta Chem. Scand.,* **11,** 913 (1957).
69. Giua, M., *Gazz. chim. ital.,* **49,** 158 (1919).
70. Birosel, D. M., *Univ. Philippines Nat. and Appl. Sci. Bull.,* **1,** 145 (1931).
71. Jackson, C. L., and Dunlap, F. L., *Am. Chem. J.,* **18,** 117 (1896).
72. Cahours, A., *Ann.,* **69,** 230 (1894).
73. Lange, M. P. de. *Rec. trav. chim.,* **45,** 19 (1926).
74. Robertson, P. W., *J. Chem. Soc.,* **81,** 1482 (1901).
75. Neville, R. H. C., and Winther, A., *Ber.,* **13,** 1949 (1880).
76. Bender, F., *Ber.,* **22,** 996 (1889).
77. Diehl, and Merz, *Ber.,* **11,** 1661 (1878).
78. Wells, F. B., and Allen, C. F. H., "Organic Syntheses," Collective Volume I, p. 221, New York, John Wiley & Sons, Inc., 1941.
79. Witt, O. N., and Witte, E., *Ber.,* **41,** 3090 (1908).
80. Swann, H., *J. Chem. Soc.,* **117,** 1 (1920).
81. Campbell, T. W., *J. Am. Chem. Soc.,* **71,** 740 (1949).

82. Forster, A., and Coulson, W., *J. Chem. Soc.,* **121,** 1988 (1922).
83. Bain, *Army Ordnance,* **VI,** p. 435 (1926).
84. Desseigne, G., *Mem. poudres,* **28,** 156 (1938).
85. Pinnow, J., *Ber.,* **31,** 2984 (1898).
86. Reverdin, F., *Ber.,* **40,** 2442 (1907); *Bull. soc. chim.,* [4], **1,** 618 (1907).
87. Bogert, M. T., and Hand, W. F., *J. Am. Chem. Soc.,* **24,** 1031 (1902).
88. Muller, H., Montigel, M., and Reichstein, T., *Helv. Chim. Acta,* **20,** 1472 (1937).
89. Brady, O. L., and Harris, S., *J. Chem. Soc.,* **123,** 484 (1923).
90. Hodgson, A. H., *J. Soc. Dyers Colourists,* **46,** 183 (1930).
91. Eichengrun, A., and Einhorn, A., *Ann.,* **262,** 136 (1891).
92. Lowy, A., and Balz, H., *J. Am. Chem. Soc.,* **43,** 343 (1920).
93. Corson, R. B., and Hazen, R. K., "Organic Syntheses," Collective Volume II, p. 434, New York, John Wiley & Sons, Inc., 1943.
94. Gerland, *Ann.,* **91,** 186 (1854).
95. Hubner, *Ann.,* **222,** 95 (1883).
96. Lehmstedt, K., and Schrader, K., *Ber.,* **70,** 1526 (1937).
97. Leonard, N. J., and Boyd, S. N., *J. Org. Chem.,* **11,** 414 (1946).
98. Culhane, P. J., and Woodward, G. E., "Organic Syntheses," Collective Volume I, p. 408, New York, John Wiley & Sons, Inc., 1941.
99. Huntress, E. H., and Shriner, R. L., "Organic Syntheses," Collective Volume II, p. 459, New York, John Wiley & Sons, Inc., 1943.
100. de Bruyn, C. A. L., *Rec. trav. chim.,* **2,** 210 (1899).
101. Montmollin, G. de, and Montmollin, M. de, *Helv. Chim. Acta,* **6,** 94 (1923).
102. Bunnett, J. F., and Zahler, R. E., *Chem. Rev.,* **49,** 273 (1951).
103. Hine, J. S., "Physical Organic Chemistry," p. 372, New York, McGraw-Hill, 1956.
104. Bunnett, J. F., McCormack, J. F., and Mckay, F. C., *J. Org. Chem.,* **15,** 481 (1950).
105. Dale, W. J., and Buell, G., *J. Org. Chem.,* **21,** 45 (1956).
106. Baeyer, *Ber.,* **7,** 964 (1874); **8,** 614 (1873).
107. Tseng, C. L., and Hu, M., *J. Chinese Chem. Soc.,* **1,** 183 (1933).
108. Henrich, F., *Ber.,* **35,** 4192 (1902).
109. Bennett, G. M., and Bell, E. V., "Organic Syntheses," Collective Volume II, p. 223, New York, John Wiley & Sons, Inc., 1943.
110. Hodgson, H. H., and Nicholson, D. E., *J. Chem. Soc.,* **1941,** 470.
111. MacMillan, W. G., and Reade, T. H., *J. Chem. Soc.,* **1929,** 2863.
112. Karrer, P., *Ber.,* **48,** 1308 (1915).
113. Fischer, O., and Hepp, E., *Ber.,* **19,** 2991 (1886).
114. Fischer, O., *Ann.,* **286,** 156 (1895).
115. Morgan, G. T., *et al., J. Chem. Soc.,* **115,** 1142 (1919); *Proc. Chem. Soc.,* **110,** 518 (1925).
116. Houben, J., *Ber.,* **46,** 3985 (1913).
117. Houben, J., *Ber.,* **42,** 2750 (1900).
118. Hickenbottom, W. J., *J. Chem. Soc.,* **1933,** 1070.
119. Cronheim, G., *J. Org. Chem.,* **12,** 1, 7, 20 (1947).

120. Coleman, G. H., McCloskey, C. M., and Stuart, F. A., "Organic Syntheses," Vol. 25, p. 80, New York, John Wiley & Sons, Inc., 1945.
121. Lutz, R. E., and Lytton, M. R., *J. Org. Chem.*, **2,** 68 (1937).
122. Barrow, F., and Thorneycroft, F. J., *J. Chem. Soc.*, **1939,** 773.
123. Francesconi, L., and Bresciani, G., *Gazz. chim. ital.*, **34,** II, 13 (1904).
124. Meisenheimer, J., and Witte, K., *Ber.*, **36,** 4164 (1903).
125. Meisenheimer, J., *Ann.*, **355,** 299 (1907).
126. Bamberger, E., *Ber.*, **36,** 836 (1903).
127. Bamberger, E., *Ber.*, **28,** 250 (1895).
128. Anderson, L. L., *et al.*, *J. Am. Chem. Soc.*, **54,** 3064 (1932); **56,** 732 (1934).
129. Bamberger, E., *Ber.*, **29,** 102 (1896).
130. Freundler, *Bull. soc. chim.*, [4], **1,** 220 (1907).
131. Hantzsch, A., *Ber.*, **38,** 2056 (1905).
132. Ehrlich, P., and Sachs, F., *Ber.*, **32,** 2341 (1899).
133. Sachs, F., *et al.*, *Ber.*, **33,** 959 (1900); **35,** 1224, 1437, 2704, 3319 (1902); **36,** 757, 1132, 3236 (1903).
134. Houben, J., *et al.*, *Ber.*, **42,** 2746, 2753, 2758 (1909); **46,** 3992, 3996 (1913); **53,** 2350 (1920).
135. Houben, J., *et al.*, *Ber.*, **42,** 2747 (1909).
136. Schmidt, O., *J. prakt. Chem.*, [2], **44,** 531 (1891).
137. Stenhouse, J., and Groves, C. E., *J. Chem. Soc.*, **32,** 51 (1877); *Ann.*, **189,** 151 (1877).
138. Boyer, J. H., *et al.*, *J. Am. Chem. Soc.*, **77,** 5688 (1955).

8. ALIPHATIC NITRO COMPOUNDS

The first nitroparaffin was prepared in 1872 by Meyer and Stuber[1] who reacted amyl iodide with silver nitrite and obtained a mixture of nitropentane and amyl nitrite. The method has been reviewed and extended by Reynolds and Adkins[2] and more recently by others. The method has been found to be suitable for the preparation of polynitroparaffins,[3] nitroalcohols[4,5] and other nitro compounds.

A mixture of nitroparaffin and alkyl nitrite is always obtained. Silver nitrite favors the production of nitroparaffins but sodium nitrite gives largely the nitrite esters. The reason for the differences in the ratio of nitroparaffin to the nitrite ester obtained with different metal nitrites is not obvious. There is apparently competition between two reaction mechanisms. Reynolds and Adkins postulate the formation of an addition complex between the two reagents and that each constituent of the complex is able to influence the further course of the reaction to give a nitrite or a nitro derivative.

Kornblum, Taub, and Ungnade[6] investigated the reaction between alkyl halides and silver nitrite. At high temperatures a number of by-products such as alcohols and ketones, presumably obtained from the intermediate nitrite ester, are formed, but if the reaction is carried out at room temperature or below the product is primarily a mixture of nitroparaffin and alkyl nitrite.

When the reaction between an alkyl halide and silver nitrite was initiated at ice temperatures and completed at room temperature the results shown in Table 8–1 were obtained. In all cases where reaction occurred the yield of nitroparaffin relative to alkyl nitrite is good.

Kornblum also found that dimethylformamide and dimethylsulfoxide are both effective solvents for the preparation of nitroparaffins from alkyl halides and silver nitrite. Dimethylsulfoxide has the advantage over dimethylformamide in that it is a better solvent for sodium nitrite.[7,8] Thus 2-iodooctane (71.2 g) was stirred for 4 hours at room temperature with 225 ml of dimethylsulfoxide and 36 g of sodium nitrite. The reaction mixture was then diluted with water and extracted with ligroin to give 14 g of 2-octylnitrite and 27 g of 2-nitrooctane. An identical experiment using dimethylformamide and sodium nitrite gave a 57 per cent yield of 2-nitrooctane.

Plummer and Drake[9] independently developed a process for making nitroparaffins from alkyl bromides and silver nitrite which they report gives

TABLE 8-1. THE REACTION OF ALKYL HALIDES WITH SILVER NITRITE

Halide	Nitro-paraffin (%)	Alkyl-nitrite (%)
n-Butyl bromide	73	13
n-Butyl iodide	74	12
n-Hexyl chloride	0	0
n-Hexyl bromide	76	10
n-Hexyl iodide	78	13
n-Heptyl bromide	79	11
n-Heptyl iodide	82	10
n-Octyl chloride	0	0
n-Octyl bromide	80	14
n-Octyl iodide	83	11

higher yields of product. The method consists of adding rapidly a five per cent excess of silver nitrite to a cold solution of the alkyl halide in about an equal volume of petroleum ether, allowing the temperature to rise to 40°C and maintaining this temperature for 6–8 hours. Yields are 65–70 per cent.

The yields of nitro compounds obtained by treating secondary bromides and iodides with silver nitrite are poor, being in the neighborhood of 15 per cent. Nitrite esters and olefin formation is considerably more important than with the primary halides. Olefin formation amounts to 25–30 per cent of the starting halide. Dehydrohalogenation is responsible for two additional side reactions: (a) the low temperature formation of nitrate esters and (b) the formation of olefin-nitrogen oxide adducts.[10]

In contrast with secondary and primary chlorides, tertiary chlorides react with silver nitrite but the yields of nitroparaffins are very low (*ca.* 5 per cent). The principal products are nitrite esters, but olefin-nitrogen oxide adducts are also formed.

Tertiary bromides and silver nitrite give 50–64 per cent yield of nitrite esters but no nitroparaffins.

Alkyl sulfates may be substituted for alkyl halides in the preparation of nitroparaffins. However, methyl and ethyl sulfates are the only ones readily available.

The optimum conditions for the preparation of nitromethane from dimethyl sulfate are reported to be a molar ratio of sodium nitrite to dimethyl sulfate of 3:1, the presence of 90 g of water for each 100 g of sodium nitrite and the addition of 0.025 mole of potassium carbonate per mole of sodium nitrite. The reaction proceeds in two steps, the first occurring at 60°C and the second at 115–120°C. Yields of nitromethane are about 65 per cent.[11] The yields are about 69 per cent when sodium methyl sulfate is used.

Nitroethane is prepared in 43 per cent yield by treating 1.5 moles of sodium nitrite with one mole of sodium ethyl sulfate at 125–130°C in the presence of 0.0625 mole of potassium carbonate.[12]

In some cases primary amines may be oxidized to nitro compounds.[13] The reaction probably proceeds as follows:

$$CH_3NH_2 \rightarrow CH_3NHOH \rightarrow CH_2{=}NOH \begin{smallmatrix} \nearrow HC(OH){=}NOH \\ \rightarrow CH_2{=}NO_2H \rightarrow CH_3NO_2 \\ \searrow HCN + H_2O \rightarrow HCOOH \end{smallmatrix}$$

Kornblum and Clutter[14] have used this procedure in the preparation of *tert*-nitroalkanes. Thus *tert*-nitrobutane has been obtained from *tert*-butyl-amine in 83 per cent yield. The oxidation is carried out with aqueous potassium permanganate at 45–55°C. Problems are encountered with higher molecular weight amines because of their insolubility in water.[15] Addition of acetic acid increases the solubility of the amines but the yields of *tert*-nitrocompounds are only 30–60 per cent. The reaction proceeds very well however, in a mixture of 80 per cent acetone and 20 per cent water.

Halonitroparaffins react with zinc alkyls with the replacement of one or more halogens. Thus tertiary nitrobutane has been prepared by treating chloropicrin, CCl_3NO_2, with dimethyl zinc.[16]

Metallic derivatives of aci-nitroparaffins react with alkyl halides to give either a nitronic ester or a higher nitro derivative.[17,18]

$$R_2C{=}NO_2Na + R'X \begin{smallmatrix} \nearrow R_2C{=}NO_2R' + NaX \\ \searrow R_2CR'{-}NO_2 + NaX \end{smallmatrix}$$

The nitronic esters are frequently unstable and decompose to give ketoximes and aldehydes.

$$R_2C{=}NO{-}OCH_2R' \rightarrow R_2C{=}NOH + R'CHO$$

The ratio of nitronic ester to nitroparaffin varies considerably with the nature of the reactants. The high yields of nitro compounds can apparently be correlated with the lability of the halogen. The method can be used for the preparation of dinitro compounds.

$$R_2C{=}NO_2Na + R_2CBr{-}NO_2 \rightarrow R_2C\underset{NO_2}{{-}}{-}\underset{NO_2}{CR_2} + NaBr$$

The first preparation of a chlorinated aliphatic nitro compound was accomplished by Mills[19] who nitrated chloroform in a sealed tube to give chloropicrin. Other liquid-phase nitrations have been reported. Beilstein and Kurbatov[20] nitrated a Caucasion petroleum to give nitrocycloparaffins. An American petroleum fraction boiling between 95 and 100°C was nitrated in the liquid phase to give nitro derivatives boiling at 193° and 197°C and having the composition $C_7H_{15}NO_2$. This product was probably a mixture of 2-nitroheptane, 3-nitroheptane and 4-nitroheptane together with small amounts of other isomers.

Worstall[21] nitrated nonane in the liquid phase and obtained a 76 per cent conversion to mono- and polynitro compounds by refluxing his reagents at atmospheric pressure. Worstall reported that the mononitro compounds obtained from hexane, heptane, octane, nonane and decane were exclusively primary nitro compounds.

The work on the liquid-phase nitration of paraffin hydrocarbons, with the exception of that of Worstall, indicates that tertiary hydrogen atoms are more reactive than secondary, which in turn are more reactive than primary hydrogens. There are two possible explanations of Worstall's apparent exceptions. He may not have been too exact in his identification of products and there is good reason to believe that the secondary nitro compounds are selectively attacked to give polynitro compounds. Henry[22] has shown that there is considerable question concerning part of Worstall's identifications.

The yield of nitrated product increases with the reaction temperature. Worstall obtained a 6.0 per cent yield of nitrated hexane products at the reflux temperature of hexane but a 70 per cent yield of product from nonane where the reflux temperature is higher. Konovalov[23] found that nitrating hexane in a sealed tube at 140°C gave a 60 per cent yield of nitrohexanes.

Dodecane has been nitrated with dinitrogen tetroxide at 175°C under nitrogen or carbon dioxide at a pressure of 25 atmospheres.[24] With a contact time of 3.75 minutes, a product is obtained containing mono- and dinitrodecanes in a ratio of 3:1.

A great deal of oxidation occurs during liquid-phase nitration with the nitric acid being reduced to elemental nitrogen. This is in contrast to vapor-phase nitration which gives primarily oxides of nitrogen which can be readily oxidized back to nitric acid.

The nitric-sulfuric acid mixture used in the nitration of aromatic hydrocarbons can not be used with alkanes because hot sulfuric acid hydrolyzes primary nitroparaffins and converts secondary and tertiary nitroparaffins to tars.

Aluminum nitrate has been recommended as a catalyst for liquid-phase nitration. However, Denison[25] reports that the principal effect of this salt is to raise the boiling point of the nitric acid so that nitration will occur at higher temperatures.

Stevens and Schiessler[26] nitrated levo-3-methyloctane in the liquid phase and obtained optically active 3-nitro-3-methyloctane. This would indicate that the reaction does not involve free radicals but proceeds probably by an S_N2 attack.

The liquid-phase nitration of hydrocarbons has not proved to be a satisfactory process for making nitroparaffins and so the availability of these compounds awaited development of a vapor-phase process.

Beginning about 1930, Hass and a group of graduate students at Purdue University[27,28] began an extensive investigation of the nitration of paraffin hydrocarbons. Inasmuch as in the liquid-phase nitrations, tertiary hydrogen atoms were most readily replaced, attempts were made to nitrate isobutane in a sealed tube. No reaction occurred at 115°C but a smooth reaction occurred at 150°C which was complete in 15 minutes to give the expected tertiary nitrobutane in good yield. Conversions, however, were only about 22 per cent. A similar experiment with *n*-butane gave similar results.

It was realized that 150°C was above the critical temperature of isobutane and consequently the reaction had occurred in the vapor phase. This observation led to the development of a continuous process for the vapor-phase nitration of paraffin hydrocarbons at essentially atmospheric pressure. Under these conditions, temperatures of 400–450°C are desirable.

The product obtained from the vapor phase nitration of isobutane is much different from that obtained in sealed-tube experiments. Instead of obtaining *tert*-nitrobutane as the principal nitrated product, the vapor-phase product contained only a small amount of this compound but relatively large amounts of 1-nitro-2-methylpropane together with 2-nitropropane and nitromethane. The latter two compounds are obtained by cleavage of the carbon chain.

Vapor phase nitration does not give dinitroparaffins at temperatures above 248°C.[29] Attempted nitration of mononitroparaffins results in pyrolysis and oxidation but not nitration. Either nitric acid or nitrogen dioxide can be used as nitrating agents, but nitric acid is somewhat more satisfactory. Nitrogen dioxide and nitric acid give the same products but the yields per mole of nitrating agent are better with nitric acid. About 40 per cent of the nitric acid is converted into nitroparaffins and the remainder serves as an oxidizing agent, being reduced to nitric oxide. No nitrogen is produced and by oxidizing the nitric oxide to nitrogen dioxide a conversion of about 90 per cent of the nitric acid to nitroparaffins can be obtained. Alcohols, aldehydes, acids, carbon monoxide and carbon dioxide are formed as by-products. There is considerable evidence that oxidation accompanies nitration but that the nitroparaffins are not themselves oxidized.

Hass has listed some general rules governing the nitration of paraffin hydrocarbons.[30] These are summarized as follows: An increase in the temperature of nitration increases (1) the velocity of reaction, (2) the production of primary nitroparaffins at the expense of secondary and tertiary nitroparaffins, (3) the yield of fission products. High pressure increase the rate of reaction without greatly affecting the conversions.

The hydrocarbons differ in the ease of nitration. For example, methane is the most difficult to nitrate while ethane and propane are progressively more easily nitrated. The nitration of a hydrocarbon, such as propane, does not give a single product and considerable carbon-carbon bond scission occurs. The nitration of propane gives 1-nitropropane, 2-nitropropane, nitroethane and nitromethane. In general, it can be said that every nitrated product will be obtained that can be formed by replacement of any hydrogen in the molecule and by the cleavage of any one carbon-carbon bond at a given time.

Nitromethane, nitroethane, 1-nitropropane, and 2-nitropropane are commercially available from the nitration of propane. The normal distribution of these compounds in the product is approximately 25 per cent 1-nitropropane, 40 per cent 2-nitropropane, 10 per cent nitroethane and 25 per cent nitromethane.

The vapor phase nitration of neopentane and neohexane give all the expected nitroparaffins.[31] These products together with the approximate distribution by volume are shown in Table 8–2.

TABLE 8–2. PRODUCTS OBTAINED FROM THE NITRATION OF NEOPENTANE AND NEOHEXANE

	Volume (%)
Neopentane	
Nitromethane	8
2-Methyl-2-nitropropane	12
2,2-Dimethyl-1-nitropropane	80
Neohexane	
Nitromethane	11
Nitroethane	9
2-Methyl-2-nitropropane	7
2-Methyl-2-nitrobutane	8
2,2-Dimethyl-1-nitropropane	3
2,2-Dimethyl-1-nitrobutane	34
2,2-Dimethyl-3-nitrobutane	17
3,3-Dimethyl-1-nitrobutane	11

Hass and Schecter[32] nitrated cyclopropane with nitric acid or nitrogen dioxide in the vapor phase and obtained nitrocyclopropane as the product. Nitrocyclopropane does not form salts with strong bases at 25°C and this has been related to the increase in internal strain resulting from the conversion of the nitrocyclopropane into its nitronate anion.

Gee[33] nitrated propane with nitrogen dioxide and reported that aluminum in the form of turnings was a catalyst for the reaction. A mixture of equal volumes of propane and nitrogen dioxide was passed over aluminum turnings at 270°C. A 10 per cent conversion to nitrated products was obtained with a reaction time of 80 seconds. About 4 per cent of the propane was oxidized to oxides of carbon.

Rottig[34] prepared mononitro compounds containing 6 to 9 carbon atoms by the direct nitration of the corresponding hydrocarbon at 200-300°C in the presence of a large surface catalyst. Thus octane and 96 per cent nitric acid were vaporized and passed at 300°C over a calcined bauxite catalyst, which had been pretreated with hydrochloric acid, to give a liquid product which contained 52 per cent mononitrooctanes.

A commercial process for the nitration of paraffin hydrocarbons has been described by Stengel and Egly.[35] A 70-80 per cent solution of nitric acid is sprayed into a stream of preheated hydrocarbon in small portions at several points. The temperature is maintained at 390-440°C. The over-all ratio of hydrocarbon to nitric acid is from 3:1 to 6:1 but at any point it is from 1:1 to 1.6:1. Thus 11,500 cubic feet of propane per hour is fed into a reactor at a pressure of 125 psi and at a temperature of 435°C while 122 pounds of 72 per cent nitric acid per hour is sprayed into the reactor, to give 185 pounds of nitroparaffins per hour.

Bishop, Denton and Nygaard[36] claim to have prepared secondary nitroparaffins from C_3, C_4, and C_5 hydrocarbons by reaction with 70 per cent nitric acid at 170-230°C and pressures of 900-1200 psi.

These same investigators[37] prepared 2,2-dinitropropane by heating an equimolar mixture of nitric acid (70 per cent) and 2-nitropropane to 200-230°C under a pressure of 900-1200 psi. Conversions were 11-14 per cent per pass with ultimate yields of 50 per cent. This compound is a valuable modifier for Diesel fuels.

A patent issued to duPont[38] describes a method for preparing dinitro compounds and nitro alcohols by the addition of N_2O_4 under pressure to olefins, diolefins, cycloaliphatic olefins, etc.

The preparation of tetranitromethane has been described by Hager.[39] Acetylene and nitric acid are converted to trinitromethane by adding the acetylene to 85 per cent nitric acid containing dissolved nitrogen dioxide and mercuric nitrate. In the second step sulfuric acid was added to the solution and on heating, tetranitromethane separated. It was purified largely by rinsing with sulfuric acid. Tetranitromethane is quite unstable but has a melting point of 13.8–14.0°C.

Tetranitromethane has also been prepared by Darzens and Levy[40] by passing a stream of ketene into cooled 100 per cent nitric acid. The reaction is very fast and the mixture is almost immediately poured onto ice whereupon the tetranitromethane separates. Yields of 90 per cent are reported.

$$4CH_2\text{=}C\text{=}O + 4HNO_3 \longrightarrow C(NO_2)_4 + CO_2 + 3CH_3COOH$$

Tetranitromethane was investigated by German chemists as an oxygen detonator in place of nitric acid for rockets.

Grundmann and Haldenwanger[41] developed a continuous liquid-phase process for the nitration of cyclohexane. The nitration is carried out at 120–125°C and a pressure of 4–5 atmospheres. A 35 per cent nitric acid solution is preferred as a nitrating agent. Higher concentrations favor oxidation. Below 110°C, formation of adipic acid becomes important. Pressure is used only to maintain the liquid phase.

Stengel[42] nitrated paraffins and alicyclic hydrocarbons by introducing sufficient oxygen to maintain the reaction temperature between 390 and 460°C as desired. This process permits the use of 40–70 per cent nitric acid.

The vapor-phase nitration of aliphatic ethers gives nitro ethers in addition to nitroparaffins formed as a result of fission of the carbon chain.[43] From the nature of the products obtained, it would seem that (1) nitro ethers are obtained having only one nitro group per molecule, (2) Any hydrogen atom in the ether except an *alpha* hydrogen is capable of being substituted by a nitro group. (3) No nitro ethers are formed as a result of fission of a carbon-carbon bond. (4) All possible nitroparaffins are formed by fission of a carbon-carbon or carbon-oxygen bond. (5) The higher aliphatic ethers give higher yields of nitro compounds than the lower ethers, probably because of the decreased probability of attack upon *alpha* positions.

Alcohols give nitroparaffins by fission of carbon-carbon bonds but no nitro alcohols are obtained.

Acetone, diisopropyl ketone and di-*n*-propyl ketone have been nitrated in the vapor phase to give the expected mononitro ketones in addition to nitroparaffins.

Saturated aliphatic hydrocarbons may be nitrated with nitric oxide in the presence of catalytic amounts of free radicals.[44] The source of the free radicals may be tetraethyl lead or azo compounds. Thus ethane is saturated with tetraethyl lead at 0°C, mixed with nitric oxide in the ratio of 2:1 by volume and passed through a tube heated to 200°C. Only a very small amount of cleavage occurs and nitroethane is the main product.

The reaction may be carried out in either the gas or liquid phase.

Dinitroparaffins having the nitro groups in the 1 and 3 positions have been prepared by the addition of an alkali metal salt of a nitroparaffin to a nitroolefin.[45] Thus the gradual addition of 2-nitro-1-butene to an alcoholic solution of the *aci*-2-nitropropane gives the crude potassium salt of 3,5-dinitro-3-methylhexane. The corresponding nitroparaffin can be obtained by treatment with dilute acid.

If only about one-fourth of the potassium hydroxide required for complete conversion of 2-nitropropane to the salt is used, a highly viscous, high molecular weight product is obtained in place of the desired nitroparaffin.

The nitration of olefins with dinitrogen tetroxide followed by hydrolysis gives nitroparaffins and carbonyl compounds in good yield.[46] Thus anhydrous dinitrogen tetroxide is added to anhydrous ether at –20°C and oxygen is bubbled through the solution until the color changes from dark to light brown. Isobutylene and oxygen are then bubbled through the solution until the color disappears. The product, which is a mixture of nitro-*tert*-butyl nitrite, nitro-*tert*-butyl nitrate and 1,2-dinitroisobutylene is hydrolyzed in two steps, first at 27°C with water containing zinc oxide then heating to 80°C while continuously distilling the product. The product contains approximately equal amounts of nitromethane and acetone.

The nitration of paraffin hydrocarbons proceeds by a free-radical mechanism and it is not surprising that oxygen, chorine or bromine accelerates the rate of reaction. Hass and Alexander[47] found that the presence of nitrogen in amounts up to 30 per cent had little or no effect upon the nitration of paraffins, but when propane was nitrated with nitric acid in the presence of excess oxygen at 410°C, the conversion was increased from 28 to 62 per cent; the acidity was not changed appreciably. At 395°C the conversion increased from 20–76 per cent by the addition of 3.8 moles of oxygen per mole of nitric acid used. When propane is nitrated with nitrogen dioxide at 410°C with the addition of 3.1 moles of oxygen for each mole of nitrogen dioxide, the conversion to nitrated products increased from 14 to 25 per cent.

Bachman, Hass and Addison[48] report that the addition of oxygen to the system increases the mole per cent conversion of nitric acid to nitroparaffins from 36–44 per cent at an optimum temperature of 425°C with a mole ratio of $C_4H_{10}:O:HNO_3$ of 15:1.6:1. This increase however, is at the expense of increased conversion of butane to by-products. Considerable amounts of butenes and propenes are obtained. Only 26 per cent of the butane was converted to nitrated products, but this conversion was greatly increased by providing more reaction surface in the reactor. By increasing the ratio of surface to volume, it was possible to obtain slightly higher conversions based on nitric acid and striking improvement in the yields of nitroparaffins based on the butane used.

The effect of oxygen on the nitration of methane has been investigated.[47] When oxygen is present in the nitration mixture to the extent of 2.6 moles per mole of nitric acid, the conversion rises from 18 to 24 per cent. When the ratio is increased to 5.0, the conversion falls to 1.4 per cent. The product is considerably more acidic when oxygen is introduced and the amount of formaldehyde formed is appreciably increased.

The nitration of propane in the presence of oxygen was appreciably different. The reaction is carried out at 395–410°C with a 1.6 second residence time. It is observed that the weight of non-aqueous product is increased by a factor of at least 3. A conversion of propane to nitrated products of 62 per cent is obtained at 410°C when a mole ratio of oxygen to nitric acid of 2.5 is used. This compares to a conversion of 28 per cent in the absence of oxygen.

Bachman, Hass and Hewitt[49] investigated the effect of oxygen on the nitration of propane with nitrogen dioxide. They report that oxygen improves the yield of nitroparaffin based on propane over that obtained without oxygen, largely by decreasing the conversion to by-products. The yield of nitroparaffins based on propane is much higher with nitrogen dioxide than with nitric acid. Optimum conditions are a contact time of 3 minutes at 285°C with a 0.75 mole of oxygen per mole of nitrogen dioxide to give a yield of 71 per cent nitrated products based on the propane and a 29 per cent yield based on nitrogen dioxide.

Bachman and Kohn[50] showed that combinations of oxygen and halogens give improved yields of, and conversions to nitroparaffins. Bachman and Pollack[51] showed that the oxygen could be eliminated and that halogens such as chlorine give improved yields of nitroparaffins based on the hydrocarbon. Furthermore in contradistinction to oxygen, halogens, are regenerated and may cause repeated formation of alkyl radicals. They therefore are required in lower concentration (about 20 per cent of the oxygen concentration) for the maintenance of an optimum rate of alkyl radical formation. A combination of chlorine and oxygen is most effective.

$$Cl_2 \longrightarrow 2Cl \cdot$$

$$RH + Cl \cdot \longrightarrow R \cdot + HCl$$

$$HCl + O(HNO_3, NO_2) \longrightarrow HO \cdot + Cl \cdot$$

Total nitroparaffin conversions may be catalytically increased as much as 32 per cent with oxygen-halogen combinations and as much as 46 per cent with chlorine alone compared to uncatalyzed nitrations.

A patent issued to Bachman and Hewitt[52] describes a process for the vapor-phase nitration of aliphatic hydrocarbons with catalytic amounts of a free halogen, either with or without oxygen, to obtain increased yields of nitrohydrocarbons. For example to nitric acid (1 mole) and a hydrocarbon (7–35 moles) was added free halogen (0.0018–0.026 mole) and oxygen (up to 3 moles) and the mixture heated 1–15 seconds at 200–500°C. Conversions were increased 50 per cent over the usual method with oxygen and as much as 150 per cent over ordinary nitrations without oxygen.

A mechanism for the free radical nitration of paraffin hydrocarbons in the presence of oxygen has been proposed by Bachman and Pollack.[51] They propose that the degradation products may be formed by the following scheme:

$$CH_3CH_2CH_2 \cdot \longrightarrow CH_2{=}CH_2 + H_3C \cdot \tag{1}$$

$$CH_3CH_2CH_2 \cdot + \cdot NO_2 \longrightarrow CH_3CH_2CH_2ONO \tag{2}$$

$$CH_3CH_2CH_2ONO \longrightarrow CH_3CH_2CH_2O \cdot + \cdot NO \tag{3}$$

$$CH_3CH_2CH_2 \cdot + O_2 \longrightarrow CH_3CH_2 \cdot + HCHO \tag{4}$$

$$CH_3CH_2CH_2 \cdot + O_2 \longrightarrow CH_3CH_2CH_2O_2 \cdot \tag{5}$$

$$CH_3CH_2CH_2O_2 \cdot + HA \longrightarrow CH_3CH_2CH_2O_2H \tag{6}$$

$$CH_3CH_2CH_2O_2H \longrightarrow CH_3CH_2CH_2O \cdot + \cdot OH \tag{7}$$

The loss of propyl radicals through reaction is controlled in part by the concentration of $\cdot NO_2$ radicals present in the reaction system. If this is high the probability is low that a propyl radical will degrade before it reacts with $\cdot NO_2$. Fortunately, the half-life of alkyl radicals seems to be sufficiently long to prevent much degradation by this process.

Equations (2), (3), and (4) represent a series of reactions over which there is no apparent control. The relative tendencies of alkyl radicals to unite with $\cdot NO_2$ to produce RONO versus RNO_2 are unknown. However, once the nitrite ester is formed its degradation to lower alkyl radicals seems to be quite rapid. Equation (4) is quite rapid compared to (1).

Quoting from this paper, "The best means of controlling degradation is derivable from Equations (4), (5), (6), and (7). The extent to which oxygen enters the system determines to a marked degree the amount of degradation that occurs. Elimination of added oxygen or air would appear to be desirable for this reason. However, oxygen is added to increase the rate of formation of alkyl radicals. A high rate of alkyl radical formation is necessary to maintain a proper balance of $\cdot NO_2$ radicals. The latter do not remain unchanged very long at nitration temperatures and dissociate to NO $+ 1/2O_2$ if sufficient alkyl radicals are not present. These arguments are based on the assumption that the actual nitration step involves the combination of alkyl radicals with $\cdot NO_2$ radicals. If, instead, the principal nitration step involves the reaction of alkyl radicals with nitric acid molecules, then the rate of formation of alkyl radicals becomes even more important, because the rate of dissociation of nitric acid is much greater than the rate of dissociation of $\cdot NO_2$ radicals under vapor phase nitration conditions. In either event oxygen is observed to increase both the conversions and the degree of degradation. Oxygen is therefore not a good catalyst for nitrations in which a high yield of nitro derivatives of the hydrocarbon nitrated is desired."

Reactions of Nitroparaffins

The nitroparaffins are very reactive compounds and undergo most of the normal reactions of the nitro group. In addition, nitroparaffins having *alpha* hydrogen atoms exist as tautomeric mixtures

$$RCH_2NO_2 \rightleftharpoons RCH{=}NO_2H$$

in which the position of equilibrium depends upon the pH of the solution. Thus primary and secondary nitroparaffins form salts with metal hydroxides which are water soluble

$$RCH_2NO_2 + NaOH \longrightarrow RCH{=}NO_2Na + H_2O$$

The hydrogen atoms *alpha* to the nitro group are reactive and undergo reactions typical of active hydrogen compounds.

Hydrogenation of Nitroparaffins. Many reagents have been found for the successful reduction of nitroparaffins to alkyl amines. These include tin and hydrochloric acid,[53] zinc and sulfuric or hydrochloric acid,[16,54] zinc and acetic acid,[55] iron and hydrochloric acid[56] and sodium amalgam with water or alcohol.[57] Catalytic hydrogenation in the presence of nickel, copper, palladium or platinum is also successful in either the vapor or liquid phase.[58,59]

Johnson[60] reported that iron and hydrochloric acid was the most satisfactory of all the chemical reducing agents for the reduction of nitroparaffins to alkylamines. Johnson and Degering[61] obtained excellent results by the catalytic hydrogenation of nitroparaffins under pressure using a Raney nickel catalyst.

On a commercial scale, Senkus[62] reports that material costs for reduction with iron and sulfuric acid and for Raney nickel catalyzed hydrogenation are comparable.

The selective reduction of nitroparaffins to hydroxylamines and oximes is also possible. Alkylhydroxylamines can be isolated as by-products from any of the processes for the reduction of nitro compounds to amines. In 1891, Meyer and Hoffmann[6] obtained methylhydroxylamine by the reduction of nitromethane with tin and hydrochloric acid. Three years later, Bamberger[64] obtained the same compound by refluxing nitromethane with zinc dust and water. In this case no measurable quantities of methylamine or ammonia were obtained. Beckman[65] and Scheiber[66] accomplished the same thing using zinc dust and an aqueous solution of ammonium chloride.

Nitroparaffins can be converted to hydroxylamines by catalytic hydrogenation. Traube and Schulz[67] hydrogenated nitromethane and some nitro alcohols to the corresponding hydroxylamines in the presence of a palladinized barium sulfate catalyst.

Addition of sodium to a solution of nitroparaffin in liquid ammonia in the presence of ammonium bromide causes evolution of hydrogen and the reduction of the nitroparaffin to the corresponding hydroxylamine. Thus nitroethane is reduced to ethylhydroxylamine.[68]

Electrolytic reduction has also proved successful. Pierron[69] reduced nitromethane, nitroethane and 1-nitropropane to hydroxylamines by the electrolysis of a 10–15 per cent alcoholic solution of the nitroparaffins containing sulfuric acid. Pierron used a nickel cathode in contact with the solution and a platinum anode in sulfuric acid separated by a porous pot. The current density at the cathode was 0.4–0.75 amps/cm^2 at a temperature of 15–20°C. Yields are 65–80 per cent. At 70°C amines are produced in about the same yields.

When concentrated hydrochloric acid is used, the main products are aldehyde and hydroxylamine.

Nitromethane, 1-nitropropane and 2-Nitropropane are reduced to N-methylhydroxylamine, N-propylhydroxylamine and N-isopropylhydroxylamine respectively at an amalgamated lead catholyte at a temperature of 5°C. Current efficiencies of 80 per cent are obtained.[70] Appreciable quantities of alkylamines are also formed.

The reduction of nitroparaffins to oximes has been reported by a number of investigators.[60,61,71,72,73] Johnson and Degering[61] reduced the nitroparaffins to oximes in 53 per cent yield with zinc dust and glacial acetic acid. The oxime formed is hydrolyzed and the yield estimated from the recovered aldehyde.

Nitroparaffins are reduced to the corresponding oxime by adding a mixture of the sodium salt of the aci-nitroparaffin in aqueous sodium hydroxide and a metal such as magnesium, iron or zinc to sulfuric or hydrochloric acid.[74] Thus nitroethane in 10 per cent sodium hydroxide solution together with powdered magnesium are added to 3 per cent sulfuric acid at 20°C. The pH is held constant at 1 during the reaction. The acetaldoxime ($CH_3CH{=}NOH$) formed is extracted with benzene to give a yield of about 68 per cent.

The conversion of nitroparaffins to aldehydes and hydroxylamines can also be accomplished by adding a salt of the aci-nitroparaffin to a strong acid in the absence of a reducing agent.

Action of Mineral Acids. When salts of nitroparaffins are warmed with concentrated mineral acids they are converted to carboxylic acids and hydroxylamine salts.

$$CH_3CH{=}NO_2Na + 2H_2SO_4 \longrightarrow CH_3COOH + H_3NOH \cdot HSO_4 +$$

$$NaHSO_4 + H_2O$$

Lippincott and Hass[75] converted nitroparaffins into carboxylic acids and hydroxylamine by the action of 85 per cent sulfuric acid. Thus equimolar amounts of nitroethane and 85 per cent sulfuric acid were refluxed for a few minutes and as the boiling subsides the mixture was again heated for 8 hours during which time the temperature rose to 117°C. The product contained acetic acid formed in 90 per cent yield, hydroxylammonium sulfate formed in 88 per cent yield and ammonium sulfate.

More concentrated sulfuric acid can be used with a corresponding decrease in the reaction time.

In a similar manner propionic acid is obtained from 1-nitropropane, butyric acid from 1-nitrobutane and isobutyric acid from 2-methyl-1-nitropropane.

Nitronic acids, $RCH{=}NO_2H$, are considered to be intermediates in the reaction. This is supported by Lowry and Magson[76] who have reported that acids serve as catalysts for the establishment of the equilibrium between the two tautomeric forms of the nitroparaffin.

It has also been suggested that hydroxamic acids are intermediates in the reaction.[77] In support of this suggestion, Hass and Lippincott,[75] by modifying the conditions somewhat were able to obtain a 44 per cent yield of propionohydroxamic acid from 1-nitropropane. Inasmuch as yields of carboxylic acids in excess of 90 per cent were ultimately obtained in similar experiments, at least part of the hydrolysis must proceed through the hydroxamic acids.

Hydroxamic acids are isolated in approximately 50 per cent yields by adding the nitroparaffin to anhydrous sulfuric acid at 60°C, pouring the product over crushed ice and neutralizing the acid with calcium carbonate. When less concentrated acid is used, the nitroparaffins are converted into aldehydes or ketones. This was first observed by Nef in 1894.[78] Hass[79] reports that yields of aldehydes or ketones of about 85 per cent are obtained by adding the salt of the aci-nitroparaffin to 50 per cent sulfuric acid at room temperature.

$$2RCH{=}NO_2Na + 2H_2SO_4 \longrightarrow 2RCHO + 2NaHSO_4 + N_2O + H_2O$$

$$2R_2C{=}NO_2Na + 2H_2SO_4 \longrightarrow 2R_2CO + 2NaHSO_4 + N_2O + H_2O$$

Johnson and Degering[61] found that calcium salts of the nitronic acids can be used as well as sodium salts. A typical procedure for the reaction is given below: One-sixth of a mole of nitroparaffin dissolved in 150 ml of a solution containing 8 g of sodium hydroxide was added dropwise to an ice-cold mixture of 25 ml of concentrated sulfuric acid in 160 ml of water. Efficient agitation is used during the addition. The aldehyde or ketone is recovered by distillation.

Nitrous Acid. Primary and secondary nitroparaffins react with nitrous acid by replacement of one of the *alpha* hydrogen atoms with a nitroso group. Tertiary nitro compounds having no *alpha* hydrogens do not react. Inasmuch as different, easily distinguishable products are obtained in each case, the reaction serves as a means of distinguishing among the three types of nitroparaffins.

Primary nitroparaffins react with nitrous acid to give nitrolic acids whose salts are red.

$$RCH_2NO_2 + HONO \longrightarrow \left[RCH{<}^{NO}_{NO_2} \right] \longrightarrow R{-}C{<}^{NOH}_{NO_2}$$

Nitrolic acid

Secondary nitroparaffins give pseudonitroles which are blue

$$R_2CHNO_2 + HONO \longrightarrow R_2C{<}^{NO}_{NO_2}$$

Pseudonitrole

Tertiary nitroparaffins do not react so the solution remains colorless

The salts of the nitrolic acids are bright red, even in solution, and are explosive when they are dry. Nitrolic acids when treated with strong acids give polymers of nitrile oxides, $R—C\equiv N\rightarrow O$. Treatment with concentrated sulfuric acid results in the formation of carboxylic acids.[80,81]

The pseudonitroles behave like typical nitroso compounds. They are blue in solution but the crystalline forms are colorless because of the formation of dimers.

Action of Bases. The acidic nature of primary and secondary nitroparaffins has already been described. Tertiary nitroparaffins, having no *alpha* hydrogen atoms, can not form salts with bases. Maron and LaMer[82] investigated the kinetics of neutralization of nitromethane, nitroethane and 2-nitropropane in water and in deuterium oxide. Maron and Shedlovsky[83] reported a value of 4×10^{-5} for the ionization constant of aci-nitroethane at 23°C.

Nitromethane, in contrast with other nitroparaffins, behaves somewhat differently. Sodium or potassium hydroxide converts nitromethane into salts of methazonic acid.[84,85] The reaction involves the loss of water from two molecules of nitromethane, one of which is in the aci-salt form.

$$\underset{NO_2K}{\overset{CH_2}{|}} + \underset{H}{\overset{CH_2NO_2}{|}} \longrightarrow \underset{HO \diagdown \quad \diagup OK}{\overset{CH_2—CH_2NO_2}{\underset{N}{|}}} \longrightarrow HON{=}CHCH{=}NO_2K \;+\; H_2O$$

A molecule of nitromethane probably adds to the potassium salt to give an intermediate which loses water and rearranges to the potassium salt of methazonic acid.

On further treatment with a strong base, methazonic acid is converted to nitroacetic acid.[86]

$$HON{=}CHCH{=}NO_2K \xrightarrow{-H_2O} N{\equiv}C—CH—NO_2K \xrightarrow[H_2O]{KOH} KOOC—CH{=}NO_2K$$

$$\xrightarrow{H^+} HOOC—CH_2NO_2$$

The sodium salt of nitroacetic acid can be obtained in one operation by dropping nitromethane into a 50 per cent aqueous solution of sodium hydroxide at 50°C, then refluxing the solution for 10 minutes and cooling. The free acid is obtained by suspending the finely divided salt in ether and acidifying with hydrochloric acid.

Nitroparaffins other than nitromethane react with bases to give isoxazoles. Lippincott[87] isolated a β-dioxime from the reaction and proposed that the isoxazoles are formed according to the following scheme:

$$RCH_2NO_2 \rightleftharpoons RCH=NO_2H$$

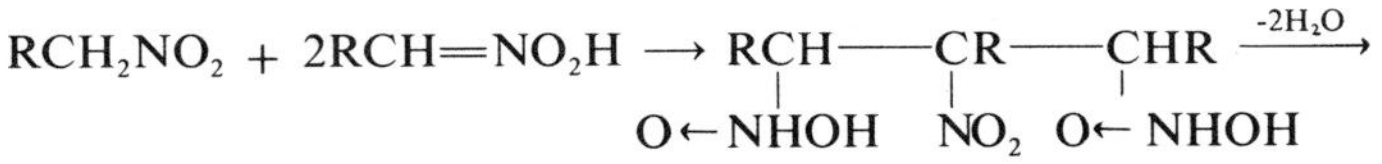

$$RCH_2NO_2 + 2RCH=NO_2H \longrightarrow \underset{O \leftarrow NHOH}{RCH} \underset{NO_2}{-CR} \underset{O \leftarrow NHOH}{-CHR} \xrightarrow{-2H_2O}$$

$$RCH(NO_2)-RCNO_2-CH(R)NO_2 \xrightarrow[-HONO_2]{H_2O} RC(=NOH)-CHR-C(=NOH)R$$

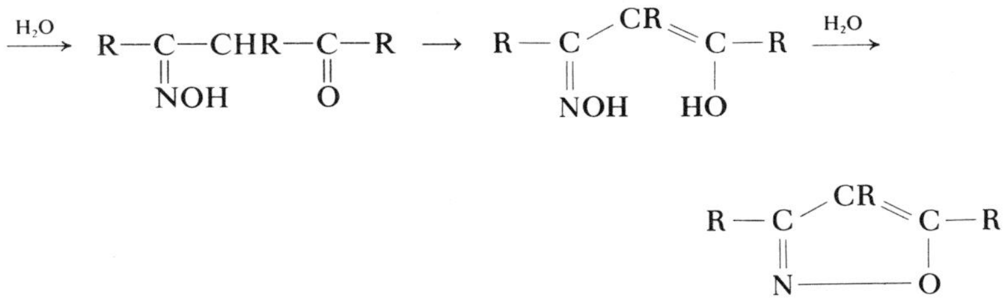

$$\xrightarrow{H_2O} \underset{NOH}{R-C}-CHR-\underset{O}{C-R} \longrightarrow R-\underset{NOH}{C}\overset{CR}{\diagup}\diagdown\underset{HO}{C-R} \xrightarrow{H_2O}$$

$$R-C\overset{CR}{\diagup}\diagdown C-R$$
$$N \underline{\hspace{2cm}} O$$

Halogenation. Nitroparaffins may be halogenated in either the normal or aci-form to give different products. Tscherniak[88] obtained a mono-chloronitromethane by adding the dry sodium salt of nitromethane to chlorine water. Chlorination of nitromethane to give chloropicrin, Cl_3CNO_2, has been accomplished by Ramage[89] in the presence of an aqueous suspension of calcium carbonate. The yields are almost quantitative. The same product was obtained by Vanderbilt[90] using an alkali or alkaline earth hypochlorite.

Henry[91] obtained the monochloro derivative of nitroethane, 1-nitropropane and 2-nitropropane by bubbling chlorine gas into an aqueous solution of the sodium salt of the nitroparaffin. The chlorination occurs on the same carbon atom to which the nitro group is attached.

Strickland[92,93] found that with the exception of chloronitromethane, the monochloride can be converted smoothly into the dichloride in good yields. The conversion of nitroparaffins to dichlorides can be accomplished in one operation by using 2 moles of chlorine to 1 of nitroparaffin.

Reaction of bromine with an aci-nitroparaffin or a salt of an aci-nitroparaffin is so rapid that the reaction has served as a method for determining the amount of the aci form in a tautomeric mixture with the normal nitroparaffin.[94] The bromine is found on the same carbon atom to which the nitro group is attached.

Direct iodination of nitroparaffins is accomplished using iodine and potassium hydroxide.[95,96]

The chlorination of nitroparaffins in the presence of bases probably proceeds by the addition of halogen to the nitronic acid or the salt of the nitronic acid followed by liberation of the hydrogen halide or metal halide

$$RCH{=}NO_2H + Cl_2 \longrightarrow \underset{\underset{Cl}{|} \quad \underset{Cl}{|}}{RCH{-}NO_2H} \longrightarrow \underset{\underset{Cl}{|}}{RCH{-}NO_2} + HCl$$

In the absence of bases but in the presence of phosphorus pentoxide and intense illumination, bromine gives the same products obtained in the presence of a base.[97] On the other hand chlorine attacks carbon atoms other than the one to which the nitro group is attached. Thus nitroethane gives almost exclusively 2-chloro-1-nitroethane; 1-nitropropane yields 2-chloro-1-nitropropane and 3-chloro-1-nitropropane; 2-nitropropane yields 1-chloro-2-nitropropane; nitrobutane gives a mixture of 2-, 3- and 4-monochloroderivatives.

Hass[98] suggested that the differences in the products obtained may be explained as follows: Chlorination proceeds by two competing mechanisms.

$$CH_3CH_2NO_2 \xrightarrow[h\nu]{Cl_2} CH_2Cl{-}CH_2NO_2 + HCl$$
$$\downarrow H^+$$
$$CH_3CH{=}NO_2H \xrightarrow{Cl_2} \underset{\underset{Cl}{|} \quad \underset{Cl}{|}}{CH_3CH{-}NO_2H} \xrightarrow{-HCl} CH_3CHClNO_2$$

Water in the presence of hydrogen chloride is a source of hydrogen (or hydronium) ions which would favor the tautomerism of the nitroparaffin to the nitronic acid. Phosphorus pentoxide would inhibit this. The presence of water therefore would favor substitution on the *alpha* carbon atom. Bromine substitutes much less rapidly than chlorine but adds to double bonds more readily. Consequently, relative to chlorine, the second mechanism is more probable for bromination even though the rate of tautomerism is less rapid.

Condensation with Aldehydes. Nitroparaffins having *alpha* hydrogen atoms react with aldehydes or ketones in the presence of bases to give nitro alcohols. Thus nitromethane having three *alpha* hydrogens reacts with one, two or three molecules of formaldehyde.

$$CH_3NO_2 + HCHO \longrightarrow HOCH_2CH_2NO_2 \xrightarrow{HCHO} (HOCH_2)_2CHNO_2$$

$$\xrightarrow{HCHO} (HOCH_2)_3CNO_2$$

This is a condensation of the aldol type in which the base promotes the formation of a nitronate ion $[CH_2{=}NO_2^{(-)} \leftrightarrow {}^{(-)}CH_2{-}NO_2]$ which attacks the aldehyde as indicated

$$^-CH_2NO_2 + HCHO \xrightarrow[-H_2O]{OH^-} O_2NCH_2CH_2O^- \xrightarrow{H_2O} O_2NCH_2CH_2OH + OH^-$$

Kamlet reports an unusually fast condensation between the sodium bisulfite addition product of the aldehyde and the sodium salt of the aci-nitroparaffin.[99] This would be expected on the basis of the above mechanism.

Boileau[100] describes a method for the preparation of trimethylolnitromethane taking advantage of its insolubility in benzene. Paraformaldehyde and a small amount of sodium sulfite is added to benzene and the mixture is heated on a water bath. Nitromethane is introduced at a rate which will maintain reflux. The triol precipitates as a liquid which solidifies on standing.

The addition of acetaldehyde to a dispersion of nitromethane in water in the presence of catalytic amounts of potassium carbonate (pH 7.5–8.0) and heating the mixture for 3–6 hours at 50°C gives a mixture of $CH_3CH(OH)CH_2NO_2$ and $(CH_3CHOH)_2CHNO_2$ in about 80 per cent yield.[101] A similar procedure is described by Hurd and Nilson.[102]

A large number of compounds are effective basic catalysts for the condensation. These include sodium and potassium hydroxides, carbonates, bicarbonates, methoxides and organic amines. Vanderbilt and Hass[103] favor the use of calcium hydroxide because it is easily removed from the reaction mixture by conversion to insoluble calcium salts. Schmidle and Mansfield[104] and Astle and Abbott[105] reported that anion exchange resins are effective catalysts for the condensation of nitroparaffins with aldehydes.

The rate of reaction varies considerably with the structure of both the nitroparaffin and the aldehyde. Nitromethane and formaldehyde are both highly reactive but the rate decreases with increasing size of both types of molecules. Even with nitromethane and formaldehyde there is a tendency for the reaction to stop when only one or two molecules of formaldehyde have reacted. Secondary nitroparaffins react much more sluggishly than primary nitroparaffins and tertiary nitroparaffins do not react at all. Nitroolefins are formed in small amounts and these tend to polymerize to form tars.

Astle and Abbott used two different anion exchange resins which differ in basic strength. "Amberlite" IRA-400 is a polystyrene resin containing quaternaryammonium hydroxide groups which makes it as strong a base as sodium or potassium hydroxide. Amberlite IR-4B contains secondary and tertiary amino groups and therefore is a much weaker base. The condensations were carried out in ethanol solutions at about 30°C. Nitromethane, nitroethane and 2-nitropropane were condensed with formaldehyde, propionaldehyde, *n*-butyraldehyde, isobutyraldehyde, heptaldehyde and benzaldehyde. The expected nitro alcohols were obtained in each case.

These aldehydes condensed with nitromethane in the presence of "Amberlite" IRA-400 in 35 to 70 per cent conversions with the exception of formaldehyde which reacted to the extent of only 16 per cent. "Amberlite" IR-4B was not an effective catalyst. In no case was any detectable amount of resin formed.

Condensations of these aldehydes with nitroethane proceeded in much the same way with slightly smaller conversions. "Amberlite" IRA-400 again was the best catalyst except for the butyraldehydes which gave higher conversions to nitro alcohols with "Amberlite" IR-4B.

"Amberlite" IR-4B was also a better catalyst for the condensation of the aldehydes with 2-nitropropane. Conversions were somewhat lower than with nitromethane and nitroethane. Formaldehyde was an exception in that better conversions were obtained in the presence of "Amberlite" IRA-400.

Conversion of acetone and cyclohexanone with nitromethane were low amounting to 19 per cent after 15 hours and 27 per cent after one week, respectively. The weak base resins would not promote these condensations.

Ketones condense satisfactorily with nitroparaffins in the presence of sodium alkoxides. Thus Kozlow, Fink and Liorber[106] added nitroethane and acetone to a 5 per cent solution of sodium methoxide in methanol and the mixture was shaken for 30 hours at room temperature. A 21 per cent yield of $(CH_3)_2C(OH)CH(CH_3)NO_2$ was obtained.

Other compounds prepared in this way are shown in Table 8–3.

TABLE 8–3. CONDENSATION OF NITROPARAFFINS WITH KETONES IN THE PRESENCE OF SODIUM METHOXIDE

Nitroparaffin	Ketone	Product	Yield (%)
Nitromethane	Acetone	$(CH_3)_2C(OH)CH_2NO_2$	37
Nitroethane	Acetone	$(CH_3)_2C(OH)CH(CH_3)NO_2$	21
1-Nitropropane	Acetone	$(CH_3)_2C(OH)CH(CH_2CH_3)NO_2$	20
2-Nitropropane	Acetone	$(CH_3)_2C(OH)C(CH_3)_2NO_2$	19
Nitromethane	Methyl ethyl ketone	$(CH_3CH_2)C(OH)CH_2NO_2$ $\quad\quad\vert$ $\quad\quad CH_3$	24
Nitromethane	Cyclopentanone	$(CH_2)_4C(OH)CH_2NO_2$	42
Nitromethane	Cyclohexanone	$(CH_2)_5C(OH)CH_2NO_2$	85
Nitroethane	Cyclohexanone	$(CH_2)_5C(OH)CH(CH_3)NO_2$	53
2-Nitropropane	Cyclohexanone	$(CH_2)_5C(OH)C(CH_3)_2NO_2$	45
1-Nitropropane	Cyclohexanone	$(CH_2)_5C(OH)CH(C_2H_5)NO_2$	39

The nitro alcohols are of considerable technological importance. Esters with nitric acid are excellent explosives. Trihydroxymethylnitromethane is nitrated at 0–20°C with 100 per cent nitric acid in sulfuric acid.

$$(HOCH_2)_3CNO_2 + 3HNO_3 \longrightarrow (O_2NOCH_2)_3CNO_2 + 3H_2O$$

This compound has perfect oxygen balance, is less sensitive to shock and has 7 per cent more explosive power than glycerol trinitrate.[107] The dinitrate of 2-methyl-2-nitro-1,3-propanediol has also been patented as an explosive.[108]

Esters of organic acids and the nitro alcohols are prepared by the action of the acid anhydrides, acid chlorides or in some cases the acids themselves. These esters are of interest as plasticizers.[109]

The reduction of the nitro alcohols gives hydroxyamines which form soaps with fatty acids which are effective emulsifying agents. The amino alcohols commercially available include $(HOCH_2)_3CNH_2$, $(HOCH_2)_2CH$-$(CH_3)NH_2$.

Mannich Reaction. Amines, formaldehyde and nitroparaffins undergo a Mannich type reaction to give nitroamines. Senkus[110] reacted formaldehyde, primary amines and primary or secondary nitroparaffins to give nitroamines. Thus formaldehyde, isopropylamine and 2-nitropropane give a 76 per cent yield of N-(2-nitro-2-methylbutyl)-isopropylamine at room temperature. Other nitroamines formed in this way are shown in Table 8–4.

Johnson[111] prepared, in a similar manner, a series of nitroamines utilizing secondary amines.

TABLE 8–4. NITROAMINES MADE FROM FORMALDEHYDE USING THE
MANNICH REACTION

Nitroparaffin	Amine	Product	Conv. (%)
2-Nitropropane	Methylamine	N-(2-Nitroisobutyl)-methylamine	48
Nitroethane	Isopropylamine	2-Nitro-2-methyl-1,3-diisopropylaminopropane	71
2-Nitrobutane	Isopropylamine	N-(2-Nitro-2-methylbutyl) isopropylamine	90
2-Nitropropane	Butylamine	N-(2-nitroisobutyl)-butylamine	85
2-Nitropropane	Benzylamine	N-(2-nitroisobutyl)-benzylamine	75

No reaction was observed with an aromatic amine, formaldehyde and a nitroparaffin because of the low basic strength of the arylamines.[112] A reaction was observed, however, in the presence of a strong base. Even in the presence of strong bases some arylamines do not undergo reactions. For example, no reaction was observed with diphenylamine or aminoanthroquinones under any conditions.

Most aromatic amines react with formaldehyde and primary or secondary nitroparaffins according to the equation

$$C_6H_5NH_2 + HCHO + (CH_3)_2CHNO_2 \longrightarrow C_6H_5NHCH_2C(CH_3)_2NO_2 + H_2O$$

$$2C_6H_5NH_2 + HCHO + CH_3CH_2NO_2 \longrightarrow C_6H_5NHCH_2\overset{\overset{\displaystyle CH_3}{|}}{\underset{\underset{\displaystyle NO_2}{|}}{C}}CH_2NHC_6H_5 + 2h_2O$$

Two procedures are used for the preparation of nitroamines. In the first the amine, formaldehyde and the nitroparaffin are mixed and permitted to react, and in the second the nitro alcohol is first formed from the nitroparaffin and formaldehyde and this product is then reacted with the amine.

Secondary aromatic amines do not undergo the reaction unless one of the groups is alkyl.

A patent issued to Senkus[113] describes the preparation of nitroalkylamines by a Mannich reaction on a nitroparaffin and the hydrogenation of these compounds to give diamines. Thus 2-nitropropane, formaldehyde and ammonia give 2-nitroisobutylamine. Hydrogenation in the presence of Raney nickel at 30–50°C under a pressure of 500 psi gives a diamine which is useful as an intermediate for the preparation of surface active agents.

Urbanski and Kolinske[114] investigated a Mannich reaction involving nitroparaffins and ethylene diamine. Thus a mixture of 1-nitropropane, formaldehyde and ethylene diamine reacts spontaneously at room temperature to give a resinous product from which 3,7-dinitro-3,7-diethyl-1,5-diazabicyclo[3.3.2]decane is obtained by recrystallization.

Olefin Oxides. Ufer[115] reported that the reaction of nitroparaffins with olefin oxides in the presence of alkaline catalysts at temperatures of 0–100°C gives oximes. Superatmospheric pressures may be used. Nitrocyclohexane treated with ethylene oxide in alcohol containing sodium methoxide and potassium carbonate at temperatures of 0–10°C gives a 70 per cent yield of cyclohexanoneoxime.

Donat[116] found that pyridine behaves differently from other basic catalysts in the reaction of nitroparaffins with olefin oxides. At room temperature, nitromethane reacted with ethylene or propylene oxides to give 1-(2-hydroxyalkyl)-pyridinium nitrite as the major product. Other products formed were tars and a trace of the expected nitro alcohol.

Nitroethane is somewhat more reactive than nitromethane and gives, with ethylene oxide, 3,4,5-trimethylisoxazole as the major product together with 1-(2-hydroxyethyl)pyridinium nitrite.

Secondary nitroparaffins such as 2-nitropropane and 2-nitrobutane are still more reactive. 2-Nitropropane and ethylene oxide gives 1-(2-hydroxyethyl)pyridinium nitrite, 3-nitro-3-methyl-1-butanol, 2,3-dinitro-2,3-di-methylbutane, acetone, acetoneoxime and tars.

Other bases were not particularly effective in promoting a reaction between nitroparaffins and olefin oxides.

Grignard Reagents. Nitroethane reacts with one mole of ethyl magnesium bromide at 0°C to form a solid complex which precipitates from solution. With the addition of two additional moles of Grignard reagent, the complex largely dissolves and one mole of gas, probably ethane, is evolved. The reaction is relatively slow and requires heating to drive it to completion and one mole of Grignard reagent remains. The main liquid product is diethylhydroxylamine. The first step in the reaction is therefore the addition of the Grignard reagent to the nitrogen-oxygen bond

$$CH_3CH_2NO_2 + CH_3CH_2MgBr \longrightarrow (CH_3CH_2)_2\underset{\underset{O}{\downarrow}}{N}\text{—}OMgBr$$

which is reduced to the hydroxylamine by a mechanism which is not understood. Similar products are obtained from 2-nitropropane and 2-nitrobutane.[117]

Addition to Activated Double Bonds. Certain unsaturated aldehydes react with nitroparaffins to give nitroaldehydes rather than the nitro alcohols obtained by the aldol condensation. These aldehydes containing a terminal CH_2=C group conjugated with the carbonyl double bond, such as acrolein or methacrolein, are especially reactive and add primary or secondary nitroparaffins readily.[118] The reactions are usually carried out in alcohol solutions containing basic catalysts.[119] Polymerization of the aldehyde is inhibited by the presence of hydroquinone.

Schecter[120] reacted nitromethane, nitroethane and 2-nitropropane with acrolein and methyl vinyl ketone to give the corresponding nitrocarbonyl compounds which may be reduced to nitro alcohols with aluminum isopropoxide.

$$CH_3NO_2 + CH_2{=}CH\text{—}CHO \longrightarrow O_2NCH_2CH_2CH_2CHO$$

$$CH_3NO_2 + H_2C{=}CH\text{—}CO\text{—}CH_3 \longrightarrow O_2NCH_2CH_2CH_2COCH_3$$

Nitromethane adds across the double bond of styryl isopropyl ketone by letting a methanol solution of the reactants, containing a little diethylamine, stand for 15 days. The yield of product is 70 per cent.

$$C_6H_5CH{=}CHCOCH(CH_3)_2 + CH_3NO_2 \longrightarrow \underset{\underset{CH_2NO_2}{\mid}}{C_6H_5CHCH_2COCH(CH_3)_2}$$

Nitromethane adds across the carbon-nitrogen double bond of benzalaniline by refluxing for 6 hours. The yield of the indicated product is 60 per cent.

$$C_6H_5CH=NC_6H_5 + CH_3NO_2 \longrightarrow \underset{\underset{CH_2NO_2}{|}}{C_6H_5CHNHC_6H_5}$$

Nitroparaffins add to the double bond of unsaturated esters. Thus nitroparaffins add to methyl acrylate.[121]

$$CH_3NO_2 + CH_2=CH-COOCH_3 \longrightarrow O_2NCH_2CH_2CH_2COOCH_3$$

Amines are effective catalysts for the reaction. Nitroparaffins (3 moles) react with diethylfumarate (1 mole) in the presence of diethylamine (1 mole) at 30°C to give the corresponding nitroalkylidene succinic ester in good yield.

Ethylnitroacetate, in anhydrous 20 per cent alcoholic potassium hydroxide, reacts with acrylonitrile at 10°C to give ethyl-2-nitro-4-cyanobutyrate in fair yield.[122]

1,5-Dinitropentane reacts with methyl vinyl ketone in the presence of a sodium hydroxide catalyst to give a di-addition product.[123]

$$CH_3CO(CH_2)_2CH(NO_2)(CH_2)_3CH(NO_2)(CH_2)_2COCH_3$$

A maximum yield of 25 per cent is obtained when the reaction is carried out in 90 per cent alcohol for 20 hours at 50°C.

Certain nitroparaffins react with vinyl pyridine to give pyridylnitroalkanes. Nitromethane did not react with 2-vinylpyridine but nitroethane refluxed for 3 hours in *tert.*-butyl alcohol containing Triton B gives a 14 per cent yield of 2-nitro-4-(2-pyridyl)butane.[124] 1-Nitropropane and 2-nitropropane give a 40 and a 71 per cent yield of the corresponding pyridylnitroalkane. 4-Vinylpyridine and 2-vinyl-6-methylpyridine behave in a similar manner.

Miscellaneous Reactions. An aqueous solution containing an *aci*-salt of a secondary nitroparaffin and an equimolar amount of sodium azide added to concentrated sulfuric acid give an N-substituted amide with a ketone and ketoxime as by-products.[125] Thus 2-nitropropane and sodium azide give a 44 per cent yield of N-methylacetamide and 4-nitroheptane gives a 62 per cent yield of N-propylbutyramide. The over-all reaction may be a combination of the Nef and Schmidt reactions.

2-Nitropropane is oxidized by air to give acetone and nitrite ion.[126] The reaction is autocatalytic in the presence of an aqueous base at room temperature. The oxidation is catalyzed by the addition of ferric ion and is completely inhibited by arsenic trioxide.

NITROOLEFINS

Preparation of Nitroolefins

One of the most widely used methods for the preparation of nitroolefins involves the dehydration of nitro alcohols obtained by the condensation of aldehydes with nitroparaffins. The dehydrations have been carried out in the presence of acid catalysts such as phosphoric acid, or potassium or sodium bisulfate. Temperatures of 25–40°C must be used for the preparation of nitroethylene or nitropropylene to prevent polymer formation. With higher derivatives, temperatures as high as 125°C are desirable.

Nitroethylene is prepared from β-nitroethanol by permitting the alcohol to stand at room temperature for 3 days in the presence of phosphoric acid.[127] Considerable polymerization occurs under these conditions but if potassium bisulfate is used as the catalyst the polymerization is suppressed.

A 66 per cent yield of nitroethylene has been obtained by heating the nitro alcohol with phthalic anhydride at 140–150°C under a pressure of 80 mm.[128] Similarly 2-nitro-1-propanol gives 2-nitro-1-propene and 1-nitro-2-propanol gives 1-nitro-1-propene.

Higher molecular weight nitro alcohols are also dehydrated successfully to nitroolefins with phthalic anhydride.[129] Thus 1-nitro-1-octene is prepared in 80 per cent yield by heating 1-nitro-2-octanol with acetic anhydride at 100°C for 8 hours.

Nitroolefins have been prepared by the vapor phase pyrolysis of acetates of the nitro alcohols.[130,131,132] The nitroacetate is passed over a catalyst such as silica gel, aluminum sulfate, aluminum phosphate or zinc chloride at temperatures of 200–500°C. Yields are 75–95 per cent. As an example, 1-nitro-1-propene is prepared by passing 2-nitro-1-methylethylacetate over a catalyst consisting of 90 per cent calcium phosphate and 10 per cent magnesium phosphate at 285°C with a reaction time of 18 minutes. The reaction is limited to acetylated nitro alcohols having no more than 8 carbon atoms in the molecule. As an alternate procedure the nitroolefins can be prepared by refluxing for 8 hours the appropriate nitroacetate in a 0.5 normal solution of sodium carbonate in methanol. Reported yields are 90–95 per cent.[133]

Nitroolefins are formed from compounds having two nitro groups, a nitro and a nitrate group, or a nitro and a nitrite group on adjacent carbon atoms by reaction with basic reagents such as ammonia, ammonium carbonate or sodium hydroxide in aqueous or non-aqueous solutions.[134,135] In some cases, merely refluxing with methanol in the absence of a catalyst is sufficient.[136] Low temperatures (0–15°C) and short reaction times are employed so that polymerization tendencies are greatly reduced. As an illustration, 2,4,4-trimethyl-1,2-dinitropentane treated with ammonia at 10°C gives a 77 per cent yield of 2,4,4-trimethyl-1-nitro-1-pentene and 2-methyl-1,2-dinitropropane gives 2-methyl-1-nitro-1-propene in 83 per cent yield.

Certain olefins (isobutylene, 2-ethyl-1-hexene, 1-octene and cyclohexene) have been nitrated by refluxing for 2–3 hours with 70–80 per cent nitric acid at 60–70°C.[137,138] If the temperature is allowed to get as high as 90–100°C a complex mixture of nitro derivatives is obtained.

α-Nitroolefins are prepared conveniently by the pyrolysis of amine hydrochlorides prepared by reacting a nitroparaffin with a Mannich base. Thus 2-nitropropene is made by the following sequence of reactions:

$$R_2NH + HCHO \longrightarrow R_2NCH_2OH \tag{1}$$

$$R_2NCH_2OH + CH_3CH_2NO_2 \longrightarrow CH_3\underset{\underset{NO_2}{|}}{C}HCH_2NR_2 + H_2O \tag{2}$$

$$CH_3\underset{\underset{NO_2}{|}}{C}HCH_2NR_2 \cdot HCl \xrightarrow{\text{heat}} CH_3\underset{\underset{NO_2}{|}}{C}{=}CH_2 + R_2NH_2Cl \tag{3}$$

Pyrolysis of the free amine gives rise to polymers and reaction products of the amine and the nitroolefin. These reactions can be suppressed by using the amine hydrochloride.

Using boron trifluoride complexes of the Mannich bases reduces the pyrolysis temperatures as much as 100°C and therefore decreases the amount of by-products formed.[139] Yields are as high as 80–90 per cent.

Bachman and Atwood[140] used this procedure for the preparation of gamma-dinitro compounds. Nitroparaffins and formaldehyde were heated in the presence of a basic catalyst. Best yields (about 30 per cent) were obtained when secondary amines were used as catalysts. The following mechanism was proposed:

$$R_2NH + HCHO + RCH_2NO_2 \longrightarrow R\underset{\underset{NO_2}{|}}{C}H{-}CH_2NR_2 \xrightarrow{-R_2NH}$$

$$R\underset{\underset{NO_2}{|}}{C}{=}CH_2 \xrightarrow{RCH_2NO_2} R\underset{\underset{NO_2}{|}}{C}HCH_2\underset{\underset{NO_2}{|}}{C}HR$$

However, a carefully purified tertiary amine and sodium carbonate also catalyze the reaction, so that at least in these cases, a different mechanism is required. The intermediate nitroolefin is probably obtained by the catalytic dehydration of the Mannich base.

$$RCH_2NO_2 + HCHO \longrightarrow RCH(NO_2)CH_2OH \xrightarrow{-H_2O} RC(NO_2)=CH_2$$

The relative ease of splitting out the secondary amine, compared to water, to form the nitroolefin probably accounts for the more effective use of secondary amines as catalysts.

Secondary and tertiary nitroparaffins do not undergo this reaction because they are incapable of forming nitroolefin intermediates.

Replacement of formaldehyde by acetaldehyde gives none of the expected gamma-dinitroparaffin. Some of the dinitroparaffins obtained are shown in Table 8-5.

TABLE 8-5. PREPARATION OF SOME DINITROPARAFFINS

	Yield (%)
$(CH_3CHNO_2)_2CH_2$	4
$(CH_3CH_2CHNO_2)_2CH_2$	20
$[(CH_3)_2CHCH_2CHNO_2]_2CH_2$	16
$(n\text{-}C_6H_{13}CHNO_2)_2CH_2$	13

The reactions were carried out at reflux temperatures and several hours were required to obtain satisfactory yields.

Aromatic aldehydes react with nitroparaffins in the presence of amines and a base to give nitroolefins.

$$ArCHO + RNH_2 \longrightarrow ArCH=NR + H_2O$$

$$ArCH=NR + RCH_2NO_2 \longrightarrow RNH_2 + ArCH=C(NO_2)R$$

ω-Nitrostyrene has been prepared from benzaldehyde and nitromethane in the presence of an amine and alcoholic potassium hydroxide,[141] or sodium methoxide.[142] This method is limited to those aldehydes in which the carbonyl group is attached directly to the benzene ring.

Reactions of Nitroolefins

Complete reduction of nitroolefins gives alkylamines but oximes are more frequently obtained. Completely anhydrous conditions are apparently required to get reduction to the amine.

Susie[143] reduced nitroolefins with iron turnings and hydrochloric acid and obtained a mixture of the corresponding ketone and ketoxime in 70 per cent yield. Thus 3-nitro-2-pentene is converted to a mixture of 3-pentanone and 3-pentanonoxime. If sufficient hydrochloric acid is used, the ketone is obtained almost exclusively and if only a small quantity of acid is used, the ketoxime is the major product.[144]

Tindall[145] proposes that the first stage of the hydrogenation forms a hydroxylamine which rearranges to the oxime. Under the influence of an acid, the oxime is hydrolyzed to the ketone and part is reduced to the amine.

Ammonia, primary and secondary amines react with α-nitroolefins to give nitroalkylamines.

$$CH_2{=}CHNO_2 + RNH_2 \longrightarrow RNHCH_2CH_2NO_2$$

This is similar to cyanoethylation reactions with acrylonitrile. The compounds formed from ammonia are aliphatic nitroamines which are in general extremely unstable but can be reduced over Raney nickel to diamines.[146] The N-(2-nitroalkyl)arylamines are somewhat more stable but are best isolated as their salts.

1-Nitro-1-propene reacts with ammonia in methanol at 0°C to give a 55 per cent yield of 1-nitro-2-aminopropane in 3 hours.[147]

Primary amines having two active hydrogens will react with two molecules of nitroethylene.[148]

$$CH_3NH_2 + 2CH_2{=}CHNO_2 \longrightarrow (O_2NCH_2CH_2)_2NCH_3$$

Secondary amines on the other hand react with only one molecule of nitroethylene. The reactions are carried out at about 5°C.

Dickey[149] prepared nitroamines by the addition of arylamines to nitroolefins.

$$p\text{-}HOC_6H_4NH_2 + CH_2{=}CHNO_2 \longrightarrow p\text{-}HOC_6H_4NHCH_2CH_2NO_2$$

Nitroolefins react with sodium bisulfite in water solution to give the sodium salt of β-nitroalkanesulfonic acids[150]

$$CH_2{=}CHNO_2 + NaHSO_3 \longrightarrow NaSO_3CH_2CH_2NO_2$$

Reduction gives aminosulfonates which are useful in the preparation of detergents. These reactions all indicate the ease of addition to the carbon-carbon double bond of nitroethylene by nucleophilic reagents.

Nitroolefins undergo Diels Alder reactions with conjugated dienes.[55] Alder, Richert and Windemuth reacted nitroethylene, 1-nitropropene and 1-nitro-1-pentene with cyclopentadiene.

$$\underset{HC\diagdown_{CH}}{\overset{HC\diagup^{CH}}{|}}\!\!\!\diagup CH_2 \;+\; \underset{CHNO_2}{\overset{CHR}{\|}} \;\longrightarrow\; \underset{HC\diagdown_{CH}}{\overset{HC\diagup^{CH}\diagdown CH-R}{\underset{CH_2}{\|}\,|}}\diagup CH-NO_2$$

Butadiene, isoprene and 2,4-hexadiene form similar Diels Alder adducts.

Hydrogen sulfide and mercaptans add to nitroolefins in the presence of a base to give nitromercaptans or nitrothioethers. Temperatures of 0–100°C are used. Examples of this reaction are:

$$2(CH_3)_2C=CHNO_2 + H_2S \xrightarrow[CH_3ONa]{25°C} [(CH_3)_2CHCH(NO_2)]_2S$$

$$\underset{NO_2}{\overset{CH_3C=CH_2}{|}} + CH_3SH \longrightarrow CH_3CH(NO_2)CH_2SCH_3$$

Nitroethers are prepared by the action of alcohols on nitroolefins.

$$CH_2=CHNO_2 + ROH \longrightarrow ROCH_2CH_2NO_2$$

The reactions are carried out at 0–20°C in anhydrous alcohol in the presence of a basic catalyst such as sodium alkoxide.[151,152] Yields are 30–50 per cent.

Salts of nitroparaffins add to nitroolefins to give dinitro compounds. Thus 2-nitropropane and 2-nitro-2-butene added to ethyl alcohol containing sodium ethoxide give 2,4-dinitro-2,3-dimethylpentane.[147,153]

$$CH_3CH(NO_2)CH_3 + \underset{NO_2}{\overset{CH_3C=CHCH_3}{|}} \xrightarrow[C_2H_5OH]{C_2H_5ONa} \underset{CH_3CH_3}{\overset{NO_2\quad NO_2}{\underset{|\quad|}{CH_3C-CH-CHCH_3}}}$$

Hydrogen chloride adds stepwise to α-nitroolefins to give 1,2-dichloronitroso compounds which rearrange, if an α-hydrogen atom is available, to give 1,2-dichlorooximes[146]

$$CH_3CH=CHNO_2 + 2HCl \longrightarrow \underset{Cl}{\overset{CH_3CHCl-C=NOH}{|}} \xrightarrow{H_2O}$$

$$CH_3CHCl-COOH + HONH_3Cl$$

1-Nitropropene treated with anhydrous hydrogen chloride in ether gives 1,2-dichloropropionaldoxime which can be isolated. On hydrolysis, α-chloropropionic acid and hydroxylammonium chloride are obtained. In aqueous solutions the dichlorooxime is not isolated.

2-Nitropropene gives the dichloronitroso compounds which can not rearrange to the oxime because no α-hydrogen is present.

$$CH_3-\underset{\underset{NO_2}{|}}{C}=CH_2 + 2HCl \longrightarrow CH_3\underset{\underset{NO}{|}}{CCl}-CH_2Cl + H_2O$$

Hydrogen bromide behaves in a much different manner. The dibromonitroso compound is not formed. Instead the nitro group is removed as ammonium bromide to give a dibromohydrocarbon derivative.[154]

$$CH_2=CHNO_2 + 9HBr \longrightarrow BrCH_2CH_2Br + NH_4Br + 2H_2O + 3Br_2$$

Alkylmagnesium halides add to nitroolefins at temperatures below 10°C to give nitroparaffins in yields up to 65 per cent. 1-Nitro-2,2-dimethylbutane has been prepared in 60 per cent yield by reacting ethylmagnesium bromide with 1-nitro-2-methyl-1-propene at 0–10°C followed by hydrolysis with dilute acid.[155]

$$CH_3-\underset{\underset{CH_3}{|}}{C}=CHNO_2 + C_2H_5MgBr \longrightarrow CH_3CH_2\underset{\underset{CH_3MgBr}{|}}{\overset{\overset{CH_3}{|}}{C}}-CH-NO_2 \overset{H^+}{\longrightarrow}$$

$$CH_3CH_2-C(CH_3)_2-CH_2NO_2$$

Similarly *n*-butylmagnesium bromide reacts with nitroethylene to give a 65 per cent yield of 1-nitrohexane. The reaction is quite general and serves as a very interesting method for preparing nitroparaffins.

1-Nitropropene in ethanol added slowly to aqueous potassium cyanide at −5 to 0°C and the mixture stirred for 4 hours at 0°C gives a 25 per cent yield of 2-methyl-3-nitropropionitrile.[156]

Frankel and Klager[157] nitrated nitroolefins with 70 per cent nitric acid under a variety of conditions. The only product isolated and identified by them was 2,3-dinitro-2-butene obtained from 2-nitro-2-butene.

Early attempts to polymerize low molecular weight nitroolefins gave only black tars. Since 1944 however, the preparation of white, flocculent, solid polymers have been reported.[158,159] The end objective was the preparation of polyvinylamines.

Schmidt and Rutz[160] polymerized 2-nitropropene using aqueous potassium bicarbonate as a catalyst to give a microcrystalline low molecular weight solid which decomposed above 200°C. Blomquist, Tapp and Johnson[159] also used this method of polymerization. Hydrogenation of this polymer can only be accomplished at 90–100°C in the presence of a Raney nickel catalyst under pressures of 1700–1750 psi. Higher temperatures cause degradation of the polymer.

References

1. Meyer, V., and Stuber, O., *Ber.,* **5,** 203 (1872).
2. Reynolds, R. B., and Adkins, H., *J. Am. Chem. Soc.,* **51,** 279 (1939).
3. Brackebusch, E., *Ber.,* **6,** 1290 (1873).
4. Demuth, R., and Meyer, V., *Ber.,* **21,** 3529 (1888).
5. Meyer, V., and Askenasy, P., *Ber.,* **25,** 1701 (1892).
6. Kornblum, N., Taub, B., and Ungnade, H. E., *J. Am. Chem. Soc.,* **76,** 3209 (1954).
7. Kornblum, N., and Powers, J. W., *J. Org. Chem.,* **22,** 455 (1957).
8. Kornblum, N., and Larson, H. O., *J. Am. Chem. Soc.,* **78,** 1497 (1956).
9. Plummer, C. W., and Drake, N. L., *J. Am. Chem. Soc.,* **76,** 2720 (1954).
10. Kornblum, N., Smiley, R. A., Ungnade, H. E., White, A. M., Raub, B., and Herbert, S. A., *J. Am. Chem. Soc.,* **77,** 5528 (1955).
11. Desseigne, G., and Giral, H., *Mem. poudres,* **34,** 13 (1952).
12. Desseigne, G., and Giral, H., *Mem. poudres,* **34,** 49 (1952).
13. Bamberger, E., and Seligman, R., *Ber.,* **35,** 4299 (1902).
14. Kornblum, N., and Clutter, R. J., *J. Am. Chem. Soc.,* **76,** 4494 (1954).
15. Kornblum, N., Clutter, R. J., and Jones, W. J., *J. Am. Chem. Soc.,* **78,** 4003 (1956).
16. Bevard, I., *Ber.,* **26,** 129 (1893); *J. prakt. Chem.,* [2], **48,** 345 (1893).
17. Brown, G. B., and Shriner, R. L., *J. Org. Chem.,* **2,** 376 (1937).
18. Thurston, J. T., and Shriner, R. L., *J. Org. Chem.,* **2,** 183 (1937).
19. Mills, E. J., *Ann.,* **160,** 117 (1871).
20. Beilstein, F., and Kurbatov, A., *Ber.,* **13,** 1818, 2029 (1880).
21. Worstall, R. A., *Am. Chem. J.,* **20,** 202 (1898).
22. Henry, L., *Rec. trav. chim.,* **24,** 352 (1905).
23. Konovalov, M., *J. Russ. Phys. Chem. Soc.,* **25,** 472 (1894).
24. Badische Anilin- & Soda-Fabrik A.-G., German Patent 864,991 (Jan. 29, 1953).
25. Denison, C., Ph.D. Thesis, Purdue University, 1940.
26. Stevens, P. G., and Schiessler, R. W., *J. Am. Chem. Soc.,* **62,** 2885 (1940).
27. Hass, H. B., and Hodge, E. B., U. S. Patent 2,071,122 (Feb. 16, 1937).
28. Hass, H. B., Hodge, E. B., and Vanderbilt, B. M., *Ind. Eng. Chem.,* **28,** 339 (1936); U. S. Patent 1,967,667 (July 24, 1934).
29. Dorsky, J., *Ind. Eng. Chem.,* **33,** 1138 (1941).
30. Hass, H. B., and Schecter, H., *Ind. Eng. Chem.,* **35,** 1146 (1943); **39,** 817 (1947).
31. Howe, A. P., and Hass, H. B., *Ind. Eng. Chem.,* **38,** 251 (1946).
32. Hass, H. B., and Schecter, H., *J. Am. Chem. Soc.,* **75,** 1382 (1953).

33. Gee, K., U. S. Patent 2,464,572 (Mar. 15, 1949).
34. Rottig, W., German Patent 902,374 (Jan. 21, 1954).
35. Stengel, L. A., and Egly, R. S., U. S. Patent 2,418,241 (Apr. 1, 1947).
36. Bishop, R. B., Denton, W. I., and Nygaard, E. M., U. S. Patent 2,511,454 (June 13, 1950).
37. Denton, W. I., Bishop, R. B., and Nygaard, E. M., *Ind. Eng. Chem.,* **40,** 381 (1948).
38. E.I. du Pont de Nemours, British Patent 603,344 (June 14, 1948).
39. Hager, K. F., *Ind. Eng. Chem.,* **41,** 2168 (1949).
40. Darzens, G., and Levy, G., *Compt. rend.,* **229,** 1081 (1949).
41. Grundmann, C., and Haldenwanger, H., *Angew. Chem.,* **62,** 556 (1950).
42. Stengel, L. A., U. S. Patent 2,512,587 (June 20, 1950).
43. Hass, H. B., and Hudgen, D. E., *J. Am. Chem. Soc.,* **76,** 2692 (1954).
44. Weghofer, H., German Patent 831,393 (Feb. 14, 1952).
45. Bahner, C. T., and Kite, H. T., *J. Am. Chem. Soc.,* **71,** 3597 (1949).
46. McKinnin, A. C., U. S. Patent 2,811,560 (Oct. 29, 1957).
47. Hass, H. B., and Alexander, L. G., *Ind. Eng. Chem.,* **41,** 2266 (1949).
48. Bachman, G. B., Hass, H. B., and Addison, L. M., *J. Org. Chem.,* **17,** 914 (1952).
49. Bachman, G. B., Hass, H. B., and Hewitt, J. V., *J. Org. Chem.,* **17,** 928 (1952).
50. Bachman, G. B., and Kohn, L., *J. Org. Chem.,* **17,** 942 (1952).
51. Bachman, G. B., and Pollack, M., *Ind. Eng. Chem.,* **46,** 713 (1950).
52. Bachman, G. B., and Hewitt, J. V., U. S. Patent 2,587,698 (May 20, 1952).
53. Henry, L., *Ber.,* **33,** 3169 (1900).
54. Bevard, I., *J. prakt. Chem.,* [2], **63,** 193 (1901).
55. Alder, K., Rickert, H. F., and Windemuth, E., *Ber.,* **71,** 2451 (1938).
56. Lyons, R. E., and Smith, L. T., *Ber.,* **60B,** 173 (1927).
57. Neyer, V., and Demuth, R., *Ann.,* **256,** 28 (1890).
58. Sabatier, P., and Senderens, J. B., *Compt. rend.,* **135,** 225 (1902).
59. Kleinfelter, H., *Ber.,* **62B,** 1582, 1590 (1929).
60. Johnson, K., Ph.D. Thesis, Purdue University, 1937.
61. Johnson, K., and Degering, E. F., *J. Am. Chem. Soc.,* **61,** 3194 (1939).
62. Senkus, M., *Ind. Eng. Chem.,* **40,** 506 (1948).
63. Meyer, V., and Hoffmann, E., *Ber.,* **24,** 3528 (1891).
64. Bamberger, E., *Ber.,* **27,** 1347 (1894).
65. Beckmann, E. B., *Ann.,* **365,** 205 (1909).
66. Scheiber, J., *Ann.,* **365,** 215 (1901).
67. Traube, W., and Schulz, A. P., *Ber.,* **56,** 1856 (1923).
68. Watt, G. W., and Knowles, C. M., *J. Org. Chem.,* **8,** 540 (1943).
69. Pierron, P., *Bull. soc. chim.,* [3], **21,** 780 (1899).
70. Leeds, M. S., and Smith, G. B., *J. Electrochem. Soc.,* **98,** 129 (1951).
71. Konovalov, J., *J. Russ. Phys. Chem. Soc.,* **30,** 960 (1898).
72. Bamberger, E., and Weiler, M., *J. prakt. Chem.,* [2], **58,** 333 (1898).
73. Braun, J. v., and Sobecki, W., *Ber.,* **44,** 2526 (1901).
74. Farbenfabriken Bayer A.-G., British Patent 722,745 (Jan. 26, 1955).
75. Lippincott, S. B., and Hass, H. B., *Ind. Eng. Chem.,* **31,** 118 (1939).

76. Lowry, T. M., and Magson, E. H., *J. Chem. Soc.*, **93**, 107, 119 (1908).
77. Bamberger, E., and Rust, E., *Ber.*, **35**, 45 (1902).
78. Nef, J. U., *Ann.*, **280**, 263 (1894).
79. Hass, H. B., *Ind. Eng. Chem.*, **35**, 1146 (1943).
80. Demole, E., *Ann.*, **175**, 142 (1875).
81. Meyer, V., *Ber.*, **7**, 432 (1874).
82. Maron, S. H., and LaMer, V. K., *J. Am. Chem. Soc.*, **60**, 2588 (1938).
83. Maron, S. H., and Shedlovsky, T., *J. Am. Chem. Soc.*, **61**, 753 (1939).
84. Friese, P., *Ber.*, **9**, 394 (1876).
85. Lecco, M. T., *Ber.*, **9**, 705 (1876).
86. Steinkopf, W., *Ber.*, **42**, 3925 (1909).
87. Lippincott, S. B., *J. Am. Chem. Soc.*, **62**, 2604 (1940).
88. Tscherniak, J., *Ber.*, **8**, 609 (1875).
89. Ramage, W. D., U. S. Patent 1,996,388 (Apr. 2, 1935).
90. Vanderbilt, B. M., U. S. Patent 2,181,410 (Nov. 28, 1939).
91. Henry, L., *Bull. acad. roy. Belg.*, [3], **34**, 547 (1898).
92. Strickland, B. R., M.S. Thesis, Purdue University, 1937.
93. Hass, H. B., and Strickland, B. R., U. S. Patent 2,256,839 (Sept. 23, 1941).
94. Junell, R., *Z. physik. Chem.*, **A141**, 71 (1929); *Arkiv Kemi, Mineral. Geol.*, **11B**, No. 34 (1934); *Svensk Kem. Tidskr.*, **46**, 125 (1934).
95. Villiers, A., *Bull. soc. chim.*, [2], **43**, 323 (1885).
96. Seigle, L. W., and Hass, H. B., *J. Org. Chem.*, **5**, 100 (1940).
97. Riley, E. F., and McBee, E. T., Abstracts of St. Louis Meeting of the American Chemical Society, April, 1941.
98. Hass, H. B., and Riley, E. F., *Chem. Revs.*, **32**, 373 (1943).
99. Kamlet, J., U. S. Patent 2,151,517 (Mar. 21, 1939).
100. Boileau, J., *Mem. poudres*, **35**, Annexe 7 (1953).
101. Eckstein, Z., and Urbanski, T., *Roczniki Chem.*, **26**, 571 (1952).
102. Hurd, C. D., and Nilson, M. E., *J. Org. Chem.*, **20**, 927 (1955).
103. Vanderbilt, B. M., and Hass, H. B., *Ind. Eng. Chem.*, **32**, 34 (1940); U. S. Patent 2,139,120 (Dec. 6, 1938).
104. Schmidle, C. J., and Mansfield, R. C., *Ind. Eng. Chem.*, **44**, 1388 (1952).
105. Astle, M. J., and Abbott, F., *J. Org. Chem.*, **21**, 1228 (1956).
106. Kozlov, L. M., Fink, E. F., and Liorber, G. B., *Trudy Kazan. Khim. Tekhnol. Inst. im. S.M. Kirova*, **23**, 148 (1957).
107. Hofwimmer, F., *Soc. Chem. Ind.*, **31**, 204 (1912).
108. Bergeim, F. H., U. S. Patent 1,691,955 (Nov. 20, 1928).
109. Tindall, J. B., *Ind. Eng. Chem.*, **33**, 65 (1941).
110. Senkus, M., *J. Am. Chem. Soc.*, **68**, 10 (1946).
111. Johnson, H. G., *J. Am. Chem. Soc.*, **68**, 12 (1946).
112. Johnson, H. G., *J. Am. Chem. Soc.*, **68**, 14 (1946).
113. Senkus, M., U. S. Patent 2,513,248 (Dec. 24, 1946).
114. Urbanski, T. U., and Kolinski, R., *Roczniki Chem.*, **30**, 201 (1950); *Bull. acad. polon. sci.*, **3**, 493 (1955).
115. Ufer, H., German Patent 877,303 (May 21, 1953).
116. Donat, F., Ph.D. Thesis, Case Institute of Technology, 1959.

117. Buckley, G. D., *J. Chem. Soc.,* **1947,** 1492.
118. N. V. Bataafsche Petroleum Maatschappij, British Patent 666,623 (Feb. 13, 1952).
119. Warner, D. T., and Moe, O. A., *J. Am. Chem. Soc.,* **74,** 1064 (1952).
120. Schecter, H., *et al., J. Am. Chem. Soc.,* **74,** 3664 (1952).
121. Kloetzel, M. C., *J. Am. Chem. Soc.,* **70,** 3571 (1948).
122. Boyd, R. N., and Lestrin, R., *J. Am. Chem. Soc.,* **74,** 2675 (1952).
123. Feuer, H., and Aguilar, C. N., *J. Org. Chem.,* **23,** 607 (1958).
124. Profft, E., *Chem. Tech. (Berlin),* **8,** 705 (1956).
125. Donaruma, L. G., and Huber, M. L., *J. Org. Chem.,* **21,** 965 (1956).
126. Russell, G. A., *J. Am. Chem. Soc.,* **76,** 1595 (1954).
127. Noma, K., Okumura, T., and Sone, T., *Chem. High Polymers (Japan),* **5,** 99 (1948).
128. Buckley, G. D., and Scaife, C. W., *J. Chem. Soc.,* **1947,** 1471.
129. Mauny, H. C. de, *Bull. soc. chim.,* **7,** 133 (1940).
130. Schwartz, H., and Nelles, J., U. S. Patent 2,257,980 (Oct. 7, 1942).
131. Gold, M. H., U. S. Patent 2,414,594 (Jan. 21, 1947).
132. Viking Corp., British Patent 593,109 (Oct. 8, 1947).
133. Nightingale, D. V., and Janes, J. R., *J. Am. Chem. Soc.,* **66,** 352 (1944).
134. Wilder-Smith, A. E., and Scaife, C. W., British Patent 580,256 (Sept. 2, 1946).
135. Scaife, C. W., Baldock, H., and Wilder-Smith, A. E., British Patent 596,303 (Jan. 1, 1948).
136. Wilder-Smith, A. E., Scaife, C. W., and Stanley, R. H., U. S. Patent 2,384,050 (Sept. 4, 1945).
137. Petrov, A. D., and Bubygina, M. A., *Doklady Akad. Nauk S.S.S.R.,* **77,** 1031 (1951).
138. Topchiev, A. V., and Fantalova, E. L., *Doklady Akad. Nauk S.S.S.R.,* **78,** 83 (1953).
139. Emmons, W. D., Cannon, W. M., Dawson, J. W., and Ross, R. M., *J. Am. Chem. Soc.,* **75,** 1993 (1953).
140. Bachman, G. B., and Atwood, M. T., *J. Am. Chem. Soc.,* **78,** 484 (1956).
141. Thiele, J., *Ber.,* **32,** 1293 (1899).
142. Boubeault, L., and Wahl, A., *Compt. rend.,* **135,** 41 (1902).
143. Susie, A. G., Ph.D. Thesis, Purdue University, 1939.
144. Heider, R. L., Ph.D. Thesis, Purdue University, 1941.
145. Tindall, J. B., U. S. Patents 2,636,901 (Apr. 28, 1953); 2,647,930 (Aug. 4, (1953).
146. Heath, R. L., and Rose, J. D., *J. Chem. Soc.,* **1947,** 1486.
147. Lambert, A., and Piggott, H. A., *J. Chem. Soc.,* **1947,** 1494.
148. Bahner, C. T., U. S. Patent 2,520,104 (Aug. 22, 1950).
149. Dickey, J. B., U. S. Patent 2,292,212 (Oct. 5, 1939).
150. Heath, R. L., and Piggott, H. A., U. S. Patent 2,465,803 (Mar. 29, 1949).
151. Lambert, A., British Patent 584,792 (Jan. 23, 1947).
152. Wilder-Smith, A. W., U. S. Patent 2,393,827 (Jan. 29, 1946).
153. Bahner, C. T., and Kete, H. F., U. S. Patent 2,477,162 (July 26, 1949).
154. Takabayashi, M., *J. Chem. Soc. Japan,* **64,** 191 (1943).

155. Buckley, G. D., and Ellery, E., *J. Chem. Soc., ***1947,** 1497.
156. Buckley, G. D., Heath, R. L., and Rose, J. D., *J. Chem. Soc.,* **1947,** 1500.
157. Frankel, B., and Klager, K., *J. Org. Chem.,* **23,** 494 (1958).
158. Mason, L. H., and Wildman, W. C., *J. Am. Chem. Soc.,* **76,** 6194 (1954).
159. Blomquist, A. T., Tapp, W. J., and Johnson, J. R., *J. Am. Chem. Soc.,* **67,** 1519 (1945).
160. Schmidt, E., and Rutz, G., *Ber.,* **61B,** 2142 (1928).

INDEX

381

Date Due

PRINTED IN U. S. A.